Forging Peace

*Intervention, Human Rights
and the Management of Media Space*

Edited by Monroe E. Price and Mark Thompson

Edinburgh University Press

To Ben Webb and the memory of Harold G. Price

Edinburgh University Press Ltd
22 George Square, Edinburgh

Typeset in Ehrhardt by
Hewer Text Ltd, Edinburgh, and
printed and bound in Great Britain by
MPG Books Ltd, Bodmin

A CIP Record for this book is available from the British Library

ISBN 0 7486 1500 8 (hardback)
ISBN 0 7486 1501 6 (paperback)

Contents

Section Four

Acknowledgements

This book was supported by Oxford University's Programme in Comparative Media Law and Policy (PCMLP). Its then-director, Stefaan Verhulst, encouraged publication and suggested that the two co-editors co-operate in producing it. Professor Price's early work on the subject occurred under the auspices of the Media Studies Center in New York City, where he was ably assisted by Stacy Sullivan. In 1999, he was asked to bring together, for UNESCO, a group of essays on particular episodes of media management in post-conflict situations. Marcello Scarone was particularly helpful in that effort. The authors worked nobly to meet their exacting commitments to the editors, despite careers that leave little time for surplus writing. Particular thanks are due to Eric Blinderman and Helen Darbishire, whose contributions to this book far transcend the chapters that bear their names. Some of the material in Chapters 7 and 9 has appeared in Mark Thompson's report, *Slovenia, Croatia, Bosnia and Herzegovina, Macedonia (FYROM) and Kosovo: International Assistance to Media*, commissioned by the Office of the OSCE Representative on Freedom of the Media and published by the OSCE in 2000. The editors gratefully acknowledge the permission of Mr Freimut Duve, the OSCE Representative on Freedom of the Media, to draw on that report. Elena Chernyavska at the European Institute for the Media and Anna Di Lellio of the OSCE mission in Kosovo were generous in supplying information. The Ford Foundation provided a grant to Oxford University's PCMLP that included financial support for this study. John Santos, the Foundation's Program Officer, was consistently helpful. Philip Taylor, in whose series this book is published, has provided different sorts of encouragement. Bethany Davis Noll, manager of publications at the PCMLP, provided invaluable editorial and co-ordination services. We are also grateful for the research assistance of Jessica Stalnaker and Milan Milenkovic of PCMLP, and for Andrew March's sharp eye.

Oxford, December 2001

Why is there so much research about the role of news media in political conflict and war and so little concerning the media and peace? . . . There is not one major study which has looked at the role of the news media in an ongoing peace process . . . Even the most casual observer cannot fail to be impressed with the ability of the news media to serve an either constructive or destructive role in the promotion of peace.

Gadi Wolfsfeld[1]

The change in the nature of military operations brought about by the end of the Cold War, along with a revolution in communications technology, has transformed information and the news media into an even more vital component of conflict and conflict management.

Warren P. Strobel[2]

Governments, international organisations, and humanitarian agencies . . . are often willing to spend hundreds of millions of dollars on humanitarian or peacekeeping operations, but are reluctant to allocate sufficient funding to ensure that people are properly and accurately informed. Normally, this does not take a great deal of money.

Edward R. Girardet[3]

The old rules of war and peace, which distinguished between internal conflicts and international ones, have been eroded, and it does not appear at all probable that they will be restored in the near future . . . [P]recisely because of the new fusion between domestic and international politics, intervention in the internal affairs of a state must respond to clearly defined rules and criteria. There needs to be a debate on this point: what are the new rules of the international system of powers?

Eric Hobsbawm[4]

Introduction

Mark Thompson and Monroe E. Price

If wars 'begin in the minds of men', it follows that they are not over until they have ended there too. There are other, more manifest reasons why the media play an essential role in societies recovering from conflict, but none is more fundamental than this one, which surely looks even more pertinent today than when it was enshrined in the UNESCO charter in 1946.[5] Today, the human mind is exposed to modes of political influence that are more pervasive, insinuating, and sophisticated than was easily imagined half a century ago. And media are prime conduits and agents of this influence.

By 1995, failures to prevent war and genocide in Somalia, the Balkans, and Rwanda had tainted if not dashed the hopes released by the end of the Cold War for a new era of international co-operation. While the more successful interventions in East Timor and Kosovo partly redeemed this record, the elation of 1989 and 1990 is long gone. In the prevailing mood of sober assessment, those landmark conflicts of the 1990s have been scrutinized in terms of security, ethnicity, history, international relations, humanitarian action – and mass communication.

A good deal has been written about the strategies of media exploitation that were used to bring about particular conflicts. It is widely accepted that media played a central role in fomenting 'ethnic' violence in, for example, Rwanda and Bosnia and Herzegovina, where government forces and rebels or other factions contested the very organization and content of the press and broadcasting.[6] The impact of international media on diplomacy, mediation, and humanitarian assistance has also been appraised.[7]

Much less study has been devoted to the relationship between the international community and local or indigenous media before, during, and after conflict.[8] As information management became central in the run-up to wars and in post-conflict reconstruction, a decade of costly experiments commenced. In 1992–3, as John Marston points out in Chapter 6 of this book, the United Nations Transitional Authority in Cambodia (UNTAC) was given more control over information than any previous UN mission. UNTAC sought ways to alter the structure and practice of information distribution before the 1993 elections. It was very much the forerunner of the three giant missions in the Balkans: the UN Protection Force (UNPROFOR) in the Balkans, the UN Transitional Authority in Eastern Slavonia, Baranja, and western Sirmium (UNTAES) in eastern Croatia, and the UN Interim Mission in Kosovo (UNMIK).

In Bosnia, after the Dayton Accords ended the war, the Office of the High Representative (OHR), the Organization for Security and Co-operation in Europe (OSCE), and a variety of non-governmental organizations (NGOs) took steps to reshape and reform the media space. The same was later attempted in Kosovo, after the United Nations took responsibility for administering that province in 1999. International administrative mechanisms were placed over media such as had not been seen for half a century. A new approach by the international community was evolving, with important constitutional, political, and structural implications.

Yet these experiments were conducted for the most part in the dark. There was little organizational awareness as to how the international community should react either to the incendiary uses of media in Rwanda before and during the perpetration of genocide, or to the systematic manipulation of public opinion in Bosnia after Dayton. International peace operations have often seemed at a loss when facing hostile propaganda that host governments emitted after 'consenting' to the operations' deployment on their soil. Such governments often proved more resourceful at devizing techniques that preserved their control over key media while paying lip service to democratic standards, than the international community did in overcoming them. The efforts of intergovernmental organizations (IGOs) and NGOs to intervene in media space as part of democratic institution-building after conflict, to support peace operations, or merely to extend the influence of powerful Western states, has gone largely unexamined.

Given this recent experience, and in light of the substantial likelihood of more such conflicts in the future, it is opportune to review, reflect, and determine whether there are practical and academic lessons to be learned.[9] Part of this book's purpose is to analyze the tension between interventive action of governments, international organizations and military forces, on the one hand, and the international legal protection of freedom of media and information, on the other.

A coherent international policy on these issues is unlikely to emerge, especially one that might involve specific duties of intervention for the international community, unless a framework is developed for assessing the information challenges and needs in conflict zones, as well as for evaluating the different techniques of what has been called 'information intervention'. We hope this book will be useful in establishing such a foundation.

Our approach is to weave theory with case study. The novelty and complexity of this issue mean that lessons have scarcely emerged from practice. An analysis of theory without looking at the facts on the ground would be dry and vacuous. A description of events without abstracting their implications for international law and acceptable international practice would be a missed opportunity.

Ultimately, what is essential for shaping doctrine and evaluating policies is an understanding of the great conflicts of the last fifteen years or so, where media and violence were closely associated. Cambodia, Rwanda, Bosnia and

Herzegovina, and Kosovo have all been laboratories where the effectiveness, moral limits, legal bases and practical possibilities for 'information intervention' have been tested. These occasions form a sequence. Each shows the interplay between pre- and mid-conflict use of media to encourage violence and the perils of peacekeeping in the post-conflict period. The sequence illustrates the differences between those societies with a history of professional media institutions, and others lacking such a history. It also shows the uncertain evolution of international responses to media in conflict.

Our contributors consider how international law is changing to encompass, reflect, and channel intervention practices. We look at 'information intervention' through the lens of human rights principles, especially those relating to restrictions on hate speech and the right to receive and impart information. We examine the distinctions between State-authorized and rogue uses of media to incite conflict; between authorized and unauthorized incidents of information intervention; and between preventive intervention as opposed to that directed towards resolving conflict. And we test some of the justifications that are articulated for different forms of information intervention, actions that range from mere monitoring of broadcasts to the total reformulation of media laws, and ultimately the seizure or bombing of transmitters, and full-blown cyberwarfare.

This book focuses primarily on the problems of media management in conflict and post-conflict situations. More specifically it examines situations where Western democracies, the United Nations, the OSCE and even the North Atlantic Treaty Organization (NATO) have attempted to transform the media sector in third party states. By examining the legal and political context of the new interest in media before, during, and after conflict, we make current trends more visible and illuminate the relationship between speech and force in international affairs.

Whether or not Gadi Wolfsfeld's statement, cited as an epigraph of this book, is still literally true, the dearth of attention to this aspect of contemporary peacemaking is itself noteworthy. Part of the explanation may be that the theme is too fresh, too plastic. Practitioners are still defining its shape and form. Simply stated, it has not yet congealed to the point where analysts can get to work.

Another reason may be the subject's nature, somewhat inchoate and contingent, defying simple categorization. This is, we hope, reflected in the unusually diverse range of contributions. It is no coincidence that most of our authors are activists and practitioners as well as scholars or academics. Our purpose has been to bring together case studies, legal analyses, and related perspectives that shed light on the present and likely future of media development in conflict zones.

This book is not about the function of media or the politics of media control in the context of purely military interventions or direct occupation, such as the USA's in Grenada and Panama or more recently Russia's in Chechnya. For that matter, Moscow's handling of both international and local media in its 'pacification' of Chechnya provides a counter-example, a photographic negative of the peace-building exercises studied in this book.

This distinction is not hard-and-fast. When the USA sent forces into Haiti in September 1994 to restore the country's democratically elected leader (and forestall shoals of desperate refugees from landing on Florida's shores), FM radio sets were dropped 'to keep the local population informed and to avoid destructive rumor-mongering'.[10] While it had nothing to do with 'managing media space' in line with democratic rights and standards, this was a plain example of external action that changed the information environment without the consent of the sovereign power, for a wider democratic purpose. The convergence between contemporary 'psyops' (psychological operations), or military propaganda, and civilian uses of information technology has important implications, some of which are explored by Philip Taylor in Chapter 11.

Antecedents: Germany, Japan, Italy

The only antecedents for contemporary efforts to modify media space in target countries were the Allied Occupation Forces' attempts to transform Germany and Japan after the World War II. Those efforts remain the prototypes of post-conflict information management. They were wholesale attempts to empty the information space of its previous political content and recast its relationship to executive government. Overwhelming media control and the transformation of press and broadcasting were used to advance democratization. In Germany, the Allied Control Council was given full powers to establish broadcasting facilities and those powers were delegated to the zone commanders.

These efforts spawned a variety of approaches. On the one hand, the Russians created a centralized network in the East Zone. On the other hand, the Western Allies expressly ruled out direct control over radio, but as they began to organize their zones, their actions belied this claim. Together, these approaches radically changed the structure of broadcasting.[11] The Allies split up and decentralized the dominant media outlets in order to prevent a dominant national voice from arising.[12] The British, replicating the BBC in form, organized Northwest German Radio so that it could become financially independent and ultimately free of government and party influence. In the United States zone, separate networks were set up in each of the Länder (provinces). The French network, set up in Baden-Baden, stayed in French hands until 1952.[13]

Denazification, meaning the removal of Nazis from public life and elimination of the influence of Nazism, was a primary responsibility of the Occupiers. It was intended to help 'pave the way for the establishment of a stable government based upon democratic institutions and procedures that guarantee fundamental human rights, a realization that the German State is the servant of the people, and a consciousness of moral and political responsibility for German policy and action'.[14]

The Potsdam Agreement of August 1945 required the occupiers to 'prevent all Nazi and militarist propaganda' and all German information services were placed under the Military Government.[15] Logically, the process had to censor and restructure German public space, not just the news media. 'Information services, including the radio, press, books and periodicals, films, theaters, concerts, and other forms of entertainment, were early placed under strict Military Government supervision.'[16] All newspapers were initially banned, and Nazi literature removed from the shelves of bookshops. Radio, 'perhaps the information medium most thoroughly infected with Nazi ideology and personnel', was the last to be returned to active German control.[17]

In Japan, the US government sought to eradicate all elements of militarism and nationalism from the media.[18] The first Memorandum of the Allies proclaimed an Allied re-establishment of freedom of speech and press.[19] Not only was the news to be 'true to facts'; it would also be 'faithful to the policies of the Allied Powers', and refrain from sceptical criticism of the Allied Forces.[20] The General Headquarters approved films and documentaries before public distribution. 'Along with Hollywood movies which cast – or threatened to cast – an unfavourable glow on America . . ., Japanese criticism of the occupation was disallowed. Correspondingly, the censors regarded any mention of the fate of Hiroshima and Nagasaki as likely to incite anti-American sentiment.' As one Japanese writer recalled, 'We were not allowed to write about the atomic bomb during the Occupation. We were not even allowed to say that we were not allowed to write about the atomic bomb.'[21]

In Italy under the Armistice, equivalent powers and responsibilities were imposed on the Italian authorities, which had to 'conform to such measures for control and censorship of press and of other publications, of theatrical and cinematograph performances, of broadcasting, and all forms of inter-communication as the Allied Commander-in-Chief may direct. The Allied Commander-in-Chief may, at his discretion, take-over radio, cable, and other communications stations.'[22]

Viewed from the present, those great experiments in building democratic media suggest both a similarity and a contrast to current efforts. The similarity lies in the broad intention then and now to construct a democratic media space by imposing appropriate legislation, regulations, and statutes, encouraging professionalism, preventing political domination, and so forth. The contrast can be found in the scope and degree of international authority dedicated to this purpose. Contemporary media interventions lack the clarity of authority and purpose that the Allied military victory provided in 1945. Then, the United States and its allies 'belligerently occupied' Germany and Japan.[23] It was under that status that the Allies refashioned the radio broadcasting systems there.[24] Their objectives in managing radio broadcasting were part of the larger mission of constructing a democratic society in the former Axis nations.[25] To do that, the Allies imposed a legal regime that transformed the structures, management, and content of existing media outlets.[26] These efforts were given a high priority because of the key role radio propaganda played in fuelling the war, both at home and abroad.[27]

While the Occupiers were legally empowered to act in lieu of a sovereign, and limited only by internationally established standards, contemporary peace-keepers cannot make the same claim.[28] Critics of the international authorities in Bosnia and Kosovo invoke undeniable norms and standards, which did not constrain the Allied powers in the 1940s. Hence these historic precedents, occurring as they did in the aftermath of 'total war' and at a time when the international machinery of human rights was in its infancy, should inform contemporary actions, but cannot instruct them.

Intervention

The meaning of the term intervention has broadened. Until recently, it meant 'coercion short of war'; it was 'always dictatorial, involving the threat if not the exercise of force';[29] it was 'dictatorial interference in the domestic or foreign affairs of a state by another, in such a way as to impair the first state's independence'.[30] Now, in normal British and American usage, intervention encompasses anything from sheer aggression to tentative mediation. In international relations, it has come to denote 'a move by a state *or an international organization* to involve itself in the domestic affairs of another state, whether the State consents or not'.[31]

In this book, we mainly address a number of occasions since 1990 when states have formally (if often disingenuously) consented to limit *pro tem* their own sovereignty by permitting an international organization – usually the United Nations – to intervene on their territory and assume responsibilities of governance.

Peace operations themselves have undergone fundamental changes since 1989. The standard definition of 'classical peacekeeping tasks' as comprising 'monitoring, interposition, or cease-fire implementation'[32] could not encompass the tasks which the United Nations began to assume in the late 1980s, beginning with Namibia and continuing first in Cambodia, then the Balkans and elsewhere.[33] Peacekeeping tasks in the new era have included assisting humanitarian agencies to carry out their mandates to deliver humanitarian aid and protect displaced persons; stabilizing failed or collapsing states; developing democratic institutions that monitor human rights; and even administrating territories with their entire populations. These tasks required the UN to expand its range of institutional resources, as well as rethink the complex forms of interaction between, on one hand, the civilian and military components of a mission, and on the other, the missions and their host governments.

A new lexicon of terms has been coined to help policy-makers map the altered landscape of conflict and intervention. 'Multidisciplinary' or 'multi-functional' peacekeeping and 'multidimensional operations' have become the norm, and seem likely to remain so.[34] So-called traditional peacekeeping has swollen and fragmented into subcategories that cover such areas as preventive deployment, peace-support operations, peace-enforcement or peace-building missions, and even MOOTW, or 'military operations other than war'.

In practice, peace operations must be able to cope with a fluid combination of challenges. Given the experiences described in this book, we should expect public opinion in the targeted society – as well as in the intervening states – to play an increasingly important role in affecting the success or failure of international interventions. For this reason, the performance of indigenous, local media will also grow in importance. While this will be most true of humanitarian interventions (see below), it will also apply to all-out military interventions, such as the unilateral US actions against Grenada or Panama or the multilateral campaign to drive Iraq out of Kuwait.

Humanitarian Intervention

Described as 'at once an immensely powerful and a terribly imprecise idea',[35] humanitarian intervention is generally accepted to incorporate 'nonconsensual humanitarian activities mounted from outside an area in crisis, sometimes involving the threat or the use of military force'.[36] As Jamie Metzl points out in Chapter 1, there is 'no working international system for humanitarian intervention'. The term has no precise legal definition, and in practice it might include the Vietnamese intervention in Cambodia, Tanzania's intervention in Uganda, the US in Somalia, the UN in Bosnia and East Timor, and even NATO's bombardment of Serbia.

In truth, it would be easier to list those international – bilateral or multi-lateral – military engagements in the 1990s that could *not* be dubbed 'humanitarian' than vice-versa. Not surprisingly, a number of quarters view the term as dangerously woolly. Critics from the left suspect humanitarian intervention, along with linked notions such as 'pro-democratic intervention', or 'liberal intervention', of cloaking the self-interest of Western powers, or indeed the denial of politics.[37] Critics from the right fear the erosion of the prerogatives of state sovereignty in the name of morality.

While the potential for cant on this subject is high, and in all likelihood there is no such thing as a purely humanitarian intervention, the humanitarian agenda in international affairs is probably here to stay. It is now necessary to eliminate that terrible imprecision as far as possible.

'Information Intervention'

An effort to create a more precise definition of humanitarian intervention would also aid attempts to develop an international legal norm for media restructuring. In the most ambitious scenario, this definition would formalize and acknowledge a right to humanitarian intervention, alongside the right to democratic government, the right of a population to be free from internal as well as external aggression, and the right of human rights' victims to receive assistance.[38] In such a context, the recognized human right freely to receive and impart information could logically also, when denied or violated, become a basis for intervention.

The term 'information intervention' has been coined to comprise the extensive external management, manipulation, or seizure of information space in conflict zones.[39] The term itself is novel. There is no automatic meaning assigned to it; rather, there is a set of practices or conditions from which a tidy definition has yet to emerge.

In the extended interview that forms the first chapter of this book, Jamie F. Metzl, who put the term into circulation, proposes that information intervention comprises several elements, undertaken by states in response to 'misuse of mass communication', especially where there is a potential for mass violation of human rights. The strategies used can encompass an aggressive reaction to information misuses, 'first to provide counter-information that opposes harmful incitement, and second to proscribe or suppress the latter if necessary'. What is generally accepted is that information intervention involves actions taken by a powerful state or a combination of states, sometimes in the name of 'the international community'. The actions may be taken to prevent conflict, as part of conflict, or as part of post-conflict reconstruction. These actions can help in the forceful creation of a more neutral environment for elections (a predominant motive in Cambodia and East Timor and, initially, in Bosnia and Herzegovina) or for the coupling of elections with a longer, more sustained process of reformulating governance patterns (as latterly in Bosnia).

The methods of information intervention can be divided under three temporal headings: pre-conflict, mid-conflict, and post-conflict. The appropriateness of a given technique depends on the stage that a potential or actual conflict has reached. At the same time, the mere possibility of using certain techniques may hinge on political will and economic resources, which moral or pro-democratic arguments cannot summon into existence. Alison Des Forges notes in Chapter 8 that the United States jammed radio stations in Iraq in 1991, but refused to do so in Rwanda during the 1994 genocide. State Department lawyers advised that jamming in Rwanda would violate international telecommunications law and international conventions protecting freedom of information and expression. But in light of the jamming done in Iraq earlier, this may have been a mask for lack of political will in high places.

If the failure to intervene against Rwandan media in 1994 was the starkest illustration of this constraint, it also applies to large-scale media sector reforms following conflict, for example the restructuring of state broadcasters and the passage of new media laws. On the other hand, some interventions, such as NATO's bombing of Serbian state television in April 1999, are driven by political will to the exclusion of clear moral or pro-democratic motives.

Finally, it should be noted that the term implies two kinds of activity that should be distinguished conceptually and practically. One kind is the enhancement of public affairs and media relations ('public diplomacy') through the use of new technology to project a certain (political) message at a certain audience with or without the sovereign's consent. The other is media development activity, which, in various ways, aims to assist in building a democratic media sphere. In some circumstances these activities are complementary; in others, not. Jamie Metzl's equal interest in 'public diplomacy' and human rights reflects an ambiguity that is intrinsic to the idea of information intervention.

Perhaps this ambiguity and its associated tensions dissolve in the forging of integrated approaches to information policy and management, as part of conflict prevention or peace-building. Yet it remains important, as Philip Taylor reminds us in Chapter 11, to keep these two dimensions separate. The pervasive expansion of civilian and military information activities makes it more important to ensure that certain operational distinctions are preserved. Psyops must be kept apart from both deception activities and media operations. If this is not done, perceptions that media are intended to serve the needs of external propaganda (for example, the interests of a United Nations mission or of a donor government such as the United States) may damage the credibility of media development efforts. And the loss of credibility with a target audience can be fatal to a peace operation.

Naturally this perception will be difficult or even impossible to avoid if, in fact, the intervening authority manipulates the media development agenda for short-term gain. NGOs perform a valuable service when they act as watchdogs to detect such stratagems, and protest loudly when they occur. The delicacies of the funding relationship between NGOs and the intervening governmental organizations may, however, silence the watchdogs, or at least muffle their barks. There are no perfect safeguards.

The Role and Rule of Law

Political, not legal considerations drive intervention. Yet the role of law and rule of law are central to any debate about information intervention. The United Nations, NATO, and Western democracies all purport to be ruled by law and to act in accordance with it. But international law has not clearly enunciated the circumstances in which the international community, or any member of it, can take steps to modify the flow of information in a zone of existing or potential conflict.

Much of this book deals with the interaction between information intervention and international law, human rights conventions, and agreements among states. Three chapters directly address questions of international law. The rule of law – compliance with accepted principles – should govern when states intervene, individually or collectively, in the media space of another sovereign state, and should govern their actions once intervention has taken place. This is particularly the case when multilateral intervention has a humanitarian motive. When the international community undertakes actions for moral purposes, it asks to be judged by the strictest legal criteria.

The rule of law does not provide yet one more vehicle by which government can wield and abuse power. On the contrary, it establishes principles that constrain government power and oblige it to behave according to a series of prescribed and publicly known rules. Adherence to the rule of law entails far more than the mechanical application of static legal technicalities; it involves an evolutionary search for those institutions and processes that will best facilitate authentic stability through justice.

Balkan and African atrocities in the 1990s encouraged a growing consensus that preventing 'ethnic cleansing' and the potential for genocidal activity are justifications for humanitarian intervention. Above all, the explosive mobilising role that Radio-Television Libre des Milles Collines (RTLM) played in Rwanda in 1994, with its explicit incitement for Hutu to slaughter Tutsi, became the common point of reference in arguments that the international community should develop a capacity to intervene against incendiary media. Alison Des Forges' material on Rwanda (Chapter 8), with its double focus on domestic media abuse abetted by international spinelessness (dressed in legalist scruple), is pivotal to the book.

The first two parts of the book reflect this growing consensus, and also explore how the obstacles to intervention might be overcome, so that a range of sanctions can be used against incendiary media in a context where massive abuses of human rights are liable to occur. The rule of law presumes that there is law, which governs. Even after the interventions of the 1990s, the contours of a legal regime are still being shaped. In Chapter 2, Stephanie Farrior explores the origins of the limitations on the freedom to receive and impart information contained in internationally agreed human rights treaties and conventions. It is not an easy jump in jurisprudential logic (though it may seem so) to argue that if these rights are subject to internal limitations that authorize or oblige the State to take action against its own media when they foment hate in certain circumstances, then the international community should be able to take similar action across sovereign borders. Nor does it follow that if states can address hate speech to protect minority populations within their boundaries, they can act in a humanitarian vein to do the same elsewhere.

Yet the body of law that has developed concerning state power over hate-related and genocide-inciting propaganda is a source for ideas that delineate the authority of international bodies and their ability to conduct multilateral actions. Farrior concludes that 'under international human rights law, . . . unilateral or multilateral intervention against media engaged in inciting racial or ethnic hatred can constitute a permissible limitation on free expression and on the right to receive and impart information and ideas', regardless of frontiers.

Even with this clearance given, the relationship between cross-border information intervention and law remains inchoate. It is not yet evident whether or how far the practices and standards analyzed by Farrior are translatable to concrete examples that indicate when intervention is legally permissible. This is why Metzl argues for an improved mode of developing legal norms that authorize and (by the same token) limit information inter-vention; and why Eric Blinderman argues (in Chapter 3) that new forms of practice need to be developed – leading to the development of new legal norms – that would allow cross-border intervention against certain kinds of media in limited contexts. In Chapter 5, Peter Krug and Monroe E. Price consider the deficit in development of legal norms from another, more operational perspective (see below).

Along with the exceptions related to the free flow of information, there are three exceptions to the non-intervention norm. Chapter VII of the United Nations Charter entitles the Security Council to determine measures against threats to international peace and security. What is more, Article 41 of the Charter explicitly provides that such measures may include 'complete or partial interruption of [. . .] postal, telegraphic, radio, and other means of communication'. Accordingly, in his analysis of the customary legal expressions of the non-intervention norm in public international law, Blinderman argues that if the Security Council assesses that 'a particular state's media outlets are creating a situation that threatens peace and security or if a particular state's media outlets threaten to impede the effect of prior Security Council resolutions, the Council may authorize member states to take any measures not involving the use of force [. . .] or it may authorize member states to interrupt transmissions.'

The second relevant exception to the non-intervention norm is the 'humanitarian assistance' exception. This exception covers action that has, as its immediate goal, the prevention of human suffering. While this condition may or may not be difficult to invoke in the context of supporting media outlets in potential or actual conflict zones, it is important that forms of information intervention fall within the parameters of international humanitarian law. As Blinderman puts it, 'international humanitarian legal obligations limit a state's sovereign right to allow individuals within the State to use media outlets to incite systematic and widespread human rights violations.'

This has very practical implications: to the extent possible, assistance to certain media should be categorized as humanitarian assistance. Blinderman again: '[A]ny unilateral information intervention strategy that merely provides humanitarian assistance . . . will not violate the non-intervention norm so long as it is given to media outlets or individuals that comply with basic human rights obligations.' As Helen Darbishire notes (Chapter 12), UNESCO quietly set a precedent during the war of Yugoslav succession by redefining humanitarian assistance to include the provision of aid to independent media.

The third exception, provided by the Genocide Convention, authorizes action to prevent incitement to commit genocide. Given the role of Nazi propaganda, the role of media must have been high among the drafters' concerns. (Farrior quotes memorably from the UN Secretariat's commentary on an early draft of the Convention. 'Genocide cannot take place', it said, 'unless a certain state of mind previously has been created.') However, the international refusal to stop the 1994 incitement in Rwanda taught a bleak lesson. The political obligations upon states that ensue from legally defining a particular human rights abuse as genocide are so daunting that this exception is likely to remain of little practical utility as a means to enjoin intervention against incendiary media.

The lack of clarity over the applicability of legal limits on media freedom is even denser with the Internet. If unscrupulous regimes or extremist groups have not yet effectively exploited this situation, it is partly because Internet dissemination is still sparse in the world's conflict zones, and partly because governments are still less able to control the Internet than traditional media. The bottom-up development of the Internet contrasts strikingly with the early history of broadcasting, though as Patrick Carmichael shows (Chapter 13), governments are adjusting to new realities and engaging in various forms of multilateral or unilateral negotiations that allow them to conserve control or influence over their information space. What is more, the new information technology makes it increasingly possible to shape the information environment in a third party state at a distance, without the use of force. For these reasons, Eric Hobsbawm's warning – quoted as an epigraph – that without a legal frame of 'clearly defined rules and criteria', intervention techniques are open to misuse by whichever state or states have the means, is highly pertinent to the media sector.

Use of Force

Under international law, states are generally prohibited from using or threatening to use force against the territorial integrity or political independence of other states unless the Security Council has authorized such use under Article 42 of the UN Charter.[40] As we saw, humanitarian intervention may include the threat or use of force duly authorized by the Security Council. This is not clearly the case with information intervention. Eric Blinderman's analysis in Chapter 3 turns precisely on the question of whether information intervention involves 'the use of force'. He concludes that many elements of information intervention implicate neither the use of force nor breaches of sovereignty. Therefore, they do not have to satisfy the legal requirements of intervention. However, this does not settle the issue.

Of course, the bombardment of transmitters, certain jamming techniques, and other sweeping techniques of information manipulation (such as cyberwar) may be, or come to be, categorized as the use of force.[41] On the intervention scale, jamming is more forceful than 'peace broadcasting'. It encompasses a variety of external tools that prevent a transmission from reaching its intended audience.[42] International legal principles that would or would not authorize jamming are quite different from those that deal with the seizure of transmitters or other steps, which involve the use of troops or arms or other forms of physical coercion to curtail or obstruct broadcasts.[43] This is so because jamming does not involve the destructive use of arms to threaten life or destroy property.

Yet the question of what standards should govern the actions of international actors when the mode of intervention *can* be characterized as the use of force does not (yet) have an automatic answer. For example, traditional international legal thought would hold, in relevant part, that no state may forcibly intervene in the domestic affairs of another state unless acting in self-defence or with prior UN authorization pursuant to its Chapter VII powers. Still others have long argued that Article 2(4) of the UN Charter contains an implied exception that allows states to use force against other states that commit systematic and widespread human rights violations.

Nevertheless, the use of force to prevent or stop the commission of human rights violations is likely to remain anomalous. Yet, the majority of techniques and instances of information-related intervention are non-forceful. This is the prime source of their attraction for the international community. As they search for intermediate measures to diffuse human rights crises before they occur, and as information technology develops further, states are likely to make increasing use of non-military technological means against other states to prevent the dissemination of messages that incite conflict, and to enhance the production and reception of countervailing messages.

Consent

Today's looser understanding of intervention places extra stress on the element of 'consent' in peace and humanitarian operations. In the complex interventions of the 1990s, the international community learned that a host government's consent often turned out to mean little more than basic permission for a mission to deploy in country. Beyond that, consent could not be taken for granted.[44] The host government would challenge the international community, whether on symbolic issues (thumbing one's nose at the great powers can boost popularity ratings), or to prevent the international community from implementing unwanted peace term provisions.[45]

Implementing the media aspects of a peacekeeping mandate is liable to be contested and qualified in practice, even though rarely challenged openly. What ensues are often games of cat and mouse between weak states with few resources other than legal sovereignty and total dedication to a certain outcome (not necessarily reducible to regime-survival), and international missions notionally endowed with political and moral strength, but usually hobbled by the lowest-common-denominator caution that characterizes multilateral operations when great power interests are not directly at stake.

There are several reasons why media and information policy are highly vulnerable to such subversion. While the intervening state might consider media and information as a 'soft' issue, the host authorities usually consider them a crucial political tool. Hence they may not hesitate to undermine public support for a mission by distorting public perception of international objectives. John Marston (Chapter 6) and David Wimhurst (Chapter 10) describe the difficulties of working in nominally-but-barely consensual environments. Although the UN's mandated control over the media in Cambodia 'should logically have meant that UNTAC could show whatever it wanted [on television],' Marston writes, 'it did not in fact really have the power.'

At the same time, intergovernmental organizations have been reluctant to insist that their field missions have suitable access to media, or that host authorities cease to disseminate hostile or incendiary propaganda via media under their control. This reticence – which is traceable to underestimation of media effects – contributed to international failures in Africa and the Balkans. Nor has the international community yet devised a standard strategy for public information (media relations) in peacekeeping or peace-building contexts.

For obvious reasons, media reform is even more controversial with host governments than a bold public information strategy. Unlike the German and Japanese reconstructions, undertaken on the basis of full-fledged occupation, the recent experiments in post-conflict areas have rested on foundation of general 'consent', without the benefit of an established media reform programme.

In Chapter 4, Julie Mertus concludes that even if a peacekeeping operation does not qualify as an occupation, where the sovereign has consented to it, international humanitarian law still provides a justification for the operation to engage in elements of 'information intervention'. One important implication of this argument is that the international community need not be so hesitant to act against media abuses, provided it does so within the limits that Mertus and Blinderman describe. Another is that the actions and issues dealt with in this book may be usefully considered in the larger context of 'humanitarian intervention'.

Before leaving the notion of consent, its other relevant meaning should be mentioned. The consent of the local population 'may be vital to a [humanitarian or peace] mission's success'.[46] Such popular consent is something quite different from governmental attitudes; it will largely reflect people's under-standing of international objectives. If a mission is not to abandon the shaping of public perception to local authorities, it has to establish credibility with that same public. This leads us back to the enhanced public affairs function of media intervention, discussed above.

Human Rights

In the tussle between rival claims of human rights and state sovereignty, the massive advantage enjoyed by the latter has been eroded in recent years. But only somewhat. Control over the flow of information within sovereign states will continue to be closely defended. While information intervention is often articulated as rights-based, it is much more likely to come about as a means of increasing the chances of international community success in a wider inter-vention, for example by protecting peacekeepers and weakening hardline factions in election campaigns. If the media can be democratized and freedom of speech increased, these are spin-off benefits of intervention rather than its mobilising objective.

Even in 1945, governments' seizure of information space to make it more democratic, using the prerogatives of absolute authority to develop media that would in the future be free of government domination, was an activity ripe with irony.[47] The growth over the subsequent half-century of 'a shared human rights culture' has deepened this irony by generating higher requirements and expectations of official accountability.[48] These virtues of accountability are especially required of states that act collectively against one or more states on broadly humanitarian grounds.

Hence the reference to human rights in our subtitle. Multilateral interventions for the purpose of achieving or strengthening peace are required to respect international human rights norms and standards that military interventions routinely flout. For example, when NATO was bombarding the Federal Republic of Yugoslavia in April 1999, a decision was taken to target the headquarters of Serbian state broadcasting. This decision was controversial even in the context of a military operation motivated by humanitarian concerns.[49]

Non-governmental organizations are both the beneficiaries of this shared human rights culture, and the agents of its expansion. During the 1990s, media freedom NGOs became an indispensable part of the international scene, whether by directly collaborating with governmental and intergovernmental bodies, complementing their efforts, chiding them, or discharging their critical duty of opposing short-term expediency.

Our chapters on Bosnia and Kosovo illustrate how tensions between NGOs and governmental bodies are at their sharpest when intervening entities breach the highest principles of media freedom. The assertion of United States First Amendment principles has provided an example. Notwithstanding the values inherent in the jurisprudence of the US Constitution's free speech clause, difficulties have arisen where primacy was claimed for its applicability. This is especially the case in environments with significant unresolved security issues and legitimate debates about competing approaches.

Applying imported rights norms, such as those of the United States First Amendment to the Balkans, brings problems which are intriguing at best, bitterly divisive at worst. Even the clearest international standards on media regulation can have a somewhat hollow resonance when brought to a conflict zone, which lacks a functioning legal framework and judicial system.

Each time the international community intervenes to shut down a media outlet, the line between information intervention and censorship becomes blurred. The real test of an information intervention is not only whether it positively transforms the host society. Rather, the intervention must also be judged according to whether it was carried out within a spirit of democratic change. Yet situations may easily arise when intervening organizations consider repressive action essential to stabilize their area of responsibility. Even more dismaying for NGOs, these organizations may plausibly argue that the longer-term good of the society requires short-term censorship of media outlets.

With any externally driven attempt to restructure the media sector in a conflict zone, the question is bound to arise: who shall guard the guardians of free media? There is no answer except to require that reformers themselves be held accountable to the same standards that they inculcate in the conflict zone. Yet, as several of our chapters show, the practical pressures and longer-term objectives of peace-building in a conflict zone may make it counter-productive to subject the intervening entity, from the outset, to the highest international standards of human rights, including media freedom.

Reflecting on his experience as the first head of the United Nations mission in Kosovo, Bernard Kouchner suggested that it may be 'a mistake to implement international norms too quickly. To arrive in a place like Kosovo after the war and to think of implementing all the latest human rights norms [. . .] is much too soon. What is a good idea, in peacekeeping and peace-building missions, is to come with a protection kit, a temporary law-and-order kit, and a press freedom kit.'[50] These ideas merit careful consideration. First, Kouchner cautions, perhaps in the same way that some economists believe the International Monetary Fund's 'shock-therapy' has done more harm than good in most transitional countries, that the quickest possible introduction of international human rights norms in post-conflict zones can be harmful.

Kits and Modules

Kouchner's second point is less provocative but equally timely: the international community should develop a set of standard procedures or options to assist media development in post-conflict contexts. This is a common-sense proposal. In Cambodia and Bosnia, media reform strategies were designed in the process of enacting them. Without a toolkit of agreed objectives and procedures, intervening organizations will keep reinventing the wheel. Also, multilateral interventions place a special premium on co-ordination. Without pre-operational agreement on ends and means, inordinate time and energy may be lost as competing agencies haggle.

To have any chance of wider acceptance, however, a press freedom kit has to combine operational realism with high international standards. Yet, part of Kouchner's point is that a post-conflict society needs an end to interethnic revenge killings more than it needs the highest standards of media freedom.[51] In the hierarchy of rights, media freedom may not occupy first place. Anybody in Kouchner's position should be ready to breach the highest standards in certain circumstances. At the same time, few media freedom NGOs will ever approve a policy that results in the deliberate lowering of media freedom standards; it seems to contradict their reason for existing.

Such differences could be eased, perhaps even reconciled, by agreement on a legal and regulatory 'module'. Krug and Price consider how norms have developed in the context of actual interventions. They inquire whether an emergent architecture of media law – such as the one that evolved in Bosnia – establishes an institutional-normative model for intervention in the wake of active belligerence and under the administration of intergovernmental organizations.

In the process, Krug and Price suggest a framework for analyzing whether the rules and decisions formulated by such processes meet international standards. With reference to situations where the international community has executive authority, the authors identify a module for peacekeeping-related information intervention that comprises a self-contained set of mechanisms with its own legislative, executive, and judicial functions separate from any domestic legal regime. Reflecting a sceptical acceptance of the need for an exceptionally vigilant regulation of media content in post-conflict societies, the authors' module is defined by the appointment of a standing, but temporary, regulatory authority operating pursuant to a set of discrete normative rules and an institutional model for the application of those norms.

Beyond Suppression: Media for Peace

While jamming may be essential in extreme circumstances, it is a crude and negative means of countering incendiary propaganda and influencing war-torn societies. Far preferable is to deliver impartial information and peace-building messages through the media. This activity, which is sometimes called 'peace broadcasting', has been attempted in three ways: by establishing international outlets for the purpose, by setting up new indigenous media, and by working with established local media.

The first approach succeeded in Cambodia, as John Marston shows. The second was tried in Bosnia, where it failed spectacularly for reasons explored by Thompson and De Luce (Chapter 7); and in West Africa, where it has achieved some remarkable results. The third method has been widely practised in the Balkans. While it incurs fewer risks to the intervener, it is worth applying only in places where the existing media system is sound enough to be developed and does not actually need to be supplanted. By the same token, the first method proved ineffective in the Balkans, where the public was too sophisticated to be impressed by UN or NATO propaganda for peace.

The logic of creating an alternative system of media outlets is simple: to disseminate content that is neutral and peace-oriented, a structure that is neutral and peace-oriented is required. To be effective, however, this structure must have credibility – an attribute that cannot be conjured by technical resources alone, and may be unattainable where government-controlled media may strive to discredit the outlets attempting to be neutral and peace-oriented.

As a rule credibility is more easily won by local journalists working for local media. When strengthening indigenous media outlets, the international community needs not only to boost particular peace-building content, but also to build professional media that can outlast the intervention which sponsors them and thereby strengthen the public sphere and civil society. Constructing a network independent of the international community would also contribute to the creation of a pluralist infrastructure, an informed electorate, and a heritage of non-partisan information.

The dilemma mentioned above also arises over peace broadcasting.

Replacing negative with positive propaganda may be necessary as a short-term measure, but does little or nothing to resolve the deeper problem of political manipulation in the media sector. As a rule, journalists should not preach 'peace' – though of course situations can arise where they should do nothing else.

Ideally, peace broadcasting consists of professional, pluralist journalism. In practice, there may often be pressures to exclude certain kinds of information and highlight other kinds. Hence there is 'a certain tension between using the news media for specific and directed purposes and, at the same time, trying to carry the message that a professional and open news media should not be controlled'.[52] The price of preventing this tension from becoming destructive is to preserve a vigilant separation between international propaganda and the development of indigenous media.

One of the most positive cases where peace broadcasting and media development coincided was STAR Radio in Liberia. It was established in July 1997 by Fondation Hirondelle, from Switzerland, shortly before the first post-conflict democratic elections.[53] It was a subspecies of international broadcasting and of the use of media in post-conflict settings and an example of an external government providing financial assistance through a non-government entity to address the sources of conflict within society.[54] Its fate also illustrated how vulnerable information intervention can be to obstruction by local authorities, untrammelled by international executive authority.

On the premise that 'impartial, independent, and factual information helps to appease socio-political tensions and challenges the culture of war', Fondation Hirondelle sought to create an independent radio station that provided 'pertinent and propaganda-free information to help create the conditions for the return to peace'. In STAR Radio's Charter, Hirondelle defined the station as an 'independent regional radio with a humanitarian vocation'. Hirondelle contended that 'the reception of essential, concrete, and independent information in circumstances of crisis [is] as necessary to survival as food and aid'. Because of its stated purpose 'to provide useful, impartial, and independent information to populations deprived of such by conflict or natural disaster' the Fondation took responsibility for transforming 'the job of informing into a tool of peace'.[55]

The US Agency for International Development (USAID) financed STAR to support 'an objective and independent press through the establishment of a locally owned FM and short wave radio station [. . .] and strengthening the media by training journalists to improve the quality of reporting and establishing a private and independent printing press'.[56] The Office of Transition Initiatives (OTI), part of USAID, provided a grant to purchase 2,640 wind-up short wave AM/FM radios for distribution to electoral polling sites and community groups to provide better information for Liberians taking part in elections.[57]

The station soon became extremely popular. Doubtless for this reason, the government closed down STAR Radio's FM broadcasts in January 1998, but through negotiations (and after intervention by the international community) rebroadcasts were permitted.[58] The following October, the short wave frequencies were withdrawn.[59] The Liberian Ministry of Posts and Telecommunications claimed that this withdrawal resulted from the Liberian government's decision to ban non-governmental shortwave outlets.[60] Furthermore, the government established a general policy that made it illegal for non-Liberian entities to operate a shortwave frequency in Liberia.[61]

On 15 March 2000, the government again ordered the closure of STAR Radio in addition to the suspension of Catholic-run Radio Veritas.[62] President Charles Taylor said the decision to close the stations was based upon 'a security threat created by agents provocateurs using the news media to abuse the unprecedented freedom of speech and press now prevailing in the country'.[63] The Ministry of Information, Culture, and Tourism accused STAR Radio of 'broadcasting and hosting political talk shows, news, interviews, and programs that have damaging political effects that tend to undermine the peace, security and stability of Liberia'.[64]

The fact that suppression of outlets such as STAR Radio cannot, in the end, be prevented does not render them less worthwhile. In some circumstances, international sponsors should even regard the likelihood of government repression as one gauge of a project's value.[65]

The Management of Media Space

Even more is at stake in information intervention than preventing hate speech; and very much more than refining the 'public diplomacy' of the great powers, however laudable those powers' political objectives may be. The longer-term motive should be to rebuild shattered societies on the bedrock of democratic institutions. If free media are essential to open societies and accountable governance, there can be no real recovery from conflict, or removal of the threat of massive human rights abuse until free media are established where, for the most part, they have never existed.

Overhauling international legal norms will not achieve this. Even if the norms missed by Metzl and Blinderman had been in place by 1990, and some international authority had existed to oversee compliance with the free-speech provisions of international conventions and treaties, the main abuses of mass media in Serbia, Croatia, and Bosnia could still have been perpetrated. For, although these abuses were intrinsic to the belligerent strategies of various factions, they were more sophisticated than those in Rwanda; the incitement was probably too oblique to be actionable outside domestic courts – which were either impotent against the regimes, or controlled by them.[66]

While international reluctance to authorize the suppression of incendiary media will remain the rule, the future is likely to bring more Balkan models than Rwandan models of media abuse, requiring responses more complex than jamming. Institutional and legal reform are necessary to develop structures and practices that will give journalists a chance to work in conditions conducive to the creation of democratic standards.

This is why the present book focuses more on media restructuring than on coercive acts of intervention. Restructuring encompasses many activities and actors. The overall purpose is to develop democratic and pluralist media, usually through a combination of economic and technical assistance backed by political incentives and pressure.

What has been called 'the post-Cold War style of instant intervention and quick exit' is not designed to provide the 'long-term, unspectacular commitment to the rebuilding of society itself'.[67] Applied to media and information, this means that interventions deal with effects or symptoms (through public information or public diplomacy) rather than causes (through media reform). Yet the interventions discussed in this book concern societies so bereft of institutions that the interveners have little option but to rebuild, reconstruct, and establish a framework for enduring stability if they are to withdraw their forces without grave risk of implosion. The effects of a quick exit can be so ruinous that the rebuilding of society has also come to be seen as serving the interests of the interveners as well as those of the receiving society. This is why the past decade – since the United Nations mission to Namibia (1989–90) – saw the growth of institution-building as a core function of peace operations where the disintegration of states posed a threat to international peace and security.

Reforming Laws and Regulations

Law reform plays a key part in legitimating and, perhaps, facilitating change. Law becomes the vehicle for articulating goals and establishing the machinery for meeting those goals. When the international community is present in post-conflict circumstances, it has reconstructed the media regime by drafting or helping to draft laws, encouraging self-regulation, and establishing broadcast licensing mechanisms.

In Rwanda, and in the former Yugoslavia, a partial liberalization of the media system worked into the dynamics of internal extremism. The attractive informality of new, ostensibly independent outlets won credibility for extremist agendas. The absence of effective regulation, transparent ownership, or genuine competition made this possible. These shortcomings must be urgently repaired when conflict is over, by establishing effective media laws and regulations and reforming media institutions. The experience in Kosovo since 1999 is particularly instructive; there, the international authorities progressed within a matter of months from imposing draconian decrees against incitement, to instituting an autonomous check on their own power, in the form of the Media Appeals Board.

The revision of media laws and regulations in conflict areas is a form of international assistance discussed in several chapters. This technique evolved remarkably in the Balkans in the late 1990s. As an activity, it perhaps appears too consensual and staid to be called intervention, yet the term is appropriate.

In many cases, governments in south-eastern Europe in the 1990s had no wish to reform their media laws and regulations in line with international standards. On the contrary, retaining influence over the media by delaying reform was the name of the game. The OSCE, the Council of Europe, and Western governments acting through these organizations as well as bilaterally, and often following the lead of non-governmental actors, made headway against this resistance by linking progress in media reform to the prospects of integration into 'Euro-Atlantic structures', a shorthand for the European Union, NATO, and international financial institutions. Where this leverage was lacking, as for example with Serbia under Slobodan Milosevic, no progress in reform could be made. In such cases, effective intervention had to be robustly political, and preferably linked to sanctions. Western emphasis on the lack of media freedom in Serbia, and the flow of economic support to politically independent outlets, did help to erode the Serbian regime.

State and Public Broadcasting

The question has arisen in post-conflict zones of what to do with the State media sector, which often dwarfs the private media and is the biggest violator of the principles of ethical journalism. Here, ideological differences between European and United States interveners have sometimes been sharp. Many American officials and donors saw little purpose in trying to reform the State sector dinosaurs and considered development of the private sector to be the first priority. While Europeans are generally less sceptical about the public sector, no single model of public service broadcasting and no coherent strategy for reforming the State giants in Europe's potential conflict zones has emerged.

Leaving the State media in the hands of repressive or violent regimes is unacceptable. Mere deregulation and dismantling, on the other hand, solves nothing and may benefit the individuals that are fomenting conflict in the regime if they also control nascent markets through patronage. Of course, the challenge of reforming the State broadcasters in all transitional countries is enormous. To quote Karol Jakubowicz of Poland: 'From both a conceptual and political point of view, it is hard to postulate the creation of a public service sector of broadcasting in a highly politicised society with a fundamentally unstable political and party system, where politics and a power struggle invade and subordinate, to their ends, practically every aspect of public life.'[68] If this is the view from Warsaw, what can be expected in Sarajevo and Pristina, let alone Kigali, Grozny, Dili or Kabul? Yet, experience in the 1990s suggests that, due in part to economic constraints and national identity concerns, no better alternative than attempting to establish some form of public service broadcasting exists for societies riddled with corrupt and feeble media markets, ruled by ineffective media regulation, and saturated by state-controlled, politicized media.

Intergovernmental Organizations

Intergovernmental organizations (IGOs) have been the main external agents of media reform in conflict zones. Four of these organizations merit particular attention. The United Nations and the OSCE have pioneered successive institution-building efforts in the Balkans and elsewhere; UNESCO and the Council of Europe have come to play central roles in officially redefining assistance to media, and developing legal standards.

The United Nations

This book's prime implied institutional readership is located in the headquarters of the United Nations, in New York. There are several reasons for this. Insofar as practical techniques of post-conflict information intervention have been established, they have done so within the framework of UN structures. The UN's role in legitimating, organizing, and implementing multilateral interventions to prevent, stop, or mitigate conflicts is irreplaceable. The organization's unexpectedly rapid recovery from the nadir of the mid-1990s reflects the lack of alternatives. Several regional organizations such as NATO or the OSCE have come to assume responsibilities in peacemaking and peace-building missions that were unimaginable only a dozen years ago; yet they have not supplanted the UN, nor could they do so.

UN officials have generally taken a cautious approach to information, whether in the context of peace operations or elsewhere. In the Department of Peacekeeping Operations (DPKO), the exceptions to this rule have sometimes had to watch their backs. David Wimhurst alludes to his difficulties in East Timor when the Indonesian government persuaded some in the UN Secretariat that he should be removed as UN spokesman there. At least two spokesmen for the UN mission in Bosnia in 1995 were threatened with removal when senior officials in New York were disturbed by their unusual (but fully justified) frankness.

Institutional conservatism is powerful at the UN, always liable to feed on the handily slow-moving procedures of multilateralism. DPKO has been reluctant to adapt its traditional concept of 'public information' in line with broader changes during the 1990s.[69] UN peace operations were no more spared by the heightened expectations of democratic transparency and accountability than were other national and intergovernmental institutions following the end of the Cold War. Advances in information technology played their part in fostering these expectations.

The Secretariat's attention to issues of 'information intervention' has grown remarkably since Boutros Boutros-Ghali, then the Secretary-General, issued his seminal report on peace operations, 'An Agenda for Peace', in 1992. That report said nothing about the salience of public information in successful peacemaking efforts, or the importance of media reform in post-conflict environments.[70] His follow-up report rightly identified the need for peace-keeping operations to have 'an effective information capacity [. . .] to enable them to explain their mandate to the population and [. . .] to counter mis-information disseminated about them, even by the parties themselves'.[71] Yet, despite eloquently identifying 'the essential goal' of post-conflict peace-building as being 'the creation of structures for the institutionalisation of peace',[72] the Secretary-General still had nothing to say about media sector reform.

Boutros-Ghali's successor, Kofi Annan, had led DPKO during the mid-1990s. As Secretary-General, he broke new ground in demonstrating institutional accountability for the United Nations' abject failure in Bosnia and Rwanda, by overseeing the preparation of reports that were both thoroughly researched and frequently critical. Annan has also shown a robust awareness of the importance of information in the context of peace operations. He argued that a peacekeeping mission's 'power of communication with the [local] population' forms one 'source of leverage' that can be used 'not only to push the parties to abide by their commitments, but also to insist on respect for themselves and their mandate'.[73] While this may seem an uncontroversial observation, it presupposes a far more engaged and pro-active, indeed 'political' understanding of public information than any previous secretary-general would have avowed.

Early in 2000, Annan set up a committee to assess the UN's ability to conduct peace operations and make practical recommendations.[74] The Brahimi Report, published the following August, contained two recommendations about public information. Recommendation twelve called for designated information specialists to join 'rapidly deployable startup teams' with 'basic start-up kits to enable team experts to work effectively in the field from the moment of arrival'.

Recommendation seventeen proposed establishment of a dedicated Planning and Support Unit 'to undertake and provide operational planning and support for information components in peace missions'. This idea had a second, ulterior purpose; it was designed to overcome, by means of the new dedicated unit, a harmful turf-battle in the UN Secretariat, where the Department of Public Information had guarded its primacy in all matters dealing with information, including in peacekeeping, despite having no particular resources or will to provide such support.

If implemented, these recommendations should improve the handling of information by UN field missions. However, as David Wimhurst explains, implementation has been blocked at the committee stage. Outsiders can only guess whether the blockage is due more to budgetary constraints or to member states' conventional reluctance to endow the Secretariat with autonomous capacity in areas linked to intelligence-gathering. Whatever the reason, these recommendations are at time of writing still gathering dust in the Secretariat.

Concerned with boosting the performance of peacekeeping missions, the Brahimi Report did not make media restructuring an element of post-conflict peace-building. This was appropriate. An international mission's efforts at media reform are not merely different from its media-relations activity; the two may be linked by mutual tension – and also, in many cases, by the fact that the host government is equally hostile to the exercise of both functions.

In its own self-interest, any organization logically seeks the most effective means of persuading the local and international media to view it positively. All of these multilateral operations – whether run by the UN, NATO, or any other organization – need to develop their public information capacity to deal with media that are less deferential and more intrusive than ever before. The management of media space in a conflict zone, however, is another matter entirely. Its purpose is to develop professionalism and improve standards in all media sectors, not in the mission's own immediate (political) interest but for the sake of fulfilling the host society's longer-term needs. This requires a different mandate and other expertise – people who can assist media restructuring, journalists' training, the drafting of laws and regulations, and so forth.

At the same time, the two functions are in practice contiguous and indeed closely related. Wimhurst's account of UNAMET shows that the mission's attempts to provide objective information to the population before an internationally supervised plebiscite placed it, necessarily, at odds with media outlets under the influence of authorities who opposed important elements of the mission's mandate. He vividly conveys the helter-skelter of crisis-management, caught between resource-deprivation and high principle, improvizing solutions to urgent problems, trying to outwit local extremists without dismaying the senior-level fainthearts in the Secretariat. Wimhurst's chapter suggests that peacekeeping operations require explicitly authorized access to local media to protect their own security, though also to build credibility with the local population.

The UNAMET Public Information Office had a very practical interest in seeing improvements in the professionalism of Indonesian and Timorese media. Yet, a full-fledged media operation – including efforts at media reform and development – could only begin *after* the vote, in the context of a mission with an institution-building mandate.[75] In practice, an extensive, pro-active media operation is only achievable when conducted within a broader institution-building mandate, which is most unlikely to be issued in pre- or mid-conflict conditions.

What was true in East Timor was also true in Cambodia, Bosnia, Kosovo – wherever the international community was involved in a complex attempt to establish democratic institutions in conflict-torn societies. From this point of view, media reform and development is fully in accord with the international community's short-term interests, as well as the host society's longer-term needs.

Deputy Secretary-General Louise Frechette's remarks on World Press Freedom Day in 2000 suggested the Secretariat's awareness of the operative links between media relations and media reform. Describing these functions in the same breath, she observed: 'Upon arrival in a post-conflict environment, our first challenge is to explain to the population at large the role of a United Nations mission [. . .] Our second, and equally important challenge, is to begin fostering a local press, by employing local media professionals, and by providing the means of broadcast and offering training programmes for journalists and technicians. [. . .] Our peacekeeping missions in Sierra Leone – and elsewhere – are doing their part to help indigenous journalists as best we can. Building a free and thriving press is an essential component of our post-conflict strategy in every mission. But often, we are not given the resources to do so.'[76]

If these comments appear more like an expression of intent than a description of practice, it is an intention that everyone interested in the development of free and independent media, where these are most urgently needed, should support.

Other Intergovernmental Organizations

The OSCE has done much to implement media reform in conflict zones – more indeed than the UN. Sometimes, as in the Balkans, this has been achieved in connection with a mandate to organize elections. The creation of the required neutral political atmosphere for an election has afforded leverage for information intervention. Given this experience, and the OSCE's roots in the Helsinki process with its commitment to human rights, it would make sense for the OSCE to systematize its knowledge and capacity in this field. To some extent the Office of the OSCE Representative on Freedom of the Media, established in 1997, does this. So slender is the OSCE's infrastructure, however, and so determined are most of its members not to see this change, that there seems little prospect of mustering extra operational resources for information.

UNESCO has played a key role in redefining assistance to media as humanitarian assistance. As Helen Darbishire notes, UNESCO worked with NGOs to get assistance to media exempted from the international sanctions imposed on Yugoslavia in the 1990s. 'This marked an important policy shift at the international level [. . .] The principle that media assistance should be included with humanitarian assistance has now become well established.' This achievement might be said to reflect UNESCO's long standing commitment to develop the autonomous media capacity of developing countries. Also, it is UNESCO that has made the best attempt yet to codify recommendations to the international community on media in conflict and post-conflict areas.[77]

The fourth relevant IGO is the Council of Europe. The Media Section in the Directorate of Human Rights organized expertise missions throughout Europe's transitional countries, offering guidance on media legislation and regulation, commenting on draft laws, meeting with government officials and NGOs, and developing the application of internationally agreed standards. These activities were conducted in the context of the transitional countries' strong aspiration to gain membership of the European Union – a goal that gave leverage to the Council of Europe and others seeking to introduce international human rights standards. Membership in the Council of Europe became a way-station to EU candidacy. As obscure conventions and ministerial agreements came to apply to would-be candidates for EU membership, the Council grew from a talking-shop into an organization helping to shape democratic standards for the continent.

Coda

Early in October 2001, a United States missile strike disabled the Taliban regime's radio station in Kabul. Shortly afterwards, the US commenced psyops from an aerial radio station circling overhead. 'Noble people of Afghanistan, the forces of the United States are passing through your area.'[78]

When the 'war on terrorism' was declared in September and bombardment of Afghanistan began the following month, the Bush administration seemed to see itself as taking America and its coalition allies across a watershed, away from the confusions of the previous decade. 'Not only is the Cold War over,' Secretary of State Colin Powell declared, 'the post-Cold War period is also over.'[79] The bombardment of Afghanistan seemed to mark the end of an era of 'limited conflicts fought largely on humanitarian grounds', where 'direct national interests are rarely at stake'.[80] No longer, it was implied, would the international community find itself trying to prevent, mitigate, or end violent conflicts in dysfunctional states.[81] Pursuing those responsible for the 11 September attacks on New York and Washington, the international community no longer served as a mediator or helpmeet, cleaving to a sometimes compro-mised impartiality.

This time, as the traditional US psyops message made clear, it was a combatant. Reverting to the international broadcasting model forged early in the Cold War, the administration pumped extra money into Voice of America, launched Radio Free Afghanistan, and planned to launch 'an Arabic-language satellite television station [. . .] aimed at winning hearts and minds in the Muslim world'.[82]

Yet, by the time psyops kicked into action, this appearance of a reversion to more traditional war-fighting strategies had already proved deceptive. On 11 October, President Bush reluctantly admitted that the US 'should not just simply leave after a military objective has been achieved'. In fact, the United Nations should *'take over the so-called nation-building.'*[83] This daunting chal-lenge – the most difficult project of post-conflict reconstruction since Germany after 1945 – led Washington policy-makers to ponder recent experiences in the Balkans.[84] The *Washington Post* counselled a 'second look' at the 'extended US and Western effort at nation building' in Bosnia, particularly.[85] In short, the peace-building agenda is here to stay. Today, radio stations are demolished with missiles. Tomorrow, they will have to be rebuilt to operate according to accepted professional standards, serving a divided society with an unstable government.[86]

In their immediate aftermath, the atrocities of 11 September seemed at a stroke to have shifted the risks and causes of major regional conflicts onto a global ideological or 'civilizational' plane that was inaccessible to mere incremental progress in interstate relations. Yet, when the first wave of shock and fear had passed, not everything had changed after all. The sources of terrorism and conflict cannot be addressed without institution-building assistance on an unprecedented scale. Sooner rather than later, the US-led international coalition will have to reckon with the fact that terrorism takes root more easily where media freedom is suppressed with impunity. The approaches developed in the Balkans and elsewhere may soon be needed, in circumstances much less propitious, across the vast swathe of territory from the Caucasus to the Chinese border, posing a scarcely imagined challenge to international will and resources.

Bibliography

Annan, Kofi (27 March 2000), Address on 'Peacekeeping in the Twenty-first Century', (UN Press Release SG/SM/7339).

Arzt, Donna E. (1995), 'Nuremberg, Denazification and Democracy: The Hate Speech Problem at the International Military Tribunal', *New York Law School Journal of Human Rights*, vol. 12, pp. 689–758.

Benvenisti, Eyal (1993), *The International Law of Occupation*, Princeton, NJ: Princeton University Press.

Berlin (Potsdam) Conference, chapter II, sub. A. pt. 10 (1945), reprinted in The Department of State, *Germany 1947–1949: The Story in Documents*, 49 (1950).

Boutros-Ghali, Boutros (31 January 1992), 'An Agenda for Peace. Preventive Diplomacy, Peacemaking and Peace-keeping.' Report of the Secretary-General Pursuant to the Statement Adopted by the Summit Meeting of the Security Council, New York: United Nations.

——— (3 January 1995), 'Supplement to an Agenda for Peace', (UN document A/50/60 S/1995/1).

Braunthal, Gerard (1962), 'Federalism in Germany: The Broadcasting Controversy', *The Journal of Politics*, vol. 24, no. 3, pp. 545–61.

'Building Nations', *Washington Post* editorial, printed in the *International Herald Tribune*, 16 October 2001, p. 6.

Campbell, Duncan, 'US Plans TV Station to Rival Al-Jazeera', *The Guardian*, 23 November 2001.

Carruthers, Susan L. (2000), *The Media at War*, Basingstoke: Macmillan Press.

Clark, Wesley K. (2001), *Waging Modern War. Bosnia, Kosovo, and the Future of Combat*, New York: PublicAffairs.

'Closure of Liberian Radio Stations Provokes Strong Reactions'. Agence France-Presse, 16 March 2000. 200 WL 2754618.

Collin, Matthew (2001), *This Is Serbia Calling*, London: Serpent's Tail.

D'Amato, Anthony (1990), 'The Invasion of Panama was a Lawful Response to Tyranny', *American Journal of International Law*, vol. 84, pp. 516–24.

Daniel, Donald C. F. and Hayes, Bradd C. with Oudraat, Chantal de Jonge (1999),

Coercive Inducement and the Containment of International Crises, Washington, DC: United States Institute of Peace Press.

Falk, Richard (1997), 'The United Nations, the Rule of Law and Humanitarian Intervention', in Mary Kaldor and Basker Vashee (eds), *Restructuring the Global Military Sector, Vol. 1: New Wars*, London: Continuum International Publishing Group/Pinter.

Feher, Michel (2000), *Powerless by Design. The Age of the International Community*, Durham and London: Duke University Press.

Franck, Thomas (1992), 'Emerging Right to Democratic Governance', *American Journal of International Law*, vol. 6, pp. 46–91.

Gag, Giorgio (1981), 'Jus Cogens beyond the Vienna Convention', *Recueil des Cours*, vol. 172, pp. 275, 287–8.

Girardet, Edward R. (1996), 'Reporting Humanitarianism: Are the New Electronic Media Making a Difference?', in Robert I. Rotberg and Tomas G. Weiss, eds, *From Massacres to Genocide. The Media, Public Policy, and Humanitarian Crises*, Washington, DC and Cambridge, MA: The Brookings Institution and the World Peace Foundation, p. 56.

Gow, James, Patterson, Richard and Preston, Alison (eds), *Bosnia by Television*, London: British Film Institute.

Gowing, Nik (1994), *Real-Time Television Coverage of Armed Conflicts and Diplomatic Crises: Does it Pressure or Distort Foreign Policy Decisions?* Cambridge, MA: Joan Shorenstein Barone Center on the Press, Politics, and Public Policy, Harvard University.

Habul, Emir (15 November 2001), 'The Media and War Crimes. Will The Hague Prosecute Journalists?', published by Media Plan Institute, Sarajevo; available at www.mediaonline.ba

Hay, Robin (8 July 1999), 'The Media and Peacebuilding. A Discussion Paper', IMPACS (the Institute for Media, Policy and Civil Society), p. 6. Available at http://www.impacs.org/media/peacebuilding.html

Hobsbawm, Eric (2000), *The New Century. In conversation with Antonio Polito*, London: Abacus.

Ignatieff, Michael (1999), *The Warrior's Honor. Ethnic War and the Modern Conscience*, London: Vintage.

International Crisis Group, Asia Report No. 26 (27 November 2001), *Afghanistan and Central Asia: Priorities for Reconstruction and Development*.

Jakubowicz, Karol (1996), 'Poland: Prospects for Public and Civic Broadcasting', in Marc Raboy (ed.), *Public Broadcasting for the Twenty-First Century*, Luton: John Libbey.

Kanuck, Sean P. (1996), 'Information Warfare: New Challenges for Public International Law', *Harvard International Law Journal*, vol. 37, pp. 272–91.

Kirschke, Linda (1996), *Broadcasting Genocide. Censorship, Propaganda & State-Sponsored Violence in Rwanda 1990–1994*, London: ARTICLE 19.

Korman, Sharon (1996), *The Right of Conquest*, Oxford: Clarendon Press.

Lehmann, Ingrid A. (1999), *Peacekeeping and Public Information: Caught in the Crossfire*, London and Portland, OR: Frank Cass.

'Liberia – Giving Peace A Chance', US Agency for International Development: Office of Transition Initiatives Country Programs. Online [June 2001], available at www.usaid.gov/hum response/oti/country/liberia.html

'Liberia Yanks Mikes at Two Radio Stations', *The Washington Times*, 16 March 2000, 2000 WL 4150899.

Mertus, Julie (May 2000), 'Special Project: Humanitarian Intervention and Kosovo: Reconsidering the Legality of Humanitarian Intervention: Lessons from Kosovo', *William and Mary Law Review*, vol. 41, pp. 1743–87.

Metzl, Jamie Frederic (1997), 'Rwandan Genocide and the International Law of Radio Jamming', *American Journal of International Law*, vol. 91, pp. 628–51.

—— (November/December 1997), 'Information Intervention: When Switching Channels isn't Enough', *Foreign Affairs*, pp. 15–20.

Minear, Larry, Scott, Colin and Weiss, Thomas G. (1996), *The News Media, Civil War, and Humanitarian Action*, Boulder, CO: Lynne Rienner Publishers Inc.

'Molding a Nation: Events Force Bush to Take Course he has Derided', *International Herald Tribune*, 13–14 October 2001, p. 3.

Murphy, Sean (1996), *Humanitarian Intervention: The United Nations in an Evolving World Order*, Pennsylvania: University of Pennsylvania Press.

Natsios, Andrew (1996), 'Illusions of Influence: The CNN Effect in Complex Emergencies', in Robert I. Rotberg and Tomas G. Weiss (eds), *From Massacres to Genocide. The Media, Public Policy, and Humanitarian Crises*, Washington, DC and Cambridge, MA: The Brookings Institution and the World Peace Foundation, p. 164.

Paris, Roland (2001), 'Wilson's Ghost. The Faulty Assumptions of Postconflict Peacebuilding', in Chester A. Crocker, Fen Osler Hampson and Pamela Aall (eds), *Turbulent Peace. The Challenges of Managing International Conflict*, Washington, DC: United States Institute of Peace Press.

Pilgert, Henry P. (1953), 'Press, Radio and Film in West Germany 1945–1953', Historical Division of the Office of the United States High Commissioner for Germany, pp. 74–5.

Plischke, Elmer (1947), 'Denazification Law and Procedure', *American Journal of International Law*, vol. 41, pp. 807–27.

Prittie, Terence (Summer 1954), 'The Progress of Broadcasting in Western Germany', *The BBC Quarterly*, IX, 74.

Reisman, W. Michael (1990), 'Comment: Sovereignty and Human Rights in Contemporary International Law', *American Journal of International Law*, vol. 84, p. 866.

Rieff, David (1999), 'Humanitarian Intervention', in Roy Gutman and David Rieff (eds), *Crimes of War: What the Public should Know*, New York: W. W. Norton.

Rotberg, Robert I. and Weiss, Tomas G. (eds), (1996), *From Massacres to Genocide. The Media, Public Policy, and Humanitarian Crises*, Washington, DC and Cambridge, MA: The Brookings Institution and the World Peace Foundation.

Schmid, Alex P. (1998), *Thesaurus and Glossary of Early Warning and Conflict Prevention Terms*, Rotterdam: Synthesis Foundation, Erasmus University.

Schwabach, Aaron (2000), '*Yugoslavia vs. NATO*, Security Council Resolution 1244 and the Law of Humanitarian Intervention', *Syracuse Journal of International Law and Commerce*, vol. 27, pp. 77–101.

Scruton, Roger (1983), *A Dictionary of Political Thought*, London: Pan Books.

Sebald, William J. and Spinks, C. Nelson (1967), *Japan: Prospects, Options and Opportunities*, p. 17, Washington, DC: American Enterprise Institute for Public Policy Research.

Simma, Bruno (1999), 'NATO, the UN and the Use of Force: Legal Aspects', *European Journal of International Law*, vol. 10, pp. 1–22.

Strobel, Warren P. (2001), 'Information and Conflict', in Chester A. Crocker, Fen Osler Hampson and Pamela Aall (eds), *Turbulent Peace. The Challenges of Managing International Conflict*, Washington, DC: United States Institute of Peace Press.

———— (1997), *Late-Breaking Foreign Policy. The News Media's Influence on Peace Operations*, Washington, DC: The United States Institute of Peace Press.

Thompson, Mark (1999), *Forging War. The Media in Serbia, Croatia, Bosnia and Hercegovina*, Luton: University of Luton Press and ARTICLE 19.

United Nations, Seminar on Public Information Policies and Practices for Field Missions. Harrison Conference Center, Glen Cove, New York, 5–6 March 1997 (October 1997), New York: United Nations Reproduction Section, p. 10.

———— 'Italian Military Armistice' (January 1946), *American Journal of International Law*, vol. 40, 1 Supplement: Official Documents 1–21 (para. 16).

Whitton, John B. and Larson, Arthur D. (1964), *Propaganda towards Disarmament in the War of Words*, Dobbs Ferry: New York.

Wight, Martin (1986), *Power Politics*, Harmondsworth: Penguin Books, (2nd edn).

Wolfsfeld, Gadi (1998), 'Promoting Peace through the News Media. Some Initial Lessons from the Oslo Peace Process', in Tamar Liebes and James Curran (eds), *Media, Ritual and Identity*, London: Routledge, p. 219.

Notes

1. Wolfsfeld, 'Promoting peace through the news media', p. 219.
2. Strobel, 'Information and Conflict', p. 691.
3. Girardet, 'Reporting Humanitarianism', p. 55.
4. Hobsbawm, *The New Century*, pp. 10, 22.
5. The Preamble of the Constitution of the United Nations Educational, Scientific and Cultural Organisation (UNESCO), adopted in November 1945, begins: 'The Governments of the States Parties to this Constitution on behalf of their peoples declare: That since wars begin in the minds of men, it is in the minds of men that the defences of peace must be constructed . . .'
6. See, for example, Kirschke, *Broadcasting Genocide. Censorship, Propaganda & State-Sponsored Violence in Rwanda 1990–1994*; Thompson, *Forging War*; Gow, Patterson and Preston (eds), *Bosnia by Television*.
7. See, for example, Gowing, *Real-Time Television Coverage of Armed Conflicts and Diplomatic Crises*; Rotberg and Weiss (eds), *From Massacres to Genocide*; and Strobel, *Late-Breaking Foreign Policy*.
8. The Institute for Media, Policy and Civil Society (IMPACS), based in Vancouver, has issued valuable material on media and peace-building. In a discussion paper issued in 1999, IMPACS noted that 'the literature on peace-building . . . scarcely mentions the media (though the relationship between the media and conflict is widely covered).' Available at http://www.impacs.org/media/peacebuilding.html
9. '[A]ny survey of the developing world will readily show that the countries most at risk of falling into complex emergencies are also the least likely to have a free and developed press'. (Natsios, 'Illusions of Influence', p. 164.) Since the contributions to this book were written, the war in and against Afghanistan has borne out this assessment. See International Crisis Group, *Afghanistan and Central Asia*.
10. Girardet, 'Reporting Humanitarianism: Are the New Electronic Media Making a Difference?', p. 56.
11. Arzt, 'Nuremberg, Denazification and Democracy', pp. 689, 727.

12. Military Government Regulations, Title 21, part 5 (1949) reprinted in The Department of State, *Germany 1947–49: The Story in Documents*, 605 (1950).

13. See Prittie, 'The Progress of Broadcasting in Western Germany'; Pilgert, 'Press, Radio and Film in West Germany 1945–1953'; pp. 74–5; Braunthal, 'Federalism in Germany', pp. 545–61.

14. See Plischke, 'Denazification Law and Procedure', p. 827.

15. Potsdam Agreement Part III, Sec. A, par. 3 (iii). Potsdam Agreement or Berlin Protocol, 2 August 1945.

16. Ibid., p. 819.

17. Ibid., p. 820.

18. Sebald and Spinks, *Japan: Prospects, Options and Opportunities*, p. 17.

19. See Berlin (Potsdam) Conference, chapter II, sub. A. pt. 10 (1945), reprinted in The Department of State, *Germany 1947–1949: The Story in Documents*, 49 (1950).

20. Ibid.

21. Quoted by Carruthers, *The Media at War*, p. 250.

22. United Nations, 'Italian Military Armistice', pp. 1–21 (para. 16).

23. Compare Korman, *The Right of Conquest*, p. 177 with Benvenisti, *The International Law of Occupation*.

24. Arzt, 'Nuremberg, Denazification and Democracy', pp. 689, 727.

25. See generally Benvenisti, *The International Law of Occupation*.

26. Military Government Regulations, Title 21, Part 5 (1949), reprinted in The Department of State, *Germany 1947–1949: The Story in Documents*, 605 (1950).

27. Ibid.

28. Regulations Respecting the Laws and Customs of War on Land (annexed to 1907 Hague Convention IV), (18 October 1907), Art. 42, 36 Stat. at 2306 [hereinafter Hague Regulations]. The Article in its entirety states: 'The authority of the legitimate power having in fact passed into the hands of the occupant, the latter shall take all the measures in his power to restore and ensure, as far as possible, public order and [civic life], while respecting, unless absolutely prevented, the laws in force in the country.'

29. Wight, *Power Politics*, pp. 191–2.

30. Scruton, *A Dictionary of Political Thought*, p. 233.

31. Stanley Hoffman, quoted by Prof. Alex P. Schmid in *Thesaurus and Glossary of Early Warning and Conflict Prevention Terms*, p. 51. (Emphasis added.)

32. Daniel and Hayes with Oudraat, *Coercive Inducement and the Containment of International Crises*, p. 9.

33. The UN Transition Assistance Group in Namibia has been described as 'the first of the "second-generation" of peacekeeping operations', and 'a model for the large multilayered peacekeeping operations' that were to follow in the early 1990s. See Lehmann, *Peacekeeping and Public Information*, p. 28.

34. 'Multidisciplinary peacekeeping' is the title of a recent report by the Department of Peacekeeping Operations (DPKO), which begins thus: 'United Nations peacekeeping in the 1990s has been characterised by multidisciplinary operations encompassing a wide range of elements to enhance peace. These include the supervision of cease-fire agreements; regrouping and demobilisation of armed forces; destruction of armed forces; destruction of weapons surrendered in disarmament exercise; reintegration of former combatants into civilian life; designing and implementation of demining programmes; facilitating the return of refugees and displaced persons; provision of humanitarian assistance;

training of new police forces; monitoring and respect for human rights; support for implementation of constitutional, judicial and electoral reforms; and support for economic rehabilitation and reconstruction.' Available at http:// www.un.org/Depts/dpko/lessons/handbuk.htm Boutros Boutros-Ghali used the term 'multifunctional peacekeeping operation' in his 'Supplement to An Agenda for Peace', para. 49. His successor, Kofi Annan, used the term 'multidimensional operations' in his address on 'Peacekeeping in the Twenty-first Century'.

35. Rieff, 'Humanitarian Intervention', p. 181. See also, in general Murphy, *Humanitarian Intervention*; Schwabach, '*Yugoslavia vs. NATO*', p. 77; Mertus, 'Special Project', p. 1743.

36. Minear, Scott and Weiss, *The News Media, Civil War, and Humanitarian Action*, p. 108.

37. A searching critique of the humanitarian agenda is Michel Feher's *Powerless by Design. The Age of the International Community*.

38. For information about the 'right to democratic government', see Franck, 'Emerging Right to Democratic Governance', p. 46. For the 'right of a population to be free from internal as well as external aggression', see Reisman, 'Comment: Sovereignty and Human Rights in Contemporary International Law', p. 866; and D'Amato, 'The Invasion of Panama was a Lawful Response to Tyranny', pp. 516–24.

39. See Metzl, 'Rwandan Genocide and the International Law of Radio Jamming', p. 628; Metzl, 'Information Intervention: When Switching Channels isn't Enough', pp. 15–20; Kanuck, 'Information Warfare: New Challenges for Public International Law', p. 272.

40. See UN Charter, Art. 2, para. 4; Case concerning Military and Paramilitary Activities in and against Nicaragua (*Nicaragua v. US*) 1986 International Court of Justice Reports 14 (Judgement), para. 188. The prohibition on the use of force against the territorial integrity or political independence of a state as declared in Article 2, paragraph 4 of the Charter is a norm of general internal law 'accepted and recognized by the international community of states as a whole as a norm from which no derogation is permitted and which can be modified only by a subsequent norm of general international law having the same character'. Vienna Convention on the Law of Treaties, Art. 53, UN Doc. A/Conf. 39/27, 1155 U.N.T.S. 331 (1969) (hereinafter 'Vienna Convention') (defining the term *jus cogens*); see also, Report of the International Law Commission on the work of the second part of its seventeenth session, *Yearbook of the International Law Commission* 2; pp. 169, 247 (1966) (stating that 'the law of the Charter concerning the use of force [. . .] constitutes a conspicuous example of a rule in international law having the character of *jus cogens*'.). The Commission reaffirmed this view in 1980. See United Nations, International Law Commission, Report of the International Law Commission on the work of its thirty-second session 108, UN Doc A/35/10 (1980), quoted in Gag, 'Jus Cogens beyond the Vienna Convention', pp. 275, 287–8 (declaring '[o]ne obligation whose peremptory character is beyond doubt in all events is the obligation of a State to refrain from any forcible violation of the territorial integrity or political independence of another State.'); Restatement of the Law (Third) Foreign Relations Law of the United States § 331 (1987); Simma, 'NATO, the Un and the Use of Force', pp. 1, 3.

41. During the NATO bombardment of Yugoslavia in 1999, US sources reportedly confirmed that the United States 'had begun to assemble a "cyber arsenal" for use in future wars, including "computer viruses or 'logic bombs' to disrupt enemy networks, the feeding of false information to sow confusion and the morphing of video images on to foreign television stations to deceive".' (Collin, *This Is Serbia Calling*, p. 166.) There is little doubt that these techniques could count as the use of force.

42. Whitton and Larson, *Propaganda towards Disarmament in the War of Words*, p. 210. Jamming has been defined as 'the deliberate use of interfering radio signals sent from one or more transmitters to garble emissions from other transmitters in order to make them unintelligible at reception'.

43. Metzl, 'Rwandan Genocide and the Law of Jamming', pp. 628, 636.

44. Richard Falk has suggested that the bad news about the degraded nature of consent was broken in Somalia in 1993: 'The reversal of the US commitment in Somalia during 1993 has turned out to be a decisive moment, disclosing that . . . *without genuine consent by indigenous forces*, the intrusion of peacekeeping missions even of a mainly humanitarian cast could be provocative in the target society and unpopular in the intervening society.' (Emphasis added.) Falk, 'The United Nations, the Rule of Law and Humanitarian Intervention', p. 115.

45. In the light of the UN's bitter experience in the Balkans and Africa in the mid-1990s, when he was running the Department of Peace-keeping Operations, UN Secretary-General Kofi Annan showed interest in ideas for 'inducing' better co-operation by host governments, through incentives or coercion. See generally Daniel and Hayes with Oudraat, *Coercive Inducement and the Containment of International Crises*.

46. Warren Strobel, *Information and Conflict*, p. 687.

47. A recent study makes the point nicely: 'As in Germany, American occupation authorities set about reconstructing Japan's media along democratic lines, with the recurrent irony that freedom of speech was tolerated so long as the American occupiers approved the speech in question.' Carruthers, *The Media at War*, p. 250.

48. 'We are scarcely aware of the extent to which our moral imagination has been transformed since 1945 by the growth of a language and practice of moral universalism, expressed above all in a shared human rights culture.' Ignatieff, *The Warrior's Honor*, p. 8.

49. General Wesley Clark, the American commander during the NATO bombardment, has recorded that his initial attempt to justify the decision to target RTS in terms of 'the military value of the transmitters' failed to convince 'some of the [NATO] ambassadors'. He eventually gained political approval for the missile strike, which he claims – irrefutably, of course – demonstrated 'NATO's resolve' to the Serbs. (Clark, *Waging Modern War*, p. 264.) In December 2001, the European Court of Human Rights ruled that a case against NATO member states for the bombing of RTS was inadmissable on the ground that Yugoslavia was not a member of the Council of Europe.

50. From Dr Bernard Kouchner's address to the Media and Peace Institute of the University for Peace, Paris, 20 April 2001. Excerpts available at http://www.mediapeace.org/paris

51. In terms used by Roland Paris, Kouchner supports the 'institutionalisers' against the 'liberalisers'. Paris writes: '[P]eacebuilders should delay liberalisation until they have constructed political and economic institutions that are capable of

managing the societal tensions that naturally arise from the process of democratisation and marketisation.' It follows that, 'before liberalising popular media in
war-shattered states, peace-builders should establish mechanisms to limit the
promulgation of inflammatory propaganda.' Roland Paris, 'Wilson's Ghost',
pp. 767 and 777.

52. Hay, 'The Media and Peacebuilding. A Discussion Paper', p. 6.
53. Fondation Hirondelle Online, Background of Star Radio. www.hirondelle.org.
    Special thanks are due to Ijeoma Okoli for much of the information about
    Fondation Hirondelle and Liberia.
54. Among STAR's funders are the United States Agency for International Devel-
    opment (USAID), the Swedish International Development Agency (SIDA), the
    Swiss Agency for Development and Co-operation (SDC) of the Swiss Confedera-
    tion, the United Nations High Commissioner for Refugees (UNHCR), the
    Humanitarian Office of the European Community (ECHO), the International
    Foundation for Election Systems (IFES), the Office of Transitional Initiatives
    (OTI) in Washington, the Netherlands Ministry of Foreign Affairs, the Search for
    Common Ground, the Association Enfants du Rwanda, Direction Politique 3 of
    the Federal Department of Foreign Affairs (Bern), UNESCO, Republic and
    Canton of Geneva, the Reuter Foundation, Edipresse (Lausanne), the Netherlands
    Development Agency (NEDA), the British Embassy in Abidjan and a few private
    donors. Fondation Hirondelle Online, About Star Radio Monrovia – Independent
    Radio Station for Liberia (www.hirondelle.org); Fondation Hirondelle Online,
    The Sponsors (www.hirondelle.org).
55. Quotations from Fondation Hirondelle Online (www.hirondelle.org)
56. Democracy Programme – Liberia, USAID Liberia – Programme Description
    (www.usaid.gov/democracy/afr/liberiaso.html viewed 9 January 2001).
57. 'Liberia – Giving Peace A Chance', US Agency for International Development:
    Office of Transition Initiatives Country Programs. Online [June 2001], available
    at: www.usaid.gov/hum response/oti/country/liberia.html
58. Liberian Daily News Bulletin Star Radio, African News Service, 11 January 2000,
    2000 WL 4128650; broadcast of Voice of America for 15 January 2000 by Kim
    Andrew Elliot, transcript provided by Communications World Script. Online
    [June 2001], available at: www.trsc.com/cw/cw 20000115.html
59. 'Closure of Liberian Radio Stations Provokes Strong Reactions'. Agence France-
    Presse.
60. Liberian Government Press Release Announcing the Withdrawal of STAR Radio
    Shortwave Frequencies, Republic of Liberia Ministry of Posts and Telecommu-
    nications, International Freedom of Exchange. Online [June 2001], available at:
    www.ifex.org/alerts/view.html?id = 3811
61. Broadcast of Voice of America for 4 March 2000 by Kim Andrew Elliot, transcript
    provided by Communications World Script. Online [June 2001], available at:
    www.trsc.com/cw/cw 20000304.html
62. Fondation Hirondelle Online. Star Radio Suspended – Fondation Hirondelle
    press release; 'Liberia Yanks Mikes at Two Radio Stations', *The Washington
    Times*. Radio Veritas, a radio service of the Catholic Media Center, opened in
    Monrovia in July 1997 and has been supported by the European Union, which
    purchased a transmitter for the station. Liberian Daily News Bulletin, STAR
    Radio, African News Service, 7 July 1998, 1998 WL 14359136.
63. 'Liberia Yanks Mikes at Two Radio Stations', ibid.

64. Letter from the Liberian Ministry of Information, Culture and Tourism to Star Radio Liberia, 14 March 2000.
65. Fondation Hirondelle is now collaborating with the UN mission in the Democratic Republic of Congo to develop a network of twelve shortwave radio stations. If this unprecedented partnership succeeds, its example should be emulated in other crisis areas.
66. Speaking in September 2001, the spokesperson of the Prosecutor's Office at the International Criminal Tribunal for the former Yugoslavia (ICTY) said that the Tribunal had found no evidence of the responsibility of journalists for offences under the ICTY Statute. This contrasts with the sister tribunal for Rwanda, which has indicted, tried and sentenced individuals for inciting killings. Habul, 'The Media and War Crimes'.
67. Ignatieff, *The Warrior's Honor*, p. 105.
68. Jakubowicz, 'Poland: Prospects for Public and Civic Broadcasting', pp. 180–1.
69. A UN seminar on public information policies and practices for field missions, in March 1997, concluded that 'The UN has failed to position public information as a "strategic" component in UN peacekeeping operations, generally speaking.' See United Nations Seminar on Public Information Policies and Practices for Field Missions, p. 10.
70. Though it could be argued that the potential need for media sector restructuring was anticipated in Boutros-Ghali's reference to 'support for the transformation of deficient national structures and capabilities, and for the strengthening of new democratic institutions' in the context of post-conflict peace-building. See Boutros Boutros-Ghali, 'An Agenda for Peace', pp. 33–4.
71. Boutros-Ghali, 'Supplement to an Agenda for Peace', para. 46.
72. Ibid., para. 49.
73. Annan, 'Peacekeeping in the Twenty-first Century'.
74. The panel was chaired by Lakhdar Brahimi, formerly a foreign minister of Algeria, and the panel's conclusions are usually known as the Brahimi Report. See United Nations, 'Report of the Panel on United Nations Peace Operations', distributed 21 August 2000, A/55/305-S/2000/9/809. Available at http://www.un.org/peace/reports/peace operations
75. The Indonesian legislature ratified the East Timorese vote on 20 October 1999, making East Timor an independent country. Since then the international community has been attempting to rebuild East Timor, including by means of aid for media development. The most difficult medium for the international effort, as in the Balkans, has been television: gaining access to relevant transmitters and obtaining editorial control over production and distribution of the UN's message. The UN television station, TV-TL, established in May 2000, is the only TV station in the country and began broadcasting on a daily basis the following March. In January 2001, journalists gathered for the inaugural Congress of the Association of Journalists of Timor Lorosea (AJTL), which pledged to co-ordinate training, provide protection, and to establish a code of ethics and professional standards in the country.
76. From United Nations Deputy Secretary-General Louise Frechette's Address to the International Press Institute World Congress, Boston, 3 May 2000.
77. The 'Recommendations for Future Actions' emerged from a UNESCO Round Table on Media in Conflict and Post-Conflict Areas, held in Geneva on 4 and 5 May 2000, attended by some sixty experts from IGOs and NGOs. The fifteen recommendations (dated 14 June 2000) are as follows:

1. Whenever the international community intervenes in a conflict or post-conflict situation, one of its main goals should be to promote the fulfilment of Article 19 of the Universal Declaration of Human Rights. Its actions should always be understandable as part of a strategy aimed at extending the right to receive and impart information.

2. In particular, it should aim to strengthen independent local media, where these exist; to rebuild them where they have been destroyed; and to establish them where they do not exist. This priority should be spelt out clearly and unequivocally in any mandate given to an intergovernmental organisation (IGO).

3. Independent media may be privately owned, or may take the form of a public service, financed through a licence fee or other form of taxation but protected by a legal statute and governed by an independent authority. The international community should aim to strengthen genuinely independent media of both types, and to establish them as vehicles for the transmission of non partisan information to all sectors of the population.

4. IGOs should undertake this task in close consultation with appropriate non-governmental organisations (NGOs). The roles of IGOs (including international military forces) and bilateral donors, in assisting independent media in conflict areas, should as far as possible be coordinated, so that they complement each other and the cooperation with NGOs should be emphasised. Advice and help should also be sought from the international and regional media.

5. Both IGOs and NGOs must be transparent in their own activities. They should make special efforts to keep local journalists informed.

6. The international community must be concerned with the establishment of the rule of law, in the media as in other sectors of society. It should therefore promote the establishment and implementation of an independent regulatory framework and an appellate system, providing full guarantees for freedom of expression.

7. IGOs themselves should set an example of respect for the rule of law in their own actions, including those aimed at reconstructing or regulating the media.

8. Any entity set up by an IGO to broadcast information on behalf of the international community, during the critical early stages of post-conflict peace-building, should as far as possible function *ab initio* as an independent public service broadcaster, and should in any case be developed as such so that responsibility can, at the appropriate time and without risk to the broadcaster's independence, be transferred to the duly constituted local authority.

9. Because the first days and months of any restructuring period are critical, the international community should be ready to act very swiftly, as much in handling local media as in other aspects of peace-building. Each situation will of course be unique, and a specific strategy for restructuring the media will have to be worked out in each case. But there should be an agreed handbook, regularly updated, setting out clear general principles, giving an inventory and evaluation of past actions in this field, and defining the main strategic choices that have to be made. There should also be an inventory of NGOs active in this field, giving their specific histories and areas of expertise.

10. Resources available from the international community for media development

should, as far as possible, be used to give direct support to free and independent local media and to create infrastructures that will enhance the eventual ability of independent media to survive economically.

11. IGOs and NGOs must be flexible enough to adapt their strategy swiftly to a changing situation, and to the real needs of the independent media.

12. Besides strengthening media enterprises themselves, attention should be given to helping individual journalists improve their professional skills, and to encouraging the establishment of professional media associations and institutions for self-regulation, as well as opportunities for training.

13. IGOs should use their influence with governments to ensure that they protect the right of journalists to engage in their profession, and that they prosecute and punish those who commit crimes against journalists.

14. The international community should give opportunities to media professionals from conflict areas, who hold different views on the merits of the conflict, to come together on neutral ground and exchange views and information, with the assistance of experienced conflict resolution facilitators.

15. International peace operations should where possible employ experienced media professionals in positions that involve working closely with the media. Professional media organisations could be asked to suggest names of suitable people who could be able and willing to undertake such tasks at short notice.

78. Information from BBC 1 television news, 10 p.m., 15 October 2001.

79. Quoted in Weekly Review, *Harper's Magazine*, 23 October 2001.

80. Strobel, 'Information and Conflict', pp. 678, 683.

81. Roland Paris counts 'twelve such operations' between 1989 and 2000: Namibia, Angola, Mozambique, Rwanda, Cambodia, Bosnia and Herzegovina, Croatia, Nicaragua, El Salvador, Guatemala, Kosovo and East Timor. See Paris, 'Wilson's Ghost', p. 766.

82. Campbell, 'US Plans TV Station to Rival Al-Jazeera'.

83. Quoted in 'Molding a Nation: Events Force Bush to Take Course he has Derided'.

84. Ibid.

85. 'Building Nations'.

86. By late October 2001, a small team from Danish and British non-governmental organizations had already visited the Pakistan–Afghanistan border to assess future needs and opportunities for international assistance to media in the region.

SECTION ONE

Defining Information Intervention

An Interview with Jamie Metzl

The following interview was
conducted by Mark Thompson in
Washington, DC, in October 2000.

*The phrase 'information intervention' appeared in your 1997 essay for Foreign
Affairs.*[1] *What should we understand by it?*

Information intervention is a soft form of humanitarian intervention. The core
of humanitarian intervention is the belief that a country gives up an element of
its sovereignty when it severely violates the human rights of its citizens. In that
situation, the international community is justified in being more aggressive,
including by using information tactics, than would otherwise be the case.
Information intervention is the use of information in that aggressive manner
when this is justified on strong human rights grounds.

When we look at the situations where humanitarian intervention might be
appropriate, we should think about the role information plays in the underlying
conflict that we are hoping to address. My thinking on information intervention
stemmed from my understanding of the limitations of the existing human rights
response structures. There were multiple conflicts around the world in the
1990s where humanitarian intervention would have been an appropriate
response to an impending or existing mass human rights violation. But in
many of those situations there were not the political will or appropriate
conceptual models or institutions to respond at an early enough stage to have
a significant impact.

There are a number of reasons for this. Many people refer to Somalia and the
difficulties that the United States and others faced there in 1993 and 1994, and
the perception of the increasing costs of humanitarian intervention, as the
watershed. The catastrophe in Rwanda in 1994 proved there was no working
international system for humanitarian intervention. United Nations reports
asserted in January 1994 that the possibility of genocide was high, yet little was
done. In the absence of a system of humanitarian intervention that would kick
in once a certain threat threshold was crossed, we need to focus on what is
achievable through current international institutions and sensibilities, even as
we work towards a more responsive and accountable system. We need to
explore what can be done between the impossible everything and the unacceptable nothing. The political cost of doing everything is usually prohibi-
tive. The moral cost of doing nothing is astronomical. If we accept that we are

not going to do everything possible to stem a given conflict, what can we do to have as much impact as we are willing to have? It would be a great shame if there were some element of political will but the response structures were not developed enough to fulfill it. Those of us in the international community and in the human rights community need to think creatively about the limits of the possible, even as we work towards what now seems impossible. We need enough structure to correspond maximally to fluctuating levels of political will.

Every one of the major humanitarian crises and human rights conflicts around the world over the past century began with a propaganda phase, where extremists took control of the means of mass communication and used them to incite conflict. In Rwanda, the media were even used to organise the conflict. Information intervention is a strategy to address those patterns of misuse of mass communications, and asks how we can use a more aggressive form of information-related action, first to provide counter-information that opposes harmful incitement, and second to proscribe or suppress the latter in extreme circumstances.

Information intervention has also come to signify a sometimes broader use of information by the international community in its peacekeeping operations. This might be termed phase two, coming after the international community has established itself in a given conflict area. How does it use information, what rights, what legal authority does it have, what techniques does it use to bring about desired democratic and human rights goals within a post-intervention framework?

This distinction between phase one and phase two information intervention is important because different legal regimes apply to each. Phase one involves weighing conflicting legal regimes, while phase two involves being more creative and expansive in how we utilize information tools in peacekeeping and other international operations – a challenging but legally less complicated task.

Information intervention, then, means both intervention with information from outside a place, and also intervention against certain kinds of information being produced inside it?

Yes. While every situation is different, we can list the three general objectives in a conflict situation where information is used to incite violence. The longest-term and most important objective is to empower voices of moderation and reason within the society. It is much more difficult to argue for more aggressive action where there is a multiplicity of voices, even if some of them are voices of incitement. If voices of moderation, reason, and objectivity aren't adequate within a given society, then the second objective is to get news and information from outside that society into it, to create a baseline of objectivity. For a number of different reasons, this doesn't always work. In some places there may be a multiplicity of voices but domination by one voice. Or it may be that the indigenous community doesn't trust international voices.

The third objective entails being much more aggressive, interfering in some way with indigenous media activity. There have to be very tough standards for this, but if the thresholds are crossed and it is deemed appropriate to have that kind of intervention, then it should be possible to suppress incendiary media in a commensurate way.

The strongest and most controversial form of intervention, short of bombardment, is jamming. Does international law currently accept the legality of jamming broadcasts through intervention in a sovereign state? If not, should it do so?

It depends on how narrowly or broadly you define the legal regime that covers this set of issues. If jamming is considered under the rubric of international radio and telecommunications law, then it is correct to conclude that states have minimal rights to engage in what we are calling information intervention. The question is, do the dictates of international human rights and humanitarian law trump those more specific legal requirements and regimes of telecommunications law? We need to have an appropriate balancing test to weigh the pros and cons in various situations. In the great majority of cases, the free flow of information standard would trump what we might call the proscription standard. Nevertheless, I think we need to develop models for situations in which international humanitarian law can, should, and must trump the more specific dictates of radio and telecommunications law.

The United States maintains a more protective standard for the freedom of speech than most other countries. My heart is with the American model; the free flow of information, with minimal censorship, is the goal. Yet, even in the United States, it is not true that anything goes. There are limits. When an individual passes those limits, his or her speech can be proscribed. The most famous case is *Brandenburg v. Ohio*, in 1969. According to the Brandenburg decision, only speech 'directed to inciting or producing imminent lawless action' that was 'likely to incite or produce such action' could be proscribed. If I am inciting someone to take action that is illegal, the State has the power to proscribe my speech.

In the international arena the United States has upheld a model of the free flow of information that is even more liberal than its domestic model, and does not carve out Brandenburg-style limits. The reason for this – perhaps justifiably – was the fear that our Cold War adversaries would abuse any loopholes by using them to justify the distortion or censorship of information, as the Soviets, Cubans, and others attempted to do.

The end of the Cold War has cleared a space for the United States and others to support an international model more equivalent to what they have domestically. This means the United States would do everything in their power to support the free flow of information, but in extreme cases of incitement to imminent mass human rights abuse, the overwhelming weight of international law should favour limited interference with people's ability to disseminate that type of information. In some conflict situations, incendiary speech becomes in many ways a form of action. It cannot be separated from action. The Convention on Genocide, for example, considers incitement an element of the crime of genocide. In the case of Rwanda, Radio-Television Libre des Milles Collines clearly incited genocide and then organized it, giving orders to various militias to go to various places or broadcasting the licence plates of cars that were subsequently stopped and their occupants murdered. The fact that something is being said on a mass communication system should not entitle it to extra protection. That would be absurd. Clearly, we need a much more nuanced intellectual model and legal analysis.

Besides jamming, what other techniques would be appropriate for stopping the incitement of massive human rights abuses?

Information deals with attitudes and opinions that are often slow in forming. This puts a premium on pro-activity in international responses to incitement. You need to get there as early as you can and be as effective as you can. And if it is to be most effective, information needs to be presented to people in ways which they are prepared to accept.

   We need to ask how people get their information. What sort of information do they trust, and how do they process it? How do they think about problems, why do they think as they do? In some situations, hiring street-theatre troupes might be the most appropriate step. There are places in Africa with one video-player in the village, and getting videos with certain messages into those places might work. The first priority is supporting people on the ground who are saying reasonable things. Moving beyond that, you need a deep analysis of how people get information. Bombarding a country with radio broadcasts doesn't achieve anything if people don't get their information from radio.

   People also need to feel they are involved in a dialogue. This is difficult to manage, because it contradicts traditional propaganda methods, such as dropping leaflets on people's heads. One of the lessons of the information revolution – the Internet being the ultimate example – is that people develop ideas and opinions through dialogue. A dialogue model allows people to form their own opinions while working to ensure that they are doing so based on multiple and reliable information sources. In some situations, simply the provision of reliable news and information is the critical contribution. This is why credibility is so important. For example, the BBC has developed a brand credibility, so that in some areas people believe the BBC more than their local news-provider. Creativity and credibility are also key assets.

Can or should states intervene with or against information only collectively or also individually? Are the legal standards different for an intervention carried out by or through the United Nations, or by a group of states, say NATO, or a single state acting unilaterally?

A standard set by the international community through the United Nations or even NATO is clearly preferable to one set by an individual state. It is difficult to envisage a model where a single state should act alone without multilateral agreement or justification from an entity broader than itself. Single-state humanitarian interventions are suspect because the international community should be able to cobble something multilateral together if the cause is just.

How do you regard the NATO bombardment of Serbian state broadcasting headquarters in Belgrade in April 1999?

While we must grieve for the people who were killed in that bombing, I believe there was some justification for that targeting decision. RTS (Radio–Television Serbia) spread propaganda that supported and arguably prolonged the war. Propaganda institutions were one of the most critical components of Milosevic's regime. Thanks to that power structure, supported by RTS, the regime was better able to engage in human rights violations in Kosovo and elsewhere. The regime also made the RTS headquarters into more of a target by suppressing independent media and making illegal the rebroadcast of international media. If there had been more widely available alternative media sources within Serbia, it would have been more difficult to make a case for targeting one of them. It is always better, however, to counter propaganda with more reliable information, even when extreme actions are taken. Simply targeting the RTS headquarters and transmitters without doing this would have been a mistake. Finally, various reports suggest there was advance warning that RTS would be targeted, and engineers and others were coerced into staying while the management left. If that was the case, it must affect our judgement of the incident.[2]

The Nuremberg trials and the Rwanda Tribunal have both asserted that propaganda activities can rise to the level of war crimes and crimes against humanity, so there are certainly situations where very strong responsive action can be justified. At the same time, information intervention is often about being effective in a context of reduced physical risk to the intervener, but perhaps also to the perpetrators, and efforts should always be made to reduce those risks whenever possible. Sometimes it may not be possible and policy-makers must balance these risks against the threat posed by the incitement.

Do you think the NATO operation against Yugoslavia reflects a new emerging norm more favourable to the types of intervention that you have advocated, and that we have been discussing?

Absolutely. There is increased recognition of the role that information and propaganda play in conflict situations, and an increased willingness to think about suppression as a last resort, but still a possibility.

When the United States interdicted the local media in Grenada and Panama, those were not information interventions, then, but coercive military interventions with an information dimension?

Information intervention is much less severe than armed intervention. Whether or not it is justified, the justification that a state would use for armed intervention would cover information intervention. It's what we call in criminal law a lesser included offence.

Do different legal standards apply when an intervention targets media outlets that are privately owned rather than government-owned?

The case for intervention is made easier when a medium is government owned, but I can imagine a situation in which a non-governmental media source was inciting to imminent lawless action, with support from government that conferred quasi-official status on the broadcasts. This would count almost as official. This was, in fact, the case with RTLM in Rwanda.[3] Alternatively, an inciting medium might be against the government, in which case it would be necessary to build a relationship with the government to help it develop other voices that would make the incitement less dangerous.

Your argument for the right to jam acknowledges both the extreme situations that have been caused by incendiary media over the past ten years, and also the likelihood that such emergencies will occur again.[4] There are occasions when certain media should be prevented from operating, and it is important to recognize that prevention cannot be achieved by graduated forms of pressure on the authorities that control the media outlet in question. In other words, circumstances can arise in which conventional forms of external or internal pressure on state authorities cannot be effective quickly enough to avert potential mass abuses of human rights. Even if this argument is granted, however, there remains the all important question of criteria for pro-active intervention. Who is to make the assessment that a situation is, so to speak, actionable, warranting interference with media in a sovereign state? And on the basis of which legal or other criteria?

This is an issue of international law, and it is going to be hard to establish the requisite criteria. The United States and the international community have been well served by the free-flow model. People in positions of authority and other opinion-makers will justifiably worry that, by carving out these sorts of exceptions, we would create pretexts for proscriptive action, such as the censorship of Internet sites. These actions could be justified with reference to a different definition of this standard.

   The definition needs to be very narrow. There are two ways of proceeding. A new mechanism could be set up to consider how information is used in conflict situations and to develop legal standards. This process might be launched with international meetings. The second way would be to create a model for action within the United Nations, possibly by thinking about information intervention as a component of Chapter VII of the United Nations Charter.[5] This would not require amending the Charter. Under Chapter VII, the Security Council can authorize actions by member states that violate or compromise the sovereignty of a state in order 'to restore international peace and security'.[6] It could be argued that the United Nations should be prepared to authorize a more aggressive information response to a developing situation, using Chapter VII, then keep the situation under close review and be ready to issue another Chapter VII resolution if there was further escalation and an armed intervention was judged appropriate. Clearly, interpretations of Chapter VII have broadened over recent years to include more proactive human rights considerations.

The most realistic, maybe the only way to develop a capacity for the United Nations to act interdictively in extreme circumstances, might be by encouraging an acceptance that an information intervention capacity, up to and including jamming, should be a standard attribute of a Chapter VII mandate.

Chapter VII has already been used to justify certain responses to and with information, and I agree that information intervention should be considered a component part of a Chapter VII mandate. There is increasing recognition that this is already the case, but such recognition has not been formalised; it hinges on the experience of individual officials, both military and civilian, in a range of conflicts who realise the importance of media and are determined to do a better job of countering abuses.

Pursuing a definition both broad enough to be usable in authorizing interventions, yet narrow enough to resist abuse by authoritarian regimes, and drawing on the Brandenburg v. Ohio *decision, you have argued that for speech to constitute incitement, it must incite 'people to commit mass abuses whose realisation appears imminent'.[7] While this helpfully opens the way to pro-active intervention, it is a highly political definition, isn't it?*

The Nuremberg standard from the Streicher case was that the incited act had to occur for the incitement to be actionable.[8] This is *de facto* the kind of standard we have now, and it apparently removes our capacity to be pro-active. It means people can be punished for incitement only after the incited act occurs. The Ferdinand Nahimana prosecution in the Rwanda Tribunal appears to confirm this standard.[9] We haven't yet reached the stage where people are being punished in a more pre-emptive or preventative manner for incitement, even if there is a high degree of imminence. We need to do better, and we need to develop practices and institutions that build credibility for making pro-active judgements that address conflicts early in their development.

How in practice would international legal norms be revised?

This is the great question in international law: how is international law made? There is overlap between members of the legal community thinking about these things, members of international organizations who deal with these conflicts, and thirdly, the governments that foot the bill for mopping up the conflicts once they emerge. Information intervention is not a big enough issue for an international convention. Perhaps a first step would be an international conference on media and conflict, bringing together governments, non-governmental organizations, media providers, and others. But it is an issue that more and more people recognize as being critical, and its centrality will only increase as the information revolution develops new ways of delivering information to people and affecting our lives.

What is the role of international legal bodies such as the United Nations (Human Rights Commission), the International Criminal Court, and the war crimes tribunals, in developing the legal standards necessary to discern when information intervention is appropriate?

If we are prepared to punish people for using media to incite violence, and if such incitement is considered an offence for which a person can be tried, there is an imperative to consider what we can do to prevent such incitement when it occurs. Legal judgements can do a great deal to develop the type of standards that allow us to know what it is that we are looking for. All the institutions you mention can and should play a role in developing these standards.

Did the Rwanda tribunal's judgement in the Akayesu case break new ground? The judges indicated that successful and unsuccessful incitements to genocide must alike be actionable.[10]

The *Akayesu* judgement is helpful but I don't know how influential it will be in developing new standards, because Akayesu was mayor of a town and was involved in ordering actual killings. Nevertheless, that case did hold that direct and public incitement to commit genocide should be punished, even when the incitement fails to produce the result expected by the perpetrators. While this is encouraging, the broader legal implications are yet to be seen. The ideal scenario for testing this holding might look like this: tensions in Burundi, let us say, are extremely high, there are reports that weapons are being distributed, and someone goes on a dominant radio station to say, 'Take out your weapons, now is the time.' This would demonstrate most clearly the need for a structure that would allow the apprehension and trial of that person for incitement even before the act took place. Better yet, we would empower people in Burundi to make the case in the responsible media against taking out your knives and doing those kinds of things, but those options aren't mutually exclusive. The imminent Nahimana decision may also have a bearing on this issue.

Are we going to see a reopening of the Great Power debates between the late 1940s and the 1960s, when definitions of incitement were hammered out among the delegates drafting the Genocide Convention, Article 19 of the Universal Declaration, the International Covenant on Civil and Political Rights, and so forth?

There is a difficult balancing act to be achieved. For this specific exception that we are talking about – incitement to imminent human rights abuses – the same types of legal models could indeed be used for censoring the Internet, or keeping cultural content out of certain national markets. On the other hand, while there is a danger in reopening these issues, it should be weighed against the benefit of creating a space where action may be required. Even on the Internet, in the United States we recognize that minimum standards are required. Our domestic legal system accepts those minimum legal standards. It will be difficult, but there is enough room for nuance in the international system for that claim to be made.

We should remember that when these issues were raised in the 1950s and 1960s, non-governmental organisations (NGOs) did not have the same role that they have today. This is another complicating factor. When you talk about limiting the absolute free flow of information, you invite the wrath of certain NGOs. I have tremendous respect for those organisations. It is critically important that there are watchdog groups that stand up for absolute principles.[11] Absolute principles are easier to uphold than principles with exceptions.

Citing the example of Rwanda in January 1994, when RTLM broadcasts were inciting a genocide, which then happened, most NGOs would probably agree that it would have been justified to interfere with those broadcasts. Others would insist that any benefit of making this exception would not be worth the loss of the principle. While the latter would be a respectable opinion, I would disagree with it. NGOs that fund, support, and promote indigenous media are the future, and we should give them all the support we can. Maybe a next step will be to bring local people who have developed indigenous media in, say, the Balkans to, say, East Timor. What are the models for developing indigenous media in a repressive society? After the wealthier nations and international organisations have helped these groups, these indigenous groups should help build the trans-national issue networks that can empower people all around the world to develop indigenous media. We need to facilitate the cross-empowerment of a global independent media movement.

Returning to the United Nations: in 1997, you proposed that 'the United Nations should establish an independent information intervention unit with three primary areas of responsibility: monitoring, peace broadcasting, and, in extreme cases, jamming radio and television broadcasts [. . .] [I]t may be necessary to provide the proposed unit with standing authority to carry out its function, with the Security Council maintaining veto power over its actions [. . .] Radio and television jamming is the most potentially controversial of the unit's proposed tasks and ideally should be used only after peace broadcasting has failed, but often there may not be time for such piecemeal escalation.'[12] Predictably, this idea drew fire in the American press.[13] Do you stand by it today?

At that time, I was trying to think how to devise an automatic tripwire so that people engaging in that sort of incitement would at least have to worry about crossing the line. I accept that in the current international climate, the popular fear of giving a standing United Nations body the ability to violate, even to this extent, the sovereign rights of a sovereign state mean that such ideas would just not be feasible. It may be an ideal of the human rights movement, but we are not there yet.

Nevertheless, the United Nations can and should play a much greater role in monitoring provocative propaganda, reporting on its occurrence, supporting independent media, and engaging in peace broadcasting to bring reliable news and information with a United Nations imprimatur to crisis areas, even when United Nations peacekeeping troops are not engaged. This is a huge growth area and deserves considerable attention.

The United Nations must be much better organised in how it addresses pre-conflict propaganda and how it utilizes information tools in peacekeeping and other operations. A cohesive unit that brings together best practices, develops guidelines, carries out training, maintains a database of skills and equipment, and serves as a United Nations focal point for information intervention-style activities would be very valuable, although it might shy away from discussing jamming, at least in earlier stages of development.

Thanks to the Brahimi Report, there seems a better chance than ever that the United Nations will establish a dedicated unit to develop and oversee information in peace operations. By the time this book comes to print, the unit may even be up and running.[14]

The Brahimi recommendations will, if realized, be an important step forward. Nevertheless, much more is needed than to improve the ability to utilize public information more effectively in peacekeeping operations. There needs to be a unit focusing on media issues, pulling together resources, planning and developing strategies for using media tools to promote peacekeeping and peacemaking. This would make a critical difference. Pro-active forms of information intervention, that is, intervention prior to humanitarian intervention, arc another and a trickier matter. Presumably any new unit within the UN Department of Peacekeeping Operations (DPKO) will steer clear of pro-active intervention issues at least at the beginning, and focus on what is more realizable. Having said that, some type of pro-active capacity at the United Nations is necessary if the international community is serious about responding effectively to the type of incitement that we saw in Rwanda.

There needs to be a forum for discussing the technical issues, resources, and challenges. First, we need to define international responsibilities for the monitoring, alert, and response functions I have just mentioned. Then, we need to develop the technology for doing what needs to be done. We should probably think in terms of community radio packages, mobile production facilities, and mobile high-power transmitters that can broadcast on FM frequencies across borders. Digital satellite radio may become critical in the future, but it will be a long time before it is usable in most crisis areas.

The right to seek, receive, and impart information and ideas through any media and regardless of frontiers has been considered for more than half a century as an elementary human right.[15] *Should the operational definition of 'humanitarian assistance' be broadened accordingly to include information-related assistance, along with food, drink, medicines, and shelter?*

It could and it should. The right to receive and impart information is critical for empowering citizens to make the decisions that determine the future of their countries, and to control their own lives. Wherever there is a need for humanitarian assistance, at least one faction on the ground is often manipulating the information system to help create the very conflicts that are causing the refugee crisis or whatever crisis it is that humanitarian assistance is responding to. This is why indigenous voices of moderation and indigenous responsible media must be supported. If a crisis has already passed the point where humanitarian assistance would be feasible, we are presumably beyond the stage where the mere provision of reliable news and information to people could avert the crisis. In such situations, stronger measures might be appropriate.

If it were accepted that reliable information was a form of humanitarian assistance, mechanisms to deliver that information would have to be developed. Those mechanisms do not exist now. It might require a dedicated unit with mobile radio stations. Right now, we have the international beg, borrow, or steal model, which does not work quickly or systematically enough. There may be technical fixes, but they will always require people and equipment. Information assistance must be a core component of humanitarian assistance because it empowers people to make better decisions that impact every aspect of their lives and livelihoods.

You mentioned changes in intervention practice that have not yet been reflected in changing precept. Can you expand on this?

Consider the Balkans. There has been a strong recognition in recent years that the media were critical in the development of conflict, and would be critical in responding to it. In Bosnia, for example, the power to intervene in the local media has grown since 1997. Look at the Sintra accords for Bosnia, or the increasing levels of investment in media activities in the Balkans, but also to a much lesser extent in East Timor and elsewhere.[16] For that matter, the targeting decisions for NATO bombings in 1999 were an implicit recognition that mass media were playing a central role in the Milosevic propaganda and war effort.

There is increased recognition of the importance of the information issue, but what is badly needed is systematization of the lessons and conclusions so far. Everywhere the international community goes to engage in peacekeeping or peacemaking operations, information should be a critical part of their mandate. There needs to be a core of people who understand these issues and who are building models for how these tools are applied. In the current structure, there is too much ad-hockery. Energy and resources are wasted in reinventing the wheel, and the time it takes to get going once a problem has been identified is much longer than it should be. In the case of information for peacekeeping operations, a single day's delay matters. You must get on the ground, explain why you're there, explain what you're doing, empower voices of moderation, and get their voices to the public. There isn't time to reconstitute ourselves for each of these conflicts.

Not only that: when the international community does this the ad-hoc way, it loses a lot of credibility because there's no plan, and expectations are not clearly delineated to local populations. This is why the international community sometimes comes into conflict with the very people they are trying to help. You must come with a framework and explain your goals. Goal number one is developing indigenous media: these are the models we use, these are the resources that we bring to bear, this is how we want to work together. Goal number two is to establish an effective mouthpiece of the international community, with a transparent structure. Goal number three is to create an environment in which everybody – ourselves included – acts responsibly, explaining that different models and frameworks have been used successfully elsewhere in the world to develop media responsibility, with a system of sanctions for those who don't abide by minimum standards. If those three points were clearly delineated in the beginning, and a dialogue was begun immediately with groups on the ground, it would help every other aspect of a peace operation.

Should the United Nations be the forum for this systematizing at operational and also conceptual or strategic levels?

Whether the United Nations should do it I cannot say, but someone has to bring all the players together and think about what makes the most sense. For United Nations peace operations, the United Nations needs its own system. But it would be a shame if others who are involved in situations where the United Nations is not the primary actor could not benefit from a shared knowledge base. A private NGO could equally well bring all the players together and compile what ultimately might be a play-book, setting out the different ways of creating responsible indigenous media, and establishing an effective co-ordination point for the international community. There are various options for developing an optimal media environment, but the set of options is not infinite and patterns repeat themselves. The development of a shared play-book and a community of experts would benefit whoever was engaged in peacekeeping or peacemaking operations.

Will situations requiring information intervention arise in the future with anything like the frequency and urgency of the 1990s? Additionally, information tools are cheap and effective. The weaker power in a conflict will always use them to seek an asymmetrical advantage, while the stronger will always utilize them to enhance legitimacy?

Absolutely. These crises will look different in different contexts, but they will recur. Increasingly powerful information and communications tools are and will be available to small and otherwise weak groups that will use them to build coalitions, disrupt relationships, mount propaganda or misinformation campaigns, and so on. These groups may never be able to raise an army, but they can in some cases go head to head with major powers – look at the Zapatistas in Mexico or the Falun Gong in China. The tools may be new but the goals are as old as politics itself.

At the same time, the need for means to address this problem might decrease as the number of outlets grows unceasingly?

Ideally, information intervention techniques will be made redundant by media proliferation and liberalization. That is the goal, and the great bulk of international efforts should go into making that the case. It is much more productive to support and empower voices of moderation within a society than to do anything else. The jamming argument, so to speak, applies only when everything else has been tried, or when an extreme crisis situation precludes more deliberate efforts.

In the Internet age it will be increasingly difficult to make the case for jamming or other proscriptive interference. As people gain more information options, it becomes more difficult to make the case that one particular television or radio station, let alone a newspaper or website, can fulfil the imminence standard – the connection between the incitement and the act. If the information connects the ideas to the action, then it is as much a part of the action as it is of the ideas. But if there are multiple outlets, then it is going to be a lot more difficult to argue that a particular outlet is a component part of an action, because many different pieces of information will be feeding into the action. Implicit in this argument is the problematic prospect that it will become more acceptable to take proscriptive action in less developed media markets than in media markets that are more developed.

Let's discuss a concrete measure of multilateral information intervention that you were involved with: the 'Ring Around Serbia'.

The 'Ring Around Serbia' should be put in the context of the broader United States approach to information issues in Serbia and Kosovo. The United States government, along with a range of inter-governmental and non-governmental bodies, has for a long time strongly supported indigenous media throughout the Balkans as a critical part of United States policy. Early in 1999, between the February and March rounds of negotiations at Rambouillet, we established a satellite television programme on Albanian television called *Agreement for Peace*. In that programme, American leaders – Secretary of State Madeleine Albright, Senator Robert Dole, and others – appeared through a satellite hook-up on prime-time Albanian television. Interviewed live by Albanian and Kosovo Albanian journalists, they made the case through dialogue for Rambouillet. We estimate these programmes reached approximately 70 per cent of the population of Kosovo. Over the ensuing months, we produced about 140 programmes for Albanian, Macedonian, Bosnian, and other regional stations. This was a central part of our information strategy, and it was something the United States had never done at this level before.

The Serbian Law on Public Information, passed in October 1998, made illegal the re-broadcast of international programming.[17] A democratic media environment depends on the overlap of different types of media. What matters is the interaction between the independent media, the international media, and other types of local media, so people hear different things from different quarters, allowing them to develop their own views based on the levels of credibility they attribute to the different sources. When the Milosevic regime cracked down on rebroadcasting the local-language services of the international media and cracked down on the indigenous independent media, a vacuum was created. This vacuum was empowering for Milosevic's propaganda, because it gave him a tool that was much more dominant than it would otherwise have been.

The international community faced a challenge. How could we get information to the population of Serbia that would allow them to make their own decisions about their future? We gave what support we could to indigenous media, but when the conflict started in March 1999 they largely fell silent. We considered a number of other options. The model we decided on was a network of radio transmitters in the countries adjoining Serbia. Starting in April, these transmitters broadcast the pooled Serbian-language programming of five international stations: BBC, Deutsche Welle, Radio France International, Voice of America, and Radio Free Europe. We believe it had a major impact. Our polling during the conflict suggested that about 40 per cent of the population was listening to those broadcasts. Subsequent assessments found an audience level of about 12 or 13 per cent, nothing like during the bombing but not bad for radio penetration.[18] It has been a monumental feat of co-ordination among the international broadcasters, and a feat of engineering as well. Some of the towers had to be built from scratch, others had to be boosted.

The 'Ring Around Serbia' was a model of international co-operation in trying to get objective and alternative information into a conflict zone. Was it legal? I believe it was, as a result of the balancing test I described earlier. The dictates of human rights law provided a justification, in my view, of more aggressive responsive action by NATO and the international community, and information intervention was a component of this broader intervention but also independent of it.

The radio station in eastern Bosnia that joined the 'Ring Around Serbia' broke the terms of its contract with the Independent Media Commission (IMC) in Sarajevo when it adjusted its transmitter to beam into Serbia. This was ironic, given the IMC's struggle to regulate the Bosnian media according to international norms of broadcast behaviour. Information intervention weaves a tangled web.

There is always a very difficult and sometimes painful balancing act to be achieved between the dictates of different legal regimes. When you suppress speech or radio broadcasts in support of the incitement provisions of the Convention on Genocide, you often violate dictates of radio or telecommunications law. Doing nothing is a choice and doing something is a choice. Whatever decision you take is part right and part wrong. Bosnia needs an adequate system of broadcasting regulation, in line with international standards, and people in Serbia needed objective information. There were issues of legal justification in a number of countries involved. In some of them, the go-ahead was given by cabinet decision. Unfortunately, these sorts of conflicts are inevitable.

The 'Ring Around Serbia' came about when you were senior co-ordinator for the International Public Information Group (IPIG), a new unit at the Department of State. What were the origins of this initiative?

During the Gulf War, there was a United States interagency co-ordination body on information issues that was run out of the White House. At the end of that time, a request was made to turn that ad-hoc committee into a more permanent one. This did not happen. When I came to the National Security Council in September 1997, I felt strongly that we needed to be more systematic about how we think about and respond to the use of malicious information in the development of conflicts and crises. We pulled together an interagency team to do a six-month study on how the United States uses information tools for the prevention and mitigation of conflict. While we were preparing this study, this interagency group got tasked with a number of different activities, co-ordinating information responses in situations like Iraq and Rwanda. When the study was complete, we made certain recommendations, including that there should be a presidential decision directive on international public information. This was done.[19] It called for all agencies to be more systematic in how they think about information projection internationally; for greater outreach to non-state actors, including NGOs; and for a central co-ordination mechanism housed at the State Department. I moved from the White House to the State Department to oversee implementation. Our IPI co-ordination group was already functioning when the Kosovo war began.

What were the obstacles to introducing a different way of looking at international information issues at the State Department?

The fundamental problem as I see it is that there are two different cultures that are sometimes complementary and at other times in conflict over the role that media-related activities can play in a conflict. The first is the traditional public-affairs function. People who are socialised within the public affairs system see everything that might bring the sanctity of information into question as inherently dangerous. Information intervention involves a much more aggressive use of information tools. These tools are more commonly associated with propaganda than with press or public affairs. Even if it is propaganda against genocide, there is sometimes a propaganda element in information intervention.

In other words, even though the primary goal of information intervention is to promote and empower the voices of moderation and objectivity in target countries, officials trained in public affairs tend to worry that once the international community or certain international actors support media on the ground, already you are potentially tainting the information from those sources. These criticisms have some validity. Some of the implementation problems that have been repeated around the world stem from the difference between these two cultures. When traditional public-affairs people see this more aggressive approach towards information tools, their alarm bells go off, because they see this as something that can undermine what they are doing. At the same time, people who are engaged in this approach need to be extremely mindful of credibility, perception, and objectivity. Institutionally, this can create conflict. This is what has happened in the United States government and in a lot of different places.

Part of the answer lies in compromise. There needs to be an informed dialogue, within but also between the institutions of government. You wouldn't want the people who think of information as an intervention tool to be running around on their own. Information intervention is a very serious action that should be placed in the context of other needs and goals, and my feeling is that we need to create an environment where every legitimate policy has a hearing, then let the chips fall where they may. But the public affairs model is much older, there is an entrenched bureaucracy doing that; while when you come into a bureaucracy trying to innovate you have no natural supporters, but you do have natural opponents. Additionally, engaging the international media requires a government culture of openness to reach out to and involve non-state actors such as independent media and NGOs. This culture is often lacking in government foreign policy institutions.

This resembles what one hears about the perennial tensions between the Department of Public Information and the Department of Peacekeeping Operations (DPKO) at the United Nations Secretariat. From the point of view of traditional diplomacy, the pro-active use of information can be deeply suspect, even more so than covert action. Let us explore a little further the risks of using information and propaganda tools in an international context. You mentioned the risk that it will become 'more acceptable to take proscriptive action in less developed media markets'. Your writing on 'openness' in government has, a critic might say, an apologetic ring. You say outright that the advertising industry should be the exemplar of effective foreign policy outreach.[20] To put the best and most persuasive face on the mandate of a multilateral humanitarian or even military intervention is one thing, but you are advocating something different: to wit, a more adroit spinning of United States foreign policy. Our critic, not necessarily a left-libertarian, might see these essays as unmasking the real political agenda behind information-intervention thinking as a whole; to wit, that it represents a fashionable means of enhancing United States predominance within the international system, using information technology, and that this sleek discourse of openness, accountability, and humanitarian intervention seeks to preserve United States hegemony.[21]

I would understand the criticism, insofar as openness can favour the largest actor in the current global information environment, and the United States is dominant. At the same time, what distinguishes electronic media is their multi-directionality. This creates the possibility of engaging in a global dialogue. It may or may not happen. The United States is still producing the majority of content (although most content will be Chinese within ten years). The messages from our society will have much less impact if we are seen as a hegemonic power. We need to overcome the perception of hegemony, and the way to do this is by supporting the efforts of people abroad, primarily in the developing world, to share their information, to get it online. The United States should make a major commitment of resources to support indigenous groups so they can engage in a global dialogue. We stand to benefit far more from having people critical of us engaged in global dialogue than from not supporting that kind of democracy of access.

Having said that, people who serve the United States government need to think how they can be most effective in achieving what they are seeking to do. If our goal is to promote democracy or to promote policies around the world, we must do the best job we can, which means building coalitions, sharing expertise, and learning from others at home and abroad. It also means utilizing the most effective tools available.

Who should pay for this United States commitment? Is it philanthropy, or farsighted pre-positioning for future market expansion?

It would be philanthropy in the same way that the Marshall Plan was philanthropic. The United States, in alliance with other nations around the world that want to participate, should commit major resources both to building the infrastructure for global dialogue – Internet access and the like – and for the human development that will allow indigenous content to be placed online in a presentable and shareable way, and for those resources to be used and shared by a broad range of people.

Can we discuss the implications of the United States free-flow model as applied to media development in recent post-conflict situations? The differences between median American and European assumptions about, for example, public service broadcasting and media regulation can be fruitful, but may also generate tension. Since NATO forces occupied Kosovo in summer 1999, the tension has become more acute there than elsewhere in the region. In Croatia and Bosnia, the gap has been bridged in the interest of preserving a united international front for media reform. In Kosovo, however, some European governments feel that the Americans undermined their efforts to restructure the former state broadcaster, while some Americans feel the Europeans have been high-handed, even 'neo-colonialist' towards local media.

This is a problem. There was concern in the United States that the only system the Kosovars know from experience is that of a single, dominant, state-controlled broadcaster. If you recreate that model, even in the name of public service, are you creating a new model that almost certainly will be abused? So the American view is that you have to develop multiple voices. My sense is that the European model will change, as the role of private media entities in Europe continues to increase. National broadcasters have played an important role in Europe, and the commitment to public service has been greater as a result, but the trend is towards an American model.

It is true that the existing public service models face mounting challenges of legitimacy, funding, and mission. Yet there is a counter-argument. Advertising revenues in most post-conflict societies cannot support a range of media that can afford to uphold high ethical standards. Therefore media are dependent on magnates, tycoons, who want to influence the outlets they own. In this context, privatization is likely to militate against the emergence of ethical journalism, because the society has no more experience of professional private media than it has of public service media. Secondly, the free-flow advocates may be confusing an end with a means in these particular post-conflict situations. Everyone agrees that the objective is to establish a liberal-democratic state of law in which freedom of expression can be as strongly upheld as it is in the United States. The best way to attain that objective, however, is not necessarily by installing it as a finished fact in societies that lack the elementary conditions of liberal democracy.

It comes down to judging which of these flawed systems seems least flawed. In my view, the possibility of abuse weighs in favour of a more American model. The level of supervision needed to ensure that a public service broadcaster won't be abused, is greater than the level of oversight and commitment required to make a private system work. But I recognize the difficulty and the fine balance needed here. The distinction between these models is not hard-and-fast. Both models need a sound legal and regulatory framework. The private model is ultimately a public-private model, because self-regulation does not function satisfactorily unless it can be overridden by official measures when it fails. Additionally, tycoons may control some private media, but there often is a market for reliable information and the costs of producing and sharing this type of information can be relatively low.

Let's stay with media development. Other chapters in this book have much to say about media development, as authorized by the mandates of international missions and regulated by the international standards and conventions that the State in question is a party to. Is media development the natural sequel to information intervention?

Media development is more palatable as a term than information intervention, which alarms some people. I would be delighted if the term information intervention could be completely subsumed within media development. But I think there is a narrow area for information intervention, and a grey area where more aggressive action in the media field is required. Some of that action might be more on the intervention side, some might be more on the development side. The goal of information intervention, of course, is to make itself unnecessary by identifying conflict situations as early as possible so that in a spirit of co-operation, support, and mutual understanding the international community can help the indigenous media to develop their own independent voices.

Is there an analogy here with the thinking in the United Nations since the failed missions of the mid 1990s, about the need for peace operations to have a 'credible deterrent capacity'? The logic being that the better prepared you are to use coercion, the less likely you are to have to exercise it, and the more likely you are to succeed?

The whole threat of jamming and suppressive action would have to be dangled so prominently to be an effective deterrent that you would be compromising your own integrity. You would have to build a system that might even be stronger than you would want it to be in order to have this deterrent effect. Hostile suppression is really the last resort.

We must be ready to respond to the most egregious situations, while knowing that this information response may never strike fear into potential perpetrators' hearts as might armed intervention. Most of our resources, however, should go into encouraging the development of open media environments that can support dialogue, understanding, and the peaceful and informed resolution of disputes.

Even so, the better prepared we were to intervene coercively, the less likely we would be to have to do so?

That's bound to be true. Developing norms and standards would ultimately be more effective than developing coercive readiness, even though you need such stand-by mechanisms for extreme situations where other more pro-active and less interventionist methods have failed.

You have written that the definition of 'foreign policy' has to widen, to include inter alia 'government information campaigns targeted at foreign populations'.[22] The Charter of the IPI, as leaked in the press, defined the group's mission 'to influence foreign audiences in ways favourable to the achievement of United States foreign-policy objectives'. This was to be done by influencing 'the emotions, motives, objective reasoning, and ultimately the behaviour of foreign governments, organisations, groups, and individuals'.[23] This was copied directly from the official United States military definition of psychological operations, or 'psyops'. Should we admit that what we've been discussing all along is white psyops, and what we need is more of the same, conceived by civilians yet carried out with military resolve?[24]

Government public communications are only effective if people think them credible. In an age of decentralized and open information systems, there is virtually no room for governments to make knowingly false or misleading statements or to engage in overt propaganda. Governments trade on their credibility, which must be steadfastly maintained. The downside of being caught in such insidious action far outweighs any short-term benefits. Having said that, however, government can and should attempt to put their best foot forward and communicate their interests in an effective manner. Governments can and should also build alliances with others of like mind to advance shared goals.

Psyops is a strange term that even military people are moving away from. Within the military, people engage in public information activities such as explaining to Haitians why US troops were arriving, or in public information campaigns for the anti-drug effort. There are also people in the military who engage in battlefield deception – trying to convince an enemy that we are about to do one thing when actually we are preparing to do another. These two functions – public information and deception – are distinct and should be kept separate. Psyops is a grab-bag term that doesn't do a good enough job of making this distinction. A number of people in the US military argue that the term should be retired. That would allow us to create another term, perhaps 'International Military Information', to describe the truthful activities carried out by the military, like other government agencies, to promote certain goals.

The United States gains from open information systems, even if these systems relatively soften our own voice, much more than we would from propagandizing the rest of the world. We need to promote global democratic access to media, which will be one of the critical foreign policy issues of this century. We all need to think systematically and creatively about how to work with media to foster global dialogue, forestall the most egregious abuses, and promote peace and understanding.

Bibliography

Bullock, Alan (1993), *Hitler and Stalin: Parallel lives*, London: Fontana Press.
Lukovic, Petar (2001), 'Balkan Crisis Report no. 220', *Institute for War and Peace Reporting*, 21 February 2001.
Metzl, Jamie F. (1996), 'Information technology and human rights', *Human Rights Quarterly*, vol. 18, no. 4., pp. 705–46.
————— (1997), 'Rwandan genocide and the international law of radio Jamming', *The American Journal of International Law*, vol. 91, no. 4, October, pp. 628–51.
————— (1997), 'Information intervention: when switching channels isn't enough', *Foreign Affairs*, vol. 76, no. 6, November/December 1997, pp. 15–20.
————— (1999), 'Popular Diplomacy' *DAEDALUS*, vol. 128, no. 2, Spring, pp. 177–92.
————— (1999), 'The International Politics of Openness', *The Washington Quarterly*, vol. 22, no. 3, Summer, p. 11.
Taylor, Philip M. (1997), *Global Communications, International Affairs and the Media since 1945*, London and New York: Routledge.

Notes

1. 'There have been an increasing number of "information interventions" in recent years. UN radio stations and programs in peace missions in Namibia, Cambodia, and eastern Slavonia have disseminated impartial, reliable news and information in conflicts rife with propaganda. Broadcasts organised by non-governmental organisations (NGOs) in Liberia, Burundi, and Bosnia have brought individuals from different sides of the conflicts together to discuss issues openly over the airwaves and develop conflict-resolution strategies.' Metzl, 'Information Intervention. When Switching Channels Isn't Enough', p. 16.
2. Mr Dragoljub Milanovic, the director of RTS, was indeed arrested in February 2001 in connection with the death of sixteen of his staff during the NATO air strike. 'Speaking about the incident during her recent visit to Belgrade, Carla del Ponte [chief prosecutor for the International Criminal Tribunal for the former Yugoslavia] said Milosevic and his regime knew in advance that RTS would be bombarded; that they sacrificed its employees, convinced their death would reverse international public opinion'. Petar Lukovic, 'Balkan Crisis Report no. 220'.
3. RTLM was Radio-Television Libre des Milles Collines, a radio station established in 1993, nominally independent but in reality under the control of Hutu governing circles and security forces.

4. 'As the great powers lose enthusiasm for addressing mass human rights abuses with large-scale armed interventions, the international community must search for less risky alternatives that accomplish more than the symbolic and generally impotent condemnations from bodies like the UN Commission on Human Rights. One such measure would be to monitor, counter, and block radio and television broadcasts that incite widespread violence in crisis zones around the world [. . .] Permitting limited radio and television jamming in defence of human rights is no magic bullet, but it is a potentially effective and relatively low-risk tool for countering dangerous messages that incite people to violence.' Metzl, 'Information Intervention. When Switching Channels Isn't Enough' pp. 15 and 20.

5. Chapter VII of the Charter of the United Nations contains Articles 39–51. It addresses 'Action with respect to threats to the peace, breaches of the peace, and acts of aggression'. Art. 41 states that 'The Security Council may decide what measures not involving the use of armed force are to be employed to give effect to its decisions, and it may call upon the Members of the United Nations to apply such measures. These may include *complete or partial interruption of economic relations and of rail, sea, air, postal, telegraphic, radio, and other means of communication*, and the severance of diplomatic relations.' (Emphasis added.)

6. See Note 1 above. Also, Art. 42 of Chapter VII: 'Should the Security Council consider that measures provided for in Article 41 would be inadequate or have proved to be inadequate, it may take such action by air, sea, or land forces as may be necessary to maintain or restore international peace and security. Such action may include demonstrations, blockade, and other operations by air, sea, or land forces of Members of the United Nations'.

7. 'Rather than establishing a traditional military intervention force, UN member states might create a well-trained and equipped rapid information response team to address and challenge media activities in a given country when those activities are inciting people to commit mass abuses whose realisation appears imminent. Such a unit would be equipped with the most advanced monitoring technology, mobile broadcast capabilities, and jamming devices and might carry out monitoring, peace, and reconciliation broadcasting, and, in the most extreme cases, jamming activities.' Metzl, 'Rwandan Genocide and the International Law of Radio Jamming', p. 649.

8. Julius Streicher was a leading Nazi who founded and edited *Die Stuermer*, which according to Alan Bullock was 'the most notorious of all anti-Semitic publications'. Alan Bullock, *Hitler and Stalin: Parallel lives*, p. 87. The Nuremburg Tribunal sentenced Streicher to death on the ground that his 'incitement to murder and extermination at the time when Jews in the East were being killed under the most horrible conditions clearly constitutes persecution on political and racial grounds in connection with War Crimes, as defined by the Charter, and constitutes a Crime against Humanity'. Metzl, 'Rwandan Genocide and the International Law of Radio Jamming', pp. 636–7.

9. Mr Ferdinand Nahimana was director of the Radio-Television Libre des Milles Collines (RTLM). At time of writing, he stands accused of conspiracy to commit genocide, genocide, direct and public incitement to commit genocide, complicity in genocide, and crimes against humanity. His trial, together with those of Mr Jean-Bosco Barayagwiza, former director of political affairs in the Rwandan Ministry of Foreign Affairs and a founding member of the board of directors of RTLM, and Mr Hassan Ngeze, the editor-in-chief of *Kangura* newspaper,

began on 23 October 2000. See Chapter 8, 'Silencing the Voices of Hate in
Rwanda' by Alison Des Forges, and Chapter 3, 'International Law and Information Intervention' by Eric Blinderman.

10. On 2 September 1998, the International Criminal Tribunal for Rwanda found
Jean-Paul Akayesu guilty on nine counts, including 'direct and public incitement
to commit genocide'. This wording is taken from Art. 3C of the 1948 Convention
on the Prevention and Punishment of the Crime of Genocide. Paragraphs 561 and
562 of the judgement contain the following remarks: '[T]he issue before the
Chamber is whether the crime of direct and public incitement to commit genocide
can be punished even where such incitement was unsuccessful. It appears from the
travaux préparatoires of the Convention on Genocide that the drafters of the
Convention considered stating explicitly that incitement to commit genocide could
be punished, whether or not it was successful. In the end, a majority decided
against such an approach. Nevertheless, the Chamber is of the opinion that it
cannot thereby be inferred that the intent of the drafters was not to punish
unsuccessful acts of incitement. In light of the overall *travaux*, the Chamber holds
the view that the drafters of the Convention simply decided not to specifically
mention that such a form of incitement could be punished. [. . .] In the opinion of
the Chamber, the fact that such acts are in themselves particularly dangerous
because of the high risk they carry for society, even if they fail to produce results,
warrants that they be punished as an exceptional measure. The Chamber holds
that genocide clearly falls within the category of crimes so serious that direct and
public incitement to commit such a crime must be punished as such, even where
such incitement failed to produce the result expected by the perpetrator.'

11. 'Because information systems are simultaneously emerging both as potential tools
of empowerment and liberation and as implements of surveillance and oppression,
and because the contours of this struggle will largely be determined by the values
and priorities of the relevant actors, human rights organisations can play a vital role
in shaping public discourse. Just as the movement has brought human rights to
greater levels of popular consciousness over past decades, so too can it weigh in to
support this vital human rights concern by making the free flow of information
and free and democratic access to it a central human rights concern'. Metzl,
'Information Technology and Human Rights', p. 743.

12. Metzl, 'Information Intervention. When Switching Channels Isn't Enough',
pp. 17, 19, 18.

13. The *Los Angeles Times* (3 December 1997) commented, 'Although the problem of
hate-filled radio broadcasts is a serious one, there are ways of dealing with it that
don't involve creating some huge, supranational censorship unit [. . .] Who would
determine exactly what kinds of radio programs should be blocked and which
programs could be aired? What would ensure that the jamming decisions were not
motivated by politics? Wouldn't the creation of such a United Nations operation
strengthen the hand of governments that want to jam radio transmissions for much
less noble reasons? [. . .] But a worldwide, UN-run jamming team? As a Hollywood script, maybe the idea has possibilities. As a foreign policy, it's a loser.' On 5
January 2000, *The Christian Science Monitor* accepted that hate-radio in Rwanda
should have been stopped by 'a UN body [making] a specific, limited jamming
effort'. 'But', the editorial goes on, 'does that mean a UN "jam squad" should be
created and sent to block broadcasts wherever incitement to violence might
be expected? No. There's too much risk that mission creep could occur.

Well-intentioned officials might decide to jam suspect stations lest they say something dangerous. The result could be blocking stations hither and yon because a soldier makes a bellicose threat, or a strongman voices defiance toward UN observers.'

14. The Report of the Panel on United Nations Peace Operations (known after its Algerian chairman as the Brahimi Report) was commissioned by UN secretary-general Kofi Annan in March 2000 and presented to the Security Council the following September. Recommendation no. 17 states that 'A unit for operations planning and support of public information in peace operations should be established.' In October 2000, Annan instructed that this unit should be set up within the Department of Peace-keeping Operations (DPKO). Unfortunately, at time of writing, implementation of this reform has been stalled at committee stage.

15. Art. 19 of the Universal Declaration of Human Rights states, 'Everyone has the right to freedom of opinion and expression; this right includes freedom to hold opinions without interference and to seek, receive, and impart information and ideas through any media and regardless of frontiers.'

16. Sintra accords for Bosnia: On 30 May 1997, the ministerial meeting of the Steering Board of the Peace Implementation Council (the PIC, the highest international body for implementing the Dayton Accords in Bosnia and Herzegovina) met at Sintra in Portugal. The PIC announced that the high representative (the most senior civilian responsible for implementation) would thenceforth have 'the right to curtail or suspend any media network or programme whose output is in persistent and blatant contravention' of the Dayton Accords. This extra authority was used later in the year to order NATO to occupy a number of Bosnian Serb-controlled transmitters, as discussed in Chapter 7.

17. This information law was repealed in February 2001 by the anti-Milosevic coalition that gained power in elections in September and then December 2000.

18. Audience interest revived during the post-electoral crisis of autumn 2000.
    A survey conducted by the Institute of Social Sciences of Belgrade University of radio listening habits of 1,104 persons [. . .] showed that RFE/RL was the most listened-to broadcaster since August 1999 and especially during the political crisis in the fall of 2000 [and] that international radio as a whole played a major role in informing the Serbian population during the recent tense period. During the days between 24 September and 3 October [2000], RFE/RL's listenership rating was 37 per cent, or nearly double that of the BBC (19 per cent) and more than state-run Radio Belgrade's 31 per cent. (Patrick Moore, Radio Free Europe/Radio Liberty's *Balkan Report*, 31 October 2000).

19. On 30 April 1999, President Clinton signed Presidential Decision Directive NSC-68. According to the text of the directive:
    Dramatic changes in the global information environment [. . .] require that we implement a more deliberate and well-developed international public information strategy in promoting our values and interests. Events in the Bosnia conflict and preceding the 1994 genocide in Rwanda demonstrated the unfortunate power of inaccurate and malicious information in conflict-prone situations. Effective use of our nation's highly-developed communications and information capabilities to address misinformation and incitement, mitigate inter-ethnic conflict, promote independent media organizations and the free flow of information, and support democratic participation will advance our interests and is a critical foreign policy objective. IPI activities address foreign audiences

only, and are designed neither to mislead audiences regarding the content or intent of US foreign policy nor to compromise in any way the integrity or independence of non-governmental organizations [. . .] It is the policy of the United States to enhance our use of IPI as a key instrument for preventing and mitigating foreign crises and advancing our interests around the world. In doing so, we will pay special attention to the collection and analysis of foreign public opinion on issues vital to US national interests [. . .] An interagency IPI core group (ICG) is hereby established to implement this PDD [. . .] Institutions outside the Administration may at times be more appropriate and effective conduits for information into an area than US Government agencies [. . .] Special attention must therefore be given to the potential contributions of a wide range of organizations now involved in providing information. These include those in the private sector – for-profit communications firms, independent media organizations, Internet providers, media conglomerates, and advertisers – as well as non-governmental organizations, which play a critical role in the development of civil society and the free exchange of ideas and information. The United States will continue to place the highest priority on supporting the development of global and indigenous media outlets that promote these objectives. It is also the policy of the United States to promote effective use of IPI by the United Nations and other international organizations in support of multilateral peacekeeping and complex contingency operations, as well as to promote cooperation on international information efforts with key allies.

20. 'To be most effective in the next century, US foreign policy must be first and foremost well conceived, but it must model itself both in formulation and promulgation along the lines of mass advertising and principled political campaigns.' Metzl, 'Popular Diplomacy', p. 188.

Although using different techniques for outreach has not been traditionally at the core of foreign policy, the models for its effective use are plainly available in political and mass advertising campaigns: state a goal, determine the audience, test messages or products with that audience, and then constructively engage with that audience [. . .] [T]hese models must be expanded to influence non-traditional and culturally dissimilar audiences across the globe. Some may argue that a foreign policy that internalises such principles is inherently amoral and manipulative. This is not the case. The most moral and just policies deserve their best chance of success by utilising proven methods that will only become more important in the future. In an open information environment, obfuscation and manipulation will eventually be uncovered, and providing reliable information will be crucial for earning the trust of populations already bombarded with multiple competing messages. Metzl, 'The International Politics of Openness', p. 11.

21. On 20 March 2000 *In These Times* newspaper reported:

There is nothing new about the US government deceiving the public about bad policies or strategic blunders. They are by nature hard to defend, even with the best PR, as one administration after another has demonstrated. What's new is that the administration is preparing to use different techniques to convince a world audience that US might makes right.

22. Metzl, 'Popular Diplomacy', p. 183.

23. As quoted by *In These Times*, 20 March 2000.

24. 'Psyops' are 'psychological operations', defined by NATO as 'planned

psychological activities in peace and war directed at enemy, friendly, and neutral audiences in order to influence attitudes and behaviour affecting the achievement of political and military objectives'. The United States military definition is only slightly different: 'Planned operations to convey selected information and indicators to foreign audiences to influence their emotions, motives, objective reasoning, and ultimately the behaviour of foreign governments, organisations, groups, and individuals. The purpose of psychological operations is to induce or reinforce foreign attitudes and behaviour favourable to the originator's objectives.' White psyops have been defined by Philip M. Taylor as information 'which is disseminated openly by clearly identifiable sources. It therefore acts as the official voice of the sender'. By contrast, 'Black activity is that which emanates from a source whose real origin is disguised [. . .] secret.' As for grey activity, it 'fails to identify any source specifically. It specialises in not telling the "whole truth" '. Taylor, *Global Communications, International Affairs and the Media Since 1945*, pp. 149, 150, 162–4.

SECTION TWO

2

Hate Propaganda and
International Human Rights Law

Stephanie Farrior

Introduction

International human rights treaties do not explicitly address multilateral intervention. This is because they are designed to govern the actions or inaction of states within their own territory or jurisdiction. This very significant body of law does, however, provide standards against which information intervention efforts might be evaluated. These laws allow – and in some cases require – states to block certain types of hate speech within their boundaries. Does this then permit the international community to take similar action? It does not necessarily follow that if a state may address hate speech to protect targeted populations within its boundaries, it may act out of humanitarian concern to do the same within another state's boundaries. Yet the body of law that has developed concerning state power over hate propaganda provides a rich source of ideas about legal authority and limits where international bodies and multilateral actions are concerned.

It is my view that, under international human rights law, unilateral or multilateral intervention against media engaged in inciting racial or ethnic hatred can constitute a permissible limitation on free expression and on the right to receive and impart information and ideas.

Hate propaganda can create and has, in fact, created conditions that foment widespread, sometimes genocidal violence. That violence can become so deeply entrenched and reinforced by propaganda that it cannot be offset solely by 'more speech' or speech advocating tolerance. Where such deeply etched speech-inspired hatred exists, the result can be the loss of thousands or millions of lives. This is the lesson that the drafters of international and regional human rights treaties drew from the Nazi regime, which led to their incorporating prohibition of hate speech into treaties whose goal it was to protect human rights. It is why human rights laws on freedom of expression often explicitly address issues of hate speech and authorize action against it.

In this essay, I explore the development of international human rights principles on speech and hate propaganda that govern individual states and that might, by extension, relate to the actions of the United Nations, NATO, or a state acting out of humanitarian concern to avoid violence and conflict in neighbouring or other states. The general principle, of course, is that international human rights law both protects the right to freedom of expression and allows certain limitations on the exercise of that right. The limitations pertinent here have been interpreted to permit the prohibition of hate speech. Indeed, three human rights instruments explicitly require governments to make advocacy of racial hatred an offence punishable by law. These are the International Covenant on Civil and Political Rights, the International Convention on the Elimination of All Forms of Racial Discrimination, and, if the advocacy constitutes incitement to violence or other similar illegal action against a person or group, the American Convention on Human Rights.

Freedom of expression is guaranteed in Article 19 of both the Universal Declaration of Human Rights and the International Covenant on Civil and Political Rights. Both documents also set out certain limits on that freedom. The Universal Declaration provides in Article 7 that everyone is entitled to protection against 'incitement' to any discrimination that is prohibited in the Declaration. The Universal Declaration also states in Article 29 that the exercise of the rights it sets forth may be restricted in order to secure recognition and respect for the rights and freedoms of others and to protect the public order. Article 30 declares that the rights in the Universal Declaration may not be interpreted as implying any right to engage in any activity aimed at the destruction of the rights in the Declaration. Nearly identical limitations clauses appear in the International Covenant on Civil and Political Rights, the European Convention on Human Rights, and the American Convention on Human Rights.

In addition to permitting certain restrictions on freedom of expression, the Covenant on Civil and Political Rights also requires states parties to prohibit by law 'any advocacy of national, racial, or religious hatred that constitutes incitement to discrimination, hostility, or violence' (Article 20.2).[1] A similar clause appears in the American Convention on Human Rights (Article 13.5), and a more detailed requirement to prohibit advocacy of racial hatred appears in the Convention on the Elimination of All Forms of Racial Discrimination (Article 4).

One of the principal theories underlying these limitations is that a right may not be used as a sword to destroy others' rights. Thus, for example, the European Commission on Human Rights has determined that it is permissible to punish someone for slurring ethnic groups and calling for their deportation, because such expression aims to convince people to violate the rights of others, in that case, members of those ethnic groups.[2] International law therefore requires a contextual analysis, wherein the right to freedom of expression is examined in relation to the other rights enumerated in a human rights instrument, and in particular to the right to equality. The use of the right to freedom of expression, if aimed to destroy the rights of others, constitutes an abuse of that right and as such may be restricted by law.

The *travaux préparatoires* of these human rights instruments reveal that the drafters recognised well the complexity of crafting a specific limitation on freedom of expression. As the drafters debated what particular form this matrix of human rights should take, issues common to human rights discourse arose: how to reconcile competing rights, how to determine permissible limits on a given right, and how to protect against the potential for government abuse of the power to limit a right.

These provisions were controversial. The clause in the Covenant on Civil and Political Rights requiring the prohibition of advocacy of racial hatred, for example, was adopted by a vote of fifty to eighteen, with fifteen abstentions.[3] It has been pointed out that the clause 'did not receive a single affirmative vote from any Member States of the Council of Europe. Indeed, ten of them voted against it'.[4] The implication that hate speech prohibitions lacked support among Western European nations, however, is misleading, as is the characterization that the debate was solely a manifestation of the Cold War struggle between the United States and the USSR. In fact, René Cassin of France was amongst those who led the push for such a clause. Several European countries voted against the provision simply because of disagreement over language added in the final debates, not because of opposition to the concept of prohibiting hate speech.

This chapter provides an overview of the provisions in international and regional human rights treaties that either permit or require states to prohibit the advocacy of racial hatred. The drafting history explains the concerns and the aims behind these provisions. Concrete examples illustrate the interpretation and application of these provisions by the bodies charged with monitoring their implementation.

The Universal Declaration of Human Rights

The right to freedom of opinion and expression proclaimed in the Universal Declaration of Human Rights includes the right 'to seek, receive, and impart information and ideas through any media and regardless of frontiers'.[5] As with all the rights in the Universal Declaration, however, this right is subject to certain restrictions. Individually and collectively, Articles 7, 29, and 30 limit the exercise of freedom of expression and provide ample support for 'information intervention' in certain circumstances.

Article 7 of the Universal Declaration requires protection against incitement to discrimination. It provides, *inter alia*, that 'All are entitled to equal protection against any discrimination in violation of this Declaration and against any incitement to such discrimination.'

Under Article 29, the Universal Declaration allows limitations on rights in order to ensure recognition and respect for the rights and freedoms of others. It states, *inter alia*, that the exercise of the rights and freedoms in the Declaration may be subject to limitations if they are 'determined by law solely for the purpose of securing due recognition and respect for the rights and freedoms of others and of meeting the just requirements of morality, public order, and the general welfare in a democratic society'.

A fundamental principle echoed in subsequent treaties on human rights appears in Article 30 of the Universal Declaration. This article states that nothing in the Declaration 'may be interpreted as implying for any state, group, or person any right to engage in any activity or to perform any act aimed at the destruction of any of the rights and freedoms set forth herein'.

The history of these provisions indicates that most drafters of the Universal Declaration understood them to allow restrictions on the advocacy of hatred. Indeed, the very first drafts of the Declaration submitted to the Commission on Human Rights showed concern over the potential abuse of the right to freedom of speech. Restrictions on 'publications aimed at the suppression of human rights and fundamental freedoms', for example, were provided for in the draft freedom of expression provision submitted by the United Kingdom.[6] The accompanying commentary stated the case for allowing such a restriction:

> It would be inconsistent for a Bill of Rights whose whole object is to establish human rights and fundamental freedoms to prevent any Government, if it wished to do so, from taking steps against publications whose whole object was to destroy the rights and freedoms, which it is the purpose of the Bill to establish.[7]

The initial full draft Universal Declaration did not include this proposal. Instead, it provided that 'Subject only to the laws governing slander and libel, there shall be freedom of speech and of expression by any means whatsoever.'[8] However, the words 'by any means whatsoever' were later deleted by the Commission on Human Rights after the representative of the Coordinating Committee of Jewish Organizations addressed the Commission, stating that in no case should the freedom of expression imply freedom to incite hatred and violence aimed at groups on the basis of race or religion.[9] The deletion of the clause strongly suggests that the Commission believed that the right to freedom of expression does not include the right to incite racial or religious hatred.

The Equal Protection Clause as Limiting Freedom of Expression

Although the Universal Declaration does not contain an explicit prohibition on hate propaganda, its equal protection clause provides a basis for restrictions on this type of expression. Article 7 proclaims the right to equality before the law and to the equal protection of the law. In its second sentence, Article 7 indicates one means by which equality is to be safeguarded: 'All are entitled to equal protection against [. . .] any incitement to [. . .] discrimination' in violation of the Declaration.

The original draft contained an equal protection clause. When the UN Commission on Human Rights was considering the draft Declaration, the International Refugee Organization (IRO) presented a statement that appears to have influenced the Commission to go further.[10] During the Commission's discussion of the draft equal protection clause, the IRO urged that equality before the law should be safeguarded not only by positive rights, but also by incorporating into civil and criminal law 'adequate safeguards against discrimination, incitement to, and advocacy of, discrimination against individuals or groups of individuals'.[11]

The IRO Executive Secretariat explained that incitement to discrimination is frequently directed against national, religious, and racial groups. Civil proceedings and criminal prosecutions against instigators of discrimination, or even violence, against such groups have sometimes failed in the past because the law provided only for the protection of individuals, but not of groups.[12]

A few days later, the Commission on Human Rights adopted a working draft containing a clause stating, '[a]ll are [. . .] entitled to equal protection of the law against any arbitrary discrimination, or against any incitement to such discrimination, in violation of this Declaration.'[13] Under this clause, incitement to discrimination in the form of hate propaganda, similar to that which was spread in Rwanda and the former Yugoslavia, would not enjoy protection.

Provisions Explicitly Limiting the Exercise of Rights

Another clause in the Universal Declaration that limits expression in the form of hate speech is found in Article 29, which provides, *inter alia*, that in the exercise of the rights and freedoms in the Declaration everyone shall be subject to:

> such limitations as are determined by law solely *for the purpose of securing due recognition and respect for the rights and freedoms of others* and of meeting the just requirements of morality, public order and the general welfare in a democratic society. [Emphasis added.]

The *travaux préparatoires* indicate that the Commission on Human Rights derived this Article from Article 4 of the French 1789 Declaration of the Rights of Man and of the Citizen:

> Liberty consists in the power of doing whatever does not injure another. Accordingly, the exercise of the natural rights of every man has no other limits than those which are necessary to secure to every other man the free exercise of the same rights; and these limits are determinable only by the law.[14]

The French Declaration also contains a clause specifically limiting free expression: 'The unrestrained communication of thought or opinions being one of the most precious rights of man, every citizen may speak, write, and publish freely provided he be responsible for the abuse of this liberty in the cases determined by law' (Article 11). Charles Malik, the Lebanese representative, proposed including this principle in the draft Declaration, explaining that people who were working to undermine the rights in the Declaration should not be protected by those rights.[15] A revised version of his proposal became Article 30 of the Universal Declaration, which states:

> Nothing in this Declaration may be interpreted as implying for any State, group, or person any right to engage in any activity or to perform any act aimed at the destruction of any of the rights and freedoms set forth herein.

When what became Article 19, the freedom of expression provision, was being debated, the drafters were unwilling to include a specific limitation in the article itself, although the decision-making process indicates that a limitation was understood. One of the drafts of the freedom of expression provision did contain a general restriction regarding abuse of that freedom. That language was deleted at the suggestion of the United States, which pointed out that another article in the Declaration (Article 29) already contained provisions that would restrain the freedom within legitimate limits.[16] Freedom of expression was thus considered subject to Article 29.

During discussion of Article 19 in the Third Committee of the General Assembly, the French and Soviet delegates reintroduced specific limitation clauses they had proposed earlier.[17] The Soviet proposal would have amended the provision to prohibit 'war-mongering and fascist speech', on the ground that 'the propagation of such ideas [had] been responsible for the horrors that the world had recently known'. The Soviets asserted that:

> It was of no use to argue that ideas should only be opposed by other ideas; ideas had not stopped Hitler making war [. . .] The mistake of not considering any measures for punishment might once again cost the world millions of lives.[18]

This proposal and a similar one introduced by the French were rejected by the majority, who said they viewed the general limitations clause (Article 29) as sufficiently covering these concerns. Article 19 of the Universal Declaration of Human Rights was therefore understood to be limited by other clauses in the Declaration, in particular by Article 29.

International Covenant on Civil and Political Rights

Article 19 of the Civil and Political Rights Covenant both protects and limits freedom of expression. It states that 'everyone shall have the right to freedom of expression', and that this right includes freedom 'to receive and impart information and ideas of all kinds, regardless of frontiers' (Article 19.2). However, because the exercise of this right 'carries with it special duties and responsibilities', it 'may therefore be subject to certain restrictions', including those 'necessary [. . .] for respect of the rights or the reputations of others' or 'for the protection of national security or of public order' (Article 19.3).

While Article 19 includes general restrictions on freedom of expression, Article 20 of the Covenant contains a specific prohibition on two types of expression. It proscribes war propaganda, as well as the advocacy of national, racial, or religious hatred that constitutes incitement to discrimination, hostility, or violence:

1. Any propaganda for war shall be prohibited by law.
2. Any advocacy of national, racial, or religious hatred that constitutes incitement to discrimination, hostility or violence shall be prohibited by law.

The drafting history shows that these articles were subjects of considerable debate. As is evident from the records of Commission meetings, many delegates appreciated the complexity of the issue and the points of view expressed by various sides.

The Drafting of Articles 19 and 20 of the Covenant

As early as 1947, the Commission on Human Rights considered 'the possibility of excluding from' the right to freedom of expression 'publications and other media of public expression which aim or tend to inflict injury, or incite prejudice or hatred, against persons or groups because of their race, language, religion, or national origin'.[19] The initial working draft of the Covenant, however, limited its prohibition of advocacy to that which constituted incitement to violence.[20] A number of drafters saw a connection between advocacy of hatred or discrimination and the war from which the world had so recently emerged. Explaining his state's proposal to prohibit advocacy of racial hostility, the Soviet representative stated:

Millions had perished because the propaganda of racial and national superiority, hatred and contempt, had not been stopped in time. Yet five years had hardly elapsed since the end of the war, and there were already signs of a revival of similar tendencies in various countries of the world.[21]

Speaking against the proposed clause, the United States representative noted that a United States Supreme Court decision had been handed down just one month earlier, in which someone accused of creating dissension between political and religious groups was freed on the ground that 'the principle of democracy was better served by allowing individuals to create disputes and dissension than by suppressing their freedom of speech'.[22] Justice

Frankfurter's lengthy dissenting opinion in *Terminiello* is indicative of the concerns being expressed during the drafting of the Covenant. He wrote:

> In the long run, maintenance of free speech will be more endangered if the population can have no protection from the abuses which lead to violence. No liberty is made more secure by holding that its abuses are inseparable from its enjoyment [. . .] There is danger that, if the Court does not temper its doctrinaire logic with a little practical wisdom, it will convert the constitutional Bill of Rights into a suicide pact.[23]

Few others supported the United States view on this point. René Cassin of France not only supported the Soviet proposal to prohibit hate propaganda, but even proposed inserting the words 'and hatred' after the word 'violence', so that the proposed article would require a prohibition of 'any advocacy of national, racial, or religious hostility that constitutes an incitement to violence and hatred'.[24]

The wording of the French proposal indicates that it was meant to prevent not only government abuse, but private abuse as well. The United States noted that its own proposal declaring the right to freedom of expression 'was deliberately framed to make it clear that the freedom to be guaranteed was against governmental interference. Extension to the field of private infringements on freedom of information would create complications and give rise to many unpredictable situations.'[25]

The Danish representative responded that the Commission must prevent infringement of freedom of information not only by the government, but also by groups outside the government. The French representative then spoke. 'Every freedom has two aspects,' he said, 'that of the protection of the individual against the State and that of the protection of the freedom itself by the enforcement of the individual's respect for it.'[26]

Article 17 is another of the articles requiring governments to take action to protect individuals against violation of their rights by private persons. Article 17 provides that 'no one shall be subjected to [. . .] unlawful attacks on his honour and reputation.' Paragraph 2 of that Article provides: 'Everyone has the right to the protection of the law against such interference or attacks.'

PROHIBIT INCITEMENT TO 'VIOLENCE' ONLY, OR 'HATRED' AS WELL?

During debates over what scope the Covenant's hate propaganda provision should take, delegates discussed whether to condemn only 'incitement to violence' against racial, national, or religious groups, or 'incitement to hatred', as well. In the view of the Polish delegate, simply condemning incitement to violence did not go to 'the root of the evil', but 'merely tackled its consequences, and [. . .] would only serve to hide the real nature of the problem'.[27] He proposed that the article go further since the danger of not doing so had been demonstrated. Nationalist propaganda in Nazi Germany, he said, 'by the constant repetition of the theory of racial domination had led not only to the curtailment of human rights, but to the destruction of entire peoples'.[28] He therefore proposed prohibiting advocacy of national or racial 'exclusiveness, hatred, and contempt or religious hostility', though he qualified that language, adding, 'particularly of such a nature as to constitute an incitement to violence'.[29]

The Chilean representative believed that the Covenant should condemn incitement to hatred.[30] In his view, 'hatred was at the root of violence', and '[t]he Commission must not await the effects of an evil before seeking to remedy it. It must take preventive action and attack the evil at its roots.'[31] He simply could not support a provision which prohibited only incitement to violence, for that would leave 'the door open to all other forms of intolerance', and 'render no service to the cause of tolerance'.[32]

Speaking in support of the Chilean amendment, the Uruguayan representative said that the reference to incitement to hatred 'would fill a gap in the text, since it was obvious that the indulgence of hatred must inevitably lead to violence'.[33]

CONCERN OVER THE POTENTIAL FOR ABUSE

Debate over the incitement to hatred proposals often centred on whether they would provide too much opportunity for government abuse. The French and Soviet incitement to hatred proposals were 'extremely dangerous', United States representative Eleanor Roosevelt argued, 'since any criticism of public or religious authorities might all too easily be described as incitement to hatred and consequently prohibited'.[34] Pointing out the difficulty of distinguishing between 'hatred' and 'ill-feeling and mere dislike', she warned against using 'such vague expressions as national hostility and religious hostility which appeared in the French text', since such terms would encourage governments to punish all criticism under the guise of protecting against religious or national hostility.

Giving a specific example of such a danger, Mrs Roosevelt spoke of the problem that arose from a similar provision contained in several peace treaties concluded after World War II. She noted that during the General Assembly debate in 1949 on the human rights problems in Hungary, Bulgaria, and Romania, the Polish representative had argued that the acts taken by those three governments were entirely justified under the peace treaties, in particular Article 4 of the treaties relating to the suppression of fascism or hostility to democracy or the United Nations.

Interestingly, a critical role had been played in crafting those treaties by the two countries now opposed to prohibiting racist or fascist propaganda – the United States and the United Kingdom.[35] As Egon Schwelb has pointed out, 'In the Peace Treaty of 1947 the Allied Powers, including the United Kingdom and the United States, imposed on Hungary the obligation not to permit Fascist-type organisations as well as other organisations conducting propaganda, including revisionist propaganda, hostile to the United Nations.'[36] Similar provisions appeared in the peace treaties with Bulgaria, Finland, Italy, and Romania, as well as in the 1955 State Treaty with Austria. Austria was also placed under the obligation to prevent 'the revival of Nazi organizations and all Nazi propaganda'.[37]

Mrs Roosevelt nevertheless cautioned against including in the Covenant 'any provision likely to be exploited by totalitarian states for the purpose of rendering the other articles null and void'.[38] She saw the peace treaties with Hungary, Bulgaria, and Romania as doing just that, for although they required those countries to safeguard basic human rights for everyone in those countries, the clause that permitted suppression of fascism and hostile propaganda was a 'loophole' for them to ignore their obligations.

The United Kingdom representative expressed a similar view. 'Unscrupulous governments like nothing better than a moral justification for their actions,' he said, and a provision such as the one proposed would provide that justification. 'Hitler had started out on a moral platform, posing as the champion of a Germany oppressed through the Treaty of Versailles.'[39]

However, a representative of the World Jewish Congress, invited to speak to the Commission, argued against the notion that the right to freedom of expression should be free from restrictions because restrictions might open the way to abuse.[40] He believed that judges should have no difficulty applying such an article:

> As a member of the minority which had suffered more than any other from the absence of provisions such as those under discussion and a third of whose members had suffered the supreme sacrifice during the Second World War, [I] would recall that for many years the words 'Down with the Jews' had appeared in the Nazi publication, the *Der Stürmer*, in letters over an inch high, and houses in Germany had been plastered with hundreds of thousands of posters calling for the death of the Jews or other minorities. It would be difficult to deny that such propaganda incited hatred or violence, and it would be doing the independent and enlightened judges of the democratic nations an injustice to suppose that they would have any difficulty in applying an article prohibiting it.[41]

Keeping the focus on a causal link between the power of such words and the Holocaust that followed, he added that 'those who had suffered most from racial and religious hatred would fail to understand how it was that the Commission on Human Rights could not find the means to prohibit explicitly the actions which engendered it'.[42]

The Swedish representative, however, expressed doubt that a provision prohibiting incitement to hatred would in fact prevent the 'fanatical persecution' that the world had witnessed. Instead, she believed that 'the effective prophylaxis lay in free discussion, information, and education'.[43]

Several representatives challenged the position taken by the United States and the United Kingdom. The Soviet bloc countries used the debates to bring attention to the serious problems of racism in the United States. One such comment came from the Ukrainian representative. Referring to a Mississippi state law then in force, which made publishing statements in favour of racial equality a crime subject to a fine or imprisonment, he asserted that 'perhaps the United States delegation was opposed to prohibiting propaganda of racial hatred because it shared that view'.[44]

The Polish representative, after pointing out that the United States was party to two conventions prohibiting the dissemination of obscene publications, said he could not see how the United States could consider such publications 'more dangerous than war propaganda, the incitement of hatred among the peoples, racial discrimination, and the dissemination of slanderous rumours'.[45]

René Cassin of France suggested that his proposal to prohibit advocacy that incited 'violence or hatred' drew a middle course between two extremes: that of the USSR proposal, which would 'silence free men', and that of the United States, which 'wished to permit full freedom of expression for the purpose of incitement to hatred and violence'.[46]

DEFINITIONAL ISSUES

The representative of Lebanon, Charles Malik, was particularly concerned that terms such as 'national hostility' and 'religious hostility' could be interpreted in a variety of ways. He thought that even the phrase 'incitement to violence' would be 'very difficult to define'.[47]

The Yugoslav representative, however, said it was clear that the ideas to which that phrase referred 'had been the cause of the death of two million Yugoslavs . . . [The Yugoslav] people knew what was meant by incitement to hatred.'[48]

The Chilean representative, addressing the criticism that the word 'hatred' would be difficult to define, noted that countries commonly use in their legislation words such as 'honour' and 'reputation' without complaining that those terms were so difficult to define that they should not be included in legislation.[49]

THE POWER OF PROPAGANDA IN FOSTERING HATRED

Much discussion during the drafting process addressed the power of propaganda in manipulating views. The United Kingdom representative argued, '[t]he power of democracy to combat propaganda lay in the last resort in the ability of its citizens to arrive at reasoned decisions in the face of conflicting appeals.'[50] The Austrian delegate, although supporting the aims of the Chilean proposal to prohibit hate propaganda, believed that legislation was not the best means for achieving that aim. 'The *practice* of tolerance could be achieved through means other than legislation,' he said.[51] Considering the danger of censorship inherent in the draft proposal, 'the remedy might be worse than the evil it sought to remove'.[52]

The Chilean representative rose to counter this argument, speaking at length about the use of organized propaganda to shape public opinion. Propaganda campaigns before World War II, he said, showed that 'skillfully directed propaganda could successfully nullify the effects or falsify the premises of education'.[53] Moreover, 'powerful media' played a considerable role in forming opinion, which when used as a tool of propaganda, could easily incite national, racial, or religious hatred.[54] He spoke of his own personal experience in this regard, living as a young person in a country 'poisoned by a hatred' that made people ready to commit violence, as a result of a propaganda that 'transformed the moral outlook of the man in the street and sometimes that of cultivated people'.[55] He thus argued that 'the principle of *laissez-faire* was indefensible'. One could certainly counter hate propaganda by urging mutual respect, he said, but that was not enough; national and international law must also prohibit incitement to hatred.[56]

The French delegate agreed with what he referred to as the 'brilliant exposition' of the Chilean in describing 'that vicious phenomenon of the modern world, propaganda, [which was a] mind-conditioning and spiritual rape of the masses'.[57] René Cassin of France noticed that those pushing for an anti-hate propaganda clause were for the most part those who had been most subjected to such hatred.[58] Similarly, the Yugoslav representative said, '[i]t was probably necessary to have been a victim of such propaganda, as the people of Yugoslavia had been, to appreciate the importance' of the hate speech article, but in his opinion, such a provision 'should figure in all relevant national instruments'.[59]

The draft Covenant on Civil and Political Rights reached the Third Committee of the UN General Assembly (UNGA) in 1961. Many of the same arguments for and against the incitement provision were raised in the Committee as had been raised in the Commission on Human Rights. However, whereas Cold War concerns were evident during the Commission on Human Rights deliberations, the discussions in the Third Committee reveal the emergence of other global issues. The Soviet Union departed from references to World War II and shifted its focus to colonialism, the racism evident in the non-self-governing and trust territories, and, of course, South Africa.[60]

Also in 1961, the clause prohibiting propaganda for war was first introduced. Never proposed or even discussed in the Commission on Human Rights, that provision was added in the Third Committee of the UNGA in large part in reaction to the looming threat of nuclear war.[61]

MEANS AND ENDS

Throughout the debate in the Commission on Human Rights and in the Third Committee of the UN General Assembly, neither side seemed to respond much to the concerns of the other. Their disagreement reflects the split in conceptions of hierarchy in the goals of free speech and non-discrimination. Opponents of Article 20 raised the spectre of the potential for abuse and the difficulty of defining 'incitement', 'hostility', and 'hatred', whereas the proponents of Article 20 continually spoke of the need to end racial hatred and discrimination and the human suffering that results from such hatred and discrimination. While the opponents rarely expressed concern over rampant racism, the proponents seemed to do better at addressing the former's concerns. Agreeing that some of the terms were difficult, they pointed out that the Covenant contained other terms, to which those countries had not objected, which could be just as difficult to define.

After several days of deliberations in the Third Committee, sixteen countries joined together to propose a text, known as the Sixteen Power Amendment, which one delegate suggested represented a compromise between those who thought that 'hatred' could not be defined and that existing proposals posed too great a threat to freedom of expression, and those who felt that prohibiting incitement to violence alone was insufficient.[62] The text of the Sixteen Power Amendment was ultimately adopted as Article 20(2).

The French delegate expressed concern that the wording of the amendment weakened the meaning of the earlier draft. The amendment would prohibit advocacy of hatred that constituted incitement to hostility, but, he said, 'hatred always resulted in hostility'. He indicated that his delegation would be unable to support the amendment, not because it opposed the principle that advocacy of hatred should be prohibited, but rather because of the particular phrasing of the amendment.[63]

The Vote to Adopt Article 20

Finally, Article 20 came to a vote. After voting to include paragraph 1 prohibiting propaganda for war, the Third Committee then took a vote on paragraph 2, prohibiting advocacy of hatred. It was adopted with fifty votes in favour, eighteen votes against, and fifteen abstentions.[64] Some countries that had been very active in the Commission on Human Rights in promoting an anti-hatred provision abstained from the vote, most notably Chile and France. The article as a whole was adopted by a roll call vote of fifty-two to nineteen, with twelve abstentions.[65] Although it had abstained in the vote on paragraph 2, Chile voted in favour of Article 20 as a whole. It was not completely satisfied with the final wording, but it nonetheless believed it important to have some provision in the Civil and Political Rights Covenant explicitly prohibiting what it viewed as an abuse of the right to free expression.

Using Rights to Destroy Others' Rights

Another basis in the Covenant for restricting hate speech is Article 5, which allows restrictions on expression aimed at destroying the rights of others. This clause, proposed by Mr Malik of Lebanon, is identical to Article 29 of the Universal Declaration of Human Rights. During debate on the article Mrs Roosevelt argued that it was open to abuse and that 'it [would be] difficult to determine' just what acts might tend to destroy the rights of others.[66]

Urging support for the proposal, Mr Malik spoke of the need to prevent fascists from using rights to suppress others' rights.[67] In typically eloquent fashion, René Cassin of France noted, '[the] edifice of liberty which was erected in the Covenant must not be capable of being used against liberty itself.'[68] Indeed, an identical clause in the European Convention on Human Rights, discussed *infra*, has been used to justify restrictions on hate propaganda.

Human Rights Committee: Review of State Reports

Statements made by the Human Rights Committee, the body charged with monitoring implementation by states parties of their obligations under the Covenant, indicate that the Committee takes very seriously the obligation under Article 20 to outlaw advocacy of racial, religious, and ethnic hatred. At one point the Human Rights Committee issued a General Comment on Article 20(2), expressing concern that a number of the reports submitted to it by states parties did not provide sufficient information on their implementation of Article 20 of the Covenant, and urging states that had not yet done so to take the measures necessary to fulfill their obligations under Article 20.[69]

The Human Rights Committee has also urged individual countries to enact laws pursuant to Article 20, during its review of those countries' periodic reports.[70] In reviewing the report from Sri Lanka, for example, a Committee member noted that it made no mention of the prohibition of racial hatred as required in Article 20. He maintained that such prohibition by law 'would be a most effective means of combating the terrorism now racking Sri Lanka'.[71]

In 1992, the Human Rights Committee became so concerned over the situation in the former Yugoslavia that it requested the government of the Federal Republic of Yugoslavia (FRY) (Serbia and Montenegro) to submit a report on, amongst other things, '[m]easures taken to combat advocacy of national, racial, or religious hatred constituting incitement to discrimination, hostility, or violence, in relation to Article 20 of the International Covenant on Civil and Political Rights'.[72]

The Committee expressed concern over mass arrests, arbitrary executions, forced disappearances, torture, rapes, and many other human rights violations, which were meant, it noted, 'to displace or eliminate Muslims, Croats, or other nationalities and thus constitute ethnically homogeneous areas'. It further recommended, among other things, that the FRY government 'do its utmost to foster public awareness of the need to combat national hatred and to crack down forcefully on the perpetrators of violations of individual rights by bringing them to justice'.[73]

Meeting with FRY representatives again the following year, the Committee continued to express these concerns, with one Committee member urging the government to 'take firm steps to put an end to advocacy of hatred, which was the root of the evil'.[74]

Human Rights Committee: Individual Petitions

Two cases illustrate the Human Rights Committee's approach to claims of freedom of expression violations in instances where the petitioner has advocated hatred. Article 20(2) was referred to in one case, while the permissible limitations on expression in Article 19(3) were the basis for finding no violation in the other.

In the first case, the Committee addressed the complaint of a Canadian, John Ross Taylor, and his political party, whose phone service was curtailed after they used the phone line to disseminate anti-Semitic statements.[75] The petitioners maintained tape-recorded messages that the public could hear by dialing a telephone number. The messages warned callers 'of the dangers of international finance and international Jewry leading the world into wars, unemployment, inflation, and the collapse of world values and principles'.[76] They claimed that the Canadian government had infringed their right to hold and maintain their opinions without interference under Article 19(1) of the International Covenant on Civil and Political Rights and their right to freedom of expression under Article 19(2) of the Covenant.

The Canadian government's decision to curtail the telephone service of the party and Taylor was based on a provision of the Canadian Human Rights Act which declares it a discriminatory practice to communicate telephonically 'any matter that is likely to expose a person or persons to hatred or contempt by reason of the fact that the person or those persons are identifiable on the basis of a prohibited ground of discrimination'.[77] Among the 'prohibited grounds of discrimination' is discrimination based on 'race, national, or ethnic origin'.

Although the Committee declared the communication inadmissible because of a failure to exhaust domestic remedies, the Committee saw fit to state:

> The opinions that Mr Taylor seeks to disseminate through the telephone system clearly constitute the advocacy of racial or religious hatred that Canada has an obligation under article 20(2) of the Covenant to prohibit. In the Committee's opinion, therefore, the communication is, in respect of this claim, incompatible with the provisions of the Covenant, within the meaning of article 3 of the Optional Protocol.[78]

In a case several years later brought by an individual who questioned the Holocaust, the Human Rights Committee found the person's criminal conviction and fine to be permissible in light of the limitations clause of Article 19, the freedom of expression provision of the Covenant.[79] In that case, the petitioner, Robert Faurisson, had been convicted and fined by France for his statements that there had been no gas chambers used in exterminating Jews in Nazi concentration camps, and calling 'the myth of the gas chambers' a 'dishonest fabrication'. The legislation under which he was convicted, known as the Gayssot Act, makes it an offence to contest the existence of the category of crimes against humanity as defined in the London Charter of 8 August 1945, on the basis of which Nazi leaders were tried and convicted by the International Military Tribunal at Nuremberg.

The Human Rights Committee determined that the restriction of the petitioner's freedom of expression met the requirements of a limitation on that freedom under Article 19(3). The restriction was provided by law, and was for a legitimate purpose – protecting the rights of others. The Committee noted that 'the statements made by the author, read in their full context, were of a nature as to raise or strengthen anti-Semitic feelings; the restriction served the respect of the Jewish community to live free from fear of an atmosphere of anti-Semitism.' As for the third requirement, whether the restriction was necessary to achieve the purpose, the Committee noted both the state party's contention that the Act 'was intended to serve the struggle against racism and anti-Semitism', and the statement by the then Minister of Justice 'characterizing the denial of the existence of the Holocaust as the principal vehicle for anti-Semitism'.[80] Several Committee members noted in a concurring statement that Holocaust denial could amount to a form of incitement to anti-Semitism.[81]

Convention on the Elimination of Racial Discrimination

Among the methods included in the International Convention on the Elimination of All Forms of Racial Discrimination (ICERD) for abolishing racial discrimination is the requirement in Article 4 that states parties prohibit incitement to racial hatred. Article 4 goes further than Article 20 of the Civil and Political Rights Covenant. It requires that states prohibit not only advocacy of hatred, but also 'all dissemination of ideas based on racial superiority or hatred', and the provision of 'any assistance to racist activities, including financing thereof'. In addition, organizations 'which promote and incite racial discrimination' are to be declared illegal and prohibited by law, and participation in such organizations or activities is to be made punishable as well. Another difference between the Covenant and the ICERD is that the latter requires that incitement be made an offence, whereas Article 20 of the Covenant only requires that incitement be punishable by law, which could be met by a civil or administrative remedy in addition to criminal sanction.

The drafting debates over Article 4 reflect the same concerns expressed during drafting of Article 20 of the International Covenant on Civil and Political Rights. The original draft of Article 4 as adopted by the UN Commission on Human Rights provided for the punishment by law of 'all incitement to racial discrimination resulting in or likely to cause acts of violence'.[82] When this language came before the UN General Assembly, an amendment was proposed that would require states to prohibit dissemination of ideas as well.[83]

Among the states that objected were the United Kingdom and Colombia. The United Kingdom announced that it would not accept punishment for expression of ideas or incitement to discrimination unless there was incitement to violence.[84] Colombia stated that the resulting Article 4 would be 'a throwback to the past, since punishing ideas, whatever they may be, is to aid and abet tyranny, and leads to the abuse of power. As far as we are concerned', the Colombian representative stated, 'and as far as democracy is concerned, ideas should be fought with ideas and reasons; theories must be refuted by arguments and not by the scaffold, prison, exile, confiscation, or fines.'[85]

Nigeria proposed a compromise text, one that was ultimately adopted as the text of Article 4 of ICERD. In addition to prohibiting 'acts of violence or incitement to such acts against any race or group of persons', as well as 'all dissemination of ideas based on superiority or hatred, incitement to racial discrimination', the proposal included what has become known as the 'due regard' clause. Under that clause of Article 4 of ICERD, parties to the Convention undertake to adopt the measures indicated 'with due regard to the principles embodied in the Universal Declaration of Human Rights and expressly set forth in Article 5 of this Convention'. This language incorporates all the rights in the Universal Declaration into a balancing test. Arguably then, freedom of expression is not given greater weight; it is one among many rights to be given 'due regard' in fashioning legislation pursuant to Article 4. The United States representative, however, interpreted the due regard clause as 'not imposing on a State party the obligation to take any action impairing the right to freedom of speech and freedom of association'.[86] The United States joined other delegations in voting in favour of Article 4, which was adopted by a vote of seventy-six to one, with fourteen abstentions.[87]

Committee on the Elimination of Racial Discrimination

In a major report on the implementation of Article 4 published by the UN in 1986, the committee of experts established by the Convention to oversee its implementation declared that states parties 'cannot construe the "due regard" clause as cancelling or justifying a departure from the mandatory obligations set forth in Articles 4(a) and (b). Otherwise, there would have been no purpose in their inclusion.'[88]

The Committee has characterized as 'the extreme position' the view that implementation of Article 4 might impair or jeopardize freedom of opinion and expression.[89] In indicating that a balance must be struck between the obligations under Article 4 and the freedoms of expression and association, it noted that those freedoms are not absolute. Limits on rights, the Committee noted, were found in Articles 29(2) and 30 of the Universal Declaration of Human Rights, and in Article 19(3) of the Civil and Political Rights Covenant. In a remark seemingly aimed at such countries as the United States and the United Kingdom, the Committee noted, '[e]ven in societies most zealous of safeguarding the right of free speech, there are laws against defamation and sedition'.[90] It opined that laws against incitement to racial discrimination or hatred 'are certainly no less necessary to protect public order or the rights of others'.[91]

The Committee acknowledges that methods other than prohibition by law may deal effectively with racist organizations and ideas, and indeed, Article 7 of the Convention requires states parties to undertake measures in the fields of teaching, education, culture, and information in order to combat prejudices that lead to racial discrimination. The Convention, however, requires a comprehensive approach that includes measures under Article 4.

The role of media in combating discrimination is noted in General Recommendation XXVII on discrimination against the Roma. Among the measures states parties are urged to take is '[t]o act as appropriate for the elimination of any ideas of racial or ethnic superiority, of racial hatred and incitement to discrimination and violence against Roma in the media [. . .]' States are also to 'encourage awareness among professionals of all media of the particular responsibility to not disseminate prejudices'.

The 'Due Regard' Clause: Limitation on a Limitation

The 'due regard' clause of Article 4 of the ICERD restricts the limitation on freedom of expression found in that Article. Because the focus of Article 4 is on protection from racial discrimination, its format has been interpreted to give greater weight to the right to freedom from racial discrimination than to the freedoms protected under the 'due regard' clause.[92] Committee members, when faced with a conflict between the right to freedom from racial discrimination and the right to freedom of expression, have tended to give greater weight to the former. In interpreting the 'due regard' clause, ICERD members have explained that it must be read with reference to the Universal Declaration as a whole, not just the freedom of expression provision.[93] Although Article 19 of the Universal Declaration protects freedom of expression, numerous other articles emphasize other rights and protections, which tends to indicate that in a balancing of rights situation, freedom from discrimination should be given very great weight indeed.[94]

State Implementation of Article 4

The Committee on the Elimination of Racial Discrimination has twice seen fit to issue a General Recommendation urging states parties to address implementation of Article 4(a) and (b) in their periodic reports, and to supplement their legislation with provisions meeting the requirements of that Article.[95] In explaining their failure to implement fully Article 4 (a) or (b), states have generally given one of several reasons. One is that they need not enact legislation outlawing racist organizations as required under paragraph (b), because there are no organizations in that country that promote or incite racial discrimination. The Committee typically responds by stating that 'the possibility that organizations might promote or incite racial discrimination [cannot] be ruled out, particularly in a multi–racial society'.[96]

A second reason states have offered for not implementing Article 4 (a) or (b) is that there is no racial discrimination in their country. Committee members either question how such statements can be made if the state has not done research inquiring into the subject, or they point out that implementing legislation is necessary because 'even if there were no racial discrimination in a country at a given time, no one could predict that unfortunate events would not alter that situation in the future'.[97]

A third reason given for not implementing legislation under Article 4 is that the treaty provisions are already part of domestic law, 'by virtue of ratification'. The Committee has emphasized time and again, however, that Article 4 is not self-executing, and thus requires implementing legislation.[98]

Enacting legislation alone is not enough. States parties also have a duty to make known the remedies provided pursuant to the Convention. Expressing surprise that, given 'the present tide of xenophobia affecting the industrialised countries of Europe', only two cases involving racial discrimination had been reported by Denmark, Committee members inquired whether this might be because those who might suffer most from discrimination, particularly new immigrants, were ill-informed about the existing remedies.[99]

The situation in the former Yugoslavia when ICERD reviewed the state's report in 1993 led the Committee to request further information from the Federal Republic of Yugoslavia (FRY) (Serbia and Montenegro). Meeting later that year with government representatives, ICERD expressed 'deep concern over reports of serious and systematic violations of the Convention occurring in the territory [. . .]. In that regard, the Committee considered that by not opposing extremism and ultra-nationalism on ethnic grounds, state authorities and political leaders incurred serious responsibility.[100] ICERD recommended that the State 'should urgently take vigorous steps to ban racist activities and propaganda'.[101]

The ICERD member serving as country rapporteur on the FRY recalled that in April 1993, the International Court of Justice had ordered provisional measures under which the Federal Republic of Yugoslavia should ensure that any armed units under its control or influence:

> do not commit any acts of genocide, of conspiracy to commit genocide, or direct or public incitement to commit genocide, or of complicity in genocide, whether directed against the Muslim population of Bosnia and Herzegovina or against any other national, ethnic, racial, or religious group.[102]

In reviewing in 1995 the supplementary information submitted by the FRY, ICERD members stressed the role of the communications media in promoting ethnic and religious hatred, and drew attention in that regard to the findings of the special rapporteur for the UN Commission on Human Rights, which they said 'clearly indicate systematic and grave violations of article 4 of the Convention'.[103]

In its concluding observations on the state's report, ICERD stated:

> Note is taken with profound concern of the large part which the media continue to play in the propagation of racial and ethnic hatred. Given the

very tight state control over the media this propagation of hatred may be attributed to the state.[104]

In its recommendations to the State party, ICERD urged, among other things:

> the immediate drafting and implementation of legislation with a view towards the outlawing of every manifestation of racial discrimination and the full implementation of the Convention. Particular attention should be paid to the legal regulation of matters such as the media and freedom of expression.[105]

ICERD members noted the role of the media in the genocide in Rwanda in 1994. Making reference to the report of the UN Commission on Human Rights' special rapporteur on the situation of human rights in Rwanda, one member drew attention to the passage in the report that addressed the role played by the media, 'or rather the way in which the politicians had used the media. One of the saddest aspects of the tragedy was that so many lies had been spread and so many people had believed them.'[106]

European Convention on Human Rights

Although the [European] Convention for the Protection of Human Rights and Fundamental Freedoms, unlike the International Covenant on Civil and Political Rights, does not require states parties to prohibit hate propaganda, its freedom of expression provision has been interpreted to permit states to prohibit such expression. As with its counterpart in the Civil and Political Rights Covenant, the right to freedom of expression in the European Convention is not an absolute right. After first proclaiming that 'Everyone has the right to freedom of expression', Article 10 states that the right 'carries with it duties and responsibilities, and may be subject to such [. . .] restrictions [. . .] as are necessary in a democratic society [. . .] for the protection of the reputation or rights of others'.

The specific limitations in Article 10, as well as the general limitations clause, Article 17, have led the European Commission on Human Rights and the European Court of Human Rights to determine that prohibitions on hate propaganda are entirely consistent with the obligations of states parties under the Convention.

Drafting History

'In drawing up this code let us not [only address] the tyrannic acts of those who misuse power, but also . . . those who misuse freedom.'[107] These words, spoken at the first meeting of the Council of Europe's Consultative Assembly as it met to consider a draft human rights treaty, reflect the theory ultimately used as a basis for finding that suppression of hate speech does not violate freedom of expression under the European Convention. The *travaux préparatoires* do not reveal discussion of hate propaganda *per se*, but they do show that the Convention's limitations provisions were included because of concerns about potential abuse of the freedoms enumerated in the Convention. In language presaging what would become Article 17 of the Convention, a speaker in that first meeting of the Consultative Assembly stated: 'Human freedom, just because it is sacred, must not become an armoury in which the enemies of freedom can find weapons which they can later use unhindered to destroy this freedom.'[108] Echoing the same sentiments, another speaker emphasized: 'We do not desire [. . .] to give evilly disposed persons the opportunity to create a totalitarian Government which will destroy human rights altogether.'[109]

A general limitations clause that corresponds to Article 29 of the Universal Declaration of Human Rights was then inserted in the draft European Convention. It allowed for the limitation of the rights in the Convention if the aim 'is to ensure the recognition and respect for the rights and liberties of others'.[110]

During early deliberations on the Convention, one representative proposed a clause authorizing states parties to restrict expression intended to incite violence. Specifically, the proponent wished to authorize 'special measures to deal with those who, under pretext of expressing their opinions, have resort to violence, or else try to provoke it'.[111] It was decided, however, that this point was already covered in the general limitations clause quoted above.

Limitations on rights were seen as 'necessary to prevent totalitarian currents from exploiting in their own interests the principles enunciated by the Convention; that is to invoke the rights of freedom in order to suppress human rights'.[112] Several articles delineating specific rights, including Article 10 on freedom of expression, ultimately contained limitations provisions. Thus, the drafters of the European Convention, while proclaiming certain rights, laid the groundwork for the European Commission's interpretation of Article 10 that was to allow restriction on the freedom of expression in the hate speech cases.

Advocacy of Hatred Cases under the European Convention

The decisions of the European Commission on Human Rights (now defunct with the advent of a full-time court) indicate that although prohibitions on hate speech are not mandated by the Convention, they are entirely consistent with the obligations of states parties under that Convention. One case addressed by the European Commission on Human Rights involved two members of a white supremacist group who claimed that their conviction violated their right to freedom of expression.[113] The two had been convicted under Dutch criminal law of possession, with intent to distribute, of leaflets which the Dutch court held constituted incitement to racial discrimination.[114]

The two petitioned the European Commission on Human Rights, alleging violation of their rights under the European Convention. The Commission declared the applications inadmissible, stating that the leaflets were indeed the expression of the political views of the applicants, but that they were not protected under the Convention.

As an expression of racial discrimination, the Commission explained, the statements in the leaflets were prohibited by both the European Convention and other international instruments, in particular, the International Convention on the Elimination of all Forms of Racial Discrimination. If the Netherlands authorities allowed the applicants to proclaim their views without penalty, that 'would certainly *encourage* the discrimination prohibited' by the European and Racial Discrimination conventions.[115]

The Commission then stated that the applicants were not protected under the freedom of expression provision, because of another provision of the Convention designed to prevent the abuse of freedoms in the Convention by groups supporting totalitarian policies – Article 17. This Article states that no provision in the Convention is to be 'interpreted as implying [. . .] any right to engage in any activity aimed at the destruction of any of the rights and freedoms set forth' in the Convention.

The Commission said that the applicants were 'clearly seeking to use Article 10' as the basis for a 'right to engage in activities which are [. . .] contrary to the text and spirit of the Convention and which right, if granted, would contribute to the destruction of the rights and freedoms', which are to be secured without discrimination. Therefore, the applicants did not suffer a violation of their right to freedom of expression.

Another case before the Commission dealt with an applicant from Germany who had posted pamphlets on a board outside a garden fence describing the Holocaust as an 'unacceptable lie and Zionist swindle'.[116] When a court order was entered prohibiting him from repeating the statements, he filed a complaint with the European Commission on Human Rights, claiming that the order violated his right to freedom of expression.

Finding that the pamphlets were defamatory and insulting to Jews, the European Commission stated that prohibition of the pamphlets was necessary to protect the reputation of others, as provided in Article 10(2) of the Convention. The Commission stated, '[t]he racialist pamphlets could properly be regarded as a defamatory attack on each individual member of the Jewish community.'[117]

Although the European Court of Human Rights never heard these cases because the European Commission had deemed them inadmissible, one hate speech case did reach the Court. In *Jersild v. Denmark*, a case involving freedom of the press in addition to freedom of expression, the Court found a violation of Article 10.[118]

The applicant in *Jersild* was a Danish television journalist who had been convicted and sentenced to a fine for aiding and abetting the dissemination of racist statements. This was because in a television documentary on a racist youth group, Mr Jersild included several minutes of an interview he had conducted with three members of the group in which they made some extraordinarily offensive statements about immigrants and ethnic groups in Denmark.

The European Court of Human Rights found by vote of twelve to seven that the journalist's conviction was a violation of his rights under Article 10. The focus of the Court's judgement was on whether the measures met the third requirement of a limitation on expression, that it be 'necessary in a democratic society'.[119]

The government argued, among other things, that by editing the interviews as he had done, the journalist had failed to counter the racist views of the interviewees, claiming that the broadcast was 'too subtle to assume that viewers would not take the remarks at their face value'.[120] The Court responded by reiterating that 'freedom of expression constitutes one of the essential foundations of a democratic society', and that in playing its vital role of 'public watchdog' the press must be free to impart information and ideas of public interest, which the public has a right to receive.[121]

The intent in disseminating the racist statements was highly important to the Court. Because of the 'vital importance' of combating racial discrimination, the Court stated, the object and purpose of the UN Convention on Racial Discrimination carry 'great weight' in determining whether the applicant's conviction was 'necessary' within the meaning of Article 10(2). In conducting this evaluation, an 'important factor' would be whether the purpose of the program in question appeared to be the propagation of racist views and ideas.

The Court determined that the context in which the interview was presented made it clear that the programme 'clearly sought – by means of an interview – to expose, analyze, and explain this particular group of youths' and thus dealt with a matter 'of great public concern'. It was for the media, not a court, to determine the news or information value of a programme.

Significantly, the Court did not say that a journalist has no duty to present counterbalancing views; it simply noted that the journalist did in fact present other views, both in the introduction to the programme as well as by various statements he made during the interview. The Court simply said it was not persuaded by the argument that the broadcast was presented with no counterbalancing views.

In language strongly protective of freedom of the press, the Court stated:

News reporting based on interviews, whether edited or not, constitutes one of the most important means whereby the press is able to play its vital role of 'public watchdog'. The punishment of a journalist for assisting in the dissemination of statements made by another person in an interview would seriously hamper the contribution of the press to discussion of matters of public interest and should not be envisaged unless there are particularly strong reasons for doing so.[122]

The judgement demonstrates that the European Court does see certain limits on states' authority to restrict hate speech. As for the law regarding the relation between Article 4 of the CERD Convention and Article 10 of the European Convention, even the dissenters, who thought the conviction did not violate Article 10, conceded that Article 4 'probably does not require' conviction of the journalist. This appears to be because of lack of evidence of ill intent behind the broadcast on the part of the journalist.

Inter-American Human Rights System

American Convention on Human Rights

The freedom of expression provision of the American Convention on Human Rights contains a hate propaganda provision similar to that of Article 20(2) of the International Covenant on Civil and Political Rights, but arguably less broad. Article 13 of the Convention first proclaims that 'everyone has the right to freedom of thought and expression', which includes the 'freedom to seek, receive, and impart information and ideas of all kinds'. The exercise of these rights is subject in paragraph 2 to limitations similar to those in Article 19 of the International Covenant on Civil and Political Rights and Article 10 of the European Convention, that is, limitations on the right are permissible if 'established by law to the extent necessary to ensure [. . .] respect for the rights or reputations of others or the protection of national security, public order, or public health or morals'.

Significantly, paragraph 3 of the Article provides that freedom of expression 'may not be restricted by indirect means', such as 'the abuse of government or private controls over newsprint, radio broadcasting frequencies, or equipment used in the dissemination of information, or by any other means tending to impede the communication and circulation of ideas and opinions'. The use of the phrase 'abuse of controls', however, indicates the permissibility of some controls, the validity of which would be determined by the limitations clauses contained in Article 13.

Paragraph 5 of the Convention's freedom of expression article declares that propaganda for war and advocacy of hatred that constitute incitements to violence 'or to any other similar illegal action' on racial or other grounds shall be considered an offence punishable by law:

> Any propaganda for war and any advocacy of national, racial, or religious hatred that constitute incitements to lawless violence or to any other similar illegal action against any person or group of persons on any grounds including those of race, color, religion, language, or national origin shall be considered as offenses punishable by law.

The drafting history of Article 13(5) is intriguing because the final language was drawn up by a traditional opponent of restrictions on expression, the United States, which worked energetically to gain support for it from the other delegations. The United States delegation's report on the conference that adopted the American Convention stated that 'the principal provision of the Article that could cause problems' was not the advocacy of hatred provision, but instead, was 'the rather broad prohibition of prior censorship in paragraph 2'.[123]

The initial draft American Convention, prepared by the Inter-American Council of Jurists (IACJ), contained an article on freedom of expression based on the free expression provisions of the European Convention on Human Rights and the ICCPR. This draft did not address advocacy of hatred or war propaganda. The Chilean government then submitted a draft which contained not only a general limitation on the freedom of expression similar to that found in the International Covenant on Civil and Political Rights, but also a separate article closely tracking the language of Article 20(2) of that Covenant, prohibiting war propaganda as well as 'every panegyric of national, racial, or religious hatred that constitutes an incitement to discrimination, hostility, or violence'.[124]

When paragraph 5 came up for consideration by the member states of the Organization of American States, the United States delegation urged its deletion because it 'requires censorship'. Instead of this approach, the United States argued, 'the remedy to be applied is more speech, not enforced silence'.[125] The United States directed its remarks more to the prohibition of war propaganda than suppression of hate speech. Brazilian delegate Carlos Dunshee de Abranches responded that the Article did not state that censorship must be established, 'but rather that the law shall prohibit a certain type of activity'.[126]

The conflict then ongoing between Honduras and El Salvador provided the catalyst for support for the proposed clause. The delegate of El Salvador spoke powerfully in favour of draft Article 13(5), stating that if such propaganda ceased there would likely be a solution to the conflict between his state and Honduras. These words brought applause in the room.[127] An account of this moment reports that Honduras also praised paragraph 5 as desirable and that both countries stated:

> The press has exacerbated the tense conditions between the two countries [. . .] The other delegates, anxious for a reconciliation between Honduras and El Salvador, warmly applauded when the Honduran and Salvadoran delegates embraced at the conclusion of their statements. It was clear that the Conference would not delete the paragraph entirely.[128]

The United States delegates realised that paragraph 5 would remain in Article 13 in some form. They reported that other delegations 'wanted to go on record in opposition to at least certain types of propaganda for war and advocacy of race hatred'.[129] The United States then proceeded to propose amendments to bring the clause into closer conformity with stricter standards of freedom of expression. The language as finally adopted was drafted and proposed by the United States after much consultation with other delegations.[130] In the view of the United States delegation, under paragraph 5 'the advocacy must not only be directed to inciting lawless action or be likely to incite such action, but it must actually constitute incitement to lawless action of a violent nature before the State is required to prohibit it'.[131]

This interpretation of paragraph 5 is highly questionable. Advocacy of hatred that actually incites violence is clearly not the only type of advocacy considered an offence punishable by law under paragraph 5, for that paragraph prohibits advocacy of hatred that constitutes incitements to violence 'or to any other similar illegal action'. The question, then, is what 'illegal action' should be deemed 'similar' to 'lawless violence'. In line with the arguments put forward by the drafters of similar clauses in the ICCPR and ICERD, incitement to the 'illegal action' of hate propaganda that does not immediately result in violence could arguably constitute an offence that should be punishable by law under paragraph 5.

ADDITIONAL LIMITATIONS ON FREEDOM OF EXPRESSION

In addition to the specific limitations on freedom of expression found in Article 13, the American Convention contains a general limitation similar to that found in the Universal Declaration, the ICCPR, and the European Convention. Article 29 states that '[n]o provision of this Convention shall be interpreted as permitting any State Party, group, or person to suppress the enjoyment or exercise of the right of freedom recognised in this Convention.'

In light of restrictions on the press in a number of countries, the Inter-American Commission on Human Rights has seen fit to:

> [r]eaffirm that freedom of expression is an essential right of every means of social communication, so as to safeguard it from governmental abuse; the Commission would also like to reaffirm the right of every person to be fully informed without arbitrary interferences from the State or international structures that deliver distorted information.[132]

The Inter-American Commission might interpret hate propaganda itself as delivering distorted information. Should it do so, it is likely that the Commission would scrutinize closely any restriction on expression, to assess whether the government was abusing its power in fashioning its limitation to the important right to freedom of expression.

For its part, the Inter-American Court of Human Rights has explained that any restrictions on freedom of expression must be 'necessary', and that a restriction is not necessary if its intended results can reasonably be achieved by less restrictive means.[133] The issue regarding transmission of hate propaganda, then, would turn on whether in the particular circumstances, less restrictive means, such as countering the hate propaganda, and/or providing a forum for others to counter the propaganda, would suffice.

American Declaration of the Rights and Duties of Man

The American Declaration of the Rights and Duties of Man does not contain a specific hate propaganda provision, but it does contain language that, if interpreted in the same manner as the freedom of expression clause of the European Convention has been interpreted, could allow restrictions on such propaganda. Adopted by the Organization of American States several months before the UN adopted the Universal Declaration of Human Rights, the American Declaration declares in Article 4 the right to freedom of 'the expression and the dissemination of ideas'. Under Article 28, however, the rights in the Declaration are 'limited by the rights of others, by the security of all, and by the just demands of the general welfare and the advancement of democracy'.

An earlier draft of the Declaration had spelled out in some detail specific limitations in each Article declaring a right. The Working Group on the draft chose to delete those limitations and replace the passages with a single Article describing the scope of rights – Article 28. The Working Group's report notes that the deleted passages simply indicated those cases 'in which the State – by the very reason of having to defend the rights of man – would be obligated to fix reasonable limitations upon those rights.'[134]

The Genocide Convention

The Convention on the Prevention and Punishment of the Crime of Genocide is a treaty whose goal is to protect racial, national, ethnic, and religious groups from the most extreme consequences of hatred – genocide. Article III(c) prohibits 'direct and public incitement to genocide'. One of the first drafts of the convention, submitted by the UN Secretariat, included a provision explicitly prohibiting hate propaganda. It read, 'All forms of hate propaganda tending by their systematic and hateful character to promote genocide, or tending to make it appear as a necessary, legitimate or excusable act shall be punished.' Explaining why it included this provision, the Secretariat stated that '[s]uch propaganda is even more dangerous than direct incitement to genocide. Genocide cannot take place unless a certain state of mind previously has been created.'[135]

The United States opposed this article on freedom of speech grounds, arguing that free speech should not be restricted 'unless there is a clear and present danger that the utterance might interfere with a right of others', which the United States said was already covered in the crime of 'incitement'.[136]

Both France and the Soviet Union urged inclusion of a hate propaganda clause. The Soviets proposed penalising 'all forms of public propaganda (press, radio, cinema, and so on) aimed at inciting racial, national, or religious enmities, or hatreds', in addition to 'provoking the commission of acts of genocide'.[137]

This and similar proposals were rejected, however, so the final language of the convention prohibits incitement to genocide but does not prohibit specific types of hate propaganda. Nonetheless, as Bill Schabas has pointed out, the absence of a hate propaganda provision in the Genocide Convention has since been corrected in later human rights treaties, treaties that are more widely ratified than the Convention and which set out obligations that are more comprehensive than those proposed during the drafting of the Convention in 1947 and 1948.[137] These are the treaties discussed earlier in this chapter.

Conclusion

Although international and regional human rights treaties do not address the issue of cross-border restriction of broadcasts and other media advocating racial or ethnic hatred, they do demonstrate that the right to freedom of expression and to receive and impart ideas 'regardless of frontiers' does not stand as a legal barrier to information intervention. These instruments do not provide detailed guidelines for determining the threshold for permitting such intervention. The drafting histories and the cases in which advocacy of hatred provisions are applied, though, do indicate that care must be used in light of the importance of the right to freedom of expression. It is because of the demonstrated dire consequences of a failure to suppress hate propaganda, however, that several of the treaties include a duty to intervene, in the national context. There is a strong argument that this duty exists *a fortiori* when necessary to ensure protection of the most fundamental rights in these instruments – including the right to life.

Bibliography

Advisory Opinion OC-5/85, 13 November 1985, Inter-American Court of Human Rights (ser. A) no. 5 (1985)

ARTICLE 19 (1996), *Broadcasting Genocide: Censorship, propaganda & state-sponsored violence in Rwanda 1990–1994*, London: ARTICLE 19.

Brandenburg v. Ohio, 395 U.S. 444 (1969).

Buergenthal, T. and R. Norris (eds) (1982–), *Human Rights: The Inter-American System*, 5 vols, Dobbs Ferry, NY: Oceana Publications. Looseleaf, updated periodically. vol. 1 (Basic documents); vol. 2 (Legislative History of the American Convention); vol. 3 (Cases and Decisions); vol. 4 (Cases and Decisions, Cont'd); vol. 5 (Cases and Decisions, Cont'd and Inter-American System and Domestic Law).

CERD General Recommendations VII and XV, in UN Doc. CERD/C/365/Rev. 1 (5 December 2000).

Coliver, Sandra (ed.) (1992), *Striking a Balance: Hate Speech, Freedom of Expression and Non-Discrimination*, Human Rights Centre: University of Essex.

Committee on the Elimination of Racial Discrimination, 'Positive Measures Designed to Eradicate all Incitement to, or Acts of, Racial Discrimination, Implementation of the International Convention on the Elimination of All Forms of Racial Discrimination, Article 4, UN Doc. CERD/2 (1985) [*CERD Report on Article 4*].

Cotler, Irwin (1986), 'Freedom of Expression', in *The Limitation of Human Rights in Comparative Constitutional Law*, Armand de Mestral et al., (eds), Montreal: Les Editions Yvon Blais.

European Consultative Assembly Debate (1949), 1st Session (17 August), in *Collected Edition of the Travaux Préparatoires of the European Convention on Human Rights* (1975), vol. 1.

Farrior, Stephanie (1996), 'Molding the Matrix: The Historical and Theoretical Foundations of International Law Concerning Hate Speech', *Berkeley Journal of International Law*, vol. 14, pp. 1–98.

Faurisson v. France, Communication No. 550/1993, UN Doc. CCPR/C/58/D/550/1993 (16 December 1996).

Genn, Rowel (1983), 'Beyond the Pale: Council of Europe Measures Against Incitement to Hatred', *Israel Yearbook on Human Rights*, vol. 13, p. 189.

Glimmerveen and Hagenbeek v. Netherlands, App. Nos. 8348/78 and 8406/78, [1980] in *Yearbook of the European Convention on Human Rights* 1980, vol. 23.

Human Rights Committee (1983), 'Advocacy of Racial Hatred and Admissibility of a Communication: Case of *Taylor v. Canada* [communication No. R. 24/104 (1981)]', *Human Rights Law Journal*, vol. 4, 1983.

Jersild v. Denmark, 298 European Court of Human Rights (ser. A) 23 September 1994.

Lerner, Natan (1980), *The UN Convention on the Elimination of All Forms of Racial Discrimination*, Alphen aan den Rijn, The Netherlands; Rockville, MD: Sijthoff & Noordhoff.

Mahalic, Drew and Mahalic, Joan Gambee (1987), 'The Limitation Provisions of the International Convention on the Elimination of All Forms of Racial Discrimination', *Human Rights Quarterly*, vol. 9, p. 74.

Schabas, William, A. (2000), *Genocide in International Law: The Crimes of Crimes*, Cambridge, New York: Cambridge University Press.

Schwelb, Egon (1966), 'The International Convention on the Elimination of All Forms of Racial Discrimination', *International and Comparative Law Quarterly*, vol. 15, p. 996.

Terminiello v. Chicago, 337 U.S. 1 (1949).

The Observer and The Guardian v. United Kingdom [The *Spycatcher* case], 216 European Court of Human Rights (ser. A) (1991), 24 October 1991.

Verdoodt, Albert (1964), *Naissance et Signification de la Declaration Universelle des Droits de L'Homme*, Louvain: Nauwlaerts.

X v. Federal Republic of Germany, App. No. 9235/81, 29 European Commission on Human Rights – Decisions & Reports 194 (1982).

Notes

1. 'States parties' to a treaty are states that have ratified (become party to) that treaty. States parties are legally bound to carry out the obligations set out in the treaty.
2. *Glimmerveen v. Netherlands*, discussed at p. 89 under heading: 'Advocacy of hatred cases under the European Convention'.
3. See p. 75 under heading 'Issues considered during drafting of Articles 19 and 20 of the Covenant'.
4. Genn, 'Beyond the Pale: Council of Europe Measures Against Incitement to Hatred', p. 190.

5. UN General Assembly Res. 217 A(III), 10 December 1948, UN Doc. A/810, p. 71 (1948).

6. UN Doc. E/CN.4/21 (1 July 1947), Annexe B, p. 5 (Article 14(3); the clause appears in square brackets). Another clause in the limitations provision allowed restrictions on 'publications intended or likely to incite persons to alter by violence the system of Government, or to promote disorder or crime'. The accompanying commentary declared that the clause should be interpreted 'as strictly confined to such publications as advocate the use of violence'. No such qualification, however, appeared in the commentary to the clause on publications aimed at suppressing others' human rights.

7. Ibid. The commentary ended by noting that 'in any case [. . .] no Government is obliged by the Bill to make use of the powers of limitation which are provided in paragraph 3'.

8. UN Doc. E/CN.4/AC.1/3/Add.1 (2 June 1947), p. 122.

9. Verdoodt, *Naissance et Signification de la Declaration Universelle des Droits de L'Homme*, p. 189.

10. The International Refugee Organization was the precursor to today's United Nations High Commissioner for Refugees. The Preparatory Commission of the IRO, along with other international human rights bodies, had been invited by the UN Commission on Human Rights to submit suggestions as to what rights should be included in the Universal Declaration, and to comment on earlier drafts that had been circulated.

11. Ibid., p. 1. UN Doc. E/CN.4/41/Rev.1 (13 December 1947), p. 2. Explaining the IRO's interest in providing input into the drafting process on this issue, he stated:
   No group of human individuals can be more interested in an International Bill of Human Rights than the large number of persons who are the concern of the International Refugee Organization – the refugees and displaced persons. The position of these persons is due, to a considerable extent, to the flagrant violation of their human rights by Nationalist-Socialist Germany, Japan and their Fascist Allies.

12. UN Doc. E/CN.4/41/Rev.1 (13 December 1947), p. 2.

13. Draft International Declaration on Human Rights, Commission on Human Rights, UN Doc. E/CN.4/77/Annexe A (16 December 1947), p. 2.

14. UN Doc. E/CN.4/AC.1/3/Add.1 (2 June 1947), p. 13.

15. UN Doc. E/CN.4/SR.41 (16 December 1947), p. 7.

16. Verdoodt, *Naissance et Signification de la Declaration Universelle*, p. 188.

17. Ibid., pp. 189–90.

18. UN General Assembly Official Records, 3d Comm., 180th plen.mtg. (9 December 1948) p. 855.

19. UN Doc. E/CN.4/77 (16 December 1947), pp. 12–13.

20. 'Any advocacy of national, racial or religious hostility that constitutes an incitement to violence shall be prohibited by the law of the State'. UN Doc. E/CN.4/77/ANNEX B (16 December 1947), p. 12. The United States had submitted to the Commission its own draft, which contained no restrictions in the freedom of expression clause itself. However, as the Report of the Working Party noted, the United States' Draft Convention did contain a general limitation clause which would apply to all articles, including the one on freedom of expression, which read as follows: 'The full exercise of these rights requires recognition of the rights of others and protection by law of the freedom, general welfare and security of all.' UN Doc. E/CN.4/56 (11 December 1947), p. 11.

21. UN Doc. E/CN.4/SR.123 (14 June 1949), p. 4.

22. Ibid., p. 5. The case referred to by the United States representative is most likely *Terminiello v. Chicago*, 337 U.S. 1 (1949) (holding unconstitutional an ordinance that 'permitted conviction of petitioner if his speech stirred people to anger, invited public dispute, or brought about a condition of unrest. A conviction resting on any of those grounds may not stand.' 337 U.S. at 7). The Soviet representative quickly pointed to the dissenting opinion in the Supreme Court case, saying that it 'amounted to an objection to allowing freedom for the dissemination of Fascist views'. UN Doc. E/CN.4/SR.123 (14 June 1949), p. 5.

23. *Terminiello*, 337 U.S. at 37.

24. The French word 'propagande' was simply translated into English as 'propaganda.' The United Kingdom representative, among others, proposed that the word 'advocacy' be used instead, as it was the 'proper legal term,' and the word 'propaganda' was both 'vague and derogatory'. UN Commission on Human Rights, UN Doc. E/CN.4/SR.174 (8 May 1950), pp. 6, 13.

25. UN Doc. E/CN.4/SR.160 (27 April 1950), p. 10.

26. Ibid., p. 13.

27. UN Doc. E/CN.4/SR.377 (16 October 1953), p. 4.

28. Ibid.

29. UN Doc. E/CN.4/L.269 (1953). No detailed discussion took place of the meaning of the words 'incitement' and 'advocacy'.

30. UN Doc. E/CN.4/SR.377 (16 October 1953), p. 4.

31. UN Doc.E/CN.4/SR.378 (19 October 1953), p. 11.

32. UN Doc.E/CN.4/SR.377 (19 October 1953), p. 14.

33. UN Doc. E/CN.4/SR.379 (19 October 1953), pp. 7–8.

34. UN Doc. E/CN.4/SR.174 (8 May 1950), p. 6.

35. The United Kingdom expressed concern over prohibiting advocacy of 'hostility', and asserted that the French proposal would suppress the writings of Voltaire, UN Commission on Human Rights, UN Doc. E/CN.4/SR.174 (8 May 1950), p. 13. 'The works of Voltaire had been intended to incite to religious hatred – and indeed they were still on the Index of the Roman Catholic Church.' UN Commission on Human Rights, UN Doc. E/CN.4/SR.379 (19 October 1953), p. 6.

36. Schwelb, 'The International Convention on the Elimination of All Forms of Racial Discrimination', p. 1022 (citing Peace Treaty with Hungary of 10 February 1947, Art. 4).

37. Ibid.

38. UN Doc. E/CN.4/SR.174 (8 May 1950), p. 7.

39. UN Doc. E/CN.4/SR.379 (19 October 1953), p. 7.

40. Ibid., p. 4.

41. Ibid.

42. Ibid.

43. UN Doc. E/CN.4/SR.378 (19 October 1953), p. 10.

44. The Mississippi law to which the delegate was apparently referring was Mississippi Code 2339 (1942). It provided:

    Any person, firm or corporation who shall be guilty of printing, publishing or circulating printed, typewritten, or written matter urging or presenting for public acceptance or general information, arguments, or suggestions in favour of social equality or of intermarriage between whites and negroes, shall be guilty of a misdemeanour and subject to a fine [. . .] or imprisonment [. . .] or both fine and imprisonment. (UN Commission on Human Rights, UN Doc. E/CN.4/SR.321 (17 June 1952), p. 4.)

45. UN Doc. E/CN.4/SR.321 (17 June 1952), p. 5.
46. UN Doc. E/CN.4/SR.174 (8 May 1950), p. 9.
47. UN Doc. E/CN.4/SR.379 (19 October 1953), p. 7.
48. Ibid., p. 9.
49. UN Doc. E/CN.4/SR.377 (19 October 1953), pp. 13–14.
50. Ibid., p. 9. One could argue, of course, that the citizens of Germany, Austria, and other countries hardly arrived at reasoned decisions in the 1930s and 1940s, to the detriment of millions of their fellow human beings.
51. UN Doc. E/CN.4/SR.377 (16 October 1953), p. 7 (emphasis in original).
52. Ibid.
53. UN Doc. E/CN.4/SR.378 (19 October 1953), p. 11.
54. Ibid., pp. 11–12.
55. Ibid., p. 12.
56. Noting that the Commission on Human Rights had recently adopted a provision protecting against defamation of character, he added: 'The libelling of a whole group or nation was an even more serious matter than the defamation of an individual.' Ibid., p. 13.
57. UN Doc. E/CN.4/SR.378 (19 October 1953), p. 12.
58. UN Doc. E/CN.4/379 (19 October 1953), p. 10.
59. Ibid., p. 12.
60. See, for example, UN Doc. A/C.3/SR.1078 (19 October 1961), paras. 15–18.
61. See, for example, UN General Assembly, 16th Sess., Third Committee, UN Doc. A/C.3/SR.1084 (26 October 1961), para. 28.
62. UN Doc. A/C.3/SR.1081 (23 October 1961), para. 11. Support for this amendment came from many quarters, prompting the Congolese representative to remark that since 1953, 'many new countries had been able to make themselves heard in the United Nations'. UN General Assembly, 16th Sess., Third Committee, UN Doc. A/C.3/SR.1083 (25 October 1961), para. 44.
63. UN Doc. A/C.3/SR.1083 (25 October 1961), para. 13.
64. Ibid., para. 58.
65. Ibid., para. 59.
66. UN Doc. E/CN.4/SR.181 (16 May 1950), pp. 6, 8.
67. UN Doc. E/CN.4/SR.123 (10 June 1949), p. 8.
68. Ibid.
69. Report of the Human Rights Committee, UN GAOR, 38th Sess., Supp. No. 40, Annex VI, UN Doc. A/38/40 (1983) p. 109–10.
70. See, for example, Report of the Human Rights Committee, UN GAOR, 38th Sess., UN Doc. A/38/40, Supp. No. 40 A (1983), p. 31 (reviewing report of Australia).
71. UN GAOR, 39th Sess., UN Doc. A/39/40, Supp. No. A (1984), p. 23.
72. See UN Doc. CCPR/C/79/Add.16 (28 December 1992), para. 1.
73. Ibid., para. 8.
74. UN Doc. CCPR/C/SR.1202 (8 April 1993), para. 64.
75. Human Rights Committee, Advocacy of Racial Hatred and Admissibility of a Communication: Case of *Taylor v. Canada*, p. 193.
76. Ibid.
77. Quoted ibid.
78. Ibid.

79. *Faurisson v. France*, 1996.
80. Ibid., para. 9.
81. Ibid.
82. Cited in CERD, 'Positive Measures Designed to Eradicate all Incitement to, or Acts of, Racial Discrimination, Implementation of the International Convention on the Elimination of All Forms of Racial Discrimination, Article 4', 1985 [*CERD Report on Article 4*], p. 1, n.3.
83. UN GAOR, 20th Sess., 1406th Plenary mtg., UN Doc. A/PV.1406 (1965), p. 6, cited in Lerner, *The UN Convention on the Elimination of All Forms of Racial Discrimination*, p. 46.
84. UN GAOR 3d Comm., 1361st mtg., paras. 3 and 4, cited in *CERD Report on Article 4*, p. 1.
85. UN Doc. A/PV.1406 (1965), cited in Lerner, *UN Convention*, p. 47.
86. UN Doc. A/C.3/SR.1318 (1965), cited in *CERD Report on Article 4*, p. 1.
87. UN Doc. A/6181 (1965).
88. *CERD Report on Article 4*.
89. Ibid., p. 37.
90. Ibid., p. 38.
91. Ibid.
92. Mahalic and Mahalic, 'The Limitation Provisions of the International Convention on the Elimination of All Forms of Racial Discrimination'. 1987, p. 89.
93. UN Doc. CERD/C/SR.189 (1974), p. 65.
94. See, for example, Universal Declaration, Article 1 (all people are equal in dignity and rights); Article 2 (right to be free from racial discrimination); Article 5 (protection against degrading treatment); Article 7 (protection against discrimination or incitement to discrimination); Article 8 (right to effective remedy for violation of fundamental rights); Article 28 (calling for an international order in which the rights and freedoms set forth in the Declaration can be fully realized); Article 29(2) (the exercise of rights and freedoms is subject to limitations for the purpose of, *inter alia*, respect for the rights and freedoms of others and for the collective good of society); Article 30 (no individual or group may invoke a right in the Universal Declaration for any activities aimed at the destruction of the rights and freedoms in that Declaration). For a discussion of this balance and the outcome, see Mahalic and Mahalic, pp. 90–3.
95. CERD General Recommendations VII and XV, in UN Doc. CERD/C/365/Rev.1 (5 December 2000).
96. Ibid., p. 32.
97. See, for example, UN Doc. A/43/18 (1988), pp. 23–4.
98. See, for example, *CERD Report on Article 4*, p. 39.
99. UN Doc. A/42/18 (1987), p. 57.
100. UN Doc. A/48/18 (15 September 1993), para. 536.
101. Ibid., para. 543.
102. UN Doc. CERD/C/SR.1003 (19 August 1993), para.32.
103. UN Doc. A/50/18 (22 September 1995), para. 230.
104. Ibid., para. 239.
105. Ibid., para. 244.
106. UN Doc. CERD/C/SR.1042 (25 July 1994), para. 22.
107. European Consultative Assembly Debate, (1949), 1975, p. 110.
108. Ibid.

109. Ibid., p. 118.
110. Ibid., p. 208.
111. Ibid., pp. 200–1.
112. Ibid., p. 136.
113. *J. Glimmerveen and J. Hagenbeek v. Netherlands* (1980), p. 366.
114. The leaflets, directed at 'white Dutch people', declared that 'the major part of our population has long since had enough of the presence in our country of the hundreds of thousands of Surinamese, Turks and other so-called guest workers, who, moreover, are not needed here at all,' and that 'as soon as the Nederlandse Volks Unie has gained political power in our country, it will set things right and, as the first item, will remove all Surinamese, Turks and other so-called guest workers from the Netherlands'. Ibid., p. 368.
115. Ibid. (Emphasis added).
116. *X v. Federal Republic of Germany*, p. 194.
117. Ibid.
118. *Jersild v. Denmark*, p. 1.
119. The Court briefly noted that the conviction and sentence met the first two requirements of a limitation of freedom of expression: it was undisputed that the interference with that freedom was prescribed by law, being based on Article 266 of the Penal Code, and that the interference pursued a legitimate aim under Article 10(2), the 'protection of the reputation or rights of others'.
120. *Jersild v. Denmark* p. 24.
121. Ibid., pp. 25–6 (citing *The Observer and The Guardian v. United Kingdom* [The *Spycatcher* case], (1991).
122. *Jersild v. Denmark*, p. 29.
123. Report of the United States Delegation to the Inter-American Conference on Protection of Human Rights, San Jose, Costa Rica, Nov. 9–22, 1969, in vol. 3 of Buergenthal (ed.), *Inter-American System*, Part II: Chap. III, Booklet 15 (August 1982), p. 27.
124. Draft Convention on Human Rights presented to the Second Special Inter-American Conference by the government of Chile, OAS Official Record OEA/Ser.E/XIII.I (1965) in vol. 3 of Buergenthal (ed.), *Inter-American System*, Part II, Appendix, Booklet 16.1 (June 1984), pp. 31–89.
125. Observations of the Governments of the Member States Regarding the Draft Inter-American Convention on Protection of Human Rights, United States (6 October 1969), in vol. 2 of Buergenthal (ed.), *Inter-American System*, Part II, Chap. II, Booklet 13 (August 1982), pp. 157.
126. Summary Minutes of the Conference of San Jose (1982), Minutes of the Eighth Session of Committee I Summary Version, Doc. 48 (15 November 1969), in vol. 2 of Buergenthal (ed.) *Inter-American System*, Part II, Chap. I, Booklet 12 (August 1982), p. 89.
127. Ibid.
128. Report of the United States Delegation to the Inter-American Conference on Protection of Human Rights, San Jose, Costa Rica, Nov. 9–22, 1969, in vol. 3 of Buergenthal (ed.), *Inter-American System*, Part II, Chap. III, Booklet 15 (August 1982), p. 26.
129. Ibid.
130. In drafting the paragraph, the US delegation said it 'was guided by the latest Supreme Court decision on the subject then available to it, *Brandenburg v. Ohio*,

395 U.S. 444 (1969)'. Ibid. In that case, the United States Supreme Court held that the Constitution does not allow a state to proscribe 'advocacy of the use of force or of law violation' unless 'such advocacy is directed to inciting or producing imminent lawless action and is likely to incite or produce such action' 395 U.S. at 44.

131. Report of the US Delegation, in vol. 3, Buergenthal (ed.), pp. 26–7.

132. IACHR, Annual Report for 1980–1981, OEA/Ser.L/V/II.54, Doc. 9 rev. 1 (16 October 1981), in vol. 4, Buergenthal (ed.), *Inter-American System*, Part III, Booklet 24 (May 1983), p. 39.

133. IACHR Advisory Opinion OC-5/85, 13 November 1985, Inter-Am.Ct.H.R. (Ser. A) No. 5 (1985). The case involved a journalist sentenced for exercising the profession of journalism without a licence, a penalty the Court determined violated Article 13.

134. 'Report of the Working Group, Novena Conferencia Internacionale Americana, Actas y Documentos, vol. 5 (Bogota: Min. de Relaciones Exteriores, 1953)' pp. 474–8; original report identified as CB-310/CIN-41, reproduced in vol. 1 of Buergenthal (ed.), *Inter-American System*, Part I, Chap. IV, Booklet 5 (April 1982), pp. 15–23.

135. UN Doc. E/447 (1947), p. 32.

136. UN Doc. A/401 Add. 2 (1947), p. 7.

137. UN Doc. A/C.6/215 (4 October 1948). The Soviet proposal would also have amended the Preamble to require states parties 'to suppress and prohibit the stimulation of racial, national and religious hatred' in addition to genocide itself. Ibid. For details of the drafting history, see William A. Schabas, *Genocide in International Law*, pp. 266–71.

138. See Schabas, ibid., pp. 482–6.

3

International Law and Information Intervention

Eric Blinderman

Introduction

Individuals, acting under the authority of a state and acting alone, have often used the media to incite human rights violations. The international community established a legal framework designed to punish, after the fact, those who use media outlets to incite systematic and widespread human rights violations;[1] but, as yet, has articulated no justification to prevent individuals from using media in this manner. For example, the Nuremberg Tribunal found Julius Streicher guilty of crimes against humanity and sentenced him to death even though, as some scholars have argued, neither the London Charter nor the indictment specifically granted the Tribunal jurisdiction over the crime of incitement.[2] The Tribunal stated, 'Streicher's incitement to murder and extermination when Jews were being killed under the most horrible conditions clearly constitutes persecution on political and racial grounds in connection with War Crimes, as defined by the Charter, and constitutes a Crime Against Humanity.'[3] The International Criminal Tribunal for the Prosecution of Persons Responsible for Genocide and Other Serious Violations of International Humanitarian Law Committed in the Territory of Rwanda (ICTR) indicted both Ferdinand Nahimana, one of the founders and leaders of Radio-Television Libre des Milles Collines (RTLM), which broadcast hate propaganda against Tutsis throughout the Rwandan genocide, and Hassan Ngeze, chief editor of *Kangura*, a virulently anti-Tutsi newspaper that played a significant role in mobilizing Hutu extremists to slaughter ethnic Tutsi for, among other counts, genocide.[4] It also convicted Georges Ruggiu, an extremist journalist of RTLM, for public incitement to commit genocide and crimes against humanity.[5]

States, in addition to prosecution, should be endowed with the legal right to take pre-emptive action designed to prevent the occurrence of systematic and widespread human rights violations. Stating this as a conclusion, however, leaves open the complicated question: What steps can a state or group of states take *to prevent* individuals acting in either their official capacity or privately from using the media to instigate a human rights crisis? Recent articles from legal scholars and policy experts have suggested that it is lawful for the United Nations Security Council to authorize the United Nations to intervene in another state's domestic jurisdiction and reshape that state's media using technological, psychological, and information warfare techniques in order to prevent the occurrence of systematic and widespread human rights violations.[6,7,8] Other articles have discussed whether it is lawful for the United Nations or another group of states to use these techniques against a target state in order to prevent the occurrence of systematic and widespread human rights violation if the target state consents to the intervention.[9,10]

Although these ideas may prove useful in preventing human rights abuses from occurring, scholars have not placed these ideas into a normative international legal framework. This chapter attempts to lay the foundation for such a framework. It focuses on whether an intervening state's pre-emptive use of technological, information, and psychological warfare techniques against incendiary media located in a target state to prevent the occurrence of a systematic and widespread human rights violation transgresses fundamental notions of state sovereignty as expressed by customary legal expressions of the non-intervention norm.[11,12,13,14]

The legal constructs underpinning the non-intervention norm are complex and, like the constructs underpinning freedom of speech, provide substantive guidelines that directly relate to the purported legality of pre-emptive information intervention. Consequently, a state wishing to engage in a policy of information intervention must ask whether the specific techniques utilized as part of that policy violate international norms regarding non-intervention in addition to those norms regarding freedom of speech. On a similar note, it is important to note that international legal norms regarding non-intervention are distinct from those that relate to freedom of speech and that just because international freedom of speech norms support the notion of information intervention, this does not mean that the non-intervention norm also supports the notion of information intervention.

Current jurisprudence regarding the non-intervention doctrine does not yet fully support the notion of information intervention. But existing limitations regarding the non-intervention norm as it relates to information intervention must be reviewed in light of recent experiences in Rwanda, Yugoslavia, and elsewhere where individuals and governments deliberately utilized the media in a conscious effort to precipitate systematic and widespread human rights violations. Alternative non-intervention legal constructs must be explored to provide states with the necessary theoretical groundwork to engage in a policy of information intervention when fundamental human rights are threatened.

To address whether a state's use of pre-emptive information tools against a target state violates the non-intervention norm, it is useful to differentiate between two types of intervention. The first type of intervention occurs when the United Nations, acting under its Chapter VII powers, determines that a 'threat to the peace, breach of the peace, or act of aggression' exists and authorizes a single state or group of states to take measures in accordance with Article 41 of the Charter to restore international peace and security. The second type occurs when a single state or group of states, acting in either a unilateral or multilateral capacity, take non-forcible action against a target state without authorization from the United Nations or the consent of the target state.

In accordance with this analytic pattern, this chapter first defines the term 'information intervention' and compares it to more traditional legal concepts of humanitarian intervention. It next places the term 'information intervention' within the contours of the non-intervention. In the middle sections, the chapter discusses the legality of United Nations-authorized pre-emptive information intervention and contrasts it to the purported legality of information intervention undertaken by a single state or group of states that do not receive authorization from the United Nations or the target state's consent. The chapter then discusses whether an intervening state or group of states may lawfully utilize the techniques of information intervention against a target state when individuals in the target state, acting in their individual or official capacity, utilize media outlets at their disposal to incite others into committing genocide. Finally, the last section argues that new international legal norms allowing for both United Nations authorized and non-authorized pre-emptive information intervention need to be created so that states are better equipped to prevent the occurrence of systematic and widespread human rights violations.

Information Intervention: the Doctrine Defined

For the purposes of this chapter, the term 'information intervention' refers to an intervening state's use of technological, informational, and psychological warfare techniques against incendiary media outlets (public or private) located in a target state. From a legal standpoint, the distinction between information intervention and other forms of intervention is the role of force. Under international law, states are generally prohibited from using or threatening to use force against the territorial integrity or political independence of other states unless the United Nations Security Council authorizes the use of force under Article 42 of the United Nations Charter.[15] Information intervention assumes that a state will not engage in a military campaign against incendiary media actors but will instead use non-forcible means to achieve the goal of preventing a human rights crisis.

As a corollary to this assumption, information intervention also presupposes that technological solutions designed to block access to incendiary messages or provide alternative sources of communication to media outlets that incite human rights violations can prevent the violation from occurring. This second supposition is partially correct, although highly simplistic. Though incendiary media outlets do play a role in instigating people to commit human rights violations, these outlets are usually part of a complex web of social, economic, historic, political, and institutional fractures within a society that lead to the occurrence of human rights violations. If these larger fractures are not addressed and the international community refuses to discern the impact of these fractures on instigating human rights violations, the effectiveness of information intervention may be limited. However, as a temporary solution to an immediate and impending crisis, the techniques of information intervention may grant the potential victims of human rights violations and the international community adequate time to attempt to diffuse a potential crisis before it occurs.

The distinction between force and non-force inherent in the definition of information intervention is important for a variety of reasons. Foremost among these is that international law, as expressed under Article (2)(4) of the United Nations Charter, prohibits a state from using force against another state unless it is acting in self-defence or receives authorization from the Security Council. Writers have long lamented that political considerations usually render the Security Council ineffective when it is called upon to prevent the occurrence of a human rights crisis. This inaction has led many legal jurists and politicians to argue that customary international law still provides certain implied exceptions to the Charter's legal prohibition on the use of force against a state.

One such exception, created in the late 1960s by Leonid Brezhnev to justify the Soviet invasion of Czechoslovakia and commonly called the Brezhnev Doctrine, asserts a general right of any socialist state to intervene in the affairs of another socialist state if socialism there became threatened. Declaring that '[t]he sovereignty of each socialist country cannot be opposed to the interests of the world of socialism, of the world revolutionary movement [. . .] the USSR and the other socialist states had to act decisively and they did act against antisocialist forces in Czechoslovakia', the Soviets relied upon the Brezhnev Doctrine to justify their later invasions of Hungary and Afganistan.[16]

Another such exception formulated by the United States during the mid-1980s became known as the 'Reagan Doctrine'.[17] Under this doctrine, the United States asserted that it could, consistent with international law, provide assistance or use military force to impose or restore democracy. In particular, the United States argued that when communism threatened the existence of a democracy, it could take military or other action to support the threatened democracy. Utilized to justify United States support for the Contras in Nicaragua, United States UN Ambassador Jean Kirkpatrick tried to paint a slippery distinction between permissible and non-permissible intervention under the Reagan Doctrine by arguing that Soviet and Cuban support for the Sandinistas was not permissible because the Sandinstas regime was totalitarian and merely a puppet of the Soviets and Cubans, whose true intent behind their support of the Sandinistas was to colonize Nicaragua. In contrast, because the Contras were democrats fighting a totalitarian regime, the United States was justified in providing support to them.

Legal scholars and jurists have long rejected the legality of both the Brezhnev Doctrine and the Reagan Doctrine concluding that both largely serve as little more than pretexts for a powerful state to justify otherwise illegal action in pursuit of its political goals. In fact, the USSR expressly disavowed the Brezhnev Doctrine in November 1989 when Mikhail Gorbachev refused to send Soviet troops into either Hungary or Poland to quell the democratic transition in those states. After Gorbachev declared that the Soviet Union 'has no moral or political right to interfere in events [in those states]', his spokesman referred to this shift in Soviet policy as reflective of the 'Sinatra Doctrine'.[18] He explained further, 'You know the Frank Sinatra song "I Did it My Way"? Hungary and Poland are doing it their way.'[19]

The exception most relevant to the doctrine of information intervention is otherwise known as humanitarian intervention. The first type of unilateral action falling under the rubric of humanitarian intervention is forcible intervention by a state to protect its own nationals. Considerable evidence exists indicating that, prior to the adoption of the UN Charter, international law accepted the right of a state to intervene in the affairs of another state to protect its own nationals in the event that a human rights or other crisis threatened the safety of the intervening state's nationals.[20] Following the adoption of the UN Charter and Article 2(4), the legality of a state using force to protect its nationals residing abroad was challenged and states that continued to use force in this manner were forced to rest their arguments about the continued vitality of the doctrine on Article 51 of the UN Charter.[21]

A second type of unilateral action falling under the rubric of humanitarian intervention is a single state's unilateral, or a group of states' collective, use of force against a target state when the target state's citizens are the victims of systematic and widespread human rights violations.[22] International law generally prohibits both a single state's unilateral and a group of states' collective use of force in this manner. The rationale is not that a state's sovereignty overrides the obligations of a state to protect human rights. Rather it is that, in the absence of such a rule, states would be able to use humanitarian intervention 'as a pretextual disguise' to fulfil national ambitions.[23] If single states were given the right to intervene forcibly in the internal affairs of another state, 'such a right would be difficult to check' and would present 'grave risks of abuse' for powerful states to use force against weaker states whenever the powerful state wished to gain an advantage over the weaker state.[24] As stated by the International Court of Justice when rejecting a proffered humanitarian intervention justification for United States support of the Contras in Nicaragua, '[w]hile the United States might form its own appraisal of the situation as to respect for human rights in Nicaragua, the use of force could not be the appropriate method to monitor or ensure such respect.'[25] Consequently, the legality of humanitarian intervention is questionable, although, in light of NATO action in Kosovo, its validity is finding increased acceptance among scholars and policy makers.[26]

The emergence of information intervention as an alternative to humanitarian intervention, although not causally linked to the controversy surrounding humanitarian intervention's legality, should be seen in the context of its questioned legality as well as the international community's failure to take preventive action in Bosnia and Rwanda towards the end of the 1990s. Designed to provide the Security Council with less drastic alternatives than authorizing the use of force to prevent human rights crises, it was hoped that the political consequences of authorizing information intervention would be less than those of authorizing conventional forms of humanitarian intervention. If this proved true, the Security Council would be empowered to take more aggressive preventive action in the face of human rights crises. As a result, writers and scholars began to reformulate the doctrine of information intervention, arguing that because information intervention techniques do not utilize force, states could legally employ them against a target state regardless of whether they were authorized by the United Nations or the target state consented to their use.[27] The following sections of this chapter test the underlying assumption of legality surrounding both forms of information intervention by analyzing the limits of a target state's sovereignty as expressed under current formulations of the non-intervention norm.

The Non-intervention Norm

Like the UN Charter's prohibition on the use of force against the territorial integrity or political independence of a state, the non-intervention principle 'derives from and supports, the idea of state sovereignty'.[28] In effect, the non-intervention norm protects state sovereignty where the UN Charter's prohibition of the use of force against the territorial integrity or political independence of a state leaves off. The United Nations Charter article 2(7) states that, '[n]othing in the present charter shall authorize the United Nations to intervene in matters which are essentially within the domestic jurisdiction of any state.'[29] The concept, although hazy, is partly clarified by the Friendly Relations Declaration.

In part, the Friendly Relations Declaration

> solemnly proclaims [that . . . n]o State or group of States has the right to intervene, directly or indirectly, for any reason whatever, in the internal or external affairs of any state [. . .] [nor may a state] use or encourage the use of economic, political, or any other type of measures to coerce another State in order to obtain from it the subordination of the exercise of its sovereign rights and to secure from it advantages of any kind.[30]

Read in tandem with the United Nations General Assembly Declaration of the Inadmissibility of Intervention in the Domestic Affairs of States and the Protection of their Independence and Sovereignty ('Non-Intervention Declaration'), which states that 'no State may use or encourage the use of economic, political, or any other type of measures to coerce another State in order to obtain from it the subordination of the exercise of its sovereign rights', it is apparent that the non-intervention norms rest on the premise that all states should enjoy the freedom to exercise their 'sovereign rights' without interference from other states.[31]

Thus, for a state's non-forcible interference in the domestic affairs of a target state to violate the non-intervention norm, two elements must be satisfied. The intervening state must take action against a target state that subordinates the target state's sovereign rights with the intent to subordinate the target state's sovereign rights.[33] Although it is difficult to measure a state's intent, as intent is essentially a subjective condition and a state is an abstract entity, it can be discerned by analyzing objective factors related to the challenged action to determine if these factors support an inference of intent. The problem with utilizing objective factors to discern a state's intent, such as whether the challenged action resulted in a loss of the target state's ability to decide matters which principles of state sovereignty dictate must be decided freely, is that it risks collapsing the first element into the second.[34]

Nevertheless, an objective approach is necessary because it minimizes an intervening state's ability to escape condemnation for a challenged intervention by arguing that its intent was not related to a desire to subordinate a state's sovereign rights. At the same time, an objective approach also allows policymakers to distinguish between accidental interference with a target state's rights[35] and deliberate interference with a state's sovereign rights. The following sections apply these two elements to United Nations authorized and unauthorized pre-emptive information intervention to determine their legality under the non-intervention norm.

United Nations Authorized Information Intervention

In order to apply the first prong of the non-intervention test to United Nations' authorized information intervention, it is necessary to understand the nature of the United Nations Charter. The Charter is the foundation of the modern international legal system and was drafted after the allied victory in World War II. As an international agreement, party states are bound to its provisions.[36] Although the Charter purports to codify existing law regarding the non-intervention norm, it contains one important exception to the absolute prohibition on a state interfering in the domestic affairs of another state. Article 2(7) declares that the principle of non-intervention 'shall not prejudice the application of enforcement measures under Chapter VII' of the Charter.[37]

Chapter VII of the Charter entrusts the Security Council with the task of maintaining international peace and security. Under its executive powers, the Security Council is entitled to 'determine the existence of any threat to the peace [. . .] and shall make recommendations, or decide what measures shall be taken in accordance with Articles 41 and 42, to maintain or restore international peace and security'.[38] Under Article 41:

> [t]he Security Council may decide what measures not involving the use of armed force are to be employed to give effect to its decisions [. . .]. These may include complete or partial interruption of economic relations and of

rail, sea, air, postal, telegraphic, radio, and other means of communication, and the severance of diplomatic relations.[39]

Thus, by its explicit terms, the Charter acknowledges that information intervention sanctioned by the Security Council and conducted under the auspices of the United Nations does not violate the non-intervention norm.

The rationale behind this rule is well settled. Once a state signs a treaty, it is bound by its terms. This is true even if the treaty strips away portions of the state's existing rights of sovereignty. In essence, that is the purpose of all treaties. If international law precluded a state from voluntarily delegating fragments of its sovereignty to a multinational treaty organization, the international system could not operate. As such, courts have long recognized that a state's consent to a particular treaty covering a specific matter forecloses its ability to claim that the matter is exclusively within its domestic jurisdiction.[40]

The applicability of this rule to United Nations authorized information intervention is straightforward. Because almost all currently recognized states are party to the UN Charter, they have agreed to be bound by the Security Council's decisions regarding threats to international peace and security.[41] As a consequence of this, they have also agreed to allow the Security Council to intervene in their domestic affairs if the Council deems such intervention appropriate and are foreclosed from claiming that such intervention violates their sovereign rights as protected under the first prong of the non-intervention test. This consent is expressed through the states' signature to the United Nations Charter.[42]

Accordingly, if the United Nations Security Council concludes that a particular state's media outlets are creating a situation that threatens peace and security or if a particular state's media outlets threaten to impede the effect of prior Security Council resolutions, the Council may authorize member states to take any measures not involving the use of force against that state and its media outlets or it may authorize member states to interrupt transmissions from those media outlets. Therefore, United Nations authorized information intervention is *prima facie* legal and the least controversial form of intervention. This is true regardless of whether the United Nations authorized information intervention includes jamming, peace broadcasting, or less coercive forms of intervention. State practice also confirms this view.

For example, in 1966 the Security Council adopted Resolution 232 declaring the institution of white minority rule in Southern Rhodesia to constitute a threat to international peace and security. Acting under its Article 41 powers, the Security Council's passage of Resolution 232 prohibited the sale or supply of all military supplies, aircraft, and oil products to Southern Rhodesia. Two years later the Security Council unanimously adopted Resolution 253, which called for the complete economic, political, and social isolation of Southern Rhodesia.

More recently, the Security Council, acting under its Chapter VII powers, passed Resolution 748 imposing economic sanctions against Libya until it complied with requests to turn over individuals suspected of bombing Pan Am flight 103. The Security Council based its decision to invoke its inherent powers under Article 41 on its conclusion that Libya's inaction constituted a threat to peace and security. When Libya challenged the legality of Resolution 748 as an abuse of the Security Council's discretion in the International Court of Justice, the Court upheld it, noting that although the Security Council's discretion was not unlimited, 'any limitation must be restrictively interpreted and is confined only to the principles and objects which appear in Chapter I of the Charter'.[43]

Finally, the Security Council's actions in the former Yugoslavia indicate that Article 41 intervention is both legal and appropriate when undertaken to prevent ethnic conflict. During the genesis of the conflict, the Security Council adopted numerous resolutions that placed a military embargo against Yugoslavia, suspended air travel, and prohibited the import and export of commodities into the region.[44] As the conflict progressed, the Security Council adopted stronger measures against Yugoslavia, including the imposition of a naval blockade around the Adriatic Sea and Danube River to support its earlier resolutions and the creation of 'no-fly zones' and 'safe havens' in Bosnia and Herzegovina.[45]

Although none of the above situations is directly analogous to United Nations authorized pre-emptive information intervention, they directly support the presumption that if the Security Council authorized pre-emptive information intervention actions against a target state, the action does not violate the non-intervention norm. Any such authorization directly buttresses the principles and objectives contained in Chapter I of the Charter, as the prevention of the occurrence of systematic and widespread human rights violations 'strengthens universal peace' and 'promote[s] and encourage[s] respect for human rights and for fundamental freedoms'.[46] Therefore, assuming the Security Council found the political willpower to pass a resolution authorizing pre-emptive information intervention against a target state, the resulting intervention would not violate the non-intervention norm.

Information Intervention Not Authorized by the United Nations

When a group of states or a single state intervenes in the domestic affairs of a target state without receiving authorization from the United Nations or the consent of the target state, the intervening states run the risk of violating the target state's sovereign rights. This is because the target state has not consented, either through treaty or otherwise, to the actions of the intervening state or states. To determine whether such intervention violates the non-intervention norm it is therefore necessary to analyze the nature of a target state's sovereign rights as they relate to an intervening state's pre-emptive use of specific technological, psychological, and information warfare techniques against the target state.

Jamming and the Non-Intervention Norm

A primary limitation on the concept of 'sovereign rights,' as understood under international law, is that 'sovereignty is territorial.'[47] As the *North Atlantic Coast Fisheries* case held, '[o]ne of the essential elements of sovereignty is that it is to be exercised within territorial limits, and that, failing proof to the contrary, the territory is co-terminous with the sovereignty.'[48] For this reason, an intervening state's attempt to jam a target state's terrestrial broadcasts poses a difficult problem, as it requires a state to direct electromagnetic energy into the airspace of a target country in order to interfere with the signals of a transmitter.[49]

As stated in the International Telecommunications Convention, states have a duty to operate international services 'in such a manner as not to cause harmful interference to the radio services or communications of other Members'.[50] Additionally, in 1950, during the height of the Cold War, the United States successfully urged the United Nations General Assembly to pass Resolution 424(V), proclaiming jamming to be a violation 'of the accepted principles of freedom of information'.[51] The United States was also able to convince the United Nations Economic and Social Council to condemn the Soviet Union for 'deliberately interfering with the reception by the people of the USSR of certain radio signals originating beyond the territory of the USSR'.[52]

However the legal significance of these anti-jamming expressions is circumspect for two reasons. First, numerous states have conducted and continue to conduct regular and repeated jamming operations against non-consensual and unwanted broadcasts from other states.[53] Second, both the United Nations General Assembly and United Nations Economic and Social Council Resolutions are non-binding and do not create international law. The combination of these two factors has led many commentators to conclude that customary international law does not prohibit a state from jamming broadcasts that enter its territory without its consent.[54] For purposes of information intervention, this legal rule allowing a state to jam unwanted broadcasts that enter its territory without its consent does not imply, as Jamie Metzl has argued, that an intervening state unilaterally can jam incendiary broadcasts in the territory of a target state.[55] Furthermore, there is no state practice indicating that because states may lawfully jam unwanted broadcasts that enter their territory from abroad, an intervening state may jam unwanted terrestrial broadcasts located in a target state.

The validity of this rule comports with the first prong of the non-intervention norm. Jamming a state's terrestrial transmitters interferes with the target state's right to control its sovereign airspace.[56] Moreover, it subordinates the sovereign's right to control the media outlets located in its territory and transfers that control to the intervening states.[57]

There is however a subtle twist that counters the legal prohibition against an intervening state jamming broadcasts located in a target state that applies to target state transmissions broadcast via either Direct Broadcasting Satellites

(DBS) or Conventional Satellite Broadcasting (CSB). DBS transmissions enable broadcasts from around the world to reach individual television sets provided the viewer has a parabolic antenna or satellite dish set to receive the broadcasts. Unlike CSB, which requires terrestrial redistribution networks to relay the satellite transmissions, DBS transmissions do not require any retransmission.

The critical aspect of both forms of satellite transmission as it relates to the law of jamming is that a target state often may not own the satellite that transmits broadcasts into its territory. As stated under Article 3 of the Treaty on Principles Governing the Activities of States in the Exploration and the Use of Outer Space Including the Moon and other Celestial Bodies ('Space Treaty'), 'a state party to the Treaty on whose registry an object is launched into outer space shall retain jurisdiction and control over such object.'[58] This means that a state owning a satellite that transmits broadcasts into the territory of a target state, may on its own volition or at the request of a third party intervening state, choose to terminate the satellite broadcasts of the target state, and in effect jam them, without violating the non-intervention norm. Although termination of a target state's broadcasts from another state's satellite does interfere with the target state's ability to control its media outlets, that right is superseded by the satellite owning state's right, established by the Space Treaty, to retain jurisdiction over its satellite. State practice also seems to accept the validity of this notion as indicated by Eutelsat's suspension of Serbian use of its satellite during the recent Kosovo conflict.

Information Intervention Techniques Not Prohibited under the Non-Intervention Norm

PEACE BROADCASTING

Although states have the sovereign right to control their air space and to choose which media outlets are heard within their territory by jamming unwanted broadcasts from abroad, these rights do not prohibit an intervening state from transmitting broadcasts into a target state's territory as long as the cross-border broadcasts do not interfere with transmissions existing in the target state. These transmissions are often called peace broadcasting.[59] As stated in Article 19 of the Universal Declaration of Human Rights and in substantially similar language in Article 19 of the International Covenant on Civil and Political Rights (ICCPR), '[e]veryone has the right to [. . .] seek, receive and impart information through any media regardless of frontiers.' The Declaration, although not binding under international law, is widely regarded as embodying general norms of customary international law, while the ICCPR, as a legally binding treaty, means that all states party to it must allow other states, individuals, organizations, and other entities to broadcast information into party states, subject to certain limitations.[60]

In addition to these declarations of international law, technical regulations such as the International Telecommunications Convention (ITC) and the

European Union's Television Without Frontiers Directive contain provisions compelling transnational broadcasting.[61] However, in an effort to protect the sovereign rights of member states to control broadcasts within their territory, the ITC assigns various frequencies to particular states and, as described before, declares that, '[a]ll stations, whatever their purpose, must be established and operate in such a manner so as not to result in harmful interference in the radio services or communications of other Members.'[62] In the event of broadcast interference, ITC regulations stipulate only that the interfering broadcast is not entitled to protection against interference from member states that wish to stop the interference.[63]

A contrary view, at least with regard to international transmissions via DBS, is found in United Nations General Assembly Resolution 37/92 which includes, in an Annexe, the 'Principles Governing the Use of Artificial Earth Satellites for International Direct Television Broadcasting'. According to Article J, paragraph 13 of the Annexe:

> [a] State which intends to establish or authorize the establishment of an international direct television broadcasting service shall without delay notify the proposed receiving State or States of such information and shall promptly enter into any consultation with any of those States which so request.

Writers, however, have argued that because the DBS Resolution was passed by 107 votes in favor, thirteen against, and thirteen abstentions –' a result reflecting the political divide between the Eastern Bloc and the Third World on the one hand, and the West on the others', the former desiring to protect state sovereignty and the latter desiring to protect freedom of speech – the resolution 'should be seen as a mere recommendation to the international community'.[64] Others have stated that, in view of the lack of consensus of states voting in favour and against the resolution and because General Assembly Resolutions are not binding under international law, the DBS Resolution, unlike the Universal Declaration of Human Rights, 'can hardly be regarded as evidence for a customary law rule of prior consent'.[65]

Moreover, 'over eighty countries broadcast some 22 thousand hours of international programming to over 250 million listeners and viewers daily.'[66] These messages are broadcast via terrestrial radio and television transmitters, satellite transmissions, and the Internet.[67] The combined weight of this state practice, when analysed in tandem with the *opinio juris* described in the prior section, indicates that unilateral 'peace broadcasting' via any medium, including the Internet, is not only legal under the non-intervention norm, but exceedingly common.

The underlying validity of a general rule allowing non-consensual cross-border broadcasting makes intrinsic sense when compared to the international rule prohibiting jamming. When an intervening state broadcasts material into a target state, it does not subordinate a target state's rights to control its airspace or the media outlets heard within its territory. The target state's ability to maintain control over its airspace is protected by the legal rule allowing it to jam the unwanted broadcasts. Also, because the intervening state cannot lawfully transmit broadcasts that interfere with the target state's indigenous media outlets, the target state does not lose the right to control those outlets.

An alternative form of peace broadcasting that does not violate the non-intervention norm exists with transmissions over the Internet. Illustrated best by the recent experience of ZaMirNet in the former Yugoslavia, peace broadcasting over the Internet neither violates the territory of a target state nor interferes with its ability to control media outlets located in its territory. Using servers based in Germany, ZaMirNet allowed beleaguered peace activists in Bosnia to communicate with other activists in Belgrade, Zagreb, Tuzla, Ljubljana, and Skopje.[68] Most important, as a tool of information intervention, ZaMirNet allowed individuals from all ethnic groups to discuss the deterioration of ethnic relations in the region without fear of reprisals from the centralized authorities, who were powerless to shut down the German server; thereby illustrating how an intervening state can use the Internet to link various ethnic groups together in a conciliatory forum across ethnic lines without violating the non-intervention norm.

DELIVERY OF HUMANITARIAN ASSISTANCE

The sovereign rights of a state do not include the right to incite or commit human rights violations.[69] Although a state does have a sovereign right to choose the media outlets that are heard within its territory, this right is qualified by the *erga omnes* obligation of all states to prevent individuals within their territory from inciting systematic and widespread human rights abuses.[70] In effect, international humanitarian legal obligations limit a state's sovereign right to allow individuals within the State to use media outlets to incite systematic and widespread human rights violations. Even more critical is the fact that these obligations apply to most states by multilateral treaty obligation as well as customary international law because, as stated above, a state's consent to a particular treaty covering a specific matter forecloses its ability to claim that the matter is exclusively within its domestic jurisdiction.

Because a state owes the international community of states an obligation to comply with international human rights, the international community of states can take action against a particular state when it does not fulfil its international obligations.[71] As stated by the Institute of International Law:

> Without prejudice to the [UN Charter] [. . .] States, acting individually or collectively, are entitled to take diplomatic, economic, and other measures towards any other State which has violated the obligation [to ensure the observance of human rights], provided such measures are permitted under international law and do not involve the use of armed force in violation of the Charter.[72]

Of course this statement begs the ultimate question of the chapter. What non-forcible information intervention measures are permitted under international law, or for purposes of this part of the chapter, what measures are permitted under the non-intervention norm? The *Nicaragua* case, supporting the idea that a limited exception to the non-intervention norm exists for purposes of transmitting humanitarian aid to specific groups within a target state, held:

> There can be no doubt that the provision of strictly humanitarian aid to persons or forces in another country, whatever their political affiliation or objectives, cannot be regarded as unlawful intervention, or as in any way contrary to international law [. . .]. An essential feature of truly humanitarian aid is that it is given 'without discrimination' of any kind. In the view of the Court, if the provision of 'humanitarian assistance' is to escape the condemnation as an intervention in the internal affairs of Nicaragua, not only must it be limited to the purposes hallowed in the practice of the Red Cross, namely 'to prevent and alleviate human suffering,' and 'to protect life and health and to ensure respect for the human being'; it must also, and above all be given without discrimination to all in need in Nicaragua, not merely to the *contras* and their dependents.[73]

Using this reasoning, it is possible to formulate a few bright-line rules regarding the legality of an intervening state's pre-emptive use of technological, psychological, and information warfare techniques against a target state to prevent the occurrence of a human rights crisis.

First, any unilateral information intervention strategy that merely provides humanitarian assistance, whether financial, legal, or professional – including printing newspapers in an alternative country and giving them to local nationals to distribute within the target country, mass faxing, training, and even air dropping alternative newspapers or information supplies from airplanes flying into the target state's airspace – will not violate the non-intervention norm so long as it is given to media outlets or individuals that comply with basic human rights obligations. More explicitly, a state cannot discriminate against individuals or media outlets that are to receive such assistance on the basis of the media outlet's or individual's ideological or political affiliation. Any discrimination in the donation of resources to media outlets or individuals based upon their political or ideological affiliation violates the non-discrimination aspect of the *Nicaragua* holding and, consequently, the non-intervention norm.

The importance of this requirement is based on the premise that a state seeking to engage in information intervention must minimize the possibility that the intervention is utilized to disrupt the balance of power among competing groups within the target state. As a practical matter, it may prove impossible for intervening states not to discriminate in the allocation of information resources during the course of an information intervention because of the nature of a target state's geography, location of threatened groups, and media structure. By their very nature, some of the information intervention techniques discussed – dropping of pamphlets and distribution of material through local sources – may not encounter discrimination problems because anyone within their zone of distribution can receive access to the information they provide. Accordingly, when an intervening state utilizes such techniques it is less likely, assuming the information provided is not slanted toward empowering one group over another, that the domestic power structure of the target state will be adversely impacted.

Often, however, a state seeking to intervene in the domestic affairs of a target state under the guise of information intervention might have the purpose (if not the expressed intent) of favouring one particular view over another. The claim, often justified, that intervening speech 'is objective' may, in part, serve the non-discrimination requirement. But an intervening state that begins to provide direct financial, logistic, and technical aid to groups within a target state in order to encourage a faction with a particular viewpoint or to destabilize an existing government will usually if not always violate the non discrimination norm. To avoid this problem, states should endeavour to provide that assistance, as resources dictate, to any group that seeks access to those resources as long as the group seeking access is in compliance with basic international human rights obligations.

In practice, however, intervening states will likely distribute discretionary funds to further their own political objectives. Ideally, any information intervention policy conducted should be in accordance with both prongs of the non-intervention norm and work to prevent an intervening state from utilizing the intervention to secure its own political advantages at the expense of the target state. That decisions must be made as to who ultimately receives such aid does not decrease the validity of the non-discrimination requirement. What it does mean is that when decisions are made as to those entities that receive aid and those that do not, those decisions should be made objectively, fairly, and transparently.

Second, it is not enough that a particular country wishing to intervene in the information space of another country perceives the target country's media as partisan or as disseminators of hate speech. Rather, to utilize certain information intervention techniques that might be characterized as providing 'humanitarian assistance', there must be an immediate goal of preventing human suffering.[74] The imminence or immediate suffering requirement of the 'humanitarian assistance' exception to the non-intervention norm raises the legal threshold that must be met before an intervention based on this justification can occur. By raising the threshold for intervention, the likelihood that an intervening state may intervene with the goal of extracting political concessions from a target state instead of preventing the occurrence of a human rights violation is decreased while traditional legal concepts against intervention are reinforced. For this reason, the legality of unilateral use of information intervention techniques under the humanitarian assistance exception to the non-intervention norm will depend on the circumstances of each case and the imminence of impending violence. Nevertheless, so long as non-discriminatory humanitarian assistance is provided to populations within a target state in furtherance of an immediate goal of preventing human suffering, the delivery of such assistance will not violate the non-intervention norm.

The existence of unilateral state practice in support of a humanitarian assistance exception to the non-intervention norm is illustrated in many different regions. For example, in 1991, France, the United Kingdom, and the United States all announced their intention to undertake airdrops of humanitarian supplies to Kurdish minority populations in northern Iraq without Security Council authorization. The Security Council only assented to the airdrops two days before they commenced, leading some commentators to conclude that state practice accepts the validity of a humanitarian assistance exception to the non-intervention norm.[75]

In Somalia, the United States conducted airdrops of humanitarian supplies prior to the passage of Security Council Resolution 794. That action was not condemned as unlawful.[76] Additionally, in 1987, five Indian jets escorted a number of cargo planes carrying food and medical supplies into Sri Lankan airspace to provide assistance to Sri Lankan civilians imperiled because of a Sri Lankan troop offensive against Tamil rebels.[77] Thus, state practice supports the idea that the non-intervention norms does not prohibit the unilateral violation of a target country's airspace in an effort to prevent the occurrence of an imminent human rights crisis and to provide humanitarian assistance.

Incitement to Commit Genocide

Particularly relevant to the legal analysis surrounding the non-intervention norm and an intervening state or group of state's commencement of a pre-emptive information intervention campaign against a target state is the Genocide Convention. Arising out of the horror and shock surrounding the 'repeated perpetration of the crime of genocide in the heyday of Nazi power', the Genocide Convention criminalizes conspiracy to commit genocide, direct and public incitement to commit genocide, and attempted genocide.[78] The Convention was adopted unanimously and its prohibition and criminalization of the crime of genocide are generally accepted as *jus cogens*.[79]

More importantly, for purposes of this chapter, under Article I, 'The Contracting Parties confirm that genocide [. . .] is a crime which they undertake to prevent and to punish.' In accordance with the plain language of this article, intervening states seeking to utilize pre-emptively the techniques of information intervention against a target state may attempt to argue that their actions do not violate legal norms against intervention because of the intervening states' duties under Article I of the Convention. In order to determine whether such a claim has any validity three questions need to be addressed.

First, the intervening state must determine whether incitement to commit genocide as expressed under Article III of the Convention is a crime that falls under the language of Article I. Second, a determination must be made as to what types of action constitute 'direct and public incitement to commit genocide' and finally, the obligations of an intervening state must be balanced against Article I and the non-intervention norm as outlined in the prior sections of this chapter. The following sections address each of these questions *seriatim*.

Article III of the Genocide Convention

Article III of the Genocide Convention declares that genocide, conspiracy to commit genocide, direct and public incitement to commit genocide, attempt to commit genocide, and complicity in genocide are all punishable. During the drafting of the Convention, the United States recognized that punishing the crimes of conspiracy, incitement, and attempt to commit genocide might impinge upon internationally protected rights regarding freedom of speech and expression. As such, it fought to limit the scope of these provisions.[80] Conversely, the Soviet Union proposed to outlaw 'all forms of propaganda (press, radio, cinema, etc.) aimed at inciting racial, national, or religious enmities or hatreds'.[81]

In an effort to reach a compromise between the two competing positions of the United States and the USSR, Belgium proposed to include the inchoate crimes eventually adopted as Article III and other delegates assured the Soviets that speech of this type was punishable under Belgium's proposal.[82] Thus, it appears that Article III's prohibitions on the commission of conspiracy to commit genocide, incitement to commit genocide, attempt to commit genocide, and complicity in genocide all include the broadcast and transmission of material which instigates people to commit genocide and, under Article I, contracting parties to the Convention must take steps to prevent the dissemination of this type of speech.

The continued vitality of the international norm requiring states to ensure that individuals do not transmit speech that incites genocide is further illustrated by the Statute of the International Criminal Tribunal for the former Yugoslavia, the Rwandan Tribunal, and the recently adopted Rome Statute of the International Criminal Court. Each of these tribunals has jurisdiction to prosecute and punish individuals who directly and publicly incite genocide.[83] The critical distinction, for purposes of information intervention that is reflected in these provisions is that incitement itself is considered part of the *actus reus* of genocide.[84]

From a legal standpoint, the dissemination of speech that incites genocide is treated exactly the same as killing members of a protected group. It therefore falls completely outside the international legal rules that protect other types of speech or expressive action. The critical problem with this black letter rule of international law is determining what types of action constitute 'direct and public incitement to genocide' and are therefore actionable under the Convention.

Direct and Public Incitement to Genocide: Interpretative Analysis

NUREMBERG HOLDINGS

The war crimes tribunal at Nuremberg tried two defendants for crimes that fall under the ambit of incitement. The first defendant, Hans Fritsche, was the head of the Radio Division of the Propaganda Ministry and was acquitted of any crime. The Court concluded that although Fritsche had made strongly anti-Semitic statements in his broadcasts, there was no evidence that Fritsche had ever made statements calling on individuals to persecute or exterminate Jews. The Court stated that Fritsche's statements were not 'intended to incite the German people to commit atrocities on conquered people [. . .]. His aim was rather to arouse a popular sentiment in support of Hitler and the German war effort.'[85]

Conversely, Julius Streicher was convicted of crimes against humanity because of his 'incitement to murder and extermination at the time when Jews in the East were being killed under the most horrible conditions'.[86] The Court also made an important link between Streicher's writings and his 'knowledge of the extermination of the Jews in the Occupied Eastern Territory',[87] thereby implying that Streicher's mental state regarding the effect of his writings or the potential effect of his writing was important to find him guilty of incitement. The Court essentially used Streicher's writings and the time in which they were published to demonstrate that he had the requisite *mens rea* for him to be found guilty of incitement. As the Court stated, Streicher clearly aimed to inject 'poison [. . .] into the minds of thousands of Germans which caused them to follow the policy of Jewish persecution and extermination'.[88]

The acquittal of Fritsche and conviction of Streicher illustrate a central point of criminal law necessary for a court to find an individual guilty of inciting genocide. The individual must have the requisite intent to arouse others 'to destroy, in whole or in part, a national, ethnical, racial or religious group'.[89] Other writers have argued that these two holdings, especially the Nuremberg Tribunal's decision to link Streicher's conviction to the timing of his broadcasts, implies that a person is not guilty of incitement unless some type of physical manifestation of the incitement appears along with the incendiary message.[90] Although a narrow reading of the Nuremberg holding may support this view, it is more plausible that the Court linked Streicher's writings to the commission of crimes in the East to demonstrate, with circumstantial evidence, Streicher's intent to destroy a protected group, since proving genocidal intent with direct evidence is extremely difficult – a point discussed in the next section.[91]

INTERNATIONAL CRIMINAL TRIBUNAL FOR RWANDA: THE AKAYESU CASE

As stated in the introduction, the ICTR has indicted at least two prominent Rwandan media figures for incitement to genocide and convicted another.[92] Although most of the remaining media trials have not yet resulted in any formal opinion, in the *Akayesu* case the Tribunal held a man guilty for incitement to genocide and sentenced him to life imprisonment.

Jean Paul Akayesu served as the bourgmestre (major) of the Taba commune from April 1993 until June 1994. On 19, April 1994, he held a meeting in Gishyeshye where he called on the population of Taba to 'eliminate the accomplices of the RPF' and provided a list of names to the crowd that contained Tutsi who allegedly wanted to kill Hutus.[93] He further stated that if these Tutsis were not destroyed first, they would take-over the country and kill Hutus. Because of these statements, and the general climate of hysteria during the Rwandan genocide, a large number of Tutsis in the Taba commune were slaughtered and the ICTR found Akayesu guilty of, among other things, direct and public incitement to genocide in violation of the Genocide Convention and the ICTR statute.

The Court ruled that the crime of incitement to genocide has three elements that comprise the *actus reus* of the crime. The language complained of must (1) constitute incitement; (2) be public; and (3) be direct. The Court borrowed from both civil law and common law traditions to conclude that 'incitement' occurs when an individual 'instigates or encourages another person to commit an offence'.[94] Next, the Court stated that the term 'public' should be understood to encompass calling for criminal action to a 'number of individuals in a public place or to members of the general public at large [. . .] in person in a public place or by technical means of mass communication, such as by radio or television'.[95] Finally, the Court addressed the definition of the term 'direct' and concluded that it 'requires specifically urging another individual to take immediate action rather than merely making a vague or indirect suggestion'.[96]

The Court also stated that it could make a determination of whether questioned speech 'directly' incited genocide only after examining it in its 'cultural and linguistic context'.[97] More importantly, the Court noted that, although the requirement of urging another to take *immediate* action seemed to require some type of physical manifestation of the incendiary message along with the message itself, this was not necessary for a person to be found guilty of incitement. Rather, the Court stated that the direct element of incitement and the immediacy of the effect were better addressed 'by focusing mainly on the issue of whether the persons for whom the message was intended immediately grasped the implication thereof'.[98] Thus, the Court held that unsuccessful acts of incitement to commit genocide were punishable as well as successful acts of incitement to commit genocide, giving credence to the assertion that physical manifestation of genocide is not, as indicated earlier, a requirement of the crime of incitement itself. Instead, it is useful to demonstrate the *means rea* of the accused.

JUDICIAL SYNTHESIS

The preceding analysis illustrates a central dilemma that an intervening state faces when making the determination to engage in a policy of information intervention against a target state. There are currently no existing bright line rules that can be utilized to determine whether a particular broadcast, newspaper article, or other media expression constitutes incitement to commit genocide. Accordingly, before an intervening state attempts to utilize those provisions of the Genocide Convention outlawing incitement to commit genocide to justify a campaign of information intervention against a target state, the intervening state should, as the *Akayesu* case suggests, conduct a deep linguistic and cultural analysis of the questioned speech in its specific context to determine if it constitutes incitement.

Obviously, if genocidal acts accompany the speech in question, it is easier to conclude that it constitutes incitement and the legal case for intervention under Article I of the Genocide Convention is strongest. Unfortunately, waiting for the genocidal acts to follow the speech decreases the effectiveness of pre-emptive information intervention techniques that block incendiary messages. This places an intervening state that wishes to use the techniques of information intervention in a legal dilemma. If an intervening state pre-emptively blocks incendiary messages before the messages constitute actual incitement, it runs the risk of violating international freedom of speech norms. Conversely, if it waits until actual genocide occurs prior to intervening, the goal of preventing a human rights crisis is thwarted.

To resolve this dilemma, an intervening state wishing to utilize information intervention techniques might focus first on 'peace broadcasting' or other information intervention techniques that provide alternative sources of information before it attempts to block messages that are at the borderline of incitement. When the particular speech in question crystallizes into a clear case of incitement, the intervening state can then employ methods of information intervention that block it.[99] Using this ordered hierarchy of intervention, a state can take positive action to prevent a human rights crisis from occurring and still keep itself within the bounds of international law, assuming Article I of the Convention empowers the intervening state to take such action.

Article I of the Genocide Convention

Article I of the Genocide Convention imposes a mandatory duty on contracting states to prevent the occurrence of the crime of genocide. Therefore, assuming a particular media outlet distributes messages that constitute incitement to commit genocide, an intervening state that is party to the Convention has a legal obligation to take specific preventive action in order to stop the relay of those messages. The only question that remains for the intervening state is the scope of preventive action it may take pursuant to Article I.

Shedding some light on this question is Article VIII of the Convention. This states that contracting parties 'may call upon the competent organs of the United Nations to take such actions under the Charter of the United Nations as they consider appropriate for the prevention and suppression of acts enumerated in Article III'. Considering this Article in light of Article I, it appears that intervening states that call upon relevant organs of the United Nations to take any preventive action falling under the rubric of information intervention will not violate the non-intervention norm as long as the intervening state and the United Nations operate within the legal guidelines (specified in those portions of this chapter dealing with United Nations' authorized information intervention). The more difficult issue to address is whether Article VIII of the Genocide Convention should be read to limit the broad language contained in Article I. In other words does Article VIII provide the only lawful means by which an intervening state can take action against speech that constitutes incitement to commit genocide?

There are a variety of reasons why such a reading of Article VIII is flawed. For example, the final drafting of the Article incorporates the permissive word 'may' rather than the mandatory terms 'must' or 'shall'. By implication, if contracting parties 'may' call upon the United Nations to take action to prevent or suppress acts of genocide there are other actions that those parties can undertake besides calling upon the United Nations. This reading of the Article is confirmed, in part, by the secretary-general's commentary on early drafts of it. According to the secretary-general, the intent behind Article VIII is to supplement the application of prevention mechanisms instead of supplanting them.[100] Moreover, during the drafting process itself a proposal by the Soviet Union to require contracting states to report all cases of genocide and breach of the Convention to the Security Council was soundly defeated, giving further credence to the assertion that the obligations imposed on contracting states to prevent the occurrence of genocide include, but are not limited to, referral to the United Nations.[101]

This expansive view of a contracting state's obligations under Article I of the Convention is also confirmed in the drafting process of that Article. In the Preamble to the 1948 Ad Hoc Committee on Genocide's draft of the Convention, the language ultimately placed in Article I was not placed in a substantive article. Instead it was incorporated into the Preamble.[102]

However, the Belgian representative felt that if the obligation to prevent genocide was listed merely in the Preamble of the final Convention, it would only carry the weight of a declaratory statement as opposed to the weight of a 'solemn commitment, of practical import, to prevent and suppress the crime'.[103] As such, when Article I was finalized, it included a provision calling on all contracting parties to 'prevent and punish' the crime of genocide without limitation. Accepting this expansive view of Article I, states that are parties to the Convention have an incumbent duty to take preventive action against individuals who utilize media outlets at their disposal to incite others to commit genocide.

The minimum extent of this duty includes the obligation of a state to take affirmative action against individuals living within the territory of that state.[104] At the same time, given that the international legal prohibition against the commission of the crime of genocide is *jus cogens*, an intervening state that is a party to the Convention can rely on Article I to justify an information intervention campaign against media outlets in a target state when those media outlets incite others to commit genocide. The limitations of the intervening state's actions, however, must be guided by the legal principles surrounding the non-intervention norm previously discussed, or the intervening state may run the risk of violating international law.

Conclusion

This chapter has analyzed the legality of information intervention as it relates to the concept of sovereignty under international law. Specifically, it has taken a fundamental rule of international law designed to protect state sovereignty, the non-intervention norm, and asked whether an intervening state's use of the tools of information intervention violates this rule. The answer to this question is, as is the case with most international legal questions, complex.

Under current international law, sovereignty is not necessarily a bar to states' intervention in the domestic jurisdiction of other states as long as the intervening state acts in accordance with the rules of intervention. Specifically, any policy of information intervention undertaken after the United Nations Security Council authorizes the action is *prima facie* legal. This presumption of legality applies to any form of United Nations authorized information intervention including coercive forms of intervention such as jamming.

Alternatively, the non-intervention norm does not prohibit a group of states or a single state from pre-emptively using most technological, psychological, and information warfare techniques against a target state to prevent the occurrence of a human rights crisis. This is true even if the United Nations does not authorize, and the target state fails to consent to, the intervention. Specifically, a group of states or a single state is entitled to direct broadcasts into another state, establish Internet sites that provide alternative messages to incendiary web sites, and suspend the broadcasts of target states from satellites not on its registry without violating the non-intervention norm. An intervening state may also train journalists, drop pamphlets or radios, and provide financial, legal, and professional assistance to alternative media outlets located in a target state under the humanitarian assistance exception to the non-intervention norm as long as the action is designed to halt an immediate and impending human rights crisis. Because of its coercive nature, and the current status of the non-intervention norm under international law, jamming of broadcasts within a target state is prohibited regardless of the nature of the human rights crisis the broadcasts incite. (The sole exception to this prohibition is provided by the Genocide Convention. However, as discussed below, legal norms regarding applications of the Convention are still underdeveloped.)

This international legal principle preventing states from jamming incendiary broadcasts in other states does not mean that states should refrain from jamming incendiary broadcasts when there is clear and convincing evidence that the broadcasts are responsible for inciting systematic and widespread human rights violations. Law is sometimes subject to modification. As circumstances change and indicate that pre-existing rules are no longer capable of coping with existing challenges, new norms must be formulated to cope with these changes. Recognizing the need for law to remain partially fluid, scholars and lawyers accept the fact that new international legal norms might be formed 'through breach of the current law and the development of state practice and *opinio juris* supporting the change'.[105] However, as stated in the *Nicaragua* case, to challenge a rule of international law, the State acting in violation of the current law must predicate its actions on a clear alternative rule.[106]

Thus, it may prove constructive to formulate international legal rules that generally prohibit states from unilaterally jamming broadcasts in other states with at least one exception. When a state's broadcasts incite individuals to commit systematic and widespread human rights violations within its borders other states should be entitled unilaterally to jam those broadcasts. In essence, states should accept a humanitarian jamming exception to the general rule prohibiting a state from unilaterally jamming broadcasts in another state.

Jamming a broadcast in a target state is not as coercive as the use of force against a target state. Consequently, when compared to the use of force against a target state, it is more difficult for an intervening state to utilize jamming in order to extract political concessions from that state. Therefore the incentive for a state to abuse such an exception is low when contrasted to the incentives for a state to abuse a more general exception to the non-intervention norm. Additionally, the consequences of a state abusing a narrowly crafted jamming exception are minimal when compared to the consequences of abusing a more broadly crafted exception to the non-intervention norm. First, if an intervening state abusively jams broadcasts in a target state, the United Nations Security Council or the International Telecommunications Union can take note of such action to prevent the continuance of the jamming. Second, and more importantly, lives are not lost if an intervening state jams broadcasts in a target state.

International legal norms regarding the Genocide Convention and incitement to commit genocide also need substantive advancement. Particularly, further jurisprudence that explores the precise contours of when particular speech ceases to be protected and instead rises to the level of incitement to commit genocide needs to be created. Until these contours are developed, intervening states that wish to fulfil their duties under Article I of the Convention by engaging in a policy of information intervention should follow an ordered hierarchy of intervention that minimizes the likelihood of silencing speech that does not necessarily rise to the level of incitement to commit genocide. If a target state's media threatens to incite genocide, the intervening state should first employ information intervention techniques that provide alternative sources of information to the incendiary media outlets. If this fails to stem an impending crisis and the level of rhetoric attributed to the target state's media is linked to the crisis, an intervening state may use information intervention techniques that seek to silence that rhetoric as long as the intervening state either predicates its actions on existing law or breaches currently existing law but advances a clear alternative to the breached law.

As a final note, intervening states wishing to engage in a policy of information intervention against a target state should take certain practical considerations into account when formulating an intervention strategy. As reiterated in the introductory portion of this chapter, no intervention technique standing alone can prevent an imminent human rights crisis from occurring. Rather, if an intervening state finds the political willpower to intervene pre-emptively in a target state's domestic affairs using the tools of information intervention, it may have to combine all or some information intervention techniques with more conventional techniques of intervention, including the use of military force.

Moreover, audiences who view alternative media outlets created as a by-product of the information intervention techniques described must view these outlets with a sense of legitimacy and loyalty. This means that the intervening state must create credible sources of alternative information that gain market share at the expense of incendiary media outlets in the target state. The intervening state is substituting itself into the target state's media market to repair a media market that, for various reasons, has failed to provide non-biased and non-incendiary media coverage. Thus the intervening state should strive to incorporate local journalists into the process of information intervention at an early stage and create programmes that appeal to specific populations in the target state.[107]

Acknowledgements

The author gratefully acknowledges the editorial and research assistance of Bethany Davis Noll, Nancy Edlin, Mic Jurgens, and Professors Guy Goodwin-Gill, Monroe Price, and David Wippman.

Bibliography

Acevedo, Domingo E. (1984), 'The U.S. Measures against Argentina Resulting from the Malvinas Conflict,' *American Journal of International Law*, vol. 78, pp. 323–44.

Arcia, Omar Javier (1996), 'War over the Airwaves: A Comparative Analysis of U.S. and Cuban Views on International Law and Policy Governing Transnational Broadcasts', *Journal of Transnational Law and Policy*, vol. 5, pp. 199–226.

Arquilla, John and Ronfeldt, David (1993), 'Cyberwar is Coming!', *Comparative Strategy* vol. 12, pp. 141–65.

ARTICLE 19 (1996), *Broadcasting Genocide: Censorship propaganda and State-sponsored Violence influenda, 1990–94*, London: ARTICLE 19 Publishing.

Arzt, Donna E. (1995), 'Nuremberg, Denazification and Democracy: The Hate Speech Problem at the International Military Tribunal', *New York Law School Journal of Human Rights*, vol. 12, pp. 689–758.

Ashworth, Andrew (1995), *Principles of Criminal Law*, Oxford: Clarendon Press.

Barendt, Eric (1993), *Broadcasting Law: A Comparative Study*, Oxford: Clarendon Press.

Brownlie, Ian (1998), *Principles of Public International Law*, Oxford: Clarendon Press.

Carter, Barry E. and Trimble, Phillip R. (1995), *International Law*, Boston: Little, Brown and Company.

Cassese, Antonio (1999), 'Ex Iniuria Ius Oritur: Are we Moving towards International Legitimation of Forcible Humanitarian Countermeasures in the World Community?', *European Journal of International Law*, vol. 10, pp. 23–50.

Charney, Jonathan I. (1999), 'Anticipatory Humanitarian Intervention,' *American Journal of International Law*, vol. 93, pp. 834–41.

Cloughley, Brian (1996), 'Peace in Mind: Will the UN Give Psyops a Chance?' in Jane's *International Defense Review*, vol. 3, pp. 59–61.

Costa, P. and Evans, P. (1988), 'The Indian Supply Drop into Sri Lanka: Non-military Humanitarian Aid and the Troubling Idea of Intervention,' *Connecticut Journal of International Law*, vol. 3, pp. 417–38.

D'Souza, Frances (20 December 1994), 'Response to Keith Spicer: the Flow of Information', *International Herald Tribune*.

Damrosch, Lori Fisler (1989), 'Politics across Borders: Non-intervention and Non-forcible Influence over Domestic Affairs', *American Journal of International Law*, vol. 83, pp. 1–50.

Diederiks-Verschoor, I. H. (1999), *An Introduction to Space Law*, The Hague: Kluwer Law International.

Five Principles of Peaceful Coexistence of the People's Republic of China, reprinted in J. Cohen and H. Chiu (1971), *People's China and International Law*, Princeton: Princeton University Press.

Franck, Thomas M. (1988), 'Legitimacy in the International System,' *American Journal of International Law*, vol. 82, pp. 705–59.

Goodwin-Gill, Guy S. (1999), 'Crime in International Law: Obligations Erga Omnes and the Duty to Prosecute,' in Guy S. Goodwin-Gill and Stefan Talmon (eds), *The Reality of International Law: Essays in Honour of Ian Brownlie*, Oxford: Oxford University Press.

Henkin, Louis (1991), 'The Invasion of Panama under International Law: A Gross Violation', *Columbia Journal of Transnational Law*, vol. 29.

——(1999), 'Editorial Comments: NATO's Kosovo Intervention: Kosovo and the Law of "Humanitarian Intervention" '. *American Journal of International Law*, vol. 93.

Jennings, Sir Robert and Watts, Sir Arthur (9th edn 1992), *Oppenheim's International Law*, Harlow: Longman.

Joyner, Christopher C. (1984), 'The United States Action in Grenada: Reflections on the Lawfulness of Invasion', *American Journal of International Law*, vol. 78, pp. 13–44.

Larson, Arthur and Jenks, Clarence Wilfied (1965) *Sovereignty Within the Law*, Dobbs Ferry: Oceana Publications.

Lauterpacht, H. (1968), *International Law and Human Rights*, London: Stevens.

Lemkin, Raphael (1944), *Axis Rule in Occupied Europe*, Washington: Carnegie Endowment for International Peace.

Levitt, Jeremy (1998), 'Humanitarian Intervention by Regional Actors in Internal Conflicts and the Cases of ECOWAS in Liberia and Sierra Leone', *Temple Journal of International and Comparative Law*, vol. 12, pp. 333–75.

Lippman, Matthew (1998), 'The Convention on the Prevention and Punishment of the Crime of Genocide: Fifty Years Later,' *Arizona Journal of International and Comparative Law*, vol. 15, pp. 415–514.

Lippman, Matthew (1994), 'The 1948 Convention on the Prevention and Punishment of the Crime of Genocide: Forty-five Years Later', *Temple International and Comparative Law Journal*, vol. 8, pp. 1–84.

McDougal, Myers S. et al. (1980), *Human Rights and World Public Order*, New Haven: Yale University Press.

Metzl, Jamie F. (1997), 'Information Intervention: When Switching Channels Isn't Enough', *Foreign Affairs*, vol. 76(6), November–December, pp. 15–21.

——(1997) 'Rwandan Genocide and the International Law of Radio Jamming,' *American Journal of International Law*, vol. 91(4), pp. 628–51.

Moscow Conference on Security and Co-operation in Europe Document of the Meeting on Human Dimension, Emphasizing Respect for Human Rights, Pluralistic Democracy, the Rule of Law and Procedures for Fact-Finding (3 October 1991), 30 *International Legal Materials* p. 1670, reprinted in Henry J. Steiner and Philip Alston (1996), *International Human Rights in Context*, Oxford: Clarendon Press.

Murphy, Sean D. (1996), *Humanitarian Intervention: The United Nations in an Evolving World Order*, Philadelphia: University of Pennsylvania Press.

Nanda, Ved P. (1990), 'US Force in Panama: Defenders, Aggressors or Human Rights Activists?: The Validity of United States Intervention in Panama under International Law,' *American Journal of International Law*, vol. 84, pp. 494–503.

Nelson, Michael (1997), *War of the Black Heavens: The Battles of Western Broadcasting in the Cold War*, London: Brassey's.

O'Connell, Daniel Patrick (1971), *International Law*.

Paust, Jordan, J. (1989), 'Congress and Genocide: They're Not Going to Get Away with it', *Michigan Journal of International Law*, vol. 11, p. 90.

Plowman, Edward Wilhelm (1982), *International Law Governing Communications and Information*, London: Pinter.

Poulon, Christine and McCafferty, Mair (1999), 'News from the International War Crimes Tribunals', *Human Rights Brief*, vol. 6.

Price, M. (2000), 'Information Intervention: Bosnia, the Dayton Accords, and the Seizure of Broadcasting Transmitters', *Cornell International Law Journal*, vol. 33, pp. 67–112.

Price, Rochelle B. (1984), 'Jamming and the Law of International Communications,' *Michigan Year Book of International Legal Studies*, vol. 5, p. 391.

Ragazzi, Maurizio (1997), *The Concept of International Obligations Erga Omnes*, Oxford: Clarendon Press.

Schachter, Oscar (1982), 'International Law in Theory and Practice,' *Recueil des Cours*, vol. 178.

Scott, Craig; Qureshi, Abid; Mitchell, Paul; Kalajdzic, Jasminka; Copeland, Peter; and Chang, Francis (1994), 'A Memorial for Bosnia: Framework of Legal Arguments Concerning the Lawfulness of the Maintenance of the United Nations Security Council's Arms Embargo on Bosnia and Herzegovina', *Michigan Journal of International Law*, vol. 16, pp. 1–135.

Simma, Bruno (1999), 'NATO, the UN and the Use of Force: Legal Aspects,' *European Journal of International Law*, vol. 10, pp. 1–22.

Smith, Sir John and Hogan, Brian (9th edn 1999), *Criminal Law*, London: Butterworth.

Sofaer, Abraham, D. (1998), 'Max Hilaire's International Law and the United States Military Intervention in the Western Hemisphere,' *American Journal of International Law*, vol. 92, pp. 586–7 (book review).

Spicer, Keith (17 December 1994), 'To Combat Hate Broadcasts, Let's Try Propaganda for Peace', *International Herald Tribune*.

Starke, Joseph Gabriel (9th edn 1984), *Introduction to International Law*, London: Butterworth.

Steiner, Henry J. and Alston, Philip (1996), *International Human Rights in Context*, Oxford: Clarendon Press.

Taylor, Phillip (1997), *Global Communications, International Affairs and the Media since 1945*, London: Routledge.

Thomas, Caroline, (1985), *New States, Sovereignty and Intervention*, Aldershot: Gower.

Thomas, Ann Van Wynen and Thomas, Jr., A. J. (1956), *Non-Intervention: The Law and its Import in the Americas*, Dallas: Southern Methodist University Press.

Verwey, Will D. (1986), 'Humanitarian Intervention,' in Antonio Cassese (ed.), *The Current Legal Regulation of the Use of Force*, London: Kluwer Academic.

Villalobos, J. H. Castro (1994), 'The DBS Declaration of 1982: The TV Marti Case,' in *Proceedings of the Thirty-Seventh Colloquium on the Law of Outer Space*, Washington, DC: American Institute of Aeronautics and Astronautics, p. 6.

Wasburn, Philo C. (1992), *Broadcasting Propaganda*, London: Praeger.

Wedgwood, Ruth (1999), 'NATO's Campaign in Yugoslavia', *American Journal of International Law*, vol. 93, pp. 828–34.

Whitton, John B. and Larson, Arthur (1964), *Propaganda: Towards Disarmament in the War of Words*, Dobbs Ferry: Oceana Publications.

Wippman, David (1995), 'Treaty Based-Intervention: Who Can Say No?', *University of Chicago Law Review*, vol. 62., pp. 607–87

Notes

1. The terms 'systematic human rights violation' and 'systematic and widespread human rights violations' are used throughout this chapter to refer to violations of human rights that are so egregious that they may serve as the basis for international intervention. See, e.g., U.N. ESCOR, 34th Sess., Supp. No. 6, P 223, p. 55, UN Doc. E/1979/36-E/CN.4/1347 (1979). See also *R v. Bow Street Metropolitan Stipendiary Magistrate and others, ex parte Pinochet Ugarte* (Amnesty International and others intervening) [1999] 2 All ER 97, 168, [1999] 2 WLR 827 HL.

2. Trial of the Major War Criminals before the International Military Tribunal, Nuremberg 365 (1947) [hereinafter 'Nuremberg Trial']. At the time of the Nuremberg Trial, genocide was not considered a distinct crime under international law so the defendants were in fact tried for crimes against humanity. Moreover, the Nuremberg Tribunal's jurisdiction over the crime of incitement to genocide did not stem from direct language in either the London Charter or the indictments submitted to the defendants. See Arzt, 'Nuremberg, Denazification and Democracy', p. 719. Rather it derived from Article 6 paragraph c of the Nuremberg Charter and Count IV of the Nuremberg Indictment, each of which used the word 'persecution', but neither of which contained the word 'incitement' Ibid. Regardless of the legitimacy of the Streicher conviction, international law now recognizes that genocide is a distinct crime under international law.

3. 'Nuremberg Trial' p. 304.

4. *Prosecutor v. Nahimana*, Int'l Crim Trib. For Rwanda, Case ICTR-96-11-T (1996); *Prosecutor v. Ngeze*, Int'l Crim Trib. For Rwanda, Case ICTR-97-27-I (1997).

5. *Prosecutor v. Ruggiu*, Int'l Crim. Trib. For Rwanda, Case ICTR-97-32-I (J 2000). Georges Ruggiu plead guilty to public incitement to commit genocide and crimes against humanity on 15 May 2000 and was sentenced to twelve years in prison on 1 June 2000. Ibid.

6. Psychological operations are defined differently by various military organizations. The United States Department of Defense defines 'psychological operations' as: planned operations to convey selected information and indicators to foreign audiences to influence their emotions, motives, objective reasoning, and ultimately the behavior of foreign government, organizations, groups, and individuals. The purpose of psychological operations is to induce or reinforce foreign attitudes and behavior favorable to the originator's objectives. Joint Pub 1-02, *Department of Defense Dictionary of Military and Associated Terms* (Washington, DC: GPO, 23 March 1994).

7. 'Information warfare' is generally defined as the use of broad tactics like 'public diplomacy measures, propaganda, and psychological campaigns, political and cultural subversion, deception of or interference with local media, infiltration of computer networks and databases, and efforts to promote dissident or opposition movements across networks'. Arquilla and Ronfeldt, 'Cyberwar is Coming!', pp. 141, 144.

8. Metzl, 'Information Intervention: When Switching Channels Isn't Enough', p. 15; Cloughley, 'Peace in Mind', p. 59'; Spicer, 'To Combat Hate Broadcasts, Let's Try Propaganda for Peace'; and D'Souza, 'Response to Keith Spicer: the flow of information'.

9. This chapter refers to a state that uses information intervention techniques against another state as the 'intervening state'. the State that is the subject of the intervention is referred to throughout this chapter as the 'target state'. Damrosch, 'Politics across Borders', pp. 1, 6.

10. Price, 'Information Intervention', p. 67.

11. The term 'pre-emptive' is used throughout this chapter to distinguish between what Jamie Metzl (see note 8) refers to as 'phase one' intervention and 'phase two' intervention. The former refers to intervention taken prior to the commission of a human rights crisis and designed to prevent its occurrence. The latter refers to intervention taken after the occurrence of a human rights crisis and is designed to prevent its recurrence. See Chapter I.

12. For the purposes of this chapter, the term 'incendiary media' or any derivative thereof, refers to media output of any type that can inflame, instigate, or possibly incite ethnic conflict or systematic and widespread human rights violations. This term was chosen deliberately because it is broader in context than the terms 'incitement' and 'hate speech' and more accurately reflects the myriad types of speech that play a role in instigating ethnic conflict or systematic and widespread human rights violations.

13. Customary international law develops when states follow a pattern of regular and repeated practice under the assumption that international law requires the State to act in such a manner. See generally North Sea Continental Cases (*Federal Republic of Germany v. Denmark; Federal Republic of Germany v. Netherlands*) 1969 I.C.J. 3, 44, 71. Regarding the first element of customary international law, regular and repeated state practice, 'there must in general be a recurrence or repetition of the acts which give rise to the customary rule.' Starke, *Introduction to International Law*, p. 36; The Paquete Habana, 175 US 677, 708 (1900). See also Restatement of

the Law (Third), foreign Relations Law of the United States, (1987) Foreign Relations Law of the United States 3rd. 2 volumes: vol. 1 xxviii; vol. 2 xxiv.

14. This chapter assumes that an intervening state's use of technological, psychological, and information warfare techniques against a target state does not constitute the use of 'force' against the target state as prohibited under Article 2(4) of the United Nations Charter. If an intervening state's use of these techniques against a target state constituted the unlawful use of 'force' against the territorial integrity or political independence of that state, the justifications for information intervention would be subsumed into the larger doctrines regarding the legality of humanitarian intervention, a topic outside the scope of this book. Verway, 'Humanitarian Intervention', pp. 57, 59.

15. See UN Charter Art. 2 para. 4; Case Concerning Military and Paramilitary Activities in and Against Nicaragua (*Nicaragua v. US*) 1986 I.C.J. Rep. 14 (Judgement) para. 188. The prohibition on the use of force against the territorial integrity or political independence of a state as declared in Article 2, paragraph 4 of the Charter is a norm of general internal law 'accepted and recognized by the international community of states as a whole as a norm from which no derogation is permitted and which can be modified only by a subsequent norm of general international law having the same character'. Vienna Convention on the Law of Treaties, Art. 53, UN Doc. A/Conf. 39/27, 1155 U.N.T.S. 331 (1969) (hereinafter 'Vienna Convention') (defining the term *jus cogens*); 'Report of the International Law Commission on the Work of the Second Part of its Seventeenth Session,' in *Year Book of the International Law Commission* 1996, vol. 2, pp. 169, 247 (stating that 'the law of the Charter concerning the use of force . . . constitutes a conspicuous example of a rule in international law having the character of *jus cogens*.'). The Commission reaffirmed this view in 1980. See United Nations, International Law Commission, Report of the International Law Commission on the Work of its Thirty-second Session 108, UN Doc A/35/10 (1980), quoted in Giorgio Gag, 'Jus cogens beyond the Vienna Convention', 172 *Recueil des Cours* 1981, vol. 172, pp. 275, 287–8; Restatement of the Law (Third), Foreign Relations Law of the United States, (1987) Foreign Relations Law of the United States 3rd. 2 volumes: vol. 1 xxviii; vol. 2 xxiv. Wippman, 'Treaty Based-intervention', pp. 607, 619 n. 50; Simma, 'NATO, the UN and the Use of Force', pp. 1, 3.

16. Carter and Trimble, *International Law*, p. 1307; see also Sofaer, 'Max Hilaire's International Law', pp. 586–7.

17. See Franck, 'Legitimacy in the International System', pp. 705, 720.

18. Carter and Trimble, *International Law*, p. 1311.

19. Ibid.

20. See generally Grande-Bretagne (Zone Espagnole du Maroc), 2. UNRIAA 615, 639–50 (1925).

21. Article 51 of the UN Charter states that '[n]othing in the present Charter shall impair the inherent right of individual or collective self-defense if an armed attack occurs against a Member of the United Nations, until the Security Council has taken measures necessary to maintain international peace and security.' UN Charter Art. 51; Nanda, 'US Force in Panama', pp. 494, 496–7; Henkin, 'The Invasion of Panama under International Law', pp. 293, 305–6.

22. For example, Will D. Verwey defines humanitarian intervention as:

    the protection by a state or group of states of fundamental human rights, in particular the right to life, of nationals of, and residing in, the territory of other states, involving the use or threat of force, such protection taking place neither upon the authorization by the relevant organ of the [United Nations] nor upon invitation by the legitimate government of the target state. ('Humanitarian Intervention', p. 59. (Emphasis added).)

NATO action in Kosovo and ECOWAS action in Liberia both fall under the collective sub-category. Wedgwood, 'NATO's Campaign in Yugoslavia', p. 828. For a description of ECOWAS action in Liberia, see generally Levitt, 'Humanitarian Intervention by Regional Actors', p. 333.

23. Wedgwood, 'NATO's Campaign in Yugoslavia', p. 833.
24. Charney, 'Anticipatory Humanitarian Intervention', pp. 834, 837.
25. See, e.g., *Nicaragua v. US*, p. 268 (Note 15).
26. Ibid. Following NATO intervention in Kosovo, scholars began to re-evaluate whether international law was shifting to permit forcible action in response to a state's commission of systematic and widespread human rights violations against its own citizens. See generally Cassese, 'Ex Iniuria Ius Oritur', p. 23; Henkin, *American Journal of International Law*, p. 828 (arguing that NATO action in Kosovo 'may reflect a step toward a change in the law, part of the quest for developing a "form of collective intervention" beyond a veto bound Security Council').
27. Metzl, 'Rwandan Genocide', pp. 622, 635.
28. Thomas, *New States, Sovereignty and Intervention*, p. 16.
29. UN Charter Art. 2, para. 7. The Charter itself does not express the non-intervention norm as embodied under current international law, as Article 2 paragraph 7 only limits the United Nations from interfering in matters which are essentially within the jurisdiction of any state. Brownlie, *Principles of Public International Law*, p. 296. However, Professor Brownlie opines that, although Article 2(7) 'lacks reference to international law', the 'provision corresponds to the principles of non-intervention and the reserved domain'. Ibid.
30. G.A. Res., 2625 (XXXV) 25 GAOR, Supp. (No. 28) 121, reprinted in 9 I.L.M. 1292 (1970) (hereinafter 'Friendly Relations Declaration'). Professor Oscar Schachter views the Friendly Relations Declaration as an authoritative interpretation of the UN Charter. Schachter, 'International Law' pp. 113, 361 n. 189. The Friendly Relations Declaration, because of the law-making intent of the General Assembly in passing it, serves as an example of *opinio juris* in favour of the norm.
31. G.A. Res. 2131, UN GAOR, 20th Sess., Supp. No. 14 at 12, UN Doc. A/6220 (1965). Although the United States voted in favor of the resolution, it stated that the resolution was 'only a statement of political intention and not a formulation of law'. UN GAOR 20th Sess. At 436, UN Doc. A/C.1/SR, 1423. Nevertheless, its language sheds light on the non- intervention norm as an example of state practice favouring the norm. It is also important to note that all regions of the world recognize the validity of the non-intervention norm. See Charter of the Organization of the American States, 30 April, 1948, 119 U.N.T.S. 3, Art. 18; Conference on Security and Cooperation in Europe, Final Act (Helsinki Accords), 1 August, 1975, 14 I.L.M. 1292 (1975), principle VI; Organization of African Unity, Charter, Art. 3, 2 I.L.M. 766 (1963); Pact of the League of Arab States, Art. 8, 22 March 1945, 70 U.N.T.S. 237; Five Principles of Peaceful Coexistence, pp. 156–201.
32. See, e.g., Lauterpacht, *International Law*, p. 168.
33. This second element is also derived from the I.C.J.'s formulation of prohibited intervention as the intent 'to *coerce* the sovereign state'. Ibid. at 205, 241.

(Emphasis added.) It also derives from the Friendly Relations Declaration. For further confirmation of this element of the non-intervention norm, see Domingo E. Acevedo, 'The U.S. Measures against Argentina Resulting from the Malvinas Conflict,' pp. 323, 325; Thomas, *Non-Intervention: The Law and its Import in the Americas*, p. 71.

34. See *Nicaragua v. US*, p. 205, 241 (Note 15).
35. Accidental interference with a state's sovereign rights can occur when, for example, a ship runs aground in the territorial waters of a target state or an aircraft inadvertently strays into the airspace of a target space.
36. See Vienna Convention, Art. 26 (Note 15).
37. UN Charter Art. 2, para. 7.
38. Under Article 42, the Security Council is entitled to 'take such action by air, sea, or land forces as may be necessary to maintain or restore international peace and security. Ibid., Art. 42. As the doctrine of information intervention presupposes that an intervening state will not use armed force to prevent the occurrence of a human rights violation, this provision is not applicable to the current discussion. Ibid. at Art. 39.
39. Ibid., Art. 41.
40. See, e.g., 'Interpretation of Peace Treaties with Bulgaria, Hungary, and Romania (Peace Treaties Case)', 1950 I.C.J. Reports 65, 70–1; see also 'Nationality Decrees in Tunis and Morocco', P.C.I.J., Ser. B, no. 4, p. 24 (1923); see also The Wimbledon, P.C.I.J., Ser A., no. 1, p. 5 (1923).
41. See UN Charter Art. 25.
42. Wippman, 'Treaty Based-intervention', p. 635.
43. 'Case Concerning Questions of Interpretation and Application of 1971 Montreal Convention Arising from Aerial Incident at Lockerbie', 1992 I.C.J. 2, 65, 175 (Weeramantry, J., dissenting).
44. See S.C. Res. 713, UN SCOR, 46th Sess., 3009th mtg. at 3, UN Doc. S/RES/713 (1991); S.C. Res. 757, UN SCOR, 47th Sess., 3082d mtg. at 3–4 UN Doc. S/RES/757 (1992).
45. See 'UN Authorizes Naval Blockade of Yugoslavia,' *Chicago Tribune*, 17 November 1992, p. 4C.; S.C. Res. 781, UN SCOR., 47th Sess., at 6, UN Doc. S/RES/781 (1992); S.C. Res. 816, UN SCOR, 48th Sess., at 6, UN Doc. S/Res/816 (1993); and S.C. Res. 819, UN SCOR 48th Sess., at 2 UN Doc. S/RES/819 (1993).
46. UN Charter Art. 1, paras. 2 and 3.
47. Larson and Jenks, *Sovereignty Within the Law*, p. 375.
48. *UK v. US*, Permanent Court of Arbitration, 11 R.I.A.A. 180.
49. See, e.g., Jennings and Watts, *Oppenheim's International Law*, sec. 225, p. 659.
50. International Telecommunications Convention (with annexes, final protocol, additional protocols, resolutions, recommendations and opinions), Art. 35, 25 October, 1973 Malaga-Torremolinos 1209 U.N.T.S. 32, 271 (1981). Annexe 2 of the Convention defines 'harmful interference' as 'any emission, radiation or induction which endangers the functioning of a radio navigation service or of any safety service, or seriously degrades, obstructs or repeatedly interrupts a radio communication service operating in accordance with the Radio Regulations'. Ibid. Annexe 2.
51. GA Res. 424 (V), UN GAOR 5th Sess., Supp. No. 20 UN Doc. A/1775 (1950).
52. UN ESCOR, 11th Sess., Supp. No. 5A, Chap. 2, at 2 (1950).
53. See generally Nelson, *War of the Black Heavens*; Whitton and Larson, *Propaganda: Towards Disarmament*, pp. 210–20.

54. See Letter from Assistant Chief of Telecommunications Policy Staff (Lebel), Department of State, to John Whitton (30 August, 1950), *Whiteman Digest*, vol. 13, pp. 1031–2, cited in Metzl, 'Rwandan Genocide', p. 638; O'Connell, *International Law*, p. 331; Price, 'Jamming and the Law of International Communications,' pp. 391, 396.

55. Metzl, 'Rwandan Genocide', p. 642.

56. See, e.g., 'Paris Convention for the Regulation of Air Navigation', Art. 1, 11 L.N.T.S. 173 (1919); 'Convention on International Civil Aviation', Art. 1, 61 Stat. 1180, T.I.A.S. 1591, 15 U.N.T.S. 295 (1957).

57. See, e.g., 'International Telecommunications Convention and Optional Protocol', 6 November 1982; see also, Villalobos, 'The DBS Declaration of 1982', pp. 6, 9. For this reason an intervening state is also precluded from jamming incendiary satellite transmissions broadcast from a target state's satellite into its territory and from interfering with Internet web sites located on servers within the target state.

58. Space Treaty, Art. 1, 18 U.S.T. 2410, T.I.A.S. No. 6346, 610 U.N.T.S. 205 (1967).

59. The term 'peace broadcasting' refers to any non-incendiary transmissions broadcast from an intervening state directly into a target state as part of the intervening state's attempt to prevent or stop a human rights crisis. Metzl, 'Information Intervention', p. 15.

60. See, e.g., *Filartiga v. Americo Norberto Pena-Irala*, 630 F.2d 876, 883 (2d Cir. 1980); McDougal et al., *Human Rights and World Public Order*, p. 274. As to the binding nature of the ICCPR, see Vienna Convention, Art. 26 (Note 15).

61. See International Telecommunications Convention, Art. 44, 25 October 1973, 28 U.S.T. 2495 [hereinafter ITC]; Council Directive 89/552 on Television without Frontiers, 1989 O.J. (L 298) 23.

62. ITC, Art. 44.

63. See ITC Radio Regulations, Final Acts of the World Administrative Radio Conference, Geneva 1979, reprinted in Plowman, *International Law*, p. 245.

64. Diederiks-Verschoor, *An Introduction to Space Law*, pp. 58–61.

65. Barendt, *Broadcasting Law*, p. 218.

66. Arcia, 'War over the Airwaves', pp. 199, 199.

67. For radio, see generally Wasburn, *Broadcasting Propaganda*. The United States alone 'broadcasts over 2,000 hours of radio programming in over 60 languages' per week to states around the globe. Statement of David M. Walker, Comptroller General of the United States General Accounting Office (Senate Budget Committee 1 February 2000); for television, see, e.g., 'Panel Urges Changes in Broadcasts to Cuba', *New York Times*, 1 April 1994, p. A8. According to recent United States figures, it broadcasts over '200 hours per week of television to support US foreign policy objectives'. Statement of David M. Walker. For satellite transmissions, see, e.g., *Commission v. United Kingdom*, C-222/94, 1996 UK Rep. 1-4025 (1996); see also http://www.ibb.gov/worldnet/thisweek.html (visited 26 March 2000); see also 'Chinese Radio Broadcasts Beamed to U.S. from Cuba', *San-Diego Union Tribune*, 15 January 2000, p. S-4; for the Internet, see, e.g., http://www.voa.gov (visited 26 March 2000).

68. See 'The Internet and the Disintegration of Yugoslavia,' *On the Record*, vol. 9, Issue 8, 5 October 1999.

69. See, e.g., Moscow Conference on the Human Dimension, p. 371.

70. An *erga omnes* obligation is an obligation of a particular state towards the

'international community as a whole . . . [and] in view of the importance of the rights involved, all states can be said to have a legal interest in their protection'. Barcelona Traction, Light and Power, Ltd. (*Belgium v. Spain*), 1970 I.C.J. Rep. 3, 32 (5 February); see also East Timor (*Portugal v. Australia.*), 1995 I.C.J. Rep. 90, 102–5 (30 June); see also Goodwin-Gill, 'Crime in International Law', pp. 199, 220; Ragazzi, *The Concept of International Obligations*; Cassese, 'Ex Iniuria Ius Oritur', p. 26.

71. See Simma, 'NATO', p. 3; Cassese, 'Ex Inuria Ius Oritur', p. 21.

72. UN Doc. E/CN.4/1990/NGO/55, reprinted in Steiner and Alston, *International Human Rights in Context*, p. 372.

73. *Nicaragua v. US*, p. 242–3 (Note 15).

74. See, e.g., Joyner, 'The United States Action in Grenada', pp. 131, 135.

75. See Ann Devroy and John Goshko, 'U.S. Shifts on Refugee Enclaves', *Washington Post*, 10 April 1991, p. A1; see also, S.C. Res. 688, UN SCOR, 46th Sess., 2982 mtg. at 31, UN Doc. S/INF/47 (1991) reprinted in 30 I.L.M. 858 (1991). For commentary, see Murphy, *Humanitarian Intervention*, p. 365.

76. See Murphy, *Humanitarian Intervention*, p. 365.

77. See Costa and Evans, 'The Indian Supply Drop into Sri Lanka', p. 417. The airdrop occurred after Sri Lanka threatened to stop an unarmed flotilla of twenty fishing boats loaded with humanitarian supplies that was destined for the Sri Lankan peninsula of Jaffna. Steven Weisman, 'Sri Lanka Threatens to Halt Indian Boats Bearing Tamil Relief,' *New York Times*, 3 June 1987, p. A1. The flotilla's supplies were to be used to alleviate the suffering of Sri Lankan civilians caught in the crossfire between Sri Lankan troops and Tamil rebels located there. Ibid.

78. Quote by Mr Alfaro Panama in 2 UN GAOR C.6, 123rd mtg. at 1288, UN Doc. A/C.6/SR/123 (1947). See also Convention on the Prevention and Punishment of the Crime of Genocide, 9 December 1948, Art. III, 78 U.N.T.S. 277 [hereinafter Genocide Convention].

79. See, e.g., Lippman, 'The Convention on the Prevention and Punishment of the Crime of Genocide', pp. 415, 467; Paust, 'Congress and Genocide', pp. 10, n.1; see also RESTATEMENT (THIRD) OF FOREIGN RELATIONS LAW §404 (Tentative Draft No. 6, 1985).

80. See 3 UN GAOR C.6, 84th mtg. at 213, UN Doc. A/C.6/SR.84 (1948) (statement of Mr Maktos, United States).

81. UN GAOR 3d sess. 6th Comm., UN Doc. A/C.6/215 (4 October 1948).

82. See UN GAOR, 3d sess. 6th Comm., UN Doc. A/C.6/217 (5 October 1948) (Belgium: Amendment to Draft Convention); 3 UN GAOR C.6., 84th mtg. at 235, UN Doc. A/C.6/SR.86 (1948) (statement of Mr Abdoh, Iran).

83. See Yugoslav Tribunal Statute, Art. (4)(3); Rwandan Tribunal Statute, Art. 2(3)(c); Rome Statute of the International Criminal Court, Art. 25(3)(e), UN GAOR, 53d Sess., UN Doc. A/Conf.183/9 (1998) reprinted in 39 *International Legal Materials* 999 (1998).

84. All crimes have two elements that the prosecution must prove in order for an individual to be found guilty of that crime. Smith and Hogan, *Criminal Law*, p. 27. The first of these elements is called the *actus reus* and the term refers to the actual conduct or event attributed to the accused. Ibid. The second element is called the *mens rea*. Ibid. It means criminal intent and is derived from the Latin expression, *actus non facit reum nisi mens sit rea*. Translated, this means, 'An act does not make a man guilty of a crime, unless his mind be also guilty.' *Haughton v. Smith*, [1975]

AC 476 at 491–2. See also Report of The International Law commission on the Work of Its Forty-Eighth Session, UN GAOR, 51st Sess., Supp. No. 10, at 87, UN Doc. A/51/10 (1996) (stating that 'the definition of the crime of genocide . . . consists of two important elements, namely the requisite intent (*mens rea*) and the prohibited act (*actus reus*)').

85. Nuremberg Trial, p. 338 (Note 2).
86. Ibid., p. 304.
87. Ibid., p. 303.
88. Ibid., p 302.
89. Genocide Convention, Art. II. Further support regarding the intent requirement can be found in the writings of Raphael Lemkin, the Polish jurist usually credited with creating the term 'genocide'. He wrote that genocide signifies, 'a coordinated plan of different actions aiming at the destruction of essential foundations of the life of national groups, *with the aim* of annihilating the groups themselves'. Lemkin, *Axis Rule in Occupied Europe*, p. 79. (Emphasis added).
90. Metzl, 'Rwandan Genocide', p. 637.
91. See, e.g., *Prosecutor v. Rutaganda*, Case No. ICTR-96-3-T, para. 424. (12 June 1999) (emphasis added) (citing *Prosecutor v. Akayesu*, Case No. ICTR-96-4-T, para. 523 (2 September 1998)) The majority in the *Rutaganda* case reaffirmed the *Akayesu* case and stated:

On the issue of determining the offender's specific [genocidal] intent, the Chamber considers that *the intent is a mental factor which is difficult, even impossible, to determine*. This is the reason why, in the absence of a confession from the Accused, his intent can be inferred from a certain number of presumptions of fact. The Chamber considers that it is possible to deduce the genocidal intent inherent in a particular act charged from the general context of the perpetration of other culpable acts systematically directed against that same group, whether these acts were committed by the same offender or by others. Other factors, such as the scale of atrocities committed, their general nature, in a region or a country, or furthermore, the fact of deliberately and systematically targeting victims on account of their membership of a particular group, while excluding the members of other groups, can enable the Chamber to infer the genocidal intent of a particular act.

Ibid. (Emphasis added).

92. See Notes 4, 5. Additionally, the tribunal has also indicted and arrested Andre Rwamakuba, the former Rwandan Minister of Education, for among other things incitement to genocide. See Poulon and McCafferty, 'News from the International War Crimes Tribunals', pp. 3, 17; see also *Prosecutor v. Rwamakuba*, Case No. ICTR-98-44-T (1998).
93. *Prosecutor v. Akayesu*, Case No. ICTR-96-4-T (1998) paras. 317, 332, 361.
94. Ibid., para. 555 (citing Ashworth, *Principles of Criminal Law*, p. 462).
95. Ibid., para. 556.
96. Ibid., para. 557 (citing Draft Code of Crimes Against the Peace and Security of Mankind, Art. 2(3)(f); Report of the International Law Commission to the General Assembly, 51 UN ORGA Supp. (No. 10), at 26, UN Doc. A/51/10(1996).
97. Ibid.
98. Ibid., para. 558.
99. ARTICLE 19, *Broadcasting Genocide*, p. 157.
100. Lippman, 'The 1948 Convention', pp. 1, 66.

101. Ibid., p. 67.
102. Ibid., p. 21.
103. Ibid. (quoting UN GAOR 6th Comm., 3d Sess., 67th mtg. p. 44).
104. Scott et al., 'A Memorial for Bosnia', pp. 1, 36.
105. See Charney, 'Anticipatory Humanitarian Intervention', p. 836.
106. *Nicaragua v. US*, p. 207 (Note 15).
107. This also means that any information intervention technique must incorporate
     material that not only counters incendiary media with hard news but with
     entertaining content as well. During the UN Intervention in Somalia, the Italian
     troops broadcast pop music and Pavarotti singing opera, thereby obtaining a larger
     audience for its broadcasts than American attempts to provide earnest news.
     Taylor, *Global Communications, International Affairs and the Media since 1945*,
     p. 182. One of the first tasks of the NATO-led Implementation Force in Bosnia
     was to create Radio IFOR which incorporated rock music into its programming,
     indicating that the United Nations had learned the lessons of Somalia. Ibid., p. 188.

4

Note on Legality of Information Intervention

Julie Mertus

Law of The Hague and the Law of Geneva

Two standards exist for examining the legality of information intervention. As one of the editors of this volume has written in reference to Bosnia:

> [I]f the United States and its Western allies acted as 'occupiers', then a particular body of norms [humanitarian law] would govern their powers and the limits on them. If they acted, on the other hand, under a consent regime, then the shape of their authority would be governed, in large part, by the conditions of their particular entry into [the country].[1]

International humanitarian law, also known as the law of armed conflict, comprises two main branches: the Law of the Hague and the Law of Geneva.[2] The Law of the Hague, codified in the Regulations respecting the Laws and Customs of War on Land annexed to the 1907 Hague Convention IV, addresses the means and methods of warfare.[3] The Law of Geneva, codified in the four Geneva Conventions of 12 August 1949,[4] protects victims of armed conflict.[5] This difference in focus between the two treaty regimes is significant for those concerned more with the rights of the population of an occupied country, as opposed to the rights of the occupier. As Theodor Meron explains, 'Whereas the Hague Convention established important limitations on the occupant's permissible activities, modern law obligates the occupant to assume active responsibility for the welfare of the population under its control.'[6] Significant portions of both branches of humanitarian law reflect or have developed into customary international law.[7]

Humanitarian law generally does not apply when there has been a cessation of hostilities. For example, the signing of the Military Technical Agreement for Kosovo in June 1999 by the International Security Forces (KFOR) and the governments of the Federal Republic of Yugoslavia and Republic of Serbia brought an end to armed combat between the parties. Nonetheless, humanitarian law would still apply if the international mission is considered an 'occupation'. In the case of an occupation, the provisions of the Fourth Geneva Convention continue to apply for one year beyond the close of military operations, and some provisions continue for the duration of the occupation.[8]

The 'law of occupation' thus regulates the relationship between the occupying power and the inhabitants of the occupied territory.[9]

As an example, were it to apply in Kosovo, the law of occupation would safeguard the rights of the local population and protect the sovereignty of Yugoslavia. At the same time, it would circumscribe the activities of The UN Mission in Kosovo (UNMIK) and the NATO Kosovo Force (KFOR). In particular, the international mission would be more restricted in its ability to promulgate laws and create new institutions for Kosovo. 'Because the belligerent occupant is viewed as merely a temporary replacement for an absent government authority, the present rules of belligerent occupation severely limit the discretion of occupying powers.'[10] Article 64 of the Fourth Geneva Convention provides that '[t]he national laws applicable in the occupied territory shall, in principle, remain in force.' Similarly, Article 43 of the Hague Regulations states the public order of the occupied territory shall remain in place and public life shall continue 'while respecting, unless absolutely prevented, the laws in force in the country'. The justification behind these restrictions is that the occupying power does not assume the rights of a sovereign state. The authority to make and pass laws and to change legal institutions is a hallmark of sovereignty. Accordingly, the lawful sovereign alone can make laws and change legal institutions of the occupied territory.

Exceptions to this limit on law-making have become the rule. Article 64 of the Fourth Geneva Convention and Article 43 of the Hague Regulations allow occupying forces to enact laws necessary for their own security and the security of others, and for the maintenance of public order. Occupying authorities are also obliged to ignore national laws that constitute 'an obstacle to the application of humanitarian law'. In addition, in Articles 13 and 27 of the Fourth Geneva Convention and Article 46 of the Hague Regulations, occupying powers are charged with adopting measures to protect the inhabitants of the occupied territory from violence from third parties. While Article 27 of the Fourth Geneva Convention outlines certain nonderogable rights of the population, there is no mention of an unfettered right to free speech, and thus restrictions of speech designed to promote other permissible goals, such as protecting civilians, are themselves legitimate.

The media have historically been seen as legitimate objects of regulation, usually as a means of protecting the occupying force, but they have also been regulated in order to return order and civility to the occupied society.[11] To the extent media regulations are aimed at supporting the existence of an administration (and encouraging conditions that will lead to a fairly elected administration), and fostering conditions of tolerance and non-discrimination, it is arguable that they exactly conform to the Hague and Geneva requirements.

But the larger question remains, which of the areas discussed in this book should be considered an occupied territory? The only code definition of what constitutes an occupation is found in Article 42 of the Hague Regulations, stating that '[t]erritory is considered occupied when it is actually placed under the authority of the hostile army.'[12] One key question is 'whether in fact the armed forces that have invaded the adversary's territory have brought the area under their control through their physical presence, to the extent that they can actually assume the responsibilities which attach to the occupying power.'[13] Another key question is whether the occupying power exercises control over a territory to which that power has no sovereign title, without the volition of the sovereign of that territory.[14]

Most of the countries involved in 1990's peacekeeping were under international control due to the physical presence of international forces. The military and civil entities of the international community had no sovereign title, yet they exercised authority to the virtual exclusion of what remains of the legally sovereign government.[15] Nonetheless, the test for occupation in most of the instances is not met because the international mission exercises control with the volition of the sovereign. For example, in Kosovo, evidence of the will of the Belgrade government may be found in the text of the G8 peace plan which specifically refers to 'deployment in Kosovo under UN auspices of effective international civil and security presences', and an 'international security presence, with substantial NATO participation', and the response of the Serbian Parliament agreeing to 'the role of the United Nations' there.[16]

The argument has been made that the law of occupation codified in the Fourth Geneva Convention applies even where the sovereign of the occupied territory grants its consent to the occupation.[17] Even if this were the case, the authority of the international mission in Kosovo to legislate media regulations would fall squarely under the exceptions to the general prohibition on law-making by occupying powers, namely the promotion of security, maintenance of public order, and furtherance of larger humanitarian goals found in Article 64 of the Fourth Geneva Convention and Article 43 of the Hague Regulations. Accordingly, even if humanitarian law were to be applied in this case, the media regulations would withstand scrutiny.[18]

The Law of Consensual Peace Operations

In the traditional peacekeeping context, consent of the sovereign is essential for the legitimate presence of a peacekeeping force.[19] Traditional peacekeeping follows from the parties to the conflict accepting a cease-fire or a withdrawal, and then agreeing to the presence of a force on their soil.[20] What is clear is that if the consent of the government concerned is not given or is withdrawn, then the peacekeeping operation cannot remain on that State's territory, unless the UN is prepared to change its mandate to one of enforcement.[21]

Some commentators have argued that once consent is given for the initial deployment of the peacekeeping operations, it cannot be withdrawn until the required tasks have been completed.[22] This view does not appear to have been adopted by most scholars in the field, probably because in practical terms the force needs co-operation from the parties in order to be successful. Thus, the prevailing view is that consent for peacekeeping can both be given and taken away. This concept was put into effect when Secretary General U Thant decided to withdraw the United Nations Emergency Force (UNEF I) when President Nasser of Egypt withdrew consent for its presence.

The requirement of consent does not cease once the peacekeeping force has been established – consent also dictates the UN's mandate and the specifics of government in areas under UN control. Simply put, 'intervention by consent must remain within the bounds of that consent.'[23] Alternatively, 'consent must be assured for the whole duration of the presence of the Force [. . .] [f]urthermore, an enlargement or any other modification of the mandate of the Force during the operation would also need the consent, at least tacit, of the host state.'[24] Even where there has been a downgrading of consent in the authorising resolutions of the UN Security Council for peace operations (for example, in Security Council resolutions pertaining to Iraq, Yugoslavia, and Somalia), day-to-day operations still require consent and peacekeeping forces must gain approval and agreement from the local military and political leaders for their actions.[25]

Consent must be attributed to the State; that is, 'it must issue from a person whose will is considered, at the international level, to be the will of the State.'[26] In some instances, one might have a collapsed state and in that case consent of the sovereign would be impossible to obtain. Amy Eckert explains:

> The requirement of consent presumes the existence of a government which is capable of functioning within the State, and interacting with the UN. In a collapsed state, no such government exists. Consent therefore is either impossible to obtain because the government does not function at all, or it is worthless because the government no longer legitimately represents the people.[27]

Particularly when a state is challenged by an internal, armed opposition, the government may not represent the State.

The collapsed state scenario puts the UN in a bind. UN negotiators could try to obtain consent from the most powerful non-state entities within the collapsed state, but these non-state entities also do not have legitimate authority to speak for their state.[28] A state has collapsed when the basic functions of the State are no longer performed. William Zartman has observed:

> As the decision-making centre of government, the State is inoperative: laws are not made, order is not preserved, and societal cohesion is not enhanced. As a symbol of identity, it has lost its power of conferring a name on its people [. . .] As a territory, it is no longer assured security [. . .] by a central sovereign organization. As the authoritative political institution, it has lost legitimacy [. . .] and so it has lost its right to command and conduct public affairs. As a system of socioeconomic organization, its functional balance of inputs and outputs is destroyed [. . .]. Where a state has collapsed and there is no sovereign as such to

provide consent, it has been argued that as an alternative to consent, the limits of the peacekeeping mission should be defined by reference to the expressions of self-determination given by the society within the collapsed state.[29]

Although there have been calls for consent to be sought from 'all concerned parties' and not just from the host-state, consent from additional parties is not accepted as a necessary legal requirement for the establishment of a peace-keeping force.[30,31]

While a model status of forces agreement has been developed, there is no legally prescribed format for the provision of consent by the host state for the mandate of a peace operation, and indeed the consent may take many forms.[32] In general, state consent may be 'expressed or tacit, implicit or explicit, provided however that it is clearly established'.[33] Consent to peace operations 'may be given by a unilateral act of the host state or by a bilateral act between the host state and the United Nations'.[34] In 1973, Egypt gave its consent via a letter from the permanent representative of Egypt to the UN secretary-general, and in 1964 Cyprus offered its consent via a letter issued by the Ministry of Foreign Affairs. Whatever the form of consent, the body entrusted with the mandate is responsible for interpreting it.

One important safeguard to consent is recognition that the host state may always withdraw its consent to the peacekeeping force if it finds that the force is operating *ultra vires*, or generally not conforming with the consent initially provided by that host state. Such a measure was put into effect by Croatia in 1995, when the Croatian president 'informed the Secretary-General of his Government's decision not to agree to a further extension of UNPROFOR's mandate beyond 31 March 1995'.[35] Thus, it appears that where interpretation of the scope of the mandate is in question, the onus is upon the host state to act if the peacekeeping measures are not to its liking.

In the case of Kosovo, as an example, it appears as if the host state gave its consent to the international mission. Peacekeeping was based upon Security Council Resolution 1244 of the Security Council, and the Kosovo peace plan accepted by the Serbian Parliament. Security Council Resolution 1244 emphasizes the observance of the requirement of consent by the host state, and the need for co-ordination by the Special Representative to ensure that the goals of the respective parties are met.

That media regulations were never specifically mentioned in any of the authorizing documents for the civil administration in Kosovo is not detrimental to the existence of consent. Yugoslavia consented to the goals outlined in the G-8 peace plan accepted on 3 June, which include 'immediate and verifiable end of violence and repression in Kosovo) [. . .] development of provisional demo-cratic and self-governing institutions to ensure conditions for a peaceful and normal life for all inhabitants in Kosovo; [. . .] the safe and free return [. . .] of all refugees and displaced persons; [. . .] economic development and stabilisation of the crisis region.' This language arguably constitutes consent to information intervention designed to promote safety, facilitate elections, and promote the building of democratic institutions. To the extent that Yugoslavia disagrees with the pursuance of information intervention under the UNMIK mandate, it has the power (as a sovereign host state) to terminate its consent and demand the withdrawal of the peacekeeping force. As Yugoslavia does not appear to have made any such demands, it may be assumed that its silence indicates acquiescence to the measures undertaken to regulate the media in Kosovo.

Conclusion

In sum, the first variable that must be taken into account in considering the legality of information intervention is whether hostilities have officially ended. If they have not, the law of armed conflict applies. If they have ended, either the law of occupation or of consensual peace operations applies. In the former use, media development, while restricted in scope, may be justified as maintenance of public order promotion of security. In the latter case, the key factor that must be examined is whether the proper authorities consented to the international presence, and whether media development is within the scope of that consent.

Bibliography

Annan, Kofi (1994), 'United Nations Operations: How the System Works', in *The United Nations, Peacekeeping And US Policy in the Post-Cold War World 17*, pp. 18–19.

Best, Geoffrey (1994), *War and Law since 1945*, Oxford, New York: Clarendon Press.

Benvenisti, Eyal (1993), *The International Law of Occupation*, Princeton: Princeton University Press.

Bothe, Michael; Partsch, Karl Josef; and Solf, A. Waldemar (1982), *New Rules for Victims of Armed Conflicts: Commentary on the Two 1977 Protocols Additional to the Geneva Conventions of 1949*, Boston: Martinus Nijhoff Publishers.

Bothe, Michael; Doerschel, Thomas (1999), *UN Peacekeeping; A Documentary Introduction*, Boston, MA: Kluwer Law International.

Eckert, Amy E. (1996), 'Comment: United Nations Peacekeeping in Collapsed States', *Journal of International Law & Practice*, vol. 5, pp. 273–303.

Gasser, Hans-Peter (1995), 'Protection of the Civilian Population', in Dieter Fleck, *The Handbook of Humanitarian Law in Armed Conflicts*, New York: Oxford University Press, p. 505.

Ghali, Boutros-Boutros (1995), 'An Agenda For Peace', United Nations Department of Public Information, New York.

Goodman, Davis P. (July 1985), 'The Need for Fundamental Change in the Law of Belligerent Occupation', *Standford Law Review*, vol. 37, pp. 1573–1608.

Graber, Doris Appel (1949), *The Development of the Law of Belligerent Occupation, 1963–1914*, New York: Columbia University Press.

Gray, Christine (1996), 'Host-state Consent and United Nations Peacekeeping in Yugoslavia', *Duke Journal of Comparative & International Law*, vol. 7, pp. 241–70.

Green, Leslie C. (1993), *The Contemporary Law of Armed Conflict*, Manchester, New York: Manchester University Press.

Kelly, Michael J. (1999), *Restoring and Maintaining Order in Complex Peace Operations: The Search for a Legal Framework*, Boston: Kluwer Law International.

Liu, F. T. (1992), 'United Nations Peacekeeping and the Nonuse of Force', *International Peace Academy Occasional Paper Series*, Boulder, CO: Lynne Rienner.

McCoubrey, Hilaire and D. White, Nigel (1996), *The Blue Helmets: Legal Regulation of United Nations Military Operations*, Brookfield, NH: Dartmouth Publishing.

Meron, Theodor (2000), 'The Humanization of International Law', *American Journal of International Law*, vol. 94, pp. 239–78.

Mertus, Julie (3 October 2000), 'Now to Create a Sovereign Kosovo', *Christian Science Monitor*, p. 11.

Price, Monroe (2000), 'Information Intervention: Bosnia, the Dayton Accords, and the Seizure of Broadcasting Transmitters', *Cornell International Law Journal*, vol. 33, no. 1, pp. 67–112.

Ratner, Steven R. (1995), *The New UN Peacekeeping: Building Peace in Lands of Conflict after the Cold War*, New York: St Martin's Press.

Schwarzenberger, George (1968), *International Law as Applied by International Courts and Tribunals*, vol. II, London: Stevens & Sons.

Shraga, Daphne and Zacklin, Ralph (1994), 'The Applicability of International Humanitarian Law to the United Nations Peacekeeping Operations: Conceptual, Legal and Practical Issues', in Unmesh Palwankar, ed., *Symposium on Humanitarian Action and Peacekeeping Operations*, pp. 39–49.

Tittemore, Brian D. (Winter 1997), 'Belligerents in Blue Helmets: Applying International Humanitarian Law to United Nations Peace Operations', *Stanford Journal of International Law*, pp. 61–117.

Tsur, Yoel Arnon (1978), 'The United Nations Peace-keeping Operations in the Middle East from 1965 to 1976', in Antonio Cassese (ed.), *United Nations Peace-keeping: Legal Essays*, Alphen aan den Rijn: Sijthoff & Hoordhoff.

von Grünigen, Marianne (1978), 'Neutrality and Peace-keeping', in Antonio Cassese (ed.), *United Nations Peace-keeping: Legal Essays*, Alphen aan den Rijn: Sijthoff & Hoordhoff.

White, N. D. (1997), *Keeping the Peace: United Nations and the Maintenance of International Peace and Security*, Manchester: Manchester University Press.

Wippman, David (1996), 'Military Intervention, Regional Organizations, and Host-state Consent', *Duke Journal of Comparative & International Law*, vol. 7, pp. 209–39.

Zartman, I. William. (1995), 'Posing the Problem of State Collapse', in I. William Zartman (ed.), *Collapsed States: The Disintegration and Restoration of Legitimate Authority*, Boulder, CO: Lynner Reinner.

Notes

1. Price, 'Information Intervention', p. 97.
2. See generally, Best, *War and Law since 1945*; Green, *The Contemporary Law of Armed Conflict*.
3. Annexe to the Convention Regulations Respecting the Laws and Customs of War

on Land, 18 October, 1907, 36 Stat. 2277, 1 Bevans 631 [hereinafter 'the Hague Regulations'].

4. Geneva Convention for the Amelioration of the Condition of the Wounded and Sick in the Armed Forces in the Field, 12 August, 1949, 6 U.S.T. 3114, 75 U.N.T.S. 31; Geneva Convention for the Amelioration of the Condition of the Wounded, Sick and Shipwrecked Members of the Armed Forces at Sea, 12 August 1949, 6 U.S.T. 3217, 75 U.N.T.S. 85; Geneva Convention Relative to the Treatment of Prisoners of War, 12 August 1949, 6 U.S.T. 3316, 75 U.N.T.S. 135; Geneva Convention Relative to the Protection of Civilian Persons In Time of War, 12 August 1949, 6 U.S.T. 3516, 75 U.N.T.S. 287 [hereinafter 'Fourth Geneva Convention].

5. Aspects of both the Hague and Geneva regimes are merged into the 1997 Protocols Additional to the Geneva Convention. See Bothe et al., *New Rules for Victims*, p. 184.

6. Meron, 'The Humanization of International Law', pp. 239, 246.

7. See Schwarzenberger, *International Law*, pp. 164–5.

8. The Fourth Geneva Convention ('Convention (IV) Relative to the Protection of Civilian Persons in Time of War') was signed on 12 August 1949. Online [July 2001] Available HTTP: http://www.us-israel.org/jsource/History/Human Rights/geneva1.html

9. See generally, Graber, *The Development of the Law of Belligerent Occupation*; Gasser, 'Protection of the Civilian Population'.

10. See generally Goodman, 'The Need for Fundamental Change'.

11. For a discussion of the development of instruments permitting the seizure of public and private means of communication, see generally Graber, *The Development of the Law of Belligerent Occupation*. For the use of media in protecting the occupying force see Kelly, *Restoring and Maintaining Order*, p. 212.

12. Article 4 of the Fourth Geneva Convention defines protected persons as 'those who, at a given moment and in any manner whatsoever, find themselves, in the case of . . . [an] occupation, in the hands of [. . .] [an] Occupying Power of which they are not nationals'. However, the Geneva Conventions do not define 'occupation'. See Kelly, *Restoring and Maintaining Order*, pp. 161, 149.

13. Gasser, 'Protection of the Civilian Population', pp. 209–88, 243.

14. See Benvenisti, *The International Law of Occupation*, p. 4. For further definition of what constitutes 'occupation', see also Kelly, *Restoring and Maintaining Order*, p. 112.

15. See Mertus, 'Now to Create a Sovereign Kosovo', p. 11 for further discussion of the role of Yugoslavia in Kosovo.

16. The text of the G8 peace plan submitted to Belgrade by EU and Russian envoys and accepted by Milosevic and the Serbian Parliament, 3 June 1999, is Online [July 2001] Available HTTP: http://jurist.law.pitt.edu/peace.htm~plan. The response of the Serbian Parliament (as reported by the Tanjug news agency), 3 June 1999, para. 3 is Online [July 2001] Available HTTP: http://news6.thdo.bbc.co.uk/hi/english/world/monitoring/newsid_360000/360059.stm

17. See Kelly, *Restoring and Maintaining Order*, p. 161.

18. For further discussion of the application of humanitarian law to peacekeeping operations, see generally Tittemore, 'Belligerents in Blue Helmets'; Shraga and Zacklin, 'The Applicability Of International Humanitarian Law'.

19. See generally Ghali, 'An Agenda For Peace'. The other two principles of traditional peacekeeping are non-use of force and impartiality. See generally Liu, 'United Nations Peacekeeping'.

20. Traditional peacekeeping is designed to keep enemy forces apart and create conditions in which political negotiations can proceed. This has given way in recent years to operations that add civilian and human rights monitors, institution building and electoral assistance. See Annan, 'United Nations Operations' pp. 18–19; Rataer generally, 'The New UN Peacekeeping'.
21. White, *Keeping the Peace*, pp. 232–3. For discussions of the necessity of consent, see also McCoubrey and White, *The Blue Helmets*, p. 69; Wippman, 'Military Intervention', pp. 209.
22. Tsur, 'The United Nations Peace-keeping Operations', p. 207, citing the Aide-Memoire of Secretary-General Dag Hammarskjöld, dated 5 August 1957.
23. Wippman, pp. 209, 234.
24. von Grünigen, 'Neutrality and Peace-keeping', p. 136.
25. Iraq: see UN Doc. S/22663, 31 May, 1991; Yugoslavia: see Security Council Resolution 743, UN Doc. S/RES/743 (1992); Somalia: see Security Council Resolution 794, UN Doc. S/RES/794 (1992); Security Council Resolution 814, UN Doc. S/RES/814 (1993).
26. Eighth Report on State Responsibility, Document A/CN.4/318, Y.B. Int'l L. Comm. vol. 2, 1979.
27. Eckert, 'Comment', pp. 273, 281.
28. Ibid., p. 282.
29. Zartman, 'Posing the Problem of State Collapse', p. 5.
30. See, e.g., 'An Agenda for Peace: Preventative Diplomacy, Peacemaking and Peacekeeping', Report of the Secretary General pursuant to the statement adopted by the Summit Meeting of the Security Council on 31 January 1992, A/47/277 – S/24111, 17 June 1992, paras 28, 29, 31 (discussing preventative deployment). Online [July 2001] Available HTTP: http://www.un.org/Docs/SG/agpeace.html
31. Gray, 'Host-state Consent and United Nations Peacekeeping in Yugoslavia', pp. 241, 243–4. Only in the case of Mozambique did a Security Council Resolution expressly refer to consent by a non-government party to the conflict to establishing a peacekeeping force. See Security Council Resolution 797, UN SCOR, 47th Sess., UN Doc. S/RES/797 (1992).
32. See Model Status-of-forces Agreement for Peacekeeping Operations, UN Doc. A/45/594 (9 October 1990), available in Michael Bothe and Thomas Doerschel, *UN Peacekeeping: A Documentary Introduction*, p. 59.
33. Eighth Report on State Responsibility, Document A/CN.4/318, Y.B. Int'l L. Comm. vol. 2, 1979, pp. 3, 35–6.
34. von Grünigen, 'Neutrality and Peace-keeping', p. 136.
35. McCoubrey and White, *The Blue Helmets*, p. 520.

5

A Module for Media Intervention: Content Regulation in Post-Conflict Zones

Peter Krug and Monroe E. Price

Introduction

In the late 1990s, an institutional structure – an 'architecture of media law' – emerged in post-conflict zones for the temporary generation and application of norms regulating mass media content during the transition from international to domestic governance.[1] The creation of this system for post-conflict information intervention, which we will call a 'module' to illustrate its incipient nature, was predicated on the belief that a self-contained set of formal rules and procedures – a system of law – is necessary in the absence of an operating domestic legal regime in order to respond adequately to purportedly abusive media content and at the same time to provide safeguards protecting the exercise of expressive rights recognized under international standards.[2,3]

The module first appeared with the establishment of the Independent Media Commission (IMC) in Bosnia and Herzegovina in 1998.[4] It was borrowed by the United Nations Mission in Kosovo (UNMIK) and has undergone refinement since the establishment in Kosovo of the office of the Temporary Media Commissioner (TMC) in June 2000.[5] In both Bosnia and Herzegovina and Kosovo, it is being phased out, to give way to yet another new structure in an interim system of governance more closely tied to local institutions and personnel.[6]

It is likely that the module will be considered for use in future post-conflict settings, as well as exerting some influence on the further development of media regulation in Bosnia and Herzegovina and Kosovo.[7] In this chapter, we examine aspects of the module's structure, normative base, and process, and seek to identify its implications for development of a law of information intervention if indeed it is gaining traction as a portable 'fix' for employment in the increasing number of transitory post-conflict environments. Because it represents a refinement of the module, we will focus on the Kosovo (UNMIK) system while making references to its predecessor in Bosnia and Herzegovina. We do not claim to have many complete answers; instead, we merely hope to raise useful questions and to suggest perspectives from which to judge whether the module's components are consistent with applicable international standards.

Constructing the Module

The Module in a Constitutional Order

The module is a component of those systems of civil governance established by international organizations in post-conflict zones.[8] It operates as an international system imposed on a post-conflict territory in the absence of a functioning domestic legal system.[9] Because it serves equivalent purposes, we seek to assess the module the way we would a domestic system of media content regulation, starting with its constitutional foundations and then analyzing its structure, rules, and procedures. It must be seen not in isolation, but instead within a larger constitutional order that presents an institutional structure and a set of fundamental norms with which all governing acts – legislative, executive, and judicial – must comply.

In Kosovo, the basic document for the UNMIK administration is Security Council Resolution 1244, enacted pursuant to Chapter VII of the UN Charter.[10] In Section 6, Resolution 1244 authorized the secretary-general to appoint a Special Representative (the SRSG) to control the implementation of the international civil presence in Kosovo. In turn, the SRSG ordered the establishment of the TMC in June 2000.[11] The nature of this structure means that the module is part of a chain of delegation and supervisory responsibility that extends back from the TMC to the SRSG, the UN secretary-general, and ultimately to the UN Security Council.[12]

In addition to structure, an essential component of the UNMIK constitutional order is the formal recognition of fundamental norms that are legally binding on its institutions. Ultimately, the basis for these lies in Articles 55 and 56 of the United Nations Charter and in recognition of the principle that international organizations are bound to observe human rights norms. Meanwhile, these general principles have received greater specificity via the SRSG's legislative enactments in UNMIK Regulations 1999/1 and 1999/24. UNMIK Regulation 1999/1, Section 2 ('Observance of internationally recognized standards'), states in full:

> In exercising their functions, all persons undertaking public duties or holding public office in Kosovo shall observe internationally recognized human rights standards and shall not discriminate against any person on any ground such as sex, race, color, language, religion, political or other opinion, national, ethnic or social origin, association with a national community, property, birth or other status.[13]

Regulation 1999/24, Section 1.3, is even more specific, stating that:

> In exercising their functions, all persons undertaking public duties or holding public office in Kosovo shall observe internationally recognized human rights standards, as reflected in particular in: The European

Convention for the Protection of Human Rights and Fundamental
Freedoms of 4 November 1950 and the Protocols thereto; The International Covenant on Civil and Political Rights of 16 December 1966 and
the Protocols thereto; . . . [and] The Convention on the Elimination of
All Forms of Racial Discrimination of 21 December 1965.

Of this list, the European Convention is particularly noteworthy, both for the
fact that it is the only regional instrument included and the fact that, at least in
the field of mass media law, the media regulatory authorities in Kosovo have
identified Article 10 of the European Convention for the Protection of Human
Rights and Fundamental Freedoms (ECHR) and, along with it, the Article 10
jurisprudence of the European Court of Human Rights (ECtHR), as the basis
for defining the parameters of their activity.[14,15,16]

We also make an assumption that is important for our analysis: that the
UNMIK institutions are bound by certain general principles of law that have
been recognized by domestic legal systems and supranational and international
organizations.[17] Of these, we are particularly concerned with separation of
powers principles, such as the independence of prosecutors from the legislative
and executive branches and provision of independent review of executive and
prosecutorial acts.

The Module as a Self-Contained System of Governance

The module is a self-contained, law-based international regulatory system
separate from any domestic legal regime, with a legislator promulgating
generally applicable binding norms, a standing authority empowered to
prosecute perceived violations of those norms, and control mechanisms
designed to supervise the prosecutor's acts.

The norms applicable to the mass media are generated from within this
structure, rather than from an outside source. In Kosovo, this legislative
function is performed by the SRSG, who issues generally-applicable normative
acts in addition to performing executive functions.[18,19] The module's essential
nature is defined by its core institution: a multi-dimensional agency that
monitors the media, performs administrative functions such as the granting
of broadcast licences, and acts as the prosecutor for imposition of sanctions for
violations of the normative base. We will call this agency, which in Kosovo has
been the Temporary Media Commissioner and in Bosnia and Herzegovina the
Director-General, the 'Regulator'. (Before March 2001, when the IMC was
merged with the Telecommunications Regulatory Agency to form the Communications Regulatory Agency, the IMC was headed by a 'Director-General'.
The focus of our study is the IMC and the TRA before the merger.)

In Kosovo, the core of the Regulator's prosecutorial duties is found in the
SRSG's authorization to the TMC to monitor media content and fashion
remedies, including the imposition of sanctions, if the normative base is
breached.[20] For example, as to print media, UNMIK Regulation 2000/37,

Section 2, authorizes the TMC to impose one or more of the following sanctions: a warning; a requirement to publish a reply, correction or apology; a fine of not less than DM 1,000 and not exceeding DM 100,000; seizure of equipment and/or printed material; or suspension or closure of operations.[21] The module's framers also have developed institutions for control of the Regulator's acts. In Kosovo, for example, the TMC cannot impose sanctions on the media without a finding by a three-member Media Hearings Board (MHB) that the normative base has been violated.[22] Also, the Kosovo and Bosnia and Herzegovina systems both provide for appellate review of sanctioning decisions. In Kosovo, the three-member Media Appeals Board (MAB) is empowered to uphold, modify, or rescind any TMC sanctioning decision.[23,24]

In all, the structural elements of the module suggest that attention has been paid to concerns about provision of safeguards against unconstrained, arbitrary acts by the prosecutorial authorities. However, further assessment of the effectiveness of the system in this regard, including the crucial question of the independence of the control mechanisms, requires evaluation of the normative base and the practical implementation of the module, to which we now turn.

Normative Base

The module is predicated on the conclusion that some form of content supervision and regulation is necessary in post-conflict zones and, further, that such action will be effective only if there is in place a body of generally applicable norms: that is, a formal system of law rather than an ad hoc approach. This conclusion reflects adherence to the general principle that prosecution can be based on no grounds other than those rules published and in existence at the time of the offence.[25]

In the module, it is accepted that the normative base is temporary (although indefinite) pending return to domestic rule. While in force, however, the rules of the normative base represent the sum total of the Regulator's enforcement mandate. The temporariness of the rules may be of only cosmetic interest when it comes to the legality of the norms. Unconscionable rules, for example, could not be justified because of their short-lived nature.

With the exception of laws in effect in Kosovo in 1989, the normative base comprises solely SRSG Regulations and supplementary acts in the form of Codes of Conduct, drafted by the TMC and promulgated as binding law by the SRSG, for the print and broadcast media.[26,27] The centrepiece of this normative base is found in provisions of SRSG Regulations 2000/36 and 2000/37, promulgated by the SRSG on 17 June, 2000. Because of the central place it has occupied in the TMC's prosecutorial activity, a key provision is Section 4.1 of SRSG Regulation 2000/37, which states in full:

> Owners, operators, publishers and editors shall refrain from publishing personal details of any person, including name, address or place of work, if

the publication of such details would pose a serious threat to the life, safety or security of any such person through vigilante violence or otherwise.

SRSG Regulation 2000/36, Section 5.1, applies exactly the same prohibition to 'Radio and Television Operators'. Another element in the normative base is the earlier SRSG Regulation 2000/4, 'On the Prohibition against Inciting to National, Racial, Religious or Ethnic Hatred, Discord, or Intolerance' promulgated on 1 February 2000 [the 'Hate Speech Regulation'].

The Codes of Conduct present more detailed rules. For purposes of examining the regulatory scheme in Kosovo, we focus on the Code of Conduct for the print media, since it is the instrument that has been applied most often in the TMC's prosecutorial practice. The Code's rules governing content and editorial practice are found in the following provisions:

Section 2 (Provocative Statements)
2.1. Publishers will not write, print, publish or distribute any material that encourages crime or criminal activities or which carries imminent risk of causing harm, such harm being defined as death, or injury, or damage to property or other violence.
2.2. Publishers will not write, print, publish or distribute any material that denigrates an ethnic or religious group or implies that an ethnic or religious group is responsible for criminal activity.

Section 3 (Privacy)
3.1. Publishers will not write, print, publish or distribute any material, that by intent or effect attributes criminal responsibility to any individual prior to a finding of guilt by a lawfully constituted tribunal.
3.2. Publishers will protect the identity of, and will not reveal the names, description, photograph, the likeness of, or specific information about any individual alleged to have committed a crime, unless authorities responsible for the administration of justice have expressly authorized the publication of such information, or unless the individual has been found guilty of the crime by a lawfully constituted tribunal.

Section 5 (Separation of News and Opinion)
Publishers, while free to express their own views, will make every effort to distinguish clearly between comment, conjecture, and fact and will clearly entitle editorials and commentaries as such.

Section 6 (False and Deceptive Material)
6.1. Publishers will not write, print, publish or distribute material that they know or ought to know to be false or deceptive.
6.2. Publishers will not write, print, publish or distribute material unless they have undertaken a prudent and reasonable inquiry to ensure the veracity of the material.

Section 7 (Right of Reply)

7.1. Publishers will extend a right of reply when they have written, printed, published, or distributed content that places a person, group or an institution in an unfavourable light, if fairness and impartiality require it. Publishers will ensure that the reply is given equal prominence to the unfavourable content.

7.2. If printed, published or distributed content proves to be false, publishers will print, publish and distribute a correction as soon as possible. Publishers will ensure that the correction is given equal prominence to the false content.

The catalogue of rules found in the normative base is gathered from a variety of sources. It includes provisions commonly found in domestic legal systems, such as those prohibiting advocacy of violence and protecting individual reputation and privacy, as well as prohibitions, such as those found in Section 2.2 and Regulation 2000/4, that are grounded in international conventions.[28,29] It might be viewed, in effect, as an incipient international, or extra-state, law of news media content regulation that embellishes norms found in existing international instruments.[30]

The SRSG and TMC made selective decisions as to the content of the normative base, not merely absorbing into the module a set of rules from any particular legal system. It was important to the SRSG to claim that input was sought from local groups and foreign organizations during the drafting process.[31]

Viewed in broad perspective, the key characteristic of the normative base is that it reflects the precarious and recurrent tension in human rights law between free expression guarantees and the validity of interferences with the right of free expression, especially where the countervailing interest is protection of individual right to physical security. Care should be taken to consider whether those elements that are contemplated as a surrogate Code of Conduct are of a different quality (from a free expression point of view) from those rules that are akin to domestic law. While the set of rules may find counterparts in domestic settings, many elements might conflict with various constitutional frameworks, such as that established by the First Amendment of the US Constitution. For the UNMIK authorities, the resolution of this tension is found in the emphasis on a particular vision of 'media responsibility', one which incorporates, along with traditional aspects of legal regulation, major elements of professional journalistic ethics as well. This is in keeping with the Kosovo normative structure itself, which makes the Codes of Conduct legally binding and enforceable.

The emphasis on this vision of media responsibility was set forth by the TMC in a lengthy statement disseminated to the public on 9 March 2001, in which the TMC defended the imposition of monetary fines on two newspapers, *Bota Sot* and *Epoka e Re*.[32] The statement includes these excerpts:

[W]hat has resulted is a general misunderstanding of the substantive issues on which these cases were argued. The editors of the newspapers concerned are failing yet again in their principal duty, that of educating and informing their readers [. . .] Achieving the right balance between freedom on the one hand and accountability on the other is difficult. It may be a cliché, but does freedom of speech allow a person to yell fire in a crowded theatre? Most people would say that it doesn't and they would acknowledge that there should be some sort of legal and ethical framework to deal with this delicate balance [. . .] [A]s most journalists will tell you, the principles that uphold freedom of expression in international law are laid out in the International Covenant on Civil and Political Rights and the European Convention on Human Rights. But, and as many conveniently forget, they also recognise that there are duties and responsibilities that come along at the same time . . . [*Bota Sot* and *Epoka e Re*] have shown a flagrant contempt for the basic tenets of professional journalism and the duties and responsibilities that are attached to the right of freedom of expression. Publishers and editors must understand that they are accountable both morally and in law for what they publish within the context of the society that they serve. Anarchy is not freedom and freedom of speech does not mean a free for all. It must be exercised with care and account must be taken of its consequences.

The scope of this vision of media responsibility has been broadened amid the particular circumstances in Kosovo. In Bosnia and Herzegovina, and in the period of regulation in Kosovo until June 2000, the focus was on the debilitating effect of hate speech on social and political stability. Thus, in February 2000, shortly after promulgation of the Hate Speech Regulation, OSCE Head of Mission Daan Everts stated:

We cannot tolerate hate speech anywhere in society – whether it is on the radio, in the classroom, in a newspaper or at a political rally. Which is why the issuing of the regulation on hate speech at the beginning of this month was so important. Most of all, the new regulation should work as a deterrent. I raise this now because while the mechanisms will exist to pull the plug on a radio or TV station, the same cannot be done to a newspaper. We have no plan to have a press law for printed media; in fact we are determined *not* to have such a law. It smacks of censorship. But if a paper publishes vitriol and bile, which incite hatred against a community or group – as some Kosovo papers have done – there is a legal route to take action against them. Anyone can lodge a complaint. It is up to the Court to decide whether the journalist, editor or publisher is guilty. And if they are they can be fined or jailed.[33]

As these remarks indicate, the international authorities were initially reluctant to take steps that went beyond sanctioning of hate speech to regulation of other content as well, to use law to promote a broader notion of media responsibility. Instead, as reflected in the comments of Daan Everts, hopes were placed on journalists' self-regulation:

> In any case, we hope that we won't have to use the Hate Speech Regulation. Instead we want to see self-regulation in Kosovo. Not self-censorship. But a mature look at what is published or broadcast and why. This is part of the role of a strong, democratic and independent media. Which is why we are pleased that all Kosovo's media have got together to form an Association. A central part of this Association is a Code of Conduct. Media outlets themselves will now be responsible to ensure that their professional colleagues and their rivals do not overstep the mark.[34]

However, later, following the events surrounding the death of Petar Topoljski, a Serbian UNMIK employee, in spring 2000, the SRSG's steps signalled a shift toward a more aggressive approach, abandoning media self-regulation and grounded in a public safety rationale.[35] As crafted in the context of lawlessness in Kosovo, this approach can be summarized to say: journalists have a responsibility, where a democratic state is not fully functioning and where violence is a regular means by which differences are resolved, not to infringe the physical rights of individuals or to increase social tension; where those duties are violated, the authority has the right to discipline.

There is the interesting suggestion, here, that greater leeway is permitted to the TMC because it is not only 'law' in the traditional sense, but Codes of Conduct in the self-regulatory sense, that are at issue. If the TMC were acting as a self-generated watchdog of the press, with its powers arising from ethical rules established by the press, then the restrictions, possibly, could be greater than if they originated from the State (or, here, its international equivalent). But, in fact, though the TMC may consider itself the substitute code-carrier incarnate, it is so only because of the origins of power in government.

The shift from hate speech to public safety as the core underlying public interest rationale is also significant. It shows that the normative base in the module can be flexible, lending itself to transfer to different post-conflict situations. The public safety rationale is grounded in the nature of the post-conflict setting in Kosovo, in which the UN administration faced a vacuum in civil institution infrastructure, most significantly in judicial institutions, and a chaotic situation marked by widespread violence and considerable potential for prolonged, on-going violence.[36] Thus, it was concluded, strong measures were viewed as necessary for protection of individuals from violence due to the absence of domestic legal authority and the existence of, or potential for, widespread lawlessness.[37]

Because of this shift from hate speech to public safety, the normative base in Kosovo extends beyond requirements imposed on domestic legal regimes in states party to instruments such as the Convention on the Prevention and

Punishment of the Crime of Genocide, International Covenant on Civil and Political Rights, and International Convention on the Elimination of All Forms of Racial Discrimination.[38,39,40] In other words, they go beyond the type of action that is required of states under international law, and rely on the type of action that is permissible under international law force.

The sum result of this dialectic, this effort to balance rights of free expression and countervailing rights, is that the scope of the normative base in Kosovo is quite narrow. In the end, the vision of media responsibility articulated in Kosovo gives wide latitude to news reporting and commentary that does not violate the public interest goals of protecting individuals and groups against incitement to violence and expressions of hatred. Thus, the issues in Kosovo are not those that typically give rise to the greatest concern among proponents of journalistic freedoms: the normative base does not equate protection of the public interest with protection of state interests, or with protection of public figures or institutions from critical commentary or with suppressing dissemination of facts unfavourable to the governing authorities. In this regard, while the normative base does proscribe the dissemination of material which journalists 'know or ought to know to be false or deceptive', it does not (in contrast to many domestic legal systems) dictate more stringent penalties when the material is injurious to particular public officials.[41] Nor does it include proscriptions against content found to be insulting to public officials or governmental entities.[42] Instead, the primary goal of the normative base, at least as applied in Kosovo thus far, has been to establish the kind of protection against incitement to violence found permissible in many domestic legal systems and the case law of the European Court of Human Rights, as well as the hate speech proscriptions found in international instruments.[43]

Implementation of the Module: Process and Accountability

It is a truism that the test of a legal system's compliance with fundamental norms, as well as fairness and effectiveness, lies in the actual application and enforcement of its laws. This is certainly the case with the module as well. Among the recurring themes in the studies appearing in this volume is not only the need to define substantive standards, but also the structural and procedural requirements satisfactory to establish legitimacy for information intervention. Of these, one of the most pressing is that of institutional and procedural safeguards against improper interference with the exercise of expressive activity.

In a complex context, most of the individuals endowed with these powers of regulation in Bosnia and Herzegovina and Kosovo have acted, generally, responsibly and have deliberately sought to maintain the balance inherent in the system of information intervention. At the same time, however, it must be recognized that the structure itself, if adopted in future situations, could lend itself to potential abuses. These are new phenomena – it is only very recently that international actors have begun to by-pass domestic legal regimes as the intermediaries of application of international human rights norms in the field of mass media regulation.[44] And the systems of accountability are also new and, if review is by the secretary-general or the Security Council, of awesome distance from the locales of post-conflict environments. That is a prominent reason for the existence and activity of 'freedom of speech' NGOs.

How does one review implementation of the module, application of the normative base and the procedures that have thus far been developed in its evolution? As before, we are guided by applicable international standards and general principles of law.[45] A number of these have received articulation in Article 6.1 of the European Convention on Human Rights and the case law of the European Court of Human Rights construing that provision.[46]

To do this, we will focus first on what we have called, bringing together the existing examples, the office of the Regulator, particularly its prosecutorial functions. Then, we will turn to questions about the module's control mechanisms; in particular, looking at issues of competence and degree of structural independence.

The Office of the Regulator: Public Relations, Investigation, Prosecution

The multi-dimensional office of the Regulator includes both extra-legal and law-based functions. In other words, in some cases, it acts to advance certain policies by means of powers of persuasion, while in others – its more sensitive role – it acts to investigate and prosecute suspected violations of legal norms. The result is a combination of a managerial theory of compliance with traditional criminal law models of forcible enforcement.[47]

Within this range of activity, it is possible to delineate several elements of the performance of duties in this office: informal/public advocacy, investigative, and prosecutorial elements. Thus, in carrying out its functions, the Regulator acts as a public advocate for media responsibility, a monitor of mass media conduct and investigator of complaints, and as a formal prosecutor.

Extra-Legal Functions

In general, the manner in which these functions are carried out can be attributed to questions of individual personal style; the very human, personal, direct management of the operation. Models are abstract, impersonal, described, usually, apart from the personnel who implement them. In the case of Kosovo, for example, the success and operation of the framework has been affected in important ways by the personal characteristics of the individual holding the office.[48]

The hallmark of the extra-legal activity has been a frank candour on the part of the Regulator, a readiness to articulate its motivations and its goals. Thus, the Regulator has been vocal in providing expressions of concern and pleas for voluntary compliance with accepted journalistic ethics. The style is open, cajoling, and clearly conscious of the public effect of the TMC's pronouncements. At times, these statements to the journalistic community and the public at large have taken on the character of general observations, perhaps warning about legal violations but without identifying specific offenders. For example, in a 20 February, 2001 news release about its sanctioning decision against the newspaper *Epoka e Re*, the TMC stated:

> The TMC remains deeply concerned about the current levels of inflammatory and potentially dangerous accusation and counter accusation in the Kosovo written press [. . .] Much of the press in Pristina serves up a daily diet of denouncement and insult. As a consequence the TMC considers that the flavour and tenor of the press at present contributes to the prevailing atmosphere of tension.[49]

Or, on other occasions, the TMC addressed concerns about individual news organs to the public and journalistic community with regard to conduct that, while considered irresponsible, was lacking in a legal basis to proceed to prosecution. An example is a TMC 26 March, 2001 news release, entitled 'Altering Photographs', which we reproduce here in full:

> Last Friday the 23rd March 2001 all of the major newspapers in Kosovo carried the story of Thursday's tragic shootings at a Macedonian military checkpoint in Tetovo. These stories were all accompanied by photographs, most of which originated from the Reuters News Agency. With the exception of *Bota Sot* all these newspapers showed a black object on the ground close to the body of one of those who was killed. Indeed there has been considerable debate as to precisely what this object was.
>
> The Office of the TMC understands that the circumstances surrounding this incident have caused considerable controversy. In this respect it is not the intention of the Office to comment on these circumstances or on the editorial line taken by any of the newspapers in their Friday editions. However, what is extremely alarming is the apparent removal, by *Bota Sot*, of a crucial piece of evidence from a photograph taken from an international source.
>
> The Office of the TMC is currently in discussions with the Senior Legal Council of the Reuters News Agency to determine conclusively whether or not *Bota Sot* altered the original Reuters image to suit the thesis of their article. We have also consulted with them on how they may wish to proceed. Additionally, we are also corresponding with other international news and press agencies, including CNN and AP TN, and have discussed with them their footage and reports of the incident. All have confirmed the presence of the object in their respective photographic or video sequences and from the eye witness accounts of their journalists.

If it were indeed the case that *Bota Sot* did manipulate the images they obtained from Reuters, this would constitute gross professional misconduct. Furthermore, their attempts to portray all the other media who carried these images, as being misleading would be a further example of deliberate distortion in the face of the overwhelming evidence. It is the duty of editors to report the facts as accurately as possible and to distinguish opinion from fact. This is particularly important when tensions are high and the subject matter is so sensitive. To alter the available evidence to support an opinion and pass it off as news is unconscionable and discredits the profession of journalism.[50]

In looking to future applications of the module, we note that the above examples present a fine line between the Regulator's legitimate use of powers of public persuasion and the exercise of a chilling effect on the exercise of rights of expression. The reason for this, of course, is that the Regulator's public statements are always backed by its power to influence media conduct by means of the threat inherent in its authority to prosecute. It will take strict adherence to the normative base, limiting such use of public relations to content falling clearly within its confines, to keep the Regulator from crossing the line into exerting a 'chilling effect' on protected news reporting and commentary.

Legal: the Authority to Investigate and Prosecute

The legal power of the Regulator lies here: in the authority to investigate suspected violations, to assess whether a violation has indeed occurred, and to proceed with the prosecution process, which can culminate in the imposition of sanctions. It is here where the most sensitive concerns about abuse of authority can be found.

The Regulator's investigative activity serves multiple purposes: it provides the regulatory authority with information with which to establish guilt, as well as to identify ameliorating or exacerbating circumstances for the purposes of crafting remedies and/or penalties. Thus, in the *Epoka e Re* newspaper case, TMC Simon Haselock made an unannounced visit to the newspaper's offices (following an unsuccessful attempt to elicit information by mail from the newspaper), and in the *Bota Sot* case he engaged in extensive correspondence with the newspaper's editors.[51,52]

These activities present both positive and potentially negative aspects. They demonstrate a human touch, an opportunity for negotiation and mediation. On the other hand, they pose the spectre of the sort of arbitrary harassment that authorities in many countries have employed to threaten the mass media if their content is considered offensive. To guard against this risk, a crucial element will be the existence of effective independent review of the Regulator's actions. As we will discuss below, this is a weak link in the TMC system.

Another dimension of the investigative mode provides the Regulator with the opportunity to construe and apply legal norms in deciding whether or not to proceed with formal prosecution. An example is the TMC's 25 April, 2001 letter to Mr Xhavit Haliti, demonstrating the TMC's willingness to construe international human rights norms in applying the normative base mandate.[53] Mr Haliti, a leading figure in the Democratic Party of Kosova (PDK), had asked the TMC to investigate the possibility of charges against the newspaper *Bota Sot*.[54] We quote an excerpt from his letter at length because of what it reveals regarding the TMC's investigative and prosecutorial style:

> I have written to *Bota Sot* concerning your complaints and have discussed your concerns with them at length. Unfortunately, given the very specific nature of the Regulation I have to tell you that I do not consider that I can proceed on this matter any further. To be sure of a successful action under the Regulation all the various criteria that it stipulates must be satisfied and this is not possible in the articles to which you refer. Nevertheless, I must say that I consider these articles to have been deliberately sensational, unsubstantiated and provocative and I have made these and other points forcefully to the Editor and will continue to do so.
>
> I also note from your letter that you understand the principle that as a public figure you will often be exposed to criticism and allegations. This is the one of the negative aspects of public political debate. In applying the conditions of the European Convention on Human Rights in regard to freedom of expression you will be aware that the European Court has taken the view that public figures are not entitled to the same measure of protection in cases of defamation than [sic] are private citizens. This is another reason why I believe that a case taken up on the basis of your complaints would not stand scrutiny by the Media Appeals Board.

This example serves as an illustration of TMC's efforts to operate within the constraints of law, including the fundamental norms in the UNMIK constitutional structure.

Formal Prosecution

In Kosovo, the prosecutorial energies of the TMC have been focused on cases involving suspected incitement of violence against individuals. At time of writing, the TMC has invoked the formal sanctioning process three times, in actions against three different newspapers.[55] In each case, the charge was the same: violation of Section 4.1 of Regulation 2000/37.

The Regulator is empowered to prosecute suspected violations of the normative base, which is rendered enforceable by means of a range of remedies, including financial penalties and suspension or termination of operations.[56] The exercise of these powers implicates a number of general principles of law. First, according to those principles, the laws and process must be transparent and 'lawful' – that is, based on existing, published, generally applicable legal norms generated by the legislature and not the executive branch. This means operating pursuant to generally applicable, published normative base. One measuring stick is to ascertain whether the norms in question have sufficient precision and clarity to satisfy the 'prescribed by law' requirement in Article 10(2) of the ECHR.[57]

As implemented in Kosovo and Bosnia and Herzegovina, the module, with its published normative base, appears to satisfy these standards. For example, in those cases in Kosovo in which prosecution has been invoked, these conditions appear to have been satisfied. In this regard, it should be noted that despite his evident opposition to *Bota Sot*'s alleged unprofessional conduct expressed in the 'Altering Photos' news release, TMC Simon Haselock did not pursue legal action against the newspaper.[58]

This contrasts with the action of the SRSG in June 2000, when it closed the office of the newspaper *Dita* for eight days on the grounds that *Dita* and its editors 'had violated the letter and spirit of Security Council resolution 1244 (1999)'.[59] The SRSG's action was taken in response to the events of spring 2000, when *Dita* identified Topoljski, as mentioned, a Serbian UNMIK employee, as a war criminal and provided both a photo of Mr Topoljski and details of his name, address and workplace information. Topoljski was found murdered on 16 May, and on 19 May, the editor of *Dita* published an open letter to the SRSG, indicating that the newspaper would continue to publish the names of individuals 'involved against Albanians'. It is doubtful that SC Resolution 1244, which does not refer to expressive activity in any way and is not directed toward private actors, contains any language that would support the conclusion that closure of a newspaper for publication of detailed information about an individual, even if done so in order to advocate violence against that person, would satisfy the 'prescribed by law' standard.[60]

Other general principles relevant to the module relate to the process itself: an accused's right to be heard, equality before the law, and opportunity for appeal.[61] The TMC's mandate in Regulation 2000/37 provides little direction on the procedures to be followed by the TMC in determining the existence of a violation and imposing sanctions.[62] However, the structure and process of prosecution have evolved quickly into a more formal set of legal rules and safeguards. In this regard, the important step was the MAB's decision in the *Dita* case, in which the MAB overturned the TMC's decision to impose sanctions on the newspaper because of procedural infirmities: violations of international norms and the law in effect in Kosovo in 1989.[63] In response to that decision, the TMC adopted measures to provide greater procedural safeguards for accused.[64] According to the Media Hearings Board Rules of Procedure, if the TMC concludes that a violation has occurred and that prosecution is warranted, the formal process must begin with the TMC's presentation of written notice (which we will call an 'Accusation'), which must inform the alleged violator of an opportunity to reply.[65] The indictment must then be presented to the MHB, which determines whether a violation has occurred and, in addition, recommends to the TMC whether there are any mitigating or aggravating circumstances that should be taken into account when the TMC decides upon the appropriate remedies and/or penalties.[66] The TMC is not permitted to impose sanctions without a finding by the MHB that the media outlet or representative in question has violated one or more rules in the normative base.[67]

At the MHB hearing, both the TMC and the respondent, who may be represented by an attorney, are allowed to address the Board for no more than forty minutes, and each member of the Board may question the parties for up to thirty minutes. The Board may invite for oral presentation third-party witnesses and experts; the Rules of Procedure do not provide the parties a right to question those persons.[68] The burden of proof upon all such issues is upon the TMC.[69] The TMC's decision as to penalties may be appealed to the Media Appeals Board.[70] The MAB is empowered to uphold, modify, or rescind the TMC's sanctioning decision.

Throughout, questions of accountability and independence loom over this process. Is there sufficient sharing and diffusion of power to guard adequately against abuses by the authorities? Is the Regulator sufficiently independent from the legislator/executive SRSG? Is the Regulator accountable only to the law? By what mechanisms are the Regulator's acts reviewed to determine their compliance with these principles?

Here, again, certain general principles (sensitive to the special needs of a post-conflict context) should apply. For example, a prosecutor is bound by law, and only the law (here, this means the fundamental norms in the UNMIK Constitution, as well as the normative base); a prosecutor must be independent from legislative and executive branch control; and, to insure observance of these standards, a prosecutor's act must be subject to review by an independent agency.[71] The last point is perhaps the key to the entire system of administrative justice. In effect, it provides that there must – again subject to the possibly special circumstances of conflict zones – be a supervisory system of control sufficiently independent to make an objective determination as to whether the administrator has acted in compliance not only with other principles of administrative justice, but with all applicable legal norms as well.

While clearly an effort to assure procedural fairness, the module's structure and procedures raise certain questions from the point of view of compatibility with these principles. First, there is the question of the TMC's independence from the SRSG, which is both the UNMIK legislature and executive. According to the TMC's organic statute, the TMC has independent status and is temporary pending the establishment of effective domestic parallel structures.[72] The meaning of 'independence' in this context is not explained. The individual TMC is named by the SRSG; however, the SRSG is not involved in the day-to-day functions of the TMC, nor is there evidence that the SRSG has exerted any direct influence on the TMC's actions.[73]

Second, and perhaps more problematic, are a series of questions related to the roles of the TMC, the MHB, and the MAB. The MHB is analogous to a trial court, with the judge or jury making the ultimate determination of guilt or innocence. However, this MHB decision is insulated from review. In addition, if a violation is found, it is the Regulator (the TMC) who decides on the nature of the penalties – definitely a judicial or jury function that should be outside the Regulator's powers. By possessing the ability to decide upon and impose sanctions, the TMC is both prosecutor and judge.

Next, the question must be asked, although it is very difficult to answer, whether the MHB and MAB are sufficiently independent to satisfy general principles and the UNMIK Constitution. In the context of ECHR Article 6.1, the ECtHR has construed 'independent' as independence from the legislative and executive branches, as well as the parties.[74] The European Court's determinations as to the independence of control bodies is very fact-intensive and, given the scope of our inquiry, we can simply cite the factors listed by the Court:

> In order to determine whether a body can be considered to be 'in-dependent' of the executive it is necessary to have regard to the manner of appointment of its members and the duration of their term of office, the existence of guarantees against outside pressures and the question whether the body presents an appearance of independence.[75]

Finally, it should be pointed out that there are three significant areas in which the Kosovo MAB lacks competence: (1) review of the Regulator's investigative acts; (2) review of the MHB's decisions as to guilt or innocence; and (3) review of the SRSG's legislative acts.[76,77,78] As to the last of these, this means that the MAB's competence also does not extend to a power of review over the normative base itself, to determine if its provisions comport with the fundamental norms of the UNMIK Constitution.

In sum, significant steps in the evolution of the module have been taken to insure adequate safeguards for the mass media. However, particularly before the module is again employed in a post-conflict situation, attention should be devoted to further analysis and structural and procedural revisions. These matters go directly to fundamental issues about the module's legitimacy.

The Quest for Legitimacy

The emerging system of information intervention, reflected in the module, rests on a thin veneer of acceptance within the global community at large: the assumption, by the UN Security Council and secretary-general, that regulation of media content is both acceptable and integral to democracy building in post-conflict societies, and that it is possible to conduct it in a way that is compatible with international free speech and free press standards.[79]

The initial emergence of the module met with intense criticism from free press advocates.[80] The significance of this lies in the reminder to the United Nations and other international organizations that this system of governance at bottom is reliant upon a public legitimacy, difficult to obtain or sustain in light of the perceived threat to news media freedoms. From a slightly different perspective, the concerns about legitimacy might also stem from a democratic deficit in international institutions.

To address these concerns, it is necessary to have safeguards against heavy-handedness, or even the appearance of such heavy-handedness, by assuring procedural fairness and objectivity. In this regard, in addition to noting the binding fundamental norms in the UNMIK Constitution, much of our discussion has been grounded in an assumption that certain general principles apply here as a matter of law. But even if they might not as a matter of law, they should be followed as a matter of policy, for the sake of establishing and maintaining legitimacy.

Even more generally, the human rights rationale for what might be called 'aggressive peacemaking' and the intrusiveness into the zone of freedom of expression is a precarious one. To achieve legitimacy, processes of information intervention need popular support from the very people and institutions from whom it faces determined opposition – media NGOs, especially free speech and free press advocates. A critical sticking point for these NGOs is the question of whether circumstances ever can exist to justify a rearticulation and reframing of widely accepted standards of free speech/free press. How norms are developed, their very entry and maturation, will have an influence on how they are received by these significant groups. The UN must find ways of engaging those who 'vote' on the question of legitimacy.

The development and presentation of free speech norms in the information intervention context is important for another reason. Peacekeeping operations are partly designed to provide a context sufficiently altered and enhanced that a more democratic society can flourish after the operation has been dissolved. Construction of a public sphere that supports a democratic society is an element of that process. When an international governmental organization engages in regulation of the press, its actions may affect the nature of the political system that follows. How a regulatory rule is shaped, how it is presented in the society, how those who will be subject to a seemingly censorial rule react and accept that rule – all these are part of the difficult process of democracy development in a conflict zone.[81]

Conclusion

The module is a work in progress, based on exigencies, which dictated not only its form and substance, but indeed its very rationale for existence. The post-conflict intervention functions within the existing organizational structure of the United Nations and is intended to be a temporary system designed to respond to an environment of lawlessness and violence and the absence of effective domestic legal institutions.

Two interlocking themes form the framework for understanding this normative base: the pervasive nature of human rights law, and the specific post-conflict circumstances in Kosovo. Because they directly affect the exercise of free expression guaranteed in international human rights instruments, and because some of the normative base exceeds what is required of states to regulate hate speech under international norms, an over-riding question becomes whether the restrictions on media content are permissible interferences with media freedoms.

These have always been complex issues in domestic legal systems. The emergence of the module now presents a new dimension for the study of these long-standing issues in the sphere of mass media law.

Bibliography

Amerasinghe, Chittharanjan Felix (1996), 'The Future of International Administrative Law', *International and Comparative Law Quarterly*, vol. 45, pp. 773–95.

Chayes, Abram and Chayes, Antonia Handler (1995), *The New Sovereignty: Compliance with International Regulatory Agreements*, Cambridge, MA: Harvard University Press.

Council of Europe (1996), *The Administration and You: Principles of Administrative law Concerning the Relations between Administrative Authorities and Private Persons*, Council of Europe Publishing.

Harris, D. J., O'Boyle, M. and Warbrick, C. (1995), *Law of the European Convention on Human Rights*, London: Butterworths.

Helfer, Laurence and Slaughter, Anne-Marie (1997), 'Toward a Theory of Effective Supranational Adjudication', *Yale Law Journal*, vol. 107, pp. 273–328.

Krug, Peter and Swann, Barbara (2000), *Supplement to ABA-CEELI Media Law Concept Paper: the European Convention on Human Rights* (American Bar Association Central and East European Law Initiative.

Matheson, Michael J. (2001), 'United Nations Governance of Post-conflict Societies', *American Journal of International Law*, vol. 95, pp. 78–95.

Palmer, Laura (2001), 'A Very Clear and Present Danger: Hate Speech, Media Reform and Post-Conflict Democratization in Kosovo', *Yale Journal of International Law*, vol. 26, pp. 179–218.

Pech, Laurent (1999/2000), 'Is Dayton Falling? Reforming Media in Bosnia and Herzegovina', *International Journal of Communications Law and Policy* 1, pp. 1–28.

Price, M. E. and Krug, P. (2000), *The Enabling Environment for Free and Independent Media*, sponsored by the Center for Democracy and Governance of the US Agency for International Development and prepared by the Programme in Comparative Media Law and Policy, Oxford University, UK.

Reinisch, August (2000), *International Organizations before National Courts*, Cambridge: Cambridge University Press.

Strohmeyer, Hansjorg (2001), 'Collapse and Reconstruction of a Judicial System: The United Nations Missions in Kosovo and East Timor', *American Journal of International Law*, vol. 95, pp. 46–63.

Van Dijk, P. and Van Hoof, G. J. H. (3rd edn, 1998), *Theory and Practice of the European Convention on Human Rights*, The Hague and Boston: Kluwer Law International.

Wilde, Ralph (2000), 'From Bosnia to Kosovo and East Timor: the Changing Role of the United Nations in the Administration of Territory', *ILSA Journal of International and Comparative Law*, vol. 6, pp. 467–71.

Notes

1. This phrase is borrowed from Thompson and De Luce's contribution to this volume: Chapter 7: 'Escalating to Success? The Intervention in Bosnia and Hercegovina'.

2. Contributions to this volume emphasize the distinctions between pre-peacekeeping ('Phase One') and post-peacekeeping ('Phase Two') forms of information intervention.

3. Thompson and De Luce. Chapter 7.

4. The Office of the High Representative established the IMC on 11 June 1998, following the Conclusions of the 1997 Bonn Peace Implementation Conference that called for establishment of a temporary agency to monitor and supervize the mass media in Bosnia and Herzegovina. Decision of the High Representative, 'Decision on the Establishment [sic] of the Independent Media Commission', Sarajevo, 11 June 1998, Online [June 2001] available at http://www.OHR.INT/mediares/d980611a. Pech, 'Is Dayton Falling?' p. 4. In March 2001 the IMC was merged with the Telecommunications Regulatory Agency to form a new entity, the Communication Regulatory Agency (CRA). The head of this new entity is the Chief Executive Officer. The module discussed in this chapter is based on the IMC before the merger. See OHR, 'Decision Combining the Competencies of the Independent Media Commission and the Telecommunications Agency' of 2 March 2001. Online [October 2001], available at http://www.ohr.int/decisions/mediadec/default.asp?content_id = 75.

5. The TMC was created pursuant to regulations promulgated on 17 June 2000 by the Special Representative of the UN secretary-general in Kosovo: Regulation No. 2000/36, 'On the Licensing and Regulation of the Broadcast Media in Kosovo', Online [July 2001] available at http://www.un.org/peace/kosovo/pages/regulations/reg036.html and Regulation No. 2000/37, 'On the Conduct of the Print Media in Kosovo', Online [July 2001] available at http://www.un.org/peace/kosovo/pages/regulations/reg037.html See Palmer, 'A Very Clear and Present Danger', p. 179.

6. In March 2001, a new entity, the Communications Regulatory Agency (CRA), was established in Bosnia and Herzegovina as a step in the transition toward local rule. The CRA's mandate includes assumption of the IMC's responsibilities. See the OHR, 'Decision Combining the Competencies of the Independent Media Commission and the Telecommunications Regulatory Agency', 2 March 2001. In Kosovo, it can be expected that significant changes in the module will be forthcoming as a result of the 'Constitutional Framework for Provisional Self-Government' signed into law by the SRSG on 15 May 2001 (UNMIK/REG/2001/9), Online [July 2001] available at http://www.un.org/peace/kosovo/pages/regulations/reg01.09.html. Sections 5.4(b) and 11.1 call for the establishment of a new media regulatory body, to be entitled the 'Independent Media Commission'. For the purposes of our contribution, we limit our description and analysis to the office of the Temporary Media Commissioner as of 15 May, 2001.

7. See, e.g., Hansjorg Strohmeyer's recent proposal for 'quick-start packages' of existing structural and substantive law models for UN-administered territories, in Strohmeyer, 'Collapse and Reconstruction', p. 62.

8. Matheson, 'United Nations Governance', p. 76; Wilde, 'From Bosnia to Kosovo', p. 467.

9. The module's normative base is a substitution of international law for a domestic legal regime. However, in contrast to traditional international regulatory systems, the subjects of regulation are not states, but private natural and legal persons. As Laurence Helfer and Anne-Marie Slaughter put it, this idea of the supranational – fulfilled by the emerging module – 'represents another departure from the bedrock assumption of traditional public international law: that states, functioning as unitary entities, are the only subjects of international rules and institutions and hence the only recognized actors in the international realm'. Helfer and Slaughter, 'Toward a Theory', p. 288.

10. UN Security Council Resolution 1244 (10 June 1999), Online [June 2001], available at http://www.un.int/usa/sres1244.htm

11. The organic acts for the TMC are UNMIK Regulations 2000/36 and 2000/37; and the IMC's organic instrument is the 'Regulation for the Independent Media Commission (IMC)', adopted by the IMC on 16 September 1998 (amended 8 September 1999, and 21 October 1999), Online [July 2001], available at http://www.imcbih.org/Download/DLRegulations/DLReg/dlreg_2

12. The secretary-general's periodic status reports to the Security Council concerning Kosovo include information on 'media affairs', available at the UNMIK website, http://www.un.org/peace/kosovo/pages/kosovo1.shtml

13. UNMIK/REG/1999/1, 25 July 1999, Online [June 2001] available at http://www.un.org/peace/kosovo/pages/regulations/reg1

14. Article 10 ('Freedom of Expression') states in full:
    1. Everyone has the right to freedom of expression. This right shall include freedom to hold opinions and to receive and impart information and ideas without interference by public authority and regardless of frontiers. This Article shall not prevent States from requiring the licensing of broadcasting, television or cinema enterprises.
    2. The exercise of these freedoms, since it carries with it duties and responsibilities, may be subject to such formalities, conditions, restrictions or penalties as are prescribed by law and are necessary in a democratic society, in the interests of national security, territorial integrity or public safety, for the prevention of disorder or crime, for the protection of health or morals, for the protection of the reputation or rights of others, for preventing the disclosure of information received in confidence, or for maintaining the authority and impartiality of the judiciary.

    Among the many secondary sources on the extensive Article 10 jurisprudence of the ECtHR, see: Harris et al., *Law of the European Convention*, pp. 372–416; Van Dijk and Van Hoof, *Theory and Practice*, pp. 557–85; Krug and Swann, *Supplement to ABA-CEELI*

15. For the European Court of Human Rights' Judgements, see http://www.echr.coe.int

16. See, e.g., decisions of the Media Appeals Board in the cases of: *Belul Beqaj and the Newspaper Dita*, Appellant and Temporary Media Commissioner, OSCE, Respondent (16 September 2000), paras 68–75, Online [July 2001], available at http://www.osce.org/kosovo/indbodies/tmc/cases/dita.php3 and *Sylejman Aliu and the Newspaper Bota Sot*, Appellant and Temporary Media Commissioner, OSCE, Respondent (19 February 2001), paras 71–5 (copy on file with the authors).

17. Reinisch, *International Organizations*, pp. 318–22.

18. In referring to the SRSG, we incorporate those consultative institutions that

function within its Joint Interim Administrative Structure (JIAS), such as the Kosovo Transitional Council (KTS) and Interim Administrative Council (IAC).

19. UNMIK Regulation 1999/1 ('On the Authority of the Interim Administration in Kosovo'), 25 July 1999, Section 1.1, states in full: 'All legislative and executive authority with respect to Kosovo, including the administration of the judiciary, is vested in UNMIK and is exercised by the Special Representative of the Secretary-General.'

20. In Bosnia and Herzegovina, similar powers were conferred on the director-general.

21. A similar list for broadcasters, but adding suspension or termination of broadcast licenses, is found in UNMIK Regulation 2000/36, Section 3.1.

22. 'Media Hearing Board Rules of Procedure' (adopted 7 November 2000) Sections 17–18. Online on the OSCE Mission in Kosovo Web site, http://www.osce.org/kosovo. The three members (two local, one international) of the MHB are appointed by the TMC, based on nominations from three organizations: the Association of Kosovo Journalists (AKJ), the Kosovo Law Center, and the Organization of Security and Cooperation in Europe (information in e-mail message from TMC Simon Haselock to the authors, 12 March 2001).

    In Bosnia and Herzegovina, a seven-member Enforcement Panel decides cases regarding the director-general's imposition of penalties, according to the Section 16.1 of the 'IMC Procedure for Handling Cases' (adopted 8 December 1998, and amended 9 June 1999, and 21 October 1999), Online [July 2001], available at http://www.imcbih.org/Download/DLRegulations/DLReg/dlreg_3.html The decision as to the penalty is also made by the Enforcement Panel. In Kosovo, this is made by the TMC alone. The Regulator in the Bosnia and Herzegovina system (the director-general) also serves as chair of the Enforcement Panel ('IMC Procedure for Handling Cases', Sections 13.1 and 15). Demonstrating somewhat greater sensitivity to separation of powers issues, the TMC in Kosovo is not a member of the MHB. In its 7 November 2000 news release announcing the issuance of the MHB Rules of Procedure and formation of the MHB, the TMC stated that the MHB would be an 'independent administrative panel'. Online [June 2001], available, http://www.osce.org/news/generate.php3?news_id = 1243 In its 19 February 2001 *Bota Sot* decision, para 69, the Media Appeals Board repeated this statement.

23. On 31 August 2000, the MAB adopted and issued two sets of procedural rules: 'Rules of Procedure (Conduct of Hearings)' 001/2000, 31 August 2000. See OSCE Mission in Kosovo web site, http://www.osce.org/kosovo and 'Rules of Procedure (Filing of Appeals), Online [June 2001], available at http://www.osce.org/kosovo/indbodies/mab.php3

24. UNMIK Regulation 2000/36, Section 4.5; UNMIK Regulation 2000/37, Section 3.1. The MAB's three members (two international and one local) are appointed by the SRSG upon nomination by the Deputy Special Representative of the Secretary-General for Institution Building (UNMIK Regulation 2000/36, Section 4.4). In Bosnia and Herzegovina, the IMC Council, the IMC's regulatory body, hears appeals from decisions of the director-general and Enforcement Panel ('IMC Procedure for Handling Cases' Sections 11.7, 16.5, and 23.1).

25. International Covenant on Civil and Political Rights (1966), Article 15.1; ECHR, Article 7.1. In the area of freedom of expression, this principle is expressed in the requirement in Article 10.2, ECHR, that any interference with the exercise of freedom of expression must be 'prescribed by law'.

26. UNMIK Regulation 1999/24, Section 1.1 ('Applicable Law'), states in full:
    The law applicable in Kosovo shall be:
    a. The regulations promulgated by the Special Representative of the Secretary-General and subsidiary instruments issued thereunder; and
    b. The law in force in Kosovo on 22 March 1989. In case of a conflict, the regulations and subsidiary instruments issued thereunder shall take precedence.
    The date 22 March 1989 is the date on which the Republic Serbia Assembly formally terminated most elements of Kosovo's autonomous status. As of June 2001, the TMC's publications and enforcement actions have never referred to any provisions from the legal base identified in Section 1.1(b).

27. See 'Temporary Code of Conduct for the Print Media in Kosovo' and the 'Code of Conduct for the Broadcast Media in Kosovo'. The codes were promulgated pursuant to SRSG Administrative Direction 2000/20 [UNMIK/DIR/2000/20] of 18 September 2000. The documents are online at the OSLE web site: http://www.osce.org/kosovo

28. Regulation 2000/37, Section 4.1; Code of Conduct Section 2.1. See, for example, the United States Supreme Court decision in *Brandenburg v. Ohio*, 395 U.S. 444, 447 (1969).

29. These international conventions include: the Convention on the Prevention and Punishment of the Crime of Genocide, International Covenant on Civil and Political Rights, and International Convention on the Elimination of All Forms of Racial Discrimination.

30. Reflecting perhaps the challenging conditions in which such drafting takes place, certain provisions in the normative base are suspect on technical drafting grounds, perhaps under the 'prescribed by law' test of Article 10.2, ECHR. For example, Section 4.1 says nothing about the State of mind of the publisher (in contrast to the *Brandenburg* test's 'directed toward . . .'). In Section 2.1, the term 'other violence' is quite vague.

31. See, for example, the speech by Ambassador Daan Everts, OSCE Head of Mission, on the occasion of the opening of the new studios of Radio Television Kosovo (RTK), 16 February 2000. Online at the OSCE Mission in Kosovo web site: http://www.osce.org/kosovo In response to critics of the Hate Speech Regulation, he comments:
    This new regulation has provoked strong reactions and some allegations that it is targeting the media specifically. This is not the case! The new regulation is absolutely in line with international covenants on freedom of speech and expression and it has been worked out after consultation with the Kosovo Joint Advisory Council of Legislative Matters, the Council of Europe and the UN.
    See also Section 1.1 of Regulation 2000/37, which states in full:
    The Temporary Media Commissioner, in special circumstances, may issue temporary Codes of Conduct. Before issuing any such code, the Temporary Media Commissioner shall consult with the Special Representative of the Secretary-General, and interested, media-related parties as appropriate.
    It is also possible that the SRSG vetted the proposed norms with consultative bodies such as the IAC and KTS.

32. Copy on file with the authors.

33. Everts, Speech on the occasion of the opening of the new RTK studios, 16 February 2000.

34. Ibid.
35. This more aggressive approach was without regard to distinctions between different forms of media (electronic or print). Despite protests to the contrary, one important consequence of this particular form of intervention is the elision of distinctions between the authority's treatment of broadcast media and its treatment of print media. It is true that licensing existed only for broadcasters, but, as it turned out, the burden of concern about violations that might upset the public order dealt with violations by the press. The authority to close down newspapers was actually used with newspapers, though not with radio and television stations.
36. Ibid. and Strohmeyer, 'Collapse and Reconstruction', pp. 48–50, 58–60. It is also important to note that much of the concern about violence stemmed from content in Kosovar publications that identified individual Kosovars, not members of other ethnic groups. For example, this was the case in the three formal prosecutions brought by the TMC.
37. TMC's Simon Haselock has been a vocal proponent of this view. In his 20 February 2001 sanctioning decision in *Epoka e Re*, for example, he stated:
    > In my decision of 1 December against *Bota Sot* I explained why the conditions in Kosovo could not yet be described as approximating a fully functioning democracy. I went on to describe that violence remained a regular means by which differences were resolved and scores settled and that the fear of violence was self-evident across the whole spectrum of society . . . [M]y main function in these cases is to uphold the rights of the individual against the threat of violence and increased tension caused by this irresponsibility. 'Sanctioning Decision on *Epoka e Re*', para. 8 Online at the OSCE Mission in Kosovo web site: http://www.osce.org/kosovo).
38. Convention on the Prevention and Punishment of the Crime of Genocide (1948). Article III(c) states that '[d]irect and public incitement to commit genocide' is one of the acts that parties shall make punishable. Article V requires the parties 'to enact, in accordance with their respective Constitutions, the necessary legislation to give effect to the provisions of the present Convention'.
39. International Covenant on Civil and Political Rights (1976). Article 20.2 requires parties to prohibit by law '[a]ny advocacy of national, racial or religious hatred that constitutes incitement to discrimination, hostility, or violence'.
40. International Convention on the Elimination of All Forms of Racial Discrimination (1966). Article 4(a) requires parties to 'declare an offence punishable by law all dissemination of ideas based on racial superiority or hatred, incitement to racial discrimination, as well as all acts of violence or incitement to such acts against any race or group of persons of another colour or ethnic origin'.
41. 'Temporary Code of Conduct for the Print Media in Kosovo', Section 6.1. We do not wish to suggest that the normative base is free of problems. For example, we note that dissemination of 'false or deceptive' material in Section 6.1 is enforceable even without any need for the TMC to demonstrate that it was injurious to an individual. This is a significant departure from traditional notions of defamation law in domestic legal systems, which could potentially be applied to infringe seriously the exercise of expression.
42. The absence of such provisions demonstrates the influence of the *Lingens v. Austria*, (1986) 8 EHRR 407, line of decisions by the ECtHR, in which the Court has ruled on numerous occasions that in public political debate, public officials are not entitled to the same measure of legal protection as are private citizens. See

Harris et al, *Law of the European Convention on Human Rights*, pp. 397–401; and van Dijk and van Hoof, *Theory and Practice*, p. 572.

43. See, e.g., *Brandenburg v. Ohio*, 395 U.S. at 447, in which the United States Supreme Court stated that:

[C]onstitutional guarantees of free speech and free press do not permit a State to forbid or proscribe advocacy of the use of force or of law violation except where such advocacy is directed to inciting or producing imminent lawless action and is likely to incite or produce such action.

Improvements to the normative base certainly can be made: while Section 2.1 of the print media Code of Conduct clearly seeks to replicate aspects of the *Brandenburg v. Ohio* rule, it does not include the element that the advocacy in question has been 'directed to' inciting or producing lawless action. This absence could expose speakers to prosecution under Section 2.1 even where they did not intend to 'produce' an actionable harm.

44. The international community since 1945 has been creating norms; what is new here is that it is international agencies that are applying these norms.

45. See, e.g., Council of Europe, *The Administration and You*; Amerasinghe, 'The Future of International Administrative Law, p. 773; Price and Krug, *The Enabling Environment for Free and Independent Media*.

46. Article 6.1 states 'In the determination of his civil rights and obligations or of any criminal charge against him, everyone is entitled to a fair and public hearing within a reasonable time by an independent and impartial tribunal established by law.' A recent ECtHR judgement construing and applying this provision is *Lauko v. Slovakia* (unreported, 2 September 1998), paras. 56–8. In our opinion, there is little doubt that the module's prosecutorial process presents a determination of a person's 'civil rights and obligations' or of 'criminal charges against him' and therefore implicates Article 6.1. For one thing, it is likely that these proceedings would be viewed as 'criminal' in nature for purposes of Article 6.1. Here, of particular note are the facts that the SRSG Regulations are generally applicable and that the TMC identifies the purposes of its monetary sanctions as 'punitive' and 'deterrent' – factors that the ECtHR has found determinative in concluding that Article 6.1 is implicated. Even if the TMC proceedings are not criminal in nature, it is likely that they would satisfy the 'civil rights and obligations' standard in Article 6.1. In its case law, the ECtHR has ruled that administrative proceedings that may result in a negative impact on a person's business, property, or conduct of a profession will implicate Article 6.1. See Harris et al., *Law of the European Convention* pp. 174–95.

Meanwhile, it is important to note as well that the MAB itself has concluded that it is bound to observe the standards of Article 6.1. See the MAB's decision in *Belul Beqaj and the Newspaper Dita, Appellant and Temporary Media Commissioner, OSCE, Respondent*, paras 62–7.

47. See Chayes and Chayes, *The New Sovereignty*, pp. 22–8. See also Helfer and Slaughter, 'Toward a Theory', p. 287.

48. Much of the tone can be attributed to the approach of Simon Haselock, who had been an architect of information intervention in Bosnia Herzegovina and then became Temporary Media Commissioner in Kosovo in August 2000.

49. TMC, 'Sanctioning Decision on *Epoka e Re*', para. 8.

50. Office of Media Appeals Board, 'Altering Photographs'. Online at the OSCE Mission in Kosovo website: http://www.osce.org/kosovo

51. TMC, 'Sanctioning Decision on *Epoka e Re*', para. 10(a).

52. MAB decision in *Sylejman Aliu and the Newspaper Bota Sot, Appellant and Temporary Media Commission, OSCE, Respondent*, paras 11–16.
53. Copy on file with the authors.
54. Regarding party affiliation, see: 'President, Kosovo Party Leader Discuss Macedonia Border Situation', BBC Summary of World Broadcasts, 16 March 2001; and David Holley, 'Yugoslavia Power Changes Hands', *Los Angeles Times*, 7 October 2000.
55. The first case was the TMC's 20 July 2000 sanctioning decision against the newspaper *Dita* and its publisher, Belul Beqaj, in which a fine of DEM 25,000 was imposed. This decision was appealed to the MAB, which reversed the TMC's decision on procedural grounds: *Belul Beqaj and the Newspaper Dita, Appellant and Temporary Media Commissioner, OSCE, Respondent*. The second case involved the TMC's sanctioning decision of 1 December 2000 (following an MHB decision dated 13 November 2000) against the newspaper *Bota Sot* and its publisher, Sylejman Aliu, in which a fine of DEM 50,000 was imposed. This decision was appealed to the MAB, which in a 19 February 2001 decision upheld the TMC's action: *Sylejman Aliu and the Newspaper Bota Sot, Appellant and Temporary Media Commission, OSCE, Respondent*. The third case was the TMC's 20 February 2000 imposition of sanctions (following an MHB decision of 6 December 2000) amounting to DEM 5,000 (along with other remedies) against the newspaper *Epoka e Re*. Sanctioning Decision on *Epoke e Re*. Online at the OSCE Mission in Kosovo website:http://www.osce.org/kosovo. To our knowledge, that decision was not appealed.
    Each of the cases has had a different procedural history. In *Dita*, there was no MHB decision. In *Bota Sot*, there was both an MHB decision and an MAB decision. In *Epoka e Re*, there was an MHB decision, but apparently not an MAB decision.
56. See, for example, Section 2.1 of UNMIK Regulation 2000/37, which authorizes the TMC to impose one or more of the following sanctions: a warning; the requirement to publish a reply, correction or apology; a fine of not less than DM 1,000 and not exceeding DM 100,000; seizure of equipment and/or printed material; and suspension or closure of operations.
57. For recent discussion, see the ECtHR decision in *Tammer v. Estonia* [Application no. 41205/98; Judgement of 6 February 2001], paras 35–8.
58. 'Sanctioning Decision on *Epoka e Re*' (Note 58).
59. Special Representative Executive Decision No. 2000/2 (UNMIK/ED/2000/2, 30 May 2000), cited in the MAB decision in *Belul Beqaj and the Newspaper Dita, Appellant and Temporary Media Commissioner, OSCE, Respondent*, para. 21.
60. It is possible that *Dita*'s acts might have been a violation of existing domestic law in effect at the time, but this was not the articulated basis for the SRSG's action.
61. The equality before the law standard requires that in addition to the right to be heard, that the defendant be placed on an equal footing with the accuser in the process. See Council of Europe, *The Administration and You*, pp. 14–16.
62. MAB decision in *Belul Beqaj and the Newspaper Dita, Appellant and Temporary Media Commissioner, OSCE, Respondent*, para. 65.
63. Ibid., para. 89.
64. Media Hearing Board Rules of Procedure (Note 24). In Bosnia and Herzegovina, of particular importance for procedural considerations is the IMC document entitled 'Procedure for Handling Cases' (adopted 8 December 1998, and amended

9 June 1999 and 21 October 1999), Online [June 2001], available at http://www.imcbih.org/Download/DLRegulations/DLReg/dlreg_3.html

65. SRSG Reg. 2000/37, Section 2.3.

66. Media Hearing Board Rules of Procedure, Section 15 (Note 24).

67. Ibid., Sections 17 ('Absent fraud or intentional malfeasance, the decision of the Board is deemed final and not subject to appeal. Both the TMC and the respondent are bound to the decision.') and 18 ('In [the] event that the ruling favors the respondent, the respondent shall be protected against double-jeopardy, and the TMC shall drop all related complaints stemming from the original complaint.').

68. Ibid., Sections 6, 8, and 11–12.

69. Ibid., Section 7.

70. In Bosnia and Herzegovina, the Enforcement Panel will rule on both the questions of liability and the nature of sanctions if the defendant is guilty. These decisions may be appealed to the IMC Council. 'Regulation for the Independent Media Commission (IMC)' (adopted 16 September 1998, amended 8 September and 21 October 1999), Section 16. Available at http://www.imcbih.org

71. Council of Europe, The Administration and You, pp. 37–43.

72. UNMIK Regulation No. 2000/36, Section 1.1.

73. Ibid., Section 1.2.

74. Harris et al., *Law of the European Convention*, p. 231.

75. Judgement in *Lauko v. Slovakia*, para. 63 (Note 49). See also the discussions of the Court's Article 6.1. case law on this question in Harris et al., pp. 231–4; and van Dijk and van Hoof, *Theory and Practice*, pp. 451–2.

76. According UNMIK Regulation 2000/36, Section 4.2(c), the MAB's power of review is limited to sanctioning decisions of the TMC; in other words, acts of the TMC after the end of the investigation and the MHB hearing. Thus, arbitrary use of the powers of pre-hearing investigation, such as unreasonable searches, are insulated from any review. This is because the MHB is also not competent to rule on these questions, but is limited to deciding the question of the accused's guilt or innocence and making recommendations as to mitigating or aggravating circumstances. 'Media Hearing Board Rules of Procedure' (adopted 7 November 2000), Section 15. Online on the OSCE Mission in Kosovo website, http://www.osce.org/kosovo/

77. The MAB's review power does not appear to extend to decisions of the MHB as to guilt or innocence. See UNMIK Regulation 2000/36, Section 4.2(c) [MAB's review limited to 'sanctions imposed by the Temporary Media Commissioner']; and 'Media Hearing Board Rules of Procedure' (adopted 7 November 2000), Section 17 [decisions of the MHB are not normally subject to appeal]. It is possible that the question of Section 4.2(c) reflects simply a failure to revise UNMIK Regulation 2000/36 following the November 2000 creation of the MHB. However, Section 17 is quite explicit.

78. The MAB, upon reviewing Regulations 2000/36 and 2000/37, has concluded that it is not competent to review acts of the SRSG. See *Belul Beqaj and the Newspaper Dita, Appellant and Temporary Media Commissioner, OSCE, Respondent*, paras 54–6; *Sylejman Aliu and the Newspaper Bota Sot, Appellant and Temporary Media Commission, OSCE, Respondent*, para. 64.

79. 'Report of the Secretary-General on the United Nations Interim Administration Mission in Kosovo', S/1999/779 (12 July 1999), Online [June 2001], available at

http://www.un.org/Docs/sc/reports/1999/s1999779.htm paras. 82–3 include the following:

> UNMIK has the unprecedented opportunity to lay the foundation for democratic and professional media in Kosovo . . . UNMIK will support the emergence of independent media and will monitor compliance with international media standards. The Special Representative will appoint a media regulatory commission to manage the frequency spectrum, establish broadcast and press codes of conduct, and issue licences . . . In facing the challenge of fostering the development of independent media in Kosovo, UNMIK will promote a media culture based on democratic principles.

80. See detailed reports in the contributions of Thompson and De Luce, and of Thompson and Mertus to this volume (Chapters 7 and 9). *The New York Times* disparagingly characterized the module as an 'international media ministry' in 'Kosovo's Incipient Media Ministry' (30 August 1999).

81. On at least one occasion, acts taken in operation of the module have had an impact outside the post-conflict zone. In April 2001, a news distributor in Switzerland, fearing violation of that country's anti-racism laws, decided to discontinue distribution of the newspaper *Bota Sot*. Reportedly, the decision was taken following the TMC's denunciation of *Bota Sot* for published statements regarding the tense situation in the Former Yugoslav Republic of Macedonia. See 'Switzerland: Albanian Paper Banned from Sale for Inciting Ethnic Hatred,' BBC Monitoring World Media Service, 10 April 2001.

SECTION THREE

6

Neutrality and the Negotiation of an Information Order in Cambodia

John Marston

Introduction

In late 1991, representatives of nineteen states participating in the Paris Conference on Cambodia signed a set of accords aimed at ending the convoluted, twenty-year-old conflict in that country. The peace plan intended to establish political reconciliation between the Phnom Penh government of State of Cambodia (SOC) and the three factions of armed resistance – the so-called Coalition Government of Democratic Kampuchea, which also claimed to be the legitimate government of the country. A Supreme National Council (SNC) was established to exercise authority and – equally important – to consent to the exercise of United Nations authority within Cambodia's boundaries. The agreements also outlined the establishment of a peacekeeping force. The force, named, United Nations Transitional Authority in Cambodia (UNTAC), would have civilian and military administrative authority under the direct responsibility of the secretary-general of the United Nations.

This chapter focuses on UNTAC's relationship to the Cambodian media. UNTAC's involvement with the media included its own extensive production of printed materials and broadcast programming, as well as its mandated control over the field of information, which brought it into contact with the SOC Ministry of Information and the different media-producing bodies in the country. Both types of involvement were aimed at facilitating the process of free and fair elections, while the second was also geared toward influencing the long-term institutional development of a free press. From the end of June 1992 to the end of July 1993, I worked in the UNTAC Information/Education Division (referred to informally as 'Info/Ed'). My duties were in the Control Unit, that is, the unit working to implement UNTAC's mandated control over the field of information. I was also in a position to follow the activities of the division's Production Unit.

Cambodian Media before UNTAC

Toward the end of 1992, at the time that the UNTAC Information Division initially attempted to create a media association, the most conspicuous obstacle to its formation was the lack of 'independent' media. The existing institutions of media were situated firmly within the administrative framework of one or another political party or faction. Despite the Paris Agreements, the factions remained hostile to each other, and there was not even sufficient neutral ground for an association to elect officers.

The media in Phnom Penh at this time still primarily consisted of the SOC organs of press, radio, and television. Political divisions still to some extent followed geographical lines. The Khmer People's National Liberation Front (KPNLF), National United Front for an Independent, Neutral, Peaceful and Co-operative Cambodia (known by its French acronym FUNCINPEC) and the Party of Democratic Kampuchea (PDK) had radio facilities broadcasting from Thailand or near the Thai border, and FUNCINPEC was still publishing a bulletin from the border.

Thus, the Cambodian media had changed little from the period 1979 until the 1991 Paris Agreements, when the socialist media based in Phnom Penh were pitted against the media of the tripartite resistance based on the Thai border.[1] The media of the People's Republic of Kampuchea (PRK, which after 1989 would be called State of Cambodia) were socialist and controlled by the State. The media were also economically and politically dependent on a group of countries that identified themselves as socialist, including the Soviet bloc countries and, especially, Vietnam. Many of its journalists belonged to a Soviet-dominated journalists' association, for instance, while Vietnam and other countries sent experts to provide training and technical expertise, and Cambodian journalists were sent to socialist countries for political or journalistic training. The State news agency, SPK, was originally designed to be part of an interlocking system of socialist-bloc news agencies, but this plan fell by the wayside as Soviet influence disintegrated. By the time UNTAC arrived, the Soviet Union no longer existed, and Vietnamese troops and advisors had left. The personnel and structures of the media were still shaped by the socialist system, and were identified with them in the public mind.

The Cambodian media were also socialist in that, following a Leninist model, they had since 1979 fallen under the direction and review of the Commission for Education and Propaganda of the Central Committee of the Revolutionary People's Party of Kampuchea and its successor, the Cambodian People's Party (CPP). Party members sometimes referred to the Commission as the 'brain' of the party. It was the branch responsible for generating and promoting the party's political philosophy. The Commission had a regular weekly meeting in Phnom Penh with representatives of the media to discuss goals. Editors who worked with the Commission now say it did not engage in *a priori* censorship. The heads of the various branches of media were responsible in the eyes of the party for guiding their institutions along the lines that the party directed. However, because of the weight of this responsibility, politically sensitive materials were at least sometimes sent to the Commission for approval prior to publication or broadcast, and major programming decisions were only made with the approval of the Commission. (In 1990, for example, the radio arts division consulted the Commission about whether it could begin broadcasting recordings of the wildly popular pre-1975 balladeer Sin Sisamut, long avoided because of his association with previous regimes.)

During the period between the signing of the Paris Agreements on 23 October 1991 and the deployment of UNTAC civil administration in July 1992, there was significant reshuffling of staff between the Commission for Education and Propaganda and the ministries with which it regularly dealt. This restructuring was aimed at streamlining the Commission and assuring that the party would still be in a position to wield influence once UNTAC assumed authority. The Paris Agreements mandated that UNTAC should have direct control over the field of information in order to ensure 'a neutral political environment for free and fair elections'. However, the Commission was never dissolved during the UNTAC period, and it continued to exert its authority over the SOC media even though the State and the party were, by the Agreements, separate. The SOC media would maintain a clear editorial slant in favour of the CPP and its leaders throughout the pre-election period.

In April 1992, shortly after UNTAC was established, most of the national media institutions that had fallen under the jurisdiction of the Commission were joined into a newly formed Ministry of Information. Dith Munty, the head of the Commission assumed the newly created position of Minister of Information while continuing his roles as head of the Commission and representative to the SNC. The move assured his continued his influence over the Ministry, even if it were forced to separate from the Commission.

Later that April, the SOC parliament passed a media law. Accounts vary as to who wrote the law, but it seems to have been drafted by the SOC Journalists Association in conjunction with the Commission for Education and Propaganda and then channelled through the Ministry of Justice. The law immediately drew fire from the other factions in the SNC, who perceived that it attempted to pre-empt UNTAC's position in relationship to the media and leave SOC in a position to exert its control. While the law did not assign the party an explicit role, it would have given existing SOC administration considerable restrictive power over the media, and, in effect, the power to block the creation of opposition media. (In general, SOC policy did not stress adhering to institutions that functioned along classic Marxist/Leninist lines so much as it tried to ensure a system where order would be maintained and its own figures could maintain their positions of power.) This SOC media law would be one of the first challenges faced by the UNTAC Information/Education Division.

UNTAC and the Structure of Control and Production

The Information/Education Division (Info/Ed) was divided into three units, the Production Unit, the Control Unit, and the Analysis/Assessment Unit. 'Control' and 'Production' are the principal areas of discussion in this essay.[2] The work of the two units constituted an early example of the patterns information intervention would take in UN missions, including what later became known as 'peace broadcasting'. This included establishing an authoritative voice as a neutral alternative; monitoring programming in the existing media; establishing journalistic norms and determining possible violations; and encouraging the development of a more independent and objective media. Despite the mandate of 'control', the goal was formulated from the beginning as 'de-control': not censoring the press but rather effecting a transformation toward greater freedom of the press. This effort at de-control took place while Cambodia was shifting to a market economy. The Division manoeuvred itself to play a role in what could be called a construction of discourse surrounding the elections and political/economic changes taking place – not just the discourse of the United Nations but the discourse of the larger Cambodian society.

Control

The Control Unit was basically trying to set up a media order that would function outside of political or personal domination. One early technique was the creation of a Media Charter, which declared basic principles of the freedom of the press, as well as its basic ethical obligations. This was directly motivated by the need to respond to the SOC press law, as mentioned above, although it was not totally clear what role the Media Charter would play. Many of us in the Unit assumed that the Media Charter would have the force of law or official policy, and might even be enacted by the SNC, to be operative in the administrative zones of all four factions during the UNTAC period and take precedent over the SOC law. It was a disappointment when, in the process of meetings with journalists, political representatives, and UN lawyers, the Charter was reduced to the level of 'guidelines', with no mechanisms for enforcement. Nevertheless, the Media Guidelines were widely distributed and represented what many journalists viewed as the UN's vision of the media's role in Cambodian society. As such they had considerable effect. Certainly they were what we as a unit continued to work for and what we used as the basis of our discussions with journalists about what was and was not appropriate.

The Media Guidelines were remembered and cited by journalists and Ministry of Information officials well into the year following the elections and stood as at least one reference point in ongoing debates. Other UN laws and rules concerning the media were put into effect when a UN penal code and electoral laws were drafted and enacted – to the distress of the Control Unit, which typically learned of the codes after it was too late to lobby for its own perspective. The articles concerning the media in the penal code, in particular, were harsh and very different in spirit from the Media Guidelines and would be used as a basis for imprisoning journalists in the post-UNTAC period. It is fair to say that in practice government bodies and journalists ignored the SOC media law, and, during the UNTAC period itself, the more restrictive measures of the UNTAC Penal Code were never acted on. Perhaps for this reason, there was increasingly room for an independent media to develop.

Another goal of Info/Ed was the creation of a journalists' association that, free from the State and drawing on the media of all factions, would put the task of regulating the media on journalists themselves. The idea was based on a report recommendation given to Info/Ed by UNESCO when UNTAC entered the country. The Control Unit's actual attempts to form a journalists' association, however, were maladroit and totally unrealistic. However, the basic operating assumption – that the formation of a journalists' association free from links to the government was the next logical step in the creation of independent journalism operating within a free-market system – does seem to have been valid. The gestures made by UNTAC in this direction may have laid some groundwork for the post-UNTAC formation of associations and their attempts to define their roles in the Cambodian media environment. Basically, the strategy for the formation of a journalists' association meant little other than the UN declaring that it was formed and calling a mass meeting of journalists to try to get them to discuss its structure and content. The meeting inaugurated the opening of a new Information Centre, where the public could go to read UNTAC materials and the campaign materials of the various parties. It was also timed to coincide with the printing of the Media Guidelines, which were distributed. A deputy director of the electoral division made one memorably eloquent speech, in which he talked about the importance of an independent press at the time of elections. He seemed oblivious to the fact that, at that time, there was virtually *no* media body that could be said to be independent, and that media still only existed within the context of political faction.

So it was not surprising that, when it came time to discuss possible officers for the association, there was no one regarded as sufficiently neutral even to stand as an officer, and no agenda for the association which could be mutually agreed on. This was so obvious to the journalists in attendance that there was not even room for debate. The conclusion of the journalists attending the meeting was that the 'association' should continue to hold meetings and present speakers, but that the UN should be responsible for the content, and no officers should be elected. In effect, they told us that they were not ready for an association but were willing to come to UN seminars. We did hold several more seminars, and on department reports claimed to have formed a journalists' association, but this had little real meaning.

The Control Unit was also, from the beginning, concerned with the task of gathering information about the media. Info/Ed tried to figure out the bureaucratic structures of the various media bodies and to establish a 'Control' presence there by regular visits and attending board meetings. This meant not only establishing a presence in relation to television, radio, and print media in Phnom Penh, but some kind of presence in relation to provincial radio and television, to the national Ministry of Information, and the provincial offices of Information and Culture. For those control officers, like me, who read Khmer, part of our job was to read and assimilate media monitor reports. 'Control' meant that UNTAC, as an outside body, designated as neutral and working to fulfil that role, met with Cambodian media institutions with the aim of making them conform to a vision of politically fair discursive behaviour, both in general terms and in terms of the particular situation of the election. Control's mandate could in theory have made it a significant arbiter of media norms; in practice, it was one authority negotiating with others a practical discursive consensus of what media said and didn't say during the UNTAC period.

For me, particularly in the early days, Control meant learning about newspapers and provincial ministries of information and culture and writing reports about them. Different Control officers were assigned radio, television, and one of two groups of newspapers. I worked with the SOC newspapers, *Kampuchea*, *Prâcheachon*, and *Nokorbal Prâcheachon*. Periodically, I would also go to provincial capitals and write up reports on the information activities there, both the activities of the Provincial Ministry of Information and Culture (the two ministries had not yet been divided as they had at the national level) and whatever information activities the smaller parties were engaged in. I tried to understand the flow of information in the country as it related to UNTAC and the promotion of a neutral political atmosphere.

For a time, at the three newspapers, I primarily devoted myself to interviewing staff and trying to understand their operations. These discussions, we hoped, also constituted something of a dialogue about the nature of media. As part of our mandated control, we asked to be able to sit in on regular editorial meetings. *Prâcheachon*, the CPP party newspaper, simply refused the request. *Kampuchea* and *Nokorbal Prâcheachon* claimed that there were no such meetings. (Months later there was an awkward moment when I stumbled in on one such meeting at Kampuchea. By that point my presence or non-presence seemed academic. I sat in long enough to maintain face, then left.)

Basic policy questions about what should be 'controlled', and in what way, were never answered for the unit as a whole. At what point should members of the Control Unit, as 'controllers' of the media, allow a clear political stance, recognising that the political stands of each party must be freely heard in an election, and at what point do we push for a stance of neutrality, for fear that the media unfairly has a capacity to bias public opinion?

SOC itself made decisions about which of its former bodies should be considered State and which should be considered party, but these distinctions always seemed somewhat arbitrary. There is some indication that CPP had anticipated that UNTAC might take much more control over State mechanisms than it did (and perhaps hoped that State employees would receive UNTAC salaries or that state bodies would be eligible for aid). As it happened, UNTAC never had the power or resources effectively to 'take over' State mechanisms. We felt, in Control, however, that the mandate of the Peace Agreements should give us authority in relation to media institutions. We never made any explicit distinction between 'State' and 'party' media in relation to this authority, perhaps because in most cases this distinction would have seemed arbitrary. Another UN administration might have chosen to distinguish between the *Kampuchea* newspaper and *Prâcheachon* or the opposition Buddhist Liberal Deomcratic Party (BLDP) *Weekly Bulletin*, simply because *Kampuchea* had, shortly before UNTAC entered the country, been declared 'State', but the problems we faced with both kinds of paper were essentially the same.

UNTAC Civil Administration argued that *Nokorbal Prâcheachon*, published by the Ministry of Public Security, should, like the police in general, be totally neutral politically. To me, in late 1992, the paper seemed like one of the few with any editorial vitality, and I would not have wanted totally to squash that energy – even though we pushed the paper when its news stories extended to the point of slanderous attacks on other parties. The situation called for decisions to be made about when we were encouraging neutrality (itself almost impossible to enforce) and when we were merely trying to discourage violations of journalistic ethics (also nearly impossible to enforce). These decisions were never made at a higher level, and those of us on the ground level were forced to flounder or guess intuitively what was appropriate.

We felt that broadcast media needed to be more neutral politically than print media. Since smaller parties had small broadcast facilities on the border, however, and eventually in Phnom Penh, one wondered to what extent it was equitable to insist that the State of Cambodia broadcast media was 'State' and therefore needed to be neutral. In any case, in practical terms the Unit did not have the force to divorce SOC media totally from having an editorial stance. We met regularly with *Nokorbal Prâcheachon* in connection with politically slanted articles that implicated opposition party members in crimes or implied that opposition party members were linked to the Khmer Rouge. The editor sometimes took the tack that what he was printing was accurate, but also gave us to understand that he was at least sometimes under pressure himself – regarding articles about crime or corruption that stepped on powerful people's toes. We came to see our role as sometimes defending him as well as negotiating with him to encourage more politically objective reporting.

My own work was primarily with SOC media, and, indeed, since SOC had the largest media, the work of Control inevitably fell most heavily on it. The Control Unit, however, worked with all parties, including BLDP and FUNCINPEC. BLDP had been the first party to form a bulletin openly in opposition to SOC/CPP. As such, it was both courageous and journalistically amateurish. We were especially concerned, with all the opposition parties, with articles that were expressly anti-Vietnamese and called for the expulsion of the Vietnamese population from Cambodia. For logistical reasons, our unit was not able to conduct much monitoring of radio broadcasting from the Thai-Cambodian border, which, unlike SOC radio, was not translated or summarized by the Foreign Broadcast Information Service. In this way we were more lax in subjecting the parties from the border to 'Control' than we were with SOC/CPP. However, the broadcast range of these stations was quite small, and we knew that they were in some ways operating from a position of weakness in the country. We did, at least, pay token visits to the stations. For example, one Khmer-speaking Control officer to the Liberal Democratic Party (LDP) station and I went to the FUNCINPEC station, which was better equipped than I would have expected (a FUNCINPEC transmitter from the border had been brought to Phnom Penh for the new FUNCINPEC station).

Voice of Democratic Kampuchea (VODC), the Khmer Rouge radio station, refused all requests by UNTAC to visit its station, and the question became irrelevant once it was clear that PDK was withdrawing from the peace process. Later, shortly before the elections, VODC broadcasts were jammed under circumstances that remain unclear. Info/Ed director Timothy Carney, who had always opposed UNTAC jamming on philosophical grounds, now writes, 'I reliably understand that jamming took place on individual, rather than policy or institutional initiative.'[3] The incident is a striking example of the degree to which the information intervention of the time could be ad hoc.

It was the philosophy of the Control Units of UNTAC Civil Administration, as well as Info/Ed, that UNTAC had pre-publication authority – that is to say, that we had the right to see what was going to be printed or broadcast before it came out and to demand that something be changed at that time. In actual practice, it was close to impossible to exercise control before the fact, and we had to be satisfied with lodging complaints about things that had already come out. As the election approached we became increasingly concerned over blatantly partisan television news reports, particularly those which reported on arrests for theft and other crimes and showed ID cards indicating that the arrestee was a member of an opposition political party. Most of these reports also made an assumption of guilt even though the persons in question had not yet been tried.

At one point, the Control officer covering television asked me to come along to broach this issue with television authorities. We decided to tell them in the most straightforward terms that they were prohibited from making broadcasts that were defamatory of other parties in this way. We specifically attempted to conduct *a priori* control, waiting until the Control officer covering television, who made regular visits to the station, had seen a tape of this kind prior to broadcast, in order very clearly and specifically to order that such programmes could not be broadcast. I recall that we very consciously did not check for approval with Info/Ed superiors in the hierarchy, because we suspected that they would not approve of such an overt confrontation, as we attempted to exercise control. We talked to the production manager who referred us to the station manager, who in turn insisted that the only person who could make the decision was the ministry official in charge of radio and television programming. By the time we were allowed to see him the programme had already been broadcast, but we continued to push our statement in no uncertain terms.

This was the start of a period when it became our specific strategy to protest aggressively programming that defamed other parties. We had little real control over this, but it meant that television staff had to confront us and openly defy our position. Our initial efforts were well received in Info/Ed, and we felt that we had clear support to continue doing this. The officer assigned to television ended up leaving UNTAC for a period of time, and in the period leading up to the election, I took over his work at the station. It was something of a cat and mouse game: my coming to the studio, trying to see as much of what was planned for the evening as possible, and to do so trying to wander through as many rooms as possible, in case something was being prepared in a room I was not monitoring. The assumption was always that if anything controversial was about to be aired, television staff would try to keep me from seeing it.

Periodically, something would come up which we could not approve, and I would go through the process of confrontation – to the point that the confrontation itself came to have something of the predictable quality of routine; a sort of agreeing to disagree. I can only remember once where something was changed prior to broadcast. In effect the change in wording we agreed on was nothing more than taking away a reference to a specific party and substituting conventional indirect language that in the socialist period had been used to refer to the party anyway. However, it seemed to us that the kinds of news broadcasts we were protesting were beginning to occur with less frequency, if never totally disappearing. We liked to believe that our tactics were having some effect; this is, of course, difficult to judge.

As the confrontations became more routine, our strategies became more refined. The next step was to begin putting our orders into writing; the step after that was to run back to the office, make a statement for a high Info/Ed official to sign, and bring the signed statement to the television station. These were obvious procedures, but it took time for the obvious to occur to us. Again, this never resulted in the station yielding on a given broadcast, but one could feel the effect of the signed, written document on the nervousness of the lower-level staff. Still, a signed, written document meant nothing unless UNTAC was willing to back it up with force, which it was not – so it was an elaborate game of bluff.

As the elections approached, control activities were often dictated by the electoral schedule itself. Once the official campaign period started, we were preoccupied with simply making sure that UNTAC production materials were played on television, including the televized statements of the different political parties and round-table discussions with representatives of different parties. As the officer in liaison with SOC television, it meant I had to be there at the hour UNTAC materials were scheduled to be broadcast, to be sure they was actually broadcast, and to keep track of which UNTAC tape was actually broadcast on which day.

SOC did not hesitate to broadcast extended speeches by its prime minister, Hun Sen; there was little we could do except send a letter of protest. FUNCINPEC by now had its own small television station which could at least broadcast to the city of Phnom Penh, which meant, on short notice, we were trying to figure out who was in control of programming, what kind of programming they were doing, and what they might be doing that would be questionable.

FUNCINPEC television itself managed to avoid playing the UNTAC tapes until the last minute, giving as an excuse that they did not understand the requirements, or that the tapes had been sent to the main FUNCINPEC office instead of to the television station. FUNCINPEC broadcasts passed the line of political acceptability more than once, when they read on the air letters to the radio which made libellous accusations against CPP figures, or when they interviewed university students on FUNCINPEC television saying that they knew that the Vietnamese controlled the CPP. When we protested they asked us why we were not controlling SOC media. SOC television officials took the similar line of asking me why I was only controlling them when the other side was getting away with murder. Our moral outrage over FUNCINPEC was not too extreme, given that SOC had control over so much more media and had been using it unconscionably against FUNCINPEC and other parties for so long.

UNTAC put up bulletin boards around the country where the various political parties could display their material. In Phnom Penh it was Control who checked the posters – mostly looking for racist, anti-Vietnamese statements and cartoons. After the official campaign period there was a four-day 'cooling off' period, in which there was to be no more campaigning and no political reporting in the broadcast media or, as we interpreted the rules, in newspapers. The large new newspaper *Rasmey Kampuchea* complied under protest and printed blank spaces where the articles had been, with bold headlines announcing that this had been censored by UNTAC. The most blatant violation was *Kâh Sântepheap* newspaper, which not only violated the order, but also printed a sensationalized front page, which made broad, libellous claims against FUNCINPEC and included early 1970s photographs of Sihanouk in the jungle with the Khmer Rouge.

FUNCINPEC staff came to see Timothy Carney immediately, to protest. After deliberating on what to do, he wrote a letter of complaint to the newspaper prohibiting it from putting out the newspaper until they had printed his letter on the front page. This letter was broadcast on Radio UNTAC. It was carefully worded in such a way that it conformed to the media law passed by SOC parliament as well as to UNTAC regulations. To those of us in Control, Carney had always seemed extremely cautious about exercising authority in responses to abuses by the media (too cautious, we felt), so it was cathartic when in this case he acted boldly. Like any such action, it had its costs, and, not too surprisingly, *Kâh Sântepheap* wrote harshly about UNTAC and Info/Ed from that point on.

Production

The other element of Info/Ed was the Production Unit. Its function was to produce UNTAC materials for dissemination to the Cambodian public: radio and television materials, pamphlets and posters, and all kinds of graphic arts needed by the mission. It also had a sub-unit devoted to the dissemination of these materials. Although previous UN missions had had divisions devoted to information, there was little precedent for the scale and the particular focus of the division in UNTAC. No mission had emphasized broadcast media to the extent that UNTAC did. Certainly no previous mission had had its own radio station. No UN mission had ever previously had the mandate to control the field of information in the way that UNTAC did.

Throughout the course of UNTAC, but particularly in the early days, as writers and artists were still determining the nature of their job, all output was extensively vetted for any sign of political bias in the use of language or the situation described or for anything which was not in accord with the wording of the Paris Agreements. Many words had taken on political overtones in the language, and a conscious attempt was made to avoid these words or somehow neutralize their effect. The most often cited examples were the different words for 'the people/the population' which were all politically marked. The word *prâcheachon* was associated with the socialist period and the word *prâcheapolrot* was associated with the Lon Nol period. In order to avoid using one or the other, the decision was made to combine them into a lengthy single compound word *prâcheachonprâcheapolrot*. (A third term, *prâcheareas*, which was associated with the period of monarchy, and literally means 'subjects' of the king, was not included in the compound. As it so happens, this is the term that eventually came into use following the elections.) The text of the Paris Agreements, as translated into Khmer, French, and English became a standard for the wording of UNTAC translations, even where the text's translation was uncolloquial or less than perfect as a translation. Eventually, all the international staff literate in Khmer would be expected to share the duties of vetting scripts.

The Production Unit was divided into sub-units focusing on radio, television, and graphics. Administratively, it was also responsible for an Information Centre that opened in late 1993 as a sort of library in Phnom Penh where the public could go to read UNTAC materials and the materials of the different political staff. Production also had staff devoted exclusively to the process of dissemination of UNTAC materials throughout the country.[4]

Posters and booklets in Khmer were sent through the different UNTAC administrative divisions to each of the districts in the country and each of the cantonment sites. (Other materials would be commissioned by the Electoral Division and sent directly to them.) The broadcast materials produced by UNTAC were made to be broadcast on the television of the existing administrative structures (before UNTAC had its own radio station, it likewise relied on the radio of the existing administrative structures). In the case of television, this meant TVK, the SOC station, and, in the last weeks before the election, FUNCINPEC television. Radio materials were also broadcast on Voice of America, under a special agreement. In addition, Video and audiotapes of UNTAC materials were sent throughout the country, where UNTAC staff in public meetings or information campaigns could use them.

The graphics sub-unit produced posters, banners, booklets, and leaflets. Booklets included comic book editions of the radio dialogues being broadcast on television, and copies, in Khmer, French, and English, of the text of the

Paris Agreements. Graphics designed circular stickers with UNTAC slogans for posting on cars and motorbikes. Later the sub-unit would design similar stickers out of materials that would reflect light and serve as a safety device for bicycle rickshaws. It designed T-shirts that would be worn by electoral staff during the elections. Early materials tended to focus on informing the general public about the general reasons for UNTAC being in Cambodia. Later materials focused more specifically on the mechanics of the election and on making the point that the ballot was genuinely secret.

One of my jobs was vetting the scripts for the video dialogues created by Production. My first week I rode along to watch the filming of a video dialogue in a village on a dirt road in the vicinity of Phnom Penh. The dialogue was filmed at a road straw stall of the sort that is used to sell cigarettes, vegetables, fruits, and sundries in Cambodia. Like all of these dialogues, the actors depicted Khmer peasants (conceived of as being the 'average' Cambodians) in conversation about the UN or issues related to the situation of the UN in Cambodia – in this case the peasants were talking about the right to form associations, with one of the characters at the end of the dialogue humorously announcing that he was going to form an association of cow tenders.

These dialogues were consciously written in simple language and intended to be accessible to Cambodians with little education, a public discourse that nevertheless made a show of relating to the private lives of Cambodians. The early dialogues focused on the reasons for UNTAC being in the country and the specific goals of the various UNTAC components. As the elections approached the dialogues would provide more and more specific information about the election process. Different components of UNTAC would each, for their scheduled weeks, provide a dialogue or the germ of an idea for a dialogue, and this would be extensively reworked until it was a usable script by the Production staff. At a public showing of UNTAC dialogues in north-western Cambodia, an UNTAC officer heard viewers making jokes about the peasant woman on the screen having such beautifully polished nails – unlikely for anyone who did manual labour. A report was written and the nail polish disappeared.

The Production Division was consciously preoccupied with maintaining a stance of neutrality in the video materials. In addition to the video dialogues, the video sub-unit produced 'news magazine' videos with short documentary items about UNTAC and developments relating to UNTAC and the elections. These were filmed in the style of Western news broadcasts they maintained a stance a presenting objective fact and were aimed at an audience with a higher level of sophistication than the dialogues were.

From the beginning, SOC/CPP monitored the contents of UNTAC materials very closely for anything they felt might be prejudicial against them. As early as August 1992, they objected to some video and radio materials that dealt with the issue of human rights, saying they showed SOC/CPP in a negative light. At least one news magazine story, addressing human rights abuses, was refused broadcast by SOC television. From the perspective of the UN, promoting human rights was a neutral agenda, and, more than that, it was part of their mandate to create a neutral political atmosphere in the country. Nevertheless, reports about human rights abuses inevitably showed SOC in a negative light. Materials of this sort, that SOC would not broadcast, nevertheless got some circulation by reason that they were sent around the country and used by UNTAC military and civilian staff in local screenings, and because parallel programming was given on Radio UNTAC.

Even though the Paris Agreements mandated direct control over the field of information, UNTAC in fact had few mechanisms with which to compel any particular course of action if the 'administrative structures' of any of the factions opposed it. While the mandated direct control over the media should logically have meant that UNTAC could show whatever it wanted, it did not in fact really have the power. As I mentioned above, one limitation of the power of UNTAC over the SOC media was the fact that Dith Munty, the Minister of Information, was also on the SNC, the one body that stood over UNTAC.

In early 1993, Info/Ed began a programme of round-table discussions where representatives of different parties (four at a time), would sit on a panel and answer questions about basic political issues that had been given to them in advance. It was a stiff format, falling far short of debate, but one that at least started the process of familiarizing the general public with the names of political parties and their platforms SOC television refused to air these round-tables, maintaining that parties could not make statements on television until the beginning of the official campaign period.

The Paris Agreements mandated that all political parties should have access to the media during the campaign period, and so, during the six-week period that constituted the official campaign period, UNTAC allotted time for the different political parties during the segments of UNTAC programming that were to be aired nightly. The parties were each given the option of submitting a five-minute (later expanded to ten-minute) campaign piece that they had filmed themselves, or to come to the Info/Ed studios to film a short talk by a representative of the party. Most did the latter.

SOC objected to having to broadcast this programming and the issue was debated in the SNC. Eventually, a compromise was reached where there would be thirty minutes (as opposed to an hour) of UNTAC programming per night. (As it turned out, constraints on production capacity made even this thirty-minute segment hard to fill.) The directive ordering television to supply thirty minutes to UNTAC did not state when this time should be supplied, and SOC refused to let UNTAC programming be broadcast at the prime 7:00 p.m. slot. SOC offered the time slot at the end of the day. When UNTAC asked for the time slot before the regular TVK programming, at 5:30 p.m., SOC readily agreed. We would later come to regret having chosen this time slot, since it was a time when most Cambodians had not yet returned from work and when, in many parts of the country, there was no public electricity with which to watch television.

The UNTAC package of campaign talks by different parties was carefully vetted to avoid content that was defamatory or racially inflammatory. There was at least one case where UNTAC asked a political party to retape their segment because of the use of the word *yuan* for Vietnamese in ways that were clearly derogatory. SOC refused to show one or two segments, and on one occasion UNTAC agreed that their complaints were justified. Once UNTAC tapes arrived at TVK, they were sent to SOC/CPP officials for previewing, a process that took time and meant that they were not broadcast according to the schedules that UNTAC had planned.

During the campaign period, SOC/CPP produced campaign dialogues that were similar in style to the UNTAC video dialogues, in what was perhaps an attempt to confuse the viewer into believing that their materials had the UN imprimatur. On the other hand, SOC very much wanted UNTAC material to be clearly identified as such, so that it did not seem to take on the imprimatur of SOC.

Radio UNTAC

From the beginning, it was the policy of UNTAC that radio was the key medium in Cambodia and that UNTAC's attempts to convey its message to the Cambodian people should rely most heavily on radio. This commitment is very much reflected in the amount of energy and resources that UNTAC put into radio. By the time of the elections UNTAC's use of radio came together in a way that captured the imagination of the public, and it became astoundingly popular. It is frequently cited as one of the success stories of UNTAC, and accounts of the period often describe Radio UNTAC as playing a key role in convincing the Cambodian population of the secrecy of the ballot.

In an October resolution the UN Security Council authorized UNTAC to proceed with the radio station, stating that it:

> emphasises, in accordance with article 12 of the Paris Agreements, the importance of the elections being held in a neutral political environment, encourages the Secretary-General and his Special Representative to continue their efforts to create such an environment, and in that context requests, in particular, that the UNTAC radio broadcast facility be established without delay and with access to the whole territory of Cambodia.[5]

It began broadcasting from an old Philips transmitter supplied by SOC on 9 November 1992, with three thirty-minute broadcasts per day. It was not until 12 February 1993 that the time was increased to three 1.5-hour broadcasts per day. On 19 April, six weeks before the election, the station went live, at the same time increasing broadcast time to nine hours a day. Finally on 12 May, less than two weeks before the elections, it increased its broadcast time to fifteen hours a day, a schedule it was able to maintain in the post-election period up until the time that the station went off the air in September 1993.

Zhou Mei writes that the total cost of the radio equipment at the UNTAC studio, its installation and maintenance, was US$3,101,647. UNTAC also set up, at great expense, three relay stations, in Siem Reap, Stung Treng, and Sihanoukville, so that Radio UNTAC could be heard in every possible corner of the country. Because of delays in the contracting process, the technicians hired to install the relay stations did not arrive until February and the relay stations were not operative until April, meaning that they served the mission a matter of weeks prior to the election, and there were times during the campaign period when one or more of the relay stations were not functioning because of technical problems. (After UNTAC left Cambodia, two of these relay stations would be looted, resulting in a loss which one former UN radio staff person estimated as US$750,000. Observers speculated that the looters were probably only interested in reselling the copper wiring for a few thousand dollars.)

Part of the strategy for using radio to get the message of UNTAC out was to distribute free radios throughout the country.[6] If there were times when Radio UNTAC seemed to represent much that was good about the mission, the problems associated with the distribution of radios seemed to represent all the strange complexities of idealism gone amok which was also very much a part of the mission. The used radios all came from Japan, donations generated in mass campaigns organized by the Soka Gakkai, the Social Democratic Party, and the Japanese government. In all they sent 347,804 radios, 849,400 batteries and 1,000 radio cassette recorders. While the staff involved in distributing the radios was dedicated to the task, it is undeniable that it turned out to be a very messy and complicated process, which resonated with the inequities and popular resentments associated with the UNTAC period. The essential irony was that a radio, freely given by Japan, was the equivalent to a month's earnings for most Cambodians. When UNTAC came to rural sites to distribute radios there would be fights for them, sometimes near riots. One report told of a confrontation at an UNTAC warehouse in Kampong Speu where armed soldiers came to demand radios when the rumour circulated that some radios had been withheld. (The rumour was generated by the fact that some non-functioning radios were still in a warehouse.) Incidents like these reminded us that at some level most Cambodians hoped that the UNTAC mission would bestow concrete, material benefit to them as individuals or their families, and there was ultimately resentment when the effects of the UNTAC presence proved to be more intangible.

Despite the problems encountered with the distribution of the radios, Radio UNTAC fared quite well. Measured by the comments of Cambodians in Phnom Penh, the enormous amount of letters to the station requesting songs, and the comments that would eventually appear in the Khmer language press, Radio UNTAC was popular. Its announcers were widely known and talked about. It is not easy to say what it was that 'clicked' with the Cambodian public. Radio UNTAC generated excitement in part because its staff felt and conveyed the excitement of the historical processing they were writing about and

announcing, historical processes which the general public genuinely recognized
as important and exciting.

Early in the mission, the acting head of radio sought interviews with
Cambodian musicians while he was struggling to formulate a plan for choosing
appropriate music, music not associated with one political period or another.
He wanted to explore the idea of whether there was a folk tradition of music
that was politically neutral and could be used for programming. He finally
decided to avoid Cambodian music and instead focus on the music of the
different countries represented by UNTAC in Cambodia. This was probably
the basis of the situation that Zhou Mei, the eventual director of Radio
UNTAC, describes when she writes:

> A potpourri of music would link the bits and pieces together to form a
> programme. In the pioneering days of Radio UNTAC, selection of music
> was very much left to the individual radio producer who very often would
> have to resort to whatever music tapes he/she had brought with him/her
> to Cambodia. The bias was obvious; one could always guess the
> nationality of the producer by the choice of music.[7]

Zhou Mei also describes the slow process of encouraging Cambodian radio
producers to act independently and confidently:

> The nurturing process had been painfully slow. Much depended on their
> receptivity and absorption capacity which seemed warped by fear and
> diffidence. We wanted them to understand why they should not allow
> others – politicians in particular – to intimidate them. If they could learn
> by example, working alongside the international radio team – at end-
> 1992, six; at the time of the election, eight – we hoped that over time, they
> would accept our reassurances why they should not be afraid [. . .] If we
> made any headway in the months before the election, it was at a snail's
> pace. Indeed, the closer we got to the election, the greater their paranoia
> and fear.[8]

No doubt part of the excitement that Radio UNTAC generated came out of
its technical sophistication, the fact that it had the equipment to do things with
radio that other stations did not have, and the ability of the international staff to
use this technical sophistication to push for a fast modern pace. Selections from
the hundreds of letters to Radio UNTAC were read on the air and the radio
encouraged listeners to request songs and dedicate them to people. Whether
because it was something novel, or because, in a tiny way, it represented
empowerment, this programming became enormously popular.

Many international staff have their own Radio UNTAC stories. One
Analysis/Assessment officer likes to tell how she was driving down the road
with the car windows up listening to Radio UNTAC and saw a young man who
was obviously moving his body to the same music she was listening to. Another

one likes to tell how delighted she was when visiting a remote village in Kampong Cham to enter a Buddhist temple and find the monks listening to Dave Brubeck. We should not underestimate the degree to which Radio UNTAC was popular because people came to believe they could trust its reporting. While its reporting was basic, it covered news frankly and tried to avoid assuming a political line. This meant that a field was opened up to say things that had not been possible to say on the radio of either SOC or the armed resistance. Radio UNTAC's programming included radio versions of the same dialogues prepared by the television sub-unit. It also featured news reports and interviews with key people involved in the peace process, both UNTAC personnel and Cambodian officials. Like television, during the official campaign period, Radio UNTAC allotted large blocks of time to give representatives of the twenty political parties equal time to put forward their political viewpoints. In the post-election period, the radio began reporting on larger social and cultural issues.

It is hard to pinpoint when exactly SOC criticism of Radio UNTAC began. Certainly SOC was sensitive to UNTAC's implicit criticism of it in its reporting of human rights abuses, on radio as on television. But it was in the period immediately before the elections that tension flared up. Two cases, in particular, relate to the three days prior to the election that were designated as a 'cooling off' period when there was to be no campaigning and no political reporting in the media.

As mentioned above, Info/Ed responded quickly to a clearly defamatory edition of *Kâh Sântepheap* newspaper during the official 'cooling off' period when political journalism was not allowed. Carney's letter to the newspaper was read over Radio UNTAC. From that time on *Kâh Sântepheap* was unfailingly critical of Radio UNTAC, at one time complaining that it 'controlled' Cambodia. Also during the cooling off period, UNTAC imposed fines on two prominent SOC political figures, Prince Norodom Chakrapong and the mayor of Sihanoukville, Khim Bo, for violations of UNTAC electoral law during the campaign period. A news report about the fines was broadcast on Radio UNTAC, and SOC declared that this itself constituted a violation of the cooling off period, since the report, they said, involved covering political news.

In the period leading up to the election, UNTAC personnel throughout the country were very aware of the vulnerability of the Production Unit and Radio UNTAC. In the aftermath of the election period, political uncertainties could easily erupt into social unrest or lead to the mobilization of the armed forces. Ever since Radio UNTAC had moved into its own building in April it had made a conscious effort to build up security in case it became subject to attacks by the Khmer Rouge or attempts to muzzle it by disgruntled political factions. These security measures were very much initiated by the radio staff themselves and not ordered by the UNTAC senior staff above them. At the request of Radio UNTAC, Ghana Battalion soldiers armed with machine guns were assigned to guard the building at all times. Sandbags were piled in front of the doors so that the building had the look of a fortress preparing for siege. A stockpile of food and water and medical supplies was kept on hand. Staff made certain they had spare generators. Contingency plans were worked out so that if UNTAC's access to radio transmitters was blocked, the radio programming could be micro-waved to Voice of America in Bangkok and broadcast from there.

In the days after the election, UNTAC reported partial returns as votes came in, much as would happen at the time of an election in a Western country. FUNCINPEC radio and television based their reports on UNTAC press releases also. SOC media, however, reported figures based on reports of its own poll observers, and these reports showed CPP at an advantage compared to UNTAC reports. As UNTAC reports came in which showed FUNCINPEC ahead of CPP, moreover, CPP objected, saying that the partial results distorted the outcome of the election in the minds of the population listening to the radio. On 3 May, three days after the election, the CPP broadcast over SOC radio its demand that UNTAC stop broadcasting the results of ballot counts. UNTAC did not comply.

The following day UNTAC received a phone call and, a little later, a hand-written letter, from a person who claimed to have knowledge that SOC troops were making preparations to attack the radio complex. Radio staff, checking on the report, found that there was indeed a tank fuelling up at the place that the caller had indicated. Some fifty UNTAC troops, with their trucks and anti-tank weapons, were called quickly to the scene, and the international press arrived in full force – and there was no attack. There is perhaps no way of knowing for sure whether an attack was averted by the show of UNTAC force, as many radio staff believe, or whether the woman's phone call was an elaborate hoax or paranoid fantasy. The incident does, however, point to the way Radio UNTAC became the locus of very real political tensions at a moment when, in realpolitik terms, the consequences of the election were being determined. Prince Ranariddh's FUNCINPEC Party won the vote with 45.5 per cent, followed by Hun Sen's Cambodian People's Party, and then Buddhist Liberal Democratic Party. After the vote, FUNCINPEC entered into a coalition with the other parties that had participated in the election and a representative 120-member Assembly proceeded to draft and approve a new constitution, which was promulgated on 24 September.

After the vote, the decision was made not to stop broadcasting Radio UNTAC immediately, but to continue through the period in which the new constitution was written. Local radio staff displayed greater and greater confidence. Zhou Mei writes:

> Then came a seemingly miraculous transformation, detectable by late June 1993. By then the post-election chaos on the political front that had threatened to undo all the hard work that went into the historic May 1993 election had been arrested. Tension eased; calm replaced anxiety. The ambivalence of Radio UNTAC's local staff rapidly vanished.[9]

When Radio UNTAC stopped broadcasting in September 1993, it was one of the last UNTAC institutions to cease its operations in the country. In this period, according to Zhou Mei, politicians who had once regarded the radio as anathema now clamoured to be interviewed by its reporters. When it stopped broadcasting, it was the subject of nostalgic articles in some of the local newspapers.

Neutrality

I have suggested, throughout, that a defining aspect of UNTAC was the pursuit of 'neutrality'. The words 'a neutral political atmosphere' was a catch phrase that defined what staff in UNTAC considered their goal, ineffable as it might have been, in preparation for the elections. Neutrality, of course, was never clear cut. The most straightforward meaning of the phrase 'neutral political atmosphere' was simply that the election should take place in an atmosphere where political intimidation was not a consideration – this in itself representing a major challenge, which was never fully achieved. The phrase was not necessarily meant to refer to the neutrality of UNTAC itself, which within UNTAC was more or less taken for granted, but was questioned by SOC and others. In UNTAC's broad usage, 'neutral political atmosphere' did not mean requiring the media to be 'balanced' in relation to the parties standing in the election (though these were also areas in which neutrality was an issue).

Neutrality, in my understanding, ultimately refers to the way, in relation to a historical political moment, societies construct a sense of what types of discourse contribute to the fray and what types stand above it. No cultural construction can be truly neutral and it will always have moral and social costs, which are not neutral to those who experience them. Nevertheless, cultural institutions and discourses can be defined by a society as being 'neutral' in relation to other institutions and discourses that the society defines as in conflict or in opposition. The interest of the particular cultural construction of UNTAC lies in the fact that it was consciously intended to be neutral and consciously strove to promote an atmosphere of neutrality in Cambodia.

The ultimate question for UNTAC was the degree to which it could sufficiently find common ground – neutral ground – among the warring factions to hold an election and help bring about or preserve peace. But to talk about neutrality with regards to the UN means ultimately looking at the question of how the UN constructed its own neutrality. The job descriptions for UNTAC staff, both expatriate and Cambodian, called for them to be above politics, and for at least one former UNTAC staff member reading a draft of this chapter, that was enough to show that the commitment to neutrality was fulfilled. Without meaning to suggest that lack of neutrality ever seriously compromised the mission, I want to suggest that finding neutrality was an active process, constantly being negotiated and redefined. There was, I believe, no perfectly natural or logical stance of neutrality, and almost any stance, if examined with sufficient scrutiny, could be subject to attack. To that extent neutrality was always an artifice; however, it was a necessary artifice.

It was UN policy, because of its stance of neutrality, that Cambodians should not be put in positions where they had to make political decisions. Inevitably, there was no way this line could be drawn in any clear-cut fashion, particularly since non-speakers of Khmer ended up being so dependent on Cambodians. Even a translator was subtly shaping policy in the process of translating. In Info/Ed the expatriate staff tended to be suspicious of the degree to which Cambodian staff had more links to the factions than they were letting on; there is little question but that the local staff at Info/Ed included Cambodians who were reporting back to different parties. We took this for granted and tried to keep more sensitive documents tucked away in locked drawers. But we had no desire to draw sharp barriers between us and Cambodian staff. We listened to what they had to say and were affected by it just as they listened to what we had to say and, presumably, were affected by it.

Production materials generated by Info/Ed were required to be 'neutral'. This meant different things in different contexts. It could mean searching for styles of language that did not seem biased in one direction or another, often a difficult task; it meant euphemizing certain tensions; it meant using 'international' styles instead of Khmer styles (of music, of writing, of graphics, of editing) or trying to find Khmer styles that could be seen as politically neutral. Other times neutrality meant letting *all* the different parties have a voice. In Control we tried to push for objectivity. We would have liked the media to present both points of view on an issue (we never accomplished that). We would have liked them to be neutral to the point of not telling blatant lies about each other. We pushed for what we thought were international standards of the press, in the hopes that this would represent a kind of objectivity. Ultimately, however necessary it was, this push towards neutrality was not without a constructed quality. The slippery quality of neutrality perhaps had to do with the degree to which it was inevitably defined by what it was not or by the fact that the politics it was defined against were constantly changing – once PDK withdrew from the peace process was UNTAC still to be neutral in relation to it? It also had to do with the fact that there was some ambiguity about UNTAC itself. Was it the instrument of SNC, of the community of nations, or a symbol of abstract justice and rationality? Was it a symbol of the march toward 'progress' and industrialized modernity? The search for a public stance of neutrality required in some fashion ignoring or distorting the ground-level realities of what simply was not and could not be neutral, but it did so for a solid and valid purpose.

Aftermath

With the withdrawal of the Party of Democratic Kampuchea, the UN-sponsored elections did not really bring about peace, and low-scale Khmer Rouge guerrilla warfare continued for several years. However, the UN mission did result in a government that the international community could recognize. This, along with the loss of its coalition partners, put the Democratic Kampuchea resistance in an increasingly weak position, and, after a series of defections by Khmer Rouge military leaders, a peace settlement was finally reached five years later, in late 1998.

While FUNCINPEC 'won' the UNTAC elections with a plurality of votes, CPP's realpolitik control of the country put it in a position to push for a power-sharing agreement. In time, serious tensions would arise between the two parties, and the FUNCINPEC first prime minister was overthrown in a 1997 coup. Elections were held again in 1998 and this time CPP won the plurality – although demonstrations after these elections put FUNCINPEC in a position to negotiate, perhaps more cynically than in 1993, for a share of the spoils as it co-operated with CPP.

The Cambodian National Election Commission (NEC), in charge of the 1998 elections, used many techniques that UNTAC had. With international funding, NEC once again produced television and radio programming explaining voting procedures, emphasizing the secrecy of the ballot, and calling on the public to resist intimidation in deciding their vote. Once again, voter information was dramatized in folksy dialogues between Cambodian peasants, with one of the principal UNTAC actresses taking the same role she had five years previously.

Paid political advertizing was not allowed and, following the format used by UNTAC, parties presented their arguments in panels with slots of equal time on State radio and television. This was highly criticized by human rights organizations and the major opposition parties, who saw it as limiting their access to the media.[10] The critics were right in that the mere possibility of opposition parties speaking on broadcast media, which had been so dramatic at the time of UNTAC, was no longer enough. The big difference in the access to the media, however, was the fact that whereas FUNCINPEC briefly had small radio and television stations in 1993, there was no broadcast media affiliated with a major party since the 1997 coup other than CPP. The most significant new political party, the Sam Rainsy Party, had specifically been denied a licence for a radio station.

The evidence of impact from Control's contact with the media is much more intangible. Two of its major projects, the creation of a journalists' association and the formulation of the Media Guidelines, probably relate in general ways to the momentum that created a journalists' association in 1993, and the debate surrounding the draft of a new press law in 1994. Neither development had direct links to UNTAC activities, except that the Media Guidelines was one document circulated and discussed at the time that journalists were lobbying against the new press law. The goals UNTAC pursued, in any case, remain elusive. The activities of the three journalists' associations in operation at the time of the 1997 coup decreased significantly when the US cut off all non-humanitarian aid to the country, which had been a major source of funding for the associations. They were minimally functional as of summer 2000.

The most profound changes in the media during the UNTAC period had to do with the shift to a free-market economy. The development of media not affiliated with the State might have occurred whether UNTAC had been there or not – but the sudden appearance of numerous small, independent newspapers during and immediately after UNTAC probably related to an understanding that, since UNTAC did not oppose this and could be appealed to for protection, independent journalism was safer than it had been. Cambodia still has dozens of ragtaggle newspapers, and despite periodic government harassment, there seems to be a general consensus that these newspapers are necessary for a vibrant and free press. On the other hand, the circulation of these diverse voices is largely limited to Phnom Penh. And the more dissident papers, having survived political harassment, show signs of succumbing to economic pressures.

Two English-language newspapers, *The Phnom Penh Post*, started during UNTAC, and *The Cambodia Daily*, started shortly after UNTAC, have been able to maintain a remarkably high level of journalistic quality with insightful and daring reporting of Cambodian politics and social problems. They are widely read by Cambodians as well as by the international community in the country. *The Cambodia Daily* includes Khmer translations of its major articles. While these papers might dispute the contention that they were, in part, shaped by UNTAC, their formation certainly occurred in a period during which the flourishing of an independent press was very much related to the policies implemented by UNTAC.

UNTAC impact on broadcast media is more debatable, except in the general ways the mission helped to speed up the transition to a market economy. Several new radio and television stations have opened. These are commercial in orientation and are frequently joint ventures between foreign companies and government or CPP officials. Since 1997 these are all dominated by CPP, with the exception of the small, eccentric Beehive radio station, originally based in a night club and oriented to pop music, whose owner/manager developed a small following when he began to expound his homespun folk wisdom on the air. The existence of this small station demonstrates that it is a very different ball game from what existed prior to UNTAC.

When UNTAC arrived, media was concretely in the hands of the Cambodian People's Party in the large part of the country under the control of SOC and under the administrative mechanisms of the resistance factions in the areas along the border, which they controlled. During the nineteen months that UNTAC was present in Cambodia, the media developed in several specific directions. Political factions and parties that had never before been permitted to function in Phnom Penh established a media presence there along with the media of State of Cambodia (SOC). Soon after that a non-State/non-party media arose which attempted to function within the framework of a free-market economy. Although there were some significant developments during 1992, such as the emergence of a range of political party bulletins, in the five months between the beginning of 1993 and the May elections many new, independent organs of media appeared. At the same time, the political changes taking place during the UNTAC period accelerated away from the influence on the media of Soviet bloc countries (and Vietnam) and toward, on the one hand, nationalism, and on the other hand, the influence of ASEAN countries and the West.

UNTAC constructed its own stance of neutrality while it tried to effect a more general discourse of neutrality in relation to the elections and long-term Cambodian institutions. In the end it could be only one player negotiating its position in relation to larger historical processes. What can be said is that, regardless of the specific effects of UN intervention, there was a process of change. An election took place that can be judged free and fair. Cambodian media remain very much embedded within the networks of personal and political power that affect all aspects of the society, but they have greater range than they did before UNTAC and, one way or another, the people who disagree without shooting each other are increasing.

Bibliography

Carney, Timothy and Tan, Lian Choo (1993), *Whither Cambodia? Beyond the Election*, Singapore: Institute for Southeast Asian Studies.

Doyle, Michael W. (1995), *UN Peacekeeping in Cambodia: UNTAC's Civil Mandate*, Boulder, CO; London: Lynne Rienner.

Ghosh, Amitav (1994), 'The Global Reservation: Notes Toward an Ethnography of International Peacekeeping', *Cultural Anthropology*, vol. 9, no. 3, pp. 412–22.

Heder, Steve and Ledgerwood, Judy (1996), *Propaganda, Politics and Violence in Cambodia: Democratic Transition under United Nations Peace-Keeping*, Armonk, NY; London: M. E. Sharpe.

Human Rights Watch (1998), 'Cambodia: Fair Elections Not Possible'. vol. 10 (4), June.

Ledgerwood, Judy L. (1998), 'Does Cambodia Exist? Nationalism and Diasporic Constructions of a Homeland', in Mortland (ed.), *Diasporic Identity*, Arlington, VA: American Anthropological Association, pp. 92–112.

Lichty, Lawrence W. and Hoffer, Thomas W. (1978), 'North Vietnam, Khmer, and Laos', in Lent (ed.) *Broadcasting in Asia and the Pacific*, Philadelphia: Temple University Press.

Marston, John (1997), *Cambodia 1991–94: Hierarchy, Neutrality and Etiquettes of Discourse*, Doctoral dissertation, University of Washington.

———— (2000), 'Cambodian News Media', in Kingsbury, Loo, and Payne (eds), *Foreign Devils and Other Journalists*, Clayton, Victoria: Monash Asia Institute, pp. 171–208.

Mei, Zhou (1994), *Radio UNTAC of Cambodia: Winning Ears, Hearts and Minds*, Bangkok: White Lotus.

Paris Conference on Cambodia (1989), 'Organisation of Work, Text Adopted by the Conference at its 4th Plenary Meeting on 1 August, Document CPC/89/4.

Peou, Sorpong (1997), *Conflict Neutralisation in the Cambodian War: From Battlefield to Ballot-Box*, Kuala Lumpur, New York: Oxford University Press.

Ratner, Steven R. (January 1993), 'The Cambodia Settlement Agreements', *The American Journal of International Law*, vol. 87, no. 1, pp. 1–41.

Shawcross, William (1994), *Cambodia's New Deal*, Contemporary Issues Paper #1, Washington, DC: Carnegie Endowment for International Peace.

United Nations (October 1991), Agreements on a Comprehensive Political Settlement of the Cambodian Conflict, Paris.

United Nations Resolution 783 (October 1992), Adopted by the Security Council at its 3,124th Meeting.

Notes

1. In describing the PRK/SOC media as based in Phnom Penh, I don't mean to imply that it was *only* in Phnom Penh. A more detailed description of the media would take into account regional radio and television stations set up in several provinces in the late 1980s as well as a long-time programme of loudspeaker programming functioning in many provinces. A fuller description of the media on the border would also include mention of a United Nations Border Relief Operation-funded newspaper printed there, which came to have a circulation as great as any of the newspapers published inside the country – in itself a comment on the strange economics of the border camps.
2. For descriptions of the Analysis Assessment Unit, see Heder and Ledgerwood, *Propaganda, Politics and Violence* and Marston, *Cambodia 1991–94*.
3. Personal communication, 8 June 2001.
4. I have also relied on Zhou Mei's book *Radio UNTAC of Cambodia* and on interviews I conducted with three radio staff in the two years after UNTAC.
5. United Nations Resolution, 1992.
6. Interestingly, Lichty and Hoffer ('North Vietnam, Khmer, and Laos', p. 119) report that the CIA also had a programme for the mass distribution of transistor radios in the Cambodian countryside in 1970.
7. Mei, *Radio UNTAC of Cambodia*, p. 29.
8. Mei, *Radio UNTAC of Cambodia*, pp. 72–3.
9. Mei, *Radio UNTAC of Cambodia*, p. 73.
10. For example, Human Rights Watch, 'Cambodia'.

Escalating to Success? The Media Intervention in Bosnia and Herzegovina[1]

Mark Thompson and Dan De Luce[2]

Introduction

Local and international witnesses agree that the media were highly influential on public opinion in the former Yugoslavia during the country's terminal crisis and violent disintegration. Regime-controlled media helped create the conditions for war by attacking civic principles, fomenting fear of imminent ethnic assault, and engineering consent. The Serbian regime of Slobodan Milosevic led the propaganda onslaught in 1987, using state television to portray federal Yugoslavia as an anti-Serb construct. These methods elicited rival propaganda in other republics, above all Croatia and Bosnia and Herzegovina (henceforth 'Bosnia' or 'BiH'). After the first multiparty elections in 1990, Bosnia – the only Yugoslav republic without a titular nation – was governed by a coalition of three nationalist parties, representing Muslims (or Bosniaks), Serbs, and Croats. But in April 1992, just before Bosnia was internationally recognized, the Serb party, armed by Belgrade, launched its attack, using terror to wrest control in the north and east of the country. By the end of the year, Croat forces had begun to carve out their own territory. The conflict lasted until September 1995.

With very few exceptions, the mass media in Bosnia were divided along national or ethnic lines throughout the war. A handful of independent outlets, concentrated in the capital Sarajevo, refused to sacrifice professional ethics to political conviction, pressure, or opportunity. The remainder more or less served the various parties to the conflict, who regarded media control as an essential form of political power. Media helped sustain the Bosnian conflict for more than three years, and continue to hinder the establishment of a stable peace.

The Western governments that reluctantly intervened in the Bosnian conflict and that sponsored the 1995 peace agreement were initially slow to recognize the pivotal role of the media in undermining ethnic co-existence. Post-war election victories by the three nationalist parties led NATO member states to invest heavily in various media initiatives in an attempt to break the dominance of the nationalists and to promote civic-minded opposition parties. How the international community sought to overturn the nationalist media monopolies, and how this effort shaped Bosnia's media landscape, is the focus of our interest.

Peacekeeping and Regime Media: Before Dayton

The international community's experience with regime media in former Yugoslavia began in 1992 with the deployment of a multinational peacekeeping mission – the UN Protection Force, known as UNPROFOR, in Croatia and Bosnia. The peacekeepers were charged with an ambitious, controversial mandate in war-torn authoritarian states with relatively sophisticated media. In such an environment, the local government often seeks to exploit formal or informal control over the most influential media outlets to frustrate the actions and purposes of the international mission. This is what happened to UN-PROFOR in the early 1990s, even though it had deployed with the consent of the local 'parties' (both elected and self-declared).

Notwithstanding the prestige of Security Council endorsement and great power support, UNPROFOR was unwilling to counter, let alone trump, the hostile propaganda techniques used against it. By not contesting the propaganda battle, or doing so faint-heartedly, the United Nations in effect pandered to the regime-controlled media, handing them easy victories for public opinion.

UNPROFOR's mission in Bosnia lasted from March 1992 until early 1996. Its relations with domestic and international media were notoriously antagonistic. Many mission members felt that the international media adopted the standpoint of the Bosnian government. For their part, the international media often criticised UNPROFOR for rationalizing a distorted view of the war, equating the sides in conflict and, in particular, palliating the crimes committed by Serb forces.

As in neighbouring Croatia, the UN mission kept local media at arm's length: a curious policy, given that the country was saturated with media-propaganda outlets and that international officials regarded the Bosnians as easily swayed. A British officer who served in the UN military spokesman's office during the winter 1994–5 recalled the lack of co-ordinated UN effort to counter the 'very effective and professional propaganda being churned out by the warring factions'. He noted that the UN needed to alter its entire approach toward media and information dissemination.[3]

This officer left UNPROFOR in March 1995, before the dramatic improvement in the mission's public information work, which began that spring and summer. Paradoxically, this was the period of the mission's greatest failure as well. Hundreds of UN personnel were taken hostage by Serb forces, and the mission was unable or unwilling to defend the country's 'safe areas'. When Serb forces captured the Srebrenica 'safe area' that July and massacred more than 7,000 captives, the mission's reputation sank to its lowest point.

The losses of the Srebrenica and Zepa 'safe areas' led to the mission's withdrawal from the most exposed locations of the country, while Washington's long-awaited entry in the settlement process further removed pressure from the mission. But according to Thant Myint-U, one of the mission's deputy spokespersons at this period, 'the big difference in 1995 was the arrival of [General] Rupert Smith [as UN commander in Bosnia in January 1995], who let the spokesman and others more or less follow this line [transparency], and who himself appreciated that it was not in UNPROFOR's interests to publicly be playing down Bosnian Serb Army harassment.' For the first time, the mission expressed itself frankly about the real situation on the ground, winning a measure of respect from journalists and public credibility though the criticisms did not cease completely. The significant question for the United Nations was why the improved transparency had not occurred during the previous three years. Institutional conservatism and personal errors of judgement provide part of the answer; the remainder must be traced to the reluctance of the great powers to revise their own assumptions about media as a political and social force.

Errors of Omission: Dayton and After

The 'General Framework Agreement for Peace in Bosnia and Herzegovina', known as the Dayton Peace Agreement (henceforth the DPA), was negotiated in November 1995 and signed the following month by the country's nominal, Bosniak-led but internationally recognized government and by the Croatian and Serbian heads of state.

The DPA established a timetable for military stabilization, initially by the separation of forces along the 'inter-entity boundary line', and later by institution-building. This latter process was to culminate in 'free, fair and democratic elections' to consolidate and legitimate the new, postwar state of 'Bosnia and Herzegovina' (no longer The Republic of), comprising two 'Entities' linked by a weak central government. The first, the 'Federation of Bosnia and Herzegovina', comprized an uneasy alliance of territory held by Bosniak and Croat forces. The second, Republika Srpska, owed its existence to massive 'ethnic cleansing' of Muslims and Croats, and was under exclusive Serb control. While a few individuals who had been indicted by the International Criminal Tribunal for the former Yugoslavia (ICTY) were banned from public life, the political parties that had prepared and waged the war, most notoriously the Serb Democratic Party (SDS) and the Croat Democratic Community (HDZ), remained in place.

The United States military's reluctance to put its soldiers at risk in the Balkans had helped prolong conflict in the former Yugoslavia, and it also shaped the flawed terms of the peace. During the negotiations in Dayton, Ohio, the focus of the United States and the rival Balkan leaders was almost exclusively on maps and military provisions. Crucial constitutional matters were neglected.[4] American diplomats devoted a disproportionate amount of time at the peace talks haggling with their own military over details of the peacekeeping mission.[5] The United States negotiators granted broad powers to the NATO-led peacekeeping force to oversee the military annexe, with the force accountable only to the North Atlantic Treaty Organization headquarters. A civilian authority, known as the High Representative, would 'monitor' the implementation of the agreement but would have no say over the military mission. A 'Joint Consultative Committee' would serve as a vague bridge between the High Representative and the peacekeeping force. The first High Representative, former Swedish Prime Minister Carl Bildt, soon discovered that he had to rely primarily on moral persuasion because he had been given no formal powers to enforce the peace agreement. It was a far cry from the Allied Control Council in Germany or the Supreme Commander Allied Powers in Japan after 1945.

The DPA contained next to no provisions about the media. Its drafters essentially chose to ignore the media problem, hoping it could be addressed along the way, or at least prevented from blocking implementation. The chief American negotiator, Richard Holbrooke, has praised the international media for spurring international intervention in Bosnia in 1995, but his own published account of the Dayton talks offers no clue why media were virtually omitted from the agreement. Nor does his own checklist of 'flaws' in the DPA make any mention of media, even though, by early June 1996, he was calling for Bosnian Serb broadcasting to be shut down.[6] The new constitution neither mentioned nor alluded to media or information systems (except, arguably, as we shall see, in the provision that the common state institutions should be responsible for establishing and operating 'common and international communications facilities'). Authority to enact media legislation lay with the Entities and also, within the Federation, with ten territorial units known as 'cantons'. Given the pernicious role played by the media before and during the war, the failure to set out clear regulations for the media sector in the peace agreement represented a drastic oversight that continues to haunt the implementation of the DPA.

The Peace Agreement contained only several assertions about freedom of information and media, related to the electoral process (such as, Annexe 3, Article 1.1). The signatories also committed themselves to 'the prevention and prompt suppression of any written or verbal incitement, through media or otherwise, of ethnic or religious hostility or hatred' (Annexe 7, Article 1.3.b). Responsibility for ensuring respect for these provisions fell to the Organization for Security and Co-operation in Europe (OSCE), charged with preparing and overseeing elections by, at the latest, mid-September 1996; and ultimately to the High Representative, the final authority for interpreting the civilian mandate of the DPA and a sort of viceroy on behalf of the powers sitting on the Peace Implementation Council (PIC).[7]

Yet another international agent, the United Nations, was charged with monitoring and training the civilian police with a staff of unarmed foreign police officers. This awkward diffusion of authority produced contradictory policies and, as this chapter demonstrates, planted the seeds for incessant territorial struggles between rival agencies and international agendas.

The inattention to media undoubtedly suited the Bosnian signatories of the DPA, as well as those from Serbia and Croatia. Although the agreement ended the fighting, it did not extinguish the political ambitions that had produced the fighting and then been radicalized by it over three and a half brutal years. Serb and Croat media in Bosnia were usually sceptical and often contemptuous toward key political obligations under Dayton – such as the right of refugees to return home, respect for electoral process, co-operation with the ICTY in The Hague, and the creation of mixed nationality institutions. They conveyed the views of both the Serb and Croat nationalist regimes inside Bosnia, and also of the neighbouring Serbian and Croatian authorities. While the Bosniak structures based in Sarajevo were less prone to challenge the DPA directly, they too stoutly resisted implementing those provisions that would undermine their own power.

The three Bosnian regimes, as well as the neighboring Serbian and Croatian leaderships, regarded the DPA more as an unwanted and provisional imposition than as a genuine solution. By not convincingly foreclosing any of the contrasting wartime options for Bosnian statehood, the DPA gave the internal regimes every incentive to preserve their control over influential mass media. It followed that the three Bosnian regimes became in some ways even more hostile to the independence of media after the war than they had been during it.

Bosnia was probably the most sophisticated media environment ever to host a major international peace-building mission. As in nearby Slovenia and Macedonia in the early 1990s, a legal and regulatory vacuum made it relatively easy to establish a television station or a newspaper. International donors supported many private media. By summer 1996, with postwar reconstruction barely under way, Bosnia had 145 news publications, ninety-two radio stations, twenty-nine television stations, and six news agencies, concentrated in Sarajevo and other Federation territory. By the end of 1998, the number of broadcasters had jumped to 280.

Despite this proliferation, the three pro-regime broadcasters retained their wartime predominance. By 1998, RTVBiH (Radio-Television Bosnia and Herzegovina) based in Sarajevo, reached some 70 per cent of the country. SRT (*Srpska radio-televizija*, Serb Radio-Television), based in Pale and Banja Luka, could be seen throughout the Republika Srpska and in parts of the Federation, as well. The third giant, Erotel, was a Bosnian Croat broadcaster that facilitated the illegal re-broadcasting of HTV (*Hrvatska televizija*), Croatia's State television network, across much of Bosnia.

In different degrees, political authorities opposed to the full implementation of the DPA controlled these networks. Yet the agreement gave little foundation for international officials to tackle this situation effectively. Still worse, organizations charged with overseeing the Peace Agreement seemed determined not to use the powers at their disposal. Under Annexe 1-A of the DPA, IFOR had 'the right to utilise such means and services as required to ensure its full ability to communicate and shall have the right to the unrestricted use of all of the electromagnetic spectrum for this purpose'. Thus, IFOR could have established regulatory authority over the frequency spectrum, or launched a television channel to support the wider humanitarian and institution-building objectives of the DPA, just as it could have shut down SRT (as Holbrooke apparently recommended in vain), or regulated the rebroadcasting of HTV.[8] These options were either rejected prematurely or not considered at all, presumably because they contradicted IFOR's guiding principle of incurring minimal risk to military personnel – a priority that entailed minimal support for civilian tasks.[9]

IFOR, SFOR, and Public Information

On 20 December 1995, the United Nations transferred its authority in Bosnia to the NATO-led Implementation Force (IFOR), which was to implement the military provisions of the DPA. A year later, IFOR became SFOR (Stabilization Force).

Relations between UNPROFOR's civilian and military media operations had sometimes been strained, with the military seeing their civilian counterparts as inefficient, and civilians feeling that the military were manipulative. According to an official United States assessment, NATO was determined to avoid a repetition of UNPROFOR's misadventures with the media, noting the need for a 'proactive [public information] policy', as well as a need to 'dissociate itself' from the UNPROFOR mission.[10] Thus, IFOR, then SFOR, mounted the biggest and costliest public information operation in Bosnia.

Nevertheless the IFOR Information Campaign (IIC) reproduced some of UNPROFOR's principal errors, in particular its reluctance to identify and criticize Bosnian leaders who undermined the Peace Agreement. Not only did the IIC 'not undertake efforts to directly refute the factions' regular disinformation efforts'; it even censored itself rather than imply criticism.[11]

One reason IFOR fell into the same errors as UNPROFOR is that both organizations used strategies that had been developed in and for contexts that were remote from the Balkans. Like the United Nations' doctrine of media relations as practised by field missions, NATO's psychological operations had originated in 'third-world countries with relatively low literacy levels [unlike] Bosnia and Herzegovina where the population is literate, relatively well-educated, and is used to most forms of media that characterise the "information society" '. Military conventions and doctrines about public information provide another explanation. For example, SFOR's effectiveness in influencing Bosnians was hampered by the reluctance to work with indigenous media, a centralized authority that prevented field personnel (who best knew what messages would be effective) from generating public information material, and a failure to co-ordinate the activity of major troop-contributing countries, especially the United States, the United Kingdom, and France.[12]

The High Representative and his press officers proved much more willing to name those political elements obstructing the implementation of the Peace Agreement and to speak bluntly about the problems facing the international community. Frustrated at NATO's approach to its peacekeeping duties, Bildt openly called on NATO states to take action to arrest indicted war criminals.

Media and Elections

The powers sponsoring the peace agreement, particularly the United States, claimed to believe that early elections would erode the influence of the nationalist leaders that had waged war and reduce the need for an expensive peacekeeping presence. The head of the OSCE mission, United States diplomat Robert Frowick, came under intense pressure for his own government to hold elections in the autumn of 1996 despite signs that conditions were not yet ripe. Although opposition parties lacked fair access to the most influential media, the OSCE mission certified that elections could take place.

As part of its remit to provide conditions for free and fair elections in Bosnia, the OSCE mission established the Media Experts Commission (MEC), as well as a network of sub-commissions (MESC), to try and ensure a less biased and manipulative media space throughout the elections. The MEC, an invention of the international agencies in Bosnia, bore no resemblance to regulators or press councils in democratic countries. As a consensus-seeking body staffed by officials with, in some cases, a woefully poor grasp of the principles of freedom of expression, and including broad local representation, the MEC was not configured to ensure equitable media coverage. Without strong backing from the OSCE mission leader and Western governments, the MEC was spineless.

The elections went ahead, according to Holbrooke, 'in an atmosphere poisoned by a media controlled by the same people who had started the war. Advocates of reconciliation in all three communities were intimidated by thugs and overwhelmed by media that carried nothing but racist propaganda.'[13]

Implementing Dayton

Before the election, donor governments had attempted to provide viable alternatives to the nationalist media. Bildt's office launched an ambitious television service, the Open Broadcast Network (OBN), that was supposed to challenge Bosnia's triple monopoly of pro-regime television networks.[14] The OSCE, with Swiss support, started a Free Elections Radio Network, known as Radio FERN, that became the only station broadcasting to the whole country without ethnic orientation. But OBN and Radio FERN could not threaten the predominant reach and influence of the controlled media and were viewed as foreign imports.

The overwhelming victory of the nationalist parties at the 1996 elections was a devastating setback for international efforts to secure a stable peace in Bosnia.

High Representative Carl Bildt and Western governments concluded that more had to be done to counter the nationalist parties' dominance over the airwaves. Dayton-friendly candidates had no chance of prevailing in such a hostile media environment. Efforts to provide alternatives had failed to meet expectations; altogether more serious efforts were needed. The OSCE mission lacked the political weight and the mandate to lead on this issue. Only the High Representative could plausibly do that. Bildt lobbied Western governments for clear authority to reform the two indigenous networks, RTVBiH and SRT, and take action if necessary against inflammatory reports.

In May 1997, the PIC met in Sintra, Portugal, and resolved that more needed to be done to 'encourage independent publishers and broadcasters', in order to prepare the ground 'for the elections [and enable] wider access to information and promote political pluralism'. The Sintra Declaration attempted to encourage independent media in a variety of ways. Crucially, the PIC also signalled that it would no longer tolerate political monopolies exercising editorial control over electronic or print media. Paragraph 70 stated that the Office of the High Representative (OHR) had 'the right to curtail or suspend any media network or programme whose output is in persistent and blatant contravention of either the spirit or letter of the Peace Agreement'. This tough wording was drafted with one propaganda organ in mind: SRT, which had kept up its attacks on the Peace Agreement, ethnic co-existence, Islam, the Pope, and the West while shamelessly promoting its political master – Radovan Karadzic and his hardline SDS. It remained unclear whether the NATO peacekeeping mission, and the cautious United States military bureaucracy that guided it, would be willing to enforce the robust wording of the Sintra Declaration.

OHR and SFOR Act against Propaganda Media

With internal elections due in Republika Srpska during the autumn, a pre-election power struggle escalated over the summer, between 'radicals' based in Pale loyal to wartime leader Radovan Karadzic, and 'moderates' based in Banja Luka under Republika Srpska President Biljana Plavsic, who advocated co-operating with the Western powers. This struggle led to a split between production centres in SRT. The international community firmly backed the Banja Luka faction, which controlled the SRT studio in that city, and awaited, or sought, opportunities to act against the virulent output of SRT's headquarters in Pale, as a way to weaken the pro-Karadzic faction.

The SFOR command remained extremely reluctant to employ its considerable military force against a local broadcaster, however tainted. Relations between SFOR and OHR grew tense, with SFOR military officers expressing fears of a nationalist Serb 'backlash' which they believed could play into the hands of the Karadzic faction. The commander of SFOR, United States General Eric Shinseki, wanted to see every political and diplomatic means exhausted before ordering the seizure of television transmitters.

International criticism of SRT propaganda increased over the summer.[15] OHR issued warnings and demanded SRT appoint a non-partisan governing board, which at the time was chaired by Momcilo Krajisnik, a Karadzic ally and the Serb member of the country's three-person presidency. SRT ignored OHR's protests and kept up vitriolic attacks on President Plavsic, comparing her to Mussolini. On 14 August 1997, a high ranking United States Senator suggested that United States planes should jam SRT signals while simultaneously transmitting 'broadcasts that depict the true reasons for [the Serb people's] isolation and poor standing in the international community'. The Republika Srpska information minister stated that any United States operation to jam SRT would be considered an act of war.

Several days later, on 18 August, the OHR requested that SRT broadcast a statement to inform the Serb public about the content of the Sintra Declaration and the obligation of leaders on all sides in Bosnia to abide by it. SRT refused. On 20 August, SFOR troops seized control of police stations in the Banja Luka area, allowing Plavsic to pre-empt a possible coup plot and appoint loyal police chiefs. In a fateful report, SRT compared SFOR with the Nazis and referred to them as 'occupying forces'. Adjusting the SFOR acronym to *SS-FOR*, the broadcast alternated images of SFOR soldiers with Second World War German stormtroopers.

In response, on 23 August 1997, the new High Representative, Carlos Westendorp, sent a letter to Krajisnik, demanding that SRT broadcast an OHR statement explaining the Sintra Declaration by 10.00 p.m. that day. Westendorp called the broadcast comparing SFOR to Nazis 'absolutely unacceptable'. He indicated that SFOR might take action by seizing television towers to stop the SRT propaganda against the peace forces. SRT promptly acceded and broadcast the statement before the deadline, though the station complained that the High Representative's actions exceeded the bounds of the DPA, and rebroadcast the clip comparing SFOR to the Nazis. SRT's portrayal of SFOR as Nazis made military intervention virtually inevitable. Now SRT was posing a direct threat to the peacekeeping soldiers and NATO could invoke 'force protection' as the rationale for taking action.

On 24 August, Republika Srpska police units loyal to Plavsic took control of the Kozara transmitter, shutting off the SRT Pale signal from the northern, most populous parts of the Republika Srpska. The same evening, SRT Banja Luka aired its own news programme for the first time. The Clinton administration hailed this move 'to provide objective information to the people of Bosnia', while the Republika Srpska prime minister denounced it as 'open treason'.[16]

A few days later, when Plavsic's faction tried and failed to gain control of police stations in the eastern half of Republika Srpska, United States soldiers in SFOR gained first-hand experience of the dangers of politically-controlled media. On 28 August, American troops deployed around police stations in key towns and seized a television transmitter tower in Udrigovo, a north-eastern town near Tuzla, on the grounds that they were preventing possible clashes between the Plavsic and Karadzic factions. Karadzic's supporters organized stone-throwing crowds that harassed United States soldiers at the transmitter site and elsewhere. In Brcko, American soldiers stationed at the main bridge over the Sava river, which borders Croatia, were hemmed in by several thousand people. Local Serb radio under Karadzic's control incited crowds to 'fight against the occupiers' and to 'kick out the [international supervisor]'. The Americans fired tear gas to try to contain the riot and several soldiers suffered minor injuries.

On 1 September 1997, pursuant to an agreement hammered out between the OHR, SFOR, and the Pale Serbs, SFOR restored the Udrigovo tower to SRT Pale. Included in the agreement were the following conditions: that the Republika Srpska media stop producing inflammatory reports against SFOR and the other international organizations implementing the Dayton Accords; that SRT Pale regularly provide an hour of prime time programming to air political views other than those of the ruling party; that SRT Pale provide the High Representative with a daily half hour of prime time programming to introduce himself and talk about recent developments; and that media in the Republika Srpska agree to abide by all the rules being prepared by a new joint international body, the Media Support Advisory Group (MSAG), to be chaired by OHR.

On 30 August, NATO's North Atlantic Council agreed to the High Representative's request for support to curtail 'any media programme [. . .] whose output is in persistent and blatant contradiction' of the DPA. Thus, NATO had confirmed the coercive potential of paragraph 70 of the Sintra Declaration. The Council also reaffirmed SFOR's intention to 'take necessary measures including the use of force against media inciting attacks on SFOR or other international organisations'. For the first time, the High Representative's warnings to SRT now had the explicit backing of military might. In a further ratcheting-up of pressure, the Pentagon announced on 11 September that it would send three specialized EC-130E aeroplanes to broadcast messages over Republika Srpska in support of peace, and possibly to disrupt SRT programming.

Tensions climaxed in late September. With the Entity elections looming nearer, and the battle for the Republika Srpska's airwaves increasingly bitter, Western diplomats feared the media conflict could lead to more violence and a victory for Karadzic's faction. Serbian President Slobodan Milosevic (the real power broker among the Serbs who clearly favoured Krajisnik) agreed to summon Plavsic and her rival Krajisnik to Belgrade, where they hammered out an agreement establishing a 'fairness doctrine' for SRT Banja Luka and SRT Pale. The two leaders agreed that news programmes should be broadcast from Pale and Banja Luka on alternate days. SRT Pale promptly violated the agreement.

On 28 September, the chief prosecutor of the ICTY, Louise Arbour, gave a press conference in Sarajevo, which was reported by SRT. The news anchor in Pale introduced the report on Arbour's press conference with a commentary claiming that the Tribunal was a political instrument and prejudiced against the

Serbs, and referring to indicted war criminals Karadzic and Mladic as 'national heroes'. The following day, the United Nations mission in Bosnia and Herzegovina (UNMIBH) and ICTY both demanded that SRT apologize to its viewers and to ICTY, and that it rebroadcast the entire press conference with an introduction provided by ICTY. On 30 September, Westendorp publicly endorsed their demands.

That same evening SRT Pale issued an apology, stating:

> SRT in this way wishes to apologise unreservedly for its misrepresentation of a news conference given by the prosecutor of The Hague Tribunal, Louise Arbour. We will read out a statement to this effect made by the prosecutor. The statement will be followed by the complete and unedited footage of the news conference given by Judge Arbour last Friday, during her visit to Bosnia and Herzegovina.

Although OHR representatives told SRT the apology was adequate, it had come too late for NATO, which had decided to act after the distorted coverage of Arbour was broadcast. NATO's Supreme Allied Commander, General Wesley Clark, ordered a reluctant SFOR to take action. The following day, 1 October, Westendorp formally requested SFOR troops to take control of four key SRT transmitters in response to 'persistent and blatant contravention' of the spirit and letter of the DPA.[17] Describing the transmitters as 'under the custody of SFOR', Westendorp said the international community would press for a 'fair editorial approach' at SRT.

No shots were fired and no casualties sustained in the SFOR operation. The much-feared 'backlash' never materialized apart from small protests in Pale by SRT employees and sympathizers elsewhere. SFOR had tolerated SRT's inflammatory programming for more than a year and took action to bolster a favoured political faction shortly before another round of elections. Some Bosnian journalists questioned why SFOR had waited so long to act and why international officials were so willing to entrust the network to another political faction that supported similarly nationalist sentiments.

The ensuing negotiations between the OHR and Plavsic's faction shifted SRT's headquarters to Banja Luka and initiated a process of restructuring the network in which it was determined that the Office of the High Representative would establish the rules for future SRT broadcasts. All politicians had to be removed from SRT's board of directors. The OHR undertook to rewrite SRT's editorial charter and to appoint a transitional international director to oversee reforms. The Pale studio resumed a limited broadcast on 16 October, and continued for two days until SFOR announced a technical inspection of the transmitter at Mount Zep in eastern Republika Srpska. The Pale engineers then sabotaged the transmitter to prevent it being used to carry the Banja Luka signal. The OHR's demands for the return of equipment removed from the transmitter were rejected, but Pale's days as the key to broadcasting influence in the Republika Srpska were over. The Karadzic faction, which had strong ties to the Milosevic regime in neighbouring Serbia, lost the television monopoly that it had used to stifle opposition and sabotage the implementation of the peace agreement. The intervention against SRT was a turning point for Bosnia's political landscape as well as for the international community's approach to the media.

A Strategy Emerges

The dramatic developments over SRT in 1997 highlighted the lack of an international strategy to democratize Bosnian media. Understanding that more was needed than ad hoc, coercive responses to anti-Dayton, anti-international propaganda, the OHR decided to reform the entire regulatory media regime by creating a framework – an architecture of media law – with objective standards and a mechanism to determine whether a media violation occurred and the proper sanction for each violation. A new legal system, with regulatory agencies and enforcement mechanisms, was necessary if the media system was to be disconnected from political parties and democratized.

The Independent Media Commission

On 16 October 1997, in a report to UN secretary-general Kofi Annan, Westendorp announced the intended creation of a new independent Media Standards and Licensing Commission, to provide an 'interim legal framework' for the broadcast media. According to Westendorp, the body would be charged with broadcast licensing and regulation. In its December 1997 meeting in Bonn, the PIC endorsed this idea.

The new framework would include codes of conduct for programme content, modelled on Western European and North American-democratic practices. The proposal provided that these codes would also apply to the press and the Internet. Local authorities had clearly failed to show an interest in reform or fair regulation and the tainted judiciary merely served its political masters. Until state agencies were established (and approved), the Intermediate Commission would establish, regulate, and enforce the codes.

A common international strategy for building a 'Fourth Estate' in Bosnia evolved gradually over the following year. The strategy called for a regulatory framework for radio and television, self-regulation of print media, the promotion of genuine public service broadcasting, legal protections for journalistic inquiry, support for journalism training, public information campaigns to counter the effects of propaganda, and continued donor assistance to independent-minded media.

The PIC's call in Bonn for an 'interim Independent Media Standards and Licensing Commission' resulted in the establishment of the Independent Media Commission, a body tasked with organizing the frequency spectrum and licensing all broadcasters, drawing up codes of practice for electronic and printed media, receiving complaints, monitoring media, and imposing sanctions, up to and including suspension. Its tasks would fall to an indigenous telecommunications agency 'at the earliest feasible time'. The IMC was to be institutionally separate from OHR, though answerable to the High Representative.[18] Symbolising the shift of responsibility for media development from the OSCE, the IMC inherited the MEC's tasks in December 1998.[19]

When the IMC started work in June 1998, Bosnia had 'what may be the densest concentration of radio and television broadcasting in the world', with 280 identified broadcasters using more than 750 transmitters.[20] There was no coherent licensing system for electronic media, no coherent regulatory or legal framework, no rigorous monitoring of content except during pre-election campaigns, no usable protection of intellectual property. Faced with such a jungle, the IMC first set about mapping the flora and fauna. It prepared the first database of broadcasters. It promulgated a Broadcasting Code of Practice and guidelines for pre-election coverage, and helped draft a Press Code for self-regulation (which was adopted by six journalists' organizations in April 1999). In December 1998, the IMC launched its licensing procedures; all broadcasters that wanted to legalize their status had to apply for six-month provisional licences by the end of February 1999. Later, the IMC developed a rule on compliance with copyright obligations (a vital measure to combat airwave piracy), guidelines on accuracy and balance, and on reporting provocative statements (likewise important, given past predominance of venomous polemics), and a definition of public service broadcasting.

The IMC was criticized even before it started work by United States and other media organisations and press, which saw regulation as a dangerous precedent in a society with no tradition of media freedom. (The OSCE's media strategy for Kosovo would be criticized in the same terms, by some of the same people, a year later.) Nationalist media seized on the criticism and wrote articles warning of a conspiracy to muzzle free speech. Fears of draconian, undemocratic intervention proved baseless. The IMC's regulations were modelled on best international practice and placed requirements on licence holders that fell well within the bounds of democratic norms. For the first time in the region, legal access to the airwaves was liberated from political control. Stations had to respect frequency allocation, divulge their financial sponsorship or ownership arrangements and provide programming that avoided incitement to ethnic hatred or violence.[21] But the international criticism raised important questions about the accountability of occupying powers and how the commission would evolve following the withdrawal of the international community.

Recognizing the relative diversity of the print media in Bosnia, the IMC chose to follow European practice and did not assert its authority over publications. Instead, it helped local journalist associations to establish a self-regulatory framework with a voluntary code of ethics and a Press Council. Some prominent editors embraced the notion of self-regulation as a way of pre-empting court battles and promoting better journalistic practice. It is too early to say whether the Council has managed to raise standards or discourage the kind of irresponsible journalism that is often practised in the region. But the IMC has succeeded in raising awareness among journalists in Bosnia that the public's trust must be earned and that professional solidarity is crucial to building press freedom.

The IMC initially avoided confrontation with propagandistic stations and focused on establishing credibility with broadcasters through clear rules of due process. Licence applications were used as an opportunity to educate the public and the broadcasters about European regulatory practice. Its emphasis on procedures and fairness sometimes infuriated other international agencies or political factions, which demanded intervention against stations promoting nationalist parties. Through its arsenal of regulatory carrots and sticks – similar to regulators in democratic countries – the IMC tended to persuade propagandistic stations that it was better to pay a fine or accept an IMC remedy rather than lose the possibility of securing a long-term licence.

The main criticism levelled against the IMC was not that it harassed broadcasters, but that it seemed too timid and too ready to accept the status quo. Too many stations were competing for frequencies, advertising, donor support, and journalistic talent. Piracy remained rampant. Some international agencies, local journalists, and donor governments complained that the IMC had failed to fulfil its promise.

The IMC had been conceived as a temporary body and it was anxious to show its patrons – the United States and the European Union – that it was ready to transfer its authority to an appropriate local agency as soon as possible. But no legitimate successor emerged. In December 1998, the PIC requested the IMC to announce by the end of 1999 a tentative date by which it would lose its international supervisory role and become an indigenous institution. In October 1999, the IMC noted that, while international staff would be reduced, national staff promoted and a successor agency or agencies established in 2000, 'a total hand-over would not be [. . .] possible for a number of years'.[22]

In October 2000, the IMC at last sought to introduce order and rationality to broadcasting, setting out elaborate procedures for the issuing of long-term licences. Only those stations that met a set of strict criteria would be granted long-term licences. Applicants would have to show their stations displayed programming balance and quality, sufficient financial resources, management and marketing skills, and adequate technical standards. Special attention would be paid to those stations that had employed audience research in their programming plans.

The aim of the new rule, the IMC stated, was to ensure the development of 'fair and effective competition' in the BiH media market.[23] In thirteen separate regions, the IMC would conduct a competitive application process that would include public comment. In February 2001, sixty-two stations applied for licences in the Tuzla region, with some stations asking to expand their operations. The IMC issued long-term licences to only twenty and rejected the remainder. At the time of writing, similar competitive procedures were under way elsewhere, and the IMC hoped to complete the process later in 2001.

Some public and private stations under partisan political control will be forced off the air as a result of IMC's new criteria, a development that is long overdue. The IMC has also adopted a tough line on piracy and has begun issuing fines to violators. The results may prove decisive in planting the seeds of a viable broadcasting sector that is more accountable to its audience.

The IMC also played an instrumental role in shaping policy discussions over the future course of the telecommunications sector. Wary of tainted political appointees who dominated the newly-formed Telecommunications Regulatory Agency, the IMC lobbied the High Representative for a single regulatory agency – under interim international supervision – that would oversee the development of both the telecommunications and broadcasting sectors. The proposal met stiff resistance from nationalist parties and from some international civil servants who favoured a more laissez-faire approach. The High Representative endorsed the concept and issued a decision in March 2001 that called for the merger of IMC and the telecommunications regulatory agency into a new body, the Communications Regulatory Agency (CRA).

Regulating HTV

With SRT out of the hands of Karadzic's faction, attention shifted to the inflammatory, ultra-nationalist Croat media broadcasting from western Mostar and neighbouring Croatia. The OHR co-ordinated political pressure on propagandistic media in western Mostar, forcing the resignations of several regime journalists from HTV Mostar – a small television station that broadcast vicious anti-Bosniak reports. The more serious problem in the Croat-controlled areas, however, was a company called Erotel, ostensibly under local ownership but in fact controlled by the Croatian authorities in Zagreb. Despite a token quantity of original programming, its real purpose was to bring all three channels of Croatian state television, HTV, into Bosnia. Using transmission equipment seized by Croatian and Bosnian Croat forces from RTVBiH, along with transmitters it had unlawfully installed, Erotel received and transmitted all three HTV channels throughout most of Bosnia. Hence HRT (*Hrvatska radio-televizija*) was illegally occupying part of the frequency spectrum, a public resource allocated to BiH by the International Telecommunications Union. Owing to this occupation, the RTVBiH signal could not be received in western Herzegovina. Additionally, there was spillover from transmitters inside Croatia, some of them positioned to maximize their penetration of the neighbouring country.

As a result, HTV had a bigger 'footprint' in western, central, and northern Bosnia than any other network serving as a propaganda machine for the Bosnian Croat regime. During the 1996 election campaign, HRT gave exclusive promotion every evening to the HDZ-BiH party, an offshoot of the ruling party in Croatia. At times, the broadcasts used inflammatory language about international organizations and bodies such as SFOR and the Hague Tribunal, portraying them as enemies of the Croat people. Moreover, HRT was violating copyright by broadcasting foreign-produced programmes purchased for transmission in Croatia only. This allowed HRT to gain an unfair share of the Bosnian advertising market, impeding the development of private broadcasting. Finally, this situation effectively deadlocked the reform of RTVBiH into a public service network for the Federation.

Despite these reasons for action, the international community turned a blind eye until the campaign for the September 1998 elections. In August, the MEC ruled that by favouring the HDZ-BiH party, the HTV campaign coverage had violated the 'equitable access' provision of the electoral Rules and Regulations. Faced with unprecedented international pressure co-ordinated between embassies and OSCE missions in Sarajevo and Zagreb, and including the removal of Bosnian Croat candidates from the electoral lists, HTV in Zagreb eventually complied with its obligations during the last four days of campaigning. Immediately after the elections, HTV broadcast an apology for having under international pressure exposed viewers to 'the content of certain [party-political] spots, which in fact reflected the political picture in Bosnia and Herzegovina and not in any way whatsoever the viewpoint of Croatia or HRT'. This statement spoke volumes about HRT's conception of its role.

Following this qualified success, the OHR and IMC worked to keep up pressure on HRT to legalize its transmission in Bosnia. Whereas the military intervention against SRT in 1997 had been improvized in a legal vacuum, international authorities now had a regulatory framework to apply to HRT's illegal practices and propagandistic reporting. Unlike the SRT case, however, there was no viable political faction in Croat community opposed to the ruling nationalist HDZ and Western governments were reluctant to enter into a confrontation that could require more military intervention. The key negotiator on Erotel's side was Jozo Curic, a Herzegovina politician who had been Croatian President Tudjman's spokesman at one period during the war. Occasionally the international negotiators alluded to SFOR, intimating that what had been done to SRT in 1997 could also be done to HRT, but the HDZ saw through the empty threats. In September 1998, the IMC placed the disputed sites, facilities and frequencies under custody, pending an acceptable solution of the issue, and warned Erotel to change its 'editorial practice to ensure that it conforms fully with the IMC Broadcasting Code of Practice'. Nothing changed on the ground.

On 16 December 1998, the IMC raised the stakes, calling for the 'direct rebroadcasting of HRT [. . .] [to] be terminated at the earliest practicable time, when and as RTVBiH is able to organise a Federal television system that meets the needs and rights of the Croat community in BiH'.[24] The IMC also foresaw that one of Federation Television's two channels would be 'predominantly Croat in content', albeit within a unified editorial structure. Despite continued delay, international pressure in Zagreb and Mostar did eventually bring a result: early in 1999, Erotel legalized its corporate status in Bosnia, applied to IMC for a licence, and indicated a readiness to withdraw from part of the frequency spectrum. The IMC said that HTV Channel 3 should be off the air by the end of January 1999, and Channel Two by the end of February. All three channels stayed on air throughout 1999.

Indeed, SFOR military officers had made it clear to the OHR that they did not want to be dragged into another military intervention against a television station, raising the spectre of a Bosnian Croat 'backlash' if such action was taken. The IMC, the SFOR officers said, should resolve the issue through regulatory and diplomatic means. The flawed arrangements in the DPA, which created separate military and civilian international missions, and the United States military's reluctance to take risks played perfectly into the hands of the Croat hardliners.

At the end of 1999, negotiations on Erotel came to a head. The IMC had identified a number of transmitters that were essential to a future Federation public television and demanded that Erotel relinquish control at these sites. At the same time, it offered to licence the rebroadcasting of HTV on one of the freed-up channels, so long as Federation Television presented the request. In effect, the IMC would legalize the transmission of HTV Channel One with its daily freight of Croatian nationalist and one-party propaganda throughout the Federation for an initial period of six months (the term of the IMC's provisional licences), and gave the promise of a 'sympathetic response' to any future request 'by Erotel to expand its operations'.

Loyal to the technique that had succeeded for years, the Croat regime stone-walled again, holding out for Erotel to be guaranteed a full five-year licence. The OHR found itself out on a limb without leverage or backing from Western capitals. Croat arguments for 'linguistic' rights won a sympathetic hearing from some European diplomats who saw parallels in Switzerland or Belgium.[25]

During the autumn, a hairline fracture in the Croat negotiating team widened into a split. Developments in Croatia were decisive: President Tudjman was terminally ill and his party was expected to lose imminent parliamentary and presidential elections. The Bosnian Croat leaders opted to accept the international terms on offer even at the cost of defying Tudjman's inner circle, which still ultimately controlled Erotel. They may have calculated that Tudjman's advisers hoped to use Erotel as a resource in the post-Tudjman era; an arrangement that would have had unforeseeable consequences for the Bosnian Croat leaders themselves. In November 1999, with Tudjman on his deathbed, the IMC took the step of ordering Erotel to 'cease all of its operating activities'. Nothing happened. The order was issued again in December. Again, HTV's three channels stayed on air in Bosnia.

Fearful of taking a step that might harm the electoral chances of the opposition parties in Croatia, United States diplomats in Sarajevo and Zagreb refused to approve cutting off Erotel, despite urgings to the contrary by the High Representative himself, the OSCE, the IMC, and Croatian opposition leaders.

In January 2000, Croatia's electorate threw out the HDZ government and then voted in a president who promised a clean break with Tudjman's policy towards Bosnia. Fortified, the IMC and the OHR pushed for switching off

Erotel's signal. SFOR remained reluctant, but when the IMC informed SFOR officers that its engineers would go ahead with or without military escort, the peacekeeping mission relented. The IMC switched off Erotel's signal on 17 February 2000 with SFOR helicopters carrying the engineers to remote transmitter sites.

Croat leaders claimed their community's cultural identity was under attack. Subsequent reports in the Croatian press claimed the move had been taken with prior agreement of Croatia's new foreign minister. Jelavic and his fellow hardliners protested but Bosnia's Croat citizens suffered no discrimination on the airwaves. Croatian cultural identity remained fully represented by Croatian state television broadcasts. HTV stayed on the air but with a new government in Zagreb, it was no longer a propaganda vehicle for the HDZ party. No violence or mass demonstrations erupted on the streets. In elections held in the autumn of 2000, the HDZ retained its strong position but the IMC action against Erotel did not play an influential role in the campaign.

The delays in acting against Erotel made a mockery of the whole attempt to introduce fair broadcasting regulation and merely strengthened the position of the Bosnian Croat hardline leadership. The episode underlined once again the lack of political will in Western capitals – especially Washington – to back their words with military action.

Towards Public Service Broadcasting

In the aftermath of SFOR's seizure of SRT towers in autumn 1997, British and other Western ambassadors had urged the High Representative to move beyond SRT and launch broadcasting reform throughout the country. Westendorp turned his attention to RTVBiH. This time, he could not invoke the threat of military action as the partisan (pro-SDA, Stranka Demokratske Akcije: Party of Democratic Action) and ethnic (pro-Bosniak) bias in the programming could not be compared to SRT's output, and international support for coercive action would never have been obtained. Westendorp's office opted to promote genuine public service broadcasting reform as a way of breaking the nationalists' control of television and radio.

Lacking concrete leverage, Westendorp spent much time trying to cajole or embarrass Izetbegovic – the Bosniak member of the collective presidency – into embracing European public broadcasting standards, with little effect. The final result of prolonged negotiations was a document that supported admirable principles but set out contradictory paths. The 'Memorandum of Understanding on the Restructuring of RTVBiH' called for the creation of a television for the Federation and the eventual establishment of a country-wide public corporation that would unify the Entity networks. The Federation would gain a 'new public Entity television [. . .] using the necessary technical infrastructure of RTVBiH'. In the longer term, RTVBiH would eventually form a single corporation with SRT, reflecting Bosnia's constitutional structure as a state with two Entities and three 'constituent peoples'. Unauthorized broadcasting of foreign programmes was also banned – a provision intended to stop the illegal rebroadcasting of Croatian and Serbian programmes. Constricted by the narrow constitutional interpretations of the OHR legal department at that time, the memorandum only allowed for a state-wide network through an agreement between the two Entities[26] – an unlikely scenario.

A split that had opened in the hitherto monolithic Bosnian Croat leadership played into Westendorp's hands. Kresimir Zubak, the Croat member of the collective presidency, began to distance himself from his party, the Croat Democratic Community (HDZ-BiH). On 10 June 1998, shortly before he broke away to form a new party, Zubak joined Izetbegovic in signing the memorandum.[27]

The memorandum focused media attention on the need to end political interference in publicly-funded broadcasting and put Izetbegovic's SDA party on the defensive. For the first time, political leaders had to address how a new public broadcasting service ought to be arranged. A process of reform, albeit tenuous, had been launched. But the document's ambiguities planted the seeds for future political conflict and contradictory international policies. Did such a small, impoverished country really require two Entity networks in addition to a state-wide service? How Federation Television would fit into the puzzle remained unclear, and Bosnian Croat nationalists in the HDZ fully exploited this opening.

Zubak's former associates in the HDZ were enraged that he had signed the document, having wanted to preserve the status quo of ethnically separate, politically controlled television. Izetbegovic's adviser, Mirza Hajric, persuaded Westendorp to water down the authority of the proposed international administrator, allowing RTVBiH to 'continue' to operate until new broadcasting services were created. There was no mechanism in the memorandum to prevent or punish political threats to RTVBiH's editorial independence. It was a recipe for delay and obstruction, encouraging Izetbegovic's SDA to believe it could preserve the existing RTVBiH indefinitely.

Momcilo Krajisnik, still the Serb member of the Bosnian presidency, had refused to participate in the negotiations for the Memorandum. He condemned the finished document as a violation of the DPA and refused to sign. The proposed country-wide service was castigated by other Bosnian Serb politicians as yet another plot to impose a centralized, 'unitary' state on the Serb community. The support of moderate Serb representatives was not sought and as a result the memorandum had no defenders in Republika Srpska.

The member states of the PIC, hoping to bolster Bosnia's weak statehood and break the dominance of the nationalist parties, endorsed the public service broadcasting reform in June 1998, calling for a single broadcasting system for the whole country. Less than a year earlier, the OHR had only sought to broadcast public information programming on the local networks. Now it had international backing to redesign the broadcasting system.

The PIC acknowledged the need to link the broadcast sectors in both Entities by something much stronger than the fragile web of the OBN. The form this linkage should take was left to the OHR to decide. In practice, SRT, and probably RTVBiH too, would only 'co-operate' in a country-wide public broadcasting system (PBS) if they were first reformed beyond recognition, removing them from political control and rendering them accountable to the public.

The June statement was amplified at the end of 1998, when the PIC adopted its fullest declaration to date on media reform. This called for legislation on public media that enshrined the principles of editorial independence, religious tolerance and financial transparency, prevented domination by political parties and ensured respect for the interests of Bosnia's three 'constituent peoples'.[28] In effect, the PIC was authorizing an even more intrusive role in media reform and development for the implementing organizations in Bosnia, above all the OHR and OSCE. The Madrid Declaration also called for the creation of a transmission system to service a single PBS.

Shortly after the Memorandum was signed, the High Representative appointed a multi-ethnic board of governors over the objections of Izetbegovic's office, which had tried to pack the board with a loyal majority. The new board, which had a Croat chairman, inherited a poisoned chalice. Insolvent and grossly inefficient, RTVBiH could only survive through the generosity of public enterprises and banks controlled by Izetbegovic's appointees. The morale of the 1,200 employees was dismal. Several members of the RTVBiH trade union leadership had supported and signed the Memorandum, against the wishes of Izetbegovic loyalists.

The board appointed a director of RTVBiH, a Bosniak by nationality, who was supposed to steer the network through the reform process, The new director proved to be an ambiguous asset. As the organizer of Sarajevo's annual film festival, Mirsad Purivatra was able to improve RTVBiH's entertainment programming and to make other cosmetic changes. But he failed to make genuine reforms in the news programming or to recruit non-Bosniaks to top posts. Purivatra opposed the idea of creating a new public broadcasting network and wanted RTVBiH to remain as the state-wide broadcaster, eliding Federation broadcasting: an approach guaranteed to antagonize Bosnian Croats. An international part-time 'adviser' appointed by the OHR, a Slovene television news producer, lacked the authority to carry out the vast restructuring that was required.

The board of governors, increasingly frustrated at their weak position, urged the director to rectify the ethnic, political bias in the news programme and bring in non-Bosniaks to management positions. Their appeals were ignored. Board members accused the OHR and donor governments of failing to support political rhetoric with substantial financial support for the reform project. But donor governments were wary of granting money to a network that had yet to prove its editorial independence. By retaining control of the murky financing of RTVBiH, Izetbegovic's party exerted influence over the editorial and managerial staff.

For their part, the Bosnian Croat leaders continued to demand a separately administered channel as the price of accepting a unified Federation network (RTV FBiH). The Bosniak and Croat politicians could not agree to adopt a law on Federation broadcasting that would turn RTVBiH into RTV FBiH. By January 1999, the board of governors of RTV-BiH fulfilled its obligations to the High Representative and prepared a draft law for a Federation network based on Slovenia's public broadcasting legislation. Neither Bosniak nor Croat nationalists embraced a proposal that would alter the status quo. In the spring of the same year, Bosniak SDA and Croat HDZ representatives in the Federation education ministry negotiated a compromise formula for the draft law in which one channel of the new network would broadcast primarily in the Croatian language. The compromise satisfied the HDZ but raised the danger of separate, partisan editorial operations. Bosniak nationalists in the SDA later disowned the compromise agreed by the education ministry and insisted that RTVBiH be nominated as the permanent state-wide broadcaster. Throughout these negotiations, both the Bosniak and Croat ruling parties in Bosnia spent large sums on the cantonal broadcasters that were under their respective thumbs.

SRT and Public Broadcasting

In Republika Srpska, progress in reforming the broadcast sector had been negligible. On 13 February 1998, under pressure from the OHR and with SFOR still controlling the main transmitters, the government of the Republika Srpska agreed to 'Interim Arrangements' for restructuring SRT in line with European standards of public broadcasting. In April 1998, use of the transmitters was restored to SRT. The following August, the government adopted a mechanism for transparent and reliable funding for SRT. These provisions were to be incorporated in a new law to be adopted by the end of 1998. No law was adopted. Since the July 1998 elections had given the presidency of Republika Srpska to an anti-Western, anti-liberal candidate, Nikola Poplasen, the political atmosphere did not favour reform.

The SFOR action in 1997 had improved the basic quality of SRT's programmes. Yet, although the blatant attacks on the international community and the DPA virtually disappeared from the screen, SRT presented itself as an exclusively Serb broadcaster. The station displayed a clear bias in favour of Plavsic's 'moderate' faction, led by Prime Minister Milorad Dodik. Seeing the Dodik government as a vital partner, the OHR and NATO states raised no objection to the biased programming. Izetbegovic's party accused the OHR of applying double standards by insisting on public service principles for RTVBiH while allowing mono-ethnic, politically-slanted programming at SRT.

The international community paid a price for such political expediency. When Plavsic's shaky coalition began to disintegrate in 1999, SRT started to promote the Socialist Party of Republika Srpska (SPRS), closely tied to Milosevic's ruling Socialist Party in Serbia (SPS). The lack of genuine reform was confirmed during NATO's bombing campaign against FRY in spring 1999, when SRT reverted to its worst practices of disinformation and nationalist propaganda.[29] Shortly after the end of the campaign, the IMC fined SRT the civilized amount of 2,000 Deutschmarks for censorship, broadcasting false information, and publicizing material potentially threatening to public order. The striking lack of progress in reforming SRT has also been attributed to a poor performance by the international supervisor appointed in spring 1998, Dragan Gasic. The station failed to recruit new journalists or non-Serbs to the staff. Bosnia's statehood and criticism of the Milosevic regime in Belgrade was played down or ignored. Given the political effort that had been required to secure SFOR's action against SRT in 1997, the United States became increasingly frustrated with the slow pace of reform and sharply criticised the supervisor's work.

On 31 August 1999 the High Representative issued amendments to the law on RTRS that renamed SRT and went some way to redefining it along public service lines. Exclusive references to the Serb nation were removed and programming would have to represent the ethnic and religious diversity of the Entity and the whole of BiH. These amendments, upholding the principles of editorial independence, financial transparency and cultural pluralism, brought RTRS into line with the commitments that had been made, but not subsequently honoured, in February 1998. RTRS subsequently failed to fulfil the spirit of the amendments and persisted with its mono-ethnic bias. The Dodik government showed no interest in genuine reform and merely competed with political rivals for control of electronic media and RTRS in particular. The Republika Srpska assembly was asked to adopt a new law on RTRS by the deadline of 29 February 2000. The fragmented assembly, which could hardly agree on its agenda, failed to take action. The Bosnian Serb authorities continued to resist any move to integrate the media space, describing it as an attempt to strip Republika Srpska of its autonomy.

The controversial supervisor was forced to resign and a new multi-ethnic board was appointed in the summer of 2000. The OHR retained its seat on the new governing board. Citing the failure of Republika Srpska assembly, High Representative Wolfgang Petritsch instructed the new board to prepare a comprehensive law for RTRS and to draft a strategic plan that would ensure RTRS programming and staff reflected the ethnic and religious diversity of Republika Srpska and BiH citizens. Petritsch's decision made clear that public service broadcasting principles would now apply equally to both Entities. The news programming showed some signs of life and its coverage of events in Serbia improved markedly in the autumn of 2000.

The Creation of PBS

With all three of Bosnia's nationalist regimes continuing to stall on elementary media reform, the OHR took action. In spring 1999, the OHR asked the board of governors at RTVBiH to advise the High Representative on possible frameworks for a new public broadcasting sector. The board submitted a report listing possible options, ranging from minimal co-operation between two separate Entity broadcasters to a modest state-level service or a large, centralized network.[30] In consultations with the OHR, the board members expressed a preference for some kind of state-wide network but acknowledged that financing such a network would be difficult given the political climate and the weak nature of the State authorities under the Dayton Peace Agreement. The OHR concluded that new organizations and laws were required to replace the existing, tainted networks. Legal arguments against state-level broadcasting needed to be extinguished once and for all. Following one of the board's recommendations, OHR decided to impose a modest state-level public broadcaster that would be financially realistic and based on the mutual interests of the Entity broadcasters.

On 30 July 1999, more than a year after Izetbegovic and Zubak had signed the 'Memorandum', the High Representative used his power of decree to establish the Public Broadcasting Service of Bosnia and Herzegovina (PBS BiH) and Radio-Television of the Federation of Bosnia and Herzegovina (RTV FBiH), and called on the national assembly of the Republika Srpska to pass a law 'establishing one public broadcaster for Republika Srpska, which will for all legal purposes succeed to SRT'.

The High Representative's decision broke new ground by ruling that the DPA Constitution for Bosnia provided for a single broadcasting system. He cited Article III.1.h of the constitution, stating, 'establishment and operation of common and international communications facilities' was a responsibility of the State institutions. He also mentioned the 'accepted principle in all established democracies' that the allocation of broadcasting licences is a prerogative of the State.[31] The decision also called for the creation of a State-wide public corporation that would manage the transmission infrastructure. The IMC and OHR hoped the body would generate revenue and foreign investment by offering access to transmission sites for mobile telephone and data transmission services, thereby allowing the new PBS to become self-sufficient. But the DPA's awkward framework, which allowed each Entity to claim ownership over infrastructure on its territory, posed a serious obstacle. The prime ministers of both entities had to agree on the body's formation, meaning the international community would have to persuade or coerce them to choose long-term economic benefit over short-term political control. By the spring of 2001, the transmission corporation had yet to be formed.

Whether the future PBS BiH would be a residual body gasping for air between powerful Entity networks, or a strong centre of unified production that might regenerate Bosnian broadcasting and even nurture civic identity, was a fundamental question that remained to be clarified. The OHR decision asserted that PBS BiH would 'lead [the] co-ordination among public broadcasters [in Bosnia] on issues of mutual interest' and inherit RTVBiH's membership of the European Broadcasting Union (EBU). To gain access to international sport and other valuable programming from abroad, the Entity broadcasters would have to defer to the new PBS – which would have exclusive membership in the EBU. The High Representative said that PBS BiH 'shall produce and broadcast a minimum of at least one hour of current affairs programming per day on radio and television'. By removing legal obstacles to a unified service and by promoting a new framework, the OHR believed that it had provided the means for liquidating the old system and planting the seeds of a new one. An overly optimistic OHR also assumed that civic-minded opposition parties would soon secure an election victory and take responsibility for building a public broadcasting service.

The decision contained a concession to real politik. Adhering to a compromise formula agreed by the Bosniak and Croat representatives in the Federation education ministry, the decision promised that one of the two Federation channels would 'as a rule use the Croatian language' – a weaker formulation than 'predominantly Croat in content', but very likely to mean the same in practice. In an attempt to prevent partisan news programmes, the OHR decision added a provision that required a single, unified news and editorial operation. Apparently desperate for progress in establishing Federation broadcasting, the OHR's cowardly compromise defined content in terms that suited the nationalist factions hostile to democratization.

Actually implementing the sweeping reforms proved much more difficult than issuing principles on paper. The Founding Board of the PBS, with the co-operation of the European Broadcasting Union, arranged for the broadcast of international football matches on the Entity networks. Both networks carried the same neutral PBS logo, an important symbolic step in Republika Srpska. PBS's exclusive coverage of the Sydney Olympic Games was reckoned a notable success, with a multi-ethnic staff of commentators and producers broadcasting to the whole country. But PBS remained an abstraction, without a budget, management or a comprehensive law. It had to rely on the generosity of sceptical Entity networks, OHR diplomacy and donor government funding. Two years after the 1999 decision, PBS had no regular evening news programme.

The nine-member Founding Board, which included three appointees from the BiH presidency, became paralyzed by incessant political pressure. A board for the Federation network was appointed in December 1999 and it named managers who were granted authority over the existing RTVBiH until property was allocated to the new networks. The July 1999 decision had called for a transfer agent, an outside expert who would decide how to transfer the assets of the outgoing RTVBiH to the new Entity Federation and state-level service. OHR struggled to obtain funding for a broadcasting expert and did not succeed until April 2000, hiring John Shearer, a former senior manager and producer at the British Broadcasting Corporation.

Frustrated with political obstruction of PBS, the High Representative, Wolfgang Petritsch, moved to assert greater international authority over the project. In October 2000, Petritsch issued the OHR's 'Second Decision on Restructuring the Public Broadcasting System in Bosnia and Herzegovina'.

This act established 'two new public corporations, the Public Broadcasting Service of Bosnia and Herzegovina, and the Radio and Television of the Federation of Bosnia and Herzegovina, (hereinafter PBS BiH and RTV FBiH)'.

The Second Decision entered into new and significant detail. Where the First Decision of July 1999 had referred offhandedly to 'the stated mission of PBS BiH', the Second Decision articulated that mission in a more ambitious public service programming schedule.[32] PBS would have 'one television channel, and one radio network'. Where the First Decision mentioned only 'a unified news service serving the whole country', Petritsch states that 'PBS BiH Television shall provide, from the outset, a statewide and international news service transmitted simultaneously to both Entities in prime time at a time to be decided seven nights a week as the heart of an evening PBS BiH network schedule'. PBS would also commission programming from Entity broadcasters.

The Second Decision also redefined the all-important matter of national identities or components in the output of Federation broadcasting. The OHR had considered scrapping the whole idea of two channels but feared this would be portrayed as a betrayal of two years of discussions with Croat representatives. The Decision stated that RTV FBiH would be:

> mandated to produce two radio networks, and two channels of television. These services shall be complementary and mixed. Each shall reflect national and cultural diversities, and shall be staffed by people chosen on the basis of the highest professional criteria in accordance with the principle of national equality as expressed by the Constitution of BiH.

This was a clear improvement over the previous definition, quoted above, which would have divided the two Federation channels along linguistic lines.[33]

For the Republika Srpska, the Decision held that 'the development of The Public Company Radio-Television of Republika Srpska Banja Luka (hereinafter RTRS) is a fundamental part of the creation of a public broadcasting system in BiH'. RTRS 'shall broadcast a single radio network, and one television channel'.

The Second Decision illustrated the new High Representative's determination to establish a strong public broadcasting network despite repeated attempts at obstruction. While the Second Decision should be welcomed, it may be over-ambitious. Trying to reconcile the Entity prerogatives and nationalist sensitivities with the broadcasting structure of a normal European democracy, the OHR has come up with a proposal that may be too elaborate and expensive for a small, impoverished country. It will require sorting out the grossly inefficient operations of both Entity networks and scaling back a massive workforce. Laying off hundreds of employees is the one step that the local political parties have studiously avoided. Even if the collection of subscriptions is improved, international assistance will make or break the reform effort. It remains to be seen whether the donor community will be persuaded to pay the €14.5 million that the OHR is seeking to restructure public broadcasting over the period 2001 to 2002. If such a level of donor support is secured, it is far from clear how the network will pay for itself in the long run.

The end of the struggle to reform the broadcast sector is not yet in sight. The OHR's initial approach aimed to set legal and political parameters for public broadcasting. Since 2000, the OHR has moved to assert managerial control over the public broadcasting sector and has employed a team of broadcasting, legal, and financial consultants to accomplish this task. Nationalist Serb and Croat political parties remain hostile to the whole concept of representing Bosnian statehood through a multi-ethnic public broadcaster and continue to insist on separate channels.

Thus far OHR has managed to stop the excesses of the Entity networks, effectively neutralizing the old propaganda. But a healthy alternative has yet to emerge. PBS has yet to launch its evening news programme two years after the High Representative's first decision. The delay raises the question whether the OHR can build a successful network out of the ashes of RTVBiH. The OHR studied the possibility of folding the editorial operation of the Open Broadcast Network (OBN) into PBS but funding collapsed for the OBN. A similar plan for Radio FERN was agreed and launched in the spring of 2001. The future health of PBS will hinge on how the new radio service fares.

International Aid and its Consequences

There is no precise estimate of the vast sums of international aid spent on media projects in Bosnia since November 1995, but it almost certainly outpaces donations for judicial reform, exhumations of mass graves, parliamentary reform, and many other projects. The sum is even larger if media assistance projects throughout former Yugoslavia are considered. The massive amount of international aid has shaped Bosnia's media landscape more than any piece of legislation imposed or amended by the High Representative. Ambitious initiatives such as OBN cost millions and sparked feuds among donor governments. The two principal donors, the United States and the European Union, and numerous smaller donors, have failed to co-ordinate their efforts, sometimes funding competing stations and publications. Further, the United States tendency to fund 'commercial' broadcasters lies in opposition to the European Union's preference to support public service systems, a difference that could have negative effects for the development of PBS.

OBN and Radio FERN

OBN received more funding than any other media project in the region. Although there are no official figures available, those familiar with the project estimate that donors (primarily the United States and the European Union) spent at least US $20 million on the project over a five-year period, and the total may be closer to US $30 million.

Izetbegovic's Bosniak nationalist SDA party made elaborate efforts to undermine OBN, attempting to block its legal registration, deny it frequencies and access to transmission sites. It took the intervention of United States presidential envoy John Kornblum to press Izetbegovic into permitting the scheme to go forward in 1996. Although the SDA's hostility enhanced the OBN's credibility as a neutral news source, it remained a controversial project.

By 1998, with continuing massive injections of assistance, OBN had improved in quality and quantity. It was even pirated by private television stations in Serbia. Yet it was still seen as a rootless import and the nationalist networks attracted much larger audiences. In 2000, donor patience ran out as OBN failed to fulfil its plans for self-sufficiency. While it did succeed in providing a platform for civic-minded and opposition parties as an alternative source of information to nationalist media, donor priorities had shifted to other troubled areas. The station continues to exist, but donor funding has collapsed and it is only a shadow of its former self. The end of international assistance to OBN reflected a shift in the policy priorities of the OHR. Instead of creating a new commercial network to compete with nationalist stations, the OHR decided to concentrate its efforts on reforming the major networks in the hope of creating a unified public broadcasting service.

Radio FERN won praise for its balanced news programming but could not attract sufficient advertising revenue, relying on donor funding to stay on the air. Unlike the OBN project, however, donors and the OSCE managed to forge a common strategy that was designed to preserve the fruits of a multi-year investment. In the spring of 2001, Radio FERN was integrated into the new Public Broadcasting Service, discussed earlier.

By channelling aid into 'media development', the donor governments had one overriding goal: to undermine the nationalist parties and to promote civic-minded opposition parties. Although support for democratization and journalistic inquiry were mentioned as policy goals as well, donor governments approved large expenditures with the hope of creating a new political reality in Bosnia. In municipal and general elections held in 2000, the civic Social Democratic Party did score substantial support and managed to prevent the Bosniak nationalist SDA from securing a majority of the Bosniak vote. But considering the amount of money and effort devoted to assisting 'independent' media, the electoral results appear disappointing. The Croat nationalist HDZ and the Serb nationalist SDS won a plurality of votes among their respective ethnic constituencies in the general elections held in the autumn of 2000. Perhaps donor governments had placed unrealistic expectations on the potential benefits of media assistance. Massive infusions of international aid did not always inspire quality journalism and instead encouraged blatantly biased reporting by media outlets catering to the international agenda.

There is no question that international funding has cultivated a degree of pluralism, however tenuous. The kiosks in the street offer Bosnians a real range of news and opinions, including fierce criticism of the government and the international community. Indeed, Bosnian journalists enjoyed more freedom than their counterparts in Croatia and Serbia until authoritarian regimes in both countries fell from power between December 1999 and October 2000. International assistance, coupled with the presence of the NATO-led peace-keeping mission and numerous international human rights monitors, has enhanced media freedom. Magazines such as *Dani* have even influenced policy decisions by the OHR and other international organizations, for example by forcing the removal of a controversial international envoy in Srebrenica.

Bosnian electronic media offer less choice, but there are alternatives there as well. Balanced news reporting, free of ethnic or political bias, has been broadcast daily on a number of radio stations that carry the local language services of the BBC, Radio Free Europe and Deutsche Welle. This relative pluralism has allowed civic opposition parties to reach voters. International assistance for alternative media may not have delivered political stability but it has killed off the media monopolies enjoyed by the nationalist parties in wartime. Bosnia has also benefited from growing pluralism in neighbouring Serbia and Croatia, where international aid to independent media played an instrumental role in defeating autocratic rule in Belgrade and Zagreb.

The problem, however, is that large sums of international aid simply created too many outlets. There has been no genuine competition for audience or readers because there are no market forces at work. Publishers and broadcasters seek funds and favours from local political authorities or they turn to donor governments for support. Donor governments must share responsibility for this chaos and should not pretend that they have created 'commercial broadcasting'. The same donor governments have had to fund a regulatory agency, the IMC (now the CRA), to make order of the disorder they have helped create. The United States in particular has placed a high priority on assisting private stations and has warned against funding public broadcasters. But tainted stations controlled by oligarchies throughout the former Soviet Union should serve as a clear warning against excessive faith in quasi-commercial broadcasting.

Apart from the confusion created by ad-hoc international aid, prospects for the development of commercial media have been hampered by Bosnia's corrupt and closed economy. Lacking economic reforms, Bosnia has yet to attract significant foreign investment (not counting international aid) in any sector. Local media outlets compete for meagre advertising revenue, with the main sources coming from politically-controlled public enterprises. The commercial aspects of the media sector have received scant attention by policy-makers but that is beginning to change. In autumn 2000, the High Representative suspended the planned privatization of local state-owned media until a thorough review could be conducted to ensure the protection of freedom of expression and fair competition.

Ethics, Defamation, and Journalistic Inquiry

Away from the spotlight of high politics, the OSCE and OHR have worked solidly to promote the rights of journalists, foster professionalism, develop laws and standards that uphold freedom of information and protect journalists, encourage inter-entity contacts, award small grants to independent media, and monitor the media.

After disbanding the MEC in 1998, the OSCE mission to Bosnia's Department of Media Affairs concentrated usefully on fostering media professionalism and the rights of journalists, as well as developing independent media and preparing legislation. In July 1999, the OSCE established a Media Ombudsman in the Federation, operating independently. In the same month, the High Representative imposed a 'Decision on Freedom of Information and Decriminalization of Libel and Defamation', which called on both Entities to adopt legislation to create civil remedies for defamation, libel and slander and repeal criminal sanctions for these offences. In addition, the Decision called for legislation on freedom of information. Both laws were to be drafted under the guidance of OHR and the OSCE.

The Entities failed to act by the end of the year and the OSCE invited foreign legal experts to oversee the drafting of new legislation in consultation with local legal experts. In the autumn of 2000, a majority in the State parliament adopted a Freedom of Information law, which was enthusiastically endorsed by journalists and human rights activists. Surpassing legal standards in many European Union states, the law guarantees open access to information held by governmental or public agencies except for narrowly defined categories. A draft law on defamation, prepared under similar circumstances, was being presented at public hearings in February 2001 and is due for submission to the State and Entity parliaments for debate. The Freedom of Information law in particular carries tremendous potential to transform Bosnia's culture of secrecy inherited from the communist era. It will take a sustained campaign by international agencies as well as a unified, active journalistic community to ensure the letter and spirit of the law are upheld.

These measures reflected concern at the continuing threats and other pressure, including politically motivated defamation cases, against journalists in both Entities and were accompanied by an array of other international community actions aimed at ensuring the protection of journalists. The worst incident was the near-fatal bomb attack on a courageous investigative journalist in Republika Srpska in October 1999. Zeljko Kopanja, the editor of *Nezavisne novine* newspaper in Banja Luka, lost his legs in the bombing after having published stories identifying Serb units involved in wartime atrocities. In February 2000, the OSCE, OHR, IMC, and UNMIBH joined forces to launch a programme intended to protect journalistic inquiry and free speech. The journalists' organisations formed a Press Council to implement the code adopted in April 1999. The OSCE and UNMIBH developed guidelines for the police on treatment of journalists and vice-versa. The OSCE and IMC monitored abuses of authority by public officials. It was the most ambitious co-operation among inter-governmental organizations over Bosnian media, and an encouraging sign of what was possible, albeit four years after Dayton.

However, this programme drew protest from the World Press Freedom Committee (WPFC), a United States-based media watchdog. The WPFC warned that:

> in countries lacking the foundations of democracy – including free and fair popular elections, a free and independent news media and independent courts – mechanisms such as press laws, media councils, and ethics codes have been used routinely as tools of restriction on the free flow of information and news. (World Press Freedom Committee press release, 14 February 2000).

By circulating their objections to the UN Secretary-General, the United States secretary of state, the OSCE Chairperson in Office, and the High Representative, the WPFC's response seemed excessive and out of touch with the harsh conditions facing Bosnian journalists. Legislation proposed and amended at the initiative of the international community has actually increased protections for journalistic freedom and removed draconian provisions. As for a Press Council, it was proposed as a way of pre-empting possible measures by meddlesome politicians, which is how such councils function in some European states.

Yet the WPFC raised a point that is likely to be important for media reform and development strategies in any post-conflict society. By planning a comprehensive framework of protection in a society with no democratic tradition and where law does not rule, international organizations in Sarajevo are wagering that democracy will prevail and that Bosnia's political culture will be transformed. The international community will need to create legal safeguards in Bosnia to ensure local authorities do not abuse its well-intentioned reforms in the future.

In this field as in others, international organizations are trying to compensate for basic flaws in Dayton's substance and implementation. Unarmed investigative reporters in Bosnia run the same physical risks every day that NATO commanders refuse to allow their well-protected professional troops to face. The international community must take a more robust approach to protecting journalists, to ensure their safety from physical, political and judicial harassment.

Conclusions

Post-conflict media restructuring in Bosnia resembles an inverted pyramid. The steadily increasing international engagement, involving the most powerful states in the world, intergovernmental and non-governmental organizations, and multimillion dollar budgets – all dedicated to inventing a democratic media sector – seems to rest on little more than a few sentences in the DPA.

The intervening powers disregarded the role of media in their belated rush to stop the war. This would not have mattered in Berlin in 1878 or Versailles in 1919. In 1995, it was a blindly optimistic or cynical omission. The architects of the DPA must have been aware that the media are a major, contested source of political and social power. The Agreement should have contained strong provisions to democratize the media, rather than simply approved the supreme powers granted to the NATO-led IFOR and the High Representative. In doing so, it reduced international media reformers to searching for loopholes in the DPA in order to foist measures of reform on the ethnically-determined, Dayton-approved Entity and cantonal authorities.

In order to wrest media from the Entity authorities and create central bodies, the High Representative revised the accepted interpretation of Bosnia's Constitution.[34] (Yet why did it take until July 1999 to reach this reinterpretation?) The three nationalist regimes now seem to accept that they can delay but not prevent restructuring of the major broadcasting networks. But they remain determined to control public media and own private media.

There was a price to pay for the years of delay over vital steps of reform. Emigration continued to drain the country's 'human resources'. The opponents of democratization extended their grip on power by adapting to gradual changes and learning from empty threats. Worse yet, the adaptation was mutual. It sometimes seemed that the local authorities were more adroit in moulding their international interlocutors than vice-versa.

Donor funding would have been more effective if it had been delivered in a more well-informed, prudent fashion. Too many quasi-commercial stations were created and remain vulnerable to hostile take-overs. Public service and commercial broadcasting should not be mutually exclusive. One balances the other.

The regulatory framework set up by the IMC was slow in coming but it is a model worth following elsewhere. Fair, non-partisan access to the airwaves is a prerequisite of media freedom. It has been sorely lacking throughout the Balkans because it is a concept that politicians dislike. Broadcasters in Bosnia have grown accustomed to due process and will not relinquish their new freedoms easily.

With privatization looming, the OHR and donor governments will have to focus more attention on the commercial side of the media. Legislation and other measures devised to protect journalistic inquiry will mean little if political mafias control the means of production. The first step in securing media freedom must be to prevent political oligarchies from exerting exclusive authority over advertizing, banking or printing presses. Much time was wasted in Bosnia monitoring inflammatory media reports instead of dismantling the entrenched interests that lay behind them.

For all the misjudgements by the international community, there is something lacking in Bosnian society as well. War without victors or vanquished, the legacy of communist rule, high unemployment and political paralysis have proved a pernicious combination.[35]

In addition, there is no such thing as the pressure of public opinion in Bosnia. There are civic organizations but they seem to be engineered and funded by, and hence to cater to, outside donors. The country remains divided ethnically in every meaningful sense and the media are no exception. A handful of news organizations have tried to defy ethnic categories, but they swim against the tide.

If it is unrealistic to expect the media to overturn the kind of ethnic segregation that dominates the rest of society, the separation of the media from direct political control is a realistic goal. Blatant political bias has been removed or neutralized at the Entity broadcasters. But the nationalist networks have not been replaced with public service broadcasting that meets European standards. It remains to be seen if the OHR and its experts can create an institution that will endure without outside life support and constant crisis management. PBS, like OBN, at times resembles a network in search of a constituency. If it is to succeed, the public broadcasting reform will need more grass roots support from civic-minded journalists and Bosnia's fledgling civil society. It is regrettable that such an ambitious endeavour was not launched immediately after the war, but at that point the international community lacked the necessary will. The temptation to cut costs should be resisted, if recent arduous gains are not to be risked. The future of the country still hangs in the balance.

Bibliography

Bildt, Carl (1998), *Peace Journey*. London: Weidenfeld & Nicolson.

Collins, Steven (summer 1999), 'Army PSYOP in Bosnia: Capabilities and Constraints', in *Parameters* (US Army War College Quarterly), pp. 57–73.

De Luce, Dan (winter 2000–1) 'Media Wars', in *NATO Review*, pp. 16–21.

Holbrooke, Richard (1998), *To End a War*, New York: Random House.

Independent Media Commission White Paper (September 2000), 'Media and Democratisation in Bosnia and Herzegovina' [prepared by Stan Markotich], submitted to the IMC Council on 25 September 2000. Available at www.imcbih.org

Interim Board of Governors of Radio Television BiH (1999), 'Possible Ways of Transforming Public Broadcasting in BiH', Report.

International Crisis Group (July 1999), 'Republika Srpska in the post-Kosovo Era: Collateral Damage and Transformation', Balkans Report no. 71.

Office of the High Representative document: Memorandum of Understanding, June 1998, signed by the High Representative, Members of the BiH Presidency, Alija Izetbegovic, Kresimir Zubak; Representatives of the RTV BiH trade union.

Price, Monroe E. (2000), 'Information Intervention: Bosnia, the Dayton Accords, and the Seizure of Broadcasting Transmitters', *Cornell International Law Journal*, vol. 33, pp. 67–112.

Ripley, Tim (1999), *Operation Deliberate Force. The UN and NATO Campaign in Bosnia 1995*, Lancaster: Centre for Defence and International Security Studies.

Rose, Gideon (January–February 1998), 'The Exit Strategy Delusion', *Foreign Affairs*, no. 77, pp. 56–67.
Siegel, Pascale Combelles (1998), *Target Bosnia: Integrating Information Activities in Peace Operations*, Washington, DC: National Defense University/Institute for National Strategic Studies.
Thompson, Mark (1999), *Forging War. The Media in Serbia, Croatia, Bosnia and Hercegovina*, Luton: University of Luton Press and ARTICLE 19.
———— (2000), *Slovenia, Croatia, Bosnia and Herzegovina, Macedonia (FYROM) and Kosovo. International Assistance to Media*, Vienna: OSCE Representative on Freedom of the Media.
von Merveldt, Lt Col Jan-Dirk (1998), 'UN Media Policy,' pp. 253–61, in Wolfgang Biermann and Martin Vadset (eds), *UN Peacekeeping in Trouble: Lessons Learned from the Former Yugoslavia* (Aldershot, UK: Ashgate, 1998), pp. 256–7.

Notes

1. The phrase 'escalate to success' is borrowed from Tim Ripley's book about the United Nations and NATO in Bosnia in 1995, when General Rupert Smith commanded UN peacekeeping forces. 'To be able to force the warring parties to take it seriously, the UN had to be ready to "escalate to success", otherwise it should leave Bosnia, thought General Smith [in March 1995]. Once embarked on this course, the UN needed to follow through to its logical conclusion, even if this was perceived as infringing the neutrality of the UN mission.' Without claiming any wider analogy with the military intervention in 1995, we believe General Smith's phrase not only explains the dynamic of the media intervention since 1996, but – if we replace the sacred cow of 'impartiality' with the golden calf of 'Dayton' – that it also prescribes how to continue and complete this task. Ripley, *Operation Deliberate Force*, p. 47.
2. This chapter draws on the authors' previous publications on media in Bosnia and Herzegovina (see bibliography).
3. von Merveldt, *UN Peacekeeping*, pp. 256–7.
4. Bildt, *Peace Journey*, pp. 130–6.
5. Holbrooke, *To End a War*, pp. 219–23.
6. Holbrooke, *To End a War*, p. 334, pp. 361–2. Nor Does Bildt's published account (*Peace Journey*) make any mention of this issue coming up at the peace negotiations.
7. The Peace Implementation Council was established in December 1995 and includes all the international signatories to the DPA, with a Steering Board comprising the United States, Russia, France, Germany, the United Kingdom, Japan, Canada, Italy, the European Union Presidency, the European Commission, and Turkey on behalf of the Organization of Islamic Countries.
8. Holbrooke, *To End a War*, p. 344.
9. 'Force protection' denotes the range of measures taken by the different national contingents within SFOR to protect themselves against risk of attack. This was the doctrine that led one commentator to observe: 'The Bosnia deployment [for the US] resembles nothing more than the moon landings, with the principal objective being to send men far away and bring them back safely.' Rose, 'The Exit Strategy Delusion', p. 66.

10. Siegel, *Target Bosnia*, p. 41.
11. Siegel, *Target Bosnia*, p. 92.
12. Collins, 'Army PSYOP in Bosnia', pp. 57–73.
13. Holbrooke, *To End a War*, p. 344.
14. The Office of the High Representative (OHR) managed to get OBN on the air a few days before the September elections but the signal failed to cover the Republika Srpska heartland. The OSCE cited the OBN as helping to fulfil conditions for media pluralism but its practical impact was negligible.
15. See, e.g., articles in *Slobodna Bosna* weekly, 13 July 1997.
16. Reuters (Washington, DC), 25 August 1997, and *Vjesnik*, 26 August 1997.
17. The formal request by the High Representative was not necessary under the terms of the DPA and SFOR could have opted to intervene without it. The United States and other NATO member states preferred this approach, possibly because NATO/SFOR did not want to be moving into what it considered a 'civilian' aspect of peace implementation.
18. This formula has not prevented, and may have encouraged, recurrent tension between the two organizations.
19. OSCE Mission to Bosnia and Herzegovina, The Media Experts Commission Final Report: Media in Elections 1998, submitted by Tanya L. Domi, chairperson (Sarajevo, December 1998). The first recommendation began: 'The OHR should vigorously continue with its broadcast restructuring plan for BiH.'
20. IMC document, 'IMC Licensing Phase II: Goals and Policies Adopted 21 October 1999'. Bosnia's nearest rival in media-density may have been Macedonia, which had some 210 registered broadcasters by 1997.
21. The IMC issued criteria for public broadcasters in 1999, defining a public station as one which: 'receives at least 51 per cent of its support from public sources, is sponsored or owned by a political party or governmental agency, or is sponsored by neighbouring states'. IMC document, 'Definition and Obligations of Public Radio and Television Broadcasting', 21 October 1999.
22. IMC document, 'Transfer and Transition Proposal', October 1999. The IMC redesignated itself as the Communications Regulatory Agency (CRA) in March 2001.
23. IMC Rule 04/2000, 'Merit-based Competitive Process for the Awarding of Long-Term Broadcasting Licenses', adopted 26 September 2000.
24. IMC Decision, 16 December 1998, re: HRT Broadcasting in BiH, III. Conclusions, 23(1), Online [July 2001], available PDF at http://www.imcbih.org/pdfs/001T_DG_981216_EN.PDF
25. Contrary to what the European diplomats apparently believed, the Croatian, Bosnian and Serbian languages – recognized as distinct under the Dayton Agreement, though not by many scholars – are mutually fully comprehensible.
26. Annexe 9 of the DPA allows for the Entities to form public corporations for utilities or other purposes. But both Entities must agree and the State's role is marginalized.
27. The term 'restructure', always used in this context, is, let it be noted, a misnomer. The OHR is trying to invent or create public service broadcasting (not 'public broadcasting', which is a simple tautology) in Bosnia and Herzegovina. The term 'public service' has been conspicuous by its absence; its use, and explanation, might have helped to infuse these debates with some needed passion.

28. Paragraphs 18–32 of the Annexe ('The Peace Implementation Agenda') to the Madrid Declaration of the Peace Implementation Council, 16 December 1998.
29. SRT broadcast one-sided reports throughout the Kosovo crisis, in many instances directly transmitting Radio Television Serbia (RTS) broadcasts without editing. In addition, it served up a steady diet of patriotic films about Serbia during the First and Second World Wars, as well as intense Serbian cultural programming. Eventually the High Representative sent a letter to SRT, demanding it adhere to journalistic principles of unbiased reporting. The inflammatory effect of the Serbian media led the Independent Media Commission to temporarily shut down the operation of the privately owned television station Kanal 'S'. This shut-down was tacitly supported by RS Minister of Information, Rajko Vasic. Although lasting only six days, the closure sent a strong message to SRT and other offending media outlets, causing them to moderate their programming content; International Crisis Group, 'Republika Srpska in the post-Kosovo Era', p. 7.
30. Interim Managing Board of RTVBiH, 'Possible Ways of Transforming the Public Broadcasters in BiH', June 1999.
31. OHR, 'Decision on the Restructuring of the Public Broadcasting System in Bosnia and Herzegovina', 30 July 1999. It should be noted that the OHR legal department had changed its interpretation of the constitution significantly. This was not due to a change in policy but to a change in personnel. On such contingencies the fate of Bosnia may hinge.
32. Ibid., Article 3.4.1 The PBS BiH mission shall be to provide informational, educational, entertainment and cultural programming for all parts of the State of Bosnia and Herzegovina. PBS BiH programming shall reflect the national, religious, historic, cultural, linguistic and other characteristics of the constituent peoples and citizens of BiH. It shall produce national news, and will move to develop an evening schedule in Television, in agreement with the Entity broadcasters, and a full broadcasting day in Radio.

    The First Decision had committed PBS to no more than 'a minimum of at least one hour of current affairs programming per day on radio and television.' (Decision on the Public Radio Television of Bosnia and Herzegovina, Article 2.)
33. A ground-breaking decision by the Constitutional Court had facilitated this emendation. On 30 June 2000, the Court found that the two Entity constitutions were unlawful insofar as they did not recognize that the three 'constituent peoples' had equal status throughout the country. Serbs gained full constitutional and legal equality with Bosniaks and Croats in the Federation, even though far outnumbered by them there, while Bosniaks and Croats gained the same in the Republika Srpska. The implications for public-service broadcasting in the Entities were unwelcome to nationalist parties.
34. 'The High Representative has in his decisions on media issues in July 1999 made a new interpretation of the Constitution and stated that there is a certain competence for media issues on the level of the Common institutions of Bosnia and Herzegovina.' IMC document, 'Transfer and Transition Proposal', October 1999.
35. The IMC White Paper speaks of 'the culture of lawlessness which plagues Bosnian society and which perpetuates public apathy', p. 64.

8

Silencing the Voices of Hate in Rwanda

Alison Des Forges

Introduction

The case could not have been clearer. The privately owned Radio-Television Libre des Mille Collines (RTLM) and the national Radio Rwanda were used to prepare and execute a genocide that killed at least half a million persons in Rwanda in 1994.[1] The victims represented an estimated three quarters of the Tutsi population of the country. Despite widespread recognition of the role of the radio, none of the major international actors present in Rwanda when the genocide began – Belgium, the United States, France, or the United Nations – took effective action to counter the impact of the genocidal broadcasts or to stop them altogether.

Months before the start of the genocide, Belgium recognized the risks of RTLM broadcasts. The Belgian ambassador in Kigali and Belgian soldiers serving in the UN peacekeeping force United Nations Assistance Mission in Rwanda (UNAMIR) noted that the radio threatened them as well as Rwandans. On the first day of genocidal violence, ten Belgian peacekeepers were killed, the murderers instigated by the radio. Belgium withdrew its troops and had no further capacity to influence the situation on the ground. It could, however, have urged the UN or others to act against the radio, but it did not, taking the position that all foreign forces should withdraw and leave the Rwandans to their fate.

In the United States, where non-governmental organizations (NGOs) worked hard to get the broadcasts interrupted, politicians and policy-makers refused to interrupt the broadcasts as they refused any other action which might lead to wider United States involvement in the crisis. Among themselves they acknowledged that they did not want to take the risks involved or pay the costs of such intervention. But they covered their decision with a veneer of commitment to legal principle – to the rights to freedom of expression and information, to the obligations of international convention, and to respect for national sovereignty. But given the readiness of the United States to jam broadcasts in Iraq three years before, few took seriously this reference to principle, probably not even those who crafted it.

In France such legal objections did not figure at all; rather it was the determination of high-ranking officials, including the president himself to continue supporting the Rwandan government that initially blocked any consideration of measures against the radio. Later, when French troops present in the area were threatened by broadcasts, French officials intervened first to oblige broadcasters to moderate their statements and later to knock out several of the relay stations of RTLM. But by that time, the genocide was already over and so the action did nothing to save lives.

The UN peacekeeping operations before and during the genocide were forced to operate within limits set by the United States and its allies on the Security Council who were determined to keep the UN role small, regardless of the cost to Rwandans. As a result, the commander of UNAMIR, General Romeo Dallaire, was prohibited by his superiors from taking any offensive action, including against the radio, which was threatening his troops as well as Rwandans.

A new Rwandan government defeated the authorities responsible for the genocide, but two million refugees had already been forced into exile. Eager to end the ensuing refugee crisis, the United States ended its opposition to jamming local broadcasts, which by then were discouraging the refugees from returning home. Still unwilling to take the lead in such actions, it agreed to assist others in doing so. It also supported the creation of a United Nations radio to beam objective news and information programmes throughout Rwanda.

A year later, when faced with the possibility of another genocide in neighbouring Burundi, United States policy-makers agreed that the United States could assist in silencing this radio, a position formalized by a presidential directive in 1999 concerning similar situations in the future.

The Context and Escalation

In 1990, Rwanda was an intensively administered state, the product of centuries of monarchical rule overlaid by decades of single-party control under an increasingly autocratic president. Juvénal Habyarimana, who had been in power seventeen years, was facing increasing challenges to his monolithic control. One of the Hutu, a group that constituted some 90 per cent of the population, Habyarimana faced charges of corruption and repression from other Hutu. Opponents claimed that he delivered disproportionate benefits to his personal circle, known as the *akazu* or 'little house', and to his home region, the north-west. Encouraged by the general rejection of single-party rule elsewhere on the continent, these political opponents demanded the right to form oposition parties and to enjoy greater freedom of expression.

After October 1990, Habyarimana also confronted a military challenge from a guerrilla movement, the Rwandan Patriotic Front (RPF), made up largely of Rwandan Tutsi refugees who had been living in neighbouring Uganda. They had fled abroad after a revolution in 1959 overthrew the Tutsi monarchy and ended Tutsi rule. Between 1959 and 1967, some of the refugees had carried out incursions into Rwanda. After each attack, local officials spurred reprisals against Tutsi still resident inside the country. Over the eight year period, some 20,000 Tutsi died and 300,000 fled abroad.[2] After twenty-three years of relative calm, the Tutsi abroad sought to take advantage of Habyarimana's slipping control. In 1990, they once again crossed the border into Rwanda, claiming as objectives the right to return home and the overthrow of the Habyarimana government.

Habyarimana tried in turn to use the RPF invasion as a way to rebuild his power base among the Hutu. He began a campaign to depict both Tutsi inside the country and members of the Hutu political opposition as 'accomplices' of the invaders. After having staged a fake attack on the capital to heighten fears, he arrested some 13,000 persons, mostly Tutsi but also Hutu who were challenging his power.

The effort to discourage further opposition among Hutu failed. Rather than driving a wedge between Tutsi and Hutu dissidents, the repression drove them closer together. In the face of mounting opposition, Habyarimana was obliged to permit the organization of opposition political parties in June 1991.

Notwithstanding this concession, Habyarimana and his circle resorted to increasing violence against those whom they saw as their enemies. From 1990 to 1993 they directed a series of massacres of Tutsi, each of which would claim hundreds of victims. They also recruited and gave military training to a party militia known as the Interahamwe, which attacked and killed political opponents as well as Tutsi.

The Radio in Rwanda

The national radio, Radio Rwanda, was the voice of the state and of its president, whose exhortations were heard daily before news broadcasts. Rwanda had a relatively good network of roads and telephone service to most local government offices, but officials depended upon the radio to reach the many Rwandans who lived scattered across the hills, distant from communal centres. The radio announced official meetings, nominations to and removal from government posts, and the results of nationally-administered school examinations. It offered ordinary people a way to inform relatives or friends of deaths so that they might attend funeral ceremonies. In 1991, some 29 per cent of all households owned radios, a number that rose to nearly 60 per cent in urban areas.[3] Many who did not own radios listened to broadcasts at the homes of friends or at neighbourhood bars.

Given the unity between state and the governing party, the National Democratic Republican Movement (MRND), it is not surprising that the national radio promoted the party just as vigorously as it served the state. It refused to air news of opposition parties until a street demonstration in November 1991 forced the government to grant them fifteen minute periods of airtime.[4]

From the start of the war, officials used Radio Rwanda to disseminate inaccurate or distorted information about the RPF, such as accusing the guerillas of massacres that had not taken place. Just weeks after the first RPF attack, the radio declared that the RPF goal 'is to exterminate and enslave us'.[5] The apparently nonsensical claim that Tutsi, a small minority of the population, intended to exterminate Hutu, the vast majority, appeared also in pamphlets and other propaganda produced by those close to Habyarimana.[6] The assertion that Tutsi intended to commit genocide may have been part of a propaganda strategy known as 'accusations in a mirror', whereby a party accuses its opponents of the actions which it itself is planning.

In March 1992, government and party officials for the first time used the radio to spur immediate attacks on Tutsi and members of the political opposition. Radio Rwanda repeatedly broadcast a fake press release from a non-existent human rights group warning that Tutsi were about to slaughter Hutu political leaders in a region known as Bugesera. Local organizers reinforced this message and soldiers and militia led ordinary people in attacking their Tutsi neighbours, killing several hundred.[7] Ferdinand Nahimana, once a historian at the National University of Rwanda, was then in charge of the Rwandan Office of Information where he supervised Radio Rwanda. Following an outcry among members of the opposition and pressure from international donors over Nahimana's role in the use of the radio in this massacre, he was forced to resign as was Jean-Baptiste Bamwanga, a radio journalist involved in the broadcast.[8]

A month after the Bugesera massacre, the opposition political parties had become strong enough to oblige Habyarimana to include them in a coalition government. There they demanded that Radio Rwanda cease its promotion of the MRND and observe neutrality towards all political parties. At first they had difficulty putting this concession into effect because many of the radio staff were stalwart supporters of the MRND. In November 1992, for example, Radio Rwanda broadcast excerpts of a diatribe by Dr Léon Mugesera, which incited violence both against members of other political parties and against Tutsi. Playing upon the theme of supposed planned aggression against Habyarimana's supporters, Mugesera closed his speech with the phrase, 'Know that the person whose throat you do not cut now will be the one who will cut yours.'[9]

The Arusha Accords

The war between the Rwandan government and the RPF was apparently settled with the signing of the Arusha Accords in August 1993. The agreement laid out a detailed plan for sharing power between Rwandan political parties – both those supporting and those opposing Habyarimana – and the RPF. As part of the agreement, all parties requested that a United Nations peacekeeping force be sent to oversee the implementation. They also agreed to end all hate propaganda against the other side.

In fact neither Habyarimana's firmest supporters nor the RPF expected the Accords to be executed. Habyarimana's backers could not accept the

anticipated loss of power and began preparing for renewed combat in hopes of a
military victory or at least new negotiations that might produce a result more
favourable to them. Aware of these preparations the RPF also continued to plan
for war, apparently not displeased at the possible opportunity to win a complete
victory.

Radio-Television Libre des Mille Collines (RTLM)

Habyarimana's supporters understood that they would eventually have to cede
control over Radio Rwanda. This prospect was all the more disturbing because
the RPF had mounted a radio called Radio Muhabura to recruit new supporters
and to spur criticism of the Habyarimana government. Groups in civil society
like the coalition of co-operatives known as *Iwacu* were also claiming the right
to establish radio stations, which officials suspected would be critical of the
government.

To assure that their own voice would continue to be heard on the airwaves,
Habyarimana's supporters began planning for RTLM in 1992. They established
the new station in April 1993, and began broadcasting in August. One of the chief
organizers was Nahimana, who was well aware of the power of the radio in inciting
violence. Sixty-six per cent of the founders of the station were from the two north-
western prefectures associated with Habyarimana and they included several
persons related to the president by marriage, two ministers in the government,
officials from the MRND party and the MRND militia, high-ranking military
officers, and important bankers. A leading figure from the Coalition for the
Defence of the Republic (CDR), a political party even more virulently anti-Tutsi
than the MRND, also numbered among the founders.[10] The new station drew
personnel from both Radio Rwanda and from the written press associated with the
MRND. The ostensibly private station received equipment from government
ministries and perhaps from Radio Rwanda itself.[11]

RTLM was allowed to broadcast on the same frequencies as the national
radio when Radio Rwanda was not transmitting, a measure which encouraged
listeners to see the station as also enjoying the support of the government.[12] In
other respects, however, RTLM distinguished itself sharply from the stodgy
national radio. It adopted a fast-paced, informal style that featured the latest
popular music. Its commentary seemed like 'a conversation among Rwandans
who knew each other well and were relaxing over some banana beer or a bottle
of Primus in a bar'.[13] Announcers created a sense of camaraderie with listeners,
inviting them to call in with their opinions or choice of music. Often they
greeted individuals or people of a particular place by name or interviewed
people on the street, giving them a chance to enjoy the kind of national visibility
ordinarily reserved for officials and politicians. Several announcers were
famous for their quick wit and command of the nuances of *kinyarwanda*,
the language used for most broadcasts. A Belgian named Georges Ruggiu did
broadcasts in French, lending credibility to the station by the mere fact of being
a foreigner delivering its messages.[14]

RTLM started broadcasting soon after the Arusha Accords were signed. Its disdain for the RPF and for Hutu parties opposed to Habyarimana was clear from the start but it began spewing out its most virulent messages only near the end of October 1993. At that time tensions between Hutu and Tutsi rose following the assassination of the president of neighbouring Burundi by Tutsi soldiers. The president was a Hutu who had been freely and fairly elected. RTLM seized the opportunity to impress upon Hutu that Tutsi could never be trusted and that any form of power-sharing, such as that specified in the Arusha Accords, could never work. In making these points, they wrongly reported that the assassinated president had been tortured and his body mutilated, knowing that this information would heighten fear among Hutu. Under the former Tutsi monarchy, slain Hutu rulers were sometimes castrated and their genitals attached to the royal drum.[15]

From November 1993 through to the start of the genocide, RTLM targeted specific individuals, including the prime minister and other ministers, leaders of civil society, journalists, and even the commander and men of the UN peacekeeping forces (UNAMIR). RTLM accused them all of being agents or at least pawns of the RPF. In some cases, the radio urged attacks on those who had been named, as on 26 November when it denounced the prime minister.[16] It delivered warnings from the Interahamwe militia to certain groups, such as taxi drivers who gave rides to RPF soldiers or supporters, saying that they might be ripped into little pieces. It stressed constantly the need for self-defence against Tutsi, warning that Hutu must be prepared to fight against them to the last person.[17]

In late February 1994, the head of an opposition party was assassinated and the next day a crowd of his supporters murdered the leader of the CDR party. In retaliation, the Interahamwe militia struck in the capital and killed some seventy people. RTLM announced that RPF troops had begun an offensive. Under the guise of urging listeners to search for RPF and their supporters in specified neighbourhoods of the city, it actually encouraged them to attack Tutsi in those areas. As with the Bugesera massacre of 1992, radio showed its capacity to encourage killing.[18]

Warnings and Reactions

As RTLM shouted the need for attacking Tutsi, print media too were feeding fears and hatred of Tutsi and all Hutu willing to associate with them. At that time, two major opposition parties split, one faction of each joining with the MRND and the CDR to form a loose coalition known as 'Hutu Power', committed to Hutu solidarity in the face of the supposed Tutsi menace. Leaders of Hutu Power parties stepped up the recruitment of militia, whose members received training from soldiers of the regular armed forces. They also began outlining a far more extensive form of organization for 'civilian self-defence', which would operate through the regular administrative system, under the supervision of soldiers and retired soldiers. Officials and soldiers distributed firearms to militia and others known to support Hutu Power and businessmen imported enormous quantities of machetes, which were delivered to local officials and leaders for distribution to ordinary people who had not received military training.

The propaganda of hate and the other preparations were too blatant to be ignored. Opposition politicians and leaders of civil society issued numerous statements and wrote many letters drawing the attention of the Rwandan government and of the foreign community to these preparations. Diplomats discussed the mounting tensions among themselves and alerted their home countries to the growing threat. General Dallaire repeatedly warned UN headquarters of the risks of violence. In early January, he reported to his superiors that the militia were reportedly ready to kill 1,000 Tutsi in the first twenty minutes of their attacks.

All observers deplored particularly the growing virulence and calls for violence by RTLM. Even the strongest critics, however, asked only for ending the incitements to hatred, not for closing down the station. The Rwandan minister of information, member of a party opposed to the MRND, criticized the RTLM leadership both face to face and in letters, pointing out that their incitements to violence violated both Rwandan law and the terms of the Arusha Accords. This had no effect. The attorney general registered several civil complaints against RTLM but, in the face of pressure from the president, delayed bringing the cases to court.

General Dallaire, who had hoped to have a broadcasting capability for UNAMIR, recognized the danger of the RTLM propaganda against himself and his troops, particularly the Belgians who were the strongest contingent among the peacekeepers. The Belgian announcer, Ruggiu, warned that the Belgians faced 'a fight without pity' and 'a hatred without mercy' if they did not go home immediately.[19] Just before the genocide began, the Belgian ambassador reported to Brussels that RTLM was broadcasting 'inflammatory statements calling for the hatred – indeed for the extermination' of Tutsi. Diplomats asked Habyarimana to stop the broadcasts, but did not press the issue when he declared that the radio was private and the right of freedom of expression protected its broadcasts.[20] Two days before the start of the genocide the German ambassador, speaking as head of the European Union community in Rwanda, publically criticized the 'unacceptable role of some media', but gave no details.

Had other radio stations existed that could have effectively challenged the incendiary propaganda of RTLM, the broadcasts might have had less effect. Radio Muhabura reached too few people and was not sufficiently attractive to challenge the hold of RTLM. During the period when multi-party politics was beginning several foreign donors had expressed interest in funding an alternative radio, which could be established by some part of civil society, but none had come up with the money. The Rwandan government too had refused to grant a licence to any new stations, a refusal that was never seriously challenged by the donor community.

The Genocide

On 6 April 1994, the airplane carrying Habyarimana back from consultations in Tanzania was shot down as it approached the Kigali airport. Within hours soldiers of the presidential guard and other units controlled by officers who supported Hutu Power began killing members of the government and other political leaders opposed to their ideology. Thus they cleared the way for a new government which would welcome the return to war against the RPF and which would accept the genocide of Tutsi civilians as one strategy to help win that war. As some military and militia eliminated leaders of the Hutu opposition, others began slaying Tutsi civilians. They sought them out in their homes and they put up barriers to catch any who tried to flee. The next day, the RPF troops resumed combat and from that point forward the war and the genocide were intertwined horrors. Following this, Tutsi civilians began gathering in churches, schools, and hospitals where they had found safety in previous crises. In some cases, local administrators obliged them to gather at such sites. Military and militia launched full-scale attacks on them involving firepower and thousands of assailants, sometimes continuing the slaughter over a period of days. In the worst of these massacres, tens of thousands of Tutsi perished at a time.

RTLM During the Genocide

The nominally private radio immediately began helping the killing campaign orchestrated by the Hutu Power advocates who had taken control of the State. It broadcast the news that Belgian soldiers had helped the RPF down Habyarimana's airplane. Incensed by this information, Rwandan soldiers captured and beat to death ten Belgian peacekeepers, causing the Belgian government to withdraw its contingent from UNAMIR. The Belgian retreat left the force so seriously weakened that the Security Council nearly withdrew the peacekeepers altogether. Only at the last minute did it decide to leave a token force in place, but ordered it to take no risks to save the lives of Rwandans.[21]

RTLM intensified its campaign to instill fear and hatred of the RPF, reporting gruesome details of supposed RPF killings and even cannibalism.[22] It insisted that the RPF troops or *inyenzi*, literally cockroaches, intended to massacre ruthlessly the Hutu population as they advanced. It told listeners that they must 'understand that the cruelty of the *inyenzi* is incurable, the cruelty of the *inyenzi* can be cured only by their total extermination'.[23]

RTLM announcers continued and reinforced earlier efforts to present all Tutsi in Rwanda as soldiers of the RPF or as their 'accomplices'. They reported repeatedly that RPF agents had infiltrated throughout the country dressed as civilians and that they could be found among crowds of displaced persons as well as among long-resident populations. They sought to convince listeners that even the neighbour next door, an acquaintance or friend of long standing, was secretly recruiting adherents for the RPF or had stocked a cache of arms for the arrival of combatants. In some cases, local officials dramatized such claims by staging raids to 'discover' previously planted lists of RPF members or firearms hidden in the bushes.[24]

Insisting that war was everywhere, that all Tutsi were the enemy, and that all Hutu were in danger, no matter how far from the combat zone, RTLM spurred listeners to take up arms in 'self-defence'. The situation was desperate, it claimed, because this was to be the 'final' war. The announcer Kantano Habimana promised that this was to be a war that would 'exterminate the Tutsi from the globe [. . .] make them disappear once and for all'.[25] Like Mugesera in 1992, RTLM warned that the person who hesitated to act would find himself a victim.

RTLM went beyond general incitation to name specific targets for attack. On 8 April, the announcer Valerie Bemeriki sent assailants to the home of Tutsi businessman Antoine Sebera. Soon after, RTLM speaker Noel Hitimana announced that Tutsi were hidden in the ceiling of the home of Joseph Kahabaye.[26] On 10 April, Bemeriki read a list of thirteen RPF 'leaders', their addresses, where they worked, and where they spent their leisure time. She said that all people concerned about their own security should 'rise up' against these 'spies'. She continued: 'You have heard their names, with their sectors and their cells [homes], so we find that these people are really plotting with the *inyenzi-inkotanyi* in order to kill [. . .] Rwandans.'[27]

Georges Ruggiu identified the area round the hill Mburabuturo as a place where 'suspect movements' had been observed and directed listeners from that area to 'go check out that woods'.[28] In another case, RTLM told listeners that a convoy was about to leave a Kigali hotel to transport dozens of Tutsi and opponents of the genocide to safety. Despite the presence of a UNAMIR escort, the convoy was promptly attacked by militia and forced to turn back, with a number of its passengers wounded.[29] In yet another instance, RTLM said that staff of the International Committee of the Red Cross were saving Tutsi. After one such announcement, a Red Cross ambulance was attacked and the wounded Tutsi inside were pulled out and slaughtered. When Tutsi began gathering in churches and other places of worship, RTLM announcer Hitimana warned that the RPF had supplied them with grenades and other arms. Soon afterwards assailants arrived to slaughter hundreds at a church and at a mosque in Kigali.[30]

RTLM praised the people of areas where many Tutsi had been killed and castigated those who hesitated to attack. Announcer Hitimana congratulated the people of one neighbourhood who had searched out all the Tutsi hidden in nearby houses. He exulted, 'The population is very vigilant [. . .] They have sacked all the houses, the rooms, the kitchens, everywhere! They have even torn out all the doors and windows [. . .] they have searched everywhere! [. . .] Force them to come out! Find them at whatever cost!'[31]

On another occasion, he exhorted his listeners, 'Fight them with the weapons you have at hand, you have arrows, you have spears [. . .] go after those *inkotanyi* [a code word for RPF and Tutsi generally], blood flows in their veins as it does in yours.'[32]

Members of the militia were among the most avid listeners of RTLM, frequently listening to radios at the roadblocks where they intercepted people who were trying to flee, or singing songs heard on RTLM as they set off to search out and kill Tutsi. Militia leaders used RTLM to dispatch assailants to various locations or to recall them to the capital.[33]

Radio Rwanda During the Genocide

Radio Rwanda adopted increasingly harsh language towards Tutsi and those associated with them during the genocide, although it never achieved the same level of vitriol as RTLM. Rather it contributed to the killing campaign through broadcasting official orders and the speeches of political leaders. On 12 April, government leaders used the national radio to inform Rwandans that the real enemy was the Tutsi and that assailants should henceforth stop attacking members of the Hutu opposition. The prefect or governor of the city of Kigali used the radio to explain to citizens how they should proceed in their attempt to extirpate Tutsi. He said:

> We ask that people do patrols, as they are used to doing, in their neighborhoods. They must close ranks, remember how to use their usual tools [weapons] and defend themselves [. . .] I would also ask that each neighborhood try to organize itself to do communal work [*umuganda*] to clear the brush, to search houses, beginning with those that are abandoned, to search the marshes of the area to be sure that no *inyenzi* have slipped in to hide themselves there [. . .] so they should cut this brush, search the drains and ditches [. . .] put up barriers and guard them, choosing reliable people to do this, who have what they need [. . .] so that nothing can escape them.[34]

As Tutsi civilians fled towards the southern border hoping to cross into Burundi, Radio Rwanda warned that they were planning to open a new front for the war in that area. It declared that the government was appealing to people in that area to 'remain vigilant and help restore order and peace'.[35] In the following days, local people attacked the displaced Tutsi and killed many of them.[37]

The national radio informed listeners that heads of political parties would use its airwaves 'to send messages to their members concerning how they should behave during these times'.[37] One such political leader, Shingiro Mbonyumutwa, declared on Radio Rwanda that Tutsi 'are going to exterminate, exterminate, exterminate, exterminate [. . .] they are going to exterminate you until they are the only ones left in this country, so that the power which their fathers kept for four hundred years, they can keep for a thousand years.'[38]

Radio Rwanda broadcast orders to assist with the logistics of the genocide. It notified retired soldiers that they should report for duty and called in all who knew how to drive bulldozers so that they could help bury the bodies.[39]

The Radio as the Voice of Authority

Both Radio Rwanda and RTLM served to reinforce orders given by local officials. In one commune in western Rwanda, the burgomaster told people that they 'have to follow all orders transmitted in meetings or on the radio'.[40] In this time of crisis, most ordinary people saw no reason to call into question their practice of taking the radio as the voice of authority. As one Rwandan said, 'After April 10, the orders were coming from above, and the radio was transmitting them.' Others commented, 'People were listening to RTLM which was telling them, "You people, ordinary people, the Tutsi killed your president. Save yourselves. Kill them before they kill you too." '[41] One person from the prefecture of Gikongoro stated: 'We found out from RTLM that it was the *inkotanyi* that were supposed to be killed.'[42]

Often officials seemed to co-ordinate the messages they delivered in public meetings with those heard on the radio. In mid-May, prime minister of the interim government Jean Kambanda told an audience at the National University in Butare that there had been no massacres of Tutsi in that region but rather that people had simply defended themselves against attack. Several days later RTLM announcer Valerie Bemeriki declared that 'the troubles in Butare are nothing but the wickedness of the Tutsi who have started it all [. . .] it is the Tutsi who tried to exterminate the Hutu.'[43]

Resistance

The extremists bent on genocide quickly took control of important units of the army and won the backing of civilian administrators in those parts of Rwanda where Hutu Power parties were strong. But in the first two weeks some military officers, as well as administrators and local leaders in the centre and the south, opposed the killing campaign. Those seeking to resist the genocide recognized that the radio was playing an essential role in promoting attacks. At one point, military officers tried to get RTLM to moderate its tone, but, backed by more important forces, the directors of the radio were able to ignore their efforts. Similarly local officials appealed to the national authorities to interrupt the barrage of incitement and directions from RTLM, also with no success. In desperation, several officials told people in their communes not to listen to RTLM and two prefects urged people to listen to the radio 'with a very critical ear'.[44]

Those who tried to halt the killings found themselves attacked on the radio. RTLM criticized the burgomaster of the commune of Mukingi, for example, saying that all the enemies had gone to hide in the area under his jurisdiction.

The prefect of Butare, himself a Tutsi, was accused on the radio of being a secret supporter of the RPF. The national authorities used harassment by radio as part of a larger strategy including face-to-face confrontations and public denunciations to pressure the reluctant into participation. They often reinforced the impact of such abuse by sending militia from places where the genocide was well advanced to attack in regions where it was being resisted. Few local officials were able to withstand this combination of pressures and during the second half of April, most gave in and permitted or even promoted the killing campaign in areas under their control.[45]

In mid-April, the most important leaders of the genocidal government, including the president and prime minister, came to Butare to replace the prefect who resisted the genocide with an appointee expected to contribute to the slaughter of Tutsi. In the course of the installation ceremony, the national authorities warned that any who continued opposing the genocide could expect to lose their positions and perhaps their lives. Thanks to Radio Rwanda, their warnings were heard throughout the country. In his speech, the president talked about 'work', the then standard euphemism for 'killing'. He declared that: '"the actors who only watch", "those who feel it's not their business", should be exposed. Let them step aside for us and let us "work". He who says, "that's not my business and I'm even afraid", let him step aside for us. Those who are responsible for getting rid of such a person, let them do it fast. Other good "workers who want to work" for their country are there.'[46]

Ordinarily used to spur killings, radio was also used to limit them on occasion, especially when authorities wanted to impress the international community. Just before the anticipated visit of the UN High Commissioner for Human Rights in May 1994, RTLM ordered listeners to interrupt the killing. After he had left, it resumed calling for slaughter of the 'enemy', pinpointing people who had thus far escaped attack, like local clergy. At one point when Rwandan authorities hoped to receive increased military aid from France, a government that had consistently supported them, French officials indicated that further help could not be assured so long as killing was so blatant. RTLM then asked listeners to ensure that there were no bodies visible on the roads and asked them not to stand around laughing at barriers when victims' throats were being cut.[47]

Attempts to Silence the Radio

In meetings with diplomats and government officials and in the press, non-governmental organizations, like Human Rights Watch and the United States Committee for Refugees, called for international intervention to halt the killing. They soon learned that neither the United States nor any other major power on the Security Council would favour sending its own troops or more UN peacekeepers to Rwanda. Although continuing to plead for military action to stop the genocide, NGOs also proposed other strategies to limit the impact of the killing, including jamming the radio. The effort to halt the broadcasts was echoed by various NGOs based in Europe, including the International Federation of Human Rights Leagues, Oxfam, Reporters without Borders, and Doctors without Borders.

The staff of Human Rights Watch argued that jamming the radio would reduce killing both by halting the incitements to violence and by disrupting the dissemination of orders for the organization of the genocide. In addition, they drew on extensive experience in the region to present an analysis of Rwandan political dynamics that buttressed their argument. According to their information, the genocidal authorities elicited readier compliance with their orders because they could present themselves as legitimate. The inaction of the international community allowed this pretence of legitimacy to continue. By silencing the voice of the genocidal authorities, international actors would demonstrate their disapproval of the genocidal agenda and thus help undermine the supposed legitimacy of the government. Such action would hearten resisters. It would also sow doubt about the long-term viability of the regime. Most Rwandans understood that international financial assistance was crucial to the functioning of any government in their poverty-stricken country. If convinced that international disapproval would hinder any future assistance to the genocidal government, they might question the wisdom of obeying its directives. They might begin to weigh the consequences for themselves personally – in terms, for example, of eventual prosecution – as well as for the country as a whole.

After more than a month of killing, international leaders finally began denouncing the slaughter. The Voice of America, the BBC, and Radio France Internationale carried this news into Rwanda. The genocidal authorities, fearful of losing their hold over the population, used Radio Rwanda and RTLM to broadcast reassurances to counter the impact of the criticism. RTLM announcers recalled past instances of crimes against humanity, such as those in Burundi, which had gone unpunished and remarked that the international tribunal set up for the former Yugoslavia had not yet convicted anyone.[48]

Following the genocide, Human Rights Watch researchers collected testimonies and discovered documents which showed that even ordinary people in remote locations had followed international opinion about events in Rwanda. This sensitivity suggests that the analysis made during the genocide was correct: that jamming the radio would have helped sap the authority of the regime and made Rwandans less ready to follow its orders.

The International Actors

The United States Government Refuses to Act

US Department of State officials who were particularly knowledgeable about Rwanda agreed with NGOs that the broadcasts had to be halted. Although there was no real support for this idea at the higher echelons of the Department, several determined members of the staff succeeded in late April in getting the issue sent both to their own legal experts and to the Department of Defense.

Also in late April, national security advisor Anthony Lake heard pleas for action by staff from Human Rights Watch and by one of their Rwandan colleagues, an activist who had been received by President Clinton at the White House several months before. Lake was sufficiently impressed to authorize publication of a press release naming the apparent leaders of the genocide and calling on them to stop the slaughter.

On 29 April, hundreds of thousands of Rwandans began streaming out of Rwanda into neighbouring Tanzania. They were not victims of genocide, but rather Hutu fleeing from the advancing Rwandan Patriotic Front. Their flight, nonetheless, underlined the gravity of the crisis and its potential for destabilizing the entire region. This news may have reinforced the impact of the information delivered to Lake shortly before by the NGO representatives. On 4 May, Lake raised the possibility of jamming Rwandan radio broadcasts with secretary of defense, William Perry.

Within twenty-four hours, the Pentagon 'concluded that jamming is an ineffective and expensive mechanism that will not accomplish the objective the NSC Advisor seeks'.[49] It noted that jamming would be difficult due to the mountainous terrain and would cost approximately US $8,500 per flight hour if done by plane. In passing, the memo mentioned that 'international legal conventions' would complicate interrupting the broadcasts. Instead of attacking the problem at its heart, the author of the memo suggested mere palliative measures – the provision of emergency assistance for refugees who fled Rwanda.

During the first weekend in May, lawyers at the State Department examined the question and they too decided that jamming the hate broadcasts would violate international telecommunications law and international conventions protecting freedom of information and expression. This position was consistent with the usual strong United States commitment to such freedoms and with its long-standing opposition to interrupting broadcasts.

During the 1991 Persian Gulf War and in 1994 in Haiti, the United States had, however, distinguished between civilian and military contexts and had not only accepted but itself had engaged in jamming radios in the immediate arena of combat.[50] The State Department lawyers could have drawn on this precedent, given that the genocide was being executed during a war. They did not do so, almost certainly because the policy decision had already been made not to intervene and they knew that they were serving merely to endorse it.

The lawyers could also have based their position on the Convention on the Prevention and Punishment of the Crime of Genocide, ratified by the United States in 1988, which prohibited 'direct and public incitement to commit genocide'. They could have cited United States domestic legislation as proof that calls for genocidal slaughter, if likely to provoke immediate and direct action, were not covered by guarantees of freedom of expression. The Proxmire Act of 1987 made such calls punishable by a fine of not more than US $500,000 or by a prison term of not more than five years.[51] They could have referred to the judgement of the Nuremberg Tribunal, which condemned Julius Streicher to death for having published calls for the annihilation of Jews at a time when the death camps were operating.[52]

To have raised the issue of genocide to justify intervention, however, would have required some recognition that the slaughter in Rwanda was in fact a genocide. This was an admission that the United States would not make until several weeks later. By the end of May, the United States representative to the emergency meeting of the UN Human Rights Commission was allowed to say that 'acts of genocide' might have been committed in Rwanda. But the Clinton administration only conceded that a genocide was taking place after it was embarrassed by a *New York Times* report on 10 June that stated that the White House had directed government spokesmen not to use the term 'genocide' when referring to Rwanda.

Members of the United States Congress also took up the Rwanda crisis during the first week of May, largely at the prodding of NGOs. At a hearing of the Subcommittee on Africa of the House Committee on Foreign Affairs on 4 May, Human Rights Watch and the United States Committee for Refugees called again for radio-jamming. George Moose, Assistant Secretary of State for African affairs, assured the Congressional representatives that the State Department had considered the jamming question 'very seriously' over the past weekend, but that the issue was moot because the broadcasts had ceased after a RPF attack on the studio of RTLM. Speaking after Moose, a representative from Human Rights Watch contradicted this information and insisted that the station continued to broadcast from a mobile facility, still calling for the extermination of Tutsi and announcing a deadline for finishing the 'work', as it was called.[53]

During the rest of May, Human Rights Watch staff continued to report on the role of radio in inciting and directing the genocide.[54] They also managed to learn more about the resources available to the United States government for jamming radios, information which they put at the disposal of Senators Edward Kennedy and Nancy Kassenbaum. On 1 June, Senator Kennedy wrote to Secretary of State Warren Christopher to ask that the United States co-operate with the United Nations in halting 'the unconscionable incitement to genocide' broadcast by radios in Rwanda. He noted that a 25 May RTLM broadcast called specifically for the killing of Tutsi children and that United States aircraft known as 'Volant Solo' which had been used in the Gulf War were capable of jamming Rwandan broadcasts.

Vincent Kern, director at the Office of the Assistant Secretary of Defense for International Security Affairs, assured his superiors that 'we've already gone through this before' and that 'even State lawyers said this was a non-starter'.[55] Thus buttressed, United States Defense Department officials again concluded that jamming the radios would be 'legally contentious'. To the previous legal arguments regarding international conventions and defence of freedom of expression, they now added a concern with loss of 'neutrality' of the executing agency. This argument was linked to the notion of national sovereignty: so long as the United States recognized the government of Rwanda, it was said, it could not violate Rwandan national sovereignty by disturbing its airwaves.

Although the military officials cited supposed legal justifications for their position, they also laid out other concerns which they knew would carry more weight with senior officials. A memorandum prepared for the Secretary of Defense stressed the risks involved in an operation that would be 'a very expensive, dangerous and open-ended prospect'. It mentioned again the cost of US $8,500 per hour flying time for the aircraft and the mountainous terrain as being obstacles. It added the information that the Rwandan military had SA-7 missiles which could be shot at the aircraft and concluded that the effectiveness of the jamming would probably be only 'approximately 50%'.[56]

In fact, these more concrete objections were no more credible than the legal principles cited. While the cost per hour was not insignificant, it was hardly a major expense. Jamming the broadcasts was indeed more complicated once the radios began broadcasting from mobile facilities and the mountainous terrain made the operation technically more difficult. But no one said that it could not be done. The Rwandan military had very few SA-7 missiles; the missiles were not sophisticated weapons, nor were Rwandans highly trained in their use. In addition, the Rwandan army was fully engaged in fighting a losing war against the Rwandan Patriotic Front and was unlikely to have devoted resources to downing a United States plane. Even if broadcasts had been interrupted only 50 per cent of the time, the jamming would still have delivered a clear message of international disapproval.

The jamming of Rwandan radio was discussed at the highest levels – between the National Security Advisor and the Secretary of Defense – as well as being recommended by at least some officials at the State Department, but consideration of the proposal was perfunctory and the issue seems to have been decided before the conversations began. Much as individual officials might regret the slaughter in Rwanda, the policy of the government was to treat the genocide of little importance to the United States. The White House was willing to make occasional small gestures, like the late April press release by Anthony Lake or a thirty second announcement by President Clinton on the Voice of America in which he called upon all Rwandans to recognize their common brotherhood. But any more vigorous action was seen as possibly leading to increasing involvement. Were the gravity of the crisis acknowledged, it would be difficult to retreat into inaction if the first measures failed to have the anticipated effect. Judging from the relative lack of interest about Rwanda among United States citizens, decision makers in Washington saw no political interest in taking any step that might lead to a larger role, even if it were one that might help mitigate the catastrophe.[57]

Change in the United States Position

In mid-July, the Rwandan Patriotic Front defeated the genocidal government and drove its army from Rwanda. Roughly two million refugees fled to squalid camps across the frontier, where some 50,000 died from cholera or other diseases, lack of water, and lack of food. The United States finally withdrew recognition from the government responsible for the genocide and showed itself eager to support the new government, in part because of a sense of guilt over lack of response to the genocide, in part because of a desire to restore stability in the region. It soon became clear that the continuing presence of vast numbers of refugees in surrounding countries would cost a great deal – at one point US$1,000,000 a day – and would also perpetuate insecurity in the area. Remnants of the former government army and militia had regrouped in the refugee camps and were continuing to launch incursions into Rwanda.

Staff of RTLM and Radio Rwanda had saved enough of their equipment during the flight from the country to be able to begin broadcasting again. The transmitter was at first located in south-western Rwanda in a zone controlled by French troops sent in a supposedly humanitarian operation near the end of the genocide. It subsequently moved and was said to be located either in Burundi or Zaire, or perhaps to move between the two countries. Although the broadcasts were intermittent and the range in which they could be heard was limited, they were thought important in encouraging refugees to fear and hate the new Rwandan government and hence in hindering their return home.

With an enormous interest in the rapid repatriation of the refugees, the United States decided to play a more active role in interrupting radio broadcasts. That diatribes against the United States had begun to be broadcast in mid-July may have spurred this decision.[58] An inter-agency working group was formed under the leadership of the Department of Defense to deal with the issue.[59]

At this point, there is no evidence of any renewed discussion of legal justifications for or against the policy. Presumably there was no longer any objection based on the argument of state sovereignty since the authorities supporting the hate radio no longer enjoyed recognition as a 'legitimate' government. The need to protect freedom of information and expression was not raised. Had it been, justifying interrupting the broadcasts on the basis of incitement to genocide would have been difficult since the radio at this point rarely called for exterminating the Tutsi.

Earlier objections concerning cost and safety of the aircraft now seemed no obstacle. The United States decided to call upon others to do the jamming if at all possible. On 17 August, Washington instructed embassies in Burundi and Zaire to request local governments 'to prevent hate mongering clandestine radios from broadcasting from their territory'.[60] In order to be prepared should the United States itself need to play a larger role in jamming broadcasts or in the destruction of radio equipment, the inter-agency working group at the Department of Defense on 18 August recommended the collection of 'definitive information' on the location and frequencies used by the Rwandan radios. It asked the joint staff to prepare 'a list of options for countering the broadcasts'.[61]

By the end of August, Department of Defense officials had decided that none of the countries in the region had the capacity to jam the radios.[62] The United States then looked instead to the UN to jam the broadcasts. The ad-hoc group of senior-level decision makers offered to provide the UN with the necessary equipment or information about how to get it.[63]

Change in the French Position

After more than two months of genocide, even those French leaders most committed to the Rwandan government recognized how international criticism was growing against the regime and its extermination campaign. In mid-June, the French government announced that it would launch a 'humanitarian intervention', known as Operation Turquoise, to save lives in Rwanda. French leaders insisted that they intended to protect both Tutsi endangered by the genocide and Hutu at risk from the advancing RPF troops. In fact, at least some of the French – particularly military officers who had assisted the Rwandan army in the past against the RPF – intended to use the supposed humanitarian operation to halt the RPF advance and to preserve a territorial base for the Rwandan government so that it could re-open negotiations with the RPF. Thus the force deployed included a heavy component of elite combat troops and intelligence agents.

Once in Rwanda, French troops saw the genocide from a new perspective. Some understood for the first time that Rwandan soldiers and militia were actually massacring Tutsi civilians in large numbers, contrary to what the Rwandan government had led them to believe. At the same time, French leaders realized how difficult it would be for the demoralized Rwandan government troops to win a war against the RPF, rapidly growing both in numbers and in confidence. They were unwilling to commit the resources needed to help the Rwandan government fight the RPF to a standstill. The French command ordered French troops to avoid confrontations with the RPF and to begin preventing Rwandan soldiers and militia from further massacres of Tutsi.

French officials had launched Operation Turquoise in part to counter increasingly effective attacks by NGOs on French policy. In accord with a policy of greater receptivity to NGO pleas for action, the adviser to the French president on African affairs, Bruno Delaye, received a delegation from Human Rights Watch and the International Federation of Human Rights Leagues on 5 July 1994. During the interview, Delaye said that France would be willing to jam Rwandan radio but that it had not been able to locate their broadcasting positions. The NGO representatives expressed some scepticism at this, given that the troops of Operation Turquoise included highly trained and well-equipped intelligence agents. Within days the head of the army general staff was personally charged with determining how best to jam the radio. Soon after French troops destroyed at least one and probably more of the radio transmitters.[64]

RTLM continued to broadcast, however, with a limited range. In response to the change in the French attitude, its announcers now began attacking the French. Officers of Operation Turquoise immediately brought pressure to bear on Rwandan government officials who saw to it that the broadcasters moderated their tone. In the meantime, the French brought in jamming equipment and prepared to silence the radio completely. In late July, they concluded that the broadcasters had moved their headquarters across the border into either Burundi or Zaire, areas beyond French responsibility. In late August, the United States asked the French if they would be willing to jam the radios and offered any technical assistance necessary, but by that time they had sent their equipment home.

The United Nations Finally Acts

The Secretary-General of the UN informed the Security Council at the very end of April that the civilian slaughter in Rwanda could not be treated as an unfortunate by-product of an internal war but had to be addressed in itself by more vigorous action. It was only on 17 May that the United States finally agreed to form a renewed peacekeeping force, UNAMIR II, with a mandate to assist in providing the necessary humanitarian assistance to civilians. But with bureaucratic delays caused by UN inefficiency as well as by uncooperative member states, the fresh troops arrived only in August, by which time the genocide had ended and the government responsible for it had fled the country.

In late June, the Security Council directed its attention to the hate broadcasts against Tutsi and UNAMIR troops. The president of the council demanded that such broadcasts cease and asked that the Rwandan government close down RTLM. The representative of Rwanda, then sitting as a nonpermanent member of the Security Council, at first responded with the old excuse that the radio was private and independent, but later he said that his government would do as requested.[65] When radio broadcasts were still being heard several months later, then urging the refugees not to return home, the United States sought to persuade UNAMIR to interrupt the broadcasts. The UN – in an ironic echo of an earlier United States position – refused, citing fears that doing so would cast doubts on its neutrality. But by 3 October, UN officials had changed their position and were requesting United States assistance in obtaining the needed equipment.[66] Before the equipment could be obtained, the radio itself apparently stopped broadcasting, perhaps handing over its equipment to Radio Rutomorangingo in Burundi.

Lessons Learned from Rwanda

Too late to help the victims of the genocide, the international community finally recognized how much radio had contributed to the slaughter of

Rwandans in 1994. This led to new positions concerning broadcasts of incitement to violence.

In August 1994, the Burundian Radio Rutomorangingo began broadcasting hate propaganda against Tutsi who constituted a minority of the population in Burundi, as they did in Rwanda. Although the recent political history of the two countries had been very different, Burundi too had seen considerable inter-ethnic slaughter beginning in 1972. Fearing that instability there might lead to another genocide against Tutsi, the United States government took a firm position reflecting the lessons learned from the Rwandan experience. An inter-agency working group agreed on 21 July 1995 that the United States government 'can technically and legally contribute to silencing the radio'.[67]

In the months that followed, Radio Rutomorangingo moderated the tones of its broadcasts, becoming more the voice of a military and political opposition to the Burundian government than a hate radio committed to inciting genocide. In 1996, nonetheless, the Burundi government jammed its FM broadcasts, apparently using equipment from the Israeli government. Its efforts limited broadcasts into the capital, although the radio continued to be heard elsewhere in Burundi and particularly from its shortwave transmitters located in Uvira, Zaire.[68]

In addition to being more ready to intervene in Burundi, President Clinton issued a policy directive in 1999 ordering that the United States be ready to act more vigorously in the future in responding to incitements to violence over the airwaves.[69] The Rwandan experience also suggested the importance of trying to prevent or avert violence by positive broadcasts. Once UNAMIR II was in place, its officers insisted on establishing a United Nations radio to broadcast objective news and to inform Rwandans about their activities. It took some months to negotiate assistance from member states, chiefly the United States, but the station began functioning several months later.

Others launched new efforts elsewhere to use radio to promote peace. In Burundi, Studio Ijambo was established with a multi-ethnic staff to produce programmes that were free from bias and hate. In places as distant as Liberia and East Timor, NGOs like the Swiss-based Fondation Hirondelle contributed to establishing radio stations that would counter the voices of hate, giving hope that calls to slaughter would no longer dominate the airwaves.

Bibliography

ARTICLE 19 (October 1996), *Broadcasting Genocide, Censorship, Propaganda and State-Sponsored Violence in Rwanda 1990–1994*, London: ARTICLE 19.

Burkhalter, Holly (winter 1994/95), 'The Question of Genocide: The Clinton Administration and Rwanda', *World Policy Journal*, pp. 44–54.

Chrétien, Jean-Pierre; Dupaquier, Jean-François; Kabanda, Marcel; and Ngarambe, Joseph (1995), *Rwanda, Les Médias du Génocide*, Paris: Editions Karthala.

Des Forges, Alison (1999), *Leave None to Tell the Story, Genocide in Rwanda*, New York: Human Rights Watch; Paris: International Federation of Human Rights.

France, Assemblée Nationale, Mission d'information commune. 'Enquête sur la Tragédie Rwandaise (1990–4)', tome I, rapport.

Government of Rwanda (July 1993), *Recensement Général de la Population et de l'Habitat au 15 Août 1991*, Kigali: Service National de Recensement.

Haq, F. (June 1994), 'Rwanda: Close Down Anti-Tutsi Radio, Says the UN Security Council', *Inter-Press Service*.

Higiro, Jean-Marie Vianney (1995), 'Distorsions et Omissions dans l'Ouvrage', in Jean-Pierre Chrétien et al., *Rwanda, Les Médias du Génocide,*' Paris: Editions Karthala , no. 190, p. 166.

Joint Evaluation of Emergency Assistance to Rwanda (March 1996), *The International Response to Conflict and Genocide: Lessons from the Rwanda Experience (Study 2: Early Warning and Conflict Management)* Denmark: Steering Committee of the Joint Evaluation of Emergency Assistance to Rwanda.

Kamanzi, Ntaribi (n.d.), *Rwanda, du Génocide à la Défaite*, Kigali: Editions Rebero.

Metzl, Jamie Frederic (October 1997), 'Rwandan Genocide and the International Law of Radio Jamming', *American Journal of International Law*, vol. 91, no. 4, pp. 628–51.

Prunier, Gérard (1995), *The Rwanda Crisis, History of a Genocide*, New York: Columbia University Press.

Notes

1. Des Forges, *Leave None to Tell the Story*, p. 15.
2. Prunier, *The Rwanda Crisis*, p. 62.
3. Government of Rwanda, *Recensement Général*, p. 31.
4. ARTICLE 19, *Broadcasting Genocide*, p. 47.
5. Ibid., p. 29.
6. See, e.g., Association des Femmes Parlementaires pour la Défense des Droits de la Mère et de l'Enfant en collaboration avec Dr Mugesera Léon, 'Respect des Droits de la Personne par le Rwanda,' Kigali, April 1991.
7. Africa Watch (later Human Rights Watch/Africa), International Federation of Human Rights Leagues, Interafrican Union for Human and Peoples' Rights, and the International Center for Human Rights and Democratic Development, 'Report of the International Commission of Investigation on Human Rights Violations in Rwanda since 1 October 1990', March 1993.
8. Des Forges, *Leave None to Tell the Story*, pp. 68, 70.
9. Ibid., pp. 85–6. The speaker was also author of the pamphlet cited in Note 6.
10. François-Xavier Nsanzuwera, manuscript on RTLM, in possession of the author.
11. Chrétien et al., *Rwanda, Les Médias*, p. 70; Higiro, 'Distorsions et Omissions', pp. 161, 164.
12. Des Forges, *Leave None to Tell the Story*, p. 69.
13. Higiro, 'Distorsions et Omissions', p. 171.
14. Des Forges, *Leave None to Tell the Story*, p. 70.
15. RTLM, 17–31 October 1994, Human Rights Watch, unpublished transcript.
16. Des Forges, *Leave None to Tell the Story*, pp. 144, 158–9, 164, 171; ARTICLE 19, *Broadcasting Genocide*, pp. 92–3.
17. Des Forges, *Leave None to Tell the Story*, pp. 158, 168; ARTICLE 19, *Broadcasting Genocide*, pp. 96–7.

18. ARTICLE 19, *Broadcasting Genocide*, p. 97.
19. Des Forges, *Leave None to Tell the Story*, pp. 149, 158–9, 170.
20. Joint Evaluation of Emergency Assistance to Rwanda, *The International Response to Conflict and Genocide*, p. 32.
21. Des Forges, *Leave None to Tell the Story*, pp. 255–6.
22. Chrétien et al., *Rwanda, Les Médias*, p. 162.
23. Ibid., p. 204.
24. Des Forges, *Leave None to Tell the Story*, pp. 295–6.
25. Chrétien et al., *Rwanda, Les Médias*, p. 205.
26. Des Forges, *Leave None to Tell the Story*, p. 206.
27. RTLM broadcast, 10 April 1994, recorded by Faustin Kagame (transcript provided by Article 19, *Broadcasting Genocide*). Note the use of 'Rwandans' to mean Hutu Rwandans.
28. Police Judiciaire près le Parquet du Procureur du Roi de Bruxelles, PV no. 30339, dossier 36/95.
29. Des Forges, *Leave None to Tell the Story*, p. 289.
30. Ibid., p. 210.
31. Ibid.
32. Chrétien et al, *Rwanda, Les Médias*, p. 193.
33. Kamanzi, *Rwanda*, p. 146.
34. Ibid., p. 298.
35. UNAAMIR, Notes, Radio Rwanda, 20:00, 16 April 1994.
36. Des Forges, *Leave None to Tell the Story*, pp. 463–5.
37. Chrétien et al., *Rwanda, Les Médias*, p. 249.
38. Ibid., p. 300.
39. Belgium. Police Judiciaire Près le Parquet, pv no. 30339, dossier 36/95; Missionnaires d'Afriques, Guy Theunis and Jef Vleugels, fax no. 5, 8 April 1994.
40. Bwakira commune, 'Inyandiko-mvugo y'inama ya Komini yateranye kuwa' 24.5.94 in Tharcisse Kabasha, Bourgmestre to Sous-préfet Birambo, no. 340/04.04/2 6 June 1994.
41. Human Rights Watch/Féderation International des Ligues des Droits de l'Homme (FIDH), interviews, Kigali, 16 July 1995; Musebeya, 7 June and 28 August 1995.
42. Human Rights Watch/Féderation International des Ligues des Droits de l'Homme (FIDH), interview, Butare, 19 October 1995.
43. Des Forges, *Leave None to Tell the Story*, p. 542.
44. Ibid., pp. 269, 271, 273, 444.
45. Des Forges, *Leave None to Tell the Story*, p. 275.
46. Ibid., pp. 459–60.
47. Des Forges, *Leave None to Tell the Story*, pp. 291, 532; Human Rights Watch press release, 11 May 1994.
48. Des Forges, *Leave None to Tell the Story*, p. 649.
49. Frank G. Wisner, memorandum for deputy assistant to the president for national security affairs, National Security Council, 5 May 1994. See also, intelligence briefing memorandum from INR/AA–Janean Mann to AF–Ms Render, of 3 May 1994, and Chas. W. Freeman, Jr., memorandum for director joint staff, 3 May 1994. These and other documents cited here were provided by the National Security Archive, an NGO that assists researchers in obtaining access to once-classified United States government documents. The author thanks William Ferroggiaro of the archive for his kind assistance.

50. Metzl, 'Rwandan Genocide', p. 1.
51. See Genocide Convention Implementation Act of 1987 (the Proxmire Act) US code as of 1 May 1999.
52. Metzl, 'Rwandan Genocide'.
53. Testimony of Alison Des Forges, Human Rights Watch. The Crisis in Rwanda: Hearings Before the Subcommittee on Africa of the House Committee on Foreign Affairs, 103rd Congress, 15 (1994).
54. See, for example, press release of 11 May 1994.
55. Vincent D. Kern, director, memorandum for Walt Slocombe, 9 June 1994.
56. Acting under Secretary of Defense for Policy, memorandum for Secretary of Defense and Deputy Secretary of Defense, 9 June 1994. Subject: Senator Kennedy letter on jamming of Rwandan radio broadcasts (U).
57. See generally Burkhalter, 'The Question of Genocide'.
58. Cable from 'Amembassy Kinshasa to Secstate, WashDC', 17 July 1994; e-mail message from Col James Collier to Robert J. Taylor, 8 August 1994.
59. Point paper, United States role in suppressing or promoting radio broadcasts in and around Rwanda, 29 August 1994, prepared by Chuck Williamson, office of the Assistant Secretary of Defense (special operations/low-intensity conflict).
60. Cable drafted by AF/C K. Aiston, KCA, from 'Secstate WashDC to Amembassy Bujumbura and Amembassy Kinshasa', 17 August 1994.
61. Rwanda Radio IWG 18 August 1994, prepared by Chuck Williamson, office of the Assistant Secretary of Defense (special operations/low-intensity conflict).
62. Summary of conclusions, ad hoc meeting on Rwanda, 30 August 1994, drafted by K. Aiston, AF/C, enclosed in memo from AF-George Moose to P-Mr Tarnoff, 9 June 1994; France, Assemblée Nationale. 'Enquête sur la Tragédie Rwandaise' pp. 329–30.
63. Summary of conclusions, ibid.
64. France, Assemblée Nationale, 'Enquête sur la Tragédie Rwandaise', pp. 329–30.
65. Haq, 'Rwanda: Close Down Anti-Tutsi Radio'.
66. Background paper, Rwanda Radio update, 20 September 1994; radio broadcast support to UNAMIR, 29 September 1994; and memorandum for the director, joint staff, 3 October 1994.
67. CdR Young to Deputy Director, Pms and Chief MEAF Div. Subject: peace-keeping core group SVTS, 21 July 1995.
68. Interview with Philippe Dahinden, Swiss journalist and Editor-in-Chief of Fondation Hirondelle, 5 June 2001.
69. On 30 April 1999, President Clinton signed Presidential Decision Directive NSC–68. This directive is extensively quoted in the endnotes to Chapter 1.

9

The Learning Curve:
Media Development in Kosovo

Julie Mertus and Mark Thompson

Context and Beginnings

On 24 March 1999, the North Atlantic Treaty Organisation (NATO) launched an aerial bombing campaign against the Federal Republic of Yugoslavia (FRY). NATO leaders wanted Yugoslav President Milosevic to accept the settlement they had designed for the Serbian province of Kosovo. After seventy-eight days of bombing, Milosevic yielded.[1] When NATO forces entered Kosovo on 14 June 1999, they took control of a province without a functioning government, administration, security or legal system. All of these would have to be provided by the international community.

Following the Yugoslav authorities' acceptance of the Kosovo peace agreement, the UN Security Council adopted a resolution setting forth the mandate of the international mission that would attempt to rebuild peace and establish 'provisional democratic self-governing institutions' in Kosovo.[2] Security Council Resolution 1244 (10 June 1999) authorized the creation of an international security presence, known as KFOR (Kosovo Force), and an international civil presence, known as UNMIK (United Nations Interim Mission in Kosovo). These twin bodies were created to operate in Kosovo on behalf of the international community for the purpose of securing and administering the territory.

The international security presence, led by and primarily composed of NATO forces, was mandated to 'deter renewed hostilities', 'demilitarise the Kosovo Liberation Army' (the KLA), and 'establish a secure environment in which refugees and displaced persons can return home in safety, the international civil presence can operate, a transitional administration can be established, and humanitarian aid can be delivered'.[3] The international security presence was also called upon to 'ensur[e] public safety and order until the international civil presence can, as appropriate, take over responsibility for this task'.[4]

According to paragraph 10 of the resolution, the international civil presence was responsible for:

[a]n interim administration for Kosovo under which the people of Kosovo can enjoy substantial autonomy within the Federal Republic

of Yugoslavia, and which will provide transitional administration while establishing and overseeing development of provisional democratic self-governing institutions to ensure conditions for a peaceful and normal life for all inhabitants of Kosovo.

The main responsibilities of the international civil presence included: 'promoting the establishment, pending a final settlement, of substantial autonomy and self-government in Kosovo', 'performing basic civilian administrative functions where and as long as they were required', 'organising and overseeing the development of provisional institutions for democratic and autonomous self-government pending a political settlement', 'maintaining civil law and order', 'protecting and promoting human rights', and 'assuring the safe and unimpeded return of all refugees and displaced persons to their homes in Kosovo'.

Paragraphs 6 and 11 of Resolution 1244 directed the UN secretary-general, in consultation with the Security Council, to appoint a Special Representative 'to control the implementation of the international civil presence'. On 2 July 1999, Kofi Anan appointed Bernard Kouchner, a former French health minister and co-founder of Médecins Sans Frontières, as his Special Representative in Kosovo. Kouchner moved quickly to solidify his power. Pursuant to the authority granted by Resolution 1244, Kouchner issued a regulation on 25 July 1999 vesting in UNMIK all legislative and executive authority in Kosovo. UNMIK Regulation 1 provided that the 'Special Representative of the Secretary-General may appoint any person to perform functions in the civil administration in Kosovo, including the judiciary, or remove such person.' Moreover, '[i]n the performance of the duties entrusted to the interim administration under United Nations Security Council Resolution 1244 (1999), UNMIK will, as necessary, issue legislative acts in the form of regulations.'[5] In this manner, the authority of the Special Representative to promulgate media regulations for Kosovo derives from Resolution 1244 and UNMIK Regulation 1.

The immense challenges facing UNMIK were to be tackled by a unique structure of four major institutional 'pillars'. Pillar one was humanitarian affairs, led by the UN High Commissioner for Refugees. Pillar two was civil administration of the province, under the United Nations itself. Pillar three was democratization and institution-building, to be led by the Organization for Security and Co-operation in Europe (OSCE), while pillar four, economic development, was primarily the responsibility of the European Union (EU).

Accordingly, the Permanent Council of the OSCE established a mission in Kosovo on 1 July 1999 as 'a distinct component within the overall framework' of UNMIK, where it would 'take the lead role in matters relating to institution- and democracy-building and human rights . . . including the development of a civil society, non-governmental organizations, political parties, and local media'.

The Media Mandate

Neither Security Council Resolution 1244 nor the so-called Rambouillet Accords addressed the issue of media.[6] The latter, indeed, was as negligent in this respect as the Dayton Peace Agreement for Bosnia and Herzegovina had been in 1995. Like Dayton, the Rambouillet document recognized international standards of freedom of expression without providing for media reform and development. As media development would naturally fall within the remit of pillar two, the OSCE commissioned three outside experts to propose what UNMIK's objectives and priorities for the media should be. This report argued that the international community had a 'clear opportunity to establish free and accountable media' in Kosovo. However, 'experience in Bosnia and Croatia confirms that democratic media cannot be established on the basis of incomplete or weakly asserted authority to regulate, monitor, and reform existing media.' Concretely, the report argued that UNMIK should establish a media affairs department within the OSCE pillar, with 'responsibility, authority, and resources to oversee regulatory matters, laws and standards, media development, and media monitoring'.[7]

The report was broadly accepted by the heads of UNMIK and OSCE in Kosovo, and soon thereafter by the head offices of OSCE in Vienna and the UN in New York. The UN and OSCE defined UNMIK's aim with local media: 'to contribute to the creation of conditions that support freedom of the press and freedom of information in Kosovo'. An 'integrated media affairs department' in the OSCE pillar would 'prepare media regulations, support for independent print and broadcast media in Kosovo, monitor the media and develop media laws and standards'. The Department's 'Concept of Operations' also foresaw the creation of a Media Monitoring Division and a Media Regulatory Commission, modelled on the much larger agency in Bosnia called the Independent Media Commission.[8] A Media Policy Board of seven members – six ethnic Albanians and one Serb – would advise on media issues.[9]

The Special Representative of the Secretary-General (SRSG) would 'appoint a media regulatory commission to manage the frequency spectrum, establish broadcast and press codes of practice, issue licences, and monitor compliance'. The UN Secretariat emphasized that the SRSG would actually issue the media regulations and appoint the members of advisory or consultative bodies. Thus, it was agreed at the outset that OSCE would, in the words of the UN's head of peacekeeping operations, perform 'all substantive and preparatory work on media issues', while the United Nations, in the person of the SRSG, would make the key decisions.

The new arrangement evolved in an informational and legal vacuum. Ownership and employment rights to the media were unclear. Kosovar Albanians refused to respect Yugoslav or Serbian laws, and hoped in many cases to wipe out the decade of Milosevic's full control by reverting to the status quo ante. Local Albanians and Serbs had nothing in common except mutual suspicion and hatred; genuine co-operation seemed out of the question for the foreseeable future. By autumn 1999, though, the media scene was busy, even crowded, with five or six daily newspapers, various magazines, and some forty radio stations. By early 2000, there were twenty-four television projects waiting for licences or equipment to start up. A small handful of these media attracted the lion's share of international funding. Others were criticized by local and international figures alike for their crudity and chauvinism. Kosovo journalists admitted that hate speech still blighted the media and that there was ample 'irresponsibility', meaning plentiful examples of unprincipled and substandard conduct.

With Kosovo under international administration, Albanian-language media enjoyed a freer reign in reporting events. The media was strictly segregated, with the Albanian-language media presenting only pro-Albanian points of view and the official Serbian media 'consistently hostile to the international community's efforts in Kosovo'.[10] Journalism remained a risky profession with sporadic acts of violence against both ethnic Serb and Albanian journalists reported throughout the province.[11] The print and broadcast media in both languages were prone to issue threats of violence against groups and individuals, spread disinformation, and otherwise incite violence.

Growing Pains

In this environment, the role of the international agencies was unclear and difficult. UNMIK faced challenges as great as any UN mission before it: governing a province not yet at peace, with an immature and divided local leadership, and a population recovering from oppression and atrocious violence. Unfortunately, if perhaps not so surprisingly, co-operation between the UNMIK leadership (henceforth UNMIK-UN) and OSCE did not run smoothly. While the distribution of tasks in the media mandate made sense on paper, it required trust between organizations that had not collaborated on such a scale before.

It appeared that Kouchner, his principal deputy and his director of public information may not have been fully informed of the terms of the media mandate agreed between the UN and OSCE secretariats. The first problems arose early in August, when UNMIK-UN sought to curb the OSCE's role, especially over media regulation, and built up a parallel media department. The basis for this move was Kouchner's insistence that management of the frequency spectrum belonged under 'civil administration', organized by UNMIK-UN, not with the OSCE in pillar three.

Kouchner and his colleagues were encouraged by harsh and largely misleading criticism of the OSCE media development strategy in the US press, apparently prompted by the World Press Freedom Committee (WPFC), an influential media watchdog group. The WPFC deplored in a letter to UN secretary-general Kofi Anan, dated 13 August 1999, what it saw as 'plans for a media control system in Kosovo' that was 'in conflict with the principles of democracy and freedom that the United Nations is pledged to uphold'.

Premised on the curious opinion that Kosovo's news media had 'once' been 'free and independent', and the no less curious assumption that UNMIK presented a grave threat to the restoration of this Utopia, the WPFC's argument was hollow. This did not prevent other international and Kosovar Albanian journalists from echoing the criticism that UNMIK's media plan would amount to improper impositions on local law by an occupying force, and violate international standards for free expression.[12] The International Federation of Journalists (IFJ) and the Committee to Protect Journalists were among the groups to express concern.

According to the *New York Times*, the Media Policy Board notably lacked media experience and would easily be controlled by OSCE. The OSCE responded that the board was modelled after other media boards in European countries where people without journalism experience frequently serve as board members.[13] As for the mooted Media Monitoring Division and the Media Regulatory Commission, they were intended not to censor the local news media, rather to 'support and monitor them consistent with Western media regulations'.[14] An OSCE spokesperson, Urdur Gunnarsdottir, clarified elements of the plan:

> The media commission will be [composed of] both international and local [officials] . . . Together with the media director, the commission will oversee things like media frequencies for radio and [television], giving out [licences], taking [licences] away, reviewing media laws, looking into a code of conduct, training journalists, trying to co-ordinate funding and donations.[15]

Some Kosovo journalists echoed these concerns, understandably wanting to deter UNMIK from limiting their newly won freedom. Others disagreed. Garantina Kraja, a local reporter for the Institute for War and Peace Reporting, claimed that 'all' senior Western journalists with experience in reforming the media in the Balkans agreed that Kosovo should not be viewed as a normal, functioning democratic state. On this analysis, Kosovo should be treated as an occupied state emerging from war and repression, where the 'occupying peacekeeping force' must work to 'plant the seeds for a free media, independent judiciary and thus create conditions for free elections'.[16]

Staff at the UN secretariat in New York were alarmed, perhaps unduly so, by the negative coverage. At this time, OSCE was arguing in line with previous agreement that the head of its Media Department, Douglas Davidson, a career officer from the US State Department, should be appointed as an 'interim media regulator', filling the regulatory vacuum while a body with appropriate international and local members was constituted. The SRSG declined to confirm this appointment. Negotiations continued between the two organizations over each nuance of the proposed interim procedures. The head of OSCE, Ambassador Daan Everts, accommodated the UN's objections, and the enforcement provision was weakened.

Meanwhile, UNMIK's own Press and Public Information Department had ceased at the end of July 1999 to issue provisional broadcasting licences. The *de facto* 'government' established by the Kosovo Liberation Army filled the void. KFOR also provided permission to broadcast in parts of the province. By early September, KFOR had allocated FM frequencies to thirty-nine radio stations. This proliferation was haphazard in technical terms, but not politically. The emerging pattern of media power in the electronic and print sectors favoured the KLA, as the strongest and best-positioned ethnic Albanian grouping.

On 19 September 1999, with the need for an overall regulatory authority ever more urgent, Kouchner and Everts finally agreed on the remit of a 'Temporary Media Commissioner' (TMC), dropping the contentious term 'regulator'. Now the OSCE spokesman objected privately to the provision that the press 'may temporarily be subject to a Code of Practice . . . until such time as professional self-regulation by the print media can be instituted'. Everts diluted the remit again.

During October 1999, distressed by ferocious press attacks on moderate Kosovo leader Veton Surroi, and reportedly also vexed by inflammatory attacks on UNMIK in the press, the SRSG referred to the possibility of imposing a press code of conduct. This provoked another revolt inside the OSCE Media Department, appealing to the principle that only self-regulation of the press was admissible. Everts agreed that the Media Department should encourage the establishment of a journalists' association that could endorse a self-regulatory code of practice for the press. Thus the appointment of a TMC was held up for a further month, until 18 October 1999.

Over the next six months, the TMC issued one temporary licence, valid for six months, and approved a further thirteen to KFOR, which still controlled the spectrum and allocated frequencies. KFOR was inhibited from allocating further frequencies by unresolved legal questions concerning Belgrade's authority over the spectrum. Local journalists simply ignored licensing requirements, resulting in a proliferation of unlicensed broadcasting. By mid-June 2000, more than twenty-five unlicensed radio stations were operating without sanction. However, by the end of the year all the broadcasters in Kosovo had received provisional licences and frequencies in accordance with a new frequency plan, and were required to respect a broadcasting code of conduct. Competitive tenders were applied to multiple applicants.

Regulation against Hate Speech

With the proposed Media Policy Board failing to garner support and international media watchdogs snapping at UNMIK's heels, the mission opted to encourage self-regulation by the journalists themselves. A voluntary 'Professional Code of Conduct' was developed with expert assistance from the Independent Media Commission in Sarajevo, the Council of Europe, COLPI (the Constitutional and Legal Policy Institute of the Open Society Institute) and the International Federation of Journalists (IFJ). Progress was hampered by the weakness of the local association of journalists. The code was never formally adopted, and the basic provisions of the code had little effect on the Albanian-language media. For the most part, Serbian journalists refused to participate in self-regulation efforts.[17]

Meanwhile, various newspapers and magazines, as well as radio stations and public figures, continued to stoke the fires of political intolerance and inter-ethnic hatred: what the international community considered to be 'hate speech'. For example, the Albanian daily *Bota sot*, supportive of the Democratic League of Kosovo (LDK), was frequently criticized by OSCE for its inflammatory and prejudicial language.[18]

In the absence of other instruments to address this deteriorating situation, the SRSG promulgated on 1 February 2000 a draconian and in parts vaguely worded 'Regulation (no. 2000/4) on the Prohibition Against Inciting to National, Racial, Religious or Ethnic Hatred, Discord or Intolerance'. The new law did not refer specifically to the media. The terms of UNMIK Regulation 2000/4 referred to 'whoever publicly incites or publicly spreads hatred, discord or intolerance . . . likely to disturb public order'. Violators were to be 'punished by a fine or by imprisonment not exceeding five years or both'. If the acts prohibited in UNMIK Regulation 2000/4 were carried out system-atically, through an abuse of position, or with the result of 'disorder, violence or other grave consequences', then the period of imprisonment could be extended to a maximum of eight years. Acts which 'disturb the public order through coercion, jeopardising of safety, exposing to derision of national, racial, ethnic or religious symbols, damaging belongings of another, or desecrating monu-ments or graves' were also subject to the higher penalty of a maximum of eight years. This term might be extended to a maximum of ten years – far exceeding European norms – where the actions were systematic or involved an abuse of position. UNMIK Regulation 2000/4 amended and applied to any criminal law and criminal procedural law already in existence.

The OSCE supported UNMIK Regulation 2000/4 as a necessary step to create a 'democratic society in which civil discussions and political debates must take place in a responsible and non-violent manner'.[19] Daan Everts emphasized that the OSCE had no intention of regulating the print media; however, he did leave a door open should it become necessary in the future:

> I raise this now because while the mechanisms will exist to pull the plug on a radio or TV station, the same cannot be done to a newspaper. We have no plan to have a press law for printed media; in fact we are determined *not* to have such a law. It smacks of censorship.[20]

While promoting Regulation 2000/4, Everts stressed the importance of self-regulation, and the preference demonstrated by the international community for a more lenient approach to media regulation.

The intention behind Regulation 2000/4 was to deter hate speech and curb communal violence. Its failure to achieve this effect was confirmed when a simmering crisis in the divided city of Mitrovica came to the boil only two days after the Regulation was promulgated (see below). Local media coverage of the crisis confirmed the dangerously irresponsible and unprofessional standard of Kosovo journalism. Two dailies, *Bota Sot* and *Rilindija*, routinely incited hatred against all Serbs in Kosovo, and portrayed UNMIK and KFOR as in league with Serbs against Albanians. One of the best illustrations of the problem occurred not in a newspaper but in a radio news bulletin, on 10 February 2000, on Radio Rilindija, a private station with international funding. The bulletin led with an objective report on Kouchner's regulation against hate speech, only to end with an item that included the following language: 'After the massacre that occurred in northern Mitrovica, where the criminal bands of the terrorist Belgrade regime killed nine and wounded a dozen others, Serb criminals celebrated in their *chetnik* style.'

Public Service Broadcasting for Kosovo?

The unhappy saga over regulation did not prevent the relaunch of broadcasting in Kosovo. Yet here, too, there was a damaging degree of confusion or misunderstanding inside UNMIK. The OSCE had argued in July 1999 that UNMIK should relaunch Radio Television Pristina (RTP) 'as a genuine public broadcaster'. (In June, KFOR forces had prevented a group of former employees from occupying the RTP premises. The leadership of this group was reportedly close to the KLA. Prompt intervention by KFOR stopped the creation of a 'fact on the ground' that would have made it difficult if not impossible to reform RTP.) The original OSCE proposal had suggested that, while this launch was prepared, UNMIK might establish an emergency service to broadcast 'vital public information . . . under a new, neutral name . . . [giving] priority to international news services in local languages and to messages essential to UNMIK'.

The OSCE's ad-hoc expert group had emphasized that this 'would be an interim measure . . . not to be confused in any way with plans to launch RTP anew'. These suggestions were not incorporated into the mandate agreed with the UN. However, as early as 21 July the SRSG had publicly committed UNMIK, 'led by OSCE', to 'lay the foundation for RTP to become a genuine public broadcaster that serves all the people of Kosovo'. RTP would resume 'under international supervision', with the 'final aim' of creating 'a modern RTP that operates with professional Kosovar management and staff'.

Following initial contacts in July 1999 between the UN and the European Broadcasting Union (EBU), the latter proposed an 'Emergency Satellite TV Service', defined as a 'new station' that 'would serve both as a relay for UNMIK public information programmes and as the nucleus of a future regional public service respecting the programme needs and expectations of the entire population of Kosovo'. Given economic and other practical constraints, this departure from the OSCE's original concept was probably inevitable and need not have been harmful.

The EBU and UNMIK-UN argued that satellite was the only way to reach the public before the coming winter, given that the terrestrial network, comprising two transmission towers and an estimated forty relays, had been shattered during the recent conflict. An early plan by OSCE to repair the network with European Commission support collapsed when the EC became aware of a similar project with US and UK funding. The Japanese government subsequently offered to restore RTP's terrestrial network. Although nobody knew how many households owned satellite dishes – estimates ran from 20 per cent to 80 per cent – satellite transmission had the advantage of covering the whole province as well as an estimated 800,000 refugees and economic migrants around Europe.

The SRSG accepted this proposal. Despite the OSCE's responsibility, contractual negotiations were conducted between the UN and the EBU, another expression of the unclear boundaries regarding remit. On 30 August 1999, the EBU undertook to start broadcasting within three weeks. Radio Television Kosovo (RTK) started up on 19 September, under the interim direction of an experienced Swiss broadcaster. A team of young trainee journalists – soon to be replaced by former RTP employees – prepared an hourly programme, later increased to two hours of current affairs, sport, and children's shows. The centerpiece was a half-hour news programme, including short films prepared by the UN's television unit.

In practice, the EBU soon exceeded the 'emergency service' that it was contracted to provide. Foreseen as a self-contained, outside-broadcast unit supplemented with purchased equipment, RTK became instead a local television station with a sizeable number of Kosovar employees (over 100 by February 2000) working in reclaimed studios under international management, spending vast sums for leased equipment and the satellite connection; according to inside sources, the latter alone cost some 600,000 Deutschmarks per month.

Far from presenting it as an interim solution, UNMIK publicly hailed RTK as 'a first step towards a new public service broadcasting service'. It also claimed that the station was 'publicly funded', which was true only in the sense that the bill was paid from taxes levied in OSCE member states initially including Norway, Switzerland, France and the Netherlands. The US government withheld funds until a business plan for the station was adopted; in 2000, the US and Japan became the key donors to RTK, with Japan providing some US$14.5 million. The station also solicited and carried advertising.

Initially, international journalists ran the newsroom. As this assistance trailed off, more former RTP employees were recruited by EBU, partly to conciliate organized pressure (see below). By January 2000, international supervision or vetting of content had ceased, even though the station was explicitly subsidized by international funds as the showcase of UNMIK's media programme. This had professional but also political consequences. The first week of February 2000 was marked by a sequence of murders in the northern town of Mitrovica, starting with an attack on a UNHCR coach carrying Serb civilians. As the violence escalated, RTK spoke loosely of 'Serb criminals' and 'Serb terror', and reported accusations against French KFOR troops without carrying any reply by KFOR.

Although RTK's references to the Serb minority were usually more neutral than those of private broadcasters monitored by OSCE, few if any Serb sources were cited during the first phase of the Mitrovica crisis. The failure to investigate the less extreme views held, for example, by Serb leaders in the community of Gracanica, on the outskirts of Pristina, helped to preserve a simplistic picture of Serb minority attitudes.

RTK was a bold idea, realized with impressive speed and technical resourcefulness. Yet it was hard to accept the head of OSCE's claim, on 16 February 2000, that RTK was 'developing as an independent public broadcaster'. Given Kosovo's history and actual situation, it was always going to be extremely difficult to establish an indigenous public service broadcaster worthy of the title. Worse, UNMIK seemed to lack the will to commit itself to this objective. Corners were cut, and unnecessary compromises made. As noted above, local political factions jostled to dominate RTK, and the station was ill equipped to resist them. In the words of an international official closely involved with RTK in March 2000: 'We are recreating the old structure, which is what they [Kosovar Albanian leaders] want, but should we be doing it?' A comprehensive 'action plan for the creation of a free and independent news division at RTK', commissioned by OSCE from a private British consultant and delivered on 1 September 1999, was disregarded.

Journalists complained that the operation was neither transparent nor accountable. Local wits construed RTK as meaning Radio-Television Kouchner. There was neither a charter nor statutes. The interim director-general, Eric Lehmann, was slow to appoint a Kosovar deputy, as had been promised. Editors and managers were appointed by the EBU without consulting OSCE and, reportedly, without public advertising. To quote a local independent journalist: 'RTK is becoming more and more private, though I don't know who the owner is.' Complaints about the station's lack of professionalism were also frequent, albeit less worrisome.

The launch of RTK exacerbated OSCE's already awkward relations with the 'Co-ordinating Council of the Former Employees of RTP', claiming to represent over 1,300 people. This organization's stated ambition was reinstatement or compensation. The unspoken political agenda, according to international officials, was to align RTK with the hard-line political faction led by Hashim Thaci. Hence the substitution by EBU of newly trained, politically unaffiliated journalists by former RTP employees was viewed with concern. The same pressures were brought to bear on *Rilindija*, formerly Kosovo's only Albanian-language daily newspaper, with considerable assets including a print works and distribution network.

A further problem with RTK was that the radio component had been developed quite separately; it had nothing to do with the EBU, even though it fell within the director-general's remit. On 24 July 1999, the SRSG announced that a local-language radio service should commence broadcasting within four days. OSCE rose to the challenge; Radio Pristina went on air on 28 July. By mid-August it was transmitting fourteen hours daily of Albanian, Serbian, and

Turkish programmes. Foreign NGOs or governments donated salaries, training, and some equipment. The station was beset by technical problems arising from the lack of terrestrial transmitters and its partial dependence on antiquated equipment salvaged from RTP.

Political manoeuvring to influence the media took place, of course, on both sides of the ethnic divide. Representatives of the Serb minority (including Radio Kontakt, perhaps the only Serbian-language station with an independent editorial line) alleged that Milosevic allies in Kosovo controlled seven local radio stations and planned to launch a television station in Pristina. Kontakt's director, Zvonko Tarle, warned that:

> the international community has done little to try to curb Milosevic's influence in Kosovo. But if he is allowed to continue to hold sway over the Serb enclaves, the minority's more moderate representatives, who are crucial to Serb integration, will find themselves increasingly marginalised and ineffectual.[21]

International Radio Stations

There were two international radio stations, UNMIK's Radio Blue Sky and KFOR's Radio Galaxy. Blue Sky was allegedly created because local radio stations were reluctant to broadcast short programmes produced by UNMIK-UN's radio unit, on the ground that their credibility among ethnic Albanians would be destroyed if they transmitted Serbian-language programmes. It also appeared that the SRSG wanted UNMIK to have its own radio station, regardless of international and local objections. Kosovar journalists were irritated that the station was launched on 2 October 1999, the day after the Media Advisory Board, comprising local members under OSCE chairmanship, had unanimously rejected the proposal for an UNMIK radio station.[22]

The OSCE had originally advised against a mission radio station on the grounds that it would deplete the pool of experienced local journalists, provoke resentment and probably fail to gain a reputation for impartiality. Kouchner's predecessor had accepted these arguments. While UNMIK's frustration at the non-co-operation by local radio stations was understandable, it was regrettable that the resources behind Blue Sky were not used to improve Radio Kosova instead, including the relaunch of its Serbian-language component.

Information Intervention Comes of Age

The Dita *Incident*

According to many analysts, it took the murder of Petar Topoljski, a 25-year-old Kosovo Serb branded as a war criminal in the Albanian-language daily *Dita*, to mobilize the international community to take media regulation in Kosovo seriously. This highly publicized and controversial incident not only led to the issuing of strict media regulations by the UN and the OSCE on local media, but also to major debates, locally, nationally and internationally, on the subject of media regulation in general and on whether or not the international community's actions were consistent with democratic principles.

On 27 April 2000, an article in *Dita* accused Topoljski of war crimes, including in its report his name, address, place of work (he was employed as a translator by UNMIK), and details of places he frequented.[23] He was found strangled and stabbed to death on 16 May, having been missing for a week. On 3 June, Bernard Kouchner temporarily shut down *Dita*'s offices after the daily refused to apologize for having printed the Topoljski article. The following day, Kosovo Albanian journalists demanded access to *Dita*'s offices. The paper's editor, Belul Beqaj, announced his intention to sue Kouchner.[24] He said he was sorry about Topoljski's death, but defended the decision to publish the article and insisted that the editors were only doing their job.[25] *Dita* printed an open letter to Kouchner indicating that it would not cease to publish the names of Serbs believed to be 'involved in anti-Albanian activities'. Beqaj warned, 'I can say that, if we reveal facts about an individual, we are not doing so out of hatred. But if we cover up those facts, we will simply provoke more hatred.'[26] Beqaj blamed the UN for not properly vetting war criminals in its screening and recruitment practices.[27]

The leading independent daily, *Koha Ditore*, offered to reserve several pages each day for *Dita*'s editorial pages while its offices were closed. The sympathy of other Albanian papers was reflected in *Koha Ditore*'s 4 June 2000 headline: '*Dita* is closed by decree, not through normal procedure'.[28] Veton Surroi, editor of *Koha Ditore*, commented, 'It seems to me that if Mr Kouchner wanted to convey a message in favour of tolerance and against ethnic violence, then in fact, he has done quite the opposite.'[29] Hacif Muliqui, head of the Kosovo Journalists' Association, also criticized the international community's reaction to the *Dita* article. He emphasized that many journalists felt compelled to print information on war criminals because of the poor legal system in Kosovo. He also pointed out that the tendency of the UN and the OSCE to hire people without carrying out proper background checks.[30] Muliqi contended that Kouchner himself had broken the law by halting publication of the newspaper without a court hearing.[31] The Kosovo Journalists' Association called the closure of *Dita* 'an arbitrary act which endangers press freedom', and asked the UN to rethink the decision that 'could set a dangerous precedent for the local media'.[32] When the paper resumed publication, its sales reportedly boomed.

Dita's suspension raised a myriad of questions over the role of the international community in regulating the media in the context of a postwar reconstruction. It also revived the tension between the OSCE and the UN Mission in Kosovo. Though the OSCE publicly condemned what came to be known as 'vigilante journalism', Everts sent a letter to Kouchner saying that a 'preferred approach' would have been to order an apology or a retraction by the newspaper.[33]

Print and Broadcast Regulations

During the period of the *Dita* case, Kosovar Albanian media accusations against Serbs working for UNMIK became so prolific that the OSCE was forced to evacuate Serb workers accused in the press of war crimes.[34] The OSCE complained about biased coverage of ethnic violence by the Albanian-language broadcasters; Serbs who attacked Albanians were deemed 'criminals' or 'extremists', while Albanians who attacked Serbs had been 'provoked'.[35] Nor were Serbs the only ethnic minority to have been included in the media assault on alleged war criminals. Early in July 2000, the magazine *Kosovarja* published an article called 'Nightmare Butchers', which accused members of the Roma community of war crimes.[36] 'Sources of information from all battlefields support the reactions of Albanian public opinion proving with facts and names the participation of Roma in the ethnic cleansing campaign against Albanians', it said, and went on to identify eleven men.[37] For their part, Kosovar journalists contended that they were only attempting to contribute to the realization of justice in a society in which all institutions of justice – police, courts, prisons – had historically been among the worst perpetrators of injustice.[38]

In this context the international community revisited the idea of instating media regulations. One prominent independent commentator, the International Crisis Group (ICG), considered that the Topoljski article could legitimately be considered an incitement to violence:

> The facts of the Topoljski case itself remained obscure, with rumours flying and little confirmed by investigators. *Dita* seems to have had valid grounds for concern about the UN employment of an individual with an alleged background of questionable activities during the war. It also appears that international authorities may have failed to pursue these concerns when *Dita* raised them informally. But by presenting these issues in an article in which Topoljski was identified with a photograph, along with a description of his employment – in contrast with the Albanian witnesses in the story, who were identified only by initials – the handling of the matter by *Dita* amounted to an incitement to violence against Topoljski.[39]

The ICG implied that the international community shared the blame for Topoljski's death as it had been very slow to formulate its response to the article. Indeed, the international community had reacted only after Topoljski was found dead.[40]

While the *Dita* lawsuit was pending, Bernard Kouchner prepared new media regulations which included monetary fines of up to US$49,000 and threatened the seizure, suspension, or closure of offending media outlets.[41] On 5 June 2000, UNMIK announced that 'emergency legislation' was pending that would be 'quite limited and very temporary'.[42] On 17 June, Kouchner signed both UNMIK Regulation 2000/36 on the Licensing and Regulation of the Broadcast

Media in Kosovo, and UNMIK Regulation 2000/37 on the Conduct of the Print Media in Kosovo. UNMIK Regulation 2000/36 related specifically to the broadcast media, and established a Temporary Media Commissioner (TMC) to develop and promote 'an independent and professional media in Kosovo . . . pending the establishment of an Interim Media Commission'. Although nominally indpendent, the TMC was also the director of the OSCE Media Affairs department. Many perceived this as a conflict of interest. The OSCE was also responsible for recommending members for selection to a new body, the Media Appeals Board (see below), with final approval resting upon the Special Representative of the secretary-general.[43]

UNMIK Regulation 2000/36 also required radio and television operators to obtain a broadcast licence from the TMC, without which they were not permitted to broadcast. Radio and television operators who applied for a licence under the new system were required to abide by the Broadcast Code of Conduct issued by the TMC. Where the TMC refused to issue a licence, the applicant had to be provided with an explanation for the denial. Operators who failed to abide by the Broadcast Code of Conduct or UNMIK Regulation 2000/36 were subject to the following sanctions by the TMC:

1. the requirement to broadcast a correction or apology;
2. a warning;
3. a fine of not less than DM1,000 and not exceeding DM100,000;
4. suspension of the broadcast licence;
5. denial of entry into premises;
6. seizure of equipment;
7. closedown of broadcast operations; or
8. termination of the broadcast licence.[44]

In applying any of the forgoing sanctions, the TMC was required to provide written notice of violation and a reasonable opportunity for reply. Sanctions were to be applied without prejudice to any applicable criminal or civil causes of action. Acting on a suggestion that had been knocking around since February, Regulation 2000/36 also established an independent Media Appeals Board, to hear appeals of decisions of the TMC.

The impact of the Topoljski case on the development of these regulations was evident in the 'Special Provisions' section of UNMIK Regulation 2000/36. This section expressly prohibited the broadcasting of 'personal details of any person, including name, address or work place', if so doing 'would pose a serious threat to the life, safety or security of any such person through vigilante violence or otherwise'. The 'Special Provisions' section also permitted the Special Representative to take 'such action as he may deem necessary for security reasons, to protect life, or to maintain civil law and order'. There were no provisions explicitly limiting what actions the Special Representative might employ in such cases.

UNMIK Regulation 2000/37 took a similar approach to the print media in Kosovo. According to the OSCE, this regulation was passed to deal specifically with 'a spate of irresponsible reports in Kosovo newspapers directly endangering lives of individuals'.[45] It gave the TMC the authority to issue a temporary code of conduct for the print media. The TMC had to act in consultation with the Special Representative and 'interested media-related parties as appropriate' in preparing the code. The regulation emphasized the right everyone had 'to expect that allegations made against them will be investigated by the proper judicial authorities and [that] everyone must be presumed innocent until proven guilty in a court of law'.[46]

Those individuals subject to the Print Code of Conduct and 'applicable law' included 'owners, operators, publishers, editors-in-chief, and/or those with ultimate and final editorial control of publications published and/or distributed within Kosovo'. Nearly identical sanctions applied under the Broadcast Code of Conduct as under the Print Code of Conduct. Also, those subject to the sanctions could appeal an adverse decision to the Media Appeals Board.

As well as complying with the temporary code of conduct, the print media had to adhere to the 'Special Provisions' section, which contained the same prohibitions on the publication of personal details as UNMIK Regulation 2000/36. Again, the Special Representative was authorized to take whatever action he deemed appropriate 'for security reasons, to protect life, or to maintain civil law and order'.

International and local journalists and editors alike opposed the UNMIK regulations as undemocratic and impermissible restrictions on the freedom of the press.[47] ARTICLE 19, for example, described the press regulation as 'completely unacceptable, since it was drawn up and will be enforced by the same body'. The International Federation of Journalists (IFJ) had reportedly tried to dissuade UNMIK from issuing the regulations by arguing that 'the OSCE is supposed to provide the building blocks of press freedom and democracy and now it is being asked to play the role of press police. None of this makes sense'. The OSCE countered that 'freedom of the press is not limitless. It ends where another basic right is trespassed, namely the right to life', and that attempts at self-regulation by the Kosovo media 'just haven't delivered'.[48]

To no one's surprise, *Dita* was the first newspaper subjected to action under UNMIK Regulation 2000/37. On 26 June 2000, after the paper printed details of two other individuals accused of war crimes, the Temporary Media Commissioner sent a warning letter to the daily, giving it until 2 July to reply before sanctions were imposed.[49] Davidson stated that the article printed by *Dita* was in violation of Section 4.1 of the Regulation on the Conduct of the Print Media (the section prohibiting owners, operators, publishers, and editors from publishing personal details which could threaten somebody's life, safety, or security). On 4 July 2000, still rebelling against the new regulations, *Dita* published the names, addresses, and photos of fifteen more Serbs accused of committing crimes against Albanians.[50]

On 12 July 2000, the Temporary Media Commissioner ordered *Dita* to publish a reply from a Serbian man, Svetislav Grujic, whom the paper had identified as a war criminal on 26 June, threatening to fine or even close the paper if the order was ignored.[51] Grujic's letter stated, 'In the most difficult of times for all Kosovars, especially Albanians, I was a humanist. I saved the lives of many Albanians and I thought I would be the last Serb in Kosovo to be accused of war crimes.' He also stated that many Serbs would label him a traitor for having made his statement.[52] However, while printing the letter, *Dita* juxtaposed it with a column in which the previous allegations were repeated.

On 21 July 2000, the OSCE issued a press release stating that the Temporary Media Commissioner had imposed a fine of DM25,000 on *Dita* and issued warnings to two other Kosovo publications for breaches of Article 4.1 of Regulation 2000/37.[53] The TMC required *Dita* to pay the fine by 25 July or face suspension. The paper refused and instead filed an appeal to the Media Appeals Board on 24 July. Three days later, on 27 July, the paper was temporarily shut down due to failure to pay the fine; it would be able to reopen once the fine had been paid.[54] In open defiance of UNMIK, *Dita* published on 1 August.[55] In view of the hostility between UNMIK, OSCE, and local and international journalists over this question, it was decided to separate the TMC from the OSCE Media Affairs department. A new TMC was appointed whose task was to improve relations with Kosovo journalists. His first action was to convene the Media Appeals Board.

On 13 and 14 September 2000, a public hearing was held on the *Dita* case. Two days later, the Media Appeals Board issued its decision. The Board found that the Commissioner's decision to impose the sanction 'had not satisfied the procedural guarantees required by internationally recognized human rights and the applicable law in Kosovo'. A majority of the Board referred the case back to the Temporary Media Commissioner for re-evaluation. In reaching its decision, the Board noted the state of flux and unrest in Kosovo, the fact that the European Court of Human Rights had recognised that restraints on freedom of expression were not prohibited as such, and that UNMIK Regulation 2000/37 was a temporary measure, promulgated with legitimate aims and a narrow focus and purpose. The Board was also concerned with the need to maintain 'appropriate procedural guarantees' which it found to be 'especially important where freedom of expression is concerned'. It noted that UNMIK Regulation 2000/37 provided no specific guidance on the imposition of sanctions, thus presenting the TMC with a dilemma. While sympathetic to the TMC, the Board concluded that the 20 July decision should be declared null and void for want of effective procedural safeguards.

The Board was particularly troubled by the imposition of sanctions after the newspaper had filed an appeal. In the opinion of the Board, any imposition of sanctions should have been stayed pending conclusion of the appeal process. In addition, the Board found that the formal reply available to the appellant 'did not permit a sufficient response to the case against him', and did not make clear what further actions were open to the appellant. Accordingly, the Board found a need for 'greater consistency and transparency . . . in relation to procedures and criteria'. The willingness of the Media Appeals Board to consider and effectively overrule a decision of the TMC demonstrated the potential for the

Board to act as an appropriate check on TMC discretion,[56] and encouraged a measure of trust in UNMIK's capacity to establish a democratic and accountable process. This made it possible for the new TMC to develop a public Media Hearings Board to evaluate complaints and alleged breaches of regulations.[57,58]

The Broadcast and Print Codes of Conduct

While the *Dita* case was pending, the Temporary Media Commissioner went ahead with plans to enact codes of conduct for the broadcast and print media operating in Kosovo. In September 2000, the TMC approved a Code of Conduct for the Broadcast Media in Kosovo.[59] In preparing the Code, the TMC consulted the Kosovo Media Policy Advisory Board, the Association of the Media of Kosovo, the International Federation of Journalists, the British non-governmental freedom of expression group, ARTICLE 19, and COLPI.[60] The Code specifically references the Universal Declaration of Human Rights, in particular Article 19 (freedom of opinion and expression) and Article 29 (exercise of rights is subject to the limitations of law needed to secure recognition and respect for the rights of others). The Code also references the European Convention on Human Rights, including Article 2 (right to life protected by law), 5 (right to liberty and security of the person), Article 6 (those accused of a crime are innocent until proven guilty, and press and public can be excluded from trials in the interests of public order, national security and justice), and Article 10 (right to freedom of expression, subject to restrictions of law necessary in the interests of society).

Under the Code, broadcasters were prohibited from making provocative statements that would fail to respect the ethnic, cultural, and religious diversity of Kosovo, encourage criminal or otherwise violent actions, or denigrate any ethnic or religious groups, or imply that such a group was responsible for criminal activity. In broadcasting individual criminal activity, broadcasters could not attribute responsibility to any individual until that individual had been found guilty by a 'lawfully constituted tribunal'. No personal details of such individuals were to be broadcast absent such a finding of guilt or the permission of an administrative authority.

In encouraging 'fairness and impartiality', the Code exhorted broadcasters to strive to ensure 'accuracy, fairness, and impartiality in all reporting', to present different points of view, and not promote the interests of only one political party or point of view. In addition, the broadcast media must respect laws relating to electoral rules, and other laws 'applicable to media-related activities'. Broadcasters had to distinguish clearly between their opinions and facts, and ensure that facts were obtained through 'prudent and reasonable inquiry', and were not false or deceptive.

In deciding what materials to publish, broadcasters were prohibited from restricting or censoring expression on the basis of the language of that expression, particularly if the language was that of an ethnic minority. Where broadcast material placed 'a person, group or an institution in an unfavourable light', members of the public were extended a right of reply 'if fairness and impartiality require it', and corrections to false broadcasts were to be given 'as soon as possible'. In both cases, the reply or correction were to be given 'equal prominence' to the unfavourable content/false content. To facilitate the reception of complaints and requests to reply, details were to be broadcast indicating where such inquiries could be sent. In addition, to facilitate the handling of complaints to the TMC, broadcasters had to keep appropriate recordings of broadcasts for 'at least 21 days', and preserve the recordings until a complaint had been resolved, if the TMC so requested.

The Temporary Code of Conduct for Print Media followed essentially the same requirements as the Broadcast Code of Conduct.[61] The same articles of the Universal Declaration of Human Rights and the European Convention on Human Rights were incorporated by reference, setting forth the rights that the Code affirmed to protect. One substantive difference between the codes was that the print media code was explicitly 'temporary'. Also, because print media did not need to obtain a licence to publish, there was no requirement for them to demonstrate support for the Code by signing it. (The Broadcast Code of Conduct, by contrast, was distributed with all licence applications, requiring each applicant's signature.)

The Print Code prohibited publishers from 'writing, printing, publishing, or distributing any material that encourages criminal activity or violence'. In addition, publishers were obliged to refrain from:

1. circulating material that denigrated an ethnic or religious group or implied that an ethnic or religious group was responsible for criminal activity;
2. attributing criminal responsibility to anyone before that person had been found guilty in a court of law;
3. publishing specific information about an individual alleged to have committed a crime, including their name or picture, unless authorization had been given by authorities responsible for the administration of justice (e.g., the police and the judiciary), or unless the individual had been indicted or found guilty of the crime in a court of law.[62]

The Code also exhorted the print media to respect other laws relevant to the media, including rules established for the elections. It outlined the basic norms and rules found in other European domestic codes for print media, including the obligation of the media to distinguish between fact and opinion, and to verify as far as possible the truthfulness of what they printed. The Code required publishers to allow the public the opportunity to reply to what was written in the publication and to make complaints. In the case of incorrect information, the publication was required to publish all corrections.

After the *Dita* ruling, the Temporary Media Commissioner established

Rules of Procedure to handle complaints. Henceforth complaints were to be reviewed by the Commissioner with her or his legal advisers, and the decision conveyed to the newspaper in question. If the paper's action was not satisfactory, the Media Hearings Board (MHB), comprising one international and two local members, would examine the case. If the MHB decided that the Temporary Code had been violated, it would recommend sanction. The paper could choose to appeal to the Media Appeals Board, comprising one local and two international members, whose ruling would be final. The combination of regulation 2000/37, the Code of Conduct, and the generally accepted procedure for addressing complaints enabled the TMC to take action against *Bota Sot*, the most egregious violator of regulation 2000/37, in autumn 2000. This move had the tacit support of many Kosovo journalists and some international journalist organizations. *Bota Sot* was eventually fined and the TMC's decision was upheld in appeal. *Bota Sot* duly paid the fine, instilling confidence in the regulatory mechanism.

Towards the First Elections

The municipal elections in Kosovo on 28 October 2000 provided an acid test for UNMIK and its new media regulations. The OSCE was responsible for organizing elections in Kosovo, as it also was in Bosnia and Herzegovina. Self-evidently, a certain standard of media freedom and responsibility would be essential to the success of the electoral process.[63]

The OSCE contended that the UNMIK hate speech regulations and the UNMIK media codes of conduct would help ensure accuracy, fairness, and impartiality in election reporting. Nonetheless, the international community feared that these measures would be insufficient to safeguard against harassment of journalists who were reporting on the elections, and was concerned that biased, inflammatory, and inaccurate reporting would endanger the electoral process.[64] To combat these dangers, the UNMIK Central Election Commission adopted specific rules as early as 13 July 2000 to govern the conduct of the media during the run-up to the elections. The 'Electoral Rule on the Media during the Election Campaign' was essentially an 'equal time' provision. It stipulated that the media must strive to ensure that all certified political parties, coalitions, citizens' initiatives, and independent candidates should receive fair and equitable news coverage, as well as fair exposure through interviews, articles, debates, and coverage of campaign activities during the entire electoral process.[65] Specifically, during the forty-five days prior to polling day, all broadcast media were to provide free and equal airtime to those certified to contest the elections. Paid political advertising was to be allowed in the print media, but not in the broadcast media. All media coverage was to cease in the twenty-four hours prior to the opening of the polling stations and no further coverage was to be allowed until after polls closed.[66]

Other measures to guard against biased election reporting included European-Union funded media monitoring by the OSCE mission in

Kosovo, the explicit prohibition in the election code of the use by political parties of language that 'incites hatred', and the decision to include media monitoring in the mandate of the Council of Europe Election Observation Mission.[67]

At the same time, the months before and after the elections brought significant progress in other areas of media development. A new Temporary Media Commissioner, with experience in Bosnia, seemed more comfortable in the position than his predecessor; and a new director-general at RTK had given the aspiring public-service broadcaster a fresh sense of purpose and cohesion. September brought the long-awaited launch of two major private television stations, Koha Vision and TV 21. A comprehensive frequency plan and a licensing process were devized and implemented, with help from KFOR; tenders for two Kosovo-wide television licences and two radio licences were opened in November and awarded the following month.[68] Reconstruction of the terrestrial broadcasting network continued apace, with massive Japanese and some US assistance. The network became partly operational in December, reaching an estimated 60 per cent of the population. (RTK continued to use satellite transmission, pending the completion of the terrestrial network.) The Media Appeals Board got into its stride, adjudicating a number of cases. The new TMC issued a 'set of Rules of Procedure [to] lay out the step-by-step rules by which infringements of regulations 2000/36 and 2000/37 and their associated codes will be determined and how sanctions will be applied'.

In the event, the municipal elections in Kosovo were conducted without incidents of violence and the grouping favoured by the international community, Ibrahim Rugova and his moderate party, the LDK, swept to victory.[69] While the Albanian-language media did not uniformly adhere to the election media regulations, and much of the press showed political bias, monitoring by a team of local analysts found that the principal electronic media 'treated the political parties neutrally'. RTK and Koha Vision, one of the two Kosovo-wide private stations, reported regularly on minority issues, with RTK in particular, as befitted a public service broadcaster, trying to rebuild inter-ethnic relations.[70]

A perceptible improvement in the conduct of the media was one of many factors credited for the easing of tensions prior to the elections and for contributing to the calm acceptance of results that certainly did not suit the most powerful ethnic Albanian faction.

Conclusion

This chapter is not comprehensive. For example, it barely touches on the growth of private media. By spring 2001, Kosovo had seven provincial daily newspapers, three provincial television stations and two radio stations, five or six local television stations and dozens of local radio stations: a remarkable array for a desperately impoverished population of under two million. Nor have we discussed the scale or pattern of donor activity that made this flourishing scene possible.

Instead, we have focused on the origins, beginning and evolution of media development by the international mission. If our account seems at times unduly critical of international officials who were usually acting with the best intentions in uncommonly difficult circumstances, we hope also to have shown in convincing detail that valuable lessons were imported from Bosnia and some important initial errors in Kosovo were rectified. In short, that the learning curve pointed in the right, upward, direction.

Notwithstanding an awareness of the power of the media in Kosovo, the international community, after quickly and firmly establishing a presence in the province in June 1999, had at first been slow and hesitant in its efforts to engage local media and shape their role in securing peace. Instead of outright regulation, the international community favoured a more hands-off approach, including voluntary training of journalists and the infusion of financial support for independent media. During this period, as has been discussed, the international mission in Kosovo developed its own broadcasting enterprises in an effort to create quality programming and promote inter-ethnic conversation. In the first year of UNMIK's administration, it also supported the introduction of voluntary codes of conduct and, later, a hate speech law and self-regulation by the media in Kosovo. None of these efforts proved successful at stemming hate speech and raising professional standards.

In the spring and summer of 2000, two events prompted a change in policy. First, the Topoljski affair galvanized a new approach towards the impact of the press. Second, the international community began to prepare for the autumn 2000 municipal elections in Kosovo. Convinced that a more professional and less hate-filled media would ease tensions, and that more stringent international controls were the only way to reach this result, in the summer of 2000 the international community imposed a system of strict regulations for the print and broadcast media. Within a matter of months, the international authorities had progressed from imposing draconian decrees against incitement to instituting an autonomous check on their own power, in the form of the Media Appeals Board. By autumn 2001 (the time of writing), the Temporary Media Commissioner had licensed ninety-seven radio and twenty-four television stations, and was due soon to be replaced by an Independent Media Commission, modelled on the identically named institution in Bosnia. RTK's status as a news and entertainment provider had risen, and it had a board which would appoint the director. The challenges of drafting media legislation lie ahead.

'Information intervention' in Kosovo was by autumn 2001 (the time of writing), a work in process, unfinished, subject to dispute as to its contribution and even as to the standards by which it should be evaluated. Despite precedents in Bosnia and Herzegovina, the intervention was still too often practised on a trial and error basis. Post-conflict information intervention has over time become a central component of this evolving strategy for building long-lasting peace in the Balkans. As with other aspects of international intervention, the timing and pace of implementation, the vague nature of certain of the regulations, and the lack of due process in certain cases have been troubling.

With hindsight, the controversies over the UNMIK media mandate in 1999 and 2000 sometimes generated more heat than light. For example, the pervasive atmosphere of intimidation in Kosovo was surely a far more significant obstacle to the exercise and development of professional journalism than the regulatory efforts of UNMIK, clumsy as these may sometimes have been. Yet journalists and media freedom organizations alike preferred to criticize UNMIK rather than dwell on the more pressing problem of physical security. A former member of the OSCE's Media Affairs Department has commented on the degree of 'self-censorship' among Kosovo journalists:

> The media are reluctant to even investigate the murder of their own reporters . . . [T]here was a deafening silence on both the murder [of Shefki Popova] and the question of intimidation of journalists . . . Not a single Albanian reporter to date has been willing to file official complaints against other Albanians threatening them.[71]

This bleak appraisal indicates how brutalized Kosovo has been by its recent history, and how long it may yet take to change people's – including journalists' – sense of acceptable professional risk.

Nonetheless, the media intervention considered in this chapter holds promise for addressing the needs of peace-building. In particular, post-conflict information intervention has provided the impetus for enhancing security among journalists and society at large, improving the fairness of the electoral process, thereby strengthening political institutions and revitalizing society. The processes and structures for regulation that have emerged from Kosovo provide an important precedent for future peacekeeping efforts.[72]

Debate will continue about the general legality of the forms of intervention that were used in Kosovo. For our part, we conclude that the measures of information intervention have fallen well within the internationally accepted and appropriate parameters. Regardless of whether the UNMIK operation is viewed as an occupation or, more likely, a consensual peacekeeping operation, the media-related aspects of the intervention conform to humanitarian law.[73]

Moreover, the restrictions on speech are permissible in human rights terms as necessary temporary measures designed to improve the overall dignity and freedom of individuals and groups. Human rights standards provide ample room for the media regulations created by UNMIK for Kosovo. In particular, the kind of hate speech regulation promulgated for Kosovo is well supported by international law and by the law of the European Court of Human Rights.[74] The other media regulations in Kosovo find support in the general limitations to free expression found in the Universal Declaration of Human Rights, the International Covenant on Civil and Political Rights, and the European

Convention on Human Rights. The regulations helped safeguard public order in an extremely tense postwar situation and deterred individuals from acting to destroy the rights of others. Moreover, in a time of post-conflict democratic institution-building, the regulations helped preserve a fragile peace and, in so doing, opened a safe space for wider participation in public life. If indeed the international community is taking a new and more assertive stance toward post-conflict media reform and development, it is a welcome one that should prove instrumental in building peaceful and just societies in the Balkans and also elsewhere.

Acknowledgements

Julie Mertus gratefully acknowledges the research assistance of Katherine Guernsey and Maryanne Yerkes. She also wishes to thank Monroe Price for encouraging her to study 'information intervention' in the Balkans.

Bibliography

Balkan Information Exchange (4 July 2000), 'Dita Defies Sanctions, Publishes more Names'. Source: Agence France Presse (AFP).
——— (4 June 2000), 'Journalists Demand Access to Closed Kosovo Newspaper'. Source: Deutsche Presse-Agentur (DPA).
——— (28 July 2000), 'Kosovo Albanian Newspaper Prints Serb Letter', Regional Politics Section. Sources: Agence France Presse (AFP), Associated Press (AP), British Broadcasting Corporation Summary of B2-92 Radio and Kosovapress News Agency, Organization for Security and Co-operation in Europe (OSCE).
——— (27 July 2000), 'Kosovo Daily Closed over Fine Payment'.
——— (10 August 2000), 'OSCE Takes Action on Kosovo Media', no. 343.
——— (15 August 2000), 'Rules Set for Kosovo Elections', no. 351.
BBC News (17 May 2000), 'Serb UN Employee found dead', Online [August 2001], available at http://news6.thdo.bbc.co.uk/hi/english/world/europe/newsid%5F752000/7526 92.stm
Defeis, Elizabeth F. (1992), 'Freedom of Expression and International Norms: A Response to Hate Speech', *Stanford Journal of International Law*, vol. 29.
Everts, Daan (16 February 2000), 'Speech Given on the Occasion of the Opening of the New Studios of Radio Television Kosovo'. Online [August 2001], available at http://www.osce.org/kosovo/hom/speeches/homspeech1_mediapolicy.htm
Farrior, Stephanie (1996), 'Molding the Matrix: The Historical and Theoretical Foundations of International Law Concerning Hate Speech', *Berkeley Journal of International Law*, vol. 14, pp. 3–98.
Hider, James (17 May 2000), 'Pressure for Kosovo Press Regulation Mounts after UN Murder', Agence France-Presse, available at 2000 WL 2795343.
Human Rights Watch (October 1998), 'Federal Republic of Yugoslavia: Humanitarian Law Violations in Kosovo', *Human Rights Watch Publications*, vol. 10, no. 9.

282   JULIE MERTUS AND MARK THOMPSON

———— (October 2000), 'Municipal Elections in Kosovo', Human Rights Backgrounder. Online [August 2001], available at www.hrw.org/backgrounder/eca/kosovo-election-bck.html

Independent International Commission on Kosovo, *The Kosovo Report*. Online [August 2001], available at www.kosovocommission.org/index.html

International Center for Journalists (22 May 2000), 'Assassination of UN Serb Employee Rekindles Debate over Press Restrictions in Kosovo', International Journalists' Network. Online [September 2001], available at http://www.ijnet.org/Archive/2000/5/26-7058.html

———— (13 September 2000) 'International media organizations condemn slaying of journalist in Kosovo', International Journalists' Network.

———— (20 August 1999), 'Media Groups Question Plans for Media Control in Kosovo', International Journalists' Network. Online [August 2001], available at http://www.ijnet.org/Archive/1999/8/20-5880.html

———— (30 September 1999), 'OSCE Media Policy Body in Kosovo Generates Debate', International Journalists' Network. Online [August 2001], available at http://www.ijnet.org/Archive/1999/9/30-6074.html

———— (14 July 2000) 'UN in Kosovo may Abandon Enforcing Press Code Opposed by Media', International Journalists' Network. Online [August 2001], available at http://www.ijnet.org/Archive/2000/7/14-7219.html

———— (12 June 2000), 'UN Mission in Kosovo to Draft Law on "Vigilante Journalism" ', International Journalists' Network. Online [September 2001], available at http://www.ijnet.org/Archive/2000/6/16-7135.html

International Crisis Group (7 July 2000), 'Elections in Kosovo: Moving Toward Democracy?' Online [August 2001], available at http://www.intl-crisis-group.org/projects/kosovo/reports/kos37emai.html

Kraja, Garantina (6 September 1999), 'Kosovo Journalists' Suspicion of OSCE Media Controls', Institute for War and Peace Reporting, *Balkan Crisis Report*, no. 72. Online [August 2001], available at http://www.nyu.edu/globalbeat/balkan/Kraja090399.html

Maliqi, Shkelzen (1 November 2000) 'Rugova Triumphs', Institute for War and Peace Reporting, *Balkan Crisis Report*, no. 191. Online [September 2001], available at www.iwpr.net

Mertens, Richard (7 August 2000), 'UN Muzzles "Vigilante" Press', *St Petersburg Times*, at 1A, available at 2000 WL 5628059.

OSCE, '*Belul Beqaj and Dita v. Temporary Media Commissioner*'. Summary of appeal and hearing online [September 2001] available at http://www.osce.org/kosovo/bodies/tmc/cases/dita_file.php3?n = 6

———— (21 June 2000), 'Broadcast and Print Regulations for Kosovo Media Approved', OSCE press release. Online [September 2001], available at http://www.osce.org/news/generate.php3?news_id = 816

———— (8 September 2000) Code of Conduct for the Broadcast Media in Kosovo. Online available on the OSCE web site http://www.osce.org

———— (19 September 2000), Code of Conduct for Print Media in Kosovo, OSCE Press Release. Online [September 2001], available at http://www.osce.org/press_rel/2000/09/1043-mik.html

———— (21 July 2000), 'Kosovo Newspaper Fined, Two Others Warned by Temporary Media Commissioner', OSCE Press Release, available at http://www.osce.org/press_-rel/2000/07/904-mik.html

—— (9 February 2000), 'Regulation Against Incitement of Hatred is Key for a Democratic Kosovo', OSCE press release. Online [October 2001], available at http://www.osce.org/news/generate.php3?news_id=206

—— (7 November 2000), 'Rules and Procedures Established for Kosovo Media', OSCE press release. Online available on the OSCE web site, http://www.osce.org

—— (18 September 2000), Temporary Code of Conduct for the Print Media in Kosovo, (pursuant to Section 1 of UNMIK Regulation No. 2000/37 On the Conduct of the Print Media in Kosovo of 17 June 2000). Online [September 2001] http://www.osce.org/kosovo/bodies/tmc/pcoc.php3?1g=e.

—— (28 June 2000), 'Temporary Media Commissioner Issues Warning Letter to Pristina-based Newspaper Dita', OSCE press release. Online [August 2001], available at http://www.osce.org/press_rel/2000/06/854-mik.html

—— (12 July 2000), 'Temporary Media Commissioner Orders "Dita" to Publish Reply', OSCE press release. Online [August 2001], available at http://www.osce.org/press_rel/2000/07/874-mik.html

—— (15 September 2000), 'Temporary Media Commissioner Implements Broadcast Code of Conduct', OSCE press release. Available at http://www.osce.org/news/generate.php3?news_id=1036

Semini, Llazar (6 June 2000), 'UN to Stamp out Vigilante Journalism', Institute for War and Peace Reporting, *Balkan Crisis Report*, no. 146.

Soloway, Colin (6 February 2001), 'Comment: Intimidation Silences Pristina Media', Institute for War and Peace Reporting, *Balkan Crisis Report*, no. 215.

Tarle, Zvonko (15 February 2000), 'Milosevic Tightens Hold on Kosovo Serbs', Institute for War and Peace Reporting, *Balkan Crisis Report*, no. 116.

Wood, Nicholas (31 July 2000), 'In Kosovo, Newspaper "Exposes" of War Criminals Led to Murder', *The Guardian*, available at 2000 WL 25042420.

Notes

1. The United Nations Security Council adopted general principles on a political solution to the Kosovo crisis on 6 May 1999 (S/1999/516, Annexe 1 to UN Security Council Resolution 1244). The Federal Republic of Yugoslavia indicated its acceptance in a paper presented in Belgrade on 2 June 1999 (S/1999/649, Annexe 2 to UN Security Council Resolution 1244).
2. S/RES/1244 (1999), available at http://www.un.org/Docs/scres/1999/99sc1244.htm
3. Ibid., para. 9.
4. Ibid.
5. UNMIK/REG/1999/1 (Section 4). Section 4 further provides that '[s]uch regulations will remain in force until repealed by UNMIK or superceded by such rules as are subsequently issued by the institutions established under a political settlement, as provided in United Nations Security Council Resolution 1244.'
6. The 'Interim Agreement for Peace and Self-Government in Kosovo', is known as the Rambouillet Accords, after the French castle where negotiations over the Agreement were conducted in February and March 1999. Milosevic's rejection of the Accords triggered the NATO bombardment. UN Security Council Resolution 1244 explicitly referenced the Rambouillet document: Article 11 (a) and (e).
7. The 'Report of the Ad-Hoc Media Experts Group Mission to Kosovo 7 to 12 July

1999' was prepared for OSCE by Mr Dan De Luce, media development officer at the Office of the High Representative in Bosnia and Herzegovina, Dr Regan McCarthy, head of media development at the OSCE Mission to Bosnia and Herzegovina, and Mr Mark Thompson, co-author of this chapter.

8. OSCE Mission in Kosovo Media Affairs Department: Concept of Operations [Online summer 1999], available at http://www.osce.org/kosovo/media/concept/ htm. In a second attempt to draw lessons from elsewhere in the Balkans, the deputy director of the Independent Media Commission in Bosnia was asked in July 1999 to suggest how media regulation might be organized in Kosovo. (See also Chapter 5 of this volume by Peter Krug and Monroe E. Price.)

9. The Media Board comprised two prominent journalists, Baton Haxhiu of *Koha ditore* daily and Aferdita Kelmendi of Radio Television 21, and five 'respectable' public figures: Mahmut Bakalli, a former communist leader of Kosovo, Pajazit Nushi, former head of the Council for the Defence of Human Rights and Freedoms in Kosovo, Lirie Osmani, a lawyer, Shkelzen Maliqi of the Soros Open Society Foundation, and Aca Rakocevic, a Serb representative.

10. See International Crisis Group, 'Elections in Kosovo: Moving Toward Democracy?'

11. For example, Shefki Popova, a well-known reporter for the Kosovo daily *Rilindja* and its radio station, was gunned down in the town of Vucitrn on 10 September 2000. The killing followed the disappearance the day earlier of Marjan Melonasi, a Serbian-Albanian journalist who worked with the Serbian-language service of RTS. Also Valentina Cukic, editor of Serbian-language programming on Pristina's Radio Kontakt, survived an assassination attempt in June 2000. See International Center for Journalists, 'International Media Organizations Condemn Slaying of Journalist in Kosovo'. See also Human Rights Watch, 'Municipal Elections in Kosovo'.

12. International Center for Journalists. 'OSCE Media Policy Body in Kosovo Generates Debate'.

13. Kraja, 'Kosovo Journalists' Suspicion of OSCE Media Controls'.

14. Ibid.

15. Gunnarsdottir added that considerable financial help would likely be given to Kosovo's independent news media; however, the goal was to make the local media self-sustaining. See International Center for Journalists, 'Media Groups Question Plans for Media Control in Kosovo'.

16. Kraja, 'Kosovo Journalists' Suspicion of OSCE Media Controls'.

17. Independent International Commission on Kosovo, 'The Kosovo Report'.

18. In Kosovo, unlike anywhere else in the former Yugoslavia at this time, the press was the most influential source of news and information, due to the devastation of the broadcast sector and the electricity utilities during 1999. International Crisis Group, 'Elections in Kosovo: Moving Toward Democracy?'

19. OSCE, 'Regulation Against Incitement of Hatred is Key'.

20. Everts, 'Speech Given on the Occasion of the Opening of the New Studios of Radio Television Kosovo'.

21. Tarle, 'Milosevic Tightens Hold on Kosovo Serbs'.

22. Blue Sky and Galaxy were also criticized for diverting resources from local broadcasting efforts and failing to promote quality programming. See the report of the Independent International Commission on Kosovo. Online [August 2001], available at http://www.kosovocommission.org/index.html

23. BBC News, 'Serb UN Employee found dead'.
24. Balkan Information Exchange, 'Journalists Demand Access to Closed Kosovo Newspaper'.
25. Quoted in: International Center for Journalists, 'Assassination of UN Serb Employee Rekindles Debate over Press Restrictions in Kosovo'.
26. Semini, 'UN to Stamp out Vigilante Journalism'.
27. Quoted in ibid.
28. International Crisis Group, 'Elections in Kosovo: Moving Toward Democracy?'
29. Veton Surroi quoted in: International Center for Journalists, 'UN Mission In Kosovo to Draft Law on "Vigilante Journalism" '.
30. International Center for Journalists, 'Assassination of UN Serb Employee Rekindles Debate over Press Restrictions'.
31. International Center for Journalists, 'UN Mission In Kosovo to Draft Law on "Vigilante Journalism" '.
32. Semini, 'UN to Stamp out Vigilante Journalism'.
33. Ibid.
34. Hider, 'Pressure for Kosovo Press Regulation Mounts after UN Murder'.
35. Ibid.
36. Wood, 'In Kosovo, Newspaper "Exposes" of War Criminals Led to Murder'.
37. Ibid.
38. Ibid.
39. International Crisis Group, 'Elections in Kosovo: Moving Toward Democracy?'
40. Ibid.
41. International Center for Journalists, 'UN in Kosovo may Abandon Enforcing Press Code Opposed by Media'.
42. UNMIK spokesperson, Nadia Younes, on 5 June 2000.
43. The regulation stipulates that the Board is to comprise two international members and one local member.
44. UNMIK/REG/2000/36 (Section 3.1).
45. OSCE, Broadcast and Print Regulations for Kosovo Media Approved'.
46. OSCE, 'Kosovo Newspaper Fined'.
47. International Center for Journalists, 'UN in Kosovo may Abandon Enforcing Press Code Opposed by Media'.
48. ARTICLE 19 press release, 30 June 2000; Mertens, 'UN Muzzles "Vigilante" Press'.
49. OSCE, 'Temporary Media Commissioner Issues Warning Letter'.
50. International Center for Journalists, 'UN in Kosovo may Abandon Enforcing Press Code Opposed by Media'. See also Balkan Information Exchange, 'Dita Defies Sanctions, Publishes more Names'.
51. OSCE, 'Temporary Media Commissioner Orders "Dita" to Publish Reply'.
52. Balkan Information Exchange. 'Kosovo Albanian Newspaper Prints Serb Letter'.
53. OSCE, 'Kosovo Newspaper Fined'.
54. Balkan Information Exchange, 'Kosovo Daily Closed over Fine Payment'.
55. Balkan Information Exchange, 'Kosovo Daily Defies UN Order'. Source: *Agence France Presse*, 1 August 2000.
56. OSCE, '*Belul Beqaj and Dita v. Temporary Media Commissioner*'.
57. This innovation was accepted by local journalists who provided representation on the panel. Without dropping their objections to press regulations, international journalists' organizations also cooperated with the TMC in developing a press code and making the process as fair and inclusive as possible.

58. OSCE, 'Rules and Procedures Established for Kosovo Media'.
59. OSCE, Code of Conduct for the Broadcast Media in Kosovo.
60. OSCE, 'Temporary Media Commissioner Implements Broadcast Code of Conduct'.
61. OSCE, Temporary Code of Conduct for the Print Media in Kosovo.
62. OSCE, Code of Conduct for Print Media in Kosovo.
63. Freedom of expression and access to the media are recognized as crucial elements of free and fair elections. See Conference for Security and Cooperation in Europe, Document of the Copenhagen Meeting of the Conference on the Human Dimension of the CSCE, 5 June–29 July 1990, available at http://www.osce.org/docs/english/1990–1999/hd/cope90e.htm
64. See Human Rights Watch, 'Federal Republic of Yugoslavia'; Human Rights Watch, 'Municipal Elections in Kosovo'.
65. Balkan Information Exchange, 'OSCE Takes Action on Kosovo Media'.
66. Balkan Information Exchange, 'Rules Set for Kosovo Elections'.
67. See Human Rights Watch, 'Municipal Elections in Kosovo'.
68. US donors insisted on sponsoring two private television stations, for the dogmatic reason that pluralism required nothing less. Post-electoral efforts by those same donors to merge the stations were in vain. As a result, Kosovar viewers can choose between two under-resourced private television operations, competing for international support, rather than having a single, adequately resourced alternative to RTK.
69. Maliqi, 'Rugova Triumphs'.
70. The 'Gani Bobi' Centre for Humanistic Studies, in Pristina, was paid by the Open Society Institute to monitor Kosovo media throughout the election campaign. Its reports are available on the Press Now webs site, http://www.press now.org. The phrase quoted is taken from the second report, covering the period 29 September to 5 October 2000.
71. Soloway, 'Comment: Intimidation Silences Pristina Media'.
72. See Chapter 5 of this volume, by Peter Krug and Monroe Price.
73. See Chapter 4 of this volume by Julie Mertus.
74. See Defeis, 'Freedom of Expression and International Norms'; Farrior, 'Molding the Matrix; and Chapter 2 of this volume by Stephanie Farrior.

10

Preparing a Plebiscite under Fire: The United Nations and Public Information in East Timor

David Wimhurst[1]

Introduction

A key element of information intervention has been the preparation of a population for a plebiscite or election that is designed to help resolve conflict. The Popular Consultation of 1999 in East Timor is one of the most dramatic examples of this process. In the space of about three months, from early June to the end of August, the United Nations Mission in East Timor (UNAMET) public information team, tasked with assisting in ensuring a fair process, produced more than 700,000 pieces of printed information, five hours of daily radio broadcasts and thirty minutes of daily television programming, all in four languages – English, Bahasa Indonesian, Portuguese, and Tetun. In addition, the mission's web site posted numerous updates, including daily audio files, text, and photographs.

On the media front, more than 700 journalists were accredited from around the world, provided daily press briefings and organized countless interviews. The Public Information Office also briefed a steady stream of visitors – parliamentarians, diplomats, trade unionists, and others – who travelled to East Timor to observe at first-hand the conditions surrounding the popular consultation.

Background

The international community's interest in and response to the plight of East Timor since the Indonesian invasion of the territory on 7 December 1975 had ebbed rather than flowed during the twenty-four years that followed the invasion. Following Portugal's decision in mid-1975 to end its 400-year colonial rule of East Timor, through a planned transition to independence over a period of three years, civil conflict had erupted in the territory. The Frente Revolucionária de Timor Leste Independente (FRETILIN) was opposed by a coalition of pro-Indonesian parties, led by the União Democrática Timorense (UDT) and the Associação Popular Democrática, (APODETI). Indonesia's attack by land, air, and sea brutally ended the argument in favour of the integrationists. The United Nations condemned the invasion and recognized the right of the East Timorese people to self-determination. Security Council Resolution 384, adopted on 22 December 1975, called on Indonesia to withdraw its forces. It also urged Portugal, which had withdrawn abruptly several months earlier, to co-operate with the UN in enabling the people of East Timor to exercise their right to self-determination. However, almost a quarter of a century was to pass before any of this came to be.

The tide of international concern for East Timor began turning in favour of self-determination after the Santa Cruz massacre on 12 November 1991, when Indonesian troops killed a large number of unarmed protesters at the Santa Cruz cemetery in Dili, the East Timorese capital. The massacre was caught on film and shown on newscasts throughout the world. Estimates of casualties ranged from 150 to 400. A 1994 report to the United Nations Economic and Social Council further estimated that 100,000 Timorese had been killed by the Indonesian armed forces between 1975 and 1980. Another 100,000 were also said to have died from disease and starvation between 1980 and 1984.

The cause of self-determination was given a distinguished boost in 1996, when the Nobel Peace Prize was awarded to Carlos Ximenes Belo, Bishop of Dili and Apostolic Administrator of East Timor, and José Ramos Horta, writer and leader of the East Timorese resistance in exile. The two men were honoured 'for their work toward a just and peaceful solution of the conflict in East Timor'. Shortly thereafter, Kofi Anan was appointed secretary-general of the United Nations and he, in turn, moved swiftly to consolidate the increasingly favourable international climate towards a resolution of the issue by naming Ambassador Jamsheed Marker of Pakistan as his Personal Representative for East Timor, early in 1997.

The tripartite talks between Indonesia, Portugal, and the United Nations, which the new secretary-general and Ambassador Marker set in motion, made little progress until mid-1998, when President Suharto of Indonesia was removed from office and replaced by Vice-President Habibie. The new incumbent provided a fresh impetus to the UN initiative by offering East Timor wide-ranging autonomy within the Indonesian Republic. While Indonesia considered this position to be the solution to the problem, Portugal saw it as a transitional arrangement until such time as the people of East Timor could truly exercize their right to self-determination. The secretary-general, however, persuaded both parties to lay aside their differences on the final status of East Timor, without prejudice to either position, and focus instead on the content of an autonomy package. Negotiations between senior officials then centred on the package itself, with an agreement that the East Timorese should be included in the process. Ambassador Marker subsequently became the first UN official to visit Xanana Gusmão, the leader of the East Timorese resistance, in his Jakarta jail, where he had been serving a twenty-year sentence since 1992.

Talks on the autonomy proposal continued through the latter half of 1998 to the point where the issue of the final status of East Timor loomed large but prospects for an agreement on this question remained small. Then, two events occurred in quick succession that shifted the entire process into the realm of the possible.

In December 1998, Australia, the only state to have formally recognized Indonesian sovereignty over East Timor, changed its policy and called for self-determination for the East Timorese people. Prime Minister John Howard sent a personal letter explaining this change of course to President Habibie, who responded one month later with a surprise announcement of his own. If the people of East Timor did not agree to integration under the terms of the autonomy plan, they could separate from Indonesia, he told the world.

The stage was thus set for a final agreement on how the people of East Timor would make their choice. However, as negotiations on this question continued through the early months of 1999, events in the territory cast long and dark shadows over the process that lay ahead.

President Habibie's offer to the East Timorese people was strongly opposed by significant forces within his own government, especially the Indonesian Armed Forces (TNI), which had controlled the territory militarily and economically for more than two decades. In the last months of 1998, the TNI began organizing militia units in East Timor, with the express purpose of ensuring that the people would accept the autonomy proposal then under discussion. Members of the National Council of Timorese Resistance, better known by its Portuguese acronym, CNRT, were targeted, along with other activists and sympathizers. Villages throughout the territory were terrorized. Killings and house burnings became weekly, if not daily, occurrences. These and harsher events formed the backdrop to negotiations under way in New York, where an agreement was being concluded for holding a popular consultation by the United Nations. The growing violence and intimidation were a cause of serious concern to the secretary-general, who sought assurances from the Indonesian authorities on security arrangements for the popular consultation itself. These included, among other conditions, that the TNI withdraw to barracks, that the police handle public security, that the militia disarm, and that anybody carrying a weapon be arrested.

The security conditions requested by the secretary-general of the United Nations were conveyed to the Indonesian government in written form but the document was diplomatically rejected, and returned 'as if unread'. They were then conveyed to both parties in a memorandum, which was not rejected.

The East Timorese leadership was consulted on the issue and effectively asked if the risks posed by the security situation in the territory were such that the popular consultation should not go ahead. Their answer, as well as the analysis offered by Portugal and by the UN itself, was that the international community was facing a single window of opportunity that could close definitively if not used. Indonesia was about to hold a general election in June and it appeared quite possible that President Habibie could not only be replaced, but would be replaced by someone opposed to the idea of offering the East Timorese self-determination.

Thus, the decision was taken to proceed, and on 5 May 1999, the foreign ministers of Indonesia and Portugal, Ali Alatas and Jaime Gama, respectively, and the secretary-general, signed the agreement in New York. The question for public consultation to be put to the voters offered the following choice:

> Do you accept the proposed special autonomy for East Timor within the Unitary State of the Republic of Indonesia? *Accept.*
> Or
> Do you reject the proposed special autonomy for East Timor, leading to East Timor's separation from Indonesia? *Reject.*

Seemingly simple, the public consultation presented dramatic information-related problems. The simple question had to be communicated as well as the meaning of the autonomy proposal. Language barriers had to be addressed and finding appropriate translations would be difficult. The public also had to understand the consultation (including the fact that a reject vote was a vote for separation), and the information had to be distributed. The date of the consultation was set for 8 August 1999, which gave the UN just three months to organize and implement the entire process.

Getting Started

According to the 5 May agreement, the public information campaign to inform the East Timorese population on all aspects of the public consultation was due to begin 10 May and run through to three days before 8 August, the date of the vote. The first date had already passed, while the second retreated the closer we got. In the event, the vote was held on 30 August, twenty-five days later than originally planned, but we were not to know that at the beginning of the mission. My concern, then, was to get the public information campaign up and running as soon as possible to make-up for lost time.

The 5 May agreement specified the content and tasks of the information campaign:

1 The United Nations will make available the text of the main Agreement and the autonomy document to be voted on, in the following languages: Tetun, Bahasa Indonesia, Portuguese, and English.
2 The United Nations will disseminate and explain the content of the main Agreement and the autonomy document in an impartial and factual manner inside and outside East Timor.
3 The United Nations will explain to voters the process and procedure of the vote, and the implications of an 'accept' or 'reject' vote.
4 The radio stations and the newspapers in East Timor, as well as other Indonesian and Portuguese media outlets, will be utilised in the dissemination of this information. Other appropriate means of dissemination will be made use of as required.

The autonomy proposal and the main agreement already existed in English, having been originally drawn up in that language. The agreement contained seven sub-sections, each relatively short, indicating the date of the vote, the question to be put to voters, the entitlement to vote, the schedule of the consultation process, the operational phases, funding, and, finally, security considerations. Translating this into the other three languages did not present a major problem, since the whole document was only four pages in length.

The autonomy proposal on the other hand represented a major challenge. It contained fifty-nine articles outlining the powers of an autonomous East Timor and its relationship with the central government. The text, drafted by lawyers, was written in the opaque style typical of legal agreements. This was, however, the key document voters had to understand before they cast their ballots, for it contained the substance of what they would be voting to accept or reject.

Our main concern was getting it translated into Tetun, the predominant national language of East Timor. This largely oral language had never previously been used to render official texts, let alone a complex document of this nature. The Portuguese and Indonesians had already prepared translations of the autonomy proposal in their own languages, and we were eventually able to use these for the information campaign. But we knew we could not start the campaign itself under the terms spelled out in the agreement until the document existed in all four languages. Thus, the search for resources to develop a Tetun translation became a priority.

While UNAMET made it clear from the outset that jobs with the mission for local staff were open to all, the militia began threatening and harassing those courageous East Timorese who offered their services. During the course of UNAMET's life, local staff had their homes attacked and burned down, and many saw their families forced into hiding. In the wave of post-ballot violence, the first fatalities were East Timorese working for UNAMET.

This campaign of orchestrated intimidation effectively discouraged pro-integrationists from working with UNAMET, although not completely. The political wing of the militia (Forum Persatuan Demokrasi dan Keadilan/Forum for Unity Democracy and Justice – FPDK), proceeded to attack the mission for its 'one-sided' employment record, claiming this was proof of bias in favour of separation.

Of course, employment with the UN meant respecting UNAMET's impartial position on the outcome of the ballot. Our job was to facilitate a process and allow the people to make their choice, not to support one option over the other, and this was made clear to all recruits. For this reason we would not employ anybody who was a direct member of any political organization. Everybody was instructed to keep their politics in their pocket for the duration of their employment with UNAMET, and for the most part they did. Unfortunately, not all respected these instructions. One particularly gifted translator in the public information section had to be dismissed after he publicly associated himself with a new political formation.

Within a few days we had a small team of students dedicated to the task of

translating the autonomy proposal into Tetun. The team members were told
that they had to translate the content of the document as faithfully as possible,
but they soon complained of difficulties. Tetun, they explained, had only
recently been developed in a written form. While they all spoke Tetun, they
discovered many differences between themselves as to how it should be written.
Besides this problem, the language itself had difficulty expressing abstract legal
ideas, such as were contained in the autonomy proposal. Tetun is a very
practical language that developed in a rural, agricultural society, and had never
encountered such concepts as 'spheres of respective judicial competence' or
'tribunals of the first instance'. The translation team struggled to render these
and other concepts into words that could be understood by Tetun speakers, but
not without misgivings.

Their valiant effort was, unfortunately, in vain as the finished version of the
text turned out to be incomprehensible. The students then recommended that
we give it to Father Ricardo, the director of the seminary in Daré. The Catholic
Church had sustained Tetun in a written form by using it in its teaching and
liturgy. Father Ricardo was the pre-eminent expert on all matters linguistic and
kindly agreed to take on the text, which he rewrote in the course of about four
days, with the assistance of Rui Hanjan, one of the original translation team.

After the initial help by Father Ricardo it was clear that we needed our own
expert. Manuel Viegas, of the Mary MacKillop Institute of East Timorese
Studies in Australia, came to help the UNAMET public information office with
its Tetun translations. Manuel supervized all of the translation work by the local
staff, ensuring both accuracy and consistency of output, as well as providing
expert advice on a whole range of issues involving East Timorese culture.

On another front, the pattern of violence and intimidation that had preceded
our arrival was not only continuing but also appeared to be escalating. Early on
16 May, we had received reports that a gang of armed militia had attacked the
village of Atara, about 100 km south of Dili. Six villagers were reported killed. I
decided on 17 May the moment had arrived to issue UNAMET's first press
statement, which, after describing pro-integrationist attacks and house burnings, read:

> The United Nations urgently reminds the Indonesian Government that
> it agreed, on 5 May 1999, to establish a secure environment devoid of
> violence or other forms of intimidation so that a free and fair ballot can be
> held in East Timor on 8 August.
>
> During the 12 days that have passed since Ali Alatas, the Minister for
> Foreign Affairs, signed this agreement in the presence of the Secretary-
> General of the United Nations, acts of violence by armed militia against
> the East Timorese civilian population, of which the outrage in Atara is
> the latest example, have continued to occur.
>
> Words by the Indonesian Government are not enough. Determined
> action must be taken by the appropriate Indonesian security authorities
> to curtail the activities of the armed militias . . .

The small press corps that had been covering events in East Timor since before our arrival gave the statement prominent coverage. They had witnessed the ongoing violence and intimidation, and interviewed the victims, as far as was possible. They knew what was going on and welcomed our efforts to draw attention to these violations of the agreement.

The Indonesians, however, did not. They were shocked that they should be publicly criticized and clearly believed that UNAMET had no business doing any such thing. Although unacceptable, in one sense, this position was understandable. The Indonesian power structure under Suharto had been completely unaccustomed to any form of public accountability, and to be suddenly exposed to it was clearly intolerable from their point of view. It became increasingly clear to us that the government of Indonesia had never realized what the invitation of a UN mission would actually mean in practice. The government in Jakarta wasted no time in making its views known to UN headquarters in New York and I was instructed to clear all future press statements through the secretariat.

The next press statement came a few days later, following our attempts to investigate the killings in Atara. Accompanied by a few journalists and a large police escort, which delayed our departure by arriving late, we set off for Gleno, the administrative centre of the district where the attack had occurred. There, I interviewed the army commander, who confirmed the incident. He said that a suspect believed to be collaborating with the guerillas and known to the authorities had been disturbing the villagers. The authorities wanted to help this suspect but he provoked a confrontation and six people were killed. We then drove to Atsabe, which was as close as we were to get to Atara. Our police escort insisted it would be too dangerous to continue as this would require returning to Dili at night, when we would be vulnerable to attack, they said, by Falintil (Forças Armadas de Libertação Nacional de Timor Leste), the East Timorese resistance guerillas. This was not very credible. Our preliminary contacts with the CNRT (Conselho Nacional de Resistência Timorense, the umbrella organization that grouped together a number of Timorese political organizations, including Falintil) had not only been extremely positive, but filled with assurances that the East Timorese resistance wished to see us complete our mission unharmed.

In Atsabe I interviewed the local military commander, who also confirmed the incident, but gave a completely different version from the account we had received earlier in Gleno. According to him, a pro-autonomy group had tried to enter the village to promote integration, which was illegal prior to the authorized campaign period, but had been prevented by a pro-independence group. Fighting broke out, spilled over into the village and six were dead.

I thought it appropriate to draw attention to these inconsistencies so I included in the press statement a short summary of each account, calling of course for an end to all violence and respect for the agreement. This text was faxed to the secretariat in New York with a request to release it there and notify UNAMET in Dili of any changes. The following day, with no word from New York, I assumed it had been issued and I released it to the local correspondents.

However, New York, for reasons that were never communicated, had chosen not to use it. The Indonesians were not only unhappy with the content of this second statement, they were also upset that the journalists who had accompanied us to Atsabe had filmed a group of militia being trained by the military at the local army headquarters. They insisted that those being trained belonged to a civil defence group, which are common throughout Indonesia. Civil defence members all wear identifiable uniforms, unlike the militia, who wear their own clothes and distinctive headbands, which were clearly visible in the images captured by the journalists.

At that point, though reporters were few in East Timor and worked under difficult conditions, from our standpoint their role was crucial. UNAMET faced serious opposition to the execution of its mandate, and one of the most effective ways we could draw attention to this situation was through the media. More than 700 journalists were to visit East Timor over the next seven months and their reporting proved vital in maintaining international pressure on Indonesia to comply with the 5 May accord, particularly during the period of post-ballot violence.

Media and Message

Having acquired the final texts, we were now ready to start disseminating and explaining them to the population. The principle medium was radio, and we needed both expertise to start broadcasting and an agreement with Radio Republik Indonesia (RRI) to get on the air. Patricia Tomé arrived from MINURSO, the United Nations Mission for the Referendum in Western Sahara, where she was spokesperson and head of public information. Her wide experience working in UN radio, from Cambodia to Haiti, was to prove invaluable.

Jenny Grant, an experienced radio and print journalist working in Indonesia, had joined the team, as had Judy Lessing from Radio New Zealand and Pedro Manuel from Radio Nacional de Angola. Together with Patricia, who was only to stay for the time it took to get the first broadcasts on the air, they formed the core of the Radio UNAMET production unit.

The director of RRI in Dili was accommodating and professional in all our dealings with him. He readily agreed to let us broadcast for three hours a day and to use some of his technical staff to help us get the programmes on the air. At no time did he request any payment for this service.

We also negotiated with Radio Kmanek for airtime. This station was operated by the Catholic Church and probably more widely listened to than RRI. The station survived on grants and subsidies, as well as broadcast fees from NGOs. Kmanek's director explained that he could not afford to allow us free airtime and requested payment for the two hours daily we would be broadcasting. After some discussion, a fee of US$20,000 was agreed for the period from June through August.

Radio Difusão Portuguesa rebroadcast our programming on their international service, which was beamed to East Timor from Lisbon. We sent them audio files of our broadcasts via the Internet, which they downloaded for use. We negotiated a deal with the owner of the *Suara Timor Timur* (*STT*), the only daily newspaper, for the back page in every issue in exchange for three months supply of newsprint. He wanted a guaranteed source of paper, as he was concerned he would be unable to print if his Indonesian supplier were to cut him off. He had good reason to be worried, as his newspaper had already been the target of militia anger early in 1999, resulting in its closure for several weeks.

UNAMET duly procured the newsprint from a company in Adelaide, Australia, which then ran into difficulties delivering the supply on time. Eventually, the co-operative owner of the *STT* began losing patience and threatened on several occasions to kick us off his back page. We pleaded for more time, pointing out that the problem lay in Australia, not UNAMET. The newsprint did arrive in the end and was of considerably higher quality than the usual stock, which mollified the owner. The *STT* took on a cleaner look for the duration of the information campaign and would have looked smarter for a lot longer afterwards had not the militia burned the newspaper's offices to the ground in the wave of post-ballot violence. At least half the newsprint, which cost the UN about US$15,000, ended up as expensive ashes.

The *STT* was under enormous pressure from the Indonesians not to support any independence campaign. The owner was a self-declared moderate integrationist who walked a tightrope every day he brought his paper out. The material UNAMET produced in print and on radio was scrupulous in avoiding any use of the word 'independence', as this angered the Indonesians and figured nowhere in the question that would be put to voters. On one occasion, our broadcast used a simple simile to describe the difference between autonomy and separation. The former was like having your own room in someone else's house, while the latter was like having your own house, we explained. The Indonesians protested strongly and repeatedly. The comparison was completely inappropriate, they argued. The difference was more like having one house and then having two houses, they claimed. We dropped the information spot immediately, having used it only once, but the Indonesians drew attention to it again and again, thus giving it much greater publicity, arguing that it showed proof of bias. This was to be the accusation of choice by Indonesia against UNAMET and individuals within the mission, but it proved to be an ineffective weapon against our radio, print, and television production.

Overall, the number of complaints from Indonesia on the public information campaign was negligible, which, considering that every word we produced was subject to the closest scrutiny, is indicative of the rigour and professionalism of the UNAMET team.

The most difficult medium for UNAMET was, without doubt, television.

Leaving aside the technical demands this placed on the public information team, gaining access to the transmitter was a feat in itself. I had contacted the director of Televisi Republik Indonesia (TVRI) fairly soon after my arrival and explained what we needed, which was thirty minutes of airtime daily. We could not produce more than this and even the one half hour we were seeking would prove to be quite a challenge. The TVRI director demanded US$120,000.

The sum he wanted for thirty minutes a day, over about two months, was clearly excessive. Fortunately, the television unit included a creative technical wizard. Ric Curnow had been recruited in Dili, where he provided assistance to visiting television crews that needed to beam their images back home by satellite. He knew the real cost of satellite transmission to TVRI, and we were able to cut the proposed fee in half. However, that was not the end of the negotiation. The TVRI director also demanded editorial control over UNAMET's production, the only such demand made by any of the media outlets we used to get out the message required by the agreement.

It is axiomatic that United Nations public information components in the field retain complete control over the contents of their production, and nowhere was this more necessary than in East Timor. The argument with TVRI went back and forth over a period of several weeks until, eventually, the Indonesians realized that they would be held responsible for holding up the public information campaign if they continued to cling to their position. While this delay was frustrating, it did allow time to produce programming in readiness for going on air.

The television unit, headed by Richard Sydenham, used every minute of this period to begin creating a series of programmes that were to prove extraordinarily popular. Television was not a major medium in East Timor, compared to radio, but there was enough of an audience, estimated at about 180,000, to warrant the effort. Each television set in the territory, and we never did learn how many were in use, would serve as a focal point for substantial numbers of people, who would gather to watch the UNAMET show.

Producer-cameraman Michele Zaccheo used a troupe of local actors to illustrate the essential themes related to registration and voting procedures. He also used non-actors with great effect. For example, registering to vote required the voter to produce two pieces of identification, one to prove identity and the other to prove eligibility. This was explained in a skit using one of the public information unit's local staff, who was filmed hunting for the required documentation before he went off to register.

Another segment, first thought of by Ric Curnow, then written and created by Michele, was widely considered the best video UNAMET produced. It featured an elderly Timorese lady who, like so many of her generation, chewed betel nuts. The astringent seed of the betel palm is a favourite stimulant in south-east Asia. Over a long period of use it ruins the teeth, and when chewed leaves the mouth and lips stained bright red. The juice is spat out, leaving the ground splattered in crimson droplets. The effect is visually quite remarkable, although somewhat disconcerting to those not used to it. The old lady was filmed chewing her betel. 'I might vote for integration,' she said, before spitting. 'Or I might vote against it.' Spit. 'But however I vote, it's nobody else's business.' Spit. 'Nobody will know how I vote.' Spit. 'Because it's a secret ballot.' Spit. And then she laughed.

This short segment proved very popular with the children, who obviously could not vote, but who nonetheless were very aware of what was at stake. They would imitate the old lady. 'I might vote for integration,' they cackled. Then they would spit. And that was that. They did not bother to repeat the other lines. Spitting, it seems, has a universal connotation, and they had already made their choice.

Ric came up with the idea of getting a group of Timorese musicians – the Lahané Smith Band – to compose a song that was to prove the hit of the season in East Timor. Popularly known as the UNAMET song, it was called 'Please Decide', and urged all Timorese to participate freely and without fear in the decision that they were to take collectively. Everybody knew the words and music. One *New York Times* reporter was astonished to hear a group of children sing it in the street, quite spontaneously, for his benefit while on a visit to Baucau, East Timor's second city.

Like all our work, television required production in four languages, and we used the same system for each medium. Thirty minutes of television allowed for seven and a half minutes in each language. One hour of radio gave each language fifteen minutes. And one back page of the *Suara Timor Timur*, divided into four columns, provided enough space for about 600 words for each linguistic group. We played with the point size of the typeface to balance legibility with maximum word count, but had to live with the insoluble problem that is caused by some languages being more verbose than others. English was used as the control language and any complaints or errors were checked against the original English version.

In addition to explaining the autonomy proposal to the East Timorese prior to the vote, UNAMET also had to ensure that everybody who was eligible could register to vote and knew how to cast their ballots. Thus, a substantial part of our work included explaining the vote registration and voting procedures.

Under the terms of the agreement the entitlement to vote belonged to everybody aged seventeen and above who was:

1. Born in East Timor;
2. Born outside East Timor but with at least one parent having been born in East Timor; or
3. Married to somebody in one of the first two categories.

The voter registration period was scheduled to run for twenty consecutive days in 200 voter registration centres across the territory and in a number of special registration centres outside East Timor. These were located in Jakarta, Yogyakarta, Surabaya, Denpasar and Ujung Pandang (Indonesia); Sydney,

Darwin, Perth and Melbourne (Australia); Lisbon (Portugal); Macau (Macau); Maputo (Mozambique); and New York (USA). The external registration and voting centres were set up by the Australian Electoral Commission and the International Organisation for Migration.

The public information team provided these organizations, to the extent possible, with all our printed material, which was to include the agreement, in four languages, about fifteen information bulletins covering the registration and voting procedures, and a series of posters and stickers.

These items were produced primarily for the domestic electorate and distributed widely across the territory in a campaign led by Brian Kelly, the deputy head of public information at UNAMET. We were able to produce the information bulletins ourselves and have them printed by local photo-copying shops. The 50,000 booklets containing the text of the agreement in four languages were printed in Australia. So were the posters, creatively designed by Simon Davies on computer and then sent electronically to the print shop in Darwin.

We distributed all this material to the regional UNAMET headquarters that had been established, and from there it was sent out to the 200 registration and polling centres. At the same time, we made the material available to all local organizations that wanted to assist in distributing it at the local level. The Church, the CNRT, and human rights organizations all took UNAMET's information kits and sent them out through their own networks. The same material was made available to the FPDK, but it showed little interest in receiving it and even less inclination to distribute it.

Among the key messages disseminated were reminders to voters to keep their registration cards in a safe place. One community hid their cards under a concrete slab in a local building, which the militia later burned. The documents escaped the flames and were recovered from beneath the ashes for use on polling day. Messages also included assurances that the vote would be secret, that there would only be a central count, so nobody would know how individual communities voted, and that the UN would stay in East Timor, no matter what the outcome of the ballot, to help implement the decision.

Of course, we all understood that distributing information in a printed form, although essential, was only useful in a largely illiterate society if it could be explained orally to the recipients. For those with no access to either radio or television, meetings were the only way to get the message across. To help the UN volunteers in the field pass on the voter education material in the most accessible form, we had made a series of audio tapes in Tetun, Bahasa Indonesian, and Portuguese explaining voting procedures and carrying these very important messages. But we also needed tape decks in all the communities so the cassettes could be played, heard, and discussed. Brian Kelly quickly pointed out that we had everything we required in our vehicles. The UN had flown in hundreds of Land Rover 'Discovery' vehicles for use by UNAMET staff. Each had a tape deck, and loudspeakers in the two front doors, making it a mobile boom-box. We distributed tapes to the civilian police, the UN volunteers, and the military observers, with instructions that every time they visited a village in their area, they were to play the tape at full volume with the doors open. Within minutes, people would gather to listen to the messages. It proved to be a simple, yet very effective strategy for reaching as many voters as possible.

The Pressure Increases

Under the terms of the agreement there was to be no campaigning by either side until after the voter registration process was completed. The pro-integration side had blatantly ignored this restriction since UNAMET's arrival. Banners were prominently displayed extolling the virtues of integration. Some even implied the UN favoured this solution.

Across the territory, pro-integration forces organized ceremonies at which members of the local population were obliged to swear an oath of loyalty and sometimes even drink a mixture of whisky and blood. Local government officials, who were explicitly forbidden from taking part in any campaign, except in a personal capacity, attended these ceremonies. Moreover, under the agreement public money could not be spent in support of either position but was being disbursed nonetheless by various government departments to assist the integrationist cause.

Ian Martin, the Special Representative of the secretary-general for East Timor and head of UNAMET duly brought all these breaches to the attention of the Indonesian authorities. The offending banners were eventually removed, but we still received reports of blood-drinking ceremonies. Nor were we able to prevent the entire East Timorese civil service from being threatened with dismissal if they did not sign a document guaranteeing they would vote for integration.

The period allowed for campaigning was initially scheduled to take place from 20 July to 5 August, but the timetable was revised following a decision by the secretary-general to delay the process owing to continuing violence. On 22 June, the secretary-general said he could not certify that the necessary security conditions existed. At the same time he made it clear that UNAMET had to be fully deployed before registration could commence. This effectively pushed back the timetable by three weeks, and gave the Indonesians ample opportunity to bring the militia under control.

Increasingly, the pro-integration forces tried to discredit UNAMET, or UNAMET staff. The attempts were both blatant and clumsy. On one occasion, a home-made gun was planted in the vehicle of a UNAMET staff member, whom the Indonesian police later tried to charge with illegal possession of a weapon. This was the only occasion the Indonesian authorities ever tried to charge anybody for such an offence, in spite of the fact that militia members were seen carrying a variety of illegal weapons every day. On another occasion, following a tip that weapons had been hidden in a private house not far from

Dili, UN civilian police informed the Indonesian police and accompanied them on a visit to the house. Nothing was found. However, some Dutch journalists who requested permission from the public information office to record the event filmed the inspection.

This detail was obviously not known to the TNI soldiers who arrived at the same house some time after the police had left, and ransacked it. The old lady who lived there was ordered to blame the 'white men' for the mess, which she did for the benefit of TVRI.

When I learned that TVRI planned to broadcast these allegations, along with images of the old lady in the midst of the debris of her personal possessions, I called the station director to my office. If he went ahead with the broadcast, I explained, we would have no choice but to air the video-tape made by the Dutch journalists on our news programme. This would then put the TNI in a very bad light, I told him, since our video tape showed a routine visit by Indonesian and UN police, who had left the house as they found it, completely intact. Ian Martin had already protested the incident and I wanted to avoid any further escalation of the issue in a climate that was increasingly tense. Wisely, the TVRI director concurred. The Indonesians now knew that we knew, and could prove, the entire episode was a se-up.

Those who sought to attack UNAMET in the media never directly criticized Ian Martin, the Special Representative of the secretary-general. Instead, they focused their hostility at the spokesman, which is not uncommon. Nonetheless, the degree and intensity of criticism levelled at me by the Indonesian authorities and their supporters in East Timor was unusually high. The objective of this campaign was to have me removed, and while it did not succeed, it came close.

As a former journalist, I am well aware of the needs of the media, and as a UN spokesman, of those of the organization I represent. Both needs coincide in the requirement for clear, truthful, and timely information. However, this very commodity was the last thing those opposed to the popular consultation wanted to see. The spokesman for the Indonesian police in East Timor tried to insist that I co-ordinate UN public statements on security-related matters through him. This would have seriously compromised the independence of UNA-MET's position on this very important matter, and needless to say, I refused.

One member of the Indonesian task force, which was ostensibly set up to assist UNAMET in the completion of its mandate but in fact created obstacles in our path, made inquiries about my background. Diplomats in Jakarta told me the aim was to prove I had prior links to East Timorese activism. Such was not the case. In fact, I was largely ignorant about East Timor before I arrived in the territory. The fact that I spoke Portuguese, the teaching of which had been banned by Indonesia following its invasion of the territory, was particularly annoying to some. It meant I could communicate directly with the leadership of the CNRT and Falintil in a language they had learned as children and still preferred to speak. And, of course, it provided the Portuguese media with a source that needed no translation.

This issue was later used publicly by Ali Alatas, the Indonesian foreign minister, who asserted that I could not be impartial because my wife, although a Canadian citizen, was of Portuguese origin.

The pressure to have me removed increased to the point that New York considered pulling me out. Such a move would have played right into the hands of the Indonesians and merely given credibility to their claim that UNAMET was biased. Fortunately, the matter was resolved with support from certain members of the Security Council. One visiting senior US official told me not to worry. 'We're defending you,' he said. Ian Martin informed New York that he wanted me to continue in the job, and he proposed that a deputy spokesman be appointed to take-over some of the daily briefings.

Registration and Voting

Voter registration began on 16 July. On 21 July, the secretary-general informed the Security Council that registration was proceeding relatively peacefully, but that the plight of thousands of East Timorese who had been forcibly relocated or intimidated into fleeing from their homes remained a matter of serious concern. However, as registration advanced, those who had been displaced returned home to register, or else registered at the centre closest to their new location. Showing great courage, they came out of hiding and disappeared again once they had their registration documents. The massive campaign we had conducted emphasizing the secrecy of the ballot and the central count seemed to be paying off. At the same time we were reminding voters through all our public information outlets that they could only cast their ballots at the same centre where they had registered, which was part of the agreement. The twenty-day registration period was extended by two days in East Timor and by four days at the external sites to ensure everybody entitled to vote could get onto the electoral list. Based on the numbers in the recent Indonesian general elections we estimated that there were potentially more than 400,000 eligible voters. By the end of the process, 451,792 had registered to vote and the Independent Electoral Commission appointed by the secretary-general certified the registration as a legitimate basis for holding the ballot.

While the level of violence had diminished encouragingly during the registration period, it was to increase again the closer we got to the day of the vote. The period set aside for political campaigning was preceded by successful negotiations for the establishment of a code of conduct that was intended to regulate activities by both sides during their campaigns. However, there were frequent attacks against CNRT offices and student groups campaigning for independence. Most of the violent clashes that occurred between pro-integration and pro-independence supporters during the sixteen days of campaigning were provoked by the militia, and deaths occurred on both sides. By this time, the violence surprised no one, even though each side had agreed to campaign on alternate days in order to avoid such incidents.

The independent Electoral Commission said on 20 August that the security situation was deteriorating by the day, and stated clearly that Indonesia had failed to fulfil its obligation to act impartially and to ensure a secure environment. The Security Council met on 27 August, just three days before the vote, to adopt a resolution increasing the number of civilian police and military liaison officers in the mission, up to the limit accepted by Indonesia. While this was in preparation for Phase II, and not simply a late reaction to the situation of the ground, it was to be moot.

On the day of the vote, the turnout was massive, with 98.6 per cent of those registered casting ballots. People too sick or incapacitated to make it on their own were assisted by others. Once votes were cast, the thousands who had come out of hiding returned to their sanctuaries.

The ballot paper was marked with symbols for each of the two options, and one of the last tasks of the public information campaign was to ensure that everybody understood them. Each symbol showed a map of East Timor. Autonomy or integration featured a red and white Indonesia flag and some traditional dwellings. Separation (leading to independence) featured the flag of the CNRT. The Bishop of Bacau, Dom Basílio, expressed his concern to us that some people were still confused about these symbols. There were stories flying around that many people were being told to cross out the Indonesian flag if they wanted to end Indonesian rule. This, of course, would have had the opposite effect. We had produced posters, stickers and leaflets indicating which symbol was which, as well as showing them on television and describing them on radio. Nonetheless, we produced an extra run of leaflets and distributed these just days before the vote.

The Storm

Almost immediately following the close of polling on 30 August, two local staff were murdered by militia in Atsabe. This brutal act marked the beginning of a serious deterioration in the overall security situation. As the sealed ballot boxes were brought to Dili from across the territory for the count, which would take place in an empty museum next to police headquarters, aggressive militia activity increased throughout East Timor. On 1 September, UN electoral officers and local staff were evacuated to Dili from Maliana following protracted violence there.

On the same day, BBC Jakarta correspondent Jonathan Head was severely beaten by militia in front of UNAMET headquarters. This attack was part of a concerted attempt by the militia to intimidate the international media into leaving the territory. The European Broadcasting Union, CNN, and the Australian Broadcasting Corporation had all installed satellite dishes on the roof of the Makhota Hotel. Through these links the violent events in East Timor were lead items on newscasts around the world. There were more than 100 international journalists in East Timor at the time of the ballot and their daily coverage was feeding the growing international pressure on Indonesia. Those who commanded the militia wanted to silence these witnesses before the next phase of their deadly campaign.

I appealed to the media representatives to stay, pointing out that their role was going to be crucial in the days that lay ahead, but the level of intimidation and the intensity of the security threat quickly became unacceptable. Gun-toting militia now entered hotels in Dili, threatening journalists directly. When the BBC decided to evacuate its staff, on 3 September, many other mainstream news organizations followed suit within a matter of days.

On the day the BBC left, UNAMET was forced to abandon its regional headquarters in Maliana following the murder there of two local staff. The next day, 4 September, five days after the vote, the announcement of the result was made simultaneously in New York and Dili. The count, including the external vote, showed that 344,580 (78.5 per cent) had opted for separation from Indonesia while 94,388 (21.5 per cent) had expressed their preference for integration. The result was clear, the margin was huge, and the outlook was very bleak. Ian Martin announced the result as early in the day as was compatible with the secretary-general's simultaneous announcement in New York, twelve hours behind, to give us all as many useful daylight hours as possible. Within a couple of hours it was clear that the storm was about to break. UNAMET's regional offices in Aileu, Ainaro, Liquiça, and Samé were abandoned as the militia began their rampage. In Liquiça, a US civilian police officer was hit three times when the vehicle he was travelling in was sprayed with gunfire. The vehicle was caught by a dozen bullets in an attack that involved not only militia, but also the TNI and the police.

International staff in Dili were given one hour to get to their residences, gather some essential supplies and get back to UNAMET headquarters. Many were unable to retrieve any belongings at all as the militia were already patrolling the streets and setting up roadblocks. Some staff found themselves trapped in their houses and unable to regain the relative safety of the compound. Three international and one local staff in the public information unit were in this situation and had been calling on the radio or by phone for help. We were particularly concerned for the safety of our Timorese colleague, who was alone in a house that was surrounded by militia. He reported constant gunfire throughout the late afternoon of 4 September, while our military liaison officers negotiated with the Indonesian army for an escort to pick up all stranded personnel. By the time it was the turn to get our colleagues, the Indonesian military escort told me that they did not have enough gasoline to make the trip. I managed to persuade the officer in charge of the escort that a journey of two miles would not overtax the army's fuel supply, and we were able to bring everybody back to safety. By nightfall, we were sleeping on the floors of our offices or in the backs of our vehicles inside the already over-crowded compound.

An empty school next door to the UNAMET compound had become home to as many as 2,000 internally displaced people. On 5 September, the militia fired repeatedly in the direction of the school, terrifying its temporary residents into fleeing over the adjoining wall, which was topped with razor wire, into the UN compound.

The reduced number of international journalists also sought shelter with UNAMET, as did the team of official Portuguese observers. The media quickly made themselves at home in the public information offices, where I let them use UNAMET computers to write and file their reports through our still-operating Internet connections.

Their presence was extraordinarily important, for it signified the failure of the militia strategy to force out witnesses. Reporters from a number of British, French, Portuguese, and Australian media outlets continued to tell the story of what was happening in East Timor. They also helped answer the phones, which by this time were ringing non-stop, twenty-four hours a day, as journalists from around the world called in for interviews and up-to-the-minute accounts of the situation.

By Sunday, 5 September, UNAMET staff from Manatuto and Suai had also joined us in the compound. The next day, the Ermera office closed, and the day after, Baucau, Viqueque, Los Palos and Oecussi were evacuated. In each case, international staff ensured that local staff too were brought out. In Baucau, the Indonesian police, mandated to provide security for UNAMET, machine-gunned the regional headquarters with all the staff inside for two hours. Our colleagues escaped injury by remaining flat on the floor. When the shooting stopped they evacuated directly to Darwin, but not before all the local staff were guaranteed passage to our compound in Dili by helicopter. The UN-chartered helicopter pilots threw out the rulebook and loaded twice the permitted number of passengers. Their courageous action that day almost certainly saved many lives.

All across the territory, buildings were on fire. Hundreds of thousands of people were being forcibly rounded up for deportation to West Timor. An unknown number of East Timorese had already been killed and more were to die in the days that lay ahead.

On 5 September, with the compound overcrowded and surrounded by constant gunfire, the decision was taken to evacuate the first group of personnel. In the public information office, we discussed at length who would stay and who would travel to Darwin, which was to be our haven for the next three weeks. We knew that sooner or later we would lose the telecommunications links in Dili, and that we needed to establish a public information function in a more secure environment. Eventually, it was decided I would go. Ian Martin agreed. He was also concerned by the fact that I might be a target, given the earlier security threat. While I was not alone in not wanting to leave, I felt particularly distressed, for as spokesman I had repeatedly assured the East Timorese that we would not leave them and that we were there to stay. All I could say to the East Timorese in the compound as I left for the airport was to assure them we would return. It was a painful moment.

Of the twelve local staff who worked for public information, only six remained within the compound. The others had opted to join their families or go up into the hills. Not all made it. At least two were picked up by the militia, and one of these was forcibly deported to West Timor. Fortunately, all survived the ordeal and eventually returned to Dili, many to continue working with UNAMET and the follow-on mission, UNTAET (United Nations Transitional Administration in East Timor).

Brian Kelly remained behind in charge of the public information unit while I established a public information office in Darwin, where more than 100 journalists had gathered. About twenty journalists had chosen to stay in Dili, and they were all at UNAMET headquarters. Some behaved professionally. Others did not. The latter were in reality more interested in activism than journalism and their behaviour caused serious problems in a situation that was already troubling enough. They told the by-now more than 2,000 displaced people in the compound that UNAMET was going to abandon them. One tried to instigate a riot, by encouraging the displaced Timorese to storm Ian Martin's office, which event he would then film. Another tried to persuade the Timorese to lie down on the ground at the entrance of the compound to prevent international staff from leaving. Others took over offices and refused to allow UNAMET staff to use the computers, which they claimed for their own.

The other group of journalists simply did their jobs. One video reporter was up in the hills near Daré with the tens of thousands of displaced who were seeking shelter there. He would report on the situation and interview those who had escaped the fury of the militia, send the tapes by courageous couriers down to the UNAMET compound, where they were put on the next flight to Darwin, and within hours were on newscasts all over the world. The ability of the media to maintain the story as the primary news event around the world for so long had an enormous effect. The Security Council decided to send a delegation to see for itself the situation on the ground. By the time they arrived in East Timor, much of downtown Dili had been destroyed, as had other major centres. The Australian meteorological service was the first to see just how widespread the destruction had become. Satellite images revealed dozens of hot spots across East Timor. On the weather map they showed up in red and each spot or patch marked a community on fire.

Great Britain's Permanent Representative to the United Nations, Sir Jeremy Greenstock, summed up the situation succinctly after arriving with the Security Council delegation in East Timor. 'This is hell on earth,' he said.

It was also hell in the compound. The situation was no longer sustainable and a further evacuation was authorized. At the same time, Ian Martin asked for a list of volunteers to be drawn up of international staff who would stay with the displaced in the compound. The evacuation of everybody, including local staff and the East Timorese who had sought shelter with UNAMET, was to be negotiated with the Indonesian military authorities over the course of the next several days when it became absolutely clear that maintaining any presence in the compound was no longer feasible.

The secretary-general had been urging the Indonesian authorities since 6

September to accept an international intervention to restore order in East
Timor, and I began explaining this during the marathon of interviews that now
dominated public information work in Darwin. Events had clearly surpassed
the mandate we had been given. Public information must always follow the
mandate, but when that is overtaken by extraordinary circumstances, such as
these, it has to articulate positions based on political and moral judgement.

The full evacuation began on 10 September. The Security Council delegation visited Dili the next day.

The airlift to Darwin of all personnel, except the twelve who volunteered to
stay behind, and East Timorese refugees was completed by 14 September.
Fourteen flights organized by the Australian and New Zealand air forces, as
well as UNAMET's own C-130 Hercules aircraft, brought everybody to safety.
The media covered the event extensively, interviewing many new arrivals and
maintaining the East Timor story in the number one spot on most news
programmes.

On 15 September, the Security Council authorized an international force
(INTERFET), led by Australia, to re-establish law and order in East Timor,
following President Habibie's decision to accept outside intervention and
withdraw all Indonesian military and police from the territory.

The first INTERFET troops arrived in Dili on 20 September, exactly three
weeks after the East Timorese went to the polls to determine their own future.
Within a week, UNAMET began the process of re-establishing its headquarters in Dili. The public information unit also returned, to work and sleep
for the next several months on the floors of our offices in the compound. Its task
this time was to support the huge international effort to rebuild East Timor and
assist it towards independence. But that is another story.

Conclusion

The terrible consequences of the vote for independence that were visited on the
East Timorese by the militia and the Indonesian military left many outside
observers believing UNAMET's mission had failed. Some UN staff arriving in
Dili to take part in the follow-on mission, UNTAET, asked those of us who
remained if we were not ashamed of what we had done. Our reaction was,
putting it mildly, incredulous. Responsibility for the intimidation and violence
before and after the ballot lay squarely with Indonesia, which had conspicu-
ously failed to respect its side of the 5 May agreement. We were angry, grieving,
distressed, but not ashamed. Thanks to UNAMET, the East Timorese people
had been able to exercize their long-withheld right to self-determination. In
addition, several thousand East Timorese, including hundreds of local staff,
had been saved from death or forced deportation by UNAMET's refusal to
abandon them.

What UNAMET did was to implement scrupulously the mandate it
had received from the Security Council. Within that context, the public

information campaign followed the very specific framework laid down in the 5 May agreement. This, plus the challenging deadline, provided the necessary focus for our work. The acknowledged success of the public information campaign, however, can be attributed to the professionalism and dedication of the team, including the courageous local staff.

Recruiting the right people with the necessary experience and qualifications is always a challenge for any UN mission. The organization's ability to do this effectively, which includes getting them into the field in time, is hampered by a structural lack of preparedness.

In the case of UNAMET, the staff was not fully deployed until mid-June, five weeks after the 5 May agreement was signed, and less than two months before the vote was supposed to have taken place. Without finance officers and procurement officers for the crucial early weeks, the mission had to fend for itself. Staff on the ground, including those in the public information unit, paid for materials out of their own pockets and used their own personal computers to get the job done. To ensure radio programmes could be aired as soon as possible we needed basic equipment, such as tape recorders, microphones, and audio-cassettes. Some US$3,000 in personal funds were used to buy the equipment. However, because these purchases took place in the absence of official procurement procedures, more than a year was to pass before the individuals who volunteered the funding were repaid. In the meantime, many of us, including myself, were not even being paid salaries. It took four months or more for us to receive a pay cheque. I recall one staff member whose wife called in tears during the middle of yet another security crisis because the mortgage could not be paid.

In September 2000, a report commissioned earlier in the year by Kofi Annan to review peace operations was issued shortly before the Millennium Summit.[2] Among the report's many recommendations, which were endorsed by the visiting heads of state, was a proposal to create a unit to plan and support public information in peace operations.[3] Within the overall context of the Brahimi Report (named after the chairman of the panel of experts who prepared it), this recommendation was relatively minor. But in making the proposal, the panel of experts recognized that the lack of a dedicated and adequately resourced structure for public information in the field was detrimental to on-going operations in this area.

As things stand, at the beginning of the new millennium, the United Nations Department of Public Information (DPI) is nominally responsible for supporting public information in the field. The Department of Peacekeeping Operations (DPKO) currently runs fifteen peacekeeping missions worldwide, with 37,000 troops, 7,500 civilian police, and 1,700 military observers, plus 12,000 civilian staff of whom 4,000 are international and 8,000 are local, on an annual budget of about US$2.7 billion. Each civilian component in a peacekeeping mission (communications, finance, personnel, transport, air operations etc.) has a corresponding dedicated support unit in DPKO at UN Headquarters in New York, with the exception of public information.

The Brahimi Report recommended that either DPI or DPKO should assume responsibility for the public information support unit, which would include ensuring that public information start-up kits were prepared for rapid deployment to the field with the requisite staff.[4] Implicit in this recommendation was the recognition that support for public information in peace operations had fallen between the departmental cracks. The Report advised that either DPI should put the necessary resources into providing the support function or DPKO should take on this responsibility. Eventually, the Member States will decide the matter and, it is to be hoped, in a manner that will ensure dedicated support for this area of activity in UN peacekeeping. Information is a vital component of all UN peacekeeping and peace-building operations. The ability to provide impartial, accurate information in a conflict situation may be as important for the afflicted population as food and shelter. There are dedicated UN agencies for the latter – the World Food Programme and the United Nations High Commissioner for Refugees, among others. But there is no comparable ability within the UN system for delivering high quality information to local populations, for targeting warring parties to a conflict with messages that encourage them to participate in the peace, or for extending a hand to local journalists and weaning them away from partisan positions. Increasingly, however, both the Reports of the secretary-general and the deliberations of the Security Council acknowledge the importance of public information in peace operations. The General Assembly is also taking a greater interest in this area of the UN's work. With the right resources and support, the quality and delivery of public information in peace missions can only improve. The development of rapidly deployable public information teams and equipment, and the elaboration of standard operating procedures to ensure consistent, high-quality performance in the field are the next steps in helping ensure the promise of the United Nations Charter can still be kept.

Acknowledgements

This short account of how the United Nations Mission in East Timor (UNAMET) organized its public information campaign for the Popular Consultation of 30 August 1999, is dedicated to the people who made it happen. From East Timor, they are Nuno Alves, Fausto Belo, Édio da Costa, César da Cruz (Big Cesar), Marciano da Silva, João das Neves, Maria Lourdes de Sousa, Sebastião Guterres, Rui Hanjan, António Mali (Little Cesar), Albertina Oliveira and Madalena Viegas. From elsewhere, Nick Birnback (United States), Ric Curnow (Australia), Simon Davies (United Kingdom), Chris de Bono (Australia), Rolando Gomez (Peru), Jenny Grant (Australia), Brian Kelly (Ireland), Judy Lessing (New Zealand), Pedro Manuel (Angola), Mako Natsume (United States), Richard Sydenham (United Kingdom), Patricia Tomé (France), Manuel Viegas (Australia) and Michele Zaccheo (Italy). Together, these twenty-six individuals constituted UNAMET's Public

Information Office, which I was privileged to lead as chief of public information and mission spokesman. Their determination, creativity, courage, and tireless efforts brought the information campaign to life through radio, television, print, and the Internet.

Bibliography

United Nations (2000), Report of the Panel on United Nations Peace Operations, distributed 21 August 2000, A/55/305-S/2000/9/809. Online [June 2001], available at http://www.un.org/peace/reports/peace_operations/

Notes

1. The views expressed herein are those of the author and do not necessarily reflect the views of the United Nations.
2. The Panel on United Nations Peace Operations was convened in March 2000, with a remit from the secretary-general to assess the United Nations ability to conduct peace operations effectively, and to offer frank, specific and realistic recommendations for ways to enhance that capacity. The Panel was chaired by Mr Lakhdar Brahimi, formerly a foreign minister of Algeria.
3. See Report of the Panel on United Nations Peace Operations, 21 August 2000. [Recommendation 12: Rapidly deployable capacity for public information: Additional resources should be devoted in mission budgets to public information and the associated personnel and information technology required to get an operation's message out and build effective internal communications links.]
   The full list of recommendations can be viewed at http://www.un.org/peace/reports/peace_operations/
4. Ibid. 'Recommendation 17: Operational support for public information: A unit for operational planning and support of public information in peace operations should be established, either within DPKO or within a new Peace and Security Information Service in DPI.'

SECTION FOUR

11

Information Warfare and Information Intervention

Philip M. Taylor

I

Several chapters in this book explore the management of information in pre-conflict and post-conflict periods by 'civilian administration' entities, like the Office of High Representative in Bosnia and Herzegovina, who represent the international community with the support of military force. What is missing from this story is the fundamental change that has taken place in the military's use of information and intervention strategies during periods of war.

'Information intervention' has been one element of the transformation of military strategies in the recent Revolution in Military Affairs (RMA).[1] Information intervention is also used, sanctioned, and supported by force, to minimize additional conflict. The argument of this chapter is that the RMA that emphasizes the importance of information to strategy during times of conflict also permeates the interplay between civilian and military administrations and has enormous effect on post-conflict governance. Cyberwar and information intervention are, in this sense, related phenomena. This chapter is a first attempt to focus on this relationship, on the tendency toward information warfare during conflict and the increased use of information campaigns by Western armed forces in the aftermath of a military intervention in order to pre-empt the need for further military force.

The extent to which many Western armed forces have professionalized their approach towards media operations has received considerable attention since the 1991 Persian Gulf War. Because conflicts like Desert Storm have high media profiles, the scholarly community interested in communications issues likewise tends to focus upon them as examples for analyzing government propaganda and official censorship, disinformation, and other so-called 'dirty tricks' like psychological warfare. In this respect, the manipulation of information in support of military or political objectives is framed in a somewhat negative sense, as a threat to democratic freedom of thought and expression. During the Gulf War, the allied coalition waged what is widely believed to have been a highly successful media war. This media war was made successful by allied domination of the global media agenda, a continued focus on minority 'smart' weaponry, and the ability of the coalition to keep 'real war' away from the television screen. In the process, the United States in particular is said to have exorcized the demons of the Vietnam War in which military failure was – erroneously – attributed to adverse coverage by hostile media.

The Gulf War was also a watershed in the conduct of psychological warfare. Almost thirty million leaflets were dropped on Iraqi forces in 1991, containing messages that were backed up by radio transmissions and other methods of information dissemination. Because more Iraqi soldiers surrendered than were killed, a phenomenon attributed in large part to the psychological operation (or 'psyop') campaign known as 'Burning Hawk', the use of psyops has since undergone something of a rebirth as a recognized 'combat force multiplier'. As a consequence, psyop campaigns accompanied the international interventions in Somalia, Bosnia, Haiti, Rwanda and Kosovo with varying degrees of success.

In the process, psyops have also had to become something more than the traditional 'surrender or die' and 'flee and live' messages disseminated to enemy soldiers, or the 'resistance is futile' messages targeted at enemy civilians, as during the Gulf War. This is because the notion of 'information as a weapon' has evolved into one of 'information as a tool' in the 'conflicts other than war' that characterized the 1990s.[2] Essentially, there were two reasons for this. The first was that international interventions, as they succeeded the peacekeeping operations of the Cold War, no longer involved merely keeping opposing warring factions apart. Soldiers were traditionally trained to fight soldiers. Now they had increasingly to interact with civilians.

The second factor was that the traditional battlefields of the past, where soldiers knew the rules of engagement and the limits of their ability to behave in certain ways, transformed into a new kind of environment where new skills were necessary to achieve the objectives of the intervention. In other words, in operations like the 'humanitarian intervention' in Kosovo, or Bosnia before it, the real work began after the battle. This has tended to receive scant media coverage and thus scant scholarly attention.

The theoretical and descriptive aspects of the shift to information warfare by the military have, by contrast, been extensively covered. The publication of *War and Anti-War* in 1993 by Alvin and Heidi Toffler, was a landmark event, triggering a preoccupation with the concept of information age warfare. Of course, the control of information as part of military strategy was always present. But the potential for information mastery and information dependence displayed during the Gulf War led, together with other factors, to continuing changes in military strategy and officer training and large-scale differences in patterns of defence expenditures in what was to be a new 'knowledge-based' military. The idea of a revolution in military affairs became so popular that it received acronymic honours (RMA), as did information warfare (IW). There is even talk now of a corresponding Revolution in Diplomatic Affairs in which 'international information' (or 'public diplomacy') is given a more prominent role in the achievement of foreign policy objectives.

Information warfare has been examined, subsequent to the work of the

Tofflers, in a number of books, including to some extent my *War and the Media, Propaganda and Persuasion in the Gulf War* and John Arquila and D. Ronfeldt's edited work, *Athena's Camp: Preparing for Conflict in the Information Age*. It is a hypothesis of the RMA that the Information Revolution, brought about by the proliferation of high-powered, networked computers and the interweaving of computers with telecommunications systems, will bring about changes in military affairs as significant as those it has wrought in other sectors of society.

In the early 1990s, after the Gulf War, I participated in the making of a *Horizon* documentary film called *The I-Bomb*.[3] There were frank contributions by military officers, in conversation with the Tofflers.[4] Some quotations indicate the enthusiasm for this deep new thinking about war and military strategy. On the notion of information dependence (by the enemy) one United States army officer (Colonel Warden) said:

> We didn't want Saddam Hussein to be able to talk, to give people instructions as to what to do, so we took away the telephone system from him. We didn't want Saddam Hussein to be able to gather with his staff, so we took away the primary command centres that Saddam Hussein and his generals and his political cronies were inclined to use.

A colleague, Colonel Campen, said that the Gulf War was the first to have been waged:

> with a notion that an enemy could be brought to his knees by denial of information. It was actually tested and proven on the battlefield . . . What is happening now is the emergence of a new, third-wave war form that has its own special characteristics and is highly dependent upon the application of knowledge. It embodies the concept of 'deep' battle – that the battle is not waged where the soldiers are, necessarily, or where the front lines are; the battle may be waged a thousand miles behind that.

Here was an instance where, Campen explained:

> the technology of precision, of stealth, of rapid information movement enabled us to do something that had never been done before: to wage an entirely different kind of a war for the first time in history. Literally in a matter of hours we were able to impose shock on the entire Iraqi system . . . We were able to do it from the inside to the outside, as opposed to the old-style Clausewitzian attrition approach of coming from the outside to the inside. We were able to fight all of the key battles of the war almost within the first 24 hours, and after that first 24 hours, even after the first hour, there was almost nothing that Iraq could do from a military standpoint to get itself out of the impossible problem in which we had put it.

The then chief of staff of the army, General Sullivan, again using Toffler-like language when looking at the process of change, argued:

> Both the First and Second World Wars were characterized by industrial-age warfare: lots of munitions, lots of men just pulverised, no manoeuvre, no movement, just industrial warfare, grinding each other into the ground. In my view the first war of the twenty-first century was operation 'Just Cause'. What you saw there was the United States of America seizing 26 to 28 objectives from midnight until daylight. We simultaneously shot the enemy down with parachutists from the air, with special operations forces, marine forces on the ground, naval forces off the ocean, all leveraged by the microprocessor.

The future, according to Sullivan, again mirroring the Tofflers, would be characterized by 'the third wave', as 'societies become more internally complex, more and more information is needed to handle routine events. Information is the central resource of the third-wave economy.'

Granting that information is 'the oil of the future', military strategy must pay special attention to its control. As Alvin Toffler states:

> You can't manage a society any longer in the way you did before – whether you're running a company, running a government or running an army. You now have far more complex problems, you need more information, and that can't be done on the back of an envelope.'

New vulnerabilities emerge, and with them new allocations of power and new military initiatives.

Information warfare has been defined as:

> actions taken to achieve information superiority by affecting adversary information, information-based processes, information systems, and computer-based networks while defending one's own information, in-formation-based processes, information systems, and computer-based networks.[5]

An essay by Arquila and Ronfeldt asserts that 'information is a bigger, deeper concept than traditionally presumed, and should be treated as a basic, under-lying and overarching dynamic of all theory and practice about warfare in the information-age'[6]. The Information Age empowers organizational networks rather than hierarchies and this has sweeping implications for warfare. Citing the examples of Vietnam and a number of low-intensity conflicts, they argue, perhaps controversially, that networks can defeat institutions[7].

Adoption of new technologies cannot by itself constitute an RMA. Tech-nologies are passive fixtures. Only if there are substantial doctrinal and organizational changes in the military will a true RMA take place. One area identified by Arquilla and Ronfeldt, among others, for the implementation of these changes is an integrated information strategy. This brings us to the connection between information intervention and IW. Both rely on a concept of society in which control of information is related to control over the outcome of critical events. Both rely on a systematic understanding of the relationship of information to action. Both rely on connectivity and systems analysis. The elaborated aspects of information warfare permeate modes of thinking about information management in the post-conflict environment. If a shift to democratic structures is the strategic goal of an intervention (diplomatic, military, or otherwise) then information management is an essential part of the process.

II

Information warfare and techniques used in information warfare are slowly becoming part of the arsenal used during post-conflict information interventions. This is why traditional thinking about free expression and human rights sometimes seems so difficult to apply during post-conflict situations. Information becomes an instrument related to a strategy, not an undifferentiated product of a public sphere. For example, since the armed intervention by NATO air power to expel the Serb armed forces from Kosovo from March to June 1999 and the establishment since then of KFOR, the NATO-led international force responsible for establishing security in Kosovo, the province tends to make the headlines only when things go wrong. Without getting distracted into debates about whether 'bad news' defines the media agenda, it seems clear that NATO is attempting to avoid such headlines by an ambitious information campaign designed to stabilize the region's ethnic hatreds and assist in the restoration of Kosovo's civic society. This involves three strands. The first is designed to 'retrain' the soldiers to operate within a difficult psychological climate in which civilian hatred runs deep and wide. The second is directed at the 'hearts and minds' of those very civilians divided by ethnic hatred and indoctrination. The third strand has an even more ambitious aim, namely the rebuilding not just of Kosovo's infrastructure but also of its psychology.

During the actual war-fighting phase of Operation Allied Force, the conduct of psyops assumed similar characteristics to Desert Storm. This time, more than 100 million leaflets were dropped against various targets. In Kosovo itself, Yugoslav Army (VJ) forces received warnings that they would shortly be attacked unless they left the area. This technique was copied from Kuwait when leaflets warning of impending attacks by Daisy Cutter bombs and B52s were successful in clearing the battlefield of enemy forces. In Kosovo, however, the VJ was a very different proposition from Iraq's largely conscripted forces. It did not flee. Highly skilled in deception and camouflage techniques, the VJ moved around with considerable skill to avoid the destructive power of the

NATO air campaign. Anyone who can recall the defiance of Serb forces as they were televized leaving Kosovo at the end of the campaign will appreciate that this psyop campaign had little or no impact.

A second target audience was the Serbian population. The psyop campaign here also had little or no impact. Leaflets were dropped over cities like Belgrade and Novi Sad suggesting that NATO was not fighting the civilian population but rather the Milosevic regime. This personalization of the campaign, if anything, prompted an outburst of patriotic support for Milosevic from people who had just months earlier been demonstrating their opposition to his regime. 'We are all targets' became a rallying cry that saw defiant civilians rally to bridges to test NATO's claim that they were targeting only military and political installations. A skilful domestic propaganda campaign which emphasized that the Kosovo Albanians were fleeing the country due to the NATO bombing rather than alleged Serb 'genocide' eventually saw Serb State television attacked, but even here RTS was off the air for barely four hours. Regular street concerts by traditional music and rock bands maintained the atmosphere of defiance against a NATO they equated with the Nazis.

Given the importance of credibility in the successful conduct of psyops, NATO's deployment of one leaflet in particular is worthy of mention. This was the leaflet depicting the Apache attack helicopter with the phrase 'Don't wait for me'. The Apache was never deployed during the air campaign because of orders to fight the war from above 15,000 feet, and the failure to deliver what was promised in the messages was symptomatic of a defective psyop campaign, which failed to break either military or civilian morale. After the Gulf War the Kurds and Shias had risen up against Saddam Hussein, only to be crushed by Iraqi armed forces. This had no equivalent in Serbia, though not much more than a year later Milosevic was removed by a 'velvet revolution' in Belgrade. Meanwhile, NATO had committed itself to an expanded Balkan occupation, and in Kosovo the real challenge of the information campaign was all too apparent.

One of the aspects of modern soldiering in these new military environments could be placed under the banner of 'civil-military relations'. Outsiders may well be surprised at the attention to detail which goes into this activity today. For example, in Kosovo, where the Information Operation is very much a joint effort with UK, Swedish, and German input, KFOR issues its soldiers with a code of conduct with four essential pieces of advice:

1. Especially respect:
   - the high rank of religion and family
   - the pride of a freedom loving and tradition conscious people
   - the vulnerability and latest experience and suffers [sic] of the people
   We are guests, not occupying forces!
2. Generally avoid:
   - Condescending and discriminating remarks
   - Undisciplined improper behaviour (especially after the consumption of alcohol)

- [*sic*] Do not get personal or make lewd remarks/gestures (a large part of the population does not understand German or English)
Gestures are ambiguous and may be understood wrong [*sic*]!
3. In talks pay attention to:
   - address (non asked familiar addressing [*sic*] of persons including Local employees is humiliating)
   - contact in the spirit of partnership and politeness
   - the wording of instructions (Please, Thank you)
Treat everybody the way you want to be treated!
4. Be at the conduct of tasks:
   - clear and understandable in your instructions
   - obliging and patient explanations [*sic*] concerning your actions
   - correct and moderate in the pushing through of your orders (No provocation, firm by [*sic*] but fair in the pushing through of your orders)
   - firm, clear, but fair and friendly.

Apart from the grammatical errors that characterize a lot of these publications, especially in the process of translation, the awareness of a need for 'host nation sensitivity' has definitely increased. In a publication issued almost ten years ago by Fort Bragg entitled 'Building Bridges: The Commander's Guide to Face to Face Communication', everything from learning 'the local etiquette' to ensuring 'there is laughter, that your soldiers are friendly, even that they wave (as the locals do)' was part of the advice. By the time of Kosovo, the United States forces also issued their troops with a credit-card sized summary of how to achieve 'positive perceptions' by six methods:

1. Weapons: Muzzle down. Know and understand the ROE [rules of engagement].
2. Ambassador: You are a representative of your country. How people view you is how they perceive your country.
3. Know: Know who you are dealing with and be aware of your surroundings. Albanians and Serbs speak different languages. Try to learn basic phrases in both languages.
4. Equality: Do not show favoritism to any ethnic group of Kosovars. Deal with all Kosovar citizens equally and fairly.
5. Uniformity. Follow the unit SOP [standard operation procedure]. Look, act like and be a professional soldier. Helmets and flak vests are to provide protection against mines and UXOs [unexploded ordnance].
6. Perception: Present a positive image. MNB(E) [Multinational Battalion (East)] is not an occupying force. Wave at people using an open hand and be courteous. It will spread among the people of Kosovo.

All this might seem quite obvious, but it does reflect a newfound sensitivity to the needs of effective communication in support of the mission objectives, including the prevention of ethnic clashes, delivery of humanitarian aid (in association with NGOs), the provision of medical facilities for the local population, the return of displaced persons and the promotion of 'interethnic co-existence'.

The last of these is an ambitious concept and will undoubtedly take time. This was why the young people of Kosovo were an important target audience. In schools throughout the province, there was a need to address both the short-term needs of the immediate post-conflict environment (such as the promotion of mine awareness) and the long-term objective of promoting a democratic 'mentality'. In support of the former, a range of specially prepared 'products' was created utilizing cartoon characters, comic books, posters, and even bumper stickers.

The American-led information campaign conducted in MNB(E) was done under the title 'Task Force Falcon'.[8] The Task Force held press conferences and produced such publications as the newspaper, *The Falcon Flier*. This had a hard copy circulation of 2,000 in July 2000 and it was available in PDF format on the web site, though web access in Kosovo itself is extremely restricted.

Insiders quietly agree that the most important element in such democracy-building exercises (even though they are not overtly labelled as such) is time. The allied campaign to 're-educate' Germany and Japan out of their militaristic tendencies after World War II arguably took a generation, plus the rewriting of constitutions, school text books, and press laws. I have seen no reference back to these remarkable transformations of societies and their psychologies by today's democracy-builders. One of the key debates of the Cold War surrounded the rights and wrongs of interfering in the internal affairs of other countries. With Kosovo branded a 'humanitarian intervention', such debates have subsided, especially since the fall of the Milosevic government. But it is possible to see NATO forces in Kosovo as an occupying force, with the OSCE's attempts to rebuild civic society there as tantamount to a 're-education' campaign. Whether the attempts succeed in reconciling Kosovar Albanians and Serbs really does depend upon how much time the information campaign is given to achieve its objectives.

That, of course, is a political decision and is very much dependent upon the longevity and attitudes of the new Serb government. In the meantime, NATO and other authorities on the ground continue their efforts to restore peace and reconciliation. The warm glow surrounding the conduct of psyops since the Gulf War has chilled in the light of the Kosovo experience but it still enjoys an increasingly central position in emerging Information Operations doctrine. Until it is replaced, the working definition of information operations remains: 'actions taken to affect adversary information and information systems while defending one's own information and information systems' (Joint Publication 3–13). This is very much a conflict variant of command and control warfare.

But central to the thinking is the importance of 'influence operations' or what is becoming known as 'perception management'. It is within this spectrum that psyop is being placed – dangerously in my view – alongside deception activities.

It is dangerous because the broadening nature of psyop in the last decade has meant an increasing interface with media operations. It is essential for psyops and Media Operations to be kept as completely separate, albeit co-ordinated, activities; a press conference is not, and never should be, a psychological operation in the strictest sense. However, credibility is critical to the success of psyops. And if psyops are lumped in with deception operations, that credibility is bound to be undermined.

One subject in the debate over the modern RMA is the place of the military in a global information environment. Operational security has become increasingly difficult, as the range of information disseminators from a conflict area has broadened out from the media to the general public. New communications technologies such as mobile phones and laptop computers are affordable and accessible to ordinary people and so it is not just the unpredictable media that need to concern the information operators. Battlefields have become conflict spaces in which assistance to civilians is frequently the reason for military intervention. It is in these spaces that the military now have to *compete* with their information; they are no longer able to monopolise or confine the information flows. As such, tactical information – such as that contained in psyop products – has a strategic significance, which merely makes the issue of credibility even more important. It is not just that citizens in Belgrade could pick up a leaflet dropped minutes earlier and turn to display it to a CNN camera crew. They can now take it home, scan it into their computer and send it as an e-mail attachment to anyone on the Internet. Hence power stations, television stations, and radio transmitters have become the primary targets of Information-Age warfare when perception is a vitally important and worldwide conflict space.

If modern, liberal, free-market capitalist democracies decide for whatever reason to deploy their armed forces, they cannot do so behind closed doors. Correspondingly, their behaviour has to reflect not just the political imperatives but also the very ideology for which they are risking their lives. Under such scrutiny, casualties – on both sides – need to be kept to a minimum, mistakes need to be admitted quickly, and credible and accurate information needs to be released as soon as operational security allows. Quite simply the world has changed and the military are still a little old-fashioned in their thinking about what their role now is or should become. Effectively, they have become heavily armed social workers and, although they may not like this new function, they need the new skills required to operate in humanitarian and other interventions. The new skills are not just required during the military phase of any such operation; they have already demonstrated that they are pretty effective at this anyway. But before the battle, considerable planning to prepare the way is required and when the information processors are brought into the planning loop – as in the Gulf – then information dominance can ease the path to victory. What is now required is an equally sustained effort once the fighting has stopped. Rehabilitation takes time and effort.

The use of psyops is an essential part of the post-conflict effort, together with other forms of 'perception management' that constitute the spectrum of persuasion which modern armed forces must undertake in support of both traditional and emerging missions. But because of the information explosion, adversary reliance on information technology also requires a need to target such communications and information systems. It should therefore come as no surprise, as already mentioned, to discover television stations, telephone exchanges, and even power stations as primary targets in modern conflict. Conversely, one's own information systems need to be protected from attack. The post Cold War shift of American military information systems into the civilian domain have thus created new vulnerabilities, encapsulated by the fear of what has been called 'an electronic Pearl Harbour'. By extension, the communications systems of former adversaries will need to be rebuilt in what could be called an 'electronic Marshall Plan'.

It should equally come as no surprise to find the instruments of 'soft' power assuming an increasingly central role in pre- and post-conflict scenarios. The reorganization of the United States Information Agency in 1999, which saw USIA and Voice of America fully reintegrated into the US State Department, is recognition of the latter. The hidden assumptions behind this, however, relate to wider political and (usually) unspoken imperatives about the need to promote democracy, in all its forms, worldwide. Many senior political figures in the Western world are very much taken by the assertion that democracies do not fight other democracies. If the enemies of democracy are therefore non-democracies, then it follows that every effort should be made to reduce the number of potential enemies, or until relatively recently what used to be called 'rogue states'. Hence the psychological warfare stations targeting specific 'enemies', such as Radio and TV Marti directed at Cuba, or Radio Free Asia directed at North Korea and China, continue their work under the umbrella of 'soft' power information campaigns. Radio Free Europe continues as well in an effort to consolidate democratic ways of thinking in the former communist countries of Eastern Europe. In what has now been labelled 'international information', the victors of the Cold War see a newly invigorated and potentially decisive instrument for consolidating a New World Information Order.

In the new terrain that has been identified for war-fighting and democracy-building alike, the emerging concept of information operations assumes strategic dimensions across the full spectrum of conflict within the Revolution in Military Affairs and diplomacy alike (prompting calls for a Revolution in Diplomatic Affairs). Old forms of thinking still prevail as this terrain continues to be mapped out. The paradigm shift for the new world is simply too great a leap in faith to make fully as yet. However, the acquisition, transmission, storage, and transformation of information make Information Operations (IO) a target, a weapon, a vulnerability, and an integrated strategy all at the same time. This strategy will continue to require the capacity for greater physical destruction than an adversary, both in traditional terms and in new ways that utilize the digital revolution to its full advantage, whether by protecting information systems from virus attack or by inserting logic bombs into adversary systems. And because of the increasing inter-relationship between civilian and military information infrastructures, homeland defence against adversarial hacker attacks has also become a prerequisite.

Within this thinking, 'influence' operations assume a central role, whether to pre-empt future adversaries, to defeat them in case of conflict, or to consolidate triumphal value systems once victory has been achieved. The objectives of influence operations are to support foreign policy, deter aggression, and support democratic reform. What raises some doubt from the sceptics who liken this thinking to Orwellian 'mind control' is indeed an old philosophical conundrum faced by psyops practitioners since World War I. To put it simply, is it better to persuade an adversary to lay down his weapon and to desert, defect, or surrender than it is to blow his head off? A hundred years ago, before the advent of the mass slaughter that characterizes industrialized warfare, there were many who would have said 'no' to this question. In the 1920s, Lord Ponsonby believed that 'the injection of the poison of hatred into men's minds by means of falsehood is a greater evil in wartime than the loss of life. The defilement of the human soul is worse than the destruction of the human body'.[9] If we rewrite this statement to ask whether the injection of democratic values into people's minds is a better guarantee of protecting human rights, respecting minorities and other peoples' differences than bombing them into thinking like 'us', then a simple choice has to be made. That choice is whether to conduct 'perception management' operations in support of one set of values at the expense of another.

This is not an easy choice to make. It is vulnerable to accusations of 'cultural imperialism' or 'coca-colonialism', especially if the choice is being made in Washington as the self-proclaimed capital of the democratic world. Non-democracies will accuse the United States of arrogance in assuming that its political system and values are superior to those of others who choose not to adopt the same system and values. No doubt the retort would be: 'whose choice? – government or people?' If non-democratic governments are not prepared to test their moral position by letting the people decide in free and fair elections, then they merely confirm their position as 'rogue' or authoritarian regimes that constitute the 'natural' enemies of democracies, in the view of the United States.

The international information effort now being conducted by the United States is founded on the premise that the United States should and can make a difference in world affairs. In attempting to shape the international environment best to serve United States interests, the programme is predicated on the assumption that democratization will continue to thrive on a worldwide basis. The campaign in Kosovo is but one small piece of this jigsaw. The bigger picture is to deter conflict whenever possible (including by high profile visible threats of use of force but preferably by avoiding the actual deployment of force). In order to achieve this, greater use of 'soft' power will be required at the cultural, political, and economic levels of inter-state relations on a local, regional, and global basis. But the choice has indeed been made. Only time will tell if the belief that democracies really do prefer trade to war is a valid universal assumption about international affairs and human nature, or whether it is in fact specific to some countries and cultures and not others.

III

One means of understanding the influence of information warfare on information intervention is to distinguish between what I have called 'our wars' and 'other peoples' wars'. 'Our wars' are those which involve 'our troops' possibly fighting alongside 'our allies' against a clearly identified enemy and 'their allies' for a clearly identified national objective. 'Other peoples' wars' are wars that are fought for or in defence of goals, ideologies, or land that is not directly owned or subscribed to by 'our people'. Other peoples' wars are also different because media in the countries not directly affected by the war cover the war in a fundamentally different and more objective manner. This is not to suggest that the media are above taking sides in other peoples' wars, but that there is a greater level of media disengagement about the issues involved in them even though they may invoke a similar emotional response about the human suffering involved. All wars are nasty, brutal affairs but other peoples' wars are about other peoples' business, which may have little or nothing to do with 'us'.

'Our wars' are wars of the greatest emotional engagement for the combatants – both military and civilian – involved. There is of course a further distinction between conventional warfare in which civilian participation is limited to observation of the conflict via the media and 'total war' in which civilians actively participate in the war. As such the sense of mutual identification between military and civilian combatant is intensified, as distinct from other types of war in which professional armies consisting of volunteers are watched most intensely by their civilian relatives and friends.

For such people, media coverage of limited wars can be intrusive, which is why there are guidelines in reporting pictures of the dead and injured casualties of war. Opponents of war who criticize media for 'sanitizing' such images miss this critical point. A rule of thumb in the two world wars was only to show pictures of enemy dead; that way, watching relatives could not discover the loss of their loved ones from media, although they could see that the war was inflicting casualties on the other side.

Equally, in 'our wars', the journalist walks a very thin tightrope attached to two cliff edges labelled 'objectivity' and 'patriotism'. His journalistic responsibility to stand back from a story and to analyze it objectively can prove incompatible with his audience's subjective desire to see everyone support the national war effort. Bad news about the progress of 'our side' invariably prompts calls to shoot the messenger. This critical capability gave rise to the birth of modern military censorship. But democracies have evolved during the course of this century cherishing notions of freedom of speech and opinions.

In wartime, most people accept the need for some restrictions upon those democratic 'rights' but the issue remains just how far should they go. Should they suppress all bad news in the name of patriotism, even though this often occurs in the name of operational security? Examples of this occurring in the past are numerous. Casualty figures have often been minimized and defeats simply omitted from the public record. Following the retreat from Mons in 1914, the British War Office withdrew the permits of film camera crews. In 1940, while still First Lord of the Admiralty, Winston Churchill refused to release news that HMS *Nelson* and HMS *Barham* had sustained serious damage. Such instances are only possible when the military are in complete control of information reaching the public domain from the war zone. Modern communications technology has weakened that control, whereas modern political imperatives have increased the likelihood of access being granted to journalists.

Access is, indeed, the key to all this. In Vietnam, media representatives were granted virtually unlimited access to go wherever they wanted, at their own risk. Tragically, as a result of war reports that were perceived as being more and more critical, various and ever more controversial ways of influencing the outside perception of a crisis in a manner beneficial to its military-political conduct have evolved since the 1970s: to exclude media altogether, as in Grenada; to delay their arrival, as in Panama; to make them totally dependent upon the military for their safety, transport, and communications, as in the Falklands; or a combination of all these, as in Desert Shield/Desert Storm.

In other peoples' wars, the role of the media is to make such conflicts more our own than would otherwise have been the case. In the Spanish Civil War (1936–9), for example, British Movietone's newsreel coverage of the bombing of Guernica showed pictures of the devastated city under a commentary which ended: 'This was a war, and these were homes – like yours.' The message then was that the aerial bombing of cities – then a new and terrifying weapon – was of concern to all citizens of all countries. Despite international efforts at non-intervention in Spain for fear of the conflict spreading, it was clear that Fascist Italy, Nazi Germany, and Soviet Russia were all contributing to the civil war. The newsreel coverage brought this home to cinema audiences in neutral Britain and France and prompted some members of that audience to volunteer for the international brigades.

Media coverage of other peoples' wars is characteristically less susceptible to censorship by militarily non-participating governments. It is, however, still subject to manipulation by the warring parties. More recently, in another European civil war, the wars of Yugoslav succession, attempts to manipulate journalists were endemic in an effort by the warring factions to secure the moral high ground for their cause. Hence, in Bosnia and Herzegovina, the Bosnian Serbs attempted to portray themselves as the victims, rather than the aggressors – as victims variously of German, Albanian, 'Islamic fundamentalist' but, above all, Croat and Bosnian 'fascist' conspiracies. One might have thought that in a global information environment, it would be much easier than before to verify or discredit such stories, but when international journalists wanted to check for themselves on one alleged atrocity about necklaces made from the fingers of Serb babies in Vukovar, they were quite simply refused access to the alleged scene. The famous ITN footage of emaciated Muslim prisoners-of-war, which caused an international outrage in 1992, was banned on Serbian television. The Croat and Bosnian factions were likewise keen to steer the media coverage in their favour, not just within areas under their control but in the international arena as well. The Bosnian Muslims, for example, provided increased foreign journalistic access to their civilians on the march from the fallen 'safe havens' of Srebrenica and Zepa in the summer of 1995 to demonstrate that they, indeed, were the victims in this conflict; while Serb protests that they were merely retaliating for Bosnian army attacks (off-camera) were drowned beneath the sea of devastating footage of Bosnian civilian suffering. It took aerial photographs from U-2 spy planes to identify the likely fate of the men captured at Srebrenica.

This example has been chosen to illustrate how the global media need to be brought into debates about information warfare. This is because IW/IO tends to blur the distinction between 'our wars' and 'their wars' in certain critical ways. By lowering the risk of death to 'our soldiers' on an assumption that casualties would incur media and therefore public hostility, these conflicts become altered and thus the options open to policy-makers become altered too.

Moreover, because the post-conflict situation involves long-term staying power against the backdrop of a likely loss of media interest, reinstitution of civic infrastructures such as a (democratic) media system and mode of operation can only be done by official actors – working, of course, alongside NGOs and other non-state actors such as journalistic organizations. When this happens, however, given the interest and the encouragement of tendencies toward democratic values, the aftermath of 'their wars' become more like the aftermath of 'our wars'. And if 'our wars' are being increasingly influenced by IW concepts, our journalists are in for a shock. This is because they see themselves as mere observers, not participants. But participants they are, whether they like it or not. What role they play, especially if they lose interest in a conflict once it has ended, has the capacity not only to create an information vacuum that needs to be filled by 'perception managers' but also, in the process, encourages the military to achieve even more information dominance.

IV

I have mentioned three pathways for information warfare, pathways that demonstrate the link between the military dominance of conflict and the civilian-military realities in post-conflict zones. Soldiers must be retrained to help them operate within the difficult psychological climate in which civilian hatred runs so deep that the health and welfare of the military is at risk. The second pathway – closer to the main aspects of information intervention – involves breaking or bridging ethnic divisions that are the consequence, often, of indoctrination. Much more complex, of course, is a systematic shift in the structure and psychology of the target society. While the management and direction of each of these three aspects may differ, some under military control, some under civilian or mixed control, the habits of information warfare will permeate.

Writing of the new forms of conflict, James Der Derian has suggested that 'Virtuous war' represents the combined ideas of Clausewitz and Sun Tzu. It is the continuation of politics by informational means.[10] If that is true, then the secret of information intervention for peacekeeping purposes could be said to be the continuation of war, also by informational means. This is especially true in the post-conflict aspects of 'nation building' and construction of a new society.

Bibliography

Arquilla, J. and Ronfeldt, D. (1997), 'Cyberwar is Coming' in J. Arquilla and D. Ronfeldt (eds), *In Athena's Camp: Preparing for Conflict in the Information Age*, Santa Monica, CA: Rand.
——— (1997), 'Information, Power and Grand Strategy', in J. Arquilla and D. Ronfeldt (eds), *In Attena's Camp: Preparing for Conflict in the Information Age*, Santa Monica, CA: Rand.
Der Derian, James (2001), *Virtuous War: Mapping the Military-Industrial-Media-Entertainment Network*, Boulder, CO: Westview Press.
Joint Publication 3–07 (12 Feb. 1999), *Joint Doctrine for Military Operations Other Than War*, Joint Chiefs of Staff. Online [July 2001], available at http://www.dtic.mil/doctrine/jel/new_pubs/jp3_07.pdf
Joint Publication 3–13, *Joint Doctrine for Information Operations*, Joint Chiefs of Staff, 9 October 1998. Online [July 2001], available at http://www.dtic.mil/doctrine/jel/new_-pubs/jp3_13.pdf
Mazaar, Michael Shaffer, Jeffrey and Ederington, Benjamin (March 1993), *The Military Technical Revolution: A Structural Framework*, Washington, DC: Center for Strategic and International Studies.
Ponsonby MP, Arthur (1928), *Falsehood in Wartime: Propaganda Lies of the First World War*, London: George Allen and Unwin.
Taylor, Philip (1992), *War and the Media, Propaganda and Persuasion in the Gulf War*, Manchester: Manchester University Press.
Toffler, A. and Toffler, H. (1993), *War and Anti-War: Survival at the Dawn of the 21st Century*. Boston, MA: Little, Brown and Co.

Notes

1. The Revolution in Military Affairs is defined as, 'A major change in the nature of warfare brought about by the innovative application of new technologies which

combined with dramatic changes in military doctrine and operational and organizational concepts, fundamentally alters the nature and the conduct of war.' Mazaar, et al., *The Military Technical Revolution*, p. 21. In this case, the term is used for to describe the multitude of technological and scientific changes going on in modern-day warfare as they were first brought to the forefront by the Gulf War. The manifestations of the Revolution, how it has specifically changed the nature and conduct of warfare, and what it means for the future of warfare have been the subjects of a heated post-cold war debate.

2. 'Conflicts other than war' or 'military operations other than war' are activities 'where the military instrument of national power is used for purposes other than the large-scale combat operations usually associated with war'. See generally Joint Publication 3–07.

3. *The I-Bomb* was a documentary produced for BBC *Horizon* by Broadcasting Support Services. Produced by Kate O'Sullivan and edited by Peter Millson, 1997.

4. Following quotes from Warden, Campen, Sullivan and Toffler all transcripts from ibid.

5. Chairman, Joint Chiefs of Staff Instr. 3210.10, Joint Information Warfare Policy, 6 (2 January 1993). See also US Department of Defense Dir.S-3600.1. Information Warfare, 1–1 (1996).

6. Arquilla and Ronfeldt, 'Information, Power and Grand Strategy', p. 154.

7. Arquilla and Ronfeldt, 'Cyberwar is Coming', p. 40.

8. Task Force Falcon. Online [June 2001], available at http://www.tffalcon.hqusar-eur.army.mil/

9. Ponsonby, *Falsehood in Wartime*, p. 18.

10. See generally, Der Derian, *Virtuous War*.

12

Non-Governmental Perspectives: Media Freedom versus Information Intervention?

Helen Darbishire

Introduction

Advocates of intervention in the media environment in situations of conflict work from the premise that true media freedom permits democratic debate and can contribute significantly to the peaceful resolution of disputes. While many non-governmental organizations (NGOs) share this premise, the concept of 'information intervention' provokes a certain anxiety that the peacemaking aims of the international community might be used to justify interference with media freedom, so raising the dreaded spectre of 'censorship'. NGOs often argue that if media freedom is so essential to preventing or resolving conflict, then it should never be compromised for the sake of making deals with warring parties, taking military action against belligerents, or administering a country during the post-conflict phase.

The conflict zones of the late twentieth century present ample evidence of the dilemmas facing media freedom NGOs. There have been heated debates over jamming and extraterritorial broadcasting, protests over the seizure or bombing of transmitters and broadcasters, controversies over prosecutions of journalists and others who engaged in 'hate-speech', resistance to the intro-duction of media regulation in post-conflict situations, and disagreements over which media outlets the donors should support. On numerous occasions, fears that media freedom was being sacrificed to political goals have put the defenders of media freedom on a collision course with the supposed bearers of freedom and democracy, the inter-governmental organizations and govern-ments (predominantly Western) which comprise the 'international commu-nity'.

This chapter examines the approaches of NGOs to intervention in the media environment in situations of actual or potential conflict and the role NGOs play in the development of policies concerning 'information intervention'.

The RTS Bombing: Promise Broken, Precedent Set

One of the most dramatic information interventions of recent conflicts – the bombing by NATO of Radio Television Serbia's (RTS) Belgrade headquarters in the early hours of 23 April 1999, which killed sixteen media workers – was also that which elicited the most uniform and united response from NGOs: this was a step too far in interfering with the media.

The main concern among NGOs which first tried to prevent the bombing of RTS and then condemned it, was that it would be used to legitimize future attacks on media and journalists in conflict situations, irrespective of whether or not they were really engaged in incitement. Thanks to this action by Western powers, 'Governments who attack media – whether in the Balkans, in central Africa or central Asia – will now feel justified in making journalists and all who work with them legitimate targets,' stated Aidan White, General Secretary of the International Federation of Journalists (IFJ), a few hours after the bombing.[1]

A second and equally pressing concern was that the RTS bombing might prompt and justify reprisals against those independent media in Serbia which were struggling to survive in an ever more repressive environment: one journalist had been murdered since the NATO bombing campaign began, others detained and harassed, and media forced off the air.

The bombing was seen by NGOs as breaking a written assurance on 12 April by NATO spokesperson Jamie Shea that efforts to avoid civilian casualties included 'of course, journalists'. In response to concerns raised by the IFJ after NATO's military spokesperson, Air Commodore Wilby, had described RTS as a 'legitimate target', Jamie Shea stated that 'there is no policy to strike television and radio transmitters as such.'[2] Two days before the bombing, a group of twenty-five leading freedom of expression organizations wrote to NATO Secretary-General Javier Solana seeking further assurances that media would not be targeted after two media stations were hit when NATO bombed the headquarters of the ruling Serbian Socialist Party.[3]

For many of these NGOs, the fact that there had indeed been a NATO policy to attack RTS and that warning had been given of the intended strike, only made the bombing a more egregious attack on media freedom. Forewarned, RTS was able to resume broadcasting from elsewhere within hours, thereby completely undermining the justification of stifling an aggressive propaganda machine which was serving to keep the repressive and genocidal Slobodan Milosevic in power.

The bombing of RTS had originally been scheduled for a few days earlier but was delayed for various reasons, including the disagreement of the French government and the presence of foreign journalists in the building. The protests by NGOs contributed to the hesitancy of some governments, but in the end not sufficiently to prevent an action which did nothing to advance NATO's cause (the propaganda coup was handed to the Serbian authorities), and which certainly damaged important principles.

Analysis of the bombing by leading human rights organizations such as Human Rights Watch and Amnesty International concluded that it was illegitimate. Human Rights Watch noted that even if it had served to stop the propaganda, as was NATO's stated aim, the bombing would not have been legitimate.[4]

Hoping to set the record straight on the RTS bombing, media freedom lawyers from the UK and Serbia helped to initiate a case to the European Court of Human Rights – the case of *Bankovic and others v. NATO*. The case, brought by relatives of four persons who died in the bombing and by one person who sustained injuries, was against the seventeen states which are both members of NATO and signatories to the European Convention on Human Rights (that is, all members of NATO except the US and Canada). The applicants argued that when bombing RTS, the NATO countries had jurisdiction over the life of people in the building, and that the use of lethal force was not strictly necessary and therefore a violation of Article 2 of the European Convention – a violation of the right to life. They also argued that it was a violation of Article 10 of the European Convention, the provision that protects the right to freedom of expression and information. On 24 October 2001, the court held that the case was not admissable, on the grounds that the applicants did not fall within the jurisdiction of the respondent states on account of the bombing.

In Serbia itself, the change of regime after 5 October 2000 also brought a criminal investigation into the deaths of those in the RTS building and on 13 February 2001, the arrest of former RTS director Dragoljub Milanovic on suspicion of responsibility. (According to widespread rumour, NATO had tipped off the Serbian authorities before the bombing, but Milanovic or his political bosses wanted sacrificial victims, so he ordered junior staff to stay at their posts during the night in question, on pain of dismissal.) In March 2001, another investigation followed this one, of charges of abuse of authority concerning financial dealings. Milanovic was released from custody on 23 April 2001 – a date determined by legal procedures but whose coincidence with the second anniversary of the bombing provoked an angry reaction among Serbian journalists, who protested by keeping the screens blank for thirty seconds just before the main evening newscast.[5] At time of going to press Milanovic was free pending a trial on charges of criminal negligence and possibly of first-degree murder.

In the European Court of Human Rights, meanwhile, questions of jurisdiction and responsibility were being argued out with the seventeen governments concerned. It may be that a ruling on the merits, including the Article 10 question, is never reached, Nevertheless, the *Bankovic and others* application has constructed some important legal arguments about the extent to which governments may interfere with media engaged in propaganda, during conflict. As debate about information intervention continues, such a court ruling may play an important part in setting the parameters.

Subsequent events have borne out the fears that NATO had set a dangerous precedent by legitimizing media as military targets. On 12 October 2000, Israeli helicopter gunships fired rockets at the Palestinian Broadcasting Corporation's technical facilities in Ramallah, West Bank – an action subsequently defended by citing the NATO bombing of RTS.[6]

Who and What are the Media Freedom NGOs?

United as they generally were in condemning the RTS bombing, NGOs that work on media freedom and media development do not always agree about which measures are appropriate in response to conflicts. To understand the different NGO perspectives that are set out in this chapter, it is essential to define who and what they represent.

The legal and moral basis from which NGOs start is the right to freedom of association, a fundamental right that can be exercised freely across frontiers and must be tolerated, if not welcomed, by national governments. NGOs working on media freedom or media development do not characterize their work as 'intervention' at all. Unlike interventions by foreign states or by intergovernmental organizations (IGOs) their work does not beg questions of sovereignty. The different perspectives of IGOs and NGOs on interventions are expressed in their differing modes of operation and conceptions of acceptable or legitimate activity.

The international media freedom NGOs generally have a mandate to defend media or journalists from control and censorship.[7] Some are membership organizations representing communities of media professionals. The International Federation of Journalists (IFJ) is a membership organization of journalists' associations from around the world, while the World Association of Newspapers (WAN) represents associations of publishers. In each case the member organizations are national or regional groupings of those involved in the running and production of media. The World Press Freedom Committee (WPFC) groups media organizations across the spectrum and defines its mandate as defending all media. The International Press Institute (IPI) also has as its primary purpose defending press freedom in individual countries and representing its global network of editors, publishers and leading journalists as well as academics from communications institutions.

The two main journalists' rights defence organizations are the Committee to Project Journalists (CPJ) formed by US journalists with a mission to respond to abuses against journalists and to promote press freedom, and Reporters Sans Frontières (RSF) which started as a defence movement by French journalists in solidarity with colleagues elsewhere.

Human rights organizations often include media freedom in their work, and these include Human Rights Watch, Amnesty International and, in Europe, the International Helsinki Federation representing member groups in many countries. The organization ARTICLE 19 is a human rights NGO taking its mandate specifically from Article 19 of the Universal Declaration of Human Rights, which sets forth the right to freedom of opinion, expression and information.

The 1990s saw significant developments in the field of monitoring and lobbying for human rights. International NGOs working on human rights and media freedom issues – many of them only founded in the late 1980s or early 1990s – developed and gained experience both in terms of individual professional staff and as institutions were establishing their identities and refining working methods. Democratic transitions in many countries have permitted the emergence of domestic NGOs whose professional development has been supported by international NGOs. The information revolution permitted networking between these groups, enabling remarkably rapid responses to human rights violations.

These developments have also seen a trend in which NGOs have moved from the dissident role of protesting against violations of human rights, to advocacy for measures protective of human rights, and even to active engagement in government policy and initiatives, such as involvement in drafting legislation. This shift from dissidence to advocacy to engagement is a measure of the maturity of civil society, both nationally and globally. In the media freedom sphere NGOs such as ARTICLE 19 regularly work on legislation and, with groups such as Interights, on submission of *amicus curiae* briefs to courts, including the European Court of Human Rights, in defence of media freedom principles. RSF even – controversially – litigated against 'journalists' alleged to have incited the genocide in Rwanda (see section below 'From Defending the Indefensible to Prosecuting Journalists').

A New Breed: The Activist-Donor NGOs

The conflicts of the 1990s, particularly those in the former Yugoslavia, gave rise to a new type of media NGO that works to distribute money to media in situations of conflict and at the same time gets involved in campaigning in defence of media freedom and for plurality. The development of these NGOs in some ways mirrors the evolution of humanitarian NGOs that now often focus on development strategies – which may include a political component – rather than merely on relief efforts.

In Europe, good examples of this small but professional band are Medienhilfe (Switzerland) and Press Now (Netherlands), founded in December 1992 and April 1993 respectively in specific response to the Yugoslav crisis. Swiss journalists who wanted to show 'professional solidarity against nationalism and chauvinism' formed Medienhilfe. It now raises and channels funds from private and governmental sources in Switzerland, conducts research in the media sphere and promotes policy at Swiss and EU levels. Press Now similarly started with emergency aid in 1994, moved to infrastructure projects in 1995, and now is an established donor-agency and policy adviser; it has disbursed a total of approximately €1.4 million.[8]

Another significant development in the donor sphere has been George Soros' Open Society Institute (OSI), which introduced the concept of the activist-donor with a solid indigenous base in each country as well as the capacity to exchange experiences and mobilize opinion at the international level. Starting in Central and Eastern Europe in the late 1980s and early 1990s, OSI now operates worldwide and pays particular attention to conflict zones, supporting media in difficult environments, aware of the centrality of freedom of expression and information to the concept of an 'open society'.[9]

Press Now and Medienhilfe are part of a co-ordinated media-donor group, which includes OSI, the Swedish Helsinki Committee, Norwegian People's Aid, Irex ProMedia and the Media Development Loan Fund. These in turn liaise with the aid agencies of Western governments and with IGOs on strategies for media development. They also get involved in economic, legal and policy issues to the extent that these impact upon the possibilities of developing a sustainable independent media.

Donor NGOs have developed criteria for which media they support. Press Now and Medienhilfe have six similar key points, which include independence of ownership and editorial policy, professional and ethical standards, and a commitment to democratic and intercommunity processes.[10]

These 'activist-donor' organizations have helped to channel government funds to media recipients but in doing so are making choices based on professional rather than political considerations. Sums are relatively small compared with governmental or IGO donors, but the impact on the ground can be significant because of professional and co-ordinated decision-making in close collaboration with local individuals and organizations. These NGOs have also been successful in ensuring that media development stays on the agenda of major international donors such as the European Commission, and have led the way in establishing the criteria for supporting the media in conflict zones.

Media freedom NGOs have supported UNESCO's drive to make media assistance a priority in conflict zones. The funds raised by UNESCO for media in conflict zones have risen from some US$500,000 in 1994 to over US$3 million in 2000. Furthermore, media assistance is now a standard feature of the agenda of any Inter-Agency Consolidated Appeal, the co-ordination body for UN agency responses to crises. UNESCO relies on its partnerships with NGOs, particularly the IFJ and WAN, and their local members to disburse the funds in an effective way.

Democratic Debate and Conflict Prevention

Conflicts take place in countries with radically dissimilar media profiles. Levels of economic development, literacy and media-audience sophistication differ significantly between Rwanda and Croatia; the peacekeeping missions in Bosnia and Kosova, Cambodia and East Timor were confronted with widely differing media infrastructures. Yet one factor is consistent: wherever media have been used to prepare the ground for battle, it is also the case that the media environment was restricted, debate controlled or stifled, and civil society was not vigorous enough to withstand the promotion of internal conflict.

Appraising the media's role in the Rwandan genocide, ARTICLE 19 noted that for a number of years prior to the genocide, the government – or, more specifically, those factions in the government resistant to democratic reforms –

maintained tight controls on the broadcast sector and print media run by or linked to the government. Journalists from independent papers suffered harassment, arbitrary detentions and criminal charges such as 'threatening state security'. Collection of information and distribution of newspapers were often hindered by restrictions on freedom of movement imposed under emergency regulations.[11]

It was into this context that the 'hate media', as RSF has labelled them, came into being: newspapers such as *Kangura* and the infamous Radio-Television Libre des Mille Collines (RTLM) – both linked to senior government cadre and to their militias who were the driving force behind the genocide.

Similarly if less blatantly, the political elites promoting ethnic conflict in the former Yugoslavia used the media under their control to inspire fear and hatred, while waging campaigns of repression and intimidation against independent media which challenged the approved agenda of irreconcilable ethnic differences and the necessity of violent solutions.[12]

The conclusion drawn by many media analysts was that the development of a plural and diverse media environment at an early enough stage could have prevented the 'ethnic cleansing' and genocides, at least in their extremes. The question then arises, how to accelerate this development in the most adverse circumstances? Recognizing that proposing to build pluralism in Rwanda in the weeks immediately before April 1994 or calling on the Rwandan authorities to take legal action against certain media, 'would have been a hopelessly idealistic and impractical position', ARTICLE 19 instead insisted that:

> If useful lessons are to be drawn from the Rwandan situation it is necessary to go back to the introduction of multi-party politics and the failure to build adequate institutional support for democracy. In one sense the Rwandan experience is not atypical. In countries like Kenya and Zambia, which also underwent rapid democratic transitions under pressure from Western donor governments, there has also been a failure to transform or replace the institutions of one-party rule in order to make them more accessible and accountable. In particular the mass media have changed very little. Broadcasting remains a virtual state monopoly, while the independent press exists in an almost permanent state of siege. Even countries which democratized later and constructed better constitutional safeguards – Malawi is a good example – nevertheless have failed to establish an independent and accountable publicly-funded state broadcasting system.[13]

There are many other examples of countries where media freedom is not strongly rooted. Even in those post-communist countries currently approaching EU membership, reform in the broadcast media sphere is worryingly incomplete – as recent crises over public broadcasting in the Czech Republic, Hungary and Bulgaria have highlighted. A quick comparison between countries with democratic reform deficits and those where it is not inconceivable that

internal conflict could develop will generate many matches. If there is to be a
serious commitment to fulfil the objective of the UN Charter 'to save
succeeding generations from the scourge of war', then concerted early action
in the media environment has to be a priority.

The Information Intervention of Choice: Internal Alternatives

Many countries around the world – particularly the increasing number in
'transition' – manifest signs of simmering or potential conflicts or are locked
into frozen conflicts. In these environments, the 'information intervention' of
choice for media freedom NGOs is timely support for indigenous plurality.

The activist-donors share the conviction that indigenous media are the
only viable counterweight to state-controlled media. This is the lesson of
direct experience, most notably the poor record of extraterritorial broadcasting projects in, or for, conflict zones. In the former Yugoslavia, some
attempts at extraterritorial broadcasting were expensive failures, which have
become notorious as examples of what not to do. First among these was
Radio Brod (Radio Boat, 1993–4) whose signal was not strong enough to
reach far over the Dalmatian Alps and which smacked of a 'Yugo-nostalgia'
out of step with realities on the ground. Another controversial project was
the Open Broadcast Network based in Bosnia but created and backed by a
range of international donors to the tune of US$20–30 million between 1996
and early 2001.

The exception to this extraterritorial broadcasting model is that of the
established international broadcasters such as the BBC World Service, Radio
France International (RFI), Deutsche Welle and Voice of America. In some
parts of the world, particularly in less developed countries and notably in sub-
Saharan Africa, there is a developed culture of listening to BBC and RFI
broadcasts. In other countries, with more sophisticated audiences habituated to
technically if not politically advanced mass media, there is a stronger need for
credible indigenous voices. This is particularly so where international community policy has engendered local hostility. As Veran Matic of Radio B92 in
Serbia and chairperson of ANEM (Association of Independent Electronic
Media) comments, such external media intervention 'cannot be sufficiently
effective, as listeners always seek to detect the political interest of the country in
which the broadcaster is based'. Considering Jamie Metzl's information
intervention proposals, Matic cautioned that:

> initiatives from the outside would surely fail as they can never do more
> than mimic local cultural patterns, this mimicry is obvious to the local
> community and the information it carries is disregarded. The only thing
> the international community should do is to closely cooperate with those
> individuals and organizations which are implementing local cultural and
> media initiatives in order to help the civil structures in society to win
> power.[14]

These views are representative of the independent donors and the media freedom community, which continues to place significant emphasis on building independent media in-country. Exceptions to this approach are rare, but on occasion NGOs have supported extraterritorial broadcasting initiatives when there was no possibility for independent or critical voices to operate inside a country. In Europe, Belarus is the sole example with stations like Radio Racyja broadcasting from Poland on medium and short wave with political, economic and social news, including viewpoints critical of President Lukashenka. Radio Baltic Waves broadcasts from Lithuania into Belarus, including rebroadcasting of Radio Liberty and Radio Racyja. Radio Baltic Waves was founded in 1999 and initially had problems securing a licence due to concerns over Lithuanian-Belarussian relations, but now has a five year licence and funding support. Donors include the Westminster Foundation for Democracy, the National Endowment for Democracy, and OSI Budapest.[15]

In May 2000, UNESCO convened a round-table on 'Media in Conflict and Post Conflict Areas' which addressed the question of internationally sponsored versus indigenous media. The participants, including IGO and NGO representatives and journalists, reaffirmed the development of independent local media as a priority, recommending that the international community should work 'to strengthen [them] where these exist; to rebuild them where they have been destroyed; and to establish them where they do not exist'. The participants also called that this priority 'be spelt out clearly and unequivocally in any mandate given to an intergovernmental organization'.[16] It remains to be seen whether these promising recommendations will be applied.

Significantly, the UNESCO round-table defined 'independent' media as including genuinely independent public service media 'financed through a licence fee or other form of taxation but protected by legal statute and governed by an independent authority' and called on the international community to work to strengthen these media as well.[17] In many transitional countries, this is an area where reforms have either failed or not been genuinely attempted. In part this is because governments are unwilling completely to let go of their traditional propaganda machines, and in part because such reform is strongly resisted by the employees of the powerful and overstaffed state broadcasters for whom a more efficient and professional operation means loss of jobs and political clout.

For NGOs to tackle reform of the state-funded media is therefore difficult whereas rapid and visible results are more likely to come from supporting private media development. Many have argued that reform of state-funded media can be precipitated by development of a healthy and competing private sector. This has happened, but at a speed that lags behind other democratic developments to such a degree that NGOs, IGOs and bilateral donors alike are being compelled to pay new and closer attention to the problem of how to create genuine public service broadcasters. This challenge is now recognized as urgent in conflict and post-conflict zones where state-funded media are often the main instigators of intolerance and can drown out alternative voices.

Crossing Bridges: Media and Conflict Prevention

Important initiatives to increase communication between alienated communities in conflict areas have been taken by organizations such as Search for Common Ground (US) and the Hirondelle Foundation (Switzerland), which get involved in the production of programmes designed to overcome ethnic divisions. In Macedonia the work of Search for Common Ground in the multi-ethnic children's programme *Nashe Malo* (Our Neighbourhood) has reached large audiences (a reported 75 per cent of children in Macedonia) and produced measurable changes in attitudes to ethnic issues among viewers.[18]

Many of the independent donor organizations support projects that promote the exchange of journalistic materials (texts and broadcast programmes) between communities and neighbouring countries. Other projects aim to steer media away from merely mirroring, or even worse, exacerbating the divisions in society. These include the 'Reporting Diversity' project that started with the IFJ and is now run by the Centre for War, Peace and the News Media. This initiative, along with others such as those run by Conciliation Resources, aims to work with journalists on raising ethical and professional standards of reporting on ethnic and other divisions, helping them to break out of the nationalistic or antagonistic paradigms and to present new perspectives on existing problems.[19]

Media Assistance as Humanitarian Aid

Even in a developed crisis, NGOs prefer to support alternative voices and greater plurality rather than take restrictive measures. This is an approach that became policy for a number of NGOs at an expert meeting on 'Propaganda Inciting to Commit Genocide in Rwanda' convened by UNESCO in 1995.[20] NGOs and UNESCO resolved: 'that genocide propaganda be countered by supporting or creating independent media, in particular radio, thus permitting the population to be informed in an non-partisan way and allowing voices of tolerance and reason to be heard'.

In pursuit of this principle, NGOs have worked with UNESCO since the early 1990s to support independent media in zones of conflict, including in Africa and in the Balkans. Aid to the media included financial aid but also assistance with equipment and newsprint. One of the earliest challenges was caused by the sanctions against the Federal Republic of Yugoslavia (Serbia and Montenegro) from which humanitarian aid was exempt but which did not include assistance to the media, such as supplies of newsprint. Lobbying by UNESCO in co-ordination with NGOs to change this policy began in early 1993; by June 1994, assistance to the media was exempted from the sanctions. This marked an important policy shift at the international level and an understanding of the importance of supporting media, particularly independent media, during crises. The principle that media assistance should be included with humanitarian assistance has now become well established and although it is not an absolute rule, UNESCO reports that there is a sufficiently well-established precedent that it is usually accepted.[21]

Before the Rain: Democratization versus Stability In Macedonia

One country where the strengths and limits of NGO action have been shown in recent years is Macedonia. It seems obvious that entrenching media freedom should have been a top priority in Macedonia, particularly considering the media's role in the conflicts in the neighbouring former Yugoslav countries. Macedonia's vulnerability to external and internal security threats, given its ethnic make-up and its regional position, has been well recognized since its independence in 1991.

Quite early in the 1990s, Western governments – and hence the IGOs – adopted a kid-glove approach to Macedonia over democratic and human rights standards. There has been international toleration of the Macedonian authorities' foot-dragging over improving the rights of the minorities (particularly Albanians but also Roma, Turks, Serbs, and Vlachs), which constitute a sizeable proportion of the population. The international community also endorsed elections that were marred by voting irregularities and increasingly by violence, and has not tackled the notorious level of corruption. Human rights were a lower priority than 'stability'.

IGOs and Western governments showed a similar tolerance towards Macedonia's chaotic media environment. When broadcasting regulation was eventually implemented in 1998, the government endorsed over 150 licences. This strategy ensured that all political and minority groups (often with overlapping interests) had 'their' media. Macedonia became the first country in Europe with two Roma television stations, although not as a result of pro-minorities policy. The resulting fragmented and ghettoized media scene and the disproportionate number of radio and television stations in a country of just two million potential viewers and listeners even met with international approval: the outcome and number of stations was judged by the Organization for Security and Co-operation in Europe (OSCE) to be 'a satisfactory level of pluralism in broadcasting'. The European Commission in October 1998 assessed that with respect to 'the electronic media, the law on broadcasting of April 1997, has been fully implemented'.[22]

The endorsements by IGOs were used by Macedonia's Broadcasting Council to rebuff concerns expressed by international NGOs about the licensing process, including the lack of transparency in decision-making, the licensing of stations that had not met the stipulated criteria, and the failure to close the pirate stations. Like many transitional governments defending themselves from criticism, the Macedonian authorities became adept at using IGOs to justify action or lack of action. There have been attempts in Central and Eastern Europe to use EU Accession criteria to this end, and most recently membership of NATO has been cited to justify state secrets laws proposed in Romania and Slovakia. Such strategies cause significant dilemmas for local NGOs because it is difficult to argue against the proposed regulations without being labelled as anti-democratic, anti-Western and intent on undermining the interests of the country.

In Macedonia, the most flagrant example of distortion of IGO advice on media freedom occurred in late 2000 and early 2001, when the government succeeded in securing an agreement from the Council of Europe to conduct an expert analysis of a confidential draft public information law to regulate the mass media. Such secrecy excluded NGOs and media from the drafting process, and prevented public debate on the issue, a matter of concern that local and international NGOs raised with the Council of Europe. Council of Europe representatives countered that, as a membership body, it had to bow to the wishes of member states and argued that a certain level of confidentiality in the diplomatic process was necessary to ensure the quality of the final law.

The issue came to a head in February 2001 when the government, without further consultation, approved and passed to the parliament for adoption a new version of the law that was significantly more restrictive than the earlier draft.[23] The quality versus transparency trade-off had not paid off. International NGOs launched a rapid and co-ordinated advocacy campaign. Analyses and protests came from ARTICLE 19, the International Federation of Journalists, the International Press Institute, the International Crisis Group, the South East Europe Media Organization (SEEMO), and Reporters Sans Frontières, and their reports circulated widely on the Internet, including via the International Freedom of Expression Exchange (IFEX) network. IREX and the European Institute for the Media (EIM) along with a Macedonian NGO called 'Pro-Media', quickly organized a round-table debate for 2 March, inviting the Skopje diplomatic corps, local civil society and government representatives. Other NGOs worked behind the scenes, alerting diplomatic channels in Brussels, Washington, and other capitals.

Each action was picked up by the NGOs and media in Skopje, demonstrating to the Macedonian government and public opinion the level of international concern about the draft law. The Macedonian Media Centre's lawyers put forward their own analysis of the draft using domestic constitutional arguments and international standards. The Macedonian authorities responded that the new draft was in line with the Council of Europe's recommendations, but local activists were unable to counter these claims because of the continuing confidentiality of the Council's report.

On 27 February 2001, the government announced the bill was being withdrawn from parliament, and promised an open and consultative process to prepare a future draft. Approximately two hours after this announcement, the Council of Europe announced that secretary-general Walter Schwimmer had decided to release the contents of its analysis. This decision was prompted by a growing concern that the analysis was being misrepresented and used for manipulation. This experience has not, however, caused the Council of Europe completely to abandon the practice of submitting confidential comments on draft laws as it argues that there may still be situations when not publishing a critical comment of an initial draft is an appropriate way of working with a member government.[24]

This episode can be seen as a culmination of a decade of activities in support of media freedom in the conflict zone of the Balkans. The ability of international and Macedonian NGOs to defeat the draft public information law did not happen by chance; it was the result of a clear strategy that had been developed and by donors and activists at the international level and inside the country, particularly by support for the Macedonian Media Centre, which co-ordinated the campaign.

Media freedom had been under increasing pressure in Macedonia throughout the 1990s. Concerns included increased physical and fiscal threats, escalating harassment by the authorities, and editorial pressures in politically-controlled media. State ownership of the major publishing house, distribution network and sales outlets combined with the on-going breaches of copyright and broadcasting piracy made it harder for professional stations to compete in the advertizing market and to support production costs, necessitating continued donor support.

Although introducing a modern regulatory framework for the media would have caused some discomfort for the Macedonian government, there is no reason to suppose it would have had a seriously destabilizing effect. Yet the lack of insistence by international partners that such reforms should be introduced, surely sent a signal that a less than democratic media environment was tolerated, hence resulting in the increased abuses of journalists' rights and the development of restrictive legislation.

Macedonian activists met difficulty in getting these problems taken up by either international NGOs or international media. Part of the reason was the myth of Macedonia as the international community's success story in the Balkans, a myth often reflected in international media coverage. Furthermore, there were other more pressing problems in the region demanding attention.

The Consequences of Failure

In times of conflict the lack of rigorous conditions and even appeasement on certain key issues can have devastating consequences. The failure of the international community to impose conditionality on Serbia with respect to media freedom joins the list of other shortcomings in the history of negotiations with Slobodan Milosevic. In early October 1998, as US special envoy Richard Holbrooke brokered an agreement for international monitoring in Kosova, media freedom NGOs appealed to the international community to keep up the pressure on Serbia to respect media freedom. These appeals became particularly urgent after a decree against fomenting 'fear' and 'defeatism' was used to close a number of newspapers.[25] ARTICLE 19 alleged that the 'international community's tolerance of a barrage of new media regulations has helped the government to generate domestic support for the assault on Kosovo'.[26]

Noting that Milosevic was not seeking international approval but was rather 'using the notion of Serbia's role as a pariah state to stir nationalistic fervor among radicals in Serbia', the World Press Freedom Committee recognized that 'normal forms of condemnation may not work', but still urged the US government to keep media freedom on the agenda, partly as moral support for Serbia's independent journalists. The WPFC stated that lack of guaranteed result was 'no reason not to speak out. Serbian journalists and broadcasters . . . are dismayed and disappointed at the silence of the US and other nations' leaders on this issue [media freedom]. Their morale is low and their fear is high. They feel abandoned by the West.'[27]

These fears were justified: on the same day as the WFPC letter was sent, 20 October 1998, the Serbian parliament enacted a public information law immediately denounced by local and international NGOs as highly repressive. Before this notorious law was repealed in February 2001, after the fall of the Milosevic regime, it was used regularly and rigorously to impose fines (which were not paid) totalling some €1.5 million from Serbian media.

Policy Questions: Bombing and Jamming

Once a conflict has broken out or is rapidly escalating, intervention of a different character may be considered necessary: actions such as jamming media and extraterritorial broadcasting, or even bombing of transmitters and stations. This may not solve the underlying problems but might help in extreme circumstances to save lives without putting other lives at risk.

NGOs are generally very reluctant to endorse either bombing or jamming, as reactions to the RTS bombing clearly showed. In addition, many NGOs protested after 27 May 1999 when Eutelsat, the European satellite broadcaster, suspended the RTS satellite transmissions under Western government pressure. Ronald Koven of the WPFC states the position bluntly:

> Propagandizing is not sufficient reason for bombardment. It is only when communications outlets are used as weapons of war that they become fair game: Goebbels radio was fair game; RTLM was fair game. RTS on the other hand, was denying atrocities in Kosovo rather than calling for human rights violations, and was therefore not fair game.[28]

One widely expressed concern is 'Who gets to decide?' Bettina Peters of the IFJ notes:

> In the case of Serbia it was NATO military and some Western governments, in the case of the Palestinian Broadcasting Corporation it was the Israeli military, in the case of Pakistan (jamming not bombing) it was the

Indian military and government . . . Mostly, it seems, these decisions are more motivated by either national interest or interest of certain (military) or other blocks and not always directly related to human rights concerns. It may make more sense to start counter-broadcasts – with key involvement of local journalists not exclusively foreign journalists – and to support independent media on the ground wherever possible.[29]

Andrew Puddephatt of ARTICLE 19 shares these concerns about the legitimacy of coercive action:

If an intervention is not supported by the UN Security Council – which it cannot always be because that mechanism has its flaws – then the intervention has to be in response to obvious and gross human rights violations in order to be justifiable. Counter-broadcasts are less contentious because they require a much lower threshold.

Bombing is irreversible, whereas jamming and other actions can at least be ceased. Generally, however, NGOs see even jamming as something 'highly damaging to the culture of freedom'. Puddephatt states that:

If a station is broadcasting incitement to murder, then there is no question that it should be jammed. The broad point is that freedom of expression is a human right alongside other rights. It is a fundamental right but not unlimited – it has to be balanced against respect for other human rights.[30]

Exactly when the balance tips is, of course, where IGOs, NGOs and others start to disagree. In April 1994 as the genocide in Rwanda got under way, RSF called on the United Nations presence in Rwanda, UNAMIR, to intervene to stop the RTLM broadcasts. The human rights community debated this call, although later consideration resulted in general agreement. ARTICLE 19 in 1996 concluded that, given the nature of the broadcasts after 6 April 1994, 'international law clearly permitted external intervention to jam the broadcasts at this stage, which is the action which should have been undertaken.'[31]

One coercive action that did not prompt widespread NGO condemnation was the seizure in 1997 of television transmitters of the Serb Radio Television (SRT) network in Bosnia. After international troops took control of the Udrigovo transmitter on 28 August, the Committee to Protect Journalists wrote to US Secretary of State Madeleine Albright that 'CPJ welcomes SFOR's original decision to protect the transmitter from an orchestrated mob attack', and went on to express distress that the transmitter was returned to supporters of indicted war criminal Radovan Karadzic. This move, CPJ suggested, was a lost opportunity to secure a space for alternative broadcasters who were 'struggling to report objectively in a violent, polarized situation'.[32] CPJ also expressed concerns that one of SFOR's conditions for the return of the transmitter was that SRT would desist from disseminating anti-NATO propaganda – a requirement characterized by CPJ as being out of step with international standards on media freedom and the mandate of the Dayton Accords.

The seizure of a further four transmitters in October 1997 elicited concern from ARTICLE 19, which again did not focus on the action itself but on whether those now overseeing broadcasting in the Republican Srpska area of Bosnia would exercise control responsibly.[33]

The IPI noted in 1998 that the seizure of transmitters had 'raised more than a few eyebrows in the media world. Many analysts however, now credit the move with accelerating the democratic process in Bosnia and consolidating the Dayton Accords.' Among those with raised eyebrows were the WPFC, which did not issue a formal protest but in public meetings questioned the seizure of the transmitters.[34]

These mild responses were seen by the international administrators in Bosnia as approval by NGOs for a tougher line on control of the media environment and hence encouraged the preparation of a coherent media policy for Bosnia, including media regulation, which would provide a more democratic solution to the problem of inciteful media. As will be seen, these later developments did not meet with the same uncritical approval.

A New NGO Policy on Bombing

In May 2001, a group of media freedom NGOs introduced a policy resolution:

> Members of the Coordinating Committee of Press Freedom Organizations, meeting in Windhoek, Namibia, on May 6, 2001, resolve that governments should not target broadcast facilities during war and conflict.
>
> Broadcast facilities are presumed to be civilian objects because they do not meet the customary definition of a military objective under international humanitarian law. Article 52 of Protocol (1) Additional to the Geneva Conventions of 1949 states, 'Military objectives are limited to those objects which by their nature, location, or use make an effective contribution to military action and whose total or partial destruction, capture or neutralization, in circumstances ruling at the time, offers a definite military advantage.'
>
> This rule is part of customary international law and is binding on all states that have not ratified the Protocol.
>
> Broadcast facilities can only lose this civilian immunity if they are used for significant military purposes, such as military communication. The broadcast of 'propaganda' does not constitute a military function. This is a highly subjective term that should never be used to justify a military attack.
>
> In the past several years, military attacks have been launched against

broadcast facilities in Serbia, Dagestan and the West Bank. Such attacks violate international humanitarian law and place all journalists covering conflicts at risk.

The adoption of this resolution by CPJ, the Inter American Press Association, the International Association of Broadcasters, the International Federation of Periodical Press, IPI and the WPFC was a significant development in a debate that began over RTLM in Rwanda and was given further impetus by the bombing of RTS. These NGOs have now drawn a line in the sand with regard to information intervention and developed a policy that seems to reflect an across-the-board policy by media freedom NGOs towards bombing broadcast stations in conflict.

While non-governmental thinking on other information intervention issues has not yet been so clearly defined, the majority of media freedom NGOs would presumably also extend the criteria proposed for bombing to jamming and to prosecutions for 'hate speech'. Namely, the media in question should be engaged in incitement to violence, meeting a clear and present danger-type test, or even being used as a tool for directing crimes against humanity, in order to qualify as targets of intervention.

It is important to note that even the most ardent defenders of freedom of expression have come to recognize that in some circumstances media may be culpable of directing violations of human rights (or being used for 'significant military purposes', as stated in this resolution). Thus far, the only clear instance when NGOs are agreed that bombing or jamming would have been appropriate has been RTLM. Those considering further violent or coercive interventions will have to provide very convincing evidence to have the media freedom NGOs – and with them, many highly influential media outlets – on their side.

Media in Erupting Conflict and Hate Speech

At time of writing (July 2001), Macedonia hangs on the brink of civil war. As violence escalated from March 2001, the problem of 'hate speech' reared its ugly and highly controversial head, accompanying the fighting rather than preceding it as had occurred in the former Yugoslavia in other conflicts.

Since the use of hate speech and, more precisely, direct incitement to fear, hatred and violence have become a distinguishing feature of modern civil wars, and the excesses perpetrated by Serbian and Croatian media in the 1990s had been widely noted and condemned, the eruption of violent conflict in Macedonia drew immediate international attention to local media coverage. Initial reports were mixed and confused. The OSCE Representative on Freedom of the Media, Freimut Duve, on 27 March 2001 congratulated the press on their restraint and for having 'demonstrated very little bravado'. By 7 May, however, he was urging media to 'refrain from "hate speech" that can only exacerbate the already precarious situation in the country'. The trends were clear, and in April 2001, the International Helsinki Federation (IHF) reported that:

> we are witnessing a fresh wave of 'hate speech' (especially in some of the State-owned printed media). Ethnic Macedonians and ethnic Albanians are demonizing one another and the government has not fulfilled its obligations to work against this intolerance.[35]

Reports later in the summer by the International Crisis Group noted the media's continuing decline.[36]

That the IHF recalled the Macedonian government's duty to work against intolerance reflected a trend in parts of the NGO community towards a greater readiness to point to and condemn hate speech, and to call for action against it. This development has been forced by the direct role some media have played in conflicts, most notoriously in Rwanda and Bosnia, but it has not been an easy transition. Less than a decade earlier, the overwhelming policy position among NGOs was that the best – perhaps the only – solution to inciteful speech was *more* speech.[37] This concurred with the dominant political liberalism of the time, and the interests of media freedom NGOs. Yet, as a position, it was to be tested by events in the early 1990s.

Early in the Yugoslav wars of succession, an academic paper by Branko Milinkovic, a Serbian lawyer familiar with NGO perspectives on media freedom, reviewed international law and European practice with respect to hate speech and concluded that prosecutions would be appropriate in Yugoslavia. In his essay, published in 1992 in the Belgrade-based *Review of International Affairs*, Milinkovic evaluated different definitions of hate speech as well as the negative changes that had taken place in the Yugoslav information space and the use of media for war-mongering. He noted that words 'do cause injury . . . In the course of the Yugoslav crisis words clearly showed their destructive power.' His conclusion compared electronic communications to actual highways: 'Rules prohibiting drunk drivers from the streets are not meant to limit traffic but to increase security. Prohibitions of "hate speech" are not meant to limit freedom of expression but to strengthen freedom of responsible communication.'[38]

NGOs generally ignored such arguments and did not call for prosecutions for hate speech or incitement to violence under domestic law. There were, however, heated discussions in NGO circles in each of the former Yugoslav republics and in the media. For example, at a seminar on Media Ethics held in Zagreb in December 1993 by the Croatian Helsinki Committee with the World Association of Newspapers and the Council of Europe, accusations of incitement flew across the conference table but the drafting work focused on a code of ethics. The preference for self-regulation, even in the face of massive state-orchestrated hate speech campaigns, held fast.

In the Yugoslav context there was a resigned acceptance by NGOs that the State-controlled media were as they were – organs of propaganda – yet, however deplorable or horrific their effect might be, they should remain entitled to the protections of freedom of expression as established by international standards. The most that should be done was to document the violations in anticipation of post-conflict debate and possibly prosecutions. The consistency of this position was reflected in the reaction to the bombing of RTS and Eutelsat suspension described above.

Hate Speech Laws: Use and Abuse

There is usually no shortage of regulation to address inciteful speech, with many countries around the world having legislation which embodies the permissible restrictions of Article 19 of the International Covenant on Civil and Political Rights (ICCPR), the mandatory restrictions of Article 20 of the ICCPR, and with some also reflecting Article 4 of the Convention on the Elimination of All Forms of Racial Discrimination.[39] Certainly, both former Yugoslavia and Rwanda had ample legislation to address incitement to violence in the electronic media. In Rwanda, for example, if the Press Law of 1991 law been enforced, RTLM should have been taken off the air within days of its first broadcasts.[40]

Media freedom NGOs generally fear that advocating application of hate speech regulations will create an impetus to act without ensuring that any steps taken are in conformity with international standards. This happened in Rwanda in early 1995 when the Ministry of Information, failing to distinguish between criticism and incitement – and perhaps erring on the side of caution after the genocide a year previously – launched an attack on the entire print media sector and impounded several papers. RSF then had to protest against the seizure of one newspaper, *Le Messager*, on account of articles that, the authorities alleged, 'sowed hatred between the population and the government'.[41]

Many NGOs argue that calling for prosecutions against hate speech is often futile because the media run by the state or directly linked to those in power are responsible for the most serious abuses in terms of incitement or propaganda for war. The fact that those in government or holding power are often unwilling or unable to end conflicts also accounts for the lack of political will to use the rule of law to sanction or restrict the incitement. The dim prospect of successfully curbing imminent or ongoing excesses through recourse to hate speech laws, combined with fears that such laws would be misused – especially when they are poorly framed and in an inadequate democratic framework – has led most NGOs to shy away from this area all together.

From Defending the Indefensible to Prosecuting Journalists

Any violation of journalistic ethics puts the defenders of media freedom in an awkward position: how to defend the indefensible? How to stand by principles when the very persons on whose behalf those principles are being defended are flouting them? For many media freedom NGOs, there has to be direct incitement to unlawful action plus a likelihood of inciting or provoking the illegal action. A distinction is made between propaganda in support of the perpetrators of crimes and direct incitement to murder and crimes against humanity (the distinction between Hans Fritsche and Julius Streicher at the Nuremberg Tribunal).[42]

The Rwandan genocide and the conflicts in Yugoslavia and elsewhere forced some media freedom NGOs to reconsider this position, particularly when it became clear that there would be international tribunals to hold accountable those responsible for war crimes and crimes against humanity. Reporters Sans Frontières (RSF) was probably the first media-defence NGO to recognize that the time had come to denounce 'so-called' media and journalists and to urge that they be held accountable for their actions. It was certainly the NGO that has most actively pursued and called for prosecutions, in the Rwandan case not only by the International Criminal Tribunal for Rwanda but also by courts in France, Belgium and Switzerland where RTLM directors had taken refuge. In August 1994, RSF even went so far as to bring a private party criminal action for genocide and crimes against humanity against the founders and presenters from RTLM then living in France. This caused not just ripples but large waves of concern and disapproval in the media freedom community.

RSF's own reflections on this episode noted the difficulty of deciding when 'journalists' have 'crossed the "red line" in calling, for example, for hatred and violence against individuals or groups'.[43] In a world where the media, particularly television, need clear narratives of good and bad, any campaigning NGO is obliged to worry about the clarity and consistency of its message. RSF had to contend with these tensions, particularly as it had intervened on behalf of the paper *Kangura* in 1991, along with Amnesty International, when the authorities had 'unfairly' closed it.[44]

What motivated RSF was not only that some media had become 'apostles of violence . . . directly contributing to the descent of these societies into unparalleled human tragedies'.[45] There was also the crucial issue that the 'mercenary' journalists had 'called, sometimes explicitly and by naming names, for the assassination of all those – in particular journalists – who refused to consider their "nation" as the unique enabling framework for the exercise of and respect for human rights'. In cases from Croatia, Serbia, Bosnia and Rwanda, RSF was called on to defend journalists against incitement and hatred transmitted through other media. This issue would arise again in Kosova in late 1999 when RSF expressed concern at the threats and incitement to violence against *Koha Ditore*'s publisher Veton Surroi and editor Baton Haxhiu, carried in a press agency with known links to the Kosova Liberation Army. To defend some journalists necessitated condemning others, even if this would be justified by arguing, as do many NGOs, that those working for media such as RTLM should not qualify as 'journalists' at all.

With regard to Rwanda, ARTICLE 19 concluded that:

the owners and broadcasters of RTLM should be indicted for crimes of genocide before the International Criminal Tribunal for Rwanda. These charges should relate to the rôle played by RTLM in directing the genocide from 6 April 1994 onwards. It is *not* recommended that charges be brought in relation to the propaganda rôle of RTLM or Radio Rwanda before 6 April.[46]

Both RSF and ARTICLE 19 provided material in their possession to the International Criminal Tribunal for Rwanda, in Arusha.

The 1995 UNESCO meeting 'On Propaganda Inciting to Commit Genocide in Rwanda' came up with a number of recommendations, the first of which was:

That competent international and national authorities be encouraged to bring to trial those allegedly held responsible for direct and public incitement to commit genocide, in accordance with already existing relevant international law (re art. 3 of the 'Convention on the promotion and punishment of the crime of genocide' – 9.12.1948). There should be no special immunity from prosecution for any category of citizens.[47]

The last sentence is significant as there are often moves by governments to introduce regulation that holds journalists to higher standards than civilians, proposals that intensify when it is clear that the power of the media has been 'abused'. On the other hand, media freedom advocates sometimes argue that journalists should be afforded special protections from prosecution because of the essential rôle they play in informing the public about matters of public importance. A European Court of Human Rights ruling has backed this latter position. The Court noted that a Danish journalist who broadcast a programme containing hate speech by racist youths should not have been prosecuted in the Danish courts because of the importance of stimulating public debate by airing controversial opinions on significant issues.[48] For media freedom NGOs, however, the general preference is that the media should not be subject to any special regulations – protective or restrictive – but rather be judged according to the same law as civilians with public interest being taken into account. Representatives of the IFJ and WPFC interviewed for this chapter were clear in maintaining this position.[49]

Over the years, RSF has criticized the slowness of the International Criminal Tribunal for Rwanda in collecting evidence against the media. When the trial against three of the leading media personalities finally opened in October 2000, RSF directly called on the Tribunal 'to sanction the three suspects with heavy prison sentences. The judgement of the Tribunal would thus constitute a precedent of the kind which would deter similar initiatives in Rwanda or in other countries.'[50] At time of going to press, the trial of Jean-Bosco Baryagwiza and Ferdinand Nahimana of RTLM and Hassan Ngeze of *Kangura* was ongoing in Arusha.

RSF noted that one RTLM presenter, Belgian national Georges Ruggiu, had already been sentenced by the Tribunal to twelve years in prison, but did not pass comment on the length or appropriateness of the sentence. Some legal experts considered the sentence harsh given the mitigating circumstances in the Ruggiu case, while NGOs interviewed for this chapter were generally reluctant to comment, saying it was up to the Tribunal to decide. Although usually only too ready to discuss sentences handed down by national courts or the jurisprudence of regional courts such as the European Court of Human Rights, NGOs are cautious when it comes to the role of media involved in crimes against humanity. This reflects the lack of case law in an area where each circumstance has been so specific that NGOs have not yet formed principled positions on what is appropriate. In addition, there remains a reluctance to condemn 'media' even when these have been clearly involved in crimes outlawed by international treaties. The next decade, particularly with the likely establishment of the International Criminal Court as well as national prosecutions, will bring further elaboration of policies with regard to the media's role in crimes against humanity and the appropriate sanctions.

Post-conflict: Lessons on Regulation From Bosnia and Kosova

NGOs that monitored media freedom in Bosnia after the Dayton Peace Agreement (December 1995) quickly highlighted problems with the regulatory environment, which permitted a continuation of war-time pressures on journalists and media ranging from political control to physical attacks, and resulted in ad-hoc responses to regulating the media, for example during elections.[51]

That media freedom NGOs did not expressly advocate media regulation for Bosnia is not as odd as it may seem. Many of the international media freedom NGOs started out working to the letters-of-protest model established by Amnesty International in the 1960s. In spite of the fact that other strategies have evolved, the first response tends to be the critical letter to the appropriate authority, normally the head of state or relevant minister, although in the case of Bosnia the letters from the WPFC and IPI were not addressed to the OHR but to the US Secretary of Defense in Washington. The WPFC representative interviewed for this chapter defended this protest strategy, arguing that the 'function of NGOs is not to propose regulations. We never engage in writing laws but, in critiquing, we make clear what is and what is not acceptable.'[52] Even ARTICLE 19, which recently has assisted in drafting a number of laws, prefers to comment on draft laws, but will exceptionally break this rule, balancing the risk of association with a bad law against the opportunity to help create a law protective of media freedom.[53]

Nevertheless, having tolerated and even condoned NATO's seizure of transmitters in autumn 1997, the hue and cry against plans to introduce relatively standard media regulation in 1998 was striking. A damning front-page *New York Times* article entitled 'Allies Creating Press-Control Agency in

Bosnia' reported concerns about plans by the 'alliance of democratic nations' to create a 'tribunal having the power to shut radio and television stations and punish newspapers'.[54] The article mirrors language in a letter from the WPFC to US Defense Secretary William S. Cohen (dated 28 April 1998) protesting plans to create 'what amounts to a censorship panel . . . which would without question set a most dangerous and unfortunate precedent for news censorship in Europe and elsewhere'. Other protests followed, including from the International Press Institute (IPI), which on 3 May 1998 also wrote to Defense Secretary Cohen echoing the fears 'that the United States should be involved in the establishment of what amounts to a censorship panel'.

The OHR's initial sketches for a media strategy could be criticized for lacking detail and making the fundamental error of referring to both broadcast and print media regulation in the same sentence. They nevertheless aspired to establish a coherent media policy meeting the needs previously identified by NGOs and commentators, consistent with Western standards and redressing the lack of a media mandate in the Dayton Peace Accords. The regulation proposed would, *inter alia*, allow Bosnia's international governors to address the issue of incendiary media with democratic guarantees that any measures be foreseen by law, applied with due process and subject to some kind of administrative or judicial appeal. This was surely preferable to soldiers seizing transmitters by night.

It should be noted that many journalists and others in Bosnia apparently favoured such regulation. The IFJ's Aidan White was quoted in the *New York Times* article as recognizing 'there is a good intention here, which is trying to create a transitional structure to allow the media to function professionally', although he cautioned that care should be taken to avoid regressive over-regulation. In a letter to the IPI, OHR media development officer Dan De Luce urged dialogue with Bosnian journalists:

> I would also ask you to consult with prominent independent journalists in Bosnia who also tend to support the idea. These journalists are tired of the legal chaos and would prefer not to be at the mercy of ruling parties. The expert team of consultants setting up the commission, who are familiar with the broadcast regulations in other post-communist countries, have consulted with station directors, editors and government officials.[55]

The debate over the introduction of media regulation in Bosnia rapidly became polarized, with little constructive dialogue. It was charged that those introducing the new regulation were not media law experts (worse, some were former soldiers) and that the media regulation plan was taken from that used by the Allies in postwar Germany. In fact media law experts were brought in to the process, with the IFJ and other organizations including ARTICLE 19 being consulted. At the same time it should be noted that some of the personalities involved were also engaged in the development of the Open Broadcast Network and the tensions created during that process also – unfortunately – affected the debate over media regulation.

In spite of the controversy, the OHR pushed ahead and established the Independent Media Commission (IMC) as the broadcasting regulatory body.[56] Within two years the IMC was primarily staffed by Bosnians and gradually became recognized as a model for a professional broadcasting regulator being promoted in other transitional countries. Although there have been controversies over its decisions, a mission of donors in May 2001 found that it was operating on a clear and transparent basis to well-defined criteria.

Relearning the Lessons from Bosnia

One of the clearest lessons in Bosnia was that 'democracy does not occur in a vacuum' and that 'early action should have been taken to reform the media'.[57] Consequently, the OSCE mission to Kosova was invested from the outset with a stronger mandate for democratization, including of the media. To this end the OSCE invited a group of media experts to Kosova in July 1999, to make specific recommendations on a media strategy for the OSCE.[58] The experts' report acknowledged that some of their recommendations could 'be viewed by some as controversial', and attempted to forestall this by stressing the necessity of a strong policy in the face of struggles for political control of media in an environment with little previous experience of democratic institutions and with continuing inter-ethnic animosities. Experience from Bosnia and Croatia 'confirms that democratic media cannot be established on the basis of incomplete or weakly asserted authority to regulate, monitor or reform existing media'.

As foreseen, the six-page report provoked the ire of some media freedom groups, particularly the World Press Freedom Committee, as well as a *New York Times* editorial on 30 August 1999, entitled 'Kosovo's Incipient Media Ministry'. Some of the report's weaknesses repeated those of its predecessor: it failed to draw a sufficient distinction between proposed short-term and long-term strategies, or to make a clear separation between broadcast and print regulation in line with international standards. It was short on detail on how exactly its recommendations would be implemented.

The controversy did not, however, take place at such a detailed level, and the NGOs' lobbying combined with the *New York Times*' hostility was to raise sufficient concern at UN headquarters in New York that the nature and extent of the OSCE's media mandate was called into question, making it impossible for the OSCE in Pristina to take decisive action. More detail of this controversy can be found in Chapter 9 of this book, but some NGO perspectives are evaluated here.

The most strident voice was that of the WPFC whose chairman James H. Ottoway Jr, in a letter to UN secretary-general Kofi Annan and OSCE chairman-in-office Knut Vollebaek (13 August 1999), claimed that:

[p]rior to Kosovo's catastrophic civil war, a free press functioned there. While financial assistance would be welcome for rebuilding printing houses and broadcasting facilities, foreign direction in how to operate them is neither needed nor desirable. It could, in fact, defeat the purpose of helping independent media to flourish once again in Kosovo.

The claim that Kosova's traditional media freedom was about to be squashed by the colonizing international community did not concur with a statement made by Ottoway in the leading article in the WPFC newsletter a few weeks earlier (1 July 1999) which – far more accurately – noted that: 'Kosova's print and broadcast media suffered assault, restrictions and reprisals under the dictatorship of Slobodan Milosevic', and went on to argue that: '[t]hey should now enjoy freedom, independence and diversity [. . .] Let it not be said that the democratic victory in Kosova simply led to more censorship, under a different guise.'

The WPFC's revised opinion about the previous condition of media freedom in Kosova strengthened the anti-regulation argument and made for a better news story. On 16 August, the *New York Times*' Prague-based correspondent Steve Erlanger wrote a lengthy article picking up on the WPFC's concerns and quoting the WPFC's European representative Ronald Koven:

There is a kind of colonialist mentality [. . .] Foreigners are going to impose their standards and codes of conduct on independent media journalists in Kosovo in a situation where before the war there was a perfectly adequate independent Albanian-language press.

The audacity of such statements in support of an anti-regulation argument was quite impressive and provoked heated debate in NGO circles.

The Committee to Protect Journalists (CPJ) sent 'veteran war correspondent' Frank Smyth to interview journalists and international officials in Kosova. He noted that 'Kosovar journalists . . . were almost unanimously in favor of press regulation. "We need rules for what is news and what is a lie," says Baton Haxhiu, the editor of Prishtina's most respected daily, *Koha Ditore*.' He also cited Aferdita Kelmendi, head of Radio/TV 21 whom he described as having 'nuanced views on press freedom issues'. Kelmendi recognized that both self-regulation and a regulatory authority might be appropriate, while underlining that the media could play a role in combating hate speech by facilitating discussion on it. Both Haxhiu and Kelmendi had joined a group of media experts convened to advise the OSCE and assist develop a self-regulatory code. The CPJ's investigator characterized this body as a censor: 'While *Koha Ditore* editor Baton Haxhiu says that he "opposes any form of censorship", he nonetheless joined an official body that will effectively help the OSCE to censor Kosovo's press.'[59]

As to the question of hate speech, Smyth's article noted the danger of hate speech in a society still on the verge of ethnic conflict, referring to the precedent of Radio-Television Libre de Mille Collines (RTLM) in Rwanda and quoting the OSCE's Director of Media Affairs in Pristina, Douglas Davidson, as saying that Kosova was 'not a benign environment'. But then, in a strange twist of argument, Smyth stated: 'Few would disagree that RTLM crossed a red line between journalism and criminal incitement. The real question is whether any society needs an additional layer of bureaucracy between journalists and the law.' This analysis of the role of the Media Advisory Board and its characterization as an unnecessary layer of bureaucracy were misleading. What was being sought was the closest approximation to democratic regulation for broadcast media and the necessary rule of law environment for all media that could be constructed, given the limits of the international mandate in Kosova.

By autumn 1999, Kosovar journalists were crying out for regulation – not bureaucratic censorship but legal solutions to the problems of defamatory statements, direct incitement to violence, hate speech, and piracy of the airwaves. They were also asking for urgent advice as to how this could be achieved in a society where the courts were not functioning. For the CPJ to characterize this as local journalists calling for 'censorship', an exclusively pejorative term, did a disservice to the cause of professional journalism in Kosova and even contributed to the eventual introduction of exactly the kind of draconian regulation which the CPJ and WPFC feared might be 'setting precedents that might justify censorship "long after the fighting is over" '.

One interesting point made by Frank Smyth was that 'European press freedom advocates, used to a relatively high degree of official press regulation, have not opposed the OSCE initiative.' He cited Kosovar Albanian intellectual and writer Shkelzen Maliqi as 'arguing that Kosovo should adopt "a European and not an American approach to this matter" '. It is true that the 'European' media freedom groups took a different line. Some engaged closely with the international community over the introduction of regulation, trying to ensure that it would promote rather than hinder media freedom. IFJ, ARTICLE 19 and OSI-Europe, in co-ordination with the OSCE, supported the creation of an Association of Kosovar Journalists, assisting with drafting its statutes and a code of ethics. As the OSCE stumbled towards media regulation, still awaiting the assignment of media lawyers, these organizations urged effective regulation acceptable in a democratic society, and provided drafting support, in particular on broadcasting regulation.

When, on 9 February 2000, the UN chief in Kosova, Special Representative of the Secretary-General Bernard Kouchner, signed into force a draconian hate speech law these groups both condemned it and continued the debate on what exactly international law permitted. The hate speech regulation, trumpeted in an OSCE press release as the 'key for a democratic Kosovo', was as much a political response to rising ethnic violence in the province as it was a reaction to incitement in the media.[60] Monitoring of the local media by the OSCE had recorded some offensive opinions but little that could fall under even broad definitions of hate speech.

Local elections in Kosova were scheduled for the end of October 2000 and by

May of that year the international community was under pressure to create the right conditions. Fears that the media would be the forum for an aggressive and inflammatory election campaign (not unreasonable fears given the Bosnian experience), created a new imperative that regulation be adopted to provide controls over the print media in line with those already in effect for broadcast media. Ironically, taking the lead in this was the US government whose ambassador to the OSCE, David T. Johnson, told the OSCE Permanent Council in Vienna on 4 May 2000 that:

> we need a similar code for print media. I do know that you will take the harshest and quickest hits when you move in this direction from the American press. I will defend you and I will remind you and them of a statement attributed to the late Justice Holmes: 'No man, no matter what free speech requires, is allowed to shout "Fire!" in a crowded theatre.' That is really what Kosovo is. I think we have to approach it that way.[61]

A few days later, US State Department officials attempted to persuade a group of independent and NGO experts assisting in drafting a long-term broadcasting law for Kosova that print media regulation should be included in that draft, a proposition rejected by the drafting team. Print media regulation was then introduced separately by UNMIK, bringing expressions of concern from even the 'European' organizations, the IFJ and ARTICLE 19 – which both described the regulation as setting a 'dangerous precedent', – as well as the World Press Freedom Committee.[62]

NGOs nevertheless continued to give advice on the broadcasting regulation that was eventually adopted in mid-2001. The NGOs' involvement facilitated co-ordination with the European Broadcasting Union, the Council of Europe and UNESCO. The IGOs backed NGO arguments against regulation of ethical standards for the print media – both the Council of Europe and UNESCO having taken clear positions that this was a matter for the profession alone.

Back to School!

What started in Bosnia and continued in Kosova was not simply a controversy over which types of regulation were appropriate. Rather these post-conflict societies became a new arena in which NGOs and governments waged their ideological debate about media control and media freedom – a debate that in the post-1989, post-communist world was more heated and urgent than ever. The alternatives are variously defined as 'European' v. 'American', pro-regulation v. 'First Amendment', or based on the 'enlightenment – and hence originally European – philosophies of Voltaire, Locke and Mill'.[63] In essence they reflect the on-going struggle over where and how to draw the line between freedom of expression and the limits placed on it by international law and standards to protect other human rights.

An analysis of the debates, particularly from Kosova, shows that they refer to outdated, out-of-context or non-existent comparative standards. These include the WPFC's assertion that Kosova had enjoyed a free press before the war; the tendency to ignore the existence of laws which have a regulatory effect on the media in many countries, including the United States; and the OSCE media commissioner's defence of proposed regulations by citing press laws and hate speech provisions in Europe without evaluating how these are curbed by constitutional court rulings or democratic tradition.[64] The debate about print media regulation often failed to draw the distinction between voluntary and mandatory codes, and discussions gave insufficient consideration to questions such as due process or appeals mechanisms – the introduction of which later proved crucial in getting Kosovar media to accept some form of supervision as a substitute for the post-publication processes normal in a democratic society.

In other words, a certain hypocrisy was manifest on both sides of the debate. The international community was prepared to introduce regulations that would never have been tolerated 'back home'. Some media freedom NGOs were ready to oppose – or to seem to oppose – regulation that is the norm in established democracies, including to a significant extent in the United States. The interest on one side was primarily to keep the peace and on the other to ensure that the international community did not promote standards lower than those most favourable to the media, but the result of these conflicting interests was a remarkably antagonistic debate which sometimes descended into mere point-scoring. Once polarized positions had been taken, it was hard to revert to a more constructive discussion about what kind of regulation would be most appropriate for a post-conflict society to address immediate problems and also to lay the foundations for a legal framework protective of media freedom in the longer term.

For those on both the IGO and NGO sides who were trying to find appropriate models of regulation for Bosnia and Kosova, these antagonisms were frustrating because the local media themselves were often caught in the middle or disregarded. As the OHR argued in Bosnia and as CPJ reported in Kosova, many local journalists favoured some kind of media regulation in preference to a chaotic environment where professionalism was squeezed by political forces. To call this censorship is a misnomer. It is true that there are differences in US and European perspectives on the media environment but these are much more nuanced than many, particularly advocates of a staunch 'First Amendment' position, are ready to concede. Like all established democracies the US has a regulatory body that issues licences for the broadcast sector and laws that sanction certain types of expression post-publication. Such regulation is essential if the media environment is to be a level playing field, if plurality and diversity in the broadcast media are to be ensured, and other rights such as the right to reputation be appropriately protected.

For the NGOs the struggle continued but for the international governmental community there came a point when other concerns (security, elections) took precedence over the ideological debate on freedom of expression to such an extent that even the US government urged such stringent regulation. This clearly illustrates a general problem for human rights and other NGOs: the challenge of seeking and keeping governmental and thus IGO support on issues of principle in the face of other conflicting and at times overriding priorities.

Accepting the Need for Media Regulation

There is increasing acceptance among media freedom NGOs of the need not only to defend against bad law but also to promote appropriate regulation. This became evident in the late 1990s as NGOs became more actively involved in promoting two particular kinds of regulation: access to information laws, and civil defamation provisions.

Access to information laws, if these are well crafted, are easy for even the most regulation-allergic media freedom activist to accept. As a wave of these laws were adopted in Central and Eastern Europe in 1999 and 2000, NGOs found themselves on the side of those advocating regulation. At the same time, NGOs started to advocate the replacement of criminal defamation laws by civil provisions. ARTICLE 19, accustomed to recommending standards on acceptable legislation, developed a set of standards called 'Defining Defamation'. The WPFC made recommendations on appropriate civil defamation laws. When in Bosnia the OSCE led a consultative group of local and international legal experts to draft a defamation law, these standards were referred to and the resulting law, presented as a public draft in February 2001 met with approval as a 'good model' (in spite of the fact that the WPFC had in late 1999 expressed concern about a new round of media regulation proposed by the OHR, which had included both an access to information law and this civil defamation provision).

There are other areas where the media freedom NGOs have still failed to grasp the nettle of media regulation, although current trends suggest that they will be addressed over time, whether in post-conflict zones or elsewhere. Current controversial issues include the role of broadcast regulators in limiting the number of broadcast stations, at least by holding all stations up to certain standards, and the enforcement of copyright laws – issues which, as the Macedonian and Bosnian cases show, are essential to ensure that there is a genuinely level playing field where a plurality of professional media can flourish.

Developing and Implementing Mandates: The Professional Approach

One lesson of the past decade is that the mandates for international post-conflict missions should take into account both short-term peacekeeping goals and longer term, democracy-building objectives. These considerations will affect decisions on the types of regulation to be introduced and on possible support for international community media, as distinct from indigenous media.

NGOs and IGOs will not always agree among themselves or with each other on the best approaches for a given country or province. If, however, NGO objections are not to scupper agreement on how to implement policies, more work needs to be done to define the essential and acceptable elements of post-conflict interventions. To this end two approaches are needed. One would use the experience of recent conflicts to resolve some of the extant controversies, particularly those on regulation, on creation of international-community media, and on the public service versus private media debate. Second, mechanisms are needed for developing a consensus on the content of the mandate. This is best done on a case-by-case basis by professionals with experience of both conflict environments and transitional societies, in consultation with NGOs and relevant local actors.

Models for pro-active and transparent consultation among NGOs, the donor community and local actors do exist. In the media sphere, initiatives by UNESCO, the Council of Europe and the OSCE have created forums for debating and developing media policy. The UNESCO round tables discussed in this chapter have helped NGOs and some IGOs to reach consensus, even if this has not always been translated into practice by missions deployed on the ground by those same, or other, IGOs.

The Council of Europe's Media Division within the Directorate of Human Rights has standing and ad-hoc consultative committees composed of media specialists and media NGOs. These have dealt with questions relating to conflict situations. For example, in 1995 the Council of Europe's Steering Committee on Mass Media held hearings with NGOs, journalists' organizations and IGOs such as the International Committee of the Red Cross (ICRC) that resulted in recommendations relating to the rights of journalists in situations of conflict and tension.[65] The OSCE in Bosnia came up with an extremely successful model for consultation on the development of access to information and defamation legislation: local and international experts engaged in a transparent process that included consultation with international NGOs and local civil society during and after the drafting process.

NGOs – increasingly national as well as international – can also provide much-needed experience from countries that have undergone transition and conflict and are able to share their experiences and recommend policy to colleagues elsewhere. Knowledge of transitional societies is particularly important in order to be able to anticipate the types of problems encountered in the media field and civil society after a period of repression when social values have been distorted and damaged. Some international agency staff working in Bosnia and Kosova were confounded by problems that seemed quite predictable to those with experience in neighbouring countries such as Albania, Bulgaria, Macedonia or Romania. The difficulty of achieving sufficient unity and common purpose in the journalistic community to establish a self-regulatory system; the sudden explosion of private media, especially broadcasters; the lack of understanding of regulatory regimes; even the style of journalism and the phases through which it passes in a transition from authoritarianism – none of these should have come as much of a surprise.

In addition to this relevant experience, an accurate knowledge of the local media environment before and during the conflict is essential to effective interventions.

To this end, NGOs need to be prepared to make realistic assessments of the needs in crisis areas. Some quick-fix, short-term measures may be needed to stabilize a situation, although the move from peacemaking to longer-term strategies for democracy-building should occur as quickly as possible. NGOs also need to evaluate and recognize the success stories of international administrations. The transfer of the Independent Media Commission in Bosnia from international supervision to largely local management within two years is a good example of what can be achieved within predicted time-frames given sufficient will and emphasis on professionalism.

Conclusions: Resolving Policy Disputes

This chapter has surveyed NGO perspectives on media support and intervention before, during and after conflict. There has been an emphasis on the need to support timely democratic development of the media sphere to help prevent the escalation of conflicts. This reflects the belief widely held among NGOs that such a result can be achieved with sufficient political will and co-ordination among IGOs, governments, donors and NGOs. Many in IGOs and governments also believe this, but too often the lip-service is not backed up with timely political support and financial conditionality. NGOs have made significant progress in putting media development onto the international policy agenda, and this is supported by IGOs such as UNESCO, but NGOs need to create wider recognition that it is imperative to address the media sphere in countries where there is danger of conflict.

The benchmark of media freedom should include measures of whether there exists a healthy media environment in which there is a plurality of views and perspectives both overall and – very importantly – *within* certain media, including especially the State-funded media. A lack of editorial independence and political control of either public or private media should give serious cause for concern, as should the ghettoization of media between different political, social, ethnic, linguistic or other groups in society. Projects which work with indigenous media to reach across ethnic or political divides are extremely important and should be the norm rather than the exception in conflict areas.

Hate speech should sound alarm bells but the concern should not centre on the language alone. Steps must also be taken to address the root causes. In terms of early warning, a struggle for political control of the media should be an alarm as significant as the actual content of the media. NGOs may also have to make special efforts to counter myths about a particular country and the fervent desire of the international community to believe that conflict will not happen – the myth of a fledgling multi-ethnic democracy for Macedonia; the myth of a 'hard-working little country' for Rwanda.[66] As Veran Matic of Radio B92 has stressed: 'Freedom of information must be a constituent part of every foreign affairs activity and cannot be relegated to the position of a minor issue.'

In post-conflict situations, NGOs need to continue to work to resolve the methodological and ideological differences which create distracting disputes over issues such as regulation. Many elements of the debate over regulation in post-conflict interventions merit further consideration. There needs to be a precise focus on standards for broadcast regulation, and on possible regulation for print media in the absence of a general regulatory framework in the post-conflict context. There is also a pressing need for common positions on the nature and responsibilities of public service and their relationship to private media, which will affect both regulation and donor decisions. Co-ordination between NGOs, donors, governments and IGOs on such issues has increased significantly. All international actors should pay close attention to the actual situation and needs in a particular country. Further initiatives could move policy and action forward to a stage where it has an increased impact on the ground.

To achieve these goals, media reform support and conditionality need to be pushed even harder by local and international NGOs. To the extent that this entails 'intervention' by the international community, it may be rejected as interference – something that NGOs should continue to anticipate and counter. The legitimacy of action to support development of free media is clear. Such action is also essential if potential sources of incitement to violence and crimes against humanity are to be eliminated – and if more radical forms of intervention are to be avoided.

Acknowledgements

The author thanks Mark Thompson for his essential support and patience. She also thanks colleagues and friends in the media freedom NGO community, particularly Sandra Coliver and Fiona Harrison. Gratitude to Gordana Jankovic and Biljana Tatomir for being inspiring colleagues. Special thanks to Ylber Mehmedaliu for encouragement and relinquishing precious evenings.

Bibliography

ARTICLE 19 (October 1996), *Broadcasting Genocide: Censorship, Propaganda & State-Sponsored Violence in Rwanda 1990–1994*, London: ARTICLE 19.

Council of Europe Recommendation No R (96) 4 of the Committee of Ministers to Member States on Protection of Journalists in Situations of Conflict and Tension, adopted 3 May 1996, at www.humansights.coe.nit/media

Deguine, Hervé (May 2000), 'Rwanda' in 'Media in Post-Conflict Areas', UNESCO, p. 45.

de la Brosse, Renaud (1995), Introduction in *Les Médias de la Haine*, Editions la Découverte, Paris: Reporters Sans Frontières / Editions; p 17.

Des Forges, Alison (1999), *Leave None to Tell the Story, Genocide in Rwanda*, New York: Human Rights Watch. Website: www.hrw.org/reports/1999/rwanda.

Domi, Tanya (10 November 2000), 'Putting Right Past Mistakes: Hard lessons learned in Bosnia must influence future international policy in the region', Institute for War and Peace Reporting, *Balkan Crisis Reports*, no. 194.

European Commission Directorate General 1A (19 October 1998), 'Commission Staff Working Paper, Regional Approaches to the countries of South-East Europe: Compliance with the conditions in the Council Conclusions of 29 April 1997', Brussels, SEC (98) 1727, at point 4.2.

Human Rights Watch (7 February 2000), 'The Crisis in Kosovo', in *Civilian Deaths in the NATO Air Campaign*, Human Rights Watch Publications, vol. 12, no. 1 (D).

International Crisis Group (27 July 2001), Balkans Briefing, 'Macedonia: Still Sliding'.

International Helsinki Federation for Human Rights and Helsinki Committee for Human Rights of the Republic of Macedonia (12 April 2001), 'Statement to UN Commission for Human Rights', 57th Session, Geneva.

Jersild v. Denmark, (case no. 36/1993/431/510) European Court of Human Rights (ser. A298) 23 September 1994, p. 1.

Matic, Veran (23 January 1999), 'The Responsibility of Media in National Conflicts and How to Guarantee the Future Process of Independent Media in Democracy and Democratization Processes', presentation at a seminar on 'The Future Architecture of Europe', Baden-Baden, Germany.

Milinkovic, Branko (1992), 'International Nongovernmental Organizations and the Yugoslav Crisis', *Review of International Affairs* (Sept.), vol. 43, no. 1009/1011, p. 31.

Reporters Sans Frontières (16 May 1995), '*Le Messager* seized and banned from publishing'.

Search for Common Ground (1999), 'Lessons from *Nashe Maalo*' Report, Common Ground Productions. Online [October 2001], Available at http://www.sfcg.org (on research conducted by Dr Mirjana Najchevska, University of Skopje and Dr Charlotte Cole, vice-president of Education and Research for Sesame Workshop).

Shenon, Philip (24 April 1998), 'Allies Creating Press-Control Agency in Bosnia,' *New York Times*.

Thompson, Mark (1999), *Forging War: The Media in Serbia, Croatia, Bosnia and Hercegovina*, 2nd edn, Luton: University of Luton Press and ARTICLE 19.

UNESCO, (4–5 May 2000), 'Recommendations for Future Action: Round Table on Media in Conflict and Post Conflict Areas', Geneva.

Notes

1. IFJ press statement (23 April 1999), 'IFJ Condemns NATO Bombing of Media: a broken promise that threatens the lives of all journalists and media staff'.
2. Letter from Jamie Shea to IFJ General Secretary Aidan White, 12 April 1999.
3. IFJ media release (21 April 1999), 'Free Expression Groups' World-wide Protest over NATO Attach on Belgrade Media', released by IFJ and others, carried by IFEX.
4. Human Rights Watch report (7 February 2000), 'The Crisis in Kosovo'.
5. Beta news agency, Belgrade, reports of 23 and 24 April 2001.
6. IFJ press release (12 December 2000), 'World Journalists Condemn Middle East Violence'.

7. More information on these and other NGOs can be found via the IFEX website www.ifex.org. IFEX is the International Freedom of Expression Exchange, an electronic clearing house of freedom of expression violation alerts by media freedom NGOs around the world.

8. See Press Now web site www.pressnow.org

9. The first Soros Foundation opened in Hungary in 1984; the Polish Foundation (Stefan Batory) opened in 1988; the regional Open Society Institutes in Budapest and New York were established in 1993. Websites www.osi.hu and www.soros.org

10. See Medienhilfe website www.medienhilfe.ch

11. ARTICLE 19, *Broadcasting Genocide*, p. 53.

12. Thompson, *Forging War*, passim.

13. ARTICLE 19, *Broadcasting Genocide*, pp. 167–8.

14. Veran Matic, presentation on 'The Responsibility of Media in National Conflicts and how to Guarantee the Future Process of Independent Media in Democracy and Democratization Processes' at a seminar on 'The Future Architecture of Europe' in Baden-Baden, Germany, 23 January 1999.

15. See Radio Racyja website www.newsbelarus.com and Radio Baltic Waves website www.is.lt/ratekona/rbw

16. UNESCO, 'Recommendations for Future Action'. Recommendation 2.

17. Ibid., Recommendation 3.

18. Search for Common Ground, 'Lessons from Nashe Malo' on research conducted by Dr Mirjana Najchevska, University of Skopje and Dr Charlotte Cole, vice-president of Education and Research for Sesame Workshop, and Search for Common Ground. Report at www.sfcg.org

19. See Conciliation Resources web site www.c-r.org and the Centre for War, Peace and the News Media web site www.nyu.edu/globalbeat

20. Experts at the meeting were: Alain Modoux of UNESCO Communication Division; J. P. Chrétien, CNRS, Paris; Frances D'Souza, ARTICLE 19, London; A. de Lestrange, UN Information Centre, Paris; Ronald Koven, World Press Freedom Committee, Paris; David Lush, Media Institute of Southern Africa, Windhoek; Jean-Paul Marthoz, IFJ, Brussels; Robert Menard, RSF, Paris; Mr T. Mshindi, Association of Journalists Unions in East Africa, Mauritius; Mr P. M. Sylla, West African Union of Journalists, Dakar; Michael Williams, International Institute for Strategic Studies; and Mlle N. Sow, Burundi Specialist, International Alert, London.

21. Interview with Klaus Schmitter of UNESCO, Division of Freedom of Expression, Democracy and Peace, April 2001.

22. European Commission Directorate General 1A, 'Commission Staff Working Paper, Regional Approaches to the countries of South-East Europe', point 4.2.

23. The English version of the new Macedonian Public Information Law obtained in February 2001 by international NGOs was dated 12 January 2001.

24. Discussion with Mario Oetheimer of the Council of Europe Media Section, 18 May 2001.

25. Letter from Frances D'Souza, executive director of ARTICLE 19, to members of the Contact Group, EU foreign ministers, ODIHR, OSCE, and UN Security Council, 9 October 1998, and ARTICLE 19 press release (14 October 1998), 'Belgrade Media to be Sacrificed for Kosovo Deal'.

26. ARTICLE 19 press release (2 October 1998), 'Council of Europe Application under Threat as Belgrade Stops Independent Media Conference'.

27. WPFC executive director Marilyn Greene in a letter to John Shattuck, US

Assistant Secretary of State for Democracy and Human Rights, 20 October 1998, following up on a meeting with press freedom representatives held on 9 October 1998.
28. Interview with Ronald Koven, April 2001.
29. Interview with Bettina Peters, April 2001.
30. Interview with Andrew Puddephatt, April 2001. A note of clarification: some NGOs referring to 'counter-broadcasts' mean alternative extraterritorial broadcasts rather than broadcasts which occupy the same frequencies as pre-existing frequencies which were engaged in incitement. The latter are seen as requiring higher standards before being initiated; the former are generally accepted (if in-country options are not available) partly through a *de facto* acceptance of 'international' broadcasters such as the BBC, RFI, Deutsche Welle, VOA, RFE, et al.
31. ARTICLE 19, *Broadcasting Genocide*, p. 167.
32. CPJ letter from William Orme to Madeleine Albright, 4 September 1997.
33. Letter from ARTICLE 19 executive director Frances D'Souza to Carlos Westendorp, 6 October 1997.
34. Given that the capture of Bosnian Serb transmitters in 1997 and the bombing of RTS in 1999 were carried out by the same NATO Supreme Allied Commander Europe (SACEUR), General Wesley Clark (US), it is intriguing to wonder if the positive response to the 1997 operation encouraged him to be even bolder in 1999.
35. Statement by IHF and Helsinki Committee, 2001.
36. International Crisis Group, 'Macedonia: Still Sliding':
    Macedonian-language television and newspapers have stopped referring to the enemy as 'Albanian terrorists' but [refer to them] simply as 'Albanians'. The State television news declined to mention when seven ethnic Albanian civilians were killed on 22 and 23 July in Poroj. Albanian-language television and newspapers, meanwhile, fail to report details of Macedonian military and civilian casualties.
37. See generally, ARTICLE 19, 'Striking a Balance'.
38. Milinkovic, 'International Nongovernmental Organizations,' p. 31.
39. See Stephanie Farrior, Chapter 2 for more details.
40. Hervé Deguine, 'Rwanda', p. 45.
41. RSF, '*Le Messager*', 1995.
42. On the Streicher and Fritsche judgements, see Eric Blindermann, Chapter 3.
43. De la Brosse, *Les Médias*, p 17.
44. Deguine, 'Rwanda', p. 45.
45. *Les Médias de la Haine*, Introduction by Renaud de la Brosse, p. 10, RSF/Editions la Découverte, Paris 1995.
46. ARTICLE 19, *Broadcasting Genocide*, p. 171. (Emphasis added.)
47. See Note 16.
48. *Jersild v. Denmark*, p. 1.
49. Interviews with Bettina Peters, deputy secretary-general of the IFJ, and Ronald Koven, WPFC European Representative, April 2001.
50. RSF press release, 23 October 2000.
51. Reporters Sans Frontières (May 1996) report, *Bosnie-Herzégovine:le bilan de Dayton*; International Crisis Group, press relsease (7 March 1997), 'Media in Bosnia and Herzegovina: How International Support Can Be More Effective'.
52. Interview with Ronald Koven, April 2001.
53. Interview with Andrew Puddephatt, April 2001.

54. Article by Philip Shenon, *New York Times*, 24 April 1998.
55. Dan De Luce, letter to IPI, 5 May 1998.
56. The IMC merged with the telecommunications regulator in March 2001 to become the Communications Regulatory Agency (CRA).
57. See Domi, 'Putting Right Past Mistakes'.
58. The group comprised Dr Regan McCarthy, director of the OSCE's Department of Media Affairs in Bosnia; and Dan De Luce and Mark Thompson, the authors of Chapter 7 on Bosnia and Herzegovina in this book.
59. Frank Smyth, 'Civility by Decree', *Dangerous Assignments Newsletter*, CPJ, posted 18 September 1999.
60. UNESCO, 'Recommendations for Future Action: Roundtable on Media in Conflict and Post Conflict Areas'.
61. This citation from the speech as delivered. The prepared speech stated:
    the United States has come to the regrettable conclusion that we must deal aggressively with the problem of hate speech in the run-up to elections [. . .] We firmly believe that effective means of acting against this destabilizing and dangerous problem must be brought into force now.
62. IFJ press release (23 June 2000), 'IFJ Accuses United Nations of "Dangerous Precedent" in Move to Control Press in Kosovo'; ARTICLE 19 press release (30 June 2000), 'UN Setting "Dangerous Precedent" with Kosovo Media Regulation'.
63. Interview with Ronald Koven, WPFC, May 2001.
64. An example of the dangers: Albania's 1993 adoption of Germany's North Rhine-Westphalia press law as its own led to serious problems for the media as the restrictive provisions were not constrained by previous court interpretations as in Germany. Thus the law functioned completely differently from the way it did in Germany, hindering media freedom rather than being the basis for it. The Albanian law was repealed in late 1997.
65. Council of Europe Recommendation No. R(96)4.
66. Des Forges, 'Propaganda and Practice' in *Leave None to Tell the Story*.

13

Information Interventions, Media Development, and the Internet

Patrick Carmichael

Introduction

This chapter focuses on the vulnerability of electronic networks in many parts of the world including post-conflict zones, the lack of strategic thinking on the part of governments and non-governmental organizations (NGOs) about the potential applications of these networks, and the particular paradox that exists, in places recovering from the consequences of enacted hatred, between extending access and maintaining control.

My approach to the field of information strategy arises from a background in networked education projects. Most of these have involved using network technologies to enable collaboration between educators, project managers, and researchers in the United Kingdom, between academic institutions worldwide and in support of a range of development education projects. The defining episode, for this study, arises from my involvement with Survivors' Fund, a United Kingdom-based non-governmental organization that supports a range of projects in Rwanda and amongst the Rwandese diasporas.[1] While there has been considerable discussion of the role of the traditional media – and Radio-Television Libre des Mille Collines (RTLM) in particular – in fomenting and co-ordinating the genocide of 1994 in Rwanda, less attention has been paid to subsequent patterns of media development, especially the Internet, and its implications for information intervention.[2] A consideration of the architecture of the Internet underscores the need to assess the implications of any organization becoming an information provider in a context where conflict and political instability continue, levels of network access are low, and the role of media remains problematic. It also necessitates thinking through the role of international organizations in assisting in the development of information technology (IT) networks in states where such resources may be used by *génocidaires* and others determined to encourage mass violations of human rights.

Most elements of the role of non-governmental organizations as information providers in conflict zones have proved relatively straightforward. Survivors' Fund, for example, provides information about capacity building, education, and housing programmes in Rwanda and acts as a conduit for information about the activities of AVEGA, the Rwanda-based Association of Widows and Orphans of the Genocide. Another recent development involves using the Survivors' Fund web site to provide donors of financial and material aid with regularly updated information about the projects to which they have contributed; this requires project managers to produce and e-mail reports to Survivors' Fund for inclusion in the site.[3]

Another element of the information provider role, on the surface non-problematic, involves the collection and archiving of the accounts of survivors of genocide. This project is designed to complement other ethnographic accounts of the genocide such as those compiled by African Rights in 1995 and seeks to document the experiences of survivors in the period since the events of 1994, particularly in the light of high levels of HIV+ infection and associated mortality rates amongst survivors.[4] Potentially huge volumes of data exist, including the personal details and testimonies of thousands of survivors, and there is no doubt that the development of an electronic archive of this material would be invaluable: as a 'community memory' project, as an educational resource, and as a means by which survivors in Rwanda and elsewhere could discover the fates of missing family members and friends.

In fact, choices of technology, location of resources, and levels of access offered are all sensitive in the Rwandan context where IT and Internet development have centred on the promotion of government and commercial concerns to a global audience (and to a lesser extent on access to the World Wide Web and e-mail) rather than on the provision of data warehousing or application services for the local population or NGOs.[5] A decision to 'host' the archive in the United Kingdom with limited public access via a web interface was reached because of concerns about the levels of access to, and security of, appropriate networked resources in Rwanda.[6] Any further development of the information provider role might also cause difficulties. There are already some government and independent web sites that provide news about Rwanda and the African Great Lakes Region and the organizations sponsoring these web sites are generally perceived as non-partisan and humanitarian.[7] Implicit in news provision in these regions is the recognition that the region and its people are involved in a continuing 'information war' conducted in the print, broadcast, and online media.

Information Warfare, Netwar, and Information Interventions

There has been increasing interest in the military and political role of the IT networks over the past decade, and analyses of the role of IT in warfare, in peacekeeping, and in post-conflict reconstruction have become progressively more sophisticated. Toffler and Toffler's characterization of information-rich modern warfare has been elaborated in the light of conflicts in the Gulf and the Balkans and in response to rapid development of publicly accessible networks over the past decade.[8] Denning identifies several taxonomies of 'information warfare' and distinguishes the 'offensive' and 'defensive' in her survey of technologies and incidents.[9] Goodman argues that outside the most developed countries, there is no clear correlation between the military and IT capabilities of states and international organizations and that furthermore 'some conflicts [. . .] have been notable for the way the technologically weaker combatants have used their opponents', or the worldwide, IT infrastructure to their advantage'.[10] Adams suggests that some nations 'know that they have fallen behind in military muscle [and] have begun to look to other methods to bolster their war-fighting and defense capacities'.[11] Rothrock cautions that rather than the United States developing military strategy geared towards high-intensity information warfare in the expectation of 'eventually need[ing] to be able to attack and defend against enemies of our own kind', what is needed is a capacity to attack and defend against what he terms 'information age neanderthals' capable of using less sophisticated but nonetheless effective technologies.[12]

Perhaps the most important and best-developed theoretical insight has been Arquilla and Ronfeldt's distinction between 'cyberwar' (associated with 'high-intensity' or 'medium-range' conflict and involving formal military forces pitted against each other) and 'netwar' which is more likely to involve non-state, paramilitary, and other irregular forces in low-intensity conflict, peace-keeping, and humanitarian operations and within civil societies not actively involved in conflict.[13] According to Harknett, 'netwar' focuses attention on 'societal connectivity' (rather than military capability) which can be attacked, disrupted, or destroyed on three different levels: the personal, the institutional, and the national.[14] As defined by Arquilla and Ronfeldt, on the other hand, 'netwar' is characterized by networked rather than hierarchical patterns of organization and interaction.[15] It is also evident that the relationships between perpetrators of 'netwar' and of associated military, political, or social action in the real world' may be complex and rapidly changing.

This is very evident in the study by Ronfeldt et al. of the 'social netwar' waged by the Zapatista movement of Mexico. They observe that, while the support base for the movement was (at least initially) drawn from the indigenous people of the Chiapas and the leadership of the EZLN (Zapatista National Liberation Army) from the educated Spanish-speaking community, the IT-capable perpetrators of 'netwar' activities on behalf of and in support of the movement are more socially diverse and geographically dispersed.[16] The information they disseminate can be rapidly and widely dispersed across international networks in what Ronfeldt et al. describe as a virtual 'geodesic dome' or 'panarchy'.[17] Furthermore, the distinction between 'offensive' and 'defensive' action is blurred in 'netwars': for example, the 'mirroring' of news content across many Internet sites might be construed as 'offensive' (in that it represents an increase in network 'territory' held), or 'defensive' (in that it is more difficult to locate, block access to, or remove, dispersed 'packetised' information).

'Information interventions' of the kind described by Metzl deal primarily with traditional broadcasting mechanisms.[18] The different categories of information intervention – 'negative' (jamming and destroying transmitters), 'positive' (supporting local alternative media), and 'preventative' (using political, economic, and legal process) – have analogies when applied to IT networks, although some redefinition is necessary.[19] There is a real danger that a concerted 'negative' intervention, aimed at the information infrastructure of a small state, for example, could be interpreted as an escalation into military action or cyberwar, particularly in those cases where the military and civil infrastructures are not clearly delineated. Any agency taking such action must be prepared for retaliatory attacks.[20]

The Internet differs from more traditional broadcast media not only in its structure and patterns of public access and interaction, but also in terms of its strengths and vulnerabilities.[21] What emerges from a review of the characteristics of current network technology is a complex situation in which strategies and software can be used both constructively and destructively, and in which IT strategies adopted by organizations or states have on occasion had diametrically opposite outcomes to those intended. In a virtual world where tools designed for the 'load-testing' web-servers can, with minimal effort, be used to prevent them from operating entirely, where some of the most effective security is that designed by former 'crackers', and where the most enthusiastic proponents of cryptography are both governments and those citizens who want to limit those same governments' powers, concepts and categories familiar from warfare and broadcast media may prove difficult to apply. At least some of the technologies and strategies identified as useful tools for media development are currently being put to effective use by anti-government insurgencies. As Arquilla and Ronfeldt state, 'Whoever masters the network form should gain major advantages in the new era.'[22]

We start with the fact that in many less economically developed country (LEDC) contexts, the impact of IT networks remains severely limited, particularly when compared with that of television, radio, or print media.[23] Most African countries were rated as having close to 'zero connectivity' in the mid-1990s and more recent surveys confirm that many have undergone little development since, particularly outside capital cities and university campuses.[24] Until Internet access becomes more common, many potential netwars will involve the 'connected' elites of the country or region in question, its politically active diasporas, interested governments and NGOs, and the 'connected' audience worldwide, rather than the mass of the citizenry.

Characteristics of the Global Network

It is an often-repeated truism that today's Internet was originally a military network appropriated by pioneers of public Internet access; the truth is rather more complicated.[25] What is clear is that military strategists have recognized the potential of distributed networks to absorb damage during conflict while remaining operational. At the same time, the rapid growth of the Internet due to the popularity of e-mail, Usenet groups and, more recently, the World Wide Web, has led to the development of a network of close to 30 million 'hosts' and hundreds of millions of users in which geographical distance is of little significance and 'multiple redundancy', broadband connections and round-the-clock availability of resources have become the norm for many Internet users in North America, Western Europe, Japan and Australasia.[26]

Networks such as the Internet are characterized by multiplicity. Data sources are duplicated, with user traffic to large web sites being routed to the least busy of a set of identical servers. Whole web sites can be replicated or 'mirrored', with services such as those offered by the 'Internet Traffic Report' allowing users to choose from which 'mirror' they wish to download software on the basis of global patterns and speeds of network traffic.[27] In the event of a single network component being unavailable or very busy, alternative routes may be used to deliver data; and the data may be received, stored, and retransmitted using an increasing range of platforms, including portable devices. It was this combination of features that allowed the Belgrade-based B92 radio station to continue broadcasting over the Internet even though their radio signals were jammed by the government in Belgrade. As long as they could get recordings of broadcasts, stored as 'RealAudio' sound files, to their main ISP in the Netherlands or one of their ten 'mirror' web sites by FTP (file transfer protocol) or e-mail, they could be duplicated and made available to audiences in Yugoslavia and globally.[28]

While in the early days of Internet development, having a legitimate presence on the Internet generally necessitated either membership of a networked organization or ownership of a networked computer in the home, the emergence of web-based services such as 'web mail' and web-based web site construction tools has removed the need for users to have permanent access to network resources or to be owners of specific hardware or software.[29] The increasing capabilities of web browsing software means that it is even possible to operate sophisticated and secure 'groupware' environm———[30]———
needed of participants and admin:
computer connected to the Internet.

Denial of Service Attacks: 'Jamming the Internet'

An important outcome of the open network architecture of the Internet and the rise of remote access facilities is the ease with which individuals or groups can put in place the components of 'swarm' attacks against even the largest institutional networks or web sites in the form of 'Denial of Service' (DOS) attacks.[31] The recent advent of Internet-enabled portable devices such as Portable Digital Assistants (PDA) and Wireless Application Protocol (WAP) phones (including those on 'pre-pay' tariffs, which are, therefore, not exclusively identifiable with any single individual) also has enormous implications for the security of networks and networked resources as they offer the potential for mobile and effectively anonymous co-ordination of such attacks.[32]

DOS attacks are currently the most obvious 'negative information interventions' possible across the Internet and provide the closest analogy to jamming radio broadcasts, although they do not require the targeting of a geographical location. These attacks do not involve breaching the target network or web site but rather overloading them with so much traffic that they become unable to cope, and legitimate users then find themselves unable to gain access to services and resources. Earlier 'brute-force' DOS attacks have been supplanted by Distributed DOS (DDOS) attacks which generate traffic from multiple points on the Internet, the identities of which are concealed or 'spoofed'.[33] This causes the target to be unable to complete transactions and makes identification of the sources of the attacks even more difficult.[34]

The CERT (Computer Emergency Response Team) Co-ordination Center at Carnegie Mellon University provides information about security breaches and identifies some of the characteristics of DDOS attacks:

> To a victim, an attack may appear to come from many different source addresses, whether or not IP source address spoofing is employed by the attacker. Responding to a distributed attack requires a high degree of communication between Internet sites. Prevention is not straight forward because of the interdependency of site security on the Internet; the tools are typically installed on compromised systems that are outside of the administrative control of eventual denial of service attack targets.[35]

While DDOS attacks are particularly effective because they exploit the structure of the Internet, another feature of the Internet – its rapid growth – has increased the number of insecure network locations from which such attacks may be launched:

> Currently, there are tens of thousands – perhaps even millions – of systems with weak security connected to the Internet. Attackers are (and will) [sic] compromising these machines and building attack networks. Attack technology takes advantage of the power of the Internet to exploit its own weaknesses and overcome defenses.[36]

CERT also draws attention to a further feature of the Internet which has allowed rapid development of DDOS tools, namely the opportunities it provides for distributed development of software, stating:

> One can draw parallels [between DDOS development and] open system development: there are many developers and a large, reusable code base. Intruder tools become increasingly sophisticated and also become increasingly user friendly and widely available.[37]

Security analysts SANS claim that network security is improving in that 'technology producers, system administrators, and users are improving their ability to react to emerging problems, *but they are behind* and significant damage to systems and infrastructure can occur before effective defenses can be implemented.'[38]

There have been some well-documented cases of victims of attacks retaliating against attackers or perceived attackers, but on the whole, system administrators are advised to concentrate their efforts on preventing and defending against attacks and to avoid involvement in escalation of netwar activities.[39] A pre-announced DOS attack by the EDT (Electronic Disturbance Theater) against the Pentagon in September 1998, using a technique known as 'Flood-Net', was repulsed by technical staff using counter-measures that deliberately 'crashed' the attackers' web browsing software.[40] Pentagon lawyers advised that this counter-attack constituted not only a federal felony but also a breach of *posse comitatus*, the legal doctrine that prohibits unilateral military action within the United States.[41] Had the counter-attack involved deliberate action against computers outside the United States, the legal implications of the Pentagon action could have been even more severe.

DDOS attacks currently represent the most likely strategy for any agency involved in the co-ordination of 'negative' information interventions. If *génocidaires* in Rwanda had been operating a net-based service in 1994, doubtless calls for a targeted DOS attack would have been made. One obvious difference between radio-jamming and launching a campaign of DDOS attacks is that the technology required for the latter is available to a very much wider set of agents and it is capable of being operated from any number of sites distributed both geographically and across the network. Governments (and their approved agents) may try to maintain a monopoly over intervention technologies but ultimately the power to intervene will depend on the ability accurately to identify the original sources of offending materials (as well as any intermediaries) and selectively prevent their operation. The implementation of DDOS attacks against targets (and, inevitably, the development of defences against counter-attacks) requires strategic and, as the name suggests, distributed, deployment of technology.[42]

This marks the dilemma for any organization wishing to maintain a constant and secure Internet presence. Such an entity must decide whether to concentrate on developing a well-defended central resource (a 'bastion host') over which they have complete administrative control and which is optimized for detection and response to possible incursions or DOS attacks; or to build a distributed network of sites offering less security on an individual basis but a more attack-proof network presence overall.[43] A simultaneous dilemma for international agencies and for countries such as the United States is whether technology allowing the construction of bastion hosts should, like cryptography software, have restricted distribution.

Building and maintaining either a bastion host or a distributed 'extranet' in a LEDC (or in many humanitarian organizations) has a further complication. It requires IT expertise and continuing financial and technical support, both of which may be at an unattainable premium. The Internet Service Provider which hosted much the East Timorese '.tp' domain and the web sites of a range of humanitarian organizations found itself a target for DOS and other attacks from Indonesian government supporters. It is likely that it would have been overwhelmed without technical support from other IT developers across the Internet who assisted in the reinforcement of their system.[44] This case is an indication of the claimed effectiveness of the 'free software' movement, which has established dissemination and support networks across the Internet. Proponents of 'free software' contend that proprietary systems are inferior on the basis of the dependency culture they instill in their users and their apparently lesser ability to respond to incidents of this type.[45]

Rwanda Online: Real and Virtual

The network architecture of the Internet in Rwanda is characteristic of smaller LEDCs, principally those at early stages of Internet connectivity. Points of entry to the global network are the Intelsat link, which connects the monopoly Internet Service Provider, RwandaTel, to the Internet and a second satellite link, installed by the United States Agency for International Development (USAID) as part of the African Global Information Infrastructure Gateway Project (the 'Leland initiative') in 1999.[46] Despite the recognition by USAID of the importance of a 'competitive Internet Service Provider industry', the organization of a tendering process, and indeed the provisional approval of a number of potential Internet Service Providers within Rwanda, a monopoly is still held by RwandaTel which operates 'a high quality digital telephone network but with limited penetration to areas outside the main cities'.[47] Recently a GSM cellular service, 'RwandaCell', was established with investment from South African cellular operator MTN.[48]

The number of web hosts operating in and administered from Rwanda is, at the time of writing, very small: in addition to web servers installed as part of the Leland initiative at the Kigali Institute of Science, Technology and Management (KIST) (http://www.kist.ac.rw) and at the National University in Butare (http://www.nur.ac.rw), RwandaTel's own server (http://www.rwandal.com) also hosts government and presidential resources. The United Nations maintains a server, which hosts three web sites: http://www.un.rw, http://www.u-nops.un.rw and the regional peacekeeping force site, http://www.monuc.un.rw. The final web server, which is located on the KIST network, hosts a single site, the Rwanda Centre for Health Communications (http://www.rchc.rw).[49] Despite the recent establishment of web-based mail services at the University and a fledgling portal, e-commerce, and web-mail service operating on a server at KIST (http://www.iwacu.rw), many of those Rwandan organizations and businesses who have a web presence have these 'hosted' outside the country. Imojo, for example, (http://www.imojo.com), is a consortium of business interests whose web site is hosted in the United States and the web site of the Kigali-based Banque de Commerce, de Développement et d'Industrie (BCDI) (http://www.bcdi.rw) is hosted in South Africa. Other businesses and organizations maintain their electronic archives and web sites elsewhere in the United States, South Africa, the United Kingdom, and France.

While 'mapping' the 'Cybergeography'[50] of Rwanda using a variety of Internet tools ('ping', 'traceroute' and 'WHOIS' utilities, the Netcraft Internet Survey and a web-crawler of my own design implemented in the Perl programming language) the fragility of the network infrastructure as a whole and the apparent lack of security on some of the connected resources became apparent.[51] There is little evidence of 'mirror' sites replicating content, and the dependence of much of the network on specific 'gateways' with limited bandwidth could make the entire national network vulnerable to a sustained denial-of-service attack. In addition, the lack of available web hosts and the concentration of IT expertise at a small number of institutions means that web resources associated with disparate organizations and serving different functions are 'co-located'. Co-location can have a number of implications: educational hosts may be swamped by network traffic directed at co-located commercial resources[52] and the impact of hardware failure, or of problems with web server or mail server software is liable to be shared across all the co-located resources.[53]

Co-location of the resources of organizations with different political roles may have far-reaching implications: non-partisan organizations, including international agencies, should be cautious about being seen to be sharing resources or placing their resources under the administrative control of political bodies, or service providers perceived to be under central government control. This is not solely because of a need to maintain public confidence in the impartiality of the organization or in the reliability of its web site content. In the event of 'netwar' activity, the capability of an agency to respond with positive information interventions across the Internet would be severely reduced by co-location either with one of the protagonists or with the victim of a campaign of DOS attacks. At the same time, the opposite strategy – that of establishing a network presence wholly independent of existing telecommunications systems[54] and dedicated to selected institutions or projects – brings its own set of challenges, entailing choices about who does and does not receive the benefits of Internet connection and risking the perception by government that the network and its operators are economic competitors or political opposition forces.[55]

Given the role of RTLM in promoting and organizing the genocide of 1994 and the continuing broadcasts of its successor 'Radio Voice of the Patriot' from the Democratic Republic of Congo, it is perhaps understandable that the current government of Rwanda is unwilling to provide winder opportunities for publishing or broadcasting on the Internet.[56] How long 'ring-fencing' the entire national network will be sustainable is, however, open to question. In addition to those businesses and other organizations who have chosen to locate their electronic resources outside Rwanda itself, increasingly sophisticated anti-government web presences exist at Iwacu http://www.iwacu.com (note the similar domain name to the Rwandan government-sponsored Internet portal, http://www.iwacu.rw) which carries news and information from the 'Organization for Peace, Justice, and Development in Rwanda' and at the web site of the 'Congo Defence Fund' (http://www.cdf.org), both of which are hosted in the United States. 'Virtual Rwanda' now extends far beyond the physical borders of the country, and military and political activity on the ground is mirrored by competition to dominate the Internet-using public's view of past and present events in Rwanda – a good example of Denning's characterization of a netwar as being 'waged between governments [. . .] by governments against groups [. . .] or by political advocacy groups against governments', and aiming to 'disrupt, damage or modify what a target population knows or thinks it knows about itself and the world around it'.[57]

Building Open Infrastructures: The ITU Telecentres Project

Rwanda and the African Great Lakes region remains a theatre in which a relatively low-technology netwar might be fought, perhaps with associated information interventions by external agencies. This raises questions about what a programme of 'positive' or ideally 'preventative' information intervention should involve in a context such as the one described in Rwanda and who should be responsible for its development. Ideally, I would argue, a programme of 'preventative' information intervention should be integrated with a broader national or regional policy of media development and participation, and with other 'BDD' (Bridging the Digital Divide) projects including those concerned with education, health and e-democracy.

Other countries in Africa (including Denin, Mali, and Uganda) have benefited from the establishment of local 'telecentres' established under the auspices of the International Telecommunications Union (ITU). While these are often connected to Internet gateways of the sort established in Rwanda under the USAID Leland initiative, they offer a different pattern of deployment of, and access to, IT resources than that currently available in Rwanda. The 'model telecentre' described by the ITU might offer e-mail Internet access, hosting of web resources and e-mail auto-responders, and e-mail, e-mail-to-fax and e-mail-to-post services while also providing educational, medical and news information.[58] In some cases, these technologies are widely used across the Internet but are currently little used in less developed networks. E-mail auto-responders are a good example: these allow the automated posting by e-mail or to a fax machine of content (including text, graphics, web pages, or material in proprietary formats such as PDF files) in response to e-mail from a user. These are mainly used on commercial web sites to send regularly updated information such as price lists; however, they offer many other opportunities for delivering a range of materials without any requirement for the information provider to operate a web server or for the user to spend long periods of time online or even to have a web browser on their computer.

With their emphasis on 'last-mile provision' and the provision of appropriate network technologies, the telecentre 'model' of deployment may provide a better framework for media development and participation than the centralized model evident in Rwanda, although recent evaluation of a pilot telecentre project in Suriname suggests that longer-term sustainability may be consequent on a higher level of initial funding than is presently available.[59] An evaluation of the Mali telecentre in Tombouctou describes a more effective implementation in which IT resources are housed in a newly built public library funded in part by the local community.[60] Inherent in the ITU model, however, is a network structure and organization which supports automated updating of content using utilities such as rsync and configuration of local web and mail servers, aided by a network of system and server administrators, while at the same time maintaining appropriate levels of security against DDOS and other attacks.[61] While allowing users to benefit from a broader range of networked facilities, such an approach has considerable financial implications in initial setting-up costs, training, and maintenance and demands support from external agencies extending beyond the initial installation phase.

What may also be perceived as a cost of such a strategy is the loss of central control on the part of government and monopoly service providers. Given the current political situation in Rwanda establishment of regional and local facilities offering not only unregulated network access but also the opportunity to publish web resources and operate mailing lists would probably be regarded as an invitation to the *génocidaires* and their apologists to establish a 'network presence' within the country's network rather than outside its borders, where it is invisible to the majority of the Rwandan population. For the government of Rwanda, the choice is whether to keep their national network under close control, perhaps making it less vulnerable to infiltration but at the cost of vulnerability to DOS attacks or military intervention; or whether to encourage broader patterns of access and to use the Internet as a means of encouraging democracy and reconciliation.

In addition to issues of access, one of the obstacles to such use of the Internet is the prevailing view of it as being a predominantly 'allocutive' publishing medium, involving one-to-many communication with only limited audience involvement in content development.[62] It in fact offers a range of opportunities for different patterns of communication: synchronous and asynchronous, one-to-one and one-to-many, private and public. Compared with other media such as radio and television, where technological development and deregulation have offered users a progressively broader range of services and opportunities for participation, the Internet has since its inception offered peer-to-peer contact and collaboration in the form of Usenet newsgroups, mailing lists and dedicated client-server applications. In my view, these have as significant a role to play as the predominantly allocutive World Wide Web, and within many LEDCs, may represent a more appropriate area for development and investment.

Bridging the Digital Divide: Participation and Development

In the model of telecentre development proposed by the ITU, web-hosting is only one of a wide range of services; if anything the emphasis is on the provision of access to asynchronous technologies more appropriate for users with only intermittent access to the Internet. How these technologies can be used in a co-ordinated strategy of media development, however, remains unresolved in the ITU documentation. A good example of what can be achieved using Internet technologies other than the World Wide Web as part of a broader development strategy are provided by the developers of 'e-Vote', an Internet-enabled client-server application allowing secure polling either from dedicated terminals or through mailing lists.[63] Recognizing that e-mail and newsgroups allow discussion across networks, the developers of e-Vote argue that 'discussions also imply decisions. With a list server, a new tool is used to enable the list members to propose motions and to also vote on them.' Their solution is a dedicated polling server ('The Clerk') with interfaces via telnet, e-mail, or the World Wide Web, of which the e-mail interface has proved most popular because it allows discussion before and after voting, and because it does not demand long periods of potentially costly Internet connection.[64] The e-Vote system has evolved since its inception in 1992 and now offers a range of options including 'fully public', 'semi-public', and 'private' polls and petitions. In addition, complex polls like 'Vote for one of the following', or 'Distribute 100 vote points over the following 8 Budget Items' are supported.

Where e-Vote has proved most useful is enabling geographically dispersed groups to establish and maintain democratic structures and procedures, including the Zapatista movement based in the Chiapas region of Mexico but drawing support from around the world. While Denning dwells on the use of disruptive technologies (including DOS attacks) by supporters of the Zapatista movement, Ronfeldt et al. draw attention to the range of constructive network technologies used to co-ordinate this geographically dispersed and politically diverse movement.[65] While the Zapatista movement is represented by many web sites,[66] more current information is provided through mailing lists operating from mail servers both inside and outside Mexico and known as 'Zapatistas Online'. This represents an advance over simple mailing lists in that it comprises:

A powerful system of mail sorters, unix accounts and scripts distributed among various machines to allow collaborating editors in any part of the world to produce edited news about events related to Chiapas. News is gathered from many sources and selected messages are forwarded to four e-mail lists [. . . produced by . . .] volunteers stationed at four 'language stations' on the Internet. A language station consists of a telnet-able login where editors read and forward mail; and an eVoted e-mail list, where each station's volunteers meet to coordinate themselves. There is also a special language station, the 'practice' station for training new volunteers.[67]

Interestingly, when Zapatistas Online used e-Vote to set up a online referendum in 1999, they were themselves subject to a series of attacks originating in Nicaragua:

> The attacker(s) tried many tricks, most of which failed. Two techniques were somewhat successful: 'stuffing the ballot box', that is, sending valid ballots with false e-mail addresses; and 'sendmail attacks', that is, initiating mail tasks with our mail server and then stalling the processes.

The architects of e-Vote provide a detailed breakdown of the attacks, which were launched remotely from university and other sites in Italy, France, Mexico, Turkey, and elsewhere. In each case, telnet access was gained to these sites and poorly configured e-mail software was exploited to allow ballots to be sent from fictitious individuals.[68]

What makes Zapatistas Online an interesting case study is that it represents a further development of the tiered 'netwar' described by Ronfeldt et al.[69] The network allows and encourages collaboration between system administrators, software developers, news-providers, editors, translators, and their audiences. Management roles are not confined to those with permanent Internet connections and administrative privileges on host servers. It would be possible for an editor located anywhere with even basic Internet connectivity to collect a set of resources, go 'offline', review, select, and reformat those items appropriate to specific audiences and, on the next occasion they have Internet access, assign them to translators, forward them to news services, or submit them for e-Voting by the networked group.

Zapatistas Online also provides opportunities for users to develop administrative and editorial skills by providing a 'practice station', which the developers describe as:

> A special e-mail list [. . .] for new volunteers, so that they can learn the ropes without the pressure of having their mistakes go to the big news lists [. . .] The new volunteer gets an assortment of mail: the fresh mail copied from the English Station early that morning, and some 'canned' mail that presents the new volunteer with some common problems.[70]

This is an example of a networked organization that uses appropriate technologies to support a distributed and developing 'real world' network through resource development and capacity building.

The approaches used by Zapatistas Online should not be seen as being at odds with other initiatives described here. Large-scale connectivity initiatives such as the Leland Initiative, and 'last-mile' local infrastructure developments such as the ITU telecentres and the United Nations Development Programmes

'Sustainable Development Networking Programme' can provide a basis for programmes of media development and both 'positive' and 'preventative' information intervention using the kinds of tools and strategies developed by successful networked organizations.[71] This may, however, involve a recognition on the part of international groups that couching the aims of projects solely in terms of 'connectivity' or 'access' may not be adequate as a basis for long-term capacity-building, either in media or other aspects of civil society.

Projects such as Industry Canada's NetCorps programme place unemployed and underemployed Canadian volunteers on short-term assignments with partners in LEDCs in the course of which 'interns' [. . .] tasks may range from establishing Internet connections, preparing manuals and documentation [. . .] to creating websites, developing databases, networking workstations, and setting up and configuring hardware'.[72] NetCorps does not necessarily demand high levels of IT qualification from its interns, unlike GeekCorps, a non-profit organization committed to 'expanding the Internet revolution internationally' by pairing 'skilled volunteers from the high-tech world [. . .] with small businesses in emerging nations'.[73] Geekcorps volunteers, who are drawn mainly from successful IT private-sector businesses, are currently active in Ghana where the organization also maintains a permanent staff and operates a technical support network for its commercial partners with whom they collaborate in developing plans for future technical development. The aims of GeekCorps, in particular, extend beyond improving 'access' and generic IT skills and have much in common with capacity-building projects in other fields.[74]

The announcement of a strategic partnership between UNITeS (United Nations Information Technology Service), UNV (United Nations Volunteers), UNDP, the Leland Initiative and Cisco Systems in July 2000 to extend provision in LEDCs and in particular in twenty-four of the world's countries classified as 'Least Developed' is significant not only because it extends existing initiatives beyond infrastructure provision into training and support, but also because it will be achieved through the Cisco Networking Academy program. The program teaches students how to design, build, and maintain computer networks through 'a 280-hour curriculum designed by Cisco and delivered in more than 4,400 locations around the world including all 50 states and 74 countries.'[75,76] While UN agencies such as the UNDP and UNITeS already have a global presence and relationships with existing 'Digital Divide' projects, the involvement of large corporate concerns – even as providers of what UNITeS describes as 'corporate volunteers'[77] – may need to be carefully monitored and training programmes tailored in order to respond to the UNDP commitment to support capacity development in response to locally identified needs.

Rights, Responsibilities and Frameworks for Action

Article 19 of the Universal Declaration of Human Rights explicitly protects freedom of expression for all and specifically the 'freedom to hold opinions without interference and to seek, receive and impart information and ideas through any media'. Despite this and other assertions of the right to 'freedom of expression', many states have qualified such absolute rights, particularly with respect to foreign nationals or political organizations adjudged to be hostile to national interests.

The imposition of legal norms across the Internet has, to date, proved difficult. In the United States, legal challenges and opposition from networked communities have overturned and undermined a series of initiatives: the Communications Decency Act of 1996 was overturned by the Supreme Court on the grounds of its being 'over broad'; legal action against the 'Napster' music web site has, if anything, encouraged the development of a range of 'peer-to-peer' network applications which will prove far more resistant to legal or technological control than the server-based Napster system; and the DeCSS algorithm used to encrypt Digital Versatile Disks, despite being comprehensively protected by law, is available on many web sites and newsgroups, as well as being distributed on baseball hats, mousemats, and coffee-mugs.[78,79,80] Any legal initiative or information intervention perceived as a restriction on freedom of expression on the Internet will have to take account not only of the political will and technical expertise of its intended target, but also of a strong libertarian tendency amongst the architects of the Internet and developers of networking software.

Additionally, there is little international agreement about the responsibilities of 'carriers' including Internet Service Providers, or ISPs. Under the Section 230 of US Communications Decency Act (1996), ISPs were not held responsible, in a broad range of circumstances, for the use of their facilities to publish content considered defamatory. The Court in *Lunney v. Prodigy Services* held that 'Prodigy [the ISP] was *not a publisher* of the e-mail transmitted through its system by a third party [. . .] the public would not be well served by compelling an ISP to examine and screen millions of e-mail communications'.[81] In other jurisdictions, courts have found against ISPs for breach of specific local laws, or, as in the United Kingdom, have classified e-mail, newsgroup postings, and webpages as 'publications' which are therefore subject to laws relating to the Defamation Act of 1996, the defence of 'innocent distribution' being rejected.[82,83] These differences in thinking about the nature of 'free speech', about what constitutes 'political propaganda', and about the rights and responsibilities of telecommunications companies and Internet Service Providers, makes application of international legislation such as the 1948 UN Convention on Genocide difficult, even when supported by national laws.[84]

The World Wide Web Consortium (W3C) regards its role as one of 'enablement' through the development of technical standards and the provision of advice. Miller states, 'We wish to provide tools which encourage all cultures to feel free to use the Web while maintaining an inter-operable network architecture that encourages diversity without cultural fragmentation or domination.'[85] Recognizing, however, that individuals, organizations, ISPs, and national networks may wish to filter the content of remote web sites or block access to them entirely, they have co-ordinated the development of the Platform for Internet Content Selection (PICS) rating system which would allow 'A government [to] assign labels to materials that are illegal or harmful. This option is most likely to be combined with government requirements that such materials be filtered.'[86] PICS ratings do not, however, have to be assigned by the producer of the materials or by, for example, a government-controlled Internet Service Provider in order to filter content. Resnick continues:

> Anyone can create a PICS label that describes any URL, and then distribute that label to anyone who wants to use that label. This is analogous to someone publishing a review of your web site in a newspaper or magazine [. . .] If a lot of people use a particular organization's labels for filtering, that organization will indeed wield a lot of power.[87]

This suggests that an independent agency with a mandate to monitor potential violations of international and national law on genocide but also with an advocacy role in which they would lobby Internet Service Providers to apply their ratings as the basis of a filtering policy could have a significant role as a labeller of Internet sites. Weinberg reviews the constitutional status of ratings systems and their application, and notes that the debate over rating and filtering has become dominated by the question of protecting children online.[88] Balkin et al., in their study of the RSACi rating system (established by the Recreational Software Advisory Council and supported by major IT concerns including AT&T, Microsoft, and Time Warner) express the same concerns and characterize the RSACi system as 'work[ing] across contexts by disregarding contextual information and grouping categories of content in a way that itself represents political choices.'[89] Historical accounts of genocide could, as a result, be classified alongside incitement to commit acts of violence, and accounts by survivors of sexual violence, along with violent pornographic materials. In light of this, the establishment of an independent non-profit body responsible for development and application of ratings, which recognizes that filtering will be used for purposes beyond protecting children is necessary.

Since the use of national law as the basis for the rating content and establishment in law of potential sanctions against either publishers or 'carriers' has proved problematic, more general solutions may be needed. Alternative, international frameworks such as the UN Convention on Genocide (1948) which under Section 3(b) prohibits 'direct and public incitement to commit genocide' could provide a starting-point for a strategy first of providing advisory ratings to Internet Service Providers and then of action against originators of offending content, accompanied by 'positive information intervention' and media development projects wherever feasible and appropriate. 'Negative' intervention would be reserved for case-by-case action against specific Internet Service Providers and web hosts found to be originators or knowing propagators of materials construed as representing incitement to genocide.

Any independent advisory body would need the resources and legal backing of international agencies and would have multiple roles including:

1. monitoring of the content of web sites, newsgroups and other Internet resources while at the same time observing legal norms about privacy;
2. compilation of a database of 'metadata' about organizations and their Internet presence leading to the development and application of an authoritative ratings extending the scope of the existing PICS and RSACi frameworks;
3. advising Internet Service Providers and other authorities on content and ratings application;
4. collation of evidence in support of legal cases brought under national or international law;
5. advising on the application of negative interventions when appropriate together with assessment of the potential effects of such intervention.

This is a broad mandate and would involve collaboration between individuals and organizations with expertise in the political, technical and legal fields, as well as knowledge of linguistic, socio-political, and cultural contexts around the world.

Guarded Openness and Capacity Building

Arquilla and Ronfeldt conclude their discussions of the present and future role of the United States and international agencies in information warfare with a call for a strategy of 'guarded openness', a 'deliberately ambivalent' term designed to express their perception of future strategy being a 'a constant balancing act in which competing goals and concerns may be at stake, involving tensions and trade-offs between whether to stress openness or guardedness'.[90] They also caution against trying to develop a generic 'information strategy' on a number of grounds. Despite the apparent liberalizing effects of an 'open' information strategy (involving improvements in infrastructure and increased access to networked resources), its application to a currently 'closed' society may risk destabilization of the region. Internal social and political upheaval may also result if non-governmental or political forces opposed to the government are sufficiently well organized.[91]

The current situation in Rwanda conforms to this characterization on both counts. The country is embroiled in civil war in the Democratic Republic of Congo, armed opposition to the current government continues, more than one million people remain displaced, and the social and economic infrastructure of the country remain blighted by the effects of genocide. A generic policy of 'openness', involving major investment in infrastructure by international agencies or private enterprise, greatly improved levels of access to telecommunications services and the Internet, and the introduction of networked practice at all levels of government seems not only highly unlikely at present, but could have unpredictable consequences at national and regional levels. At the same time, there is a need not only for better information services and support for infrastructure recovery, but for capacity building, including the training of IT-capable professionals and administrators.

Just as Arquilla and Ronfeldt see 'openness' and 'guardedness' as complementary elements in information strategy, so the different elements of an information intervention strategy may need to be considered carefully. While (as in Rwanda) levels of IT expertise and connectivity remain low and there is the danger of a pre-emptive netwar espousing genocide being launched by *génocidaires* or their apologists, there will remain a role for a monitoring and advocacy organization of the kind described above. In the longer term, however, more universal access to the Internet will make it essential for local capacity to be developed either by international agencies, national and local governments, or the private sector. It is at this stage that 'positive' information intervention, using the kinds of networked applications discussed here, will be needed to develop not only expertise but also a culture of participation and collaboration amongst government representative, non-governmental organizations, practitioners in health, education and other sectors, and members of the public. This pattern of 'citizen-to-citizen' networking is characterized by Korac-Kakabadse and Korac-Kakabadse as being designed to 'strengthen connections between citizens, thereby providing a robust and autonomous site for public discourse', although they caution that this involves broader transformation of political culture.[92]

The development of such a networked 'civil society' will certainly involve training technical staff to a level of expertise where they, rather than representatives of external agencies, are capable of running secure networks. It will also necessitate new patterns of communication, collaboration and accountability, and new kinds of partnership between governments, international agencies, and commercial concerns. Just as the recipients of aid and support may have to undergo structural changes in order to play a role in the information society, so too may international organizations such as the United Nations. While the various agencies and projects of the United Nations have, in the past, had clear and distinct mandates – education, refugees, networking, and so on – a more integrated, networked approach may be required in response to changing political circumstances and technological developments. This is evident in the recent UNITeS/UNDP collaboration with USAID and Cisco Systems, but even this broadly based initiative has a specific set of aims related to networking, access and training. While network security and content management will inevitably form part of the Cisco Network Academy program, the establishment of civil society structures and the enforcement of legal frameworks is likely to remain outside the responsibility either of Cisco Systems' trainers or their UN partners in this specific initiative.

Heeks and Davies suggest that a common cause of failure of IT-based reform in civil society projects is a lack of co-ordination between strategic planners and managers, 'mainstream users' and IT professionals, underscored by differences in 'knowledge, culture [. . .] worldviews, and [. . .] interests'.[93] This often leads to piecemeal development with little strategic oversight and can result in overspending and the disillusionment of some or all of those involved. IT projects can have little impact on political reform or the strengthening of civil society unless they are carefully staffed, organized, and legally empowered to achieve those aims, and the resources and networks developed are both scalable and secure. If robust civil society structures are to be developed using IT networks, either as a part of a policy of positive information intervention or more generally, there will be a need for international organizations to provide more than technical assistance. What will be needed is strategic advice and direction based on agreed national and regional priorities, rather than 'technology-led' policies which may lead either to over-dependence on proprietary solutions or external consultants.

Realistically, there will also remain a need for a legal framework, couched in international law, which may be implemented in the event that the Internet is used to promote and organize genocide. Such a framework will need to be regularly elaborated in order to respond to technological developments: it is difficult to predict what the capabilities of network technology will be in, say, ten years' time, and even more difficult to assess what pattern of development will be observed in LEDCs. If predictions about the onset of 'netwars' prove accurate, then the United Nations may soon find itself establishing new agencies. Some of these may be charged with guiding IT development within civil society; others with the development of 'swarm' technologies capable of accurate monitoring and precise intervention against networked targets, conducted in accordance with specific mandates based in international law.

Bibliography

ACLU v. Reno (1996), 929 F. Supp. 824 (E.D. Pa. 1996) striking down the Communications Decency Act.
A + M Records v. Napster Inc. (2000), US District Court in the District of California No. C 99–50183 MHP (5 March 2001).
AISI-Connect (n.d.), AISI-Connect National ICT Profiles for Africa. Online [July 2001], available at http://paradigm.sn.apc.org/africa/
Adams, J. (2001), 'Virtual Defense' *Foreign Affairs* vol. 80(3) May–June; pp. 98–112.
African Rights (1995), *Rwanda: Death, Despair and Defiance*, London: African Rights.
Akdeniz, Y. (1999), 'Case Analysis: Lawrence Godfrey v. Demon Internet Ltd, *Journal of Civil Liberties*, 4(2), July 1999, pp. 260–7.
Anderson R., Bikson, Tora K., Law, Sally Ann, and Mitchell, Bridger M. (1995), *Universal Access to E-Mail: Feasibility and Social Implications*, Santa Monica, CA: Rand.
Arquilla, J. and Ronfeldt, D. (1997), 'The Advent of Netwar', in Arquilla, J. and Ronfeldt, D. (eds) *In Athena's Camp*, Santa Monica, CA: Rand.

—— (1997), 'Looking Ahead: Preparing for Information-Age Conflict', in Arquilla, J. and Ronfeldt, D. (eds) *In Athena's Camp*, Santa Monica, CA: Rand.

BBC (1998), 'The Sound of Hatred'. BBC Online Network. Online [July 2001], available at http://news6.thdo.bbc.co.uk/hi/english/world/monitoring/newsid_71000/71524.stm

Balkin, J. M., Noveck, B. S. and Roosevelt, K. (1999), 'Filtering the Internet: A Best Practices Model', Yale Law School Information Society Project. Online [July 2001], available at http://www.copacommission.org/papers/yale-isp.pdf)

Bauer, M. (2001), 'Battening down the Hatches with Bastille', *Linux Gazette* no. 84, p. 30.

Bavaria v. Somm (1996), Local Court [Artsgericht] Munich, File No.: 8340 Ds 465 Js 173158/95.

Benjamin, P. (2001), 'Community Development through IT', in R. Heeks (ed.), *Reinventing Government in the Information Age: International Practice in IT-enabled Public Sector Reform*, London: Routledge.

Bentley, R., Appelt, Wolfgang, Busbach, Uwe, Hinrichs, Elke, Kerr, David, Sikkel, Klaas, Trevor, Jonathan, Woetzel, Gerd (1997), 'Basic Support for Cooperative Work on the World Wide Web', *International Journal of Human-Computer Studies* vol. 46(6): Special Issue on Innovative Applications of the World Wide Web; pp. 827–46.

Bordewijk, J. L. and van Kaam, B. (1986), 'Towards a New Classification of Tele-information Services', *Intermedia* vol. 14(1); p. 1621.

CERT (1999), 'Distributed Denial of Service Attacks' (CERT Incident Note IN-99-07), CERT Co-ordination Center Software Engineering Institute, Carnegie Mellon University, Pittsburgh, PA. Online [July 2001], available at http://www.cert.org/incident_notes/IN-99-07.html

—— (1999), 'Results of the Distributed-Systems Intruder Tools Workshop', CERT Co-ordination Center, Software Engineering Institute, Carnegie Mellon University, Pittsburgh, PA. Online [July 2001], available at http://www.cert.org/reports/dsit_-workshop-final.html

Chemla, L., Davis, M., Jacq, J. and MacElroy, C. (1997), 'Features for Freedom' paper presented at First European Conference on Voting, Rating, Annotation, Vienna, 21–2 April. Online [July 2001], available at http://www.deliberate.com/w4g/conf97/full-freedom.html

Cleaver, H. M. (n.d.), 'Zapatistas in Cyberspace: A Guide to Analysis and Information'. Online [July 2001], available at http://www.eco.utexas.edu/Homepages/Faculty/Cleaver/zapsincyber.html

Collin, M. (2001), *This is Serbia Calling*, London: Serpent's Tail.

Curtin, M. (2000), 'On Guard: Fortifying your Site against Attack', *Web Techniques* vol. 5(4) April; pp. 46–50.

Denning, D. E. (1999), *Information Warfare and Security*, New York: ACM Press/Addison-Wesley.

Des Forges, A. (1999), *Leave None to Tell the Story: Genocide in Rwanda*, New York: Human Rights Watch; and Paris: International Federation of Human Rights.

Diallo, B. and Engvall, L. (2000), 'Telecentres for Developing Countries: The Mali Case Study – Tombouctou. Online [July 2001], available, http://www.itu.int/ITU-D-Universal Access/pilots/Malicasestudy.doc

DiBona, C., Ockman, Sam and Stone, Mark (eds) (1999), *Open Sources: Voices from the Open-Source Revolution*, Sebastopol, CA: O'Reilly Associates.

Dodge, M. and Kitchin, M. (2000), *Mapping Cyberspace*, London: Routledge.

Emberg, J. (1998), 'Integrated Rural Development and Universal Access: Towards a

Framework for Evaluation of Multipurpose Community Telecentre Pilot Projects Implemented by ITU and its Partners. Paper presented at 'Partnerships and Participation in Telecommunications for Rural Development: Exploring What Works and Why', University of Guelph, Guelph, Ontario, Canada, 26–7 October Online [July 2001], available at http://www.itu.int/ITU-D-UniversalAccess/johan/papers/guelph.doc

Goodman, S.E. (1996), 'War, Information Technologies, and International Asymmetries', Proceedings of the ACM, vol. 39(12) December, pp. 11–15.

Guest, I. (1999), 'Wiring Up Kosovo 1 – The Internet and the Disintegration of Yugoslavia', On the Record: Kosovo vol. 9(8). Online [July 2001], available at http://www.advocacynet.org/news_158.html

—— (1999), 'Wiring Up Kosovo 3 – Online at Last!', On the Record: Kosovo vol. 9(10). Online [July 2001], available at http://www.advocacynet.org/news_160.html

Hafner, K. and Lyon, M. (1996), Where Wizards Stay up Late: The Origins of the Internet, New York: Simon and Schuster.

Harknett, R. J. (1996), 'Information Warfare and Deterrence', Parameters (US Army War College Quarterly), Autumn, pp. 93–107.

Heeks, R. and Davies, A. (1999), 'Different Approaches to Information Age Reform IT', in R. Heeks (ed.), Reinventing Government in the Information Age: International Practice in IT-enabled Public Sector Reform, London: Routledge.

Human Rights Watch (1996), Shattered Lives: Sexual Violence during the Rwandan Genocide and its Aftermath, New York: Human Rights Watch. (Summary version: Online [July 2001], available at http://www.hrw.org/hrw/summaries/s.rwanda969.html

ITU (1997), 'Proposal for International Cooperation on Multipurpose Community Telecentre Pilot Projects in Africa'. Online [July 2001], available at http://www.itu.int/ITU-D-Universal Access/pilots/pilotdetails.htm

Korac-Kakabadse, A. and Korac-Kakabadse, N. (1999), Information Technology's Impact on the Quality of Democracy: Reinventing the Democratic Vessel', in R. Heeks (ed.), Reinventing Government in the Information Age: International Practice in IT-enabled Public Sector Reform, London: Routledge.

Laurence Godfrey v. Demon Internet Ltd (1999), High Court Of Justice, Queen's Bench Division 1998-G-No 30 (26 March 1999).

Levy, S. (1984), Hackers: Heroes of the Computer Revolution, Harmondsworth: Penguin.

Lunney v. Prodigy Services (1999), 94 N.Y.2d 242 (2 December 1999).

MPAA v. Reimerdes, Kazan, Corley and 2600 Enterprises Inc. (2000), 17 USC 1201(a)(2).

McQuail, D. (2000), Mass Communication Theory (3rd edn), London: Sage.

Meese vs. Keene (1987) 481 U.S. 465.

Melvern, L. (2000), A People Betrayed: the Role of the West in Rwanda's Genocide, London: Zed Books.

Metzl, J. F. (1997), 'Rwandan Genocide and the International Law of Radio Jamming', American Journal of International Law vol. 91(4), pp. 628–51.

—— (1997), 'Information Intervention: When Switching Channels isn't Enough' Foreign Affairs, vol. 76(6) November–December, pp. 15–21.

Northcutt, S. and Novak, J. (2001), Network Intrusion Detection: An Analyst's Handbook (2nd edn), Indianapolis, IN: New Riders.

Olson, A. (2001), 'Keeping your Web Content in Sync', Systems Administrator vol. 10(2) February; pp. 37–8.

Prunier, G. (1995), The Rwanda Crisis: History of a Genocide 1959–1994, London: Hurst.

Radio Free Europe/Radio Liberty (2001), 'On Europe's Future Rapid Reaction Force or: Why Belgrade's Banking System Survived The NATO Campaign', *Balkan Report* vol. 5(6) (January). Online [July 2001], available at http://www.rferl.org/balkan-report/2001/01/6-230101.htm

Radio Netherlands Media Network (30 October 2000), 'Counteracting Hate Media' Edition 3.02. Online [July 2001], available at http://www.rnw.nl/realradio/dossiers/html/hateinfo.html

Raymond, E. (1999), *The Cathedral and the Bazaar*, Sebastopol, CA: O'Reilly Associates.

Resnick, P. (ed.) (1999), '*PICS, Censorship, and Intellectual Freedom.*' Online [July 2001], available at http://www.w3.org/PICS/PICS-FAQ-980126.html

Rheingold, H. (1994), *The Virtual Community: Homesteading on the Electronic Frontier*, New York: HarperPerennial.

Ronfeldt, D., Arquilla, J., Fuller, G. E. and Fuller, M. (1999), *The Zapatista 'Social Netwar' in Mexico*. Santa Monica, CA: Rand.

Rothrock, J. (1997), 'Information Warfare: Time for some Constructive Skepticism?', in Arquilla, J. and Ronfeldt, D. (eds) *In Athena's Camp*, Santa Monica, CA: Rand.

SANS (23 February 2000), 'Consensus Roadmap for Defeating Distributed Denial of Service Attacks: A Project of the Partnership for Critical Infrastructure Security', SANS Institute, Bethesda, MD. Online [July 2001], available at http://www.sans.org/ddos_roadmap.htm

Schwartz, A. (1998), *Managing Mailing Lists*, Sebastopol, CA: O'Reilly Associates.

Stein, L. (1999), 'How shall I measure thee? Let me count the ways', *Web Techniques* vol. 4(7) July, pp. 16–19.

——— (2001), 'Secure Internet Voting with Perl', *The Perl Journal* vol. 5(4); pp. 18–27.

Toffler, A. and Toffler, H. (1993), *War and Anti-War: Survival at the Dawn of the 21st Century*, Boston MA: Little, Brown and Co.

UNDP (1997), 'Capacity Development and UNDP: Supporting Sustainable Human Development'. United Nations Development Programme. Online [July 2001], available at http://magnet.undp.org/Docs/cap/bkmorg/1.htm)

UNITeS (2000), 'Internet Leader Forges First Private Sector Partnership with UNI-TeS'. United Nations Information Technology Services. Online [July 2001], available at http://www.unites.org/prerels/2000/220700.html

——— (2000), UNITeS Update. United Nations Information Technology Services. Online [July 2001], available at http://www.unites.org/updates/up1200.html

USAID (n.d.), 'The USAID Leland Initiative and Rwanda'. Online [July 2001], available at http://www.usaid.gov/regions/afr/leland/rwaindex.htm

US House of Representatives Committee on the Judiciary (2000), 'Internet Denial of Service Attacks and the Federal Response'. Online [July 2001], available at http://www.house.gov/judiciary/na022800.htm

Weinberg, J. (1997), 'Rating the Net' *Hastings Communications and Entertainment Law Journal*, vol. 19, p. 453. Online [July 2001], available at http://www.law.wayne.edu/weinberg/rating.htm Prior version appeared in Comm/Ent L. J. 19(1), fall 1996.

Wildt, R. (2000), 'Should you Counter-Attack when Network Attackers Strike?' SANS Institute, Bethesda, MD. Online [July 2001], available at http://www.sans.org/infosecFAQ/infowar/counter-attack.htm

Yee, D. (1999), 'Development, Ethical Trading, and Free Software', Community Aid Abroad. Online [July 2001], available at http://www.caa.org.au/

Zapatistas Online (n.d.), Zapatistas Online News Project. Online [July 2001], available at http://www.deliberate.com/zo

Notes

1. Survivors Fund. Online [July 2001], available at http://www.survivors-fund.org.uk
2. The role of the traditional media in co-ordinating the genocide in Rwanda has been treated for example in, Prunier, *The Rwanda Crisis*; Metzl, 'Rwandan Genocide and the International Law of Radio Jamming'; Melvern, *A People Betrayed*; Des Forges, *Leave None to Tell the Story*.
3. While Survivors' Fund and AVEGA receive general funds from a number of large charities including Comic Relief they also receive many smaller donations for specific projects such as education of girls, house-building, medical relief and trauma counselling.
4. African Rights, *Rwanda: Death, Despair and Defiance*; Human Rights Watch, *Shattered Lives*.
5. Application services include a wide range of server-based services such as data-storage and retrieval, 'webmail', mailing-list management, collaborative tools and workflow management tools. What they have in common is that the user is able to maintain control over data without having to take administrative control of an entire network server, and that multiple users can take advantage of the same server-based tools.
6. The choice of a non-proprietary but well-supported data format provides a degree of 'future-proofing' of the resources so that they could be made available in future, should circumstances change and a different dissemination policy be adopted. The testimonies are kept as XML (Extensible Markup Language) data, which is 'parsed' to generate web pages. XML allows the separation of original data from descriptive metadata and formatting information, unlike proprietary formats such as Microsoft Word or Adobe's Portable Document Format (PDF).
7. http://rwanda.free.fr/ [July 2001] is a French-language web site providing information and links to other web sites with news about Rwanda. Other organizations such as One World (http://www.oneworld.net) provide coverage of world events with a development focus and regularly have information about the region.
8. Toffler and Toffler, *War and Anti-War*.
9. Denning, *Information Warfare and Security*, pp. 21–42.
10. Goodman, 'War, Information Technologies and International Asymmetries', p. 12ff.
11. Adams, 'Virtual Defense', pp. 98–9.
12. Rothrock, 'Information Warfare: Time for some Constructive Skepticism?', p. 226.
13. Arquilla and Ronfeldt, 'The Advent of Netwar', p. 275.
14. Harknett, 'Information Warfare and Deterrence'.
15. Arquilla and Ronfeldt, 'The Advent of Netwar', p. 286ff.
16. Ronfeldt et al., *The Zapatista 'Social Netwar' in Mexico*, pp. 24–6.
17. Ibid., p. 13.
18. Metzl, 'Information Intervention'.
19. Radio Netherlands, 'Counteracting Hate Media'.
20. General Klaus Naumann, who headed NATO's military affairs committee during the initial air strikes on Yugoslavia, expressed concerns about the readiness of European institutions to cope with such an escalated netwar:

    General Naumann pointed out [in Munich on 29 November 2000] that information warfare must be an important component of future military thinking. Already during NATO's bombing of Serbia in 1999, Naumann thought about destroying Yugoslavia's banking system by a hacker attack. NATO knew about Milosevic's vital financial transactions and that the banking system is, in any event, a sensitive point of the national economy. But in the end, General Naumann decided not to propose an attack on Belgrade's banking system. He was afraid that Serbian hackers – who showed what they could do to some Western and Albanian web sites – would start to do the same to the computer systems of European banks. In other words: Europe was vulnerable and not prepared to counteract information attacks or counter-disinformation. (Radio Free Europe/Radio Liberty's Balkan Report, 'On Europe's Future Rapid Reaction Force')

21. See generally Bordewijk and van Kaam, 'Towards a New Classification of Tele-information Services' summarized and updated further in McQuail, *Mass Communication Theory*, p. 1621ff., p. 129ff.
22. Arquilla and Ronfeldt, 'The Advent of Netwar', p. 276.
23. Throughout this chapter the terms LEDC and MEDC are used for 'less economically developed countries' and 'more economically developed countries' respectively.
24. Anderson et al., *Universal Access to E-mail: Feasibility and Social Implications*. The AISI – Connect database of connectivity data is at http://paradigm.sn.apc.org/Africa
25. See for example, Levy, *Hackers*; Rheingold, *The Virtual Community*; Hafner and Lyon, *Where Wizards Stay up Late: The Origins of the Internet*.
26. The web site of Netcraft offers the user the chance to search close to 30 million web sites and look up the software run on them. Online [3 July 2001], available at http://www.netcraft.com
27. http://www.Internettrafficreport.com
28. Guest, 'Wiring up Kosovo'. Collin, *This is Serbia Calling* pp. 160–8, describes the role of B92 in more general terms from its launch until the defeat of Milosevic, including a discussion of the information war that accompanied NATO military action in 1999.
29. Rheingold, *The Virtual Community* provides a good account of the Internet at the early stage of its development, when the World Wide Web had yet to become established.
30. Bentley et al., 'Basic Support for Cooperative Work on the World Wide Web'.
31. Arquilla and Ronfeldt, 'Looking Ahead: Preparing for Information-Age Conflict', p. 465ff.
32. It is possible to run a 'telnet' session on PDA such as a Palm III or Psion Organizer, and WAP phones can be used to initiate programmes on remote web servers via the Common Gateway Interface (CGI).
33. Northcutt and Novak, *Network Intrusion Detection* pp. 251–4 provides an overview of the most common DDOS tools and strategies.
34. DDOS attacks came to public attention during a number of well-reported incidents in February 2000 on some of what Stein, 'How shall I measure thee' calls the 'landmarks of cyberspace' including the 'Yahoo' catalogue, e-mail and web-host, the 'eBay' auction service, and 'Amazon', the online bookstore. These attacks prompted a Senate oversight committee later that month (US House of Representatives Committee on the Judiciary, Internet Denial of Service Attacks and the Federal Response).
35. CERT, 'Distributed Denial of Service Attacks'.

36. SANS, 'Consensus Roadmap'.

37. CERT, 'Results of the Distributed-Systems Intruder Tools Workshop'.

38. SANS, 'Consensus Roadmap'.

39. A primary role of system administrators is the maintenance of the integrity of networked resources, ensuring that systems are available round-the-clock. As such their role includes detection of and defence against intrusion, but not what Denning (*Information Warfare and Security*, pp. 392–3) describes as 'in-kind responses'. This is reflected in regular articles in specialist periodicals like *Sysadmin* and in Wildt's article *Should you Counter-Attack when Network Attackers Strike?*

40. Denning, *Information Warfare and Security*, p. 74. Wildt, *Should you Counter-Attack when Network Attackers Strike?* provides a more detailed account and is aimed at systems administrators rather than strategists.

41. Wildt, *Should you Counter-Attack when Network Attackers Strike?* describes the lawyers' response to the Pentagon programmers' actions as going 'ballistic'.

42. Also inevitable is involvement in a constant round of hardware and software development. Denning, *Information Warfare and Security* pp. 235–6, cites the example of Syn_Flooder, a DOS tool designed to flood Internet hosts with bogus synchronization packets (used to initiate connections). This can be countered by the use of detection programme called synkill, which 'watches' for the patterns of network activity characteristic of an attack. However, this too, can be circumvented or 'spoofed' (p. 366).

43. Curtin, 'On Guard', p. 46. See also, in the same vein, Bauer, 'Battening down the Hatches with Bastille'. Bastille is a popular security application that allows systems administrators to disable all but the essential services on their web servers. The use of terminology derived from siege warfare is deliberate and revealing.

44. Yee, 'Development, Ethical Trading, and Free Software'.

45. See for example Raymond, *The Cathedral and the Bazaar* and DiBona et al., *Open Sources* for discussion of the merits of 'free' software and the more recently developed concept of 'open-source' software. Advocates of 'free' software contend that the 'free' is meant as in the French *libre* rather than *gratuit*. For non-Francophones they distinguish between 'free as in free speech' rather than 'free as in free beer'.

46. USAID, 'The USAID Leland Initiative and Rwanda'. Online [July 2001], available at http://www.usaid.gov/regions/afr/leland/rwaindex.htm together with much of the original documentation from the project. Interestingly, the web servers installed by USAID run 'open-source' rather than proprietary web server software.

47. The 'Present Accepted List of Rwandan Isps'. Online [July 2001], available at http://www.usaid.gov/regions/afr/leland/rwandisp.htm

48. AISI-Connect's online review of telecommunications in Rwanda. Online [July 2001], available at http://www2.sn.apc.org/africa

49. This situation is subject to change, and the schematic diagram of a typical Leland Initiative network at http://www.usaid.gov/regions/afr/leland/techdsgn.htm may not completely represent the situation 'on the ground'. For example, some users or institutions may use dial-up connections into neighbouring countries to access the Internet via other Internet Service Providers.

50. Dodge and Kitchin, *Mapping Cyberspace*, review not only the tools available for conducting this kind of survey work, but also maintain the online 'Atlas of

Cyberspace' at http://www.cybergeography.org This is a collection of visualiza-
tions of network and information architectures, conceptual maps and traffic flow,
as well as physical maps showing the extent and interconnectedness of the Internet
and other networks.

51. 'Ping' tests to see if servers are 'up' and available to the outside world; 'Traceroute'
    maps the stages in the journey across the Internet from a server to the client;
    'WHOIS' establishes the ownership of domains and the 'administrative contact'
    responsible for web resources. Netcraft (http://www.netcraft.com) automates some
    of the preceding tasks and allows the user to find out what server software is being
    used by a web site, where it is hosted and in some cases how reliable it is. Perl
    (http://www.perl.com) is an interpreted 'scripting language' used for a wide variety
    of tasks including server management, text processing and network programming.
    In this case I used it to build a 'web robot', which followed links on web pages and
    built a map of each web site it visited.

52. The best-known case of this is probably that of 'Jennicam'. Jennifer Ringley, a
    student at Dickinson College in Pennsylvania set up a 'webcam' in her room,
    pictures from which appeared on her 'home page' hosted at the university. When it
    became apparent that hundreds of thousands of web users were viewing it for
    hours at a time, the university took action and Ringley had to set up her own web
    server dedicated to hosting her site. Online [July 2001], available at http://
    www.jennicam.org. Many universities now prohibit staff and students hosting
    commercial services on university resources and prevent the 'mapping' of .com and
    .co addresses to home pages on university servers.

53. Despite the apparent administrative control enjoyed by web site or mailing-list
    'owners', the software used to manage and 'serve' content is in fact shared between
    all users, with higher-level administrative functions being the responsibility of the
    server administrator. Schwartz, *Managing Mailing Lists*, p. 16, gives a good
    explanation of this in the context of mailing list software and distinguishes
    between the 'list administrator', whose control extends only to the lists for which
    they are responsible and the server administrator who is responsible for the
    'maintenance' of the software used to manage all the lists.

54. This is possible using dedicated landlines but is more likely to make use of VSATs
    (Very Small Aperture Terminals), which connect users via a hub or 'central earth
    station' to a geostationary satellite.

55. Guest, 'Wiring Up Kosovo 3' describes the problems faced in the establish-
    ment of IPKO, an Internet Service Provider in Kosovo. These included
    technical problems (the telephone system was largely non-functional), funding
    issues and also broader questions about the status of the project and its
    relationships to the international aid effort, local government and specific
    partner projects.

56. BBC, 'The Sound of Hatred'; Radio Netherlands, 'Counteracting Hate Media'.

57. Denning, *Information Warfare and Security*, p. 73.

58. ITU, 'Proposal for International Cooperation on Multipurpose Community
    Telecentre Pilot Projects in Africa'.

59. Emberg, 'Integrated Rural Development and Universal Access'.

60. Diallo and Engvall, 'Telecentres for developing countries'.

61. rsync's capabilities are reviewed by Olson, 'Keeping your Web Content in Sync'.

62. Benjamin, 'Community Development through IT', p. 204, reviews a number of IT
    initiatives concerned with information provision in South Africa and is particularly

critical of 'technology-led' projects, which were 'an exercise in public relations rather than something that provided a community service'.

63. Chemla et al., 'Features for Freedom'. Stein, 'Secure Internet Voting with Perl' describes another electronic voting system which operates rather differently from e-Vote in that it involves two servers operated by separate agencies, one of which is dedicated to voter registration, the other to conducting polls. Stein explains that 'the privacy of the ballot is ensured by the separation of the [agencies]. One knows the identity of voters, but not whom they voted for. The other has access to their vote, but not their identity.' (p. 19). Voters are assigned a 'confirmation number' on voting, which they can use after the polls close to check that their vote has been tallied correctly.

64. Telnet sessions demand continuous connection to a remote server and are prone to connection problems; web browsers can be used for 'offline browsing' but any more complex interactions or administrative tasks necessitate continuous connection. E-mail can be sent or received as a 'batch' after which the user can disconnect from the network.

65. Denning, *Information Warfare and Security*, pp. 73, 237; Ronfeldt et al., *The Zapatista 'Social Netwar' in Mexico*, pp. 52–3.

66. Cleaver's 'Zapatistas in Cyberspace' provides an annotated listing of web sites representing and supporting the movement. The EZLN website. Online [July 2001], available at http://www.ezln.org

67. Zapatistas Online, Zapatistas Online News Project. Online [July 2001], available at http://www.deliberate.com/zo (Most information about this project and the 'home' of e-vote.)

68. Accounts of the attempt to attack the Zapatistas Online *Consulta*. Online [July 2001], available at http://www.deliberate.com/consulta/results/details.html

69. Ronfeldt et al., *The Zapatista 'Social Netwar' in Mexico*, pp. 24–6.

70. Zapatistas Online, Zapatistas Online News Project.

71. The UNDP Sustainable Development Networking Programme. Online [July 2001], available at http://www.sdnp.undp.org (provides technical advice and training, supports other projects with networking elements and runs its own 'telecentre' programme).

72. Online [July 2001], available at http://www.netcorps-cyberjeunes.org/english/faq_e.htm

73. Online [July 2001], available at http://www.geekcorps.org

74. UNDP, 'Capacity Development and UNDH' characterizes capacity development as supporting individuals and organizations in 'develop[ing] their [existing] abilities, individually and collectively, to perform functions, solve problems, and set and achieve objectives'.

75. UNITeS, 'Internet Leader Forges First Private Sector Partnership with UNITeS'.

76. UNITeS, UNITeS Update.

77. UNITeS, UNITeS Update.

78. *ACLU v. Reno*, p. 824.

79. *A + M Records v. Napster Inc.*

80. *MPAA v. Reimerdes et al.*

81. *Lunney v. Prodigy Services* p. 242; section II para 5–6.

82. Most notably *Bavaria v. Somm*, in which legislation against child pornography was used against the Compuserve ISP on the grounds that it had a responsibility to

ensure that no illegal content was held on its servers or transmitted across its network. The ruling was overturned in 1999.

83. *Laurence Godfrey v. Demon Internet* Ltd
84. Cited and discussed in Akdeniz, Y. (1999), 'Case Analysis: Laurence Godfrey v. Demon Internet Ltd', *Journal of Civil Liberties*, 4(2), July 1999, pp. 260–7.
85. Miller, quoted in Resnick, 'PICS, Censorship, and Intellectual Freedom'.
86. Resnick, 'PICS, Censorship, and Intellectual Freedom'.
87. Resnick, 'PICS, Censorship, and Intellectual Freedom'.
88. Weinberg, 'Rating the Net'.
89. Balkin et al., 'Filtering the Internet: A Best Practices Model'
90. Arquilla and Ronfeldt 'Looking Ahead', p. 478.
91. Ibid. pp. 486–8.
92. Korac-Kakabadse and Korac-Kakabadse pp. 213–5, identify four patterns of 'electronic democracy': 'electronic bureaucracy', 'information management', 'populist' and 'civil society'.
93. Heeks and Davies, p. 39.

Notes on the Contributors

Eric Blinderman
Eric Blinderman has a B.S. in Communications from Cornell University and a J.D. *cum laude* from Cornell Law School. At Cornell, he was awarded the CALI Excellence for the Future Award in two categories: (1) United Nations, Elections and Human Rights, and (2) Media and Globalization. Besides acting as the symposium editor for the *Cornell International Law Journal*, Eric was awarded a grant to study international law at the University of Oxford where he recently received his M.St. with distinction. In addition to his academic pursuits, he has served as a law clerk to United States District Court Judge Lawrence E. Kahn and worked at the United Nations Development Program. He is currently an associate at the New York Ofice of Proskauer Rose LLP.

Patrick Carmichael
Patrick Carmichael is Lecturer in IT and Education at Reading University in the UK, where he is involved in the pre-service and in-service training of primary and secondary teachers. His research is primarily concerned with the development of electronic networks for education and other civil society projects around the world and he has particular interests in information architecture and data-security issues. Dr Carmichael is also a member of 'Learning to Learn', an ESRC research project, as part of which he is developing technologies to allow the representation of 'professional knowledge' across electronic networks.

Helen Darbishire
Helen Darbishire is a human rights activist and researcher specializing in the field of freedom of expression and information. She is currently at the Open Society Institute (Soros Foundation), Budapest as Media Law Program Manager. Previously she worked with ARTICLE 19 (London) and as a freelance consultant. Specializing in countries in transition in Europe, she has also worked in Africa and in Palestine. Publications include 'Media in Transition' in *Central and Southeastern Europe in Transition* (Praeger, 2000); 'Media and Elections' in *Media and Democracy Handbook* (Council of Europe, 1998); 'Albania' in *Extremism in Europe* (Centre Européen 1998); *Critical Analysis of Media Legislation in Europe*, (UNESCO, 1997); and 'Freedom of Expression, An Historical Right' in *UNESCO Courier* 1994). She holds a degree in Natural Sciences (History and Philosophy of Science/Psychology) from the University of Durham, UK.

Dan De Luce

Dan De Luce is the deputy director and director of technical assistance at the Programme in Comparative in Media Law and Policy, Oxford University. Previous to his work at the Programme, he was the media affairs adviser and the director of media development for the Office of the High Representative, the international authority implementing the Dayton Peace Agreement in Sarajevo, Bosnia-Herzegovina. He also has extensive journalistic experience. From 1996 to 1998, he was bureau chief for Reuters in Sarajevo, Bosnia-Herzegovina and before that, correspondent for Reuters in Belgrade, Yugoslavia. He has also worked as correspondent for the *Washington Post*, the *Sacramento Union*, the *Sacramento Bee*, and the Associated Press.

Alison Des Forges

Alison Des Forges, a historian by training, has served as a consultant on Rwanda and Burundi to Human Rights Watch since 1991. She has testified as an expert witness before the International Tribunal for Rwanda in Arusha, Tanzania.

Stephanie Farrior

Stephanie Farrior is Professor of law at Pennsylvania State University, Dickinson School of Law. She has also taught courses at the University of Oxford and New York University School of Law, and is former visiting researcher at Harvard Law School and visiting scholar at Georgetown University Law Center. From 1999 to 2000 she served as legal director of Amnesty International at its international secretariat in London. She has served on the board of directors of the Center for Justice and Accountability and of a state chapter of the American Civil Liberties Union. Professor Farrior's publications on international human rights law have appeared in such journals as the *Harvard Human Rights Journal* and the *Berkeley Journal of International Law*. She has served as legal expert on human rights missions to Yemen, India, Malawi and Pakistan. She also wrote the *amicus curiae* brief for Human Rights Watch in the hate speech/freedom of the press case before the European Court of Human Rights, *Jersild v. Denmark*. Professor Farrior holds an LL.M. degree from Harvard Law School, an M.A. from the University of Pennsylvania, and a J.D. degree from The American University, Washington College of Law.

Peter Krug

Peter Krug is an associate professor at Oklahoma University School of Law, which he joined in 1991. Before that, he served for six years as an associate with the Madison, Wisconsin, firm of Foley and Lardner. Professor Krug teaches courses in communications law, comparative law, international business transactions, and public international law. He is a member of the Order of the Coif, the American Bar Association, and the International Law Section of the Oklahoma Bar Association. He is the author of a number of publications on the topics of comparative mass media law, particularly in the former Soviet Union.

John Marston
Dr Marston is a professor/researcher at the Center for Asian and African Studies at Colegio de México in Mexico City. He completed his doctorate in anthropology at the University of Washington in 1997. In the 1980s he worked in refugee camps in Thailand and the Philippines, and he has been conducting research in Cambodia regularly since 1989. His chapter in this book is based on his experiences working for the United Nations in Cambodia in 1992 and 1993.

Julie Mertus
Julie Mertus has taught at New York University, Emory University, Tufts University, Cardozo School of Law, Smith College, York University (Canada) and the University of Bucharest (Romania). Prior to her academic career, she clerked for the federal judge John M. Walker; litigated civil rights and constitutional cases for the ACLU and the City of New York; and served as counsel to Helsinki Watch, working on the international war crimes tribunal and issues arising out of the war in Bosnia. She presently is a consultant with the Humanitarianism & War Project at the Watson Institute for International Affairs, Brown University, and the Women's Commission for Refugee Women and Children. She is a term member of the Counsel on Foreign Relations and is active in numerous international law organizations. A noted speaker on ethno-national conflict, international law and gender issues, over the last two years she has spoken at Yale, Harvard, Columbia, George Washington University, the University of Miami, West Point, Moscow State University, and the School of International Affairs in Hanoi, Vietnam, as well as at the annual meeting of the American Society of International Law. She has been a frequent commentator in the national media on international law and the Balkans. Professor Mertus graduated from Yale Law School and Cornell University.

Jamie Metzl
Jamie Metzl has served as Director for Multilateral and Humanitarian Affairs on the US National Security Council at the White House, as Senior Coordinator for International Public Information at the US Department of State, and as a human rights officer for the United Nations Transitional Authority in Cambodia. He is currently a visiting scholar at the Carnegie Endowment for International Peace. His is author of the book *Western Responses to Human Rights Abuses in Cambodia, 1975–80* (St Martin's Press, 1995) as well as numerous articles on human rights, diplomacy, information techonology and other issues in journals such as *Foreign Affairs*, *Daedalus*, and *The American Journal of International Law*. His 1997 *Foreign Affairs* article coined the term 'Information Intervention'. Dr Metzl holds a doctorate in south-east Asian history from the University of Oxford, and a J.D. from Harvard Law School.

Monroe E. Price
Monroe E. Price is the founder and co-director of the Programme in Comparative Media Law and Policy at the University of Oxford. He is also the Joseph and

Sadie Danciger Professor of Law and Director of the Howard M. Squadron Program in Law Media and Society at the Benjamin N. Cardozo School of Law, Yeshiva University, of which he was the dean from 1982 to 1991. He was a member of the School of Social Science at the Institute for Advanced Study, Princeton, in 2000–1, and a fellow of the Media Studies Center of the Freedom Forum in New York City in 1998. Professor Price was Professor of Law at UCLA from 1967 to 1982. His recent and forthcoming publications include *Media Reform: Democratizing Media, Democratizing the State* (Routledge, 2001) (edited with Beata Rozumilowicz and Stefaan G. Verhulst); *Parental Control of Broadcasting* (Lawrence Erlbaum Associates, 2001) (edited with Stefaan Verhulst); and *Media and Sovereignty Law Identity and Technology*.

Philip M. Taylor

Philip M. Taylor is Professor of international communications and director of the Institute of Communications Studies at the University of Leeds. He is also chairman of the InterUniversity History Film Consortium, associate editor of the *Historical Journal of Film, Radio and Television*, and a fellow of the Royal Historical Society. Professor Taylor's research interests include the history and conduct of international communications, military–media relations, psychological warfare/operations, and international film and television.

Mark Thompson

Mark Thompson is the author of *A Paper House: The Ending of Yugoslavia* (Hutchinson, 1992) and of *Forging War: The Media in Serbia, Croatia, Bosnia and Hercegovina* (John Libbey/ARTICLE 19, 1999), which was chosen as a 'book of the year' in *The Guardian* and *The Observer*. He worked in the 1990s as a media analyst, spokesperson and political officer for several missions of the United Nations and the Organization for Security and Co-operation in Europe (OSCE) in the Balkans. Most recently, he has been Balkans Program Director for the International Crisis Group, a non-governmental organisation based in Brussels.

David Wimhurst

David Wimhurst worked in Canadian media for fifteen years before joining the United Nations in 1996. He has been spokesman for the UN peace operations in Angola, East Timor and Sierra Leone. He has also worked as an associate spokesman and as acting deputy spokesman for the secretary-general. He currently works in the Department of Peacekeeping Operations at UN headquarters in New York, where he is a political affairs officer. Although born in Canada, where he currently resides, in Montreal, David Wimhurst was raised and educated in the United Kingdom. He has a master's degree from the Graduate School of Journalism at Columbia University in New York.

Index